Current Studies
in Social Psychology

Current Studies
in Social Psychology

Edited by
IVAN D. STEINER
MARTIN FISHBEIN
University of Illinois

Published for
the Society for the Psychological
Study of Social Issues

HOLT, RINEHART AND WINSTON, INC.
New York, Chicago, San Francisco, Toronto, London

Foreword

Many of the members of the Society for the Psychological Study of Social Issues (SPSSI) identify themselves primarily as social psychologists. The Society's membership also includes, however, many psychologists in a variety of other areas of specialization as well as social scientists from other disciplines. All share the conviction that psychological analyses can contribute to the understanding and solution of pressing social problems. It is reasonable to assume that Society members—regardless of their own specialties—view social psychology as the central body of knowledge from which systematic psychological contributions to the study of social issues can be derived. Understandably, therefore, the Society has taken an active interest for many years in the development of social psychology as a discipline and in the improvement of teaching, empirical research, and theory-building in this field.

A major contribution to this enterprise was the publication, under the sponsorship of the Society, of *Readings in Social Psychology* in 1947. This volume, edited by Theodore M. Newcomb and Eugene L. Hartley, soon became widely recognized as a valuable tool in the teaching of social psychology. A revised edition, edited by Guy E. Swanson, along with Newcomb and Hartley, was published in 1952. A third edition was prepared by Eleanor E. Maccoby, again together with the original editors. All three editions have been, to quote Nevitt Sanford's foreword to the third edition, "a continuing source of pride and satisfaction" to the Society.

The field has continued to grow, however, and at an increasingly rapid rate. A committee, chaired by Theodore Newcomb and including Martin Hoffman, Edward Jones, Robert Kahn, Harold Proshansky, and M. Brewster Smith, was appointed to consider the possibility of a new edition and the general policy questions that this raised. In considering a new volume, the Committee was faced with two apparently contradictory requirements: inclusion of enough of the classical studies in the field so as to provide historical continuity and inclusion of enough of the current research so as to reflect the present state of the field. To do justice to both of these needs, the committee recommended replacement of the original *Readings* with two companion volumes: *Basic Studies in Social Psychology*, edited by Harold Proshansky and Bernard Seidenberg, which is designed to illustrate the type of research—mostly published before 1958—in which current work in the field is rooted; and the present volume, *Current Studies in Social Psychology*, which is designed to exemplify very recent developments.

The Society owes an enormous debt of gratitude to Ivan Steiner and Martin Fishbein who undertook the arduous task of editing this volume and who performed it with great dedication. They made an extensive survey of the field as a basis for selecting the readings and also solicited several new contributions, prepared especially for this volume. We are also grateful to Morton Deutsch, Daniel Katz, Theodore Newcomb, and M. Brewster Smith who served as the Editorial Committee for this volume, as well as for its companion, and who were always ready to share their considerable wisdom with the editors.

March 1965

Herbert C. Kelman, President
Society for the Psychological Study
of Social Issues

Preface

Social psychologists are an active and growing band of behavioral scientists; they have expanded the field of social psychology tremendously in the past decade. Their research efforts are too diverse and too plentiful to be sampled adequately within a single volume. And, although the scope of *Current Studies in Social Psychology* is limited to the recent and contemporary developments within the discipline, many excellent articles that reflect significant current interests have had to be excluded.

The selection of articles has been guided by several criteria. We have deliberately emphasized controlled studies dealing with basic theoretical problems and have regretfully slighted large-scale field studies and investigations of applied social psychology. In an effort to make the book maximally useful to undergraduate students, we have omitted many commendable articles that involve extremely complex research techniques or statistical analyses. But to have insisted on a uniformly high level of readability would have resulted in the virtual exclusion of papers reporting the simultaneous treatment of several variables within a single study. Many of the problems attacked by modern social psychology are very complex, and a book containing only that which is easily understood is unlikely to provide an accurate picture of contemporary research. Consequently, we have included a number of papers that will tax the intellect of even the best undergraduate students.

In order to sample a wide range of research topics, we have devoted less attention to certain problems than would seem to be justified by their current popularity. Thus, for example, papers dealing with the merits of balance theory are included in this book but not with a frequency that would reflect their prevalence in the current literature.

Within the limits established by these criteria, choices have been influenced by the recommendations of numerous colleagues who have given us their views of the current literature both in oral discussion and in response to written inquiry. Especially significant has been the counsel of Professors M. Deutsch, D. Katz, T. M. Newcomb, and M. B. Smith. But the final decisions have been made by us, and we assume full responsibility for having in-

vii

cluded sections that some instructors may find of little value and for the omission of others that some of our associates will regard as indispensable.

Social psychology courses vary tremendously from college to college. Even within a single university, different instructors impose quite different structures upon the subject matter and emphasize different facets of the total area. For these reasons, we have not attempted to organize the articles in this book according to any single systematic principle. Instead, articles are grouped into familiar categories that seem to parallel those employed by many teachers. It is our expectation that some instructors will regroup the reading assignments to bring them into closer harmony with their own preferred way of organizing the subject matter.

We are indebted to the half dozen authors who wrote special reports of their research activities for this book. Thanks are also due to the many other authors and the publishers who granted permission to reprint their articles. The sponsorship of the Society for the Psychological Study of Social Issues has been a great boon; it was the Society that stimulated our interest in editing this volume and supported our activities as the work progressed.

Urbana, Illinois   I. D. S.
March 1965   M. F.

Contents

4. COMMUNICATION AND PERSUASION

5. INTERPERSONAL PERCEPTION AND ATTRACTION

6. INTERPERSONAL INFLUENCE

11. *SOCIAL BEHAVIOR IN STRESSFUL SITUATIONS*

INTRODUCTION

The early work of social psychologists tended to emphasize man's dependence upon his fellow men. Human beings were believed to be linked to one another by mysterious but compelling processes called imitation, suggestion, or empathy. Sometimes an instinctive basis was claimed for these interpersonal connections. At other times they were described as inevitable consequences of social organization. Although there were disagreements concerning the origins of the bonds that united men, early social psychologists generally agreed that the connections were strong. Human behavior was guided by coercive social forces. Man was seen as the servant of his human environment.

During the 1920s and 1930s man's responsiveness to his immediate social situation was a subject for reexamination. The automatic mechanisms by which social influences were said to be exerted could not account for the bewildering multiplicity of human responses. Moreover, the doctrine of instinct on which some of these mecha-

nisms were thought to rest had come into disfavor. Psychologists were impressed by Watsonian behaviorism and Freudian theory, both of which put the essential dynamic processes within the individual. While it may be conceded that neither of these viewpoints accorded man much more autonomy than he had been granted earlier, both at least emphasized the role of learning and contended that man acquires habits, attitudes or motives. The learning experiences of the individual as he progresses through infancy and childhood were said to establish enduring predispositions that tend, in turn, to determine reactions to later situations. Personality and attitudes permit the individual to resist his immediate social environment.

This conception of human dynamics encouraged social psychologists to focus their attention upon the socialization process. Textbooks of this period usually emphasized three major topics: the socialization process; the nature and effects of personality; and the acquisition and consequences of attitudes.

1

These themes were sometimes linked to the learning theories of the day. Often there were long anthropological accounts of the effects of child-rearing practices on members of various preliterate societies. Man's susceptibility to his immediate environment had been reduced, but his dependence upon his earlier environment had been increased.

The Great Depression and World War II created intellectual as well as social ferment. It became increasingly difficult for scholars to view the individual as a comparatively independent agent, doing what his personal history had taught him to do. Rapidly changing economic, occupational, and family situations led people to behave in new and often bizarre ways. It was apparent that the human predicament was shaped by contemporary as well as historical forces. Attitudes changed; personalities took new shapes. The groups in which people enacted their roles exerted strong and undeniable influences upon beliefs, values, and actions.

The basic characteristics of current social psychology became apparent during the period following World War II. Personality, though it remained an exceedingly critical factor in social psychological thought, became only one of many determinants of human behavior. Conditions under which attitudes do, or do not, change came to be considered fully as important as the consequences that attitudes have on overt actions. The role of the socialization process became less central. Greater concern was shown for the immediate influence of social situations and for the processes by which members of groups shape one another's thoughts and actions. This latter concern stimulated numerous laboratory studies of communication channels, conformity behaviors, interpersonal perceptions, role systems, and social comparison processes. As never before, the ongoing behaviors of group members were subjected to careful observation and analysis; and systematic manipulations of group characteristics were carried out.

Investigation of group processes led, of course, to new insights into the nature and extent of the effects groups have on their members. It also had other consequences. The theorists of the early 1900s had sometimes pictured groups as "emergent systems" having an existence independent of their members. As the emphasis on individuals grew during the 1920s and 1930s, these exaggerated conceptions of group reality were largely discarded and many scholars avoided all thoughts about "systems of people." But the 1950s brought a resurgence of interest in groups and, with it, a growing belief that interacting human beings may sometimes constitute a system with dynamics that cannot easily be understood through a piecemeal examination of the behaviors of individuals. Based as it was upon the foundation provided by scientific studies of interpersonal influences, this renewed interest in groups may someday create a bridge connecting the psychology of the individual with the social science of collectivities.

The most recent developments in social psychology have generally involved theoretical or methodological refinements of the work that was under way fifteen or twenty years ago. With few exceptions, the major concerns of a decade ago are still active issues today; although they are viewed from an altered perspective. As social psychology passed from the postwar period to the present, it tended to re-examine its earlier views of human behavior and to replace them with more complicated conceptions. By 1954 research had demonstrated that a wide variety of social influences shape man's responses to his fellow men; and that these influences are at times the most critical determinants of human thought, perception, emotion, and action. But, by 1964 it had become apparent that these social influences operate within an extremely complex network of relationships. Subtle changes in situations may determine whether a persuasive message evokes compliance or rejection. Interpersonal perceptions within a group may determine whether group failure leads to feelings of hostility or to intensified feelings of loyalty. Personality variables, which have long been known to affect human interaction, reveal an unmistakable ability to augment behaviors in some situations and to suppress behaviors in others. The importance of every social variable that loomed large in 1954 seems in 1964 to depend upon the larger constellation of circumstances within which it operates. Critical residues of the individual's past vie with the forces of the present, as attitudes and personality interact with innumerable situational variables to produce outcomes that express the consequences of unique combinations of conditions.

That variables interact with one another is not a recent discovery. Long before World War II some social psychologists were aware of this complication, and the research of the postwar years often involved explicit attempts to deal with it. But the social psychology of today is preoccupied with problems of multiple influences. Current research and theory are increasingly focused upon the task of discovering the laws that

express the consequences of many simultaneous determinants of human behaviors. More than anything else, this preoccupation is the hallmark of current social psychology. Its influence is evident in many of the articles in this book.

Other current trends in social psychology will be evident to the reader of this volume. There is a continuing effort to sharpen the meaning of concepts and to develop new operational techniques for defining them. The measurement of attitudes and beliefs is the subject of an uncompleted dialogue; the concept of social distance is being reevaluated; power is viewed as a generic term that subsumes several types of social influence; and the concepts of norm and role are receiving firmer meanings.

The several articles dealing with balance theories reflect a tendency on the part of many contemporary social psychologists to endow man with a kind of subjective rationality in which perceptions, expectations, and actions maintain close and harmonious relationships to one another. Underlying this approach is the assumption that a desire for self-consistency is one of man's major motives. By no means do all social psychologists accept balance theory as a working view of man. Probably the majority of them do not, but acceptance of one or another version of balance theory has been very widespread, and these theories have become virtual trademarks of the time.

In addition to the self-consistency motive that is evident in balance theory, other human incentives have received attention. As Freudian conceptions declined in popularity, social psychologists tended to re-examine the needs of man. The basic biological drives were increasingly found to be an incomplete list of human urges. Today, some writers accord curiosity and the need for social stimulation a role that rivals that of hunger, thirst, or sex. Articles in this book dealing with the effects of social isolation, and with the functional autonomy of motives, are indicative of this trend.

During the postwar era, social psychologists made frequent use of anthropological reports. Descriptions of preliterate communities were used to demonstrate the extent and range of social influences upon behavior patterns. Current practice more often involves parallel empirical, or even laboratory, investigations conducted in different societies. This procedure permits a much more thorough appraisal of the consequences of linguistic, social, or economic factors; for it includes a deliberate effort to "hold constant" as many kinds of variables as possible. To an even greater extent than is indicated by the articles in this book, the orientation of social psychology has become international and cross-cultural.

For many decades, social psychologists have attempted to create laboratory replicas of social situations. The complexity of the situations that have been brought into the laboratory has increased steadily during recent years. Studies of coalition formation, negotiation processes, transmission of cultural traditions, jury deliberations, and obedience to authority are now performed in miniature experimental groups. Other research, not reported in this book, has employed electronic computers to simulate extremely complicated social systems such as nations and international organizations.

Few articles in this volume deal explicitly with the solution of immediate, practical problems. Social psychologists *are* concerned with such matters; their research has always had a special relevance to the tribulations of mankind. Not infrequently, they have investigated the psychological aspects of intensely political, moral, or ethical issues. Recent studies of desegregation, the backgrounds of extremism, and the roots of war are illustrative of this deep concern for the dilemmas of our time. Few examples of this aspect of the social psychologist's role have been reported here. These activities are less indicative of his mode of thought and his techniques of investigation than are his more basic research endeavors.

Current social psychology is not dramatically different from the social psychology of eight or ten years ago. It does, however, show a greater sensitivity to, and ability to cope with, the tremendously complex maze of factors that simultaneously influence collective behaviors. Concepts that seemed clear enough in the recent past, and relationships that seemed unassailable, are falling continuously before the attack of a more sophisticated methodology and a more mature conceptualization of human behavior. It is an exciting time to be a student of social psychology.

1

Some Aspects of Social Motivation

---

1. THE STRUCTURE OF FUNCTIONAL AUTONOMY *

John P. Seward

Like many others, I first turned to psychology with questions about motivation. I remember when it happened. I had just graduated from Cornell, where my only contact with psychology had been a 1-semester course in my sophomore year taught by Karl Dallenbach (Titchener's section was already full). Titchener's textbook left me cold. For me the only spark was struck by Dallenbach's lecture on how magicians deceive audiences.

Having left economics for literature, I hoped, of course, to write. But since I had nothing to say, I would have to write about Life, and since I knew nothing about life it would have to be fiction. And before I could write fiction I would have to find out how my characters would probably act. So I went to the library and found a book by Troland called *The Mystery of Mind*. I divided that summer between beginning Greek and struggling with nociceptors, beneceptors, cortical conductance, and retroflex action—also largely Greek. Troland had a quasi-neurological model of Thorndike's law of effect that tantalized me; at least it did not discourage me from entering the graduate psychology department at Columbia in the fall.

By 1926 instincts had had their day and biological drives were invoked to supply the energy for behavior. But hunger, thirst, and sex, even with the help of fear and rage, could hardly fill the gap left by constructive, destructive, filial, parental, acquisitive, inquisitive, self-assertive, and self-abasing instincts. If not innate, how were these undeniable motives, social or antisocial, to be accounted for? John B. Watson had

* Reprinted from the *American Psychologist*, 1963, 18: 703–710, with permission of the author and the American Psychological Association.

5

already suggested the answer that became orthodox. You recall his three primary emotions of fear, rage, and love, and his experiment—perhaps the most famous in psychology—in which the clang of a steel bar probably prevented an 11-months infant from ever becoming a student of rat behavior. The answer, of course, was to be found in the principle of conditioning. But no one was altogether happy with the solution. Why, it was objected, if a mother's face is loved because it was perceived along with mild tactile stimulation, wouldn't a pillow do just as well? At that time, 30 years before Harlow's experiments with terry-cloth "mothers" for orphaned monkeys, the objection carried more weight than it would today.

In 1937 Gordon Allport proposed a new solution: the functional autonomy of motives. In his own words:

Each motive has a definite point of origin which may possibly lie in instincts, or, more likely, in the organic tensions of infancy . . . but as the individual matures the tie is broken. Whatever bond remains is historical, not functional [p. 143].

Allport expressed his idea more clearly by paraphrasing Woodworth's (1918) earlier suggestion that a mechanism might become a drive: "activities and objects that earlier in the game were *means* to an end, now became *ends* in themselves [1937, p. 144]."

The trouble was that although Allport gave many examples of what he meant, he made no attempt to analyze how it worked. So his principle stood as a statement of faith rather than an explanation. Before accepting it, learning theorists (e.g., McClelland, 1942; Rethlingshafer, 1943) insisted on proof that Allport's examples were not simply

cases of long-delayed extinction of instrumental acts. But no acceptable form of proof was specified, and since none was forthcoming the principle has lived on in a sort of limbo, never openly acknowledged but never finally renounced.

It is conceivable, of course, that there is no real problem here, that social motives are not autonomous, and that they will be extinguished if not biologically reinforced. A hen low in the pecking order may need an occasional peck to keep her in line. A friendship may not survive many months without an invitation to dinner. Another way to evade the issue would be to draw a Cartesian dichotomy between infrahuman species goaded by bodily needs and Homo sapiens somehow capable of emergent values.

I prefer to resort to neither of these dodges. Without severing kinship with our fellow creatures, let us assume that human adults are not exclusively concerned with eating and sleeping and excreting and fighting and copulating, and that all their remaining activities will not necessarily be extinguished, even if repeated indefinitely. First, I want to make sure that traditional learning theory cannot derive such activities from bodily deficits and disturbances. Second, I shall invite you to consider some recent developments in the study of animal and human motivation. Third, we shall return to the question of functional autonomy and re-examine Allport's notion in the light of newer concepts.

ORTHODOX BEHAVIOR THEORY

Behavior theory has invented two constructs to deal with acquired motives: learned drives, and learned rewards or secondary reinforcement. Let us start with the first construct.

A drive is presumably learned by being conditioned to stimuli present when it is aroused. A child badly frightened in a dark room may thereafter insist on keeping the light on when he goes to bed. A rat that has escaped from a shock box by dashing through a door will learn new ways to open the door even after the shock has been turned off (Miller, 1948). Theoretically its efforts will continue as long as they succeed in reducing fear. But what keeps the fear alive? By the laws of classical conditioning, unless it is reinstated from time to time by more shocks, the fear must eventually be extinguished.

On the whole, empirical findings support the theory. Rats and dogs have been known to avoid a nonexistent shock for hundreds of trials, but under most conditions they finally quit (Solomon & Brush, 1956). Solomon and Wynne's (1954) traumatized dogs stand as possible exceptions; to explain their remarkable tenacity the authors finally had to postulate a principle of "partial irreversibility," logically equivalent to functional autonomy itself. But even if the theoretical scene changed and some psychologist invented a nonextinguishable fear, it is doubtful if Allport would consider it adequate to the functions he had in mind.

So much for aversive behavior; what of appetites? If fear can be conditioned, so might hunger and thirst. At first thought, the ubiquitous advertising of foods and drinks would seem to exploit some such tendency. But we must be careful to distinguish between genuine hunger and a desire for sugar-cured ham. For a more definitive test we might half starve an animal repeatedly in a certain closet, always feeding him somewhere else; then see if we could make him hungry just by putting him back in the closet when his stomach was full. Such experiments in one form or another have been tried many times with varying results, but so far they have failed to prove that the so-called homeostatic drives can be "externalized" (Hall, 1961, pp. 45–49).

Secondary reinforcement looks more promising. It has already played a prominent role in bolstering Hull's learning theory, based on the satisfaction of bodily needs. According to this theory a response is learned if it is closely followed by the reduction of a drive; this is known as primary reinforcement. But the response can also be strengthened if it produces a stimulus *associated* with drive reduction; i.e., a *secondary reinforcer*. So a hungry rat at a choice point will learn to choose the path to a food box even if it is prevented from eating by a wire screen (Schlosberg & Pratt, 1956). So, too, a hostess may keep her hungry guests hanging around an extra hour if she lets the aroma of a casserole waft from the kitchen.

Our concern is whether a secondary reinforcer can achieve independence of its origins. That means, first of all, continuing to function in the absence of the original class of drives. The rats I just mentioned dropped to chance scores after they were fed. More experiments are needed, but so far we have no convincing evidence that satiated animals find food signals rewarding (Myers, 1958).

Second, an autonomous secondary reinforcer, unlike ordinary conditioned stimuli, would have to maintain itself indefinitely after the primary satisfier was withdrawn. Serious attempts have been made to render secondary reinforcers immune to extinction. At the empirical level Zimmerman (1959) first trained rats at a starting signal to go down a runway to food on a partial reinforcement schedule. He then removed the food and trained them in the start box on a bar pressing response that occasionally produced the signal and opened the door to the runway. This procedure resulted in thousands of responses over 10 to 14 daily sessions after food rewards had been discontinued. Such persistence, he ventured, "offers a close approximation at the animal level to the 'functional autonomy' . . . hypothesized as sometimes characteristic of human behavior [p. 353]."

Further studies of the "Zimmerman effect" (Wike, Platt, & Knowles, 1962; Wike, Platt, & Scott, 1963), however, have cast serious doubt on the role of secondary reinforcement in his results. Untrained control groups given the same partial reinforcement for bar pressing responded as persistently as those that had been previously trained to food. It would seem that release from the box, not a food-associated runway, was the effective reward. I mention these studies in some detail because in a sense they epitomize the thesis to follow shortly.

At the theoretical level Skinner (1953) has proposed another solution, the "generalized reinforcer." *Multiconditioned reinforcer* would be more accurate, since Skinner is talking about a learned reinforcer based on more than a single unlearned one. An obvious example is money; equally pertinent are social favors such as attention, approval, affection, and submissiveness. Such stimuli generally accompany the satisfaction of assorted needs. They remain effective because they can draw on a pool of deprivations; on any given occasion we are likely to have at least one complaint— flu or frustration or fatigue or an itch. But the flaw in this argument is clear: In the long run, after the generalized reinforcer has failed to satisfy all the needs it was based on, it must lose its power. Skinner himself seems aware of the defect and tries to remedy it by fiat. "Eventually," he writes, "generalized reinforcers are effective even though the primary reinforcers on which they are based no longer accompany them. . . . We get attention or approval for its own sake [p. 81]." Functional autonomy again!

Earlier in his discussion, however, Skinner makes a more cogent conjecture. Speaking of the "sensory feedback" from controlling the environment, he suggests that some of its reinforcing effect may be innate. A baby shaking its rattle is getting all the reinforcement it needs simply from "making the world behave."

I shall try to convince you that Skinner's guess carries more weight today than it did when he made it. Since you are probably already convinced that neither drive conditioning nor secondary reinforcement can transform visceral needs into social motives, I may as well start now.

"NEW LOOK" IN MOTIVATION THEORY

The development I speak of was foreshadowed years ago by Woodworth's (1918) contention that capacity provides its own motivation and by Karl Bühler's (1924) concept of "function pleasure." In the same vein Diamond

(1939) pointed out "a neglected aspect of motivation," proposing that the demand for stimulation was a fundamental property of organisms. Woodworth (1947) asserted a "will to perceive" at the same time that Murphy (1947) was making a strong case for adding activity drives and sensory drives to the visceral variety. But it was not until experimenters began to produce supporting evidence that the idea took hold. Today we can work with a broader base of unconditioned motivation. We look to the external rather than the internal milieu for many of the instigators and reinforcers of behavior; it is easier to think of responses as directed outward rather than merely pushed from within. In case you doubt this statement let me run over briefly some of the evidence I have in mind.

Evidence

1. CONTACT RECEPTORS A number of stimuli not obviously drive reducing have been nominated for the list of primary positive reinforcers. (*a*) Saccharine, a nonnutritive substance, has proved rewarding to rats (Sheffield & Roby, 1950). It would seem that it must taste good. (*b*) Motherless infant monkeys find comfort in clinging to terry-cloth models that have never provided milk (Harlow & Zimmerman, 1959). (*c*) Sexually naive male rats are reinforced by intromission with a female without reducing drive through ejaculation (Whalen, 1961). Aside from the question of secondary reinforcement, however, these stimuli may strike you as too "biological" to carry us far. Tastes and touches are likely to be loaded with affect. So let us look further.

2. DISTANCE RECEPTORS Mounting evidence shows that distance receptors can also supply unconditioned positive reinforcement. A striking example is *imprinting*, most clearly demonstrated in birds. As you all know, newly hatched goslings, ducklings, and chicks are prone to follow the first moving object they see, whether it is their mother or a red cube or Konrad Lorenz. What is more, their following increases for a while in vigor and persistence (Jaynes, 1956), and this implies positive reinforcement. But imprinting is so close to instinct that one tends to put it in a special category. Another example is *sensory reinforcement*. Mice and rats show a marked rise in rate of bar pressing when its only effect is to turn on a weak light that has never been paired with need reduction (Kish, 1955; Marx, Henderson, & Roberts, 1955). Mice with four platforms to choose from prefer to step on the one that moves and clicks (Kish & Antonitis, 1956).

3. MANIPULATION AND EXPLORATION The rising flood of experiments on inquisitive behavior has been better publicized. Harlow's (1953b) monkeys needed no reward to induce them to pull mechanical puzzles apart. Köhler's genius ape Sultan had great difficulty in joining two sticks *to reach a banana*, but when Schiller (1957) gave adult chimpanzees two sticks *to play with*, 19 out of 20 joined them within 15 minutes. Butler's (1953) monkeys in solitary confinement learned which colored card would let them look out of the window. Nor are primates the only explorers. Since the work of Montgomery (1952) and Glanzer (1953) we know why rats so frequently alternate at a choice point. It is not to exercise a fresh set of muscles

but to examine a fresh set of stimuli.

4. "IRRATIONAL" FEARS   Not all stimulus patterns are attractive, however; some appear to be aversive, even though never paired with pain. Rats hesitate to come out of holes into strange places (Welker, 1957). Some of Hebb's (1946) chimpanzees were thrown into a panic by the sight of a clay model of a chimpanzee's head. Melzack's (1952) dogs showed fear of a horse skin, especially if it was draped over a sofa.

5. STIMULUS DEPRIVATION   Finally let me remind you of the recent studies, starting in Hebb's laboratory, on the effects of severe sensory restriction in human adults (cited by Fiske, 1961). Subjects were required to spend many consecutive hours in isolation, lying on a bed, with external stimulation reduced to a minimum. All bodily needs were provided for. Yet most subjects found the experience extremely unpleasant and some found it so distressing that they asked to be released. Ordinarily we find ways of relieving boredom, like hunger, before it becomes acute. If all outlets are cut off the drive may become almost intolerable.

Theory

Naturally these findings have released a wave of activity on the theoretical front. Harlow (1953a) launched a vigorous attack on the doctrine that traced all motives to metabolic drives. Woodworth (1958) now had fresh ammunition for his "behavior-primacy" theory: "that all behavior is directed primarily toward dealing with the environment [p. 102]." After years of observing primate behavior, Nissen (1954) held that every tissue has a primary drive to perform its function, the eyes to see, the brain to know. More recently White (1959) proposed that much of behavior is motivated solely by its *effectance* in changing the environment. These and other writers urge us to recognize that there are extraorganic needs as basic as those arising from the viscera.

It is interesting to see that behavior theorists are not alone in this movement. White noted a parallel trend in psychoanalytic theory. Freud's idea of a reality-oriented ego subservient to the erotic and aggressive drives of the id could be considered a counterpart of Hull's concept of habits energized by primitive drives. On the other hand, Hartmann's (1958) version of the ego, with its adaptive functions, developing independently of instinctual conflicts, is comparable with Woodworth's emphasis on interaction with the external environment. So, too, is Erikson's (1950) interpretation of the stages of development in childhood: The oral, anal, and phallic zones represent not so much successive outlets of the libido as means of relating to parent figures.

In behavior theory, as in psychoanalysis, the old guard has yielded ground but slowly. For all its defects, Hull's system contained a definite mechanism for the conditioning of drives to new stimuli and of new goals to drives. We cannot afford to discard an inadequate theory unless a more promising one can be found. What does the New Look have to offer? A cluster of theories has appeared; they overlap quite a bit and are more or less rudimentary, but they represent a healthy beginning. This is not the place to review them, especially since they have been treated elsewhere (Fiske & Maddi, 1961; Glanzer, 1958; White, 1959). Instead I should like to give you my present view of this matter, quite informally and without claiming originality or crediting all sources.

As we have seen, many of the activities of organisms appear to be aroused by and directed toward the environment with little help from the viscera. These activities may be grouped along several dimensions, that serve both to order the data and to identify possible mechanisms. They suggest, that is, a number of mediating processes—let us call them *exogenous motives*—each process or motive having a different function in dealing with the environment. The three dimensions I have in mind, with the motives and functions they subsume, are as follows:

1. A *perceptual-motor* dimension. Instead of lumping the exploratory behaviors I suggest that we distinguish between tendencies to explore and to manipulate the environment. An unfamiliar situation may move an organism to inspect it more closely, or novel objects may induce it to lift or squeeze or pound or rearrange them. We may call the first motive *curiosity* and assign it the function of *learning* the environment (Woodworth, 1958). The second motive is what White (1959) called *effectance*, and its function is to *control* the environment.

2. An *affective* dimension. No matter how we try to evade the issue, it is hard to pretend that animals do not find some perceptual experiences preferable to others. What experimental work there is (for example, Pfaffmann, 1961; Schneirla, 1959; Warren, 1963; Young, 1955) confirms our homemade convictions. There is little doubt that cats prefer soft cushions to hard floors, warm hearths to cold baths, and head rubbing to tail pulling. To make the assumption explicit let us borrow from common usage the terms *attraction* and *aversion*, and assign to them the function of *improving* the environment.

3. A *quantitative* dimension. We have seen that extraordinary stimulus patterns, such as a head without a body or a body without movement, may disturb a chimpanzee to the point of attack or flight. On the other hand, severely restricted or monotonous stimulation, if prolonged, can be a form of torture. A number of writers (Berlyne, 1963; Fiske & Maddi, 1961; Hebb, 1955; Leuba, 1955) have advocated the principle, more inclusive than drive reduction, of an optimal level of excitation. Such a concept could be a handy tool for explaining why rats turn on lights, monkeys open windows, children play, and adults visit museums—or why so many people read about space flights and so few volunteer.

There are two difficulties with the hypothesis, at least in some versions. For one thing, it implies a positive feedback that engineers tell us could cause serious trouble. For another, if reduced stimulation lowers the drive level below its optimum, whence comes the energy for the subject's increasing complaints? Berlyne (1963) has met these objections by assuming that below some middle value falling stimulation sends the arousal level *up*, not down.

However this question is settled, we may designate two more exogenous motives: *emotional shock*, aroused when stimulation exceed's the organism's tolerance; and *boredom*, produced when it falls below the level required for smooth functioning. Together the two motives serve to regulate the impact of the environment.

The foregoing treatment raises a basic question: Is there some property of stimulation common to the exogenous motives? Students of exploratory behavior attribute it to novelty, which they go on to define in different words. Information theorists would call it uncertainty (Dember & Earl, 1957) and behavior theorists, conflict (Berlyne, 1963), but both would agree that the crucial feature is a discrepancy between what is expected and what is observed. The same property takes care of the quantitative dimension, for if the discrepancy is too great the result is emotional shock, and if it is too little the result is boredom. As to effectance, its essential condition may also be reduced to a discrepancy, in this case between the situation now and the situation after a response.

That leaves the affective dimension. With so many likes and dislikes to be accounted for, it is not obvious how a common factor of discrepancy could play much part. But the hypothesis is well worth testing. We are reminded of Schneirla's (1959) view that mild stimulation leads to approach and intense stimulation, to withdrawal. Directly pertinent, of course, is McClelland and Clark's (McClelland, Atkinson, Clark, & Lowell, 1953) theory of affect, in which pleasantness and unpleasantness depend on the discrepancy between a sensory quality and the adaptation level of the organism.

To give this picture a biological frame, let us assume that the central nervous system has the primary function of correlating stimuli and integrating appropriate responses. Its business is, as Woodworth (1958) put it, to "learn the environment." In the course of life it does so by interiorizing the external world, both as perceived and as altered by the organism's own reactions. Here I refer to what Bartlett (1932) called a *schema*; call it a life space (Lewin, 1936) if you prefer, or a situation-set (Woodworth, 1937), or a cognitive map (Tolman, 1948), or an image (Miller, Galanter, & Pribram, 1960). By any name, such a construct can be built and maintained only by a continuing transaction with the environment. To do its job the brain must have materials to work with, sensory input to organize, information to process (Glanzer, 1958). It is at critical points in this transaction that exogenous motives arise: when novel stimuli call for revision of the schema, or when radical incongruities threaten its stability, or when a routine conforms too closely to the schema for too long.

IMPLICATIONS FOR FUNCTIONAL AUTONOMY

It is time to return to Allport's problem to see if we are now in a better position to solve it. The question is whether exogenous motives have the properties Allport sought to embody in the concept of functional autonomy. Let us look at three such properties with that question in mind.

1. Functional autonomy stressed the importance of social motives; the need for approval, prestige, superiority, belonging, and the like. This is just what the concept of exogenous motives would lead us to expect. The most varied and consequently most exciting stimulation comes from other organisms. As far as we know, this may be true for all species.

On the whole, though it is hard to give the statement precise meaning, social interactions probably become more important as we go up the phylogenetic scale. More is probably involved here than varied stimulation, but this factor should be recognized. In the long infancy and childhood of primates, mothers give nourishment, parent figures caress and slap, playmates provide reciprocal response. As the human child approaches maturity and no longer needs parental care, he finds himself no less dependent on other persons in his efforts to predict, to control, and to improve his environment. Backed by vast powers of reward and punishment, small wonder if social agents are the most compelling source of exogenous motivation in his life.

2. "Functionally autonomous motives" were by definition learned. They started as subgoals or instrumental acts and later were supposed to become ultimate objectives in their own right. No such transmutation is imputed to exogenous motives. On the contrary, there is enough evidence of their independence of hunger and fear (Harlow 1953b; Montgomery, 1953, 1955; Schiller, 1957) to make it extremely unlikely that investigatory behavior was originally a search for food or security. But in another sense curiosity, effectance, and boredom *are* learned, or at least are products of learning. We have assumed that they are evoked, essentially, by some kind or degree of departure from a learned schema. Hebb (1949, 1955) emphasized this point in his discussion of fear, citing the infant chimpanzee frightened by seeing one familiar attendant wearing the equally familiar coat of another. So whenever an individual "builds a new wing" on his schema he sets the stage for a new interest, aversion, or indifference.

3. Functionally autonomous motives, as their name implies, were not subject to extinction. In this respect exogenous motives are fully qualified to take their place. Play is intrinsically rewarding; so is finding a bird's nest or solving an equation. Trips to the candy jar will cease when the jar is empty, but the desire for candy lives on. True, all the exogenous motives except boredom can be satiated to some extent as new learning reduces whatever discrepancy aroused them. So it might seem that we have merely exchanged one frailty for another. But the argument would hold only if we had exhausted the possible varieties of experience, an extremity seldom reached outside of concentration camps and zoos. Most of the earth's human inhabitants, cheerfully ignoring the specter of overpopulation, do not face psychic satiation as an immediate threat. Artists, composers, and advertisers continue to explore their media for fresh combinations to titillate or appall us. Scientists race one another into the unknown. Ordinary people find that even the companion of a lifetime is never completely predictable.

SUMMARY

To summarize, we have seen that traditional drive theory could account for only a fraction of animal and human motivation. Its innate drives were too few and its acquired rewards too transitory. The concept of functional autonomy of motives did little more than stress the inadequacy of established doctrine.

We have noted the increasing acceptance of a class of exogenous motives, long recognized but ignored, concerned with attempts of organisms to predict and control their environments. We have adopted the view that an organism approaches and withdraws, explores and manipulates, as a function of specific differences between the present situation and the expectancies built into his schema of the world. I believe this view deserves consideration as a substitute for Allport's. In a literal sense exogenous motives *are* functionally autonomous; since they began that way, a *theory* of functional autonomy becomes superfluous.

A final word: At first glance terms like curiosity and effectance look like instincts revisited. At second glance I see no cause for alarm in this "return of the repressed." The instincts of old were stigmatized as barriers to research; today's "instincts" have opened up a new and exciting area to investigation. They give me a twinge of hope that we may have, if not a key, then the mold of a key to unlock one mystery of mind: the persistence and individuality of human motives.

REFERENCES

ALLPORT, G. W.   The functional autonomy of motives. *Amer. J. Psychol.*, 1937, 50, 141–156.

BARTLETT, F. C.   *Remembering: A study in experimental and social psychology.* New York: Macmillan, 1932.

BERLYNE, D. E.   Motivational problems raised by exploratory and epistemic behavior. In S. Koch (Ed.), *Psychology: A study of a science.* Vol. 5. New York: McGraw-Hill, 1963. Pp. 284–364.

BÜHLER, K.   *Die geistige Entwicklung des Kindes.* (4th ed.) Jena: Gustav Fischer, 1924.

BUTLER, R. A.   Discrimination learning by rhesus monkeys to visual-exploration motivation. *J. comp. physiol. Psychol.*, 1953, 46, 95–98.

DEMBER, W. N., & EARL, R. W.   Analysis of exploratory, manipulatory, and curiosity behaviors. *Psychol. Rev.*, 1957, 64, 91–96.

DIAMOND, S.   A neglected aspect of motivation. *Sociometry*, 1939, 2, 77–85.

ERIKSON, E. H.   *Childhood and society.* New York: Norton, 1950.

FISKE, D. W.   Effects of monotonous and restricted stimulation. In D. W. Fiske & S. R. Maddi (Eds.), *Functions of varied experience.* Homewood, Ill.: Dorsey Press, 1961. Pp. 106–144.

FISKE, D. W., & MADDI, S. R.   A conceptual framework. In D. W. Fiske & S. R. Maddi (Eds.), *Functions of varied experience.* Homewood, Ill.: Dorsey Press, 1961. Pp. 11–56.

GLANZER, M.   The role of stimulus satiation in spontaneous alternation. *J. exp. Psychol.*, 1953, 45, 387–393.

GLANZER, M.   Curiosity, exploratory drive, and stimulus satiation. *Psychol. Bull,* 1958, 55, 302–315.

HALL, J. F.   *Psychology of motivation.* Chicago: Lippincott, 1961.

HARLOW, H. F.   Mice, monkeys, men, and motives. *Psychol. Rev.*, 1953, 60, 23–32. (a)

HARLOW, H. F.   Motivation as a factor in the acquisition of new responses. In, *Current theory and research in motivation: A symposium.* Lincoln: Univer. Nebraska Press, 1953. Pp. 24–49. (b)

HARLOW, H. F., & ZIMMERMAN, R. R. Affectional responses in the infant monkey. *Science*, 1959, 130, 421–432.

HARTMANN, H.   *Ego psychology and the problem of adaptation.* New York: International Universities Press, 1958.

HEBB, D. O.   On the nature of fear. *Psychol. Rev.*, 1946, 53, 259–276.

HEBB, D. O.   *The organization of behavior.* New York: Wiley, 1949.

HEBB, D. O.   Drives and the C.N.S. (conceptual nervous system). *Psychol. Rev.*, 1955, 62, 243–254.

JAYNES, J.   Imprinting: The interaction of learned and innate behavior. *J. comp. physiol. Psychol.*, 1956, 49, 201–206.

Kish, G. B.   Learning when the onset of illumination is used as reinforcing stimulus. *J. comp. physiol. Psychol.*, 1955, 48, 261–264.

Kish, G. B., & Antonitis, J. J.   Unconditioned operant behavior in two homozygous strains of mice. *J. genet. Psychol.*, 1956, 88, 121–129.

Leuba, C.   Toward some integration of learning theories: The concept of optimal stimulation. *Psychol. Rep.*, 1955, 1, 27–33.

Lewin, K.   *Principles of topological psychology*. New York: McGraw-Hill, 1936.

McClelland, D. C.   Functional autonomy of motives as an extinction phenomenon. *Psychol. Rev.*, 1942, 49, 272–283.

McClelland, D. C., Atkinson, J. W., Clark, R. A., & Lowell, E. L.   *The achievement motive*. New York: Appleton-Century-Crofts, 1953.

Marx, M. H., Henderson, R. L., & Roberts, C. L.   Positive reinforcement of the bar-pressing response by a light stimulus following dark operant pretests with no aftereffect. *J. comp. physiol. Psychol.*, 1955, 48, 73–76.

Melzack, R.   Irrational fears in the dog. *Canad. J. Psychol.*, 1952, 6, 141–147.

Miller, G. A., Galanter, E., & Pribram, K. H.   *Plans and the structure of behavior*. New York: Holt, Rinehart and Winston, 1960.

Miller, N. E.   Studies of fear as an acquirable drive: I. Fear as motivation and fear-reduction as reinforcement in the learning of new responses. *J. exp. Psychol.*, 1948, 38, 89–101.

Montgomery, K. C.   A test of two explanations of spontaneous alternation. *J. comp. physiol. Psychol.*, 1952, 45, 287–293.

Montgomery, K. C.   The effect of the hunger and thirst drives upon exploratory behavior. *J. comp. physiol. Psychol.*, 1953, 46, 315–319.

Montgomery, K. C.   The relation between fear induced by novel stimulation and exploratory behavior. *J. comp. physiol. Psychol.*, 1955, 48, 254–260.

Murphy, G.   *Personality: A biosocial approach to origins and structure*. New York: Harper & Row, 1947.

Myers, J. L.   Secondary reinforcement: A review of recent experimentation. *Psychol. Bull.*, 1958, 55, 284–301.

Nissen, H. W.   The nature of the drive as innate determinant of behavioral organization. In M. R. Jones (Ed.), *Nebraska symposium on motivation: 1954*. Lincoln: Univer. Nebraska Press, 1954. Pp. 281–321.

Pfaffmann, C.   The sensory and motivating properties of the sense of taste. In M. R. Jones (Ed.), *Nebraska symposium on motivation: 1961*. Lincoln: Univer. Nebraska Press, 1961. Pp. 71–108.

Rethlingshafer, D.   Experimental evidence for functional autonomy of motives. *Psychol. Rev.*, 1943, 50, 397–407.

Schiller, P. H.   Innate motor action as a basis of learning. In C. H. Schiller (Ed.), *Instinctive behavior: The development of a modern concept*. New York: International Universities Press, 1957. Pp. 264–287.

Schlosberg, H., & Pratt, C. H.   The secondary reward value of inaccessible food for hungry and satiated rats. *J. comp. physiol. Psychol.*, 1956, 49, 149–152.

Schneirla, T. C.   An evolutionary and developmental theory of biphasic processes underlying approach and withdrawal. In M. R. Jones (Ed.), *Nebraska symposium on motivation: 1959*. Lincoln: Univer. Nebraska Press, 1959. Pp. 1–42.

Sheffield, F. S., & Roby, T. B.   Reward value of a non-nutritive sweet taste. *J. comp. physiol. Psychol.*, 1950, 43, 471–481.

Skinner, B. F.   *Science and human behavior*. New York: Macmillan, 1953.

Solomon, R. F., & Brush, E. S.   Experimentally derived conceptions of anxiety and aversion. In M. R. Jones (Ed.), *Nebraska symposium on motivation: 1956*. Lincoln: Univer. Nebraska Press, 1956. Pp. 212–305.

Solomon, R. L., & Wynne, L. C.   Traumatic avoidance learning: The principles of anxiety conservation and partial irreversibility. *Psychol. Rev.*, 1954, 61, 353–385.

Tolman, E. C.   Cognitive maps in rats

and men. *Psychol. Rev.*, 1948, **55**, 189–208.

WARREN, R. P. Preference aversion in mice to bitter substance. *Science*, 1963, **140**, 808–809.

WELKER, W. I. "Free" versus "forced" exploration of a novel situation by rats. *Psychol. Rep.*, 1957, **3**, 95–108.

WHALEN, R. E. Effects of mounting without intromission and intromission without ejaculation on sexual behavior and maze learning. *J. comp. physiol. Psychol.*, 1961, **54**, 409–415.

WHITE, R. W. Motivation reconsidered: The concept of competence. *Psychol. Rev.*, 1959, **66**, 297–333.

WIKE, E. L., PLATT, J. R., & KNOWLES, J. M. The reward value of getting out of a starting box: Further extensions of Zimmerman's work. *Psychol. Rec.*, 1962, **12**, 397–400.

WIKE, E. L., PLATT, J. R., & SCOTT, D. Drive and secondary reinforcement: Fur-

ther extensions of Zimmerman's work. *Psychol. Rec.*, 1963, **13**, 45–49.

WOODWORTH, R. S. *Dynamic psychology*. New York: Columbia Univer. Press, 1918.

WOODWORTH, R. S. Situation-and-goal set. *Amer. J. Psychol.*, 1937, **50**, 130–140.

WOODWORTH, R. S. Reënforcement of perception. *Amer. J. Psychol.*, 1947, **60**, 119–124.

WOODWORTH, R. S. *Dynamics of behavior*. New York: Holt, Rinehart and Winston, 1958.

YOUNG, P. T. The role of hedonic processes in motivation. In M. R. Jones (Ed.), *Nebraska symposium on motivation: 1955*. Lincoln: Univer. Nebraska Press, 1955. Pp. 193–238.

ZIMMERMAN, D. W. Sustained performance in rats based on secondary reinforcement. *J. comp. physiol. Psychol.*, 1959, **52**, 353–358.

2. THE EFFECTIVENESS OF SOCIAL REINFORCEMENT FOLLOWING TWO CONDITIONS OF SOCIAL DEPRIVATION *

Harold W. Stevenson and Richard D. Odom

Gewirtz and Baer (1958a, 1958b) have demonstrated that the effectiveness of social reinforcement in modifying children's performance is increased by a brief period of social isolation preceding the experimental task. The results are interpreted as indicating that the effectiveness of a social reinforcer is increased by its own deprivation.

Another interpretation of these findings is possible. Isolation resulted in the deprivation of not only social but also of other types of stimuli. The chil-

dren, therefore, may have been subjected to general stimulus deprivation rather than merely to deprivation of social stimuli. As a consequence, the effectiveness of social stimuli as reinforcers may be reduced when other types of stimuli are available during the deprivation period. One approach to determining the degree to which the increased effectiveness of social reinforcement is due specifically to the deprivation of social stimuli would be to isolate subjects in a setting providing a wide variety of other types

* Reprinted from the *Journal of Abnormal and Social Psychology*, 1962, 65: 429–431, with permission of the senior author and the American Psychological Association. This research was supported by a grant from the National Institute of Mental Health.

of stimuli and to compare their performance with that occurring in a condition where other subjects were isolated without such stimuli.

This study investigates the effect of social reinforcement on children's performance in a simple operant task following three conditions: a control condition with no isolation; a "toy" condition in which the subject is left alone in a room filled with unusual and interesting toys with which he can play freely for a 15-minute period; an isolation condition in which the subject is left alone in the room with no toys for 15 minutes.

METHOD

Subjects

The subjects were 30 boys and 30 girls attending kindergarten, first, and second grades of the Laboratory School of the University of Minnesota. The subjects were above average in intelligence and socioeconomic status.

Apparatus

EXPERIMENTAL TASK The apparatus was a red rectangular box, 22 inches long, 16 inches wide, and 12 inches deep. Two 8-inch square sunken bins were located on the top of the box. The right bin was covered by a Masonite plate with six ⅝-inch holes randomly placed on its surface. The floor of the right bin was covered with foam rubber and sloped toward a small aperture. As a marble passed through the aperture it activated a microswitch which in turn activated an electric counter. The left bin was filled with approximately 600 marbles of different colors.

The apparatus was placed on a child-sized table in an 8 foot × 7 foot room. The only other furnishing in the room was a chair for the experimenter behind the apparatus.

PRETRAINING TASK The pretraining room was 10.5 feet long and 10 feet wide and was located two rooms away from the experimental room. It contained two tables, two chairs, a sink, windows with drapes drawn and a one-way vision mirror.

For subjects in the Toy condition the tables and chairs were filled with toys. The toys included a drumming clown, a drinking rabbit, a rocking-tele-phoning bear, a balloon-blowing bear, a typewriting doll, a bouncing bird, a butterfly-chasing duck, a spiral shooting gun, a large stuffed bear, a stuffed rabbit, a beach ball, and a xylophone. All except the last seven toys were powered by batteries and were equipped with 2-foot extension cords with switches which could be easily operated by the children.

Procedure

The subjects were randomly divided into three groups with an equal number of boys and girls in each group. For the two pretraining groups a 15-minute period in the pretraining room proceded the experimental task. In the Toy group the pretraining room contained the toys described above. In the Isolation group no toys were present. The preliminary 15-minute period was eliminated for the control group.

The subjects were obtained individually by the experimenter from their classroom. While the experimenter escorted the subject to the laboratory room, the experimenter attempted to gain rapport with the subject by talking about school and related matters. The experimenter was a female elementary teacher trained for the experiment.

PRETRAINING TASK   For subjects in the Toy and Isolation groups the experimenter approached the experimental room and told the subject:

Now the game is in that room right there, but I have to get it ready. You wait in here and I will come and get you when the game is ready.

The experimenter walked with the subject into the pretraining room.

For the Isolation group the experimenter told the subject:

As soon as I get the game ready I will come back and get you. You wait in here until I get the game ready.

The experimenter went out of the room leaving the door partly open.

For the Toy group the experimenter told the subject:

I have a lot of toys in here and you can play with them while you are waiting. Play with any of the toys you want to and have fun.

The experimenter demonstrated how one of the mechanical toys worked. Again, the experimenter left the door partly open.

As the experimenter left the pretraining room she started a stopwatch and went to a hallway from which she could observe the subject's behavior through the one-way mirror of the pretraining room. At the conclusion of the 15-minute period the experimenter re-turned to the pretraining room and told the subject:

The game is ready. You can come with me now.

EXPERIMENTAL   TASK   The experimenter took the subject to the experimental room and said:

This is a game called Marble-in-the-Hole. I'll tell you how to play it. See these marbles. Well, they go in these holes like this. [The experimenter demonstrated.] You pick up the marbles one at a time and put them in these holes. I'll tell you when to stop. Remember, pick them up one at a time, and I'll tell you when to stop.

The task was concluded after 7 minutes.

After an average of every 15 responses the experimenter made a supportive comment about the subject's performance. The comments were delivered after every tenth, fifteenth, or twentieth response according to a prearranged random schedule. Six statements were used in a random order: Fine, Very good, That's fine, You're really good, Good, and Swell.

The experimenter counted the subject's responses in order to follow the reinforcement schedule, but the responses were also recorded electrically for each successive minute.

RESULTS

The score used in the analysis of the results was a difference score obtained by subtracting the number of responses made during the first minute of the task from that for each successive minute. This procedure was adopted to reduce the effect of individual differences in response rate.

The average number of responses during the first minute of the game was 25.8. A 2×3 analysis of variance with entries for sex of subject and condition resulted in no significant main effects and in a nonsignificant interaction ($Fs < 1.00$). Performance during the first minute of the game may be assumed to be approximately the same in all conditions.

The major results of the study are summarized in Figure 1, which presents

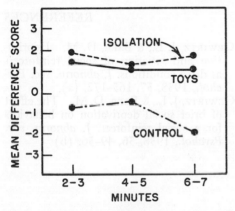

Figure 1. The average difference score for each group for 2-minute intervals following the first minute.

the average difference score obtained by each group for 2-minute intervals after the first minute of the task. The highest scores occur in the Isolation group and the lowest in the Control group. The scores of subjects in the Toy group were slightly below those of the Isolation subjects. A facilitating effect, which persisted throughout the task, was evident in the Isolation and Toy groups. The subjects in the Control group showed a decrement in performance after the first minute of the task which increased during the last 2 minutes.

These data were subjected to a 2×3 analysis of variance. The F associated with condition was significant at the .05 level ($F = 3.76$, $df = 2/54$). The F associated with sex of subject was not significant ($F < 1.00$), nor was the interaction term ($F = 2.64$, $df = 2/54$, $p > .05$).

DISCUSSION

The toys appeared to be very attractive to the subjects and they played with them with enthusiasm. When no toys were present the subjects sat quietly, sighed, peered around the room, and showed other indications of impatience and boredom. Although some subjects in the Toy group showed some of these types of behavior towards the end of the 15-minute period, the behavior of the two groups was in general quite dissimilar.

The greater effectiveness of social reinforcement in modifying performance in the Isolation group compared to the Control group corroborates the results of Gewirtz and Baer (1958a, 1958b). The greater effectiveness of a female experimenter with boys than with girls found by Gewirtz and Baer was not obtained; however, older subjects were used in the present study.

The presence of other stimuli during the isolation period did not result in a significant decrease in the effectiveness of social reinforcement over that obtained when no toys were present. Although the difference scores for the subjects in the Toy group are consistently below those in the Isolation group, the difference is not significant ($t < 1.00$). Perhaps with a larger number of subjects or with a more sensitive measure of performance a significant difference would emerge. For the present, however, it may be tentatively concluded that the greater effectiveness of social reinforcement following isolation is primarily dependent upon deprivation of social stimuli, rather than on more general stimulus deprivation.

SUMMARY

Three groups of elementary school children were presented with a simple operant task in which the insertion of marbles into a series of holes was verbally reinforced. The first group of subjects played alone for 15 minutes in a room containing a variety of interesting toys. The second group was left alone for 15 minutes with no toys. A control group received no pre-experimental treatment. Analysis of variance indicated a significant difference among conditions. The Isolation group showed the greatest increase in response rate after the first minute of the task and the Control group the lowest. The performance of the Toy group did not differ significantly from that of the Isolation group. The results are interpreted as tentatively supporting the hypothesis that the increased effectiveness of social reinforcement following isolation is primarily dependent upon the deprivation of social stimuli rather than upon more general stimulus deprivation.

REFERENCES

GEWIRTZ, J. L., & BAER, D. M.   Deprivation and satiation of social reinforcers as drive conditions. *J. abnorm. soc. Psychol.*, 1958, **57**, 165–172. (a)

GEWIRTZ, J. L., & BAER, D. M.   The effect of brief social deprivation on behaviors for a social reinforcer. *J. abnorm. soc. Psychol.*, 1958, **56**, 49–56. (b)

3.   VOLUNTEERING AND THE RECALL OF INTERRUPTED TASKS *

Donald Ross Green

The purpose of this study was to clarify the circumstances which promote or inhibit the Zeigarnik effect.

One common explanation of the results obtained in studies using Zeigarnik's technique is that "task involved" subjects tend to recall a larger proportion of interrupted than completed tasks (the Zeigarnik effect) whereas this tendency is reversed among "ego involved" subjects. Taken at face value the data do not entirely support this interpretation. For example, Zeigarnik (1927), Marrow (1938), and Lewis and Franklin (1944) each obtained a strong Zeigarnik effect under circumstances that may be considered task orienting, but Glixman (1949), and Gilmore (1954) did not. However, following a suggestion made by Atkinson (1955)

* Reprinted from the *Journal of Abnormal and Social Psychology*, 1963, 66: 397–401, with permission of the author and the American Psychological Association.

it may be that the differences in results stem from the differing ways in which the services of the subjects were obtained. Glixman and Gilmore both used students who were required to participate as part of a course. Marrow's subjects were all volunteers. Apparently some of Zeigarnik's subjects were volunteers while other like those of Lewis and Franklin were unaware that they were subjects in an experiment. If volunteers in contrast to nonvolunteers tend to become task involved more readily and ego involved less readily the difficulties created by the data for such an explanation would be reduced.

A task involved subject is generally described as one whose goal during performance is the solution of the problem or completion of the task, not primarily as a means to some other goal but as an end in itself. Conditions tending to increase the prominence of this goal in a subject's hierarchy of goals may be called task orienting. It seems quite reasonable to assume that many volunteers are curious about and interested in the things that they are going to be asked to do; many of the tasks given experimental subjects are interesting and even the duller or more unpleasant ones frequently can be thought of as challenging. It is suggested that among volunteers this view of psychological experiments is common, pretty much regardless of the specific circumstances they envisage. If so, it is logical to assert that volunteers are particularly likely to respond to task orienting cues, that is, they are particularly likely to become task involved.

By the same token one can argue that some individuals do not volunteer because of a lack of interest in such things, or an antipathy toward them.

To the extent this is important, nonvolunteers should become task involved less readily than volunteers.

A description of the ego involved subject as one whose dominant goals include defending, maintaining, or enhancing his private self-esteem and/or his public prestige, encompasses most of the attributes of ego involvement cited in the relevant studies. Thus, one may call ego orienting those conditions which make it appear to a subject that a poor performance will be a reflection on his standing in his own eyes or in the eyes of others. Such concerns may be one reason some people do not volunteer; one might expect more nonvolunteers than volunteers to be suspicious of the experimenter's motives and to perceive threat of this sort more readily. Therefore it is probable that nonvolunteers are particularly likely to respond to ego orienting cues.

It should be noted that when a whole group is drafted to serve as subjects, some of these "nonvolunteers" can be considered volunteers since they would have volunteered if given a chance. Hence these involuntary "volunteers" may behave like actual volunteers.

However, a subject required to serve, even one who would have volunteered if given a chance, has more reason to suspect he is in a threatening situation than a subject free to participate or not as he chooses. For example, if during the experiment the experimenter suggests performance scores may become part of the subject's permanent records, the vounteer, who knows that some members of the class are not participating, has the choice of assuming that the experimenter is being gratuitously unfair or that the experimenter is trying to deceive him for experimental purposes. The subject meeting a course requirement may still consider it unfair, but he has much less reason to doubt the experimenter's assertion and, in fact, may suspect some such thing whether implied or not. In short, being drafted can be an ego orienting cue and may reinforce other cues of this sort.

Thus, three categories of subjects may be distinguished: volunteers serving freely, volunteers required to serve, and nonvolunteers; these groups will be labeled F, R, and N, respectively. It is proposed that these three groups arranged in the order volunteers, required volunteers, and nonvolunteers will exhibit decreasing responsiveness to task orienting cues and increasing responsiveness to ego orienting cues.

It is further claimed that task involvement tends to induce the Zeigarnik effect and ego involvement its reverse. Therefore, of the three groups, the free volunteers should have the highest recall ratios (that is, number of interrupted tasks recalled to total number of tasks recalled) and the nonvolunteers the lowest ratios—regardless of orientation; the mean for Group R would then fall between those for F and N (first hypothesis). Also, task orienting situations should produce higher ratios than ego orienting situations within each of these three groups (second hypothesis). In general, task orientation should lead to ratios greater than .5 and ego orientation to ratios less than .5.

METHOD

Subjects

All subjects, 30 males and 66 females, were drawn from students in eight sections of an undergraduate course in Child Development at the University of California, Berkeley. In two sections of the course in the Fall semester and again in the Spring semester, the experimenter who was not known by the students, appeared in class and asked for volunteers for a psychological experiment which would take an hour at a time to be mutually determined. No further information was given. Sign-up sheets requesting name and choice of time were passed out. When they had all been collected a questionnaire asking for reasons for volunteering or not volunteering was distributed. These were collected, sign-up sheets were given to the nonvolunteers, and the class was told that participation was actually a course requirement. The whole procedure took about 20 minutes. When questioned about the volunteering routine the experimenter said only that it had been necessary in order to find out who would have volunteered. Group R was drawn from those draftees willing to serve, and Group N from those not willing to volunteer.

Those who had objection to participation were invited to see the experimenter privately. Five students in the Group N pool did so and were excused; the 15 from this same pool who missed their appointments were not pursued. No Group R student protested and the 7 who missed appointments were rescheduled. Results from 32 students in each of these two groups were used.

The 32 volunteers serving freely (Group F) were drawn from the four remaining sections of the course. Nine of these missed appointments but were rescheduled, some of them several times. Thus, although the subjects in this group were supposed to be left entirely free to participate or not as they chose, a number of them may have felt some pressure.

Testing occurred during a 4-week period beginning 5 days after the experimenter's appearance in class. The average delay for each group was a little over 2 weeks.

Materials

Twenty heterogeneous paper-and-pencil tasks taken with minor modifications from MacKinnon and Henle (1948) were used. Each task was on a separate sheet of paper with ample space for the subject to write or draw as directed.

Three different task orders were used in each experimental group. By dint of some juggling, equal numbers of interruptions and completions for each task in each group were achieved. Many subjects simply could not complete certain tasks as scheduled with the result that a perfect balance for each serial position could not be maintained in four of the six groups. A comparison with expected serial position effects on recall suggests this may have reduced the differences reported below very slightly. Alteration of the tasks during trial runs to reduce this problem proved unsuccessful.

Procedure

Subjects were tested individually seated across a table from the experimenter who questioned the subject about age, academic interests, major subject, and future plans; gave orienting instructions; presented tasks and task instructions one at a time; asked for verbal recall of the tasks; questioned the

subject about his perceptions of situation, tasks, interruptions, and recall; and explained the experiment to the subject. The procedure took an average of 50 minutes, about 40 of which were spent on the tasks.

For each subject, performance was interrupted on half the tasks scattered through the list by placing the next sheet over the one on which the subject was working and immediately giving the new directions. After the last task all sheets were picked up by the experimenter, stacked, and put in a drawer creating a brief pause after which recall began.

The subject could see that the experimenter was keeping a record but not what was being noted. Most subjects said they thought each task was being scored.

Orientation

Two different general instructions were used.[1] Both were modifications of the instructions used by Marrow (1938).

The task orienting instructions were almost the same as Marrow's Group I instructions but the word task was substituted for test and no mention of total score was made. These instructions emphasized that "We are interested in how rapidly and accurately each of these exercises can be completed . . ." and repeatedly mentioned speed, accuracy, and completion.

Ego orientation was also accomplished with Marrow's Group I instructions—but with some additions. A probable relationship between test

---

[1] A third set of instructions was also used with an additional 48 subjects. The data for these groups are not directly relevant to the hypotheses being considered here.

performance and success in various professions was asserted and the experimenter added that "Since you will probably be going into teaching or some professional field, you can see why we are interested in how successful you will be on these tests." A large majority of all subjects were, in fact, planning to teach. For task oriented, but not ego oriented, subjects the initial questions about plans and interests were accompanied by the statement that they were asked "only because one never knows what may be important."

The groups given these instructions will be called Group T and Group E, respectively. Sixteen subjects from each of the three volunteering groups (F, R, and N) were arbitrarily assigned to each of these orientation groups. Thus, a 3×2 design was obtained and the six subgroups may be labeled FT, NE, and so forth according to volunteering status and orientation.

Analysis of the Data

If degree of task involvement versus degree of ego involvement is a major variable in the determination of recall, the appropriate measure is the ratio of interrupted tasks recalled to total tasks recalled (Rosenzweig, 1952). Since for each subject 10 tasks were interrupted and 10 tasks were completed, a ratio greater than .5 indicates more interrupted tasks recalled. Comparisons among mean recall ratios using a variance analysis provide evidence relevant to the hypotheses.

The method of orthogonal comparisons, weighting Groups F, R, and N as $+1$, 0, -1, respectively, provides a test of the first hypothesis. This procedure assumes Group R is distinct from the other two groups. A comparison treating R like the other volunteers would use weights $+1$, $+1$, -2 and a comparison treating Group R like the other draftees would use weights $+2$, -1, -1. The test of the orientation main effects is a test of the second hypothesis. No significant interaction is suggested by the hypotheses.

RESULTS

Mean recall ratios are shown in Table 1 and the results of the analysis of variance in Table 2.

TABLE 1. MEAN RECALL RATIOS

Orien-tation	Volunteering			
	Free	Required	Non-volun-teers	Total
Task	.572	.554	.524	.550
Ego	.493	.480	.437	.470
Total	.533	.517	.480	

The orientation differences are reasonably large, consistent, and as predicted. Task orientation does tend to lead to the recall of more interrupted than completed tasks and ego orientation reverses this tendency. Needless to say, these are only tendencies; all six distributions overlap a great deal.

The differences among the volunteering groups are consistent, as predicted, and quite small. In fact, to claim significant variation due to volunteering differences involves a fair amount of risk. If one is willing to accept that risk then one can assert $F > R > N$ with

TABLE 2. ANALYSIS OF VARIANCE OF RECALL RATIOS

Source	SS	df	MS	F
Between groups	.1997	5	.0399	4.87[c]
Within groups	.7375	90	.0082	
Total	.9372	95		
Between groups				
Orientation	.1530	1	.1530	18.66[c]
Volunteering	.0460	2	.0230	2.80[a]
Interaction	.0007	2	.0004	0.05
Total	.1997	5		
Volunteering				
Predicted trend	.0436	1	.0436	5.32[b]
Deviations	.0024	1	.0024	0.29
Total	.0460	2		

[a] $p \leq .10$
[b] $p \leq .025$
[c] $p \leq .005$

some confidence since Table 2 indicates that almost all the volunteering variance is accounted for by the comparison used. However, it may be added that the comparison treating $F = R > N$, that is, using weights $+1, +1, -2$, would have been just about as good since the mean square for this comparison is .0421 ($F = 5.13$, $p < .05$), leaving only .0039 for deviations. On the other hand the comparison treating the draftees alike in contrast to Group F, that is, using weights $+2, -1, -1$, gives a mean square of .0245 ($F = 2.99$, $p > .10$) with a deviation mean square of .0215.

DISCUSSION

That orientation is an important variable has been demonstrated repeatedly (for example, Eriksen, 1952; Glixman, 1949; Lewis & Franklin, 1944; Rosenzweig, 1943). That the degree of a subject's task involvement or ego involvement is the major factor affecting

his recall has not been demonstrated by these data, however suggestive they may be. None of these studies, including this one, has used any direct measure of this involvement. What has been needed is some demonstration that task involvement and ego involvement result from the orienting instructions.

The present study offers considerable support for this idea. In addition to the claim that task orientation led to task involvement and ego orientation to ego involvement which in turn led to the orientation differences in recall, the differences in recall among the volunteering groups can be explained using these same constructs. If, as seems reasonable, volunteers are more likely to be interested in the tasks and less likely to be afraid of experimental and test situations than is the case among nonvolunteers, then volunteers in contrast to nonvolunteers will probably respond more readily to task orientation and less readily to ego orientation. Thus, the differences in recall among volunteering groups can be attributed to differences in degree of task involvement and ego involvement. The fact that these differences are small is not surprising since the relevant variables were not directly manipulated. The major strength of this view is that the psychological forces responsible for the recall differences among the volunteering groups are asserted to be the same as those acting in the orientation groups. This interpretation of the data also permits a reconciliation of the differences in results among the studies cited in the introduction.

It should be added that people almost certainly do or do not volunteer for a variety of reasons not included in the preceding discussion. The present data indicate that volunteers differ in recall from nonvolunteers but do not indicate which reasons, if any, are factors in this difference.

Actually, an attempt to determine the reasons for choosing or refusing to volunteer was made through a badly designed questionnaire completed by all subjects immediately after the volunteer sign-up sheets were collected. The nonvolunteers referred to "lack of time" frequently and lack of interest occasionally, along with a heterogeneous set of other reasons. Fear of being manipulated was acknowledged only once and fear of adverse judgment of performance and the like not at all. The volunteers responded in an even more heterogeneous manner with references to service and duty being most frequent. Responses loosely interpreted as indicating curiosity, interest, and anticipated pleasure ran second and can be ascribed to about one in six of the volunteers. Since the responses were anonymous all one can say is that the questionnaire data do not

prevent the interpretations offered above.

While explanations of the data using the notions of task involvement and ego involvement are defensible, it remains true that these constructs are rather vaguely defined. For example, it is not clear whether ego involvement refers to fears, hopes, or both, and to concerns about private self-esteem or about public prestige. As long as such large uncertainties remain the use of recall ratios as indications of personality does not seem justified.

REFERENCES

ATKINSON, J. W.   The achievement motive and recall of interrupted and completed tasks. In D. C. McClelland (Ed.), *Studies in motivation.* New York: Appleton-Century-Crofts, 1955. Pp. 494–506.

ERIKSEN, C. W.   Individual differences in defensive forgetting. *J. exp. Psychol.*, 1952, **44**, 442–446.

GILMORE, J. L.   Recall of success and failure as a function of subjects' threat interpretations. *J. Psychol.*, 1954, **38**, 359–365.

GLIXMAN, A. F.   Recall of completed and incompleted activities under varying degrees of stress. *J. exp. Psychol.*, 1949, **39**, 281–295.

LEWIS, HELEN B., & FRANKLIN, MURIEL.   An experimental study of the role of the ego in work: II. The significance of task-orientation in work. *J. exp. Psychol.*, 1944, **34**, 195–215.

MACKINNON, D. W., & HENLE, MARY.   *Experimental studies in psychodynamics: A laboratory manual.* Cambridge: Harvard Univer. Press, 1948.

MARROW, A. J.   Goal tensions and recall: I. *J. gen. Psychol.*, 1938, **19**, 3–35.

ROSENZWEIG, S.   An experimental study of "repression" with special reference to need-persistive and ego-defensive reactions to frustration. *J. exp. Psychol.*, 1943, **32**, 64–74.

ROSENZWEIG, S. The investigation of repression as an instance of experimental idiodynamics. *Psychol. Rev.*, 1952, 59, 339–345.

ZEIGARNIK, BLUMA. Das Behalten erledigter und unerledigter Handlungen. *Psychol. Forsch.*, 1927, 9, 1–85.

4. THE CONCEPTS OF BALANCE, CONGRUITY, AND DISSONANCE *

Robert B. Zajonc

Common to the concepts of balance, congruity, and dissonance is the notion that thoughts, beliefs, attitudes, and behavior tend to organize themselves in meaningful and sensible ways.[1] Members of the White Citizens Council do not ordinarily contribute to NAACP. Adherents of the New Deal seldom support Republican candidates. Christian Scientists do not enroll in medical schools. And people who live in glass houses apparently do not throw stones. In this respect the concept of consistency underscores and presumes human *rationality*. It holds that behavior and attitudes are not only consistent to the objective observer, but that individuals try to appear consistent to themselves. It assumes that inconsistency is a noxious state setting up pressures to eliminate it or reduce it. But in the *ways* that consistency in human behavior and attitudes is achieved we see rather often a striking lack of rationality. A heavy smoker cannot readily accept evidence relating cancer to smoking;[2] a socialist, told that Hoover's endorsement of certain political slogans agreed perfectly with his own, calls him a "typical hypocrite and a liar."[3] Allport illustrates this irrationality in the following conversation:

MR. X: The trouble with Jews is that they only take care of their own group.

MR. Y: But the record of the Community Chest shows that they give more generously than non-Jews.

MR. X: That shows that they are always trying to buy favor and intrude in Christian affairs. They think of nothing but money; that is why there are so many Jewish bankers.

MR. Y: But a recent study shows that the percent of Jews in banking is proportionally much smaller than the percent of non-Jews.

[1] The concepts of balance, congruity, and dissonance are due to Heider, Osgood and Tannenbaum, and Festinger, respectively. (F. Heider, "Attitudes and Cognitive Organization," *Journal of Psychology*, Vol. 21, 1946, pp. 107–112. C. E. Osgood and P. H. Tannenbaum, "The Principle of Congruity in the Prediction of Attitude Change," *Psychological Review*, Vol. 62, 1955, pp. 42–55. L. Festinger, *A Theory of Cognitive Dissonance*, New York: Harper & Row, 1957.) For purposes of simplicity we will subsume these concepts under the label of consistency.

[2] Festinger, *op. cit.*, pp. 153–156.

[3] H. B. Lewis, "Studies in the Principles of Judgments and Attitudes: IV, The Operation of 'Prestige Suggestion'," *Journal of Social Psychology*, Vol. 14, 1941, pp. 229–256.

* Reprinted from the *Public Opinion Quarterly*, 1960, 24: 280–296, with permission of the author and Princeton University Press.

MR. X: That's just it. They don't go in for respectable business. They would rather run night clubs.[4]

Thus, while the concept of consistency acknowledges man's rationality, observation of the means of its achievement simultaneously unveils his irrationality. The psychoanalytic notion of rationalization is a literal example of a concept which assumes both rationality and irrationality—it holds, namely, that man strives to understand and justify painful experiences and to make them sensible and rational, but he employs completely irrational methods to achieve this end.

The concepts of consistency are not novel. Nor are they indigenous to the study of attitudes, behavior, or personality. These concepts have appeared in various forms in almost all sciences. It has been argued by some that it is the existence of consistencies in the universe that made science possible, and by others that consistencies in the universe are a proof of divine power.[5] There is, of course, a question of whether consistencies are "real" or mere products of ingenious abstraction and conceptualization. For it would be entirely possible to categorize natural phenomena in such a haphazard way that instead of order, unity, and consistency, one would see a picture of utter chaos. If we were to eliminate one of the spatial dimensions from the conception of the physical world, the consistencies we now know and the consistencies which allow us to make reliable predictions would be vastly depleted.

The concept of consistency in man is, then, a special case of the concept of universal consistency. The fascination with this concept led some psychologists to rather extreme positions. Franke, for instance, wrote, ". . . the unity of a person can be traced in each instant of his life. There is nothing in character that contradicts itself. If a person who is known to us seems to be incongruous with himself that is only an indication of the inadequacy and superficiality of our previous observations." [6] This sort of hypothesis is, of course, incapable of either verification or disproof and therefore has no significant consequences.

Empirical investigations employing the concepts of consistency have been carried out for many years. Not until recently, however, has there been a programmatic and systematic effort to explore with precision and detail their particular consequences for behavior and attitudes. The greatest impetus to the study of attitudinal consistency was given recently by Festinger and his students. In addition to those already named, other related contributions in this area are those of Newcomb, who introduced the concept of "strain toward symmetry." [7] and of Cartwright and Harary, who expressed the notions of balance and symmetry in a mathematical form.[8] These notions all assume inconsistency to be a painful or at least psychologically uncomfortable state, but they differ in the generality of applica-

---

[4] G. W. Allport, *The Nature of Prejudice*, Cambridge, Mass., Addison-Wesley, 1954.

[5] W. P. Montague, *Belief Unbound*, New Haven, Conn., Yale University Press, 1930, pp. 70–73.

[6] R. Franke, "Gang und Character," *Beihefte, Zeitschrift für angewandte Psychologie*, No. 58, 1931, p. 45.

[7] T. M. Newcomb, "An Approach to the Study of Communicative Acts," *Psychological Review*, Vol. 60, 1953, pp. 393–404.

[8] D. Cartwright and F. Harary, "Structural Balance: A Generalization of Heider's Theory," *Psychological Review*, Vol. 63, 1956, pp. 277–293.

tion. The most restrictive and specific is the principle of congruity, since it restricts itself to the problems of the effects of information about objects and events on the attitudes toward the source of information. The most general is the notion of cognitive dissonance, since it considers consistency among any cognitions. In between are the notions of balance and symmetry, which consider attitudes toward people and objects in relation to one another, either within one person's cognitive structure, as in the case of Heider's theory of balance, or among a given group of individuals, as in the case of Newcomb's strain toward symmetry. It is the purpose of this paper to survey these concepts and to consider their implications for theory and research on attitudes.

THE CONCEPTS OF BALANCE AND STRAIN TOWARD SYMMETRY

The earliest formalization of consistency is attributed to Heider,[9] who was concerned with the way relations among persons involving some impersonal entity are cognitively experienced by the individual. The consistencies in which Heider was interested were those to be found in the ways people view their relations with other people and with the environment. The analysis was limited to two persons, labeled P and O, with P as the focus of the analysis and with O representing some other person, and to one impersonal entity, which could be a physical object, an idea, an event, or the like, labeled X. The object of Heider's inquiry was to discover how

relations among P, O, and X are organized in P's cognitive structure, and whether there exist recurrent and systematic tendencies in the way these relations are experienced. Two types of relation, liking (L) and so-called U, or unit, relations (such as possession, cause, similarity, and the like) were distinguished. On the basis of incidental observations and intuitive judgment, probably, Heider proposed that the person's (P's) cognitive structure representing relations among P, O, and X are either what he termed "balanced" or "unbalanced." In particular, he proposed, "In the case of three entities, a balanced state exists if all three relations are positive in all respects or if two are negative and one positive." Thus a balanced state is obtained when, for instance, P likes O, P likes X, and O likes X; or when P likes O, P dislikes X, and O dislikes X; or when P dislikes O, P likes X, and O dislikes X (see Figure 1). It should be noted that within Heider's conception a relation may be either positive or negative; degrees of liking cannot be represented. The fundamental assumption of balance theory is that an unbalanced state produces tension and generates forces to restore balance. This hypothesis was tested by Jordan.[10] He presented subjects with hypothetical situations involving two persons and an impersonal entity to rate for "pleasantness." Half the situations were by Heider's definition balanced and half unbalanced. Jordan's data showed somewhat higher unpleasantness ratings for the unbalanced than the balanced situations.

[9] Heider, *op. cit.*

[10] N. Jordan, "Behavioral Forces That Are a Function of Attitudes and of Cognitive Organization," *Human Relations*, Vol. 6, 1953, pp. 273–287.

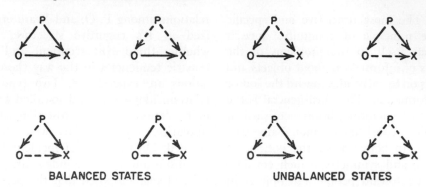

BALANCED STATES   **UNBALANCED STATES**

Figure 1. Examples of balanced and unbalanced states according to Heider's definition of balance. Solid lines represent positive, and broken lines negative, relations.

Cartwright and Harary [11] have cast Heider's formulation in graph-theoretical terms and derived some interesting consequences beyond those stated by Heider. Heider's concept allows either a balanced or an unbalanced state. Cartwright and Harary have constructed a more general definition of balance, with balance treated as a matter of degree, ranging from 0 to 1. Furthermore, their formulation of balance theory extended the notion to any number of entities, and an experiment by Morrissette [12] similar in design to that of Jordan obtained evidence for Cartwright and Harary's derivations.

A notion very similar to balance was advanced by Newcomb in 1953.[13] In addition to substituting A for P, and B for O, Newcomb took Heider's notion of balance out of one person's head and applied it to communication among people. Newcomb postulates a "strain toward symmetry" which leads to a communality of attitudes of two people (A and B) oriented toward an object (X). The strain toward symmetry influences communication between A and B so as to bring their attitudes toward X into congruence. Newcomb cites a study in which a questionnaire was administered to college students in 1951 following the dismissal of General MacArthur by President Truman. Data were obtained on students' attitudes toward Truman's decision and their perception of the attitudes of their closest friends. Of the pro-Truman subjects 48 said that their closest friends favored Truman and none that their closest friends were opposed to his decision. Of the anti-Truman subjects only 2 said that their friends were generally pro-Truman and 34 that they were anti-Truman. In a longitudinal study, considerably more convincing evidence was obtained in support of the strain-toward-symmetry hypothesis. In 1954 Newcomb set up a house at the University of Michigan which offered free rent for one semester for seventeen students who would serve as subjects. The residents of the house were observed, questioned, and rated for four to five hours a week during the entire semester. The study was then

[11] Cartwright and Harary, *op. cit.*
[12] J. Morrissette, "An Experimental Study of the Theory of Structural Balance," *Human Relations*, Vol. 11, 1958, pp. 239–254.
[13] Newcomb, *op. cit.*

repeated with another set of seventeen students. The findings revealed a tendency for those who were attracted to one another to agree on many matters, including the way they perceived their own selves and their ideal selves, and their attractions for other group members. Moreover, in line with the prediction, these similarities, real as well as perceived, seemed to increase over time.[14]

Newcomb also cites the work of Festinger and his associates on social communication [15] in support of his hypothesis. Festinger's studies on communication have clearly shown that the tendency to influence other group members toward one's own opinion increases with the degree of attraction. More recently Burdick and Burnes reported two experiments in which measures of skin resistance (GSR) were obtained as an index of emotional reaction in the presence of balanced and unbalanced situations.[16] They observed significant differences in skin resistance depending on whether the subjects agreed or disagreed with a "well-liked experimenter." In the second experiment Burdick and Burnes found that subjects who liked the experimenter tended to change their opinions toward greater agreement with his, and those who disliked him, toward greater disagreement. There are, of course, many other studies

to show that the attitude toward the communicator determines his persuasive effectiveness. Hovland and his co-workers have demonstrated these effects in several studies.[17] They have also shown, however, that these effects are fleeting; that is, the attitude change produced by the communication seems to dissipate over time. Their interpretation is that over time subjects tend to dissociate the source from the message and are therefore subsequently less influenced by the prestige of the communicator. This proposition was substantiated by Kelman and Hovland,[18] who produced attitude changes with a prestigeful communicator and retested subjects after a four-week interval with and without reminding the subjects about the communicator. The results showed that the permanence of the attitude change depended on the association with the source.

In general, the consequences of balance theories have up to now been rather limited. Except for Newcomb's longitudinal study, the experimental situations dealt mostly with subjects who responded to hypothetical situations, and direct evidence is scarce. The Burdick and Burnes experiment is the only one bearing more directly on the assumption that imbalance or asymmetry produces tension. Cartwright and Harary's mathematization of the concept of balance should, however, lead to important empirical and theoretical develop-

[14] T. M. Newcomb, "The Prediction of Interpersonal Attraction," *American Psychologist*, Vol. 11, 1956, pp. 575–586.

[15] L. Festinger, K. Back, S. Schachter, H. H. Kelley, and J. Thibaut, *Theory and Experiment in Social Communication*, Ann Arbor, Mich., University of Michigan, Institute for Social Research, 1950.

[16] H. A. Burdick and A. J. Burnes, "A Test of 'Strain toward Symmetry' Theories," *Journal of Abnormal and Social Psychology*, Vol. 57, 1958, pp. 367–369.

[17] C. I. Hovland, I. L. Janis, and H. H. Kelley, *Communication and Persuasion: Psychological Studies of Opinion Change*, New Haven, Conn., Yale University Press, 1953.

[18] H. C. Kelman and C. I. Hovland, " 'Reinstatement' of the Communicator in Delayed Measurement of Opinion Change," *Journal of Abnormal and Social Psychology*, Vol. 48, 1953, pp. 327–335.

ments. One difficulty is that there really has not been a serious experimental attempt to *disprove* the theory. It is conceivable that some situations defined by the theory as unbalanced may in fact remain stable and produce no significant pressures toward balance. Festinger once inquired in a jocular mood if it followed from balance theory that since he likes chicken, and since chickens like chicken feed, he must also like chicken feed or else experience the tension of imbalance. While this counterexample is, of course, not to be taken seriously, it does point to some difficulties in the concepts of balance. It is not clear from Heider's theory of balance and Newcomb's theory of symmetry what predictions are to be made when attraction of both P and O toward X exists but when the origin and nature of these attractions are different. In other words, suppose both P and O like X but for different reasons and in entirely different ways, as was the case with Festinger and the chickens. Are the consequences of balance theory the same then as in the case where P and O like X for the same reasons and in the same way? It is also not clear, incidentally, what the consequences are when the relation between P and O is cooperative and when it is competitive. Two men vying for the hand of the same fair maiden might experience tension whether they are close friends or deadly enemies.

In a yet unpublished study conducted by Harburg and Price at the University of Michigan, students were asked to name two of their best friends. When those named were of opposite sexes, subjects reported they would feel uneasy if the two friends liked one another. In a subsequent experiment subjects were asked whether they desired their good friend to like, be neutral to, or dislike one of their strongly disliked acquaintances, and whether they desired the disliked acquaintance to like or dislike the friend. It will be recalled that in either case a balanced state obtains only if the two persons are negatively related to one another. However, Harburg and Price found that 39 percent desired their friend to be liked by the disliked acquaintance, and only 24 percent to be disliked. Moreover, faced with the alternative that the disliked acquaintance dislikes their friend, 55 percent as opposed to 25 percent expressed uneasiness. These results are quite inconsistent with balance theory. Although one may want one's friends to dislike one's enemies, one may not want the enemies to dislike one's friends. The reason for the latter may be simply a concern for the friends' welfare.

OSGOOD AND TANNENBAUM'S PRINCIPLE OF CONGRUITY

The principle of congruity, which is in fact a special case of balance, was advanced by Osgood and Tannenbaum in 1955.[19] It deals specifically with the problem of *direction* of attitude change. The authors assume that "judgmental frames of reference tend toward maximal simplicity." Thus, since extreme "black-and-white," "all-or-nothing," judgments are simpler than refined ones, valuations tend to move toward extremes or, in the words of the authors, there is "a continuing pressure toward polarization." Together with the notion of maximization of simplicity is the assumption of identity as being less complex than the

[19] Osgood and Tannenbaum, *op. cit.*

discrimination of fine differences. Therefore, related "concepts" will tend to be evaluated in a similar manner. Given these assumptions, the principle of congruity holds that when change in evaluation or attitude occurs it always occurs in the direction of increased congruity with the prevailing frame of reference. The paradigm of congruity is that of an individual who is confronted with an assertion regarding a particular matter about which he believes and feels in a certain way, made by a person toward whom he also has some attitude. Given that Eisenhower is evaluated positively and freedom of the press also positively, and given that Eisenhower (+) comes out in favor of freedom of the press (+), congruity is said to exist. But given that the *Daily Worker* is evaluated negatively, and given that the *Daily Worker* (−) comes out in favor of freedom of the press (+), incongruity is said to exist. Examples of congruity and incongruity are shown in Figure 2. The diagram shows the attitudes of a given individual toward the source and the object of the assertion. The assertions represented by heavy lines imply

either positive or negative attitudes of the source toward the object. It is clear from a comparison of Figures 1 and 2 that in terms of their formal properties, the definitions of balance and congruity are identical. Thus, incongruity is said to exist when the attitudes toward the source and the object are similar and the assertion is negative, or when they are dissimilar and the assertion is positive. In comparison, unbalanced states are defined as having either one or all negative relations, which is of course equivalent to the above. To the extent that the person's attitudes are congruent with those implied in the assertion, a stable state exists. When the attitudes toward the person and the assertion are incongruent, there will be a tendency to change the attitudes toward the person and the object of the assertion in the direction of increased congruity. Tannenbaum obtained measures on 405 college students regarding their attitudes toward labor leaders, the *Chicago Tribune*, and Senator Robert Taft as sources, and toward legalized gambling, abstract art, and accelerated college programs as objects. Some time after the

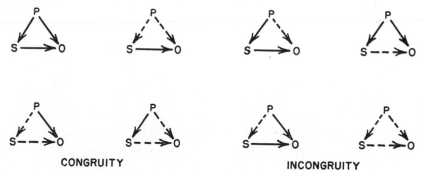

CONGRUITY   INCONGRUITY

Figure 2. Examples of congruity and incongruity. Heavy lines represent assertions, light lines attitudes. Solid heavy lines represent assertions which imply a positive attitude on the part of the source, and broken heavy lines negative attitudes. Solid light lines represent positive, and broken light lines negative, attitudes.

TABLE 1. CHANGE OF ATTITUDE TOWARD THE SOURCE AND THE OBJECT WHEN POSITIVE AND NEGATIVE ASSERTIONS ARE MADE BY THE SOURCE

Original Attitude Toward the Source	Positive Assertion About an Object Toward Which the Attitude Is		Negative Assertion About an Object Toward Which the Attitude Is	
	Positive	Negative	Positive	Negative
CHANGE OF ATTITUDE TOWARD THE SOURCE				
Positive	+	– –	– –	+
Negative	+ +	–	–	+ +
CHANGE OF ATTITUDE TOWARD THE OBJECT				
Positive	+	+ +	– –	–
Negative	– –	–	+	+ +

attitude scores were obtained, the subjects were presented with "highly realistic" newspaper clippings involving assertions made by the various sources regarding the concepts. In general, when the original attitudes toward the source and the concept were both positive and the assertion presented in the newspaper clippings was also positive, no significant attitude changes were observed in the results. When the original attitudes toward the source and the concept were negative and the assertion was positive, again no changes were obtained. As predicted, however, when a positively valued source was seen as making a positive assertion about a negatively valued concept, the attitude toward the source became less favorable, and toward the concept more favorable. Conversely, when a negatively valued source was seen as making a positive assertion about a positively valued concept, attitudes toward the source became more favorable and toward the concept less favorable. The entire gamut of predicted changes was confirmed in Tannenbaum's data; it is summarized in the accompanying table, in which the direction of change is represented by either a plus or a minus sign, and the extent of change by either one or two such signs.

A further derivation of the congruity principle is that incongruity does not invariably produce attitude change, but that it may at times lead to incredulity on the part of the individual. When confronted by an assertion which stands in an incongruous relation to the person who made it, there will be a tendency not to believe that the person made the assertion, thus reducing incongruity.

There is a good deal of evidence supporting Osgood and Tannenbaum's principle of congruity. As early as 1921, H. T. Moore had subjects judge statements for their grammar, ethical infringements for their seriousness, and resolutions of the dominant seventh chord for their dissonance.[20] After two and one-half months the subjects returned and were presented with judgments of "experts." This experimental manipulation resulted in 62 percent reversals of judgments on grammar, 50 percent of ethical judgments, and 43

[20] H. T. Moore, "The Comparative Influence of Majority and Expert Opinion," *American Journal of Psychology*, Vol. 32, 1921, pp. 16–20.

percent of musical judgments. And in 1935 in a study on a similar problem of prestige suggestion, Sherif let subjects rank sixteen authors for their literary merit.[21] Subsequently, the subjects were given sixteen passages presumably written by the various authors previously ranked. The subjects were asked to rank-order the passages for literary merit. Although in actuality *all* the passages were written by Robert Louis Stevenson, the subjects were able to rank the passages. Moreover, the correlations between the merit of the author and the merit of the passage ranged from between .33 to .53. These correlations are not very dramatic, yet they do represent some impact of attitude toward the source on attitude toward the passage.

With respect to incredulity, an interesting experiment was conducted recently by Jones and Kohler in which subjects learned statements which either supported their attitudes or were in disagreement with them.[22] Some of the statements were plausible and some implausible. The results were rather striking. Subjects whose attitudes favored segregation learned plausible prosegregation statements and implausible antisegregation statements much more rapidly than plausible antisegregation and implausible prosegregation statements. The reverse was of course true for subjects whose attitudes favored desegregation.

While the principle of congruity presents no new ideas, it has a great advantage over the earlier attempts in its precision. Osgood and Tannenbaum have formulated the principle of congruity in quantitative terms allowing for precise predictions regarding the extent and direction of attitude change—predictions which in their studies were fairly well confirmed. While balance theory allows merely a dichotomy of attitudes, either positive or negative, the principle of congruity allows refined measurements using Osgood's method of the semantic differential.[23] Moreover, while it is not clear from Heider's statement of balance in just what direction changes will occur when an unbalanced state exists, such predictions can be made on the basis of the congruity principle.

FESTINGER'S THEORY OF COGNITIVE DISSONANCE

Perhaps the largest systematic body of data is that collected in the realm of Festinger's dissonance theory. The statement of the dissonance principle is simple. It holds that two elements of knowledge ". . . are in dissonant relation if, considering these two alone, the obverse of one element would follow from the other."[24] It further holds that dissonance ". . . being psychologically uncomfortable, will motivate the person to try to reduce dissonance and achieve consonance" and ". . . in addition to trying to reduce it, the person will actively avoid situations and information which would likely increase the dissonance."[25] A number of rather interest-

[21] M. Sherif, "An Experimental Study of Stereotypes," *Journal of Abnormal and Social Psychology*, Vol. 29, 1935, pp. 371–375.

[22] E. E. Jones and R. Kohler, "The Effects of Plausibility on the Learning of Controversial Statements," *Journal of Abnormal and Social Psychology*, Vol. 57, 1958, pp. 315–320.

[23] C. E. Osgood, "The Nature and Measurement of Meaning," *Psychological Bulletin*, Vol. 49, 1952, pp. 197–237.

[24] Festinger, *op. cit.*, p. 13.

[25] *Ibid.*, p. 3.

ing and provocative consequences follow from Festinger's dissonance hypothesis.

First, it is predicted that all decisions or choices result in dissonance to the extent that the alternative not chosen contains positive features which make it attractive also, and the alternative chosen contains features which might have resulted in rejecting it. Hence after making a choice people seek evidence to confirm their decision and so reduce dissonance. In the Ehrlich experiment cited by Cohen in this issue the finding was that new car owners noticed and read ads about the cars they had recently purchased more than ads about other cars.[26]

Post-decision dissonance was also shown to result in a change of attractiveness of the alternative involved in a decision. Brehm had female subjects rate eight appliances for desirability.[27] Subsequently, the subjects were given a choice between two of the eight products, given the chosen product, and after some interpolated activity (consisting of reading research reports about four of the appliances) were asked to rate the products again. Half the subjects were given a choice between products which they rated in a similar manner, and half between products on which the ratings differed. Thus in the first case higher dissonance was to be expected than in the second. The prediction from dissonance theory that there should be an increase in the attractiveness of the chosen alternative and decrease in the

attractiveness of the rejected alternative was on the whole confirmed. Moreover, the further implication was also confirmed that the pressure to reduce dissonance (which was accomplished in the above experiment by changes in attractiveness of the alternatives) varies directly with the extent of dissonance.

Another body of data accounted for by the dissonance hypothesis deals with situations in which the person is forced (either by reward or punishment) to express an opinion publicly or make a public judgment or statement which is contrary to his own opinions and beliefs. In cases where the person actually makes such a judgment or expresses an opinion contrary to his own as a result of a promised reward or threat, dissonance exists between the knowledge of the overt behavior of the person and his privately held beliefs. Festinger also argues that in the case of noncompliance dissonance will exist between the knowledge of overt behavior and the anticipation of reward and punishment.

An example of how dissonance theory accounts for forced-compliance data is given by Brehm.[28] Brehm offered prizes to eighth-graders for eating disliked vegetables and obtained measures of how well the children liked the vegetables. Children who ate the vegetables increased their liking for them. Of course, one might argue that a simpler explanation of the results is that the attractiveness of the prize generalized to the vegetable, or that, even more simply, the vegetables increased in utility because a reward came with them. However, this argument would also lead one

[26] D. Ehrlich, I. Guttman, P. Schönbach, and J. Mills, "Post-decision Exposure to Relevant Information," *Journal of Abnormal and Social Psychology*, Vol. 54, 1957, pp. 98–102.

[27] J. Brehm, "Post-decision Changes in the Desirability of Alternatives," *Journal of Abnormal and Social Psychology*, Vol. 52, 1956, pp. 384–389.

[28] J. Brehm, "Increasing Cognitive Dissonance by a *Fait Accompli*," *Journal of Abnormal and Social Psychology*, Vol. 58, 1959, pp. 379–382.

to predict that the increment in attraction under such conditions is a *direct* function of the magnitude of the reward. Dissonance theory makes the opposite prediction, and therefore a test of the validity of the two explanations is possible. Data collected by Festinger and Carlsmith [29] and by Aronson and Mills [30] support the dissonance point of view. In Festinger and Carlsmith's experiment subjects were offered either 20 dollars or 1 dollar for telling someone that an experience which had actually been quite boring had been rather enjoyable and interesting. When measures of the subjects' private opinions about their actual enjoyment of the task were taken, those who were to be paid only 1 dollar for the false testimony showed considerably higher scores than those who were to be paid 20 dollars. Aronson and Mills, on the other hand, tested the effects of negative incentive. They invited college women to join a group requiring them to go through a process of initiation. For some women the initiation was quite severe, for others it was mild. The prediction from dissonance theory that those who had to undergo severe initiation would increase their attraction for the group more than those having no initiation or mild initiation was borne out.

A third set of consequences of the theory of dissonance deals with exposure to information. Since dissonance occurs between cognitive elements, and since information may lead to change in these elements, the principle of dissonance should have a close bearing on the individual's commerce with information. In particular, the assumption that dissonance is a psychologically uncomfortable state leads to the prediction that individuals will seek out information reducing dissonance and avoid information increasing it. The study on automobile-advertising readership described above is a demonstration of this hypothesis.[31] In another study Mills, Aronson, and Robinson gave college students a choice between an objective and an essay examination.[32] Following the decision, the subjects were given articles about examinations presumably written by experts, and they were asked if they would like to read them. In addition, in order to vary the intensity of dissonance, half the subjects were told that the examination counted 70 percent toward the final grade, and half that it counted only 5 percent. The data were obtained in the form of rankings of the articles for preference. While there was a clear preference for reading articles containing positive information about the alternative chosen, no significant selective effects were found when the articles presented arguments against the given type of examination. Also, the authors failed to demonstrate effects relating selectivity in exposure to information to the magnitude of dissonance, in that no significant differences were found between subjects for whom the examination was quite important (70 percent of the final grade) and those for whom it was relatively unimportant (5 percent of the final grade).

[29] L. Festinger and J. M. Carlsmith, "Cognitive Consequences of Forced Compliance," *Journal of Abnormal and Social Psychology,* Vol. 58, 1959, pp. 203–210.

[30] E. Aronson and J. Mills, "The Effect of Severity of Initiation on Liking for a Group," *Journal of Abnormal and Social Psychology,* Vol. 59, 1959, pp. 177–181.

[31] Ehrlich *et al., op. cit.*

[32] J. Mills, E. Aronson, and H. Robinson, "Selectivity in Exposure to Information," *Journal of Abnormal and Social Psychology,* Vol. 59, 1959, pp. 250–253.

Festinger was able to account for many other results by means of the dissonance principle, and in general his theory is rather successful in organizing a diverse body of empirical knowledge by means of a limited number of fairly reasonable assumptions. Moreover, from these reasonable assumptions dissonance theory generated several nontrivial and nonobvious consequences. The negative relationship between the magnitude of incentive and attraction of the object of false testimony is not at all obvious. Also not obvious is the prediction of an increase in proselytizing for a mystical belief following an event that clearly contradicts it. Festinger, Riecken, and Schachter studied a group of "Seekers"—people who presumably received a message from outer space informing them of an incipient major flood.[33] When the flood failed to materialize on the critical date, instead of quietly withdrawing from the public scene, as one would expect, the "Seekers" summoned press representatives, gave extended interviews, and invited the public to visit them and be informed of the details of the whole affair. In a very recent study by Brehm, a "nonobvious" derivation from dissonance theory was tested.[34] Brehm predicted that when forced to engage in an unpleasant activity, an individual's liking for this activity will increase more when he receives information essentially berating the activity than when he receives information promoting it. The results tended to support Brehm's prediction.

[33] L. Festinger, J. Riecken, and S. Schachter, *When Prophecy Fails*, Minneapolis, University of Minnesota Press, 1956.

[34] J. W. Brehm, "Attitudinal Consequences of Commitment to Unpleasant Behavior," *Journal of Abnormal and Social Psychology*, Vol. 60, 1960, pp. 379–383.

Since negative information is said to increase dissonance, and since increased dissonance leads to an increased tendency to reduce it, and since the only means of dissonance reduction was increasing the attractiveness of the activity, such an increase would in fact be expected.

CONCLUSIONS

The theories and empirical work dealing with consistencies are mainly concerned with intra-individual phenomena, be it with relationships between one attitude and another, between attitudes and values, or information, or perception, or behavior, or the like. One exception is Newcomb's concept of "strain toward symmetry." Here the concern is primarily with the interplay of forces among individuals which results in uniformities or consistencies among them. There is no question that the concepts of consistency, and especially the theory of cognitive dissonance, account for many varied attitudinal phenomena. Of course, the various formulations of consistency do not pretend, nor are they able, to account completely for the phenomena they examine. Principles of consistency, like all other principles, are prefaced by the *ceteris paribus* preamble. Thus, when other factors are held constant, then the principles of consistency should be able to explain behavior and attitudes completely. But the question to be raised here is just what factors must be held constant and how important and significant, relative to consistency, are they.

Suppose a man feels hostile toward the British and also dislikes cricket. One might be tempted to conclude that if one of his attitudes were different he would experience the discomfort of incongruity. But there are probably many people whose attitudes toward the British and cricket are incongruent, although the exact proportions are not known and are hardly worth serious inquiry. But if such an inquiry were undertaken it would probably disclose that attitudes depend largely on the conditions under which they have been acquired. For one thing, it would show that the attitudes depend at least to some extent on the relationship of the attitude object to the individual's needs and fears, and that these may be stronger than forces toward balance. There are in this world things to be avoided and feared. A child bitten by a dog will not develop favorable attitudes toward dogs. And no matter how much he likes Popeye you can't make him like spinach, although according to balance theory he should.

The relationship between attitudes and values or needs has been explored, for instance, in *The Authoritarian Personality*, which appeared in 1950.[35] The authors of this work hypothesized a close relationship between attitudes and values on the one hand and personality on the other. They assumed that the ". . . convictions of an individual often form a broad and coherent pattern, as if bound together by a mentality or spirit." They further assumed that ". . . opinions, attitudes, and values depend on human needs and since personality is essentially an organization of needs, then personality may be regarded as a determinant of ideological preference." Thus the *Authoritarian Per-*

sonality approach also stresses consistency, but while the concepts of congruity, balance, and dissonance are satisfied with assuming a general tendency toward consistency, the *Authoritarian Personality* theory goes further in that it holds that the dynamic of consistency is to be found in personality, and it is personality which gives consistency meaning and direction. Attitudes and values are thus seen to be consistent among themselves and with one another because they are both consistent with the basic personality needs, and they are consistent with needs because they are determined by them.

The very ambitious research deriving from the *Authoritarian Personality* formulation encountered many difficulties and, mainly because of serious methodological and theoretical shortcomings, has gradually lost its popularity. However, some aspects of this general approach have been salvaged by others. Rosenberg, for instance, has shown that attitudes are intimately related to the capacity of the attitude object to be instrumental to the attainment of the individual's values.[36] Carlson went a step further and has shown that, if the perceived instrumentality of the object with respect to a person's values and needs is changed, the attitude itself may be modified.[37] These studies, while not assuming a general consistency principle, illustrate a special instance of consistency, namely that between attitudes and utility, or instru-

[35] T. W. Adorno, E. Frenkel-Brunswik, D. J. Levinson, and R. N. Sanford, *The Authoritarian Personality*, New York, Harper & Row, 1950.

[36] M. J. Rosenberg, "Cognitive Structure and Attitudinal Affect," *Journal of Abnormal and Social Psychology*, Vol. 53, 1956, pp. 367–372.

[37] E. R. Carlson, "Attitude Change through Modification of Attitude Structure," *Journal of Abnormal and Social Psychology*, Vol. 52, 1956, pp. 256–261.

mentality of attitude objects, with respect to the person's values and needs.

The concepts of consistency bear a striking historical similarity to the concept of vacuum. According to an excellent account by Conant,[38] for centuries the principle that nature abhors a vacuum served to account for various phenomena, such as the action of pumps, behavior of liquids in joined vessels, suction, and the like. The strength of everyday evidence was so overwhelming that the principle was seldom questioned. However, it was known that one cannot draw water to a height of more than 34 feet. The simplest solution of this problem was to reformulate the principle to read that "nature abhors a vacuum below 34 feet." This modified version of *horror vacui* again was satisfactory for the phenomena it dealt with, until it was discovered that "nature abhors a vacuum below 34 feet only when we deal with water." As Torricelli has shown, when it comes to mercury "nature abhors a vacuum below 30 inches." Displeased with the crudity of a principle which must accommodate numerous exceptions, Torricelli formulated the notion that it was the pressure of air acting upon the surface of the liquid which was responsible for the height to which one could draw liquid by the action of pumps. The 34-foot limit represented the weight of water which the air pressure on the surface of earth could maintain, and the 30-inch limit represented the weight of mercury that air pressure could maintain. This was an entirely different and revolutionary concept, and its consequences had drastic impact on physics. Human

[38] James B. Conant, *On Understanding Science*, New Haven, Conn., Yale University Press, 1947.

nature, on the other hand, is said to abhor inconsistency. For the time being the principle is quite adequate, since it accounts systematically for many phenomena, some of which have never been explained and all of which have never been explained by one principle. But already today there are exceptions to consistency and balance. Some people who spend a good portion of their earnings on insurance also gamble. The first action presumably is intended to protect them from risks, the other to expose them to risks. Almost everybody enjoys a magician. And the magician only creates dissonance—you see before you an event which you know to be impossible on the basis of previous knowledge —the obverse of what you see follows from what you know. If the art of magic is essentially the art of producing dissonance, and if human nature abhors dissonance, why is the art of magic still flourishing? If decisions are necessarily followed by dissonance, and if nature abhors dissonance, why are decisions ever made? Although it is true that those decisions which would ordinarily lead to great dissonance take a very long time to make, they are made anyway. And it is also true that human nature does not abhor dissonance absolutely, as nature abhors a vacuum. Human nature merely avoids dissonance, and it would follow from dissonance theory that decisions whose instrumental consequences would not be worth the dissonance to follow would never be made. There are thus far no data to support this hypothesis, nor data to disprove it.

According to Conant, *horror vacui* served an important purpose besides explaining and organizing some aspects of physical knowledge. Without it the discomfort of "exceptions to the rule" would never have been felt, and the important developments in theory might have been delayed considerably. If a formulation has then a virtue in being wrong, the theories of consistency do have this virtue. They do organize a large body of knowledge. Also, they point out exceptions, and thereby they demand a new formulation. It will not suffice simply to reformulate them so as to accommodate the exceptions. I doubt if Festinger would be satisfied with a modification of his dissonance principle which would read that dissonance, being psychologically uncomfortable, leads a person to actively avoid situations and information which would be likely to increase the dissonance, except when there is an opportunity to watch a magician. Also, simply to disprove the theories by counterexamples would not in itself constitute an important contribution. We would merely lose explanations of phenomena which had been explained. And it is doubtful that the theories of consistency could be rejected simply *because* of counterexamples. Only a theory which accounts for all the data that the consistency principles now account for, for all the exceptions to those principles, and for all the phenomena which these principles should now but do not consider, is capable of replacing them. It is only a matter of time until such a development takes place.

2
Socialization

5. THE MAMMAL AND HIS ENVIRONMENT *
D. O. Hebb

The original intention in this paper was to discuss the significance of neurophysiological theory for psychiatry and psychology and to show, by citing the work done by some of my colleagues, that the attempt to get at the neural mechanisms of behavior can stimulate and clarify purely behavioral—that is, psychiatric and psychological—thinking. The research to be described has, I think, a clear relevance to clinical problems; but its origin lay in efforts to learn how the functioning of individual neurons and synapses relates to the functions of the whole brain and to understand the physiological nature of learning, emotion, thinking, or intelligence.

In the end, however, my paper has simply become a review of the research referred to, dealing with the relation of the mammal to his environment. The question concerns the normal variability of the sensory environment and this has been studied from two points of view. First, one may ask what the significance of perceptual activity is during growth; for this purpose one can rear an animal with a considerable degree of restriction, and see what effects there are upon mental development. Secondly, in normal animals whose development is complete, one can remove a good deal of the supporting action of the normal environment, to discover how far the animal continues to be dependent on it even after maturity.

THE ROLE
OF THE ENVIRONMENT
DURING GROWTH

The immediate background of our present research on the intelligence and personality of the dog is the work of

* From the *American Journal of Psychiatry*, 1955, CXI: 826–831. Reprinted by permission of the author and the publisher.

Hymovitch [1] on the intelligence of rats. He reared laboratory rats in two ways: (1) in a psychologically restricted environment, a small cage, with food and water always at hand and plenty of opportunity for exercise (in an activity wheel) but with no problems to solve, no need of getting on with others, no pain; and (2) in a "free" environment, a large box with obstacles to pass, blind alleys to avoid, other rats to get on with, and thus ample opportunity for problem-solving and great need for learning during growth. Result: the rats brought up in a psychologically restricted (but biologically adequate) environment have a lasting inferiority in problem-solving. This does not mean, of course, that environment is everything, heredity nothing: here heredity was held constant, which prevents it from affecting the results. When the reverse experiment is done, we find problem-solving varying with heredity instead. The *same* capacity for problem-solving is fully dependent on both variables for its development.

To take this further, Thompson and others have been applying similar methods to dogs.[2] The same intellectual effect of an impoverished environment is found again, perhaps more marked in the higher species. But another kind of effect can be seen in dogs, which have clearly marked personalities. Personality —by which I mean complex individual differences of emotion and motivation— is again strongly affected by the infant environment. These effects, however, are hard to analyze and I cannot at present give any rounded picture of them.

[1] B. Hymovitch, in *J. Comp. Physiol. Psychol.*, 1952, XLV, 313.
[2] W. R. Thompson and W. Heron, *Canad. J. Psychol.*, 1954, VIII, 17, 1954.

First observations during the rearing itself are significant. A Scottish terrier is reared in a small cage, in isolation from other Scotties and from the human staff. Our animal man, William Ponman, is a dog lover and undertook the experiment with misgivings, which quickly disappeared. In a cage 30 by 30 inches, the dogs are "happy as larks," eat more than normally reared dogs, grow well, are physically vigorous: as Ponman says, "I never saw such healthy dogs—they're like bulls." If you put a normally-reared dog into such a cage, shut off from everything, his misery is unmistakable, and we have not been able to bring ourselves to continue such experiments. Not so the dog that has known nothing else. Ponman showed some of these at a dog show of national standing, winning first-prize ribbons with them.

Observations by Dr. Ronald Melzack on pain are extremely interesting. He reared two dogs, after early weaning, in complete isolation, taking care that there was little opportunity for experience of pain (unless the dog bit himself). At maturity, when the dogs were first taken out for study, they were extraordinarily excited, with random, rapid movement. As a result they got their tails or paws stepped on repeatedly— but paid no attention to an event that would elicit howls from a normally reared dog. After a few days, when their movements were calmer, they were tested with an object that gave electric shock and paid little attention to it. Through five testing periods, the dog repeatedly thrust his nose into a lighted match and, months later, did the same thing several times with a lighted cigar.

A year and a half after coming out of restriction they are still hyperactive.

Clipping and trimming one of them is a two-man job; if the normal dog does not stand still, a cuff on the ear will remind him of his duty; but cuffing the experimental dog "has as much effect as if you patted him—except he pays no attention to it." It seems certain, especially in view of the related results reported by Nissen, Chow, and Semmes [3] for a chimpanzee, that the adult's perception of pain is essentially a function of pain experience during growth—and that what we call pain is not a single sensory quale but a complex mixture of a particular kind of synthesis with past learning and emotional disturbance.

Nothing bores the dogs reared in restriction. At an "open house," we put two restricted dogs in one enclosure, two normal ones in another, and asked the public to tell us which were the normal. Without exception, they picked out the two alert, lively, interested animals—not the lackadaisical pair lying in the corner, paying no attention to the visitors. The alert pair, actually, were the restricted; the normal dogs had seen all they wanted to see of the crowd in the first two minutes and then went to sleep, thoroughly bored. The restricted dogs, so to speak, do not have the brains to be bored.

Emotionally, the dogs are "immature," but not in the human or clinical sense. They are little bothered by imaginative fears. Dogs suffer from irrational fears, like horses, porpoises, elephants, chimpanzees, and man; but it appears that this is a product of intellectual development characteristic of the brighter, not the duller, animal. Our dogs in restriction are not smart enough to fear

strange objects. Things that cause fear in normal dogs produce only a generalized, undirected excitement in the restricted. If both normal and restricted dogs are exposed to the same noninjurious but exciting stimulus repeatedly, fear gradually develops in the restricted; but the normals, at first afraid, have by this time gone on to show a playful aggression instead. On the street, the restricted dogs "lead well," not bothered by what goes on around them, while those reared normally vary greatly in this respect. Analysis has a long way to go in these cases, but we can say now that dogs reared in isolation are not like ordinary dogs. They are both stupid and peculiar.

Such results clearly support the clinical evidence, and the animal experiments of others,[4] showing that early environment has a lasting effect on the form of adjustment at maturity. We do not have a great body of evidence yet and before we generalize too much, it will be particularly important to repeat these observations with animals of different heredity. But I have been very surprised, personally, by the lack of evidence of emotional instability, neurotic tendency, or the like, when the dogs are suddenly plunged into a normal world. There is, in fact, just the opposite effect. This suggests caution in interpreting data with human children, such as those of Spitz [5] or Bowlby.[6] Perceptual restriction in infancy certainly produces a low level of intelligence, but it may not, by itself, produce emotional disorder. The observed results seem to

[3] H. W. Nissen, R. L. Chow, and Josephine Semmes, *Am. J. Psychol.*, 1951, LXIV, 485.

[4] F. A. Beach and J. Jaynes, *Psychol. Bull.*, 1954, LI, 239.

[5] R. A. Spitz, "Hospitalization," in *Psychoanalytic Study of the Child*, 1946, II, 113.

[6] J. Bowlby, *Maternal Care and Mental Health* (Geneva: WHO Monogr. #2, 1951).

mean, not that the stimulus of another attentive organism (the mother) is necessary from the first, but that it may become necessary only as psychological *dependence* on the mother develops. However, our limited data certainly cannot prove anything for man, though they may suggest other interpretations besides those that have been made.

THE ENVIRONMENT
AT MATURITY

Another approach to the relation between the mammal and his environment is possible: that is, one can take the normally reared mammal and cut him off at maturity from his usual contact with the world. It seems clear that thought and personality characteristics develop as a function of the environment. Once developed, are they independent of it? This experiment is too cruel to do with animals but not with college students. The first stage of the work was done by Bexton, Heron, and Scott.[7] It follows up some work by Mackworth on the effects of monotony, in which he found extraordinary lapses of attention. Heron and his co-workers set out to make the monotony more prolonged and more complete.

The subject is paid to do nothing 24 hours a day. He lies on a comfortable bed in a small closed cubicle, is fed on request, goes to the toilet on request. Otherwise he does nothing. He wears frosted glass goggles that admit light but do not allow pattern vision. His ears are covered by a sponge-rubber pillow in which are embedded small speakers by which he can be communicated with,

[7] W. H. Bexton, W. Heron, and T. H. Scott, *Canad. J. Psychol.*, 1954, VIII, 70.

and a microphone hangs near to enable him to answer. His hands are covered with gloves and cardboard cuffs extend from the upper forearm beyond his fingertips, permitting free joint movement but with little tactual perception.

The results are dramatic. During the stay in the cubicle, the experimental subject shows extensive loss, statistically significant, in solving simple problems. He complains subjectively that he cannot concentrate; his boredom is such that he looks forward eagerly to the next problem, but when it is presented he finds himself unwilling to make the effort to solve it.

On emergence from the cubicle the subject is given the same kind of intelligence tests as before entering and shows significant loss. There is disturbance of motor control. Visual perception is changed in a way difficult to describe; it is as if the object looked at was exceptionally vivid, but impaired in its relation to other objects and the background—a disturbance perhaps of the larger organization of perception. This condition may last up to 12 or 24 hours.

Subjects reported some remarkable hallucinatory activity, some which resembled the effects of mescal or the results produced by Grey Walter with flickering light. These hallucinations were primarily visual, perhaps only because the experimenters were able to control visual perception most effectively; however, some auditory and somesthetic hallucinations have been observed as well.

The nature of these phenomena is best conveyed by quoting one subject who reported over the microphone that he had just been asleep and had a very vivid dream and although he was awake, the dream was continuing. The study of dreams has a long history and is clearly important theoretically, but is hampered by the impossibility of knowing how much the subject's report is distorted by memory. In many ways the hallucinatory activity of the present experiments is indistinguishable from what we know about dreams; if it is in essence the same process but going on while the subject can describe it (not merely hot but still on the griddle), we have a new source of information, a means of direct attack, on the nature of the dream.

In its early stages the activity as it occurs in the experiment is probably not dream-like. The course of development is fairly consistent. First, when the eyes are closed the visual field is light rather than dark. Next there are reports of dots of light, lines, or simple geometrical patterns, so vivid that they are described as being a new experience. Nearly all experimental subjects reported such activity. (Many, of course, could not tolerate the experimental conditions very long and left before the full course of development was seen.) The next stage is the occurrence of repetitive patterns, like a wallpaper design, reported by three-quarters of the subjects; next, the appearance of isolated objects, without background, seen by half the subjects; and finally, integrated scenes, involving action, usually containing dream-like distortions and apparently with all the vividness of an animated cartoon, seen by about a quarter of the subjects. In general, these amused the subject, relieving his boredom, as he watched to see what the movie program would produce next. The subjects reported that the scenes seemed to be out in front of them. A few could, apparently, "look at" different parts of the scene in central vision, as one could with a movie, and up to a point could change its content by "trying." It was not, however, well under control. Usually, it would disappear if the subject were given an interesting task, but not when the subject described it nor if he did physical exercises. Its persistence and vividness interfered with sleep for some subjects and at this stage was irritating.

In their later stages the hallucinations were elaborated into everything from a peaceful rural scene to naked women diving and swimming in a woodland pool to prehistoric animals plunging through tropical forests. One man saw a pair of spectacles, which were then joined by a dozen more, without wearers, fixed intently on him; faces sometimes appeared behind the glasses, but with no eyes visible. The glasses sometimes moved in unison, as if marching in procession. Another man saw a field onto which a bathtub rolled: it moved slowly on rubber-tired wheels, with chrome hub caps. In it was seated an old man wearing a battle helmet. Another subject was highly entertained at seeing a row of squirrels marching single file across a snowy field, wearing snowshoes and carrying little bags over their shoulders.

Some of the scenes were in three dimensions, most in two (that is, as if projected on a screen). A most interesting feature was that some of the images were persistently tilted from the vertical and a few reports were given of inverted scenes, completely upside down.

There were a few reports of auditory phenomena—one subject heard the people in his hallucination talking. There was also some somesthetic imagery, as when one saw a doorknob before him, and as he touched it felt an electric shock; or when another saw a miniature rocket ship maneuvering around him and discharging pellets that he felt hitting his arm. But the most interesting of these phenomena the subject, apparently, lacked words to describe adequately. There were references to a feeling of "otherness," or bodily "strangeness." One said that his mind was like a ball of cotton wool floating in the air above him. Two independently reported that they perceived a second body, or second person, in the cubicle. One subject reported that he could not tell which of the two bodies was his own and described the two bodies as overlapping in space—not like Siamese twins, but two complete bodies with an arm, shoulder, and side of each occupying the same space.

THEORETICAL SIGNIFICANCE

The theoretical interest of these results for us extends in two directions. On the one hand, they interlock with work using more physiological methods of brain stimulation and recording and, especially, much of the recent work on the relation of the brain stem to cortical "arousal." Points of correspondence between behavioral theory and knowledge of neural function are increasing, and each new point of correspondence provides both a corrective for theory and a stimulation for further research. A theory of thought and of consciousness in physiologically intelligible terms need no longer be completely fantastic.

On the other hand, the psychological data cast new light on the relation of man to his environment, including his social environment, and it is this that I should like to discuss a little further. To do so I must go back for a moment to some earlier experiments on chimpanzee emotion. They indicate that the higher mammal may be psychologically at the mercy of his environment to a much greater degree than we have been accustomed to think.

Studies in our laboratory of the role of the environment during infancy and a large body of work reviewed recently by Beach and Jaynes [8] make it clear that psychological development is fully dependent on stimulation from the environment. Without it, intelligence does not develop normally and the personality is grossly atypical. The experiment with college students shows that a short period—even a day or so—of deprivation of a normal sensory input produces personality changes and a clear loss of capacity to solve problems. Even at maturity, then, the organism is still essentially dependent on a normal sensory environment for the maintenance of its psychological integrity.

The following data show yet another way in which the organism appears psychologically vulnerable. It has long been known that the chimpanzee may be frightened by representations of animals, such as a small toy donkey. An accidental observation of my own extended this to include representations of the chimpanzee himself, of man, and of parts of the chimpanzee or human body. A model of a chimpanzee head, in clay, produced terror in the colony of the Yerkes Laboratories, as did a life-like representation of a human head, and a number of related objects such as an actual chimpanzee head, preserved in formalin, or a colored representation

[8] Beach and Jaynes, *op. cit.*

of a human eye and eyebrow. A deeply anesthetized chimpanzee, "dead" as far as the others were concerned, aroused fear in some animals and vicious attacks by others.[9]

I shall not deal with this theoretically. What matters for our present purposes is the conclusion, rather well supported by the animal evidence, that the greater the development of intelligence the greater the vulnerability to emotional breakdown. The price of high intelligence is susceptibility to imaginative fears and unreasoning suspicion and other emotional weaknesses. The conclusion is not only supported by the animal data but also agrees with the course of development in children, growing intelligence being accompanied by increased frequency and strength of emotional problems—up to the age of five years.

Then, apparently, the trend is reversed. Adult man, more intelligent than chimpanzee or five-year-old child, seems not more subject to emotional disturbances but less. Does this then disprove the conclusion? It seemed a pity to abandon a principle that made sense of so many data that had not made sense before, and the kind of theory I was working with—neurophysiologically oriented—also pointed in the same direction. The question then was, is it possible that something is concealing the adult human being's emotional weaknesses?

From this point of view it became evident that the concealing agency is man's culture which acts as a protective cocoon. There are many indications that our emotional stability depends more on our successful avoidance of

emotional provocation than on our essential characteristics: that urbanity depends on an urbane social and physical environment. Dr. Thompson and I [10] reviewed the evidence and came to the conclusion that the development of what is called "civilization" is the progressive elimination of sources of acute fear, disgust, and anger, and that civilized man may not be less, but more, susceptible to such disturbance because of his success in protecting himself from disturbing situations so much of the time.

We may fool ourselves thoroughly in this matter. We are surprised that children are afraid of the dark or afraid of being left alone and congratulate ourselves on having got over such weakness. Ask anyone you know whether he is afraid of the dark and he will either laugh at you or be insulted. This attitude is easy to maintain in a well-lighted, well-behaved suburb. But try being alone in complete darkness in the streets of a strange city or alone at night in the deep woods and see if you still feel the same way.

We read incredulously of the taboo rules of primitive societies; we laugh at the superstitious fear of the dead in primitive people. What is there about a dead body to produce disturbance? Sensible, educated people are not so affected. One can easily show that they are, however, and that we have developed an extraordinarily complete taboo system—not just moral prohibition, but full-fledged ambivalent taboo—to deal with the dead body. I took a poll of an

[9] D. O. Hebb, "On the Nature of Fear," *Psychol. Rev.*, 1946, LIII, 259.

[10] D. O. Hebb and W. R. Thompson, "The Social Significance of Animal Studies," in G. Lindzey (ed.), *Handbook of Social Psychology* (Cambridge, Mass.: Addison-Wesley Co., Inc., 1954).

undergraduate class of 198 persons, including some nurses and veterans, to see how many had encountered a dead body. Thirty-seven had never seen a dead body in any circumstances, and 91 had seen one only after an undertaker had prepared it for burial; making a total of 65 percent who had never seen a dead body in, so to speak, its natural state. It is quite clear that for some reason we protect society against sight of, contact with, the dead body. Why?

Again, the effect of moral education, and training in the rules of courtesy, and the compulsion to dress, talk and act as others do, adds up to ensuring that the individual member of society will not act in a way that is a provocation to others—will not, that is, be a source of strong emotional disturbance, except in highly ritualized circumstances approved by society. The social behavior of a group of civilized persons, then, makes up that protective cocoon which allows us to think of ourselves as being less emotional than the explosive four-year-old or the equally explosive chimpanzee.

The well-adjusted adult, therefore, is not intrinsically less subject to emotional disturbance: he is well-adjusted, relatively unemotional, as long as he is in his cocoon. The problem of moral education, from this point of view, is not simply to produce a stable individual but to produce an individual that will (1) be stable in the existing social environment and (2) contribute to its protective uniformity. We think of some persons as being emotionally dependent, others not; but it looks as though we are all completely dependent on the environment in a way and to a degree that we have not suspected.

6. THE MISBEHAVIOR OF ORGANISMS *

Keller Breland and Marian Breland

There seems to be a continuing realization by psychologists that perhaps the white rat cannot reveal everything there is to know about behavior. Among the voices raised on this topic, Beach (1950) has emphasized the necessity of widening the range of species subjected to experimental techniques and conditions. However, psychologists as a whole do not seem to be heeding these admonitions, as Whalen (1961) has pointed out.

Perhaps this reluctance is due in part to some dark precognition of what they might find in such investigations, for the ethologists Lorenz (1950, p. 233) and Tinbergen (1951, p. 6) have warned that if psychologists are to understand and predict the behavior of organisms, it is essential that they become thoroughly familiar with the instinctive behavior patterns of each new species they essay to study. Of course, the Watsonian or neobehavioristically oriented ex-

* Reprinted from the *American Psychologist*, 1961, 16: 681–684, with permission of the authors and the American Psychological Association.

perimenter is apt to consider "instinct" an ugly word. He tends to class it with Hebb's (1960) other "seditious notions" which were discarded in the behavioristic revolution, and he may have some premonition that he will encounter this bête noir in extending the range of species and situations studied.

We can assure him that his apprehensions are well grounded. In our attempt to extend a behavioristically oriented approach to the engineering control of animal behavior by operant conditioning techniques, we have fought a running battle with the seditious notion of instinct.[1] It might be of some interest to the psychologist to know how the battle is going and to learn something about the nature of the adversary he is likely to meet if and when he tackles new species in new learning situations.

Our first report (Breland & Breland, 1951) in the *American Psychologist*, concerning our experiences in controlling animal behavior, was wholly affirmative and optimistic, saying in essence that the principles derived from the laboratory could be applied to the extensive control of behavior under nonlaboratory conditions throughout a considerable segment of the phylogenetic scale.

When we began this work, it was our aim to see if the science would work beyond the laboratory, to determine if animal psychology could stand on its own feet as an engineering discipline. These aims have been realized. We have controlled a wide range of animal be-

[1] In view of the fact that instinctive behaviors may be common to many zoological species, we consider *species specific* to be a sanitized misnomer, and prefer the possibly septic adjective *instinctive*.

havior and have made use of the great popular appeal of animals to make it an economically feasible project. Conditioned behavior has been exhibited at various municipal zoos and museums of natural history and has been used for department store displays, for fair and trade convention exhibits, for entertainment at tourist attractions, on television shows, and in the production of television commercials. Thirty-eight species, totaling over 6,000 individual animals, have been conditioned, and we have dared to tackle such unlikely subjects as reindeer, cockatoos, raccoons, porpoises, and whales.

Emboldened by this consistent reinforcement, we have ventured further and further from the security of the Skinner box. However, in this cavalier extrapolation, we have run afoul of a persistent pattern of discomforting failures. These failures, although disconcertingly frequent and seemingly diverse, fall into a very interesting pattern. They all represent breakdowns of conditioned operant behavior. From a great number of such experiences, we have selected, more or less at random, the following examples.

The first instance of our discomfiture might be entitled, What Makes Sammy Dance? In the exhibit in which this occurred, the casual observer sees a grown bantam chicken emerge from a retaining compartment when the door automatically opens. The chicken walks over about 3 feet, pulls a rubber loop on a small box which starts a repeated auditory stimulus pattern (a four-note tune). The chicken then steps up onto an 18-inch, slightly raised disc, thereby closing a timer switch, and scratches vigorously, round and round, over the disc for 15 seconds, at the rate of about two scratches per second until the automatic feeder fires in the retaining compartment. The chicken goes into the compartment to eat, thereby automatically shutting the door. The popular interpretation of this behavior pattern is that the chicken has turned on the "juke box" and "dances."

The development of this behavioral exhibit was wholly unplanned. In the attempt to create quite another type of demonstration which required a chicken simply to stand on a platform for 12–15 seconds, we found that over 50 percent developed a very strong and pronounced scratch pattern, which tended to increase in persistence as the time interval was lengthened. (Another 25 percent or so developed other behaviors—pecking at spots, and so forth.) However, we were able to change our plans so as to make use of the scratch pattern, and the result was the "dancing chicken" exhibit described above.

In this exhibit the only real contingency for reinforcement is that the chicken must depress the platform for 15 seconds. In the course of a performing day (about 3 hours for each chicken) a chicken may turn out over 10,000 unnecessary, virtually identical responses. Operant behaviorists would probably have little hesitancy in labeling this an example of Skinnerian "superstition" (Skinner, 1948) or "mediating" behavior, and we list it first to whet their explanatory appetite.

However, a second instance involving a raccoon does not fit so neatly into this paradigm. The response concerned the manipulation of money by the raccoon (who has "hands" rather similar to those of the primates). The contingency for reinforcement was picking up the coins and depositing them in a 5-inch metal box.

Raccoons condition readily, have good appetites, and this one was quite tame and an eager subject. We anticipated no trouble. Conditioning him to pick up the first coin was simple. We started out by reinforcing him for picking up a single coin. Then the metal container was introduced, with the requirement that he drop the coin into the container. Here we ran into the first bit of difficulty: he seemed to have a great deal of trouble letting go of the coin. He would rub it up against the inside of the container, pull it back out, and clutch it firmly for several seconds. However, he would finally turn it loose and receive his food reinforcement. Then the final contingency: we put him on a ratio of two, requiring that he pick up both coins and put them in the container.

Now the raccoon really had problems (and so did we). Not only could he not let go of the coins, but he spent seconds, even minutes, rubbing them together (in a most miserly fashion), and dipping them into the container. He carried on this behavior to such an extent that the practical application we had in mind—a display featuring a raccoon putting money in a piggy bank —simply was not feasible. The rubbing behavior became worse and worse as time went on, in spite of nonreinforcement.

For the third instance, we return to the gallinaceous birds. The observer sees a hopper full of oval plastic capsules which contain small toys, charms, and the like. When the S_D (a light) is presented to the chicken, she pulls a rubber loop which releases one of these capsules onto a slide, about 16 inches long, inclined at about 30 degrees. The capsule rolls down the slide and comes to rest near the end. Here one or two sharp, straight pecks by the chicken will knock it forward off the slide and out to the observer, and the chicken is then reinforced by an automatic feeder. This is all very well—most chickens are able to master these contingencies in short order. The loop pulling presents no problems; she then has only to peck the capsule off the slide to get her reinforcement.

However, a good 20 percent of all chickens tried on this set of contingencies fail to make the grade. After they have pecked a few capsules off the slide, they begin to grab at the capsules and drag them backwards into the cage. Here they pound them up and down on the floor of the cage. Of course, this results in no reinforcement for the chicken, and yet some chickens will pull in over half of all the capsules presented to them.

Almost always this problem behavior does not appear until after the capsules begin to move down the slide. Conditioning is begun with stationary capsules placed by the experimenter. When the pecking behavior becomes strong enough, so that the chicken is knocking them off the slide and getting reinforced consistently, the loop pulling is conditioned to the light. The capsules then come rolling down the slide to the chicken. Here most chickens, who before did not have this tendency, will start grabbing and shaking.

The fourth incident also concerns a chicken. Here the observer sees a chicken in a cage about 4 feet long which is placed alongside a miniature baseball field. The reason for the cage is the interesting part. At one end of the cage is an automatic electric feed hopper. At the other is an opening through which the chicken can reach and pull a loop on a bat. If she pulls the loop hard enough the bat (solenoid operated) will swing, knocking a small baseball up the playing field. If it gets past the miniature toy players on the field and hits the back fence, the chicken is automatically reinforced with food at the other end of the cage. If it does not go far enough, or hits one of the players, she tries again. This results in behavior on an irregular ratio. When the feeder sounds, she then runs down the length of the cage and eats.

Our problems began when we tried to remove the cage for photography. Chickens that had been well conditioned in this behavior became wildly excited when the ball started to move. They would jump up on the playing field, chase the ball all over the field, even knock it off on the floor and chase it around, pecking it in every direction, although they had never had access to the ball before. This behavior was so persistent and so disruptive, in spite of the fact that it was never reinforced, that he had to reinstate the cage.

The last instance we shall relate in detail is one of the most annoying and baffling for a good behaviorist. Here a pig was conditioned to pick up large wooden coins and deposit them in a large "piggy bank." The coins were placed several feet from the bank and the pig required to carry them to the bank and deposit them, usually four or five coins for one reinforcement. (Of course, we started out with one coin, near the bank.)

Pigs condition very rapidly, they have no trouble taking ratios, they have ravenous appetites (naturally), and in many ways are among the most tractable animals we have worked with. However, this particular problem behavior developed in pig after pig, usually after a period of weeks or months, getting worse every day. At first the pig would eagerly pick up one dollar, carry it to the bank, run back, get another, carry it rapidly and neatly, and so on, until the ratio was complete. Thereafter, over a period of weeks the behavior would become slower and slower. He might run over eagerly for each dollar, but on the way back, instead of carrying the dollar and depositing it simply and cleanly, he would repeatedly drop it, root it, drop it again, root it along the way, pick it up, toss it up in the air, drop it, root it some more, and so on.

We thought this behavior might simply be the dilly-dallying of an animal on a low drive. However, the behavior persisted and gained in strength in spite of a severely increased drive—he finally went through the ratios so slowly that he did not get enough to eat in the course of a day. Finally it would take the pig about 10 minutes to transport four coins a distance of about 6 feet. This problem behavior developed repeatedly in successive pigs.

There have also been other instances: hamsters that stopped working in a glass case after four or five reinforcements, porpoises and whales that swallow their manipulanda (balls and inner tubes), cats that will not leave the area of the feeder, rabbits that will not go to the feeder, the great difficulty in many species of conditioning vocalization with food reinforcement, problems in conditioning a kick in a cow, the failure to get appreciably increased effort out of the ungulates with increased drive, and so on. These we shall not dwell on in

detail, nor shall we discuss how they might be overcome.

These egregious failures came as a rather considerable shock to us, for there was nothing in our background in behaviorism to prepare us for such gross inabilities to predict and control the behavior of animals with which we had been working for years.

The examples listed we feel represent a clear and utter failure of conditioning theory. They are far from what one would normally expect on the basis of the theory alone. Furthermore, they are definite, observable; the diagnosis of theory failure does not depend on subtle statistical interpretations or on semantic legerdemain—the animal simply does not do what he has been conditioned to do.

It seems perfectly clear that, with the possible exception of the dancing chicken, which could conceivably, as we have said, be explained in terms of Skinner's superstition paradigm, the other instances do not fit the behavioristic way of thinking. Here we have animals, after having been conditioned to a specific learned response, gradually drifting into behaviors that are entirely different from those which were conditioned. Moreover, it can easily be seen that these particular behaviors to which the animals drift are clear-cut examples of instinctive behaviors having to do with the natural food getting behaviors of the particular species.

The dancing chicken is exhibiting the gallinaceous birds' scratch pattern that in nature often precedes ingestion. The chicken that hammers capsules is obviously exhibiting instinctive behavior having to do with breaking open of seed pods or the killing of insects, grubs, etc. The raccoon is demonstrating so-called "washing behavior." The rubbing and washing response may result, for example, in the removal of the exoskeleton of a crayfish. The pig is rooting or shaking—behaviors which are strongly built into this species and are connected with the food getting repertoire.

These patterns to which the animals drift require greater physical output and therefore are a violation of the so-called "law of least effort." And most damaging of all, they stretch out the time required for reinforcement when nothing in the experimental setup requires them to do so. They have only to do the little tidbit of behavior to which they were conditioned—for example, pick up the coin and put it in the container—to get reinforced immediately. Instead, they drag the process out for a matter of minutes when there is nothing in the contingency which forces them to do this. Moreover, increasing the drive merely intensifies this effect.

It seems obvious that these animals are trapped by strong instinctive behaviors, and clearly we have here a demonstration of the prepotency of such behavior patterns over those which have been conditioned.

We have termed this phenomenon "instinctive drift." The general principle seems to be that wherever an animal has strong instinctive behaviors in the area of the conditioned response, after continued running the organism will drift toward the instinctive behavior to the detriment of the conditioned behavior and even to the delay or preclusion of the reinforcement. In a very boiled-down, simplified form, it might be stated as "learned behavior drifts toward instinctive behavior."

All this, of course, is not to disparage the use of conditioning techniques, but is intended as a demonstration that there are definite weaknesses in the philosophy underlying these techniques. The pointing out of such weaknesses should make possible a worthwhile revision in behavior theory.

The notion of instinct has now become one of our basic concepts in an effort to make sense of the welter of observations which confront us. When behaviorism tossed out instinct, it is our feeling that some of its power of prediction and control were lost with it. From the foregoing examples, it appears that although it was easy to banish the Instinctivists from the science during the Behavioristic Revolution, it was not possible to banish instinct so easily.

And if, as Hebb suggests, it is advisable to reconsider those things that behaviorism explicitly threw out, perhaps it might likewise be advisable to examine what they tacitly brought in— the hidden assumptions which led most disastrously to these breakdowns in the theory.

Three of the most important of these tacit assumptions seem to us to be: that the animal comes to the laboratory as a virtual *tabula rasa*, that species differences are insignificant, and that all responses are about equally conditionable to all stimuli.

It is obvious, we feel, from the foregoing account, that these assumptions are no longer tenable. After 14 years of continuous conditioning and observation of thousands of animals, it is our reluctant conclusion that the behavior of any species cannot be adequately understood, predicted, or controlled without knowledge of its instinctive patterns, evolutionary history, and ecological niche.

In spite of our early successes with

the application of behavioristically oriented conditioning theory, we readily admit now that ethological facts and attitudes in recent years have done more to advance our practical control of animal behavior than recent reports from American "learning labs."

Moreover, as we have recently discovered, if one begins with evolution and instinct as the basic format for the science, a very illuminating viewpoint can be developed which leads naturally to a drastically revised and simplified conceptual framework of startling explanatory power (to be reported elsewhere).

It is hoped that this playback on the theory will be behavioral technology's partial repayment to the academic science whose impeccable empiricism we have used so extensively.

REFERENCES

BEACH, F. A. The snark was a boojum. *Amer. Psychologist,* 1950, **5,** 115–124.
BRELAND, K., & BRELAND, M. A field of applied animal psychology. *Amer. Psychologist,* 1951, **6,** 202–204.
HEBB, D. O. The American revolution. *Amer. Psychologist,* 1960, **15,** 735–745.
LORENZ, K. Innate behaviour patterns. In *Symposia of the Society for Experimental Biology.* No. 4. *Physiological mechanisms in animal behaviour.* New York: Academic Press, 1950.
SKINNER, B. F. Superstition in the pigeon. *J. exp. Psychol.,* 1948, **38,** 168–172.
TINBERGEN, N. *The study of instinct.* Oxford: Clarendon, 1951.
WHALEN, R. E. Comparative psychology. *Amer. Psychologist,* 1961, **16,** 84.

7. THE CHOICE OF VARIABLES IN THE STUDY OF SOCIALIZATION *

Eleanor E. Maccoby

Perhaps the greatest change that has occurred in the field of child development in the past 15 years has been the increasing emphasis on socialization.

What are the important variables in parental behavior that ought to make a difference in the development of the child? The process of selecting and defining variables is, of course, the very heart of theory-making. There are as many possible variables as there are ideas about what causes what in human development. I cannot attempt here to give any sort of roster of variables; the task would be too great and might not prove very useful. I simply want to point out some of the major classes of variables that have been used and give a little of the history of the reasons why we have chosen to measure these things and not others and perhaps point to a few ways in which we could clarify the meaning of the dimension we are using.

In my opinion, it *is* valuable to carry

* Excerpted from *Sociometry,* 1961, 24: 357–371, with permission of the author and the American Sociological Association.

out at the human level studies which attempt to employ the standard variables that have grown out of laboratory study on learning, where most of the work has been done on subhuman species. But, in the process of applying such variables to socialization studies, the variables almost perforce undergo certain modifications and elaborations, with the result that translating traditional behavior theory variables into the socialization setting sometimes results in the addition of something new, and the possibility of getting new kinds of principles.

Let me give an example. Suppose we wanted to study the effects of a particular schedule of reward. What do we mean by reward? The traditional approach to reward has been to produce a physiological drive, such as hunger or thirst, through deprivation; and then to reinforce the desired behavior by presenting a drive-relevant reinforcing stimulus. But even in fairly young children, a rapid development of complex motivation occurs, and this changes the nature of the reinforcements to which children will be responsive. B. F. Skinner encountered this fact when he was developing his teaching machines. The early models were devised so as to emit little pieces of chocolate candy whenever a child made the correct response. But it was soon evident that a child progressed through a series of arithmetic or spelling problems just as readily without the candy; in fact, the giving of candy sometimes disrupted the learning process. Skinner, therefore, abandoned the candy rewards, and the current models of his machine rely upon no other reward than the child's interest in doing his work correctly—buttressed, no doubt, by a certain amount of pressure from the teacher and parents. This incident illustrates a major question about the definition of variables: what happens to the variable "amount of reward" when it is translated into situations of teacher-child, or parent-child, interaction? In modern societies, children's physiological drives are regularly and quite fully satisfied and are seldom used as a basis for training. That is, most parents do not let the child get hungry, thirsty, wet, or overtired, and then make the satisfaction of these needs conditional on good behavior. Rather, the rewards used are money, a trip to the zoo, being allowed to stay up for a special TV program, etc. A gift of candy for some children becomes symbolic of affection instead of vice versa. Very commonly, behavior is reinforced simply through the giving of approval, affection, or attention. So the concept "reward," when it refers to the rewards which parents use in socializing their children is not directly comparable to the concept as it was originally developed in studies of animal learning. Of course, it is not really a new idea to point out that different kinds of organisms are capable of being rewarded by different kinds of things. It is clear enough that there are as many kinds of rewards as there are distinguishable motives, and that both motives and rewards vary between species and within species. But the new idea that has been added in socialization studies is that there may be distinguishable *classes* of rewards which may have different effects. The primary distinction made in studies so far has been between material reward and praise. Material reward covers all instances of giving the child some object or privilege that he wants, conditional upon good behavior. Praise depends to some degree upon the previous establishment of a relationship between the socializing agent and the child, such that the approval of this particular adult is something the child wants. That is, the effectiveness of praise ought to depend upon the identity of the person doing the praising and upon this person's being someone the child loves, fears, or must depend upon for the satisfaction of needs.

The same kind of differentiation of a variable has occurred with respect to punishment. Students of the socialization process have been working under the assumption that not all kinds of aversive events following a child's act will have the same effect. The distinction most commonly made is that between physical punishment and so-called love-oriented discipline, or withdrawal of love. There are other categories of punishment, too, such as withdrawal of privileges and ridicule, which are less interesting than the first two because there are fewer hypotheses about their probable effects. Let us concentrate for a moment on the distinction between physical punishment and withdrawal of love. Physical punishment is easy enough to define, although in rating its frequency and severity, the researcher is always troubled about the problem of how to weigh slaps and shakings in relation to formal spankings. More tricky by far is the matter of defining withdrawal of love. Sears and his associates (19) have defined it as any act or statement on the part of the parent that threatens the affectional bond between the parent and child. This would include the mother's turning her back on the child, refusing to speak to him or smile at him or be in the same room with him, saying she doesn't like him when he does

disapproved things, etc. The system of classification of techniques of discipline presented by Beverly Allinsmith in her chapter in Miller and Swanson's book, *Inner Conflict and Defense* (1), similarly emphasizes the distinction between "psychological" and "corporal" punishment, but defines psychological discipline somewhat differently. This classification for Allinsmith includes manipulating the child by shaming the child, appealing to his pride or guilt, and expressing disappointment over his misdeeds. But there is another dimension considered in the rating: namely, the amount of emotional control the mother displays in administering her discipline. Thus, if a mother shouts angrily at the child, "I hate you for doing that," Allinsmith would *not* classify this as psychological discipline, while Sears *et al.* would. But the mother who says calmly and perhaps coldly, "Now, dear, you know I don't like little boys who do that," would be classified as using psychological discipline in both systems. The difference in these two classification systems stems in part from two different views of the nature of the process which gives psychological discipline its effect. Sears *et al.* view it as a technique which arouses the child's anxiety over whether he is loved and approved of, and thereby elicits efforts on the child's part to regain his parents' approval by conforming, apologizing, or making amends. Allinsmith, on the other hand, emphasizes two things: (a) the *modeling* function of discipline, pointing out that a mother who loses her temper at the same time she is trying to teach the child to control his, will have a child who will do as the mother *does* rather than as she *says*; and (b) the target the child chooses for the aggressive impulses aroused in him as a consequence of punishment. The reasoning here is that the openly angry mother becomes a more legitimate target for the child's counter-aggression. The distinction between the two definitions of the dimension is further brought out when we consider the kinds of findings reported in the studies using them: Sears *et al.* found that withdrawal of love was associated with high development of conscience, physical punishment with low; Allinsmith found that psychological discipline, as she defined it, was associated with *indirect* fantasy expressions of aggression in the children they studied, corporal punishment with *direct* expression of aggression. All this illustrates the fact that fairly subtle differences in the definition of a dimension can affect the nature of child behavior that can be predicted from it. But more importantly, both these studies illustrate the fact that when we attempted to take over the variable "punishment" from the learning laboratories, we found it necessary to subdivide and differentiate the variable and gained predictive power by doing so.

I have been attempting to cite ways in which I think that socialization studies have improved upon some of the standard variables employed in laboratory studies. There are instances, alas, in which we have not taken note of the differences which exist between the laboratory and the standard socialization settings, and thus have failed to identify and make use of some potentially promising variables. For example, in laboratory studies, we can take it for granted that the experimenter is there during training sessions, administering either reinforcements or aversive stimuli in some orderly relationship to the subject's

responses. In the parent-child relationship, the parent is by no means always functioning as a trainer, and parents differ greatly in the degree to which they do so. Some parents keep track quite continuously of what the child is doing, and engage in a constant flow of interaction, both verbal and non-verbal, with the child. Other parents, for a substantial portion of the time they are with their children, are bored, busy, withdrawn, intoxicated, watching television, or subject to some other state or activity which precludes their responding to the child unless he becomes very insistent. In such a household the children are, of course, in a very different learning situation than children growing up with more wholly attentive parents. I think the sheer amount of interaction may in some cases be a more important variable for predicting characteristics of the child than the nature of the interaction that does occur. Let me give an example. In a study Dr. Lucy Rau and I are now doing at Stanford, we have selected groups of children who show discrepancies in their intellectual abilities. That is, we have one group of children who are good at verbal tasks but poor at number, another group who are good at spatial tasks but poor at verbal, and so on. One of our students, Mrs. Bing, has interviewed the mothers of the children, and has also conducted some observation sessions in which the mother presents achievement tasks to the child while the observer records the kind and amount of the mother's involvement with the child's work. Mrs. Bing has found that it is the *amount*, rather than the *kind*, of mother-child interaction that best predicts what the child's pattern of intellectual skills will be. That is, the mothers of the highly verbal children use more praise, but also more criticism, than do the mothers of equally bright children whose area of special skill is nonverbal. Their total level of interaction with the child is greater, and this interaction includes the administration of what we would regard as aversive stimuli as well as reinforcements. The variable "amount of interaction" emerged in our factor analysis of the scales in the *Patterns of Child Rearing* study (19)—we titled this variable "responsible child-rearing orientation" for lack of a better name, but we never made much use of the variable because it did not fit in with the theoretical formulation of our study. But I suspect that for any future work in which we are trying to predict such things as the child's cognitive maturity level or his achievement motivation, we may find that this variable is a better predictor than the less global variables (such as amount of praise) that we have been relying on up till now.

So far, I have been discussing the process of translating variables from laboratory studies of learning to the socialization setting, and have pointed out that we have been successful in employing such variables as reward and punishment, but that in the process of using these variables, we have found useful ways of subdividing them. Let us consider the theoretical meaning of the elaborations of these variables that have occurred.

When we make the distinction between material reward and praise, and the distinction between love-oriented punishment and punishment that depends for its effect upon producing direct physical pain, we are really taking note of the fact that the effect of discipline, and in fact the very nature of the discipline that is possible to use with a child, depends upon the history of the relationship that has been developed between the child and the person who is training him. And here is a new class of variables that socialization studies have added to the list of variables derived from classical studies of learning. In laboratory studies of learning, it has not been found necessary (at least until very recently) to ask whether the experimental subject loved or hated the machine that was emitting pellets of food and drops of water, or whether the characteristics of the machine or person presenting the rewards made any difference in the effectiveness of the reinforcement. Socialization studies, on the other hand, have found the identity of the socializing agent, and certain of his personality characteristics, to be important.

The emphasis on the importance of the relationship between trainer and learner came, of course, out of psychodynamic theories of personality development. Learning theory and psychoanalytic theory differ, I think, with respect to what they believe the basic nature of the socialization process is. This is an oversimplification, but I believe it would be reasonably accurate to say that a learning theorist would regard socialization as a learning process in which certain actions of the child's are selected out by virtue of reinforcement, others tried and dropped because they are in some way punished or nonreinforced. The parents have a primary role in administering the rewards and punishments for the child's actions, although they do not necessarily do this deliberately and consciously as a teaching effort. And, of course, there are other sources of reward and punishment than the parents' reactions which will help to determine what behavior the child retains.

The psychoanalytic approach, on the other hand, would emphasize not the detailed learning of specific actions on the basis of their outcome, but the providing of conditions which will motivate the child to take on spontaneously the socialized behavior the parent wants him to have. The terms introjection, internalization, learning through role-playing, and identification have been used in this connection; they all refer to the child's tendency to copy, to take on as his own, the behavior, attitudes, and values of the significant people in his life, even when the socializing agents have not said "that's a good boy" or given him a piece of candy for performing these acts or holding these values. I will not go into the controversy concerning which so much has been written as to whether the child is more likely to identify with the person who is powerful and feared or with the person who is loved; nor will I discuss the several thoughtful efforts by personality theorists to reconcile the two points of view. The only important point for our consideration here is that the psychoanalytic view of socialization has led to an exploration of such variables as the warmth or hostility of the socializing agent toward the child.

There can be no doubt that measures of the warmth of the parent-child relationship have turned out to be enormously useful in socialization studies, in a number of ways. In some studies, warmth has been found to have a direct relationship to some dependent variable. For example, McCord and McCord (14) have found that warmth in fathers was associated with low crime rate in sons.

In other studies, warmth has turned out to be a useful crosscutting variable which interacts with other variables in such a way that other variables only begin to show their effects when the sample is first sub-divided into groups differing in parental warmth. For example, in the *Patterns of Child Rearing* study, Sears *et al.* (19) found that withdrawal of love is associated with rapid development of conscience, but only if this technique is employed by a warm mother; also that punishment for toilet accidents disrupts the toilet-training process, but that the greatest disruption occurs if punishment is administered by a cold mother.

Warmth also occupies a central role in socialization studies in its relationship to other measures of child-training variables. There have been, to my knowledge, three factor analyses carried out on sets of socialization variables. One of these was on the Fels parent behavior rating scales (17), one on the PARI (24), and one on the dimensions employed by Sears *et al.* in the *Patterns* study (19). In the latter two, warmth emerged as a fairly clear factor. In the first, there were two factors, one called "concern for the child" and the other called "parent-child harmony," which taken together are probably close to what is meant by warmth in the other two studies. It is clear then, that both in terms of its predictive value for the child's behavior and its central place among the other interrelated child-training variables, warmth is a variable to be taken seriously. Why is it so important? I have already pointed out why the psychodynamic theorists believe it to be so—because of its role in producing identification. But the laboratory learning theorists can acknowledge its importance for another very simple reason. Before a parent can socialize a child, he must have established a relationship with the child such that the child will stay in the vicinity of the parent and orient himself toward the parent. A warm parent keeps the child responsive to his directions by providing an atmosphere in which the child has continuous expectations that good things will happen to him if he stays near his parent and responds to his parent's wishes. Fear of punishment can also make the child attentive to the parent, of course, but it establishes as well the conflicting motivation to escape out of reach of the punisher.

I'm sure I needn't belabor any further the notion that warmth is an important variable. But to say this is not enough. We still are faced with considerable difficulty in definition. It has been the experience of a number of people working with child-training data that they find themselves able to make reliable distinctions between mothers they call warm and mothers they call cold, and they find it possible to train others to make similar distinctions, but find it difficult indeed to define exactly what cues they are using to make the rating.

I suspect one source of difficulty is that the behavior we look for as indicating warmth varies with the age of the child the mother is dealing with. When the child is an infant, we are likely to label a mother as warm if she gives a good deal of the contact comfort that Harlow (8) has described. As the child grows older, the part played by the giving of contact comfort in the total constellation of warmth undoubtedly declines. When a child is ten, a mother seldom expresses her warm feelings for

him by holding him on her lap. Rather, they are more likely to be expressed by the mother showing interest in the child and what he is doing, by helping unconditionally when help is needed, by being cordial and relaxed. Now warmth as expressed this way is not the same thing as giving contact comfort, and it is not to be expected that the same individuals would necessarily be good at both. Those of you who have read Brody's fascinating, detailed descriptions of mothers' behavior toward their infants (4) will perhaps have noted that the mothers who gave effective contact comfort, in the sense of holding the child comfortably and close, stroking it occasionally, imparting some rocking motion, handling it skillfully and gently in the process of caring for the child—the women who could do all these things well were not necessarily the same women who expressed delight and pride in their children, who noticed their little accomplishments, or who looked upon their infants as individuals. We should therefore not be surprised if there are low correlations between a mother's warmth toward her infant and her warmth toward the same child when it is older. If a primary ingredient of warmth is being able to gratify the child's needs unconditionally, and if the child's needs change from the infantile needs for being fed and being given contact comfort to the more mature needs for various kinds of ego support, then it is necessary for a mother to change considerably as her child changes, in order to be warm towards him at all ages. Some mothers make this change more easily than others. It is true that Schaeffer and Bayley (18), in their longitudinal study of a group of mothers, did find a substantial degree of continuity in the degree of warmth displayed by a given mother toward a given child as the child grew older. There were undoubtedly individual differences in the ways warmth was manifested, and in the appropriateness of a mother's particular style of warmth-giving to the needs of her child at each developmental stage.

From the standpoint of making use of the variable in research, it appears that we should recognize that measuring the mother's current warmth at the time the child is, say, in nursery school or in the primary grades may not be an especially good index of how warm she was to the child as an infant. Furthermore, her warmth in infancy might predict quite different characteristics of the child than her warmth in middle childhood. If there is any relation at all between nurturance to an infant and its later personality traits, infant nurturance ought to relate only to those aspects of personality that presumably have their foundation in infancy—such as Erikson's dimension of trust (6), or various aspects of orality. Achievement motivation, on the other hand, if it is related to the mother's warmth at all, ought to be related to measures of this variable taken when the child is older. A finding of Bronfenbrenner's (5) seems to support this point about the importance of warmth-giving being appropriate to the developmental level of the child. He was studying high-school-aged children and employed several variables relating to the kind and amount of affectionate interchange between these adolescents and their parents. He measured the parents' affection-giving (in the sense of direct demonstrativeness), use of affective rewards, nurturance, and affiliative companionship. Among these variables, it was only the last one, affiliative com-

panionship, that correlated with the child's current level of responsibility taking. We can speculate that this particular aspect of warmth is the one that fits in much better with an adolescent's needs than either giving him kisses or peanut butter sandwiches. All this means that warmth has to be defined in terms of parental responsiveness to the changing needs of the child.

I have referred to socialization variables that came originally from laboratory studies of learning, and that have been adapted for use in studying the socialization process. I have also referred to variables that originated in psychodynamic thinking. There is a set of variables that is difficult to classify in terms of these two theoretical systems; I am referring to the dimension "permissiveness vs. restrictiveness," which emerged in our factor analysis of the *Patterns* variables, and to the related dimension of "control vs. laissez-faire" which has come out of the factor analysis of the PARI scales. The theoretical status of these variables is confusing because they relate to both psychoanalytic and learning theory, but the predictions from the two theories as to the probable effects of "permissiveness" or "control" are sometimes quite different. To cite a familiar example, there is the issue of what ought to be the effects of permissive treatment of the infant's sucking responses. The question is complex, but a simplified version of the opposing positions would be this: the learning theorist would argue that if an infant is permitted extensive sucking, his sucking habit will be strengthened, and he will be more likely to suck his thumb, pencils, and so on, at a later stage. The psychodynamic theorist would argue that permitting extensive infantile sucking satisfies oral needs and reduces the likelihood of excessive oral behavior at a later age. The same kind of difference of opinion can be found concerning whether permissive treatment of a child's aggressive or dependent responses should increase or decrease those responses. Now, of course, the fact that different theories produce different predictions concerning the effects of a variable is no reason for abandoning the variable. On the contrary, it is cause for rejoicing, and we should by all means continue to use the variable so that we can get data which will bear upon the validity of the theories. The trouble is that when we arrive at the point of trying to get agreement on the interpretation of findings, it sometimes turns out that the two schools of thought did not mean the same thing by "permissiveness." If a study shows that the more permissive parents are toward their children's aggression the more aggressive the children become, the psychodynamic theorist may say, "Well, by permissiveness I didn't mean *license*; the child must have limits set for him but he must also be allowed to express his feelings." If, on the other hand, a study shows that children heavily punished for aggression are more aggressive on the playground, or prefer aggressive TV programs, the learning theorist may say, "Well, of course, if the parents' methods of stopping aggression are such as to provide additional instigation to aggression, then their nonpermissiveness won't eliminate the behavior." We begin to see that there are some hidden meanings in such a term as "permissiveness" and that we are dealing with several dimensions. Continuing with the example of aggression, we can see that permissiveness for

aggression could mean the following things:

1. The mother holds the attitude that aggression is an acceptable, even desirable, form of behavior.
2. The mother does not like aggressive behavior and expects to limit it in her children, but feels that it is natural and inevitable at certain ages and so does not react strongly when her young child displays anger. A related definition of permissiveness would be pacing the demands for self-control placed upon the child to correspond with his development level.
3. The mother is not especially interested in the child or is otherwise occupied, and does not act to stop or prevent his aggression because she does not notice what he is doing.
4. The mother does not act early in a sequence of her child's aggressive behavior, but waits till the behavior has become fairly intense.

And at the other end of the scale, the effect of *non*permissiveness ought to depend upon how the nonpermitting is done—whether by punishment, by reinforcing alternative behavior, by environmental control that removes the instigations to undesired behavior, or some other means. The basic point I wish to emphasize is that I believe "permissiveness" is not a unitary variable, and that we need to work more directly with its components.

So far I have discussed several classes of variables: the ones translated as directly as possible from laboratory studies of learning (e.g., amount and kind of reward and punishment), and variables such as warmth and permissiveness of the socializing agent, which have their origins more in psychodynamic theories. There is another class of variables which has been emerging as more and more important, namely the "social structure" variables. These variables have their origin largely in sociological thinking. I do not have time to give them more than the most cursory attention, but I do not believe they can be omitted if we are to do any sort of justice to the scope of significant variables employed in current socialization studies. One has only to list a few findings which have come out of the investigation of social structure factors to see how essential it has become to take them into account. Here is a brief sampling of such findings:

1. With adolescents, parents are most strict with children who are of the same sex as the dominant parent (16).
2. A mother's use of strongly dominant child-rearing techniques (called "unqualified power assertion" in this study) is related to her husband's F score (authoritarian personality score), but not to her own (11).
3. A mother's behavior toward her children is more closely related to her husband's education than her own, and her behavior is more closely related to her husband's education than is *his* behavior to his own education. Thus it appears that it is the family's social status, as indicated by the husband's education, that influences the mother's socialization practices (5).

4. Sons are more intra-punitive if their mothers are primarily responsible for discipline than they are if their fathers are the primary disciplinarians (10).
5. Aspects of social organization such as whether residence is patrilocal, matrilocal, or neolocal, and whether marriage is polygamous or monogamous, determine such aspects of culture as the length of the postpartum sex taboo, the duration of exclusive mother-child sleeping arrangements, and the amount of authority the father has over the child; these factors in turn influence such socialization practices as the age of weaning, the severity of the socialization pressures which are directed toward breaking up the child's dependency upon the mother, and the existence and nature of puberty rites at adolescence. These socialization practices then in their turn influence certain aspects of personality, including certain culturally established defense systems (21, 22, 23).
6. When offered a choice between a small piece of candy now vs. a large one later, children from father-present homes can postpone gratification more easily than children from father-absent homes (15).

These findings all represent efforts to put socialization practices into a cultural or social-structural context. In each case, socialization practices are regarded as a link in a several-step chain, and consideration is given to the factors which determine the socialization practices themselves, as well as to the effects these practices in their turn have upon the child. It is clear that the way parents treat their children will be a function of their relationship to each other (especially of the distribution of authority between them), of the place the family has in the status system of the society in which the family resides, of the society's kinship system, etc. Of course, not every student of socialization need concern himself with all the steps in the complex sequence; he may, and often does, select a set of socialization practices and relate them to the child's behavior without going back to the conditions which led to these practices. But he needs to be aware of the degree to which socialization practices are embedded in a cultural context, and even needs to be alert to the possibility that the "same" socialization practice may have different effects when it is part of different cultural settings. So far, few studies have been planned or analyzed with this possibility in mind, but it might be worth some empirical examination.

It is time to make explicit an assumption that has been implicit so far about the constancy of personality from one situation to another and from one time to another. When we select aspects of parental behavior to study, and try to relate these to measured characteristics of the child, we usually measure what we believe to be reasonably pervasive, reasonably enduring "traits" of the parent and child. Orville Brim (3) in a recent paper, has leveled a direct attack at the notion of trait constancy. He has asserted that there is no such thing as a "warm" person, nor an "aggressive" person, nor a "dependent"

person, but that behavior is specific to roles. This would mean that the same individual may be aggressive with his subordinates and dependent toward his boss; that a child may be emotionally expressive with his same-sexed age mates, but not with his teachers or his parents. The question of exactly how general personality traits are, is, of course, a matter that personality theorists have struggled with for many years. But our view of this matter will have some bearing upon our selection and definition of socialization variables. For if a child's behavior is going to be entirely specific to roles, then there is no point in trying to predict any generalized traits in the child; rather, we should be looking for those aspects of the socialization situation that will determine what behavior will be adopted by the child in each different role relationship in which he will find himself. If we wanted to find what socialization practices were associated with the child's becoming dominant or submissive, for example, we would have to study how his dominant behavior had been reacted to when he was playing with same-sexed siblings, and study this separately from the socialization of the same behavior when he was playing with opposite-sexed siblings. Only thus could we predict, according to Brim, how dominant he would be with other boys in the classroom; and we would have to make a separate prediction of his dominance with girls in the classroom. We have already been following Brim's advice, in essence, when we do studies in which we test how the child's behavior varies with the role characteristics of the person with whom he is interacting. A good example is Gewirtz' and Baer's study on the interaction between the sex of the experimenter and the effects of interrupted nurturance (7). But to follow Brim's point further, we would have to investigate the ways in which the child's behavior toward specific categories of "others" was conditioned by differential socialization in these role relationships.

I do not believe that either socialization or the child's reaction tendencies are as role-specific as Brim claims; but obviously role differentiation does occur, and he is quite right in calling our attention to the fact that, for some variables at least, we should be studying socialization separately within roles. Actually, role is only one aspect of situational variability; we have known ever since the days of Hartshorne and May (9) that trait behavior like "honesty" is situation-specific. They found, for example, that the child who will cheat on the playground is not necessarily the same child who will cheat in the classroom, and that cheating is a function of the specific task presented to the child. This means that, in studying the effects of socialization, we either have to abandon efforts to predict characteristics like "honesty" and attempt to study only those characteristics of the child that are at least somewhat constant across situations, or we have to choose socialization variables that are themselves much more situation-specific, and make much more detailed predictions. An example of the utility of making socialization variables more specific to the situations they are intended to predict is provided in a study by Levy (13), in which it was found that a child's adjustment to a hospital experience was *not* a function of the parents having trained the child generally to meet many different kinds of stress situations; rather, the child's response to

hospitalization was predicted only from the amount of training the parent gave in advance for the meeting of this *particular* stress situation.

The same sort of situation prevails with respect to trait constancy over time. In their recent article on dependency, Kagan and Moss (12) were able to present repeated measurements of dependency in the same group of individuals—measurements which began at the age of three and continued into the late twenties. The most notable feature of their findings was the absence of continuity in this trait. The children who were dependent at age three and four were not the same individuals who emerged as dependent in adulthood. There was simply no continuity at all for boys, while there was some, but not a great deal, for girls. Let us consider Kagan's findings from the standpoint of efforts to study the socialization practices that are related to dependency. The first and obvious point is that we cannot expect to find any characteristic of the parent's behavior that will correlate with dependency in the young child and also correlate with dependency when the child is an adolescent or adult. This is not to say that the only correlations we can hope for are those between socialization practices and child characteristics measured at the same point in time. It is of course most likely that we shall be able to find aspects of a parent's current behavior that correlate with characteristics his child is displaying at the same time. But it is also possible that we could find aspects of the parent's current behavior whose effects will not show up until later. That is, perhaps there were things the parents of Kagan's sample of children were doing when these children were three and four that had some bearing upon how dependent the children became at the age of ten or eleven. But it is clear enough that whatever these delayed-action variables are, they could hardly be the same variables as the ones which determined how dependent the children were at age three, since it was not the same children who were displaying large amounts of dependency behavior at the two ages.

I have pointed to the way in which different theoretical systems, and different social-science disciplines, have converged to define and elaborate some of the variables which have been used in studies of socialization. In some cases this convergence has produced useful new knowledge; in others it has produced confusion over the meaning of variables. More importantly, it has produced a startling range of findings which have not yet been integrated into a theory of socialization. This is a major task that remains to be done.

REFERENCES

1. ALLINSMITH, B. "Directness with which Anger is Expressed," in D. R. Miller and G. E. Swanson, eds., *Inner Conflict and Defense*, New York: Holt, Rinehart and Winston, 1960.
2. BALDWIN, A. L., J. KALHORN, & F. H. BREESE. "The Appraisal of Parent Behavior," *Psychological Monographs*, 1949, 63, No. 4.
3. BRIM, O. G. "Personality Development as Role Learning," in I. Iscoe and H. Stevenson, eds., *Personality Development in Children*, Austin, Texas: University of Texas Press, 1960.
4. BRODY, S. *Patterns of Mothering*, New York: International Universities Press, 1957.
5. BRONFENBRENNER, U. "Some Famil-ial Antecedents of Responsibility and Leadership in Adolescents," (dittoed paper) Cornell University, 1959.
6. ERIKSEN, E. H. *Childhood and Society*, New York: Norton, 1950.
7. GEWIRTZ, J. L., & D. M. BAER. "Does Brief Social 'Deprivation' Enhance the Effectiveness of a Social Reinforcer ('Approval')?" *American Psychologist*, 1956, 11, 428–429.
8. HARLOW, H. F. "On the Nature of Love," *American Psychologist*, 1958, 13, 673–685.
9. HARTSHORNE, H., & M. A. MAY. *Studies in Deceit*, New York: Macmillan, 1928.
10. HENRY, A. F. "Family Role Structure and Self-Blame," *Social Forces*, 1956, 35, 34–38.
11. HOFFMAN, M. L. "Power Assertion by Parents and Its Impact on the Child," *Child Development*, 1960, 31, 129–144.
12. KAGAN, J., & H. A. Moss. "The Stability of Passive and Dependent Behavior from Childhood through Adulthood," *Child Development*, 1960, 31, 577–591.
13. LEVY, E. "Children's Behavior Under Stress and Its Relation to Training by Parents to Respond to Stress Situation," *Child Development*, 1959, 30, 307–324.
14. McCORD, W., & J. McCORD. *The Origins of Crime*, New York: Columbia University Press, 1959.
15. MISCHEL, W. "Preference for Delayed Reinforcement: An Experimental Study of Cultural Observation," *Journal of Abnormal and Social Psychology*, 1958, 56, 57–61.
16. PAPANEK, M. L. "Family Structure and Child-Training Practices," Ph.D. dissertation (unpublished), Radcliffe College, 1954.
17. ROFF, M. "A Factorial Study of the Fels Parent Behavior Scales," *Child Development*, 1949, 20, 29–45.
18. SCHAEFFER, E. S., & N. BAYLEY. "Consistency of Maternal Behavior from Infancy to Pre-Adolescence," *Journal of Abnormal and Social Psychology*, 1960, 61, 1–6.

19. SEARS, R. R., E. E. MACCOBY, & H. LEVIN. *Patterns of Child Rearing*, New York: Harper & Row, 1957.

20. SHOBEN, E. J. "The Assessment of Parental Attitudes in Relation to Child Adjustment," *Genetic Psychology Monographs*, 1949, **39.**

21. WHITING, J. W. M. "Sin, Sorcery and the Superego," in M. R. Jones, ed., *Nebraska Symposium on Motivation*, Lincoln, Nebraska: University of Nebraska Press, 1959.

22. WHITING, J. W. M., E. H. CHASDI, H. F. ANTONOVSKY, & B. C. AYRES. "The Learning of Values," in F. Kluckhohn and E. Vogt, eds., *The Peoples of Rimrock: A Comparative Study of Values Systems*, (in press).

23. WHITING, J. W. M., R. KLUCKOHN, & A. ANTHONY. "The Function of Male Initiation Rites at Puberty," in E. E. Maccoby, T. M. Newcomb, and E. L. Hartley, eds., *Readings in Social Psychology*, New York: Holt, Rinehart and Winston, 1958.

24. ZUCKERMAN, M., B. BARRETT-RIBBACK, I. MONASHKIN, & J. NORTON. "Normative Data and Factor Analysis on the Parental Attitude Research Instrument," *Journal of Consulting Psychology*, 1958, **22,** 165–171.

8. A COMPARISON OF AUGMENTATION AND REDUCTION AS MODES OF INFLUENCE *

Kenneth Ring and Harold H. Kelley

If a teacher or trainer is to be effective in a social learning situation, he must provide a consistent schedule of reinforcements, rewarding the behavior he considers correct and/or punishing that which he considers incorrect. Being consistent is sometimes made difficult for him by the fact that the student or trainee has ways of preventing his responses from coming under the trainer's surveillance. For this reason, it is necessary for the trainer to consider the effects of his reinforcement schedule not only upon the particular response discrimination he is trying to teach but also upon the trainee's tendency to conceal or reveal his responses.

A fact that seems likely to be important in affecting concealment (and subsequent learning) is the relative magnitude of the rewards and punishments the trainer delivers when he does have information about the trainee's choices. We consider two cases: The trainer delivers large rewards for the trainee's performance of the desired behavior but only very small punishments for "errors," or he delivers only small rewards for correct responses but massive punishments for incorrect ones.

These two procedures correspond closely to two modes of influence described by McGregor (1948). The first is similar to the method of *augmentation* wherein a powerful person (the trainer, to whom we will refer as A) provides rewards in order to induce the trainee, B, to perform the desired behavior,

* Reprinted from *Journal of Abnormal and Social Psychology*, 1963, 66: 95–102, with permission of the senior author and the American Psychological Association. This study was performed under Grant G-5553 from the National Science Foundation.

while the second is similar to the method of *reduction* under which, for the same purpose, A applies negative sanctions whenever B performs a behavior other than the desired one. McGregor was concerned with the relative effectiveness of these two influence methods, arguing that the judicious use of augmentation would be more likely to bring about the desired behavior in a subordinate than would the reliance upon reductive techniques. He did not, however, mention the implications of augmentation versus reduction for response concealment, a factor which we believe cannot be disregarded in accounting for the differences in learning and influence attributable to these two techniques.

With respect to the effect of these methods upon B's concealment of his responses, Thibaut and Kelley (1959) point out that in the case of augmentation B will, if necessary, present evidence to A of his compliance with A's wishes in order to insure receiving his reward. If, however, A employs reduction as his technique, B may find it advantageous to conceal his behavior or in other ways to make it difficult for A to monitor it. The reason, of course, is that B can get the best outcomes the relationship has to offer (i.e., he can avoid punishment) through either compliance or concealment. He will be especially likely to choose the latter if he has difficulty in complying as when, for example, he simply does not know how to meet A's behavioral standards or prefers not to conform to them. In sum, augmentation should lead to showing which in turn will insure consistent feedback from A with the result that B should soon learn A's behavioral standards. In contrast, reduction should, when compliance is diffi-

cult, lead to concealment and, hence, continued ignorance of A's behavioral standards.

These two modes of influence not only have different implications for self-monitoring and the learning of A's behavioral standards, but also for B's acceptance of the standards. Where augmentation is used B should, in time, show a tendency to accept A's standards and to adopt them as his own. This would be expected on the grounds that as a consistent source of reward to B, A would take on positive value for B. Hence B will come to value what A values and to disvalue what A disvalues. Where reduction is used, however, one would expect that while public conformity might be elicited, B will not accept privately A's standards—at least not to the same extent that he would if A were employing the mode of augmentation. Thus, under reduction training, even though B might eventually learn what A's standards are (despite his concealment tendencies), he would be less likely to accept them.

Let us consider further the question of how the differences predicted above will be affected by the difficulty B experiences in complying with the behavioral standard A regards as correct. Let us assume that, at first, B has a bias to reveal rather than conceal his responses. Such tendencies would be expected in the numerous everyday relationships which are affected by norms which encourage commitment and candidness. Person B will, then, tend to reveal his responses to A unless actively discouraged from doing so. The augmentation procedure will not increase this incidence of "showing," but the reduction technique should depress it. Furthermore, the extent to which B will be discouraged from "showing" will depend on how often he makes mistakes and is punished. If he makes them infrequently (as when A's standard or criterion—as we shall henceforth call it—is an "easy" one in the sense that B already tends to share it or for some other reason prefers to make "correct" responses), B will rarely be punished and will tend to maintain his initial bias to "show." The augmentation procedure will yield much positive feedback to B as compared to the relatively neutral reactions obtained under the reduction procedure, and while this may make for more favorable attitudes toward A, B should be able to learn A's criterion as readily in the one case as in the other.

On the other hand, if A's criterion is a difficult or implausible one for B and he makes many mistakes, he will receive a good deal of punishment under reduction in contrast to fairly neutral treatment under augmentation. The former will encourage B's tendency to conceal and thereby produce a large difference between the two procedures with respect to the degree of learning what A's criterion is. The punishment which derives from the conjunction of the reduction technique and the implausible criterion will also be expected to produce disliking of the trainer and rejection of his criterion, following the argument given earlier.

In the present study we have evaluated the effects of augmentation versus reduction as they interact with a behavioral criterion of high versus low intuitive plausibility. The plausibility of the criterion influences the probability that B will select it of his own accord without A's intervention. We have also used an interaction situation in which it would be natural for B to reveal his responses to A, at least at first. According to the reasoning outlined above, we would expect that the reduction procedure would have a particularly pronounced effect when it is combined with the low plausibility criterion.

METHOD

Subjects

Eighty males, all enrolled in introductory psychology classes at the University of Minnesota, were used in this experiment.

Procedure

Each experimental session involved one subject as a trainee and a confederate serving as the trainer. Each subject was greeted by the experimenter (KR) who informed him that he was conducting a study of conceptions of mental illness. The subject was asked to participate, he was told, in order that the experimenter would be able to teach more effectively about the subject in introductory psychology classes such as that in which the subject himself was enrolled. The experimenter said that his assistant was actually carrying out most of the work on the project and that the subject would be interviewed by him (the confederate, of course). This person was represented as being a graduate student in clinical psychology who was, naturally, interested in the problem of mental illness himself. He was also described as someone who had pretty strong opinions on the subject of mental illness and who would not be hesitant to express them. This behavior was justified on the grounds that it "tends to stimulate persons to think more critically about the subject of mental illness than perhaps they've done in the past." At this point, the subject was told that afterwards he would be rated by the interviewer on either one of two characteristics: half the subjects were told the rating would be based on "how likable you seemed to be, how cooperative and agreeable and so on" while the other half were told that they would be rated on "how frankly and honestly you express your own opinions." Everyone was encouraged to get as high a rating as possible. This manipulation was intended to affect the subject's willingness to express his opinions and his responsiveness to the confederate's praise or reproof. However, subsequent analysis showed that it did not have the desired effect; indeed, it seemed to exert no effect whatever. Consequently, we shall discuss the results of this experiment without considering it further.

The subject was then taken to another room where he was introduced to the confederate. The latter explained the experimental task to the subject. He was asked simply to go through a series of cards on each of which were printed two statements describing symptoms of maladjustment, MMPI-style. For example, the statements on Card Number 5 read:

1. "I become pretty depressed when I fail at something important."

2. "I have nightmares every few nights."

For each pair of items on each of the cards, the subject was asked to indicate which item indicated "the greater degree of mental illness." Where he could not decide or did not know, he was encouraged to say so. (The trainer always responded to a "don't know"

response with the noncommittal comment, "Go on to the next card, please.") Hence it was not necessary for the subject to commit himself on every pair of statements. There were thirty cards in all.

As the subject proceeded through the series, making choices, the trainer responded in one of two ways. If a subject had been assigned to an augmentation condition, the trainer responded very generously when the subject's choice was "correct" ("That certainly shows a lot of insight, Mr. _____; most persons don't get that one" or "For a beginning psychology student, Mr. _____, you're certainly doing very well.") Naturally, all these comments and others were made at a time when they would seem reasonable to the subject and would have a good effect. When the choice was "incorrect," the trainer would pass it off lightly ("Well, I guess I can't go along with you there" or "No, I'm inclined to choose the other one."), the comment being made in a friendly, corrective fashion without a trace of irritation. If a subject had been assigned to a reduction condition, he would get token praise for being correct such as a simple nodding of the trainer's head or a passive "um hum." If, however, the subject did not agree with the trainer, he was made to know it ("We have been conducting this survey for 3 months and in all that time I think you're only the second person who made that choice" or "Well, I'm sure you must have a reason for that choice, Mr. _____, but I'm darned if I can see what it could possibly be.") In such instances, the trainer would be sarcastic, critical, and—toward the end—take on an attitude of resigned exasperation.

When the subject had finished

going through the stack of (30) cards, he was taken back to the experimenter's room by the confederate and the experimenter, presumably interrupting himself from his other work, asked the subject if he would be willing to do several further tasks. When he invariably consented, the experimenter had him complete the following tasks in this order:

1. Go through a series of forty-two cards (thirty were ones he had already seen before—although in a scrambled order—and twelve were new, but similar) and indicate which item of each pair the trainer himself would select as representing the greater degree of mental illness.

2. Go through the original set of items—again in a new order—and indicate his own opinions (both Tasks 1 and 2 were done silently in writing).

3. Fill out a post-experimental questionnaire.

These chores completed, the subject was given a full explanation of the experiment, and before he departed was requested not to talk about it with other students.

The statements printed on the cards were constructed in such a way that for any given pair, one could be characterized as an *anxiety* statement while the other was a *depression* statement. Previous research (Kelley & Ring, 1961) using these items has shown that the probability of a subject's selecting the depression item on any given card is substantially greater than that of his choosing the anxiety item (depression items received about 65 percent of the choices, anxiety items, 35 percent).

In this experiment, the confederate regarded as correct the anxiety statements for half the subjects; for the other half, he deemed the depression items correct. Thus, in the first case, he was choosing items in accordance with a criterion of mental illness which had been viewed by previous subjects as relatively implausible. In the second case, his criterion was a relatively plausible one.

Altogether, then, there were four conditions which may be labeled as follows, giving first the trainer's criterion and then his method of influence: plausible-augmentation (Plaus-Aug), plausible-reduction (Plaus-Red), implausible-augmentation (Implaus-Aug), implausible-reduction (Implaus-Red). The N in each condition was twenty.

RESULTS

Effectiveness of the Manipulations

PLAUSIBILITY OF THE CRITERIA If what we have asserted about the relative plausibility of the criteria is true, we should expect to find that agreement with the depression criterion is significantly higher during the trainer-trainee interaction. The first row of Table 8.1 presents the relevant data giving the average number of agreements with the criterion for each condition.[1] (On trials when a subject failed to express an opinion he was given half-credit for agreement.) By analysis of variance, the criterion difference is significant at better than .001. The interaction term is not significant. (Two-tailed tests are used throughout this paper.)

AUGMENTATION-REDUCTION If our manipulation of this variable has been

[1] The difference between the Plaus-Red and Implaus-Red conditions in number of agreements is clear and unmistakable even by the end of the first ten trials.

TABLE 1. TESTS OF EFFECTIVENESS OF THE MANIPULATIONS

Dependent variable	Experimental condition			
	Plaus-Aug	Plaus-Red	Implaus-Aug	Implaus-Red
Agreement with trainer during interaction	19.4	19.8	15.1	12.6
Ratings of trainer's criticalness	−1.8	+0.7	−1.6	+0.8

successful, we should expect to find that the subject perceives the augmentative trainer as more generous and the reductive trainer as more critical. On the post-experimental questionnaire, we included items to elicit the subject's perception of the trainer with respect to these characteristics. For each subject the difference between his ratings of the trainer's criticism and generosity was determined. The averages of these differences are given in the second row of Table 1, a positive score indicating that the trainer was judged relatively more critical than generous. The only significant effect is the augmentation-reduction difference which is significant at better than the .0001 level. Also relevant to this manipulation is the item on the post-experimental questionnaire which asked the subject to indicate how much he liked the trainer. The ratings made by the augmentation subjects were significantly higher ($p < .001$) on this dimension and there were no other significant effects.

Experimental Hypotheses

CONCEALMENT OF OPINION   The frequency with which the subjects refused to express their opinions is indicated in the first row of Table 2 which presents the mean number of trials on which this occurred for the subjects in each condition. Since there were 30 trials altogether, it can be seen that the absolute level of failure to disclose opinions was very low—less than 10 percent—for both the plausible groups and the Implaus-Aug group. For the Implaus-Red group, however, the percentage is substantially higher—close to 25 percent. An analysis of variance shows both a significant criterion and trainer orientation effect, but, as is apparent, this is

TABLE 2. TESTS OF THE EXPERIMENTAL HYPOTHESES

Dependent variable	Experimental condition			
	Plaus-Aug	Plaus-Red	Implaus-Aug	Implaus-Red
Refusals to state opinion	2.65	2.25	2.45	6.95
Knowledge of the trainer's choices	33.0	32.6	32.8	26.7
Adoption of the trainer's opinions	+.30	+.23	+.27	−.14
Disagreement with opinions attributed to trainer	6.90	5.68	9.45	15.56

largely due to the high mean of the Implaus-Red group. The interaction sum of the squares is, in fact, greater than that of either main effect and is significant at the .01 level. As anticipated, the method of influence makes the greatest difference when the trainer uses a criterion of low plausibility.

LEARNING THE TRAINER'S CRITERION
The reader will remember that after the "interview" had concluded, the subject was returned to the experimenter who asked him to state which item of each pair he thought the trainer would select. In some cases he was reporting on items about which the trainer might already have revealed his opinion; in other cases, he was "guessing" how the trainer would answer a "new" item. (The two sets of items give identical results and are, therefore, combined.) The index of knowledge of the trainer's criterion (average number of correct statements about how the trainer would have made his choices) is presented for each condition in the second row of Table 2. Inspection of the table reveals that all groups but the Implaus-Red have learned pretty well (a perfect score would be 42). Unfortunately, an analysis of variance showed neither main effect to be significant (the criterion effect reaches a level of significance between .05 and .10), nor was the interaction significant (.10 < p < .20), contrary to our predictions. Nevertheless, the trend of the data is as expected, even though the significance levels leave much to be desired.

In support of our assumption that concealment acts to retard learning, there was obtained, over all conditions, a significant negative correlation between frequency of concealment and the index of learning $(r = -.33, p < .01)$.

ACCEPTANCE OF TRAINER'S CRITERION
Another of the post-experimental chores imposed on the subject after his interview was again to indicate which item of each pair on the original thirty cards he regarded as representing "the greater degree of mental illness." When compared with the answers he gave during the interaction, these data give us some idea of the degree of adoption of the trainer's opinions. An index of this was derived by computing the difference between the number of times the subject was in agreement with the trainer on this task and the number of times he had actually voiced agreement while being interviewed, and dividing this difference by the extent of possible change in the direction of the difference. For example, if a subject agreed on twenty items afterward, but on only ten during his interview with the trainer, his adoption score would be $\dfrac{20-10}{20}$ = .50. A positive score indicates the subject is closer to the trainer in his opinions after the interview than he was during it; a negative score means the reverse.

The pattern of results yielded by the average adoption scores, shown in the third row of Table 2, is by now familiar. All groups except the Implaus-Red are influenced in a favorable direction. An analysis of variance results in a significant criterion effect $(p < .025)$, a significant effect due to method of influence $(p < .01)$, and a borderline interaction $(p = .06,$ approximately$)$. In summary, the pattern of results is very much like what one would anticipate from the data presented previously.

Another analysis was performed which sought to get at the matter of acceptance from a different angle. It could be argued that the preceding analysis unfairly penalizes subjects in the Implaus-Red condition, yielding low adoption scores simply as a reflection of their lack of knowledge of the trainer's criterion and not as any indication of their tendency to reject it. To eliminate any possible effect of amount of knowledge of the trainer's criterion, actual agreement with it was disregarded and instead each person was scored in terms of his agreement with the opinions he imputed to the trainer, whether correct or not. Accordingly, the subject's own post-experimental choices on the original thirty items were compared with those attributed to the trainer and a count made of the number of instances of disagreement. The results are given in the last row of Table 2.[2] As can be seen, rejection is much greater when the criterion of low plausibility is being employed, as one would expect. However, the greatest amount of rejection occurs in the Implaus-Red group ($p < .01$ for the comparison with the Implaus-Aug group). The results of this analysis are therefore consistent with the preceding ones which show the powerful effect of the reduction procedure when coupled with an implausible criterion.

DISCUSSION

This study is the second in a series investigating the effects of certain training schedules on the performance of trainees. We wish, in this section, not only to consider the findings of the current study, but to relate them to those of the first experiment. In that experiment (Kelley & Ring, 1961), we compared "trusting" and "suspicious" training schedules in terms of their effects on the trainee's tendency to reveal his responses and his learning to conform to the trainer's behavior standard. On each occasion during the training when the trainee made a choice between the two response categories with respect to which the trainer was trying to teach him a particular preference, he also had the option of showing or hiding his choice. The two schedules differed in the actions the trainer took when he knew that the trainee had concealed his response (but, of course, did not know what the response was). A suspicious trainer who assumed the trainee had made the incorrect choice when he hid was compared with a trusting one who under similar circumstances assumed the trainee had made the correct response. The former procedure was found to be more effective in encouraging showing and produced a higher final rate of adherence to the trainer's behavior criterion.

These results can probably be generalized to a number of real-life situations. Particularly important are their implications about the disadvantages of a trainer's providing uncontingently posi-

[2] For this analysis, the few subjects who concealed their opinions very frequently during the "interview" were eliminated because the rejection indices computed for them would have been highly unreliable, being based on few instances. One subject had to be dropped from the Plaus-Red group and four from the Implaus-Red group. It should also be noted that inasmuch as the subjects were forced to indicate what they thought the trainer's opinions were, to the extent that the Implaus-Red subjects were less *confident* of their "guesses" than the subjects in other conditions, this method of analysis does not adequately control for differences in lack of knowledge of the trainer's criterion.

tive feedback (as in the trusting condition) when the trainee makes some response analogous to hiding. Some cases likely to involve such feedback would include the winsome child who says something disarming just before the parent's evaluative comment is forthcoming, the boss who in presenting his ideas to a subordinate unwittingly emphasizes his status so that the subordinate tends to become a "yes man," the disabled person who emphasizes his handicap at appropriate times in a way that makes it difficult to make any but favorable comments about his performance, and the insecure person who by his extreme self-deprecation tends to extract a perfunctory compliment no matter what his performance. Under circumstances such as these, the trainer, (parent, subordinate) may be tempted to act in a manner similar to the trusting trainer, giving positive feedback regardless of the performance as long as it is accompanied by the appropriate auxiliary response (hiding in the experiment; the charming comment, allusion to status, etc., in the examples). The results of the first experiment suggest that if the trainer succumbs to this temptation, the auxiliary response may be learned and this will operate to the detriment of the trainee's learning the true evaluations others place upon his behavior.

Both the earlier study and the present one show that it is desirable for a trainer to consider whether his trainee has opportunities to make relevant choices while not under the former's surveillance. If so, he must take account of possible effects of his training schedule on encouraging the trainee to attempt such concealment. The first study deals with the case where the trainer knows about all the occasions on which the trainee has made a relevant choice. Under these conditions the suspicious schedule, which assumes the worst of the trainee, is equivalent to punishing all instances of hiding and dealing with instances of showing in terms of their merits. This method is more effective, as we have said, both in encouraging showing and learning of the trainer's criterion, than is the trusting procedure which tends to reward hiding.

The present study has application to a broader range of training situations because it involves schedules which permit the trainer to make no response or merely a noncommittal one when he fails to detect a relevant choice. Thus, he need not be aware of many of the instances on which the trainee confronts such choice situations. Our evidence suggests that as long as he uses an augmentation technique, providing large rewards for revealed compliance and being tolerant of revealed noncompliance, the trainee will tend to maintain an adequate rate of showing his responses and will, then, satisfactorily learn the trainer's criterion. On the other hand, a reduction method with its emphasis on punishment for errors will discourage showing and interfere with learning the criterion.

What are the implications of these two studies considered together? The first suggests the value of using punishment to discourage hiding and the second, the value of reward to encourage showing. Perhaps the best overall strategy which would combine the advantages of the suspicious and augmentation schedules would be one that provides punishment for the detected instances of concealment, is only very mildly punishing (merely to let the trainee know he is wrong) for revealed errors, and is strongly approving for revealed correct behaviors. When it is not clear that a relevant response has been made, a neutral reaction from the trainer is probably best. To attempt any other treatment is to run the risk of providing a reinforcement schedule that affords no basis for learning either to show or to make the desired choice.

Perhaps the most important finding of the present study relates to the interaction between the trainer's influence method and the plausibility of his criterion. Specifically there was a tendency for the combination of the reduction mode of influence with the implausible criterion to depress considerably the level of revealing one's opinions, learning the trainer's criterion, and accepting the trainer's criterion. We would explain this outcome as follows. The probability that the subject would select the same items as the trainer was made deliberately small by using an implausible criterion. Finding himself often in error and being rather harshly criticized for it, the subject comes to feel rather anxious and confused about having to make any kind of choice at all—his expected outcome is not very enticing. If he refuses to make a choice he can avoid the censure of the trainer. It is true that in so doing he passes up the opportunity for a small reward (in the form of mild praise), but the probability of his receiving this small reward is substantially lower than that of his receiving condemnation from the trainer. So he begins to conceal his opinions (at least, relatively speaking, more than subjects in the other conditions do). This results, of course, in a noncommittal response from the trainer. Thus, to the extent the subject refuses to commit himself,

he fails to find out anything from the trainer concerning his (the trainer's) opinions. So the trainee's learning is impaired. There are two reasons why the trainee does not adopt the trainer's opinions. One obviously derives from the fact that, because of his refusal to express his own opinions, the trainee simply does not know what the trainer's opinions are. The second factor is the negative affect that is generated by the reduction technique. The trainee just does not *care* very much what the trainer's opinions are and when he does have some ideas about them, he has no motivation whatever to accept them. It is quite possible, of course, that a lowered motivation to learn (as well as the anxiety associated with making a choice) might in part account for the low level of learning manifested by this group of subjects.

The interaction between the trainer's method and his criterion which our results so clearly indicate has one possible implication that is of considerable interest, especially as concerns practical applications of these results. Reduction is least effective, indeed most detrimental, when the trainer's standard is such that the trainee makes many errors at the outset of their interaction. Consider now a real trainer—not one who is programed to follow consistently one method or another, but one who is free to change his technique when he feels like it. Is it not likely that whatever method he starts with, a high rate of mistakes by the trainee will tend to frustrate him and cause him to turn to reduction? The point is not that this will happen every time but simply that the spontaneous adoption of reduction as an influence technique may be most likely under those very conditions where our results show it to be least effective.

A finding of some interest in this experiment is that relating to the performance of the Implaus-Aug subjects. This group learned the criterion of the trainer as well as any group and they used it (that is, accepted it) virtually to the same extent that subjects in the plausible conditions used that criterion. This was so despite the fact that the plausibility of the anxiety criterion was decidedly lower than that of the depression criterion. Apparently, after the augmentation mode of influence these subjects received when they used this criterion, they found that it was not so implausible after all. This result seems similar to that described by Kelman (1956 unpublished) as following from the process of identification. This process requires that the influencing agent be attractive to the influencee. Kelman presents evidence that the resulting influence is manifested only in situations where the influencing agent is salient in the thinking of the influencee. The present evidence is entirely consistent with this view though we have no evidence that the influence exhibited by the Implaus-Aug group would appear only under conditions of "salience." In general, the results of this experiment are consistent with the assertion by Thibaut and Kelley (1959) that the distinction between augmentation and reduction parallels two of Kelman's influence processes, identification and compliance. The former is thought to yield conformity whenever the relationship with the influencer is brought to mind, as is probably the case with our augmentation data. The latter is thought to yield conformity, if at all, only under the influencer's surveillance. In the present case, the reductive influencer did not insist on compliance. He in fact permitted the influencee to avoid the consequences of his surveillance by not taking a stand. The main purpose of this study has been to demonstrate the consequences of the trainer's so doing.

REFERENCES

KELLEY, H. H., & RING, K. Some effects of "suspicious" versus "trusting" training schedules. *J. abnorm. soc. Psychol.*, 1961, 63, 294–301.

McGREGOR, D. M. The staff function in human relations. *J. soc. Issues*, 1948, 4(3), 5–22.

THIBAUT, J. W., & KELLEY, H. H. . *The social psychology of groups*. New York: Wiley, 1959.

9. A CROSS–CULTURAL STUDY OF CORRELATES OF CRIME *

Margaret K. Bacon, Irvin L. Child, and Herbert Barry, III

A number of researchers have analyzed the sociological and psychological background of delinquents and criminals and compared them with a noncriminal control population, in order to discover what conditions give rise to criminal

* Reprinted from *Journal of Abnormal and Social Psychology*, 1963, 66: 291–300, with permission of the senior author and the American Psychological Association. This research was supported by grants from the Social Science Research Council, the Ford Foundation, and the National Institutes of Mental Health, United States Public Health Service (M-2681).

behavior; for a recent review, see Robison (1960). The present paper reports on variations among a sample of preliterate societies in the frequency of crime, in order to determine what other known features of these societies are associated with the occurrence of crime. The cross-cultural technique (Whiting, 1954), in which each society is taken as a single case, is a unique method for studying crime and has certain advantages: The index of frequency of crime in a society represents the average among its many individuals and over a span of many years, so that the measure is likely to be more stable and reliable than a measure of criminal tendency in a single individual. Some of the cultural features which may be related to crime show wider variations among societies than within a single society, permitting a more comprehensive test of their significance. Results which are consistent in a number of diverse societies may be applied to a great variety of cultural conditions instead of being limited to a single cultural setting.

If certain cultural features foster the development of criminal behavior, they should be found preponderantly in societies with a high frequency of crime; factors which inhibit crime should be found largely in societies which are low in crime. Thus the cross-cultural method may help us discover psychological and sociological variables which have a causal relationship to the development of crime; the importance of these variables may then also be tested intraculturally. On the other hand, variables identified as possible causes of crime within our society may be tested for broader significance by the cross-cultural method.

The possible causal factors which we have explored are principally concerned with child training practices, economy, and social structure. Hypotheses concerning these factors, as they have been presented by other writers or as they have occurred to us, will be described in connection with the presentation of our results.

METHOD

Sample

The sample used in this study consists of 48 societies, mostly preliterate, scattered over the world. They were taken from a larger group of 110 societies which were selected on the basis of geographical diversity and adequacy of information on aboriginal child training practices. The present sample of 48 consists of those societies whose ethnographies were searched and found to provide sufficient information to permit comparative ratings on criminal behavior by three independent research workers.

Ratings

We have included two types of crime in our study: *theft* and *personal crime*. These two were chosen because they are relatively easy to identify and almost universal in occurrence. Also, they represent two quite different types of behavior. Thus we are able to clarify antecedents common to both types of crime and those characteristic of only one. Judgments were always made in relation to the norms of the culture under consideration. Theft was defined as stealing the personal property of others. Property included anything on which the society placed value, whether it was a whale's tooth or a song. Personal crime was defined by intent to injure or kill a person; assault, rape, suicide, sorcery intended to make another ill, murder, making false accusations, etc., were all included.

The method of comparative ratings was used to obtain measures of frequency. Three raters independently analyzed the ethnographic material on each society and made ratings on a seven-point scale as to the relative frequency of the type of crime under consideration. Thus a rating of 4 on theft would mean that the frequency of theft in a given society appeared to be about average for the sample of societies. Ratings of 5, 6, and 7 represented high frequencies and those of 3, 2, and 1 were low. Societies in which the behavior did not occur were rated as 0. Each rating was classified as confident or doubtful at the time that it was made. No rating was made if the analyst judged the information to be insufficient. We have included all societies on which all three analysts made a rating, whether it was confident or doubtful, and we have used the pooled ratings of all three analysts. The reliability of these pooled ratings is estimated as $+.67$ for Theft and $+.57$ for Personal Crime. These estimates were obtained by averaging (using a z transformation) the separate interrater reliabilities, and entering this average into the Spearman-Brown correction formula.

Most writers in this field make a distinction between delinquency and crime, largely on the basis of the age of the offender. The nature of our evidence does not permit us to make such a clear distinction. Ratings were made in terms of the relative frequency of specific types of criminal behavior in the adult population. Since the age at which adulthood is considered to have begun varies from one society to another, ratings may in some cases have included individuals young enough to be considered adolescent in our society and therefore delinquent rather than criminal. The distinction does not appear to be crucial in this study.

The measures of possible causal variables consist of ratings which have been derived from several sources. Each will be described in the following section. Except where noted (for certain variables in Tables 3 and 4), none of the three people who made the crime ratings participated in any of the other ratings.

HYPOTHESES, RESULTS, AND DISCUSSION

Our results will be presented under three main headings: Correlates of Crime in General, Correlates Specific to Theft, and Correlates Specific to Personal Crime. As this classification suggests, we have found it useful to consider the antecedents of crime as either general or specific, i.e., leading to a general increase in criminal behavior, or associated with only one major category of crime. A correlation of $+.46$ was found between frequency of Theft and frequency of Personal Crime. This indicates that the two variables show a significant degree of communality ($p < .01$) and also some independence.

Correlates of Crime in General

Our principal findings concerning common correlates of both Theft and Personal Crime are relevant to a hypothesis that crime arises partly as a defense against strong feminine identification.

We will begin with an account of this hypothesis.

In our society crime occurs mostly in men, and we have no reason to doubt that this sex difference characterizes most societies. Several writers have called attention to the sex role identification of males as especially pertinent to the development of delinquency in our society. It is assumed that the very young boy tends to identify with his mother rather than his father because of his almost exclusive contact with his mother. Later in his development he becomes aware of expectations that he behave in a masculine way and as a result his behavior tends to be marked by a compulsive masculinity which is really a defense against feminine identification. Parsons (1954, pp. 304–305) notes further that the mother is the principal agent of socialization as well as an object of love and identification. Therefore, when the boy revolts he unconsciously identifies "goodness" with femininity and hence accepts the role of "bad boy" as a positive goal.

Miller (1958) has made a study of lower-class culture and delinquency which is also pertinent in this connection. He points out that some delinquent behavior may result from an attempt to live up to attitudes and values characteristic of lower-class culture. He also notes that many lower-class males are reared in predominantly female households lacking a consistently present male with whom to identify. He feels that what he calls an almost obsessive lower-class concern with masculinity results from the feminine identification in preadolescent years.

Whiting, Kluckhohn, and Anthony (1958), in a cross-cultural study of male initiation rites at puberty, found these rites tended to occur in societies with prolonged, exclusive mother-son sleeping arrangements. Their interpretation of this relationship is that the early mother-infant sleeping arrangement produces an initial feminine identification, and later control by men leads to a secondary masculine identification. The function of the initiation ceremony is to resolve this conflict of sexual identification in favor of the masculine identification. The authors further predict that insofar as there has been an increase in juvenile delinquency in our society, "it probably has been accompanied by an increase in the exclusiveness of mother-child relationships and/ or a decrease in the authority of the father."

The hypothesis that crime is in part a defense against initial feminine identification would lead to the expectation that all factors which tend to produce strong identification with the mother and failure of early identification with the father would be positively correlated with the frequency of crime in the adult population. The factor that is easiest to study is the presence of the father. It seems reasonable to suppose that successful identification with the father is dependent on his presence. Therefore, societies which differ in the degree to which the father is present during the child's first few years should differ correspondingly in the degree to which the boy typically forms a masculine identification.[1]

Whiting (1959) has made use of

---

[1] The whole problem of the mechanism whereby identification occurs has been omitted from this study. In all theories it would appear that identification with the father would be in some degree a function of the frequency of the presence of the father.

Murdock's (1957) classification of household structure and family composition to distinguish among four types of households which provide a range from maximal to minimal degree of presence of the father. They are as follows:

MONOGAMOUS NUCLEAR This household is the usual one in our society. The father, mother, and children eat, sleep, and entertain under one roof. Grandparents, siblings of the parents, and other relatives live elsewhere. The effective presence of the father in the child's environment is thus at a maximum.

MONOGAMOUS EXTENDED Here two or more nuclear families live together under one roof. A typical extended family consists of an aged couple together with their married sons and daughters and their respective families. In such a household, the child's interaction with his father is likely to be somewhat less than in the single nuclear household.

POLYGYNOUS POLYGYNOUS The polygynous household consists of a man living with his wives and their various children. Here the child is likely to have even less opportunity to interact with his father.

POLYGYNOUS MOTHER-CHILD This type of household occurs in those polygynous societies where each wife has a separate establishment and lives in it with her children. In these societies the father either sleeps in a men's club, has a hut of his own, or divides his time among the houses of his various wives. The husband usually does not sleep in the house of any wife during the 2 to 3 years when she is nursing each infant. Thus the mother may become the almost exclusive object of identification of the first two years of life.

Table 1 shows the number of societies with low and high frequency of Theft and Personal Crime within each of the four categories of household type. As the opportunity for contact with the father decreases, the frequency of

TABLE 1. FREQUENCY OF THEFT OR PERSONAL CRIME IN RELATION TO FAMILY STRUCTURE AND HOUSEHOLD

Family Structure and Household [a]	Frequency of Theft		Frequency of Personal Crime	
	Low	High	Low	High
Monogamous Nuclear	7	2	5	4
Monogamous Extended	7	3	6	3
Polygynous Polygynous	7	6	3	7
Polygynous Mother-Child	1	11	3	9

Note.—Each entry in the table gives the number of societies in our sample which have the particular combination of characteristics indicated for that row and column.

The total number of cases in the left-hand and right-hand parts of this table and in the various divisions of succeeding tables varies because lack of information prevented rating some societies on some variables. In testing each relationship we have of course been able to use only those societies for which the relevant ratings are available. The division into "low" and "high" was made as near the median as possible.

[a] See Murdock (1957).

both Theft and Personal Crime increases. This result agrees with our hypothesis. If the family structure and household is treated as a four-point scale, it yields a correlation of +.58 with frequency of Theft and of +.44 with frequency of Personal Crime; both correlations are statistically significant ($p < .01$). If we compare the extremes of the distribution—contrasting Monogamous Nuclear households (which provide the maximum opportunity for identification with the father) with Polygynous Mother-Child households (which provide the minimum opportunity for identification with the father) —this relationship is clearly demonstrated; 18 of the 21 societies fall in the predicted quadrants for Theft, and 14 out of 21 for Personal Crime.

Several results of empirical studies in our society appear consistent with this finding. One is the frequently reported relationship between broken homes and delinquency, since in the majority of cases broken homes are probably mother-child households. Robins and O'Neal (1958), for example, in a follow-up study of problem children after 30 years, refer to the high incidence of fatherless families. Glueck and Glueck (1950) report that 41.2 percent of their delinquent group were not living with their own fathers, as compared with 24.8 percent of a matched nondelinquent group. These data suggest that a relatively high proportion of the delinquents came from what were essentially "mother-child" households.

A recent book by Rohrer and Edmonson (1960) is also relevant. Their study is a follow-up after 20 years of the individuals described in *Children of Bondage* by Davis and Dollard (1941). The importance of the matri-archal household typical in a Southern Negro lower-class group, and its effect on the emotional development of the young boy and his eventual attitudes as an adult, are stressed throughout. The following passage summarizes, in its application to their (Rohrer & Edmonson) particular data, an interpretation consistent with those we have cited in introducing this hypothesis.

Gang life begins early, more or less contemporaneously with the first years of schooling, and for many men lasts until death. . . . Although each gang is a somewhat distinct group, all of them appear to have a common structure expressing and reinforcing the gang ideology. Thus an organizational form that springs from the little boy's search for a masculinity he cannot find at home becomes first a protest against femininity and then an assertion of hypervirility. On the way it acquires a structuring in which the aspirations and goals of the matriarchy or the middle class are seen as soft, effeminate, and despicable. The gang ideology of masculine independence is formed from these perceptions, and the gang then sees its common enemy not as a class, nor even perhaps as a sex, but as the "feminine principle" in society. The gang member rejects this femininity in every form, and he sees it in women and in effeminate men, in laws and morals and religion, in schools and occupational striving (pp. 162–163).

Correlates of Theft

Although we shall consider correlates of Theft in this section and correlates of Personal Crime in the next section, each table will show in parallel columns the relation of a set of variables both to Theft and to Personal Crime. This will facilitate comparison and avoid repetition. How each of these variables was measured will be described in the section to which it is most pertinent.

The first variables to be considered are concerned with child training practices. Most of the child training variables have been developed in our research and described in an earlier paper (Barry, Bacon, & Child, 1957). These variables may be briefly described as follows:

OVERALL CHILDHOOD INDULGENCE
The period of childhood was defined roughly as covering the age period from 5 to 12 years, or to the beginning of any pubertal or prepubertal status change. In making ratings of childhood indulgence, factors relevant to indulgence in infancy—such as immediacy and degree of drive reduction, display of affection by parents—if operative at this later age, were taken into account. In addition, the raters also considered the degree of socialization expected in childhood and the severity of the methods used to obtain the expected behavior.

ANXIETY ASSOCIATED WITH SOCIALIZATION DURING THE SAME PERIOD OF CHILDHOOD This was rated separately for each of five systems of behavior: Responsibility or dutifulness training; Nurturance training, that is, training the child to be nurturant or helpful toward younger siblings and other dependent people; Obedience training; Self-reliance training; Achievement training, that is, training the child to orient his behavior toward standards of excellence in performance and to seek to achieve as excellent a performance as possible.

In rating the training in these areas, an attempt was first made to estimate the Total Pressure exerted by the adults in each society toward making the children behave in each of these specified ways (Responsible, Nurturant, Obedient, Self-Reliant, and Achieving). The *socialization anxiety* measures were based on an estimate of the amount of anxiety aroused in the child by failing to behave in a responsible, self-reliant, etc. way, and they reflect primarily the extent of punishment for failure to show each particular form of behavior. The measures of Total Pressure reflect both this and the extent of reward and encouragement.

Wherever boys and girls were rated differently on any of the above variables of socialization, we used the ratings for boys.

The relation of the crime ratings to these and other variables of child training is presented in Table 2. It is clear that Theft is significantly related to several variables of child training.

First, Theft is negatively correlated with Childhood Indulgence, that is, societies with a high rating of Childhood Indulgence tend to have a low frequency of Theft in the adult population; and, conversely, societies with a low rating of Childhood Indulgence show a high frequency of Theft.

Frequency of Theft is also positively correlated with socialization anxiety during the period of childhood with respect to the following areas of training: Responsibility, Self-Reliance, Achievement, and Obedience. It should be emphasized that Total Pressures toward those four areas of socialization are not significantly correlated with Theft. Therefore it is apparently not the area or level of socialization required which is significant, but rather the punitive and anxiety provoking methods of socialization employed.

These findings on child training in relation to Theft may be summarized and interpreted by the hypothesis that theft is in part motivated by feelings of

TABLE 2. CHILD TRAINING FACTORS ASSOCIATED WITH THEFT OR PERSONAL CRIME

Factor	Theft		Personal Crime	
	N	r	N	r
1. Childhood indulgence [a]	45	−.41**	42	−.10
2. Responsibility socialization anxiety [a]	43	+.48**	41	+.20
3. Self-reliance socialization anxiety [a]	43	+.35*	41	+.24
4. Achievement socialization anxiety [a]	36	+.41*	35	+.20
5. Obedience socialization anxiety [a]	40	+.32*	39	+.06
6. Dependence socialization anxiety [b]	31	+.14	28	+.56**
7. Mother-child sleeping [c]	20	+.40	19	+.46*
8. Infant indulgence [a]				
9. Age of weaning [a]				
10. Oral socialization anxiety [b]				
11. Anal socialization anxiety [b]				
12. Sex socialization anxiety [b]				
13. Aggression socialization anxiety [b]				
14. Nurturance socialization anxiety [a]				
15. Total pressures toward responsibility, nurturance, self-reliance, achievement, and obedience [a]				

Note.—In this and the following tables the correlations are Pearsonian coefficients, thus reflecting all available degrees of gradation in score rather than simply classifying societies as high and low.

Factors 8–15 showed no significant relationship with either Theft or Personal Crime.

[a] See Barry, Bacon, and Child (1957).

[b] See Whiting and Child (1953).

[c] See Whiting, Kluckhohn, and Anthony (1958).

* $p \leq .05$.

** $p \leq .01$.

deprivation of love. Our data indicate that one source of such feelings is punitive and anxiety provoking treatment during childhood. Such treatment during infancy may tend to have a similar effect, as suggested by a correlation of −.25 between frequency of Theft and Infant Indulgence. This correlation falls slightly short of significance at the 5 percent level. It is of special interest that substantial correlations with socialization anxiety in childhood tended to occur in the areas of training in Responsibility, Achievement, and Self-Reliance. These all involve demands for behavior far removed from the dependent behavior of infancy and early childhood and close to the independent behavior expected of adults. If we assume that lack of adequate indulgence in childhood leads to a desire to return to earlier means of gratification and behavior symbolic of this need, then we would expect that pressures toward more adult behavior might intensify this need and the frequency of the symbolic behavior. Theft, from this point of view, would be seen as rewarded partly by its value as symbolic gratification of an infantile demand for unconditional indulgence irrespective of other people's rights or interests.

The results of the early study by Healy and Bronner (1936) seem directly pertinent to our findings and interpretation. They found that a group of delinquents differed from their nondelinquent siblings primarily in their relationships with their parents; the delinquent child was much more likely to give evidence of feeling thwarted and rejected. It seems reasonable to assume that such feelings would often, though not always, indicate a real deprivation of parental love. Glueck and Glueck (1950) also found that their delinquents, compared with matched nondelinquents, had received less affection from their parents and siblings and had a greater tendency to feel that their parents were not concerned with their welfare. It was also noted that fathers of the delinquents had a much greater tendency to resort to physical punishment as a means of discipline than fathers of the nondelinquents. This agrees with our observation that more punitive methods of socialization are associated with an increased frequency of theft.

Compulsive stealing (kleptomania) has been interpreted by psychoanalysts (see Fenichel, 1945, pp. 370–371) as an attempt to seize symbols of security and affection. Thus this form of mental illness, in common with more rational forms of stealing, may be regarded as being motivated by feelings of deprivation of love.

Table 3 summarizes the relationship between our two measures of crime and a number of aspects of economy and social organization on which we were able to obtain ratings. Theft shows a significant relationship with only three

TABLE 3. SOCIOECONOMIC FACTORS ASSOCIATED WITH THEFT OR PERSONAL CRIME

Factor	Theft		Personal Crime	
	N	r	N	r
1. Social stratification [a]	44	+.36*	40	+.16
2. Level of political integration [a]	43	+.34*	39	+.02
3. Degree of elaboration of social control [b]	43	+.46**	40	+.04
4. Accumulation of food [c]				
5. Settlement pattern [a]				
6. Division of labor by sex [a]				
7. Rule of residence (patrilocal, matrilocal, etc.) [a]				
8. Extent of storing [b]				
9. Irrationality of storing [b]				
10. Severity of punishment for property crime [b]				
11. Severity of punishment for personal crime [b]				

Note.—Ratings of Factors 3, 10, and 11 were made in connection with the analysis of crime by two of the three raters (H. Maretzki and A. Rosman). Ratings of Factors 8 and 9 were made by one of the raters (H. Maretzki) but in connection with an analysis of food and economy.

Factors 4–11 showed no significant relationship with either Theft or Personal Crime.

[a] See Murdock (1957).

[b] Bacon, Child, and Barry (unpublished).

[c] See Barry, Child, and Bacon (1959).

* $p \leqslant .05$.

** $p \leqslant .01$.

of these features: Social Stratification, Level of Political Integration, and Degree of Elaboration of Social Control. Social Stratification was treated as a five-point scale ranging from complex stratification, that is, three or more definite social classes or castes exclusive of slaves, to egalitarian, i.e., absence of significant status differentiation other than recognition of political statuses and of individual skill, prowess, piety, etc. Level of Political Integration was also treated as a five-point scale ranging from complex state, e.g., confederation of tribes or conquest state with a king, differentiated officials, and a hierarchical administrative organization to no political integration, even at the community level.[2] Elaboration of Social Control is concerned with the degree to which a society has law making, law enforcing, and punishing agencies.

Our findings indicate that theft is positively correlated with each of these three measures. In other words, with an increased Level of Political Integration, Social Stratification, and Elaboration of Social Control there is an increase in the frequency of Theft. These variables show no significant relationship with frequency of Personal Crime. Each of these institutional conditions seems capable of arousing feelings of insecurity and resentment, and hence may be similar in this respect to parental deprivation. Therefore the correlation of these institutional conditions with Theft might be tentatively interpreted as consistent with our hypothesis about motivational influences on Theft. It is obvious that other interpretations might be made from the same data. For example, a high frequency of crime may give rise to increased elaboration of social control.

Table 4 presents the relation of both Theft and Personal Crime to certain adult attitudes on which we were able to obtain ratings. Frequency of Theft is positively related to Sense of Property and negatively related to Trust about Property. This may indicate merely that the greater the importance of property, the greater the variety of acts which will be classified as Theft, or that a high frequency of Theft gives rise to an emphasis on property. But it may also mean that the greater the importance of property, the more effectively does Theft serve the personal needs to which it seems to be related.

Frequency of Theft is also negatively correlated with Environmental Kindness in Folk Tales. This folk tale measure requires some explanation. It was taken from an analysis of folk tales made by one of the authors (MKB) without knowledge of the societies from which the sample of folk tales was taken. In making the analysis, each folk tale was divided into units of action or events as they related to the principal character or the character with whom the listener would be expected to identify. Each unit was then classified in one of a number of different categories including that of environmental kindness. Classification in this category means that the particular unit involved action or state of affairs definitely friendly or nurturant to the principal character. Thus our results show that societies high in frequency of Theft tend to have folk tales which do not represent the environment as kind. Thinking of the environment as lacking in friendly nuturance seems entirely consistent with

[2] Both variables are taken from Murdock (1957). Our manner of treating his data is described in Barry, Child, and Bacon (1959).

TABLE 4. ADULT ATTITUDES ASSOCIATED WITH THEFT OR PERSONAL CRIME

Attitude	Theft		Personal Crime	
	N	r	N	r
1. Sense of property	43	+.45**	40	+.25
2. Trust about property	43	−.31*	40	−.27
3. General trustfulness	42	−.28	40	−.40**
4. Environmental kindness in folk tales	23	−.47*	21	−.30
5. Environmental hostility in folk tales	23	+.36	21	+.56**
6. Communality of property				
7. Competition in the acquisition of wealth				
8. Generosity				
9. n Achievement in folk tales [a]				

Note.—Attitude 3 was rated by one of the three raters (A. Rosman) in connection with the analysis of crime. Attitudes 1, 2, 6, 7, and 8 were rated by another of the three raters (H. Maretzki) in connection with the analysis of food and economy.

Attitudes 6–9 showed no significant relationship with either Theft or Personal Crime

[a] See Child, Veroff, and Storm (1958).

* $p \le .05$.

** $p \le .01$.

the relative absence of parental nurturance which we have already found to be correlated with frequency of theft.

Correlates of Personal Crime

Inspection of Tables 2, 3, and 4 reveals that the significant correlates of Personal Crime are different from those for Theft. In no instance does a variable in these tables show a significant correlation with both Theft and Personal Crime.

Frequency of Personal Crime shows a significant positive correlation with Dependence Socialization Anxiety, a rating taken from Whiting and Child (1953). In making this rating, an estimate was made of the amount of anxiety aroused in the children of a given society by the methods of independence training typically employed. This estimate was based on the following factors: abruptness of the transition required, severity and frequency of punishment, and evidence of emotional disturbance in the child.

Ratings on mother-child sleeping are taken from Whiting et al. (1958). In this study societies were placed into two categories: those in which the mother and baby shared the same bed for at least a year to the exclusion of the father, those in which the baby slept alone or with both the mother and father. According to our results there is a high positive relationship between prolonged, exclusive mother-child sleeping arrangements and frequency of Personal Crime.[3]

Inspection of the child training factors associated with frequency of Personal Crime suggests that the conditions in childhood leading to a high

[3] The variable of mother-child sleeping might be considered to favor feminine identification. In that event, the fact that it shows correlations in the positive direction with both types of crime tends toward confirmation of the findings in our earlier section on Correlates of Crime in General.

frequency of personal crime among adults are as follows: a mother-child household with inadequate opportunity in early life for identification with the father, mother-child sleeping arrangements which tend to foster a strong dependent relationship between the child and the mother, subsequent socialization with respect to independence training which tends to be abrupt, punitive, and productive of emotional disturbance in the child.

We would predict that this pattern of child training factors would tend to produce in the child persistent attitudes of rivalry, distrust, and hostility, which would probably continue into adult life. The results obtained with ratings of adult attitudes (Table 4) support this view. Frequency of Personal Crime is negatively correlated with General Trustfulness. Frequency of Personal Crime is also positively correlated with Environmental Hostility in Folk Tales. Classification of a folk tale unit in this category means that the particular unit involved definite deception, aggression, or rejection in relation to the principal character. This variable was not highly related to that of environmental kindness, although the results obtained with the two are consistent with each other. The correlation between them was only −.34, most folk tale units not falling in either of these categories. Our results indicate that societies which are rated as relatively high in the frequency of Personal Crime have folk tales with a high proportion of events representing the environment as hostile. If we may infer that the content of folk tales reflects the underlying attitudes of the people who tell them, then this finding, as well as those with our other measures of adult attitudes, supports the view that personal crime is correlated with a suspicious or distrustful attitude toward the environment.

An analysis by Whiting (1959) of the socialization factors correlated with a belief in sorcery is relevant to this aspect of our results. He points out that a belief in sorcery is consistent with a paranoid attitude. According to Freudian interpretation, paranoia represents a defense against sexual anxiety. Whiting presents cross-cultural data in support of a hypothesis, based on Freud's theory of paranoia, that a belief in sorcery is related to a prolonged and intense contact with the mother in infancy followed by a severe sex socialization. The same hypothesis might be applied to frequency of Personal Crime, since we have evidence that Personal Crime is correlated with a suspicious, paranoid attitude in adult life, and sorcery is after all one form of Personal Crime. Our results for Personal Crime, in common with Whiting's for sorcery, show a correlation with mother-child household and prolonged mother-child sleeping. However, we found no significant correlation with severe sex socialization but rather with severe dependence socialization. We do not feel that these findings negate the Freudian interpretation, because dependence socialization, bearing as it does on the child's intimate relation with his mother, necessarily is concerned with the child's sexual feelings in a broad sense.

GENERAL DISCUSSION

We would like to emphasize the value of the cross-cultural method for exploring the possible determinants of crime. When each society is used as a single case, and is classified according to crime and other variables for the entire society over a period of years, the measures are likely to be reliable; comparison among societies provides great diversity in frequency of crime and in the other variables to be related with it.

The cross-cultural method may help us to identify variables with a causal relationship to crime. For example, our cross-cultural data suggest that high differentiation of status within a society is a favorable condition for a high frequency of Theft, and that a high frequency of Personal Crime is associated with a generalized attitude of distrust. These relationships should be subjected to more systematic and intensive tests within our own society than has hitherto been done.

Variables which have been suggested, whether in empirical studies or theoretical discussions, as possible causes of crime within our society may be tested for broader significance by the cross-cultural method. It has been argued, for example, that within our society delinquent or criminal behavior is likely to develop if the boy has been raised without adequate opportunity to identify with the father. These suggestions have often been made in connection with family patterns that are said to characterize certain classes or groups within our society; the cross-cultural findings indicate that a high frequency of both Theft and Personal Crime tends to occur in societies where the typical family for the society as a whole creates lack or limitation of opportunity for the young boy to form an identification with his father. Therefore the cross-cultural method supports the theory that lack of opportunity for the young boy to form a masculine identification is in

itself an important antecedent of crime.

Another instance of such confirmation in a broader sense is the following: In our society delinquents have been reported to express feelings of alienation from their parents. It is unclear, however, whether this reflects their parents' actual treatment of them, or merely their own subjectively determined perceptions. Our cross-cultural data (in common with some of the findings within our own society) indicate that a high frequency of Theft is correlated with an actual low degree of indulgence during childhood.

Other theories about the antecedents of crime, when tested with the cross-cultural method, have not been confirmed in this broader framework. For example, pressures toward achievement were not significantly related to frequency of crime, although such a relationship is implied by theories of delinquency which emphasize the discrepancy between culturally induced aspirations and the possibility of achieving them. This negative result in our sample of societies does not deny the existence of such a relationship within our society, but it does indicate a limitation on its generality.

REFERENCES

BARRY, H., III, BACON, MARGARET K., & CHILD, I. L. A cross-cultural survey of some sex differences in socialization. *J. abnorm. soc. Psychol.*, 1957, **55**, 327–332.

BARRY, H., III, CHILD, I. L., & BACON, MARGARET K. Relation of child training to subsistence economy. *Amer. Anthropologist*, 1959, **61**, 51–63.

CHILD, I. L., VEROFF, J., & STORM, T. Achievement themes in folk tales related to socialization practice. In J. W. Atkinson (Ed.), *Motives in fantasy, action, and society*. Princeton: Van Nostrand, 1958. Pp. 479–492.

DAVIS, A., & DOLLARD, J.   *Children of bondage*. Washington: American Council on Education, 1941.

FENICHEL, O.   *The psychoanalytic theory of neurosis*. New York: Norton, 1945.

GLUECK, S., & GLUECK, ELEANOR.   *Unraveling juvenile delinquency*. New York: Commonwealth Fund, 1950.

HEALY, W., & BRONNER, A. F.   *New light on delinquency and its treatment*. New Haven: Yale Univer. Press, 1936. (Republished 1957)

MILLER, W. B.   Lower class culture as a generating milieu of gang delinquency. *J. soc. Issues*, 1958, **14**, 5–19.

MURDOCK, G. P.   World ethnographic sample. *Amer. Anthropologist*, 1957, **59**, 664–687.

PARSONS, T.   *Essays in sociological theory*. (Rev. ed.) New York: Free Press, 1954.

ROBINS, L. N., & O'NEAL, PATRICIA.   Mortality, mobility and crime: Problem children thirty years later. *Amer. sociol. Rev.*, 1958, **23**, 162–171.

ROBISON, SOPHIA M.   *Juvenile delinquency: Its nature and control*. New York: Holt, Rinehart and Winston, 1960.

ROHRER, J. H., & EDMONSON, M. S. (Eds.).   *Eighth generation: Cultures and personalities of New Orleans Negroes*. New York: Harper & Row, 1960.

WHITING, J. W. M.   The cross-cultural method. In G. Lindzey (Ed.), *Handbook of social psychology*. Vol. 1. *Theory and method*. Cambridge, Mass.: Addison-Wesley, 1954. Pp. 523–531.

WHITING, J. W. M.   Sorcery, sin and the superego: A cross-cultural study of some mechanisms of social control. In M. R. Jones (Ed.), *Nebraska symposium on motivation: 1959*. Lincoln: Univer. Nebraska Press, 1959. Pp. 174–195.

WHITING, J. W. M., & CHILD, I. L.   *Child training and personality*. New Haven: Yale Univer. Press, 1953.

WHITING, J. W. M., KLUCKHOHN, R., & ANTHONY, A.   The function of male initiation ceremonies at puberty. In Eleanor E. Maccoby, T. Newcomb, & E. L. Hartley (Eds.), *Readings in social psychology*. (3rd ed.) New York: Holt, Rinehart and Winston, 1958. Pp. 359–370.

3

Language, Cognition, and Attitude

——————— ◆ ———————

10. SPEAKING IN GENERAL *

George A. Miller

Presumably, psychologists aspire to the discovery of general laws. Many of our most cherished descriptive principles are assumed, either explicitly or implicitly, to hold true not only across different cultures, but even across different species. In the area of social psychology, however, and especially where linguistic phenomena become involved, it is all too easy to fall into an ethnocentric fallacy—to explain too much because we confuse our own social conventions with universal laws of human nature. Fortunately, our anthropological friends have not been reticent about correcting such errors; by now enough psychological theories have been punctured by ethnological shrapnel to make us all properly self-conscious in our generalizations.

One of the best publicized of these anthropological injunctions—at least among psycholinguists—is the Whorf-Sapir hypothesis of linguistic relativity. The notion that a person's whole conception of the world he lives in is, to use Whorf's phrase, "controlled by inexorable laws of pattern . . . , the unperceived intricate systematizations of his own language," was often taken to mean that men in different cultures, speaking different languages, must organize and think about their worlds in very different ways. Psychological principles established in one linguistic community, therefore, cannot be automatically generalized beyond that community. Teamwork between ethnology and psychology is obviously necessary.

* Excerpted from G. A. Miller's review of *Universals in Language,* a book edited by Joseph H. Greenberg and published by the MIT Press, Cambridge, Mass., 1963. Professor Miller's review appeared in *Contemporary Psychology,* 1963, 7: 417–418. This portion is reprinted here with the permission of the author and the American Psychological Association.

As this teamwork has developed, however, it has become increasingly clear that there is not as much difference between men in different societies as we had been led to expect. This is not to say that the Whorf-Sapir hypothesis has been discredited—a Scottish verdict of "not proven" is as much as we can presently say on that score—but rather that, even if the hypothesis were true, the conceptual differences between cultures could scarcely be *greater* than the differences between their languages. And these differences, apparently, are not as enormous as Whorf had feared. The fact seems to be that there are uniformities of surprising scope among the many diverse languages that have developed in different societies, uniformities that are probably of greater psychological significance than the differences we had expected to find.

This conclusion should not come as a complete surprise. In a sense, the very existence of educational programs that prepare linguists to cope with any new language they might encounter in their field work argues that a human language is not a completely plastic product of whimsical imagination, but that there are features common to all languages that an anthropologist can learn to expect and to recognize. Every human society has a language; every human language has both a lexicon and a syntax; the principles of organization underlying every lexicon and syntax are remarkably similar from one language to the next. If it is true, as Whorf and Sapir believed, that our language shapes our psychology, then it is at least equally true that our psychology shapes our language. The strongest evidence supporting this converse proposition comes from the existence of language universals; it is this evidence that the pres-ent volume attempts to survey and evaluate.

What are some of these language universals? They come in all sizes and varieties. There are phonological universals: all languages are spoken and can be analyzed into sequential patterns of phonemes; about a dozen phonological features serve to mediate all the phonemic distinctions that any language requires. (Charles Ferguson and Sol Saporta contributed chapters on these matters.) There are grammatical universals: all languages can be analyzed into sequential patterns of morphemes, where the morphemes fall into a few basic categories ("parts of speech") and the sequential patterns that are admissible ("sentences") can be generated by a finite set of grammatical rules. All languages have subject-predicate constructions, and in declarative sentences with a nominal subject and object, the dominant order is almost always one in which the subject precedes the object. (Greenberg lists 45 universals of this latter sort, based on a survey of 30 different languages.) There are semantic universals: all languages are capable of expressing the basic logical operations, all deal in some way with the concepts of number and time, all have systems of pronouns at least rich enough to distinguish "I," "you," and "him," all share the property of combining signs to produce new but intelligible semantic compounds, etc. (Uriel Weinrich and Stephan Ullman explore these semantic universals.) There is even (according to H. M. Hoenigswald and to Warren Cowgill) some hope of finding universal generalizations that can be made about changes that occur in the history of a language.

Many of these language universals— and the more important ones in particular—seem, by their very universality, to be almost trivial, as if no successful communication system could be conceived that would not share them. This failure to appreciate how very arbitrary and improbable are our human solutions of the communication problem is probably what leads some of us to expect that, if intelligent life has developed anywhere else in the universe, we will be able to communicate with it. One way to appreciate how peculiarily human language really is, is to consider some of the alternative communication systems that have evolved in other species; Charles Hockett has looked at human language in this wider biological context, and his impressions form part of the clear and helpful essay that is the first chapter of this book.

One wonders, of course, how complete this catalogue of universals really is. There is such variety and richness among the language universals listed here—each painstakingly documented by studies in many different languages— that one hestitates to suggest that anything might be missing. But consider, for example, the remarkable fact that conversational partners alternate between talking and listening. This reciprocity, which I assume is universal, is not a necessary consequence of any auditory or physiological inability to speak and hear simultaneously; one voice is a poor masking noise for another. There is no a priori reason why two people who have questions to ask one another could not question simultaneously and answer simultaneously. Nevertheless, we alternate. There are several interesting lines of speculation one might pursue from such a language universal—if it is indeed universal. Perhaps there is some limit imposed by the agility and attention, perhaps some critical component of the speech apparatus must be actively involved in the process of understanding speech, etc.

But, complete or not, the book makes a good beginning. It is difficult to read it and not acquire an impression that these universals fit into a pattern, that someday they will be derivable from a few basic propositions central to all the others. When that day comes, when we are ready to describe the underlying principles that explain why all human languages are so much alike in so many ways, we will undoubtedly understand human psychology a great deal better than we do today.

11. CROSS-CULTURAL COMPARABILITY IN ATTITUDE MEASUREMENT VIA MULTILINGUAL SEMANTIC DIFFERENTIALS *

Charles E. Osgood

The world is rapidly shrinking—politically, socially, and psychologically. Recent developments in the technology of transportation and communication are annihilating both space and time. These same developments are making it

* Slightly abridged from a paper read before the International Congress of Psychology, August 23, 1963. Professors William K. Archer, ethnolinguist, and Murray S. Miron, psycholinguist, were coinvestigators in this research, which was supported by the Human Ecology Fund.

possible to conduct social and behavioral science research on an international scale that is certainly rewarding scientifically and perhaps essential practically, if we are to survive along with our technology. Indeed, there are many hypotheses about human nature that demand cross-national designs, if we are to successfully disentangle what is common to the human species from what is specific to a particular language or culture.

But comparisons across cultures are extremely difficult for what anthropologists call nonmaterial traits—things such as values, customs, attitudes, feelings, and meanings. Many years ago Edward Sapir and Benjamin Lee Whorf phrased what would now be called the hypothesis of psycholinguistic relativity. According to this hypothesis, how we perceive, how we think and even how we formulate our basic philosophies depend upon the structure of the language we speak. If this were literally and completely true, then comparisons across language barriers would be impossible. The Sapir-Whorf hypothesis has been shown to apply to certain aspects of language—for example, the way in which the lexicon of any language arbitrarily carves up the world denotatively does influence the perceptual and conceptual processes of its users. But, our research is making it clear that there are other aspects of language—particularly the way it represents affect and the way affect mediates metaphor and symbolism—for which universality rather than relativity seems to be the rule.

Let me begin by asking you to do the impossible—to imagine a space of some unknown number of dimensions. This will be our hypothetical semantic space. Just like all self-respecting spaces,

this one has an origin, which we define as complete "meaninglessness"—this is like the neutral grey center of the color space. If we think of the meaning of any word or concept as being some particular point in this space, then we could represent it by a vector out from the origin to that point (for example, x and y in Figure 1). The longer the vector, the further out in semantic space (concept x), the more "meaningful" the concept; the shorter the vector, the nearer the origin of the space (concept y), the less intensely meaningful the concept—this being analogous to saturation in the color space. Vectors may also vary in their direction within this n-dimensional space, and we equate direction with the "quality" of meaning—like the way colors may vary in hue, including the white to black axis. It should also be noted that if we are dealing with an Euclidean space—which is the simplest assumption about Nature to start with—then the less the distance between the endpoints of vectors in our semantic space, the more similar in meaning should be the concepts they represent.

One more analogy with the color space will prove useful to us: Just as complementary colors are defined as points equidistant and in opposite directions from the origin of the color space, which when mixed together in equal proportions cancel each other out to neutral grey, so we may think of verbal opposites as defining straight lines through the origin of the semantic space and cancelling each other out to meaninglessness when mixed. As a matter of fact, this is exactly the way dictionary-makers define pure or logical opposites in language—their meanings cancel each other out, component for component.

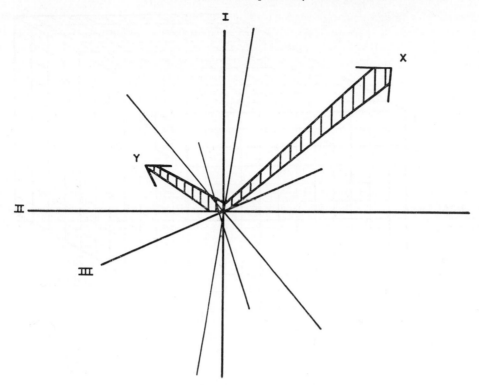

Figure 1. Hypothetical semantic space

Now imagine a whole set of different straight-line "cuts" through this space, as suggested by the fine lines in Figure 1. Each would be defined by a different pair of opposites—*hard-soft*, *excitable-calm*, *good-bad*, *fair-unfair*, *hot-cold*, *noisy-quiet*, *large-small*, and so forth—creating a veritable pincushion of qualitative dimensions. In order to locate a particular person's meaning of a particular concept, say "white rose buds," we might now play a special game of "Twenty Questions" with him: (1) Is this concept *beautiful* or *ugly*? It is *beautiful*—so it must be in the upper half of the total space. (2) Is it *hard* or *soft*? It is *soft*—so it must be upward and to the right. (3) Is it *noisy* or *quiet*? It is *quiet*—so it must be in the

octants away from us rather than near us in Figure 1. Thus, with only three binary questions, we could decide in which of eight octants of the space was "—white rose buds"; or, if each straight-line "cut" were scaled into seven discriminable steps, for example, from *extremely beautiful* through neutral to *extremely ugly*, as we have actually done in our work, then each decision would reduce uncertainty by six-sevenths, and only three "cuts" would differentiate a space having 343 discrete regions.

But to talk about "directions" in any space one has to have some reference coordinates. Is the up-down, north-south, east-west of the semantic space to be completely arbitrary, or is there some "natural" built-in structuring, analogous

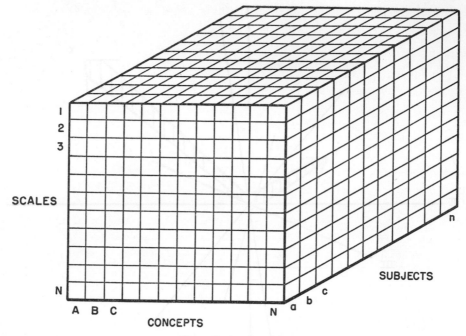

Figure 2. A cube of data

to the gravitational and magnetic determinants of geophysical space? This question is an empirical one, and the logical tool is some variant of factor analysis. We need to take large and representative samples of scales defined by verbal opposites, determine their patterns of correlation when used in judging varied samples of concepts by large and varied samples of subjects, and see if in fact they do fall into "natural" clusters or factors. We will want to determine if these factors are orthogonal, at right angles to each other, and if they are stable, that is, repeatable over independent samples of people, concepts and scales.

When a group of people judge a set of concepts against a set of semantic scales, a cube of data is generated, as shown in Figure 2. The rows are defined by scales, the columns by the concepts being judged, and the "slices" from front to back by the subjects doing the judging. Each cell represents with a single value how a particular subject rated a particular concept against a particular scale. We are usually, but not necessarily, interested in the correlations among the scales; we may obtain these correlations across subjects or across scales or across both simultaneously. We may do separate analyses for single subjects or single concepts, or we may collapse either the subject dimension (if we are interested in cultural meanings) or the concept dimension (if we are interested in concept class characteristics). In other words, there are many ways we can slice this semantic cake, and each is appropriate for answering a different kind of question.

During the past decade or more we have analysed many such data cubes collected from English-speaking Americans. Much of this work has been summarized by Osgood, Suci, & Tannenbaum (1957). Despite deliberate and independent variations in the rules for sampling scales and concepts and in the kinds of subjects used, three dominant, orthogonal factors have kept reappearing: An "evaluative" factor (represented by scales like *good-bad, kind-cruel,* and *honest-dishonest*), a "potency" factor (represented by scales like *strong-weak, hard-soft* and *heavy-light*) and an "activity" factor (represented by scales like *active-passive, fast-slow* and *hot-cold*). What this means is that there are at least three "directions" in the semantic space that are regions of relatively high density, in the sense of containing many highly correlated scales representing similar modes of qualifying. Evaluation, potency and activity appear to be the most salient modes of qualifying experience. Of course, there are additional factors, other dimensions of the semantic space—indeed, a long train of them of decreasing importance and increasing uniqueness.

Is this basic evaluation-potency-activity framework common to all people? Within the English-speaking American community we have made many comparisons—between old people and young, between males and females, between Eisenhower Republicans and Stevenson Democrats, and even between schizophrenics and normals. The results of all these and many more comparisons can be stated quite succinctly: In no case has there been convincing evidence for differences in the underlying factors. But is it possible that this semantic system is restricted to Americans who speak the English language? Let me now tell you some-

thing about our attempt to determine if this affective meaning system varies with language and culture or is, indeed, panhuman.

In the course of our earlier work we had already made a number of cross-cultural comparisons—involving Japanese, Koreans, Greeks, and Navajo, Zuni, and Hopi Indians in the American Southwest—and the similarities in factor structure were striking. But, for the most part, these studies involved simply translating American English scales into the various languages under investigation, and we were open to the criticism that we were forcing people of other language/culture communities to operate within the limits imposed by our own semantic system. During the past four years we have been trying to test the generality of the affective semantic system under the most rigorous conditions we could devise. With the cooperation of senior social scientists and their associates in some fifteen countries around the world and a staff at the University of Illinois, we have been collecting basic semantic data cubes "from scratch," so to speak, testing the generality of the factor systems, and, on the basis of the generality revealed, constructing comparable semantic measuring instruments.

We start with a list of 100 familiar concepts that have been selected by linguists and anthropologists as being "culture fair" and that have survived a stringent translation test with bilinguals in all of the six language families represented in our sample. (We have been working with Japanese, Cantonese in Hong Kong, Kannada in Southern India, Hindi in Northern India, Farsi in Afghanistan and Iran, Arabic in Lebanon, Turkish, Finnish, Serbo-Croatian in

Yugoslavia, Polish, and a number of Western Indo-European languages: Dutch, Flemish, French, Swedish, and English.) This original list of 100 translation-equivalent concepts, like "house," "man," "sky," "hand," "future," "dog," and "anger," is the only point at which translation is involved and could influence the results. From this point on, everything is done in the native language, with native monolingual subjects and with indigenous research personnel.

The first step is to have 100 young high-school-level boys in each country give the first qualifiers (adjectives, in English) that occur to them when each of the 100 concepts is given as a stimulus—for example, to the word for "tree" in his language one boy might say *tall*, another *green*, another *big*, and so forth. This basketful of 10,000 qualifiers (100 subjects times 100 concepts) is shipped to Illinois, where, using IBM and Illiac high-speed computers, we determine a rank order of these various ways of qualifying experience in terms of their total frequency of usage, diversity of usage across the 100 nouns, and independence of usage with respect to each other—in other words, we are looking for the most characteristic, productive and independent qualitative dimensions in each language. Even at this level, similarities begin to emerge. Not only are the rank-frequency distributions of qualifiers statistically similar, but when the ranked qualifiers in various languages are translated into English and correlated, the correlations are all in the .50 to .70 range and highly significant. In other words, despite the difficulty of "mapping" one language into another in translation, the dominant modes of qualifying experiences, of describing aspects of objects and events, tend to be

very similar, regardless of what language one uses or what culture he happens to have grown up in.

The 60 or 70 highest ranked qualifiers are shipped back to the field, where their opposites are elicited and they are made into bipolar scales—the highest ranked 50 surviving this process being kept. Then another group of young males rate the original 100 concepts against these 50 scales, 200 subjects being divided into subgroups of 20 judging subsets of 10 concepts because this task is so time-consuming. Thus we generate a cube of semantic data, 100 concepts times 50 scales times 20 subjects, in each language/culture community. These data are returned to Illinois, where standard correlation, factor analysis and rotation procedures are applied by our computers. Such analyses of each cube of data yield a unique solution for each language/culture community; nevertheless, it is gratifying to be able to report that for the 12 communities carried through this stage so far, evaluation, potency and activity are identifiable as the first three factors in magnitude—and usually in that order.

The most crucial test of factorial similarity is to put the data from all countries into the same mathematical space. Since we have neither identical subjects nor identical scales, we must do this by assuming that our 100 translation-equivalent concepts are identical, and by correlating across them. To the extent that these 100 concepts are *not* identical in meaning across our language/culture communities—and we can be sure that they are not identical— then all this can do is introduce "noise" into our system and reduce our correlations, that is, work against us. In the first such test that we ran, we selected the three highest-loading scales on the first three factors of the unique analysis of seven countries (63 scales in all), intercorrelated them across 100 common concepts, and then factored the correlation matrix by usual procedures. The results clearly indicated that evaluation, potency, and activity factors are truly pancultural. The three dominant factors do not represent particular language/culture communities, but rather common semantic dimensions.

What is the purpose of all this busy work in many lands and many tongues? The first, purely scientific purpose has been to demonstrate that human beings the world over, no matter what their language or culture, do share a common meaning system, do organize experiences along similar symbolic dimensions. In contradiction to Benjamin Lee Whorf's notion of "psycholinguistic relativity," here is at least one aspect of language behavior that is universal. A second, more practical purpose of this research is to develop and apply instruments for measuring "subjective culture"—meanings, attitudes, values, customs and the like—instruments that can be shown to be comparable across languages and thereby break through the language barrier. The demonstration of common semantic factors makes it completely feasible to construct efficient "semantic differentials" for measuring the meanings of critical concepts cross-culturally, with reasonable confidence that the yardstick being employed is something better than a rubber band. It is now possible to ask questions like: "How does the meaning of the self vary from culture to culture?" "How do attitudes toward leadership and authority vary around the world?" "Is a common sub-

jective culture developing among the world's elites?"—and be reasonably sure that the answers are not artifacts of translation.

Now, given this long introduction, let me turn directly to the matter of measuring attitudes cross-culturally. Despite the plethora of definitions of "attitude," there seems to be general consensus that (a) they are learned and implicit, (b) that they may be evoked either by perceptual signs or linguistic signs (c) that they are predispositions to respond evaluatively to these signs, and (d) that the evaluative predisposition may fall anywhere along a scale from "extremely favorable" through "neutral" to "extremely unfavorable."

In all of the general factor analyses of affective meanings we have done to date, the first and dominant factor usually accounting for about twice as much variance as any other—has always been clearly identifiable as Evaluation. Furthermore, being a bipolar factor, graded in intensity in both directions from a neutral point, it meets the criterion of reflecting predispositions from "extremely favorable" through "neutral" to "extremely unfavorable." It is also clear that, in the general mediation theory of meaning of which our semantic differential measuring operations are part, meanings of concepts are implicit reactions to either perceptual or linguistic signs, and they are learned. The evaluative factor of semantic differentials thus seems to meet all the criteria for a measure of attitude, and it is therefore tempting to simply define "attitude" toward any concept as its projection onto the evaluative factor in the total meaning space.

We do have some empirical justification for this identification. My colleague during the early development of semantic differential technique, Dr. Percy Tannenbaum, compared E-factor scores for subjects judging the concepts "the Negro," "the church," and "capital punishment" with their scores on special Thurstone attitude scales devised to tap each of these attitudes. Reliabilities of the E-factor scores proved to be slightly higher, actually, than those of the Thurstone scales. More important, the E-factor scores for the concepts correlated with their corresponding Thurstone scale scores as highly as reliabilities could allow. In other words, it would appear that whatever the specific Thurstone scales were measuring—and they were designed to measure attitude—the E factor was measuring equally well.

But if this is the case, then the E factor of the semantic differential has an obvious advantage: it applies exactly the same set of evaluative scales to all three concepts, "Negro," "church" and "capital punishment," whereas in the Thurstone technique unique statements must be selected and scaled for each concept whose attitude is being assessed. The E factor of the semantic differential thus has the advantage of being potentially general across the concepts being studied. If such generality is an advantage within a single language/culture community it becomes absolutely essential if we are to measure attitudes comparably, across differences in both languages and cultures. One can imagine the difficulties there would be in trying to translate and show scale equivalence for statements like "I would not admit a Negro to my social club," or "I go to church every Sunday."

You will recall that the factors obtained from different language/culture communities were found to be truly pan-cultural in the direct, mathematical sense that the scales from these different language/culture communities were found to be highly correlated when used in rating the standard 100 concepts. We will now take the four scales for each community which load highest and most purely on the pancultural evaluative factor and use their composite value for each concept, transposed to a + 3 to − 3 scale, as an *SD-attitude-score*— that is, a semantic-differential-determined attitude score for each concept. The scales used in this analysis, both in the native language and in approximate English translation, are given in Table 1. You will note that although they are not—in many cases translation equivalents, they do maintain a common evaluative feeling-tone.

Before presenting some illustrative results, I would like to offer a few words of caution about interpretation. First, these data were collected in the course of the "tool-making" phases of our work and hence the concepts were not selected for their relevance to attitude measurement. Second, due to the large number of judgments involved in the concept-on-scale task, subgroups of 20 subjects judged subgroups of 10 concepts; therefore, the N in each case is only 20. In our work with American subjects we have found factor-score differences as small as half a scale unit to be significant at beyond the .05 level for N's of this magnitude, but to be on the safe side I would use a full scale unit as a significance criterion here. Third, there appear to be real differences in scale-checking style between language/culture groups; in the present case, the Flemish-speaking Belgians have SD-attitude-scores beyond plus or minus 1.5 in po-

TABLE 1. SCALES CONTRIBUTING TO SD-ATTITUDE-SCORES FOR SEVEN
LANGUAGE/CULTURE COMMUNITIES

	Native Language	English Translation
American English	nice-awful sweet-sour good-bad happy-sad	
Dutch	prettig-naar gezellig-ongezellig mooi-lelijk gelukkig-ongelukkig	pleasant-unpleasant cozy-cheerless pretty-ugly happy-sad
Belgian Flemish	aangenaam-onaangenaam plezierig-vervelend gezellig-ongezellig prachtig-afschuwelijk	agreeable-disagreeable pleasant-boring cozy-cheerless magnificent-horrible
French	sympathique-antipathique rassurant-effrayant gai-triste gentil-méchant	likeable-repugnant calm-frightened happy-sad nice-awful
Finnish	hauska-ikava valoisa-synkka makea-hapan onneton-onnellinen	nice-awful light-gloomy sweet-sour happy-sad
Japanese	気持よい－気持悪い 快よい－不快な 有難い－迷惑な ようこばしい－悲しい	pleasant-unpleasant comfortable-uncomfortable thankful-troublesome happy-sad
Indian Kannada	ದಯಾಳು－ಕ್ರೂರ ಒಳ್ಳೆಯ－ಕೆಟ್ಟ ಸುಂದರ－ವಿಕಾರ ನಾಜೂಕು－ಒರಟು	merciful-cruel good-bad beautiful-ugly delicate-rough

larization for 56 of the 100 concepts, whereas the Finns and the Kannada-speaking Indians have only 6 and 9 concepts respectively reaching this degree of polarization. It is also true that inconsistencies in attitudinal direction among the individual subjects in a group will tend to cancel the composite scores toward neutrality, but since we are here interested in *cultural meanings*, not individual, this will not concern us. Finally, you should keep in mind the fact that the subjects are unmarried males of junior high-school age.

With these caveats in mind, let us turn to some results. Table 2 reports SD-attitude-scores for some concepts among our sample of 100 that are usually considered objects of attitude. Attitude toward "work" is most favorable for the Kannada-speaking Indians of Mysore and the Japanese, but actually slightly negative for the Flemish-speaking Belgians. The concept of "wealth"

TABLE 2. SD-ATTITUDE-SCORES FOR SOME "ATTITUDE OBJECTS"
AMONG STANDARD 100 CONCEPTS

Concepts	Language/Culture Communities						
	American	Dutch	Flemish	French	Finnish	Japanese	Kannada
Work	0.5	0.7	−0.2	0.9	0.3	1.0	1.0
Wealth	1.3	0.5	1.2	0.9	−0.1	0.9	0.4
Doctor	1.6	1.0	−0.7	0.8	0.3	1.0	1.0
Luck	1.6	1.6	1.6	1.5	1.2	2.5	1.0
Peace	2.0	1.4	2.3	2.1	1.1	2.3	0.8
Policeman	0.8	−0.4	−0.3	−0.4	−0.5	0.0	1.0

is quite positive in evaluation for Americans and Flemings but negative for Finns. Flemish and Finnish subjects have neutral or slightly negative attitudes toward "doctor," in contrast to the very favorable American attitude. For some reason—unknown to me at least—the Japanese have an extremely positive feeling about "luck." "Peace" is favored highly by everyone, and about equally if we take into account the differences in average polarization; but only for Indians and Americans is "policeman" a positive concept.

Table 3 presents sets of concepts that are universally favorable, neutral, or unfavorable—insofar as our small sample of seven language/culture communities can be considered an adequate sample of the universe! "Girl," "love," "marriage" and "mother" are highly favorable notions, as are "pleasure," "freedom," "success," "sympathy," and "friend"—all of which is not too surprising. The list of universally unfavorable concepts reads like a catalogue of human misery: the emotional states of "pain," "anger," "guilt," and "fear"; the conditions of "danger," "punishment," and "crime"; the specific threats posed by "thief," "snake," and "poison";

and then, at last, "battle," "defeat" and "death." Yet, among these generally unfavorable notions, there are some interesting deviations: note the rather mild disapproval registered by the Indians (even taking into account their generally reduced polarization), as compared with the intensely negative attitudes of the Japanese; note also the relative lack of concern of the French for things like "pain," "danger," and "death" as compared with the Flemish-speaking Belgians.

It is interesting, but perhaps not surprising, that the evaluatively neutral concepts are all natural objects and phenomena. "Stone," "root," "rope," "knot," and "cloud" surely are not objects about which people are likely to have strong attitudes, nor are the natural phenomena of "wind" and "heat" (unless they are in excess, in which case they usually have special names like "tornado"). But this is not necessarily the case. The first set of concepts in Table 4 might have been expected to be attitudinally neutral, too, but they are not for all people in our sample. The linguistically and culturally close Dutch and Flemings have a highly favorable attitude toward "Wednesday"; all

Indo-European language communities (Americans, Dutch, Flemish, and French) place a high valuation on "chair," in contrast to the non-Indo-European groups (Finnish, Japanese and Kannada); the Kannada-speaking Indi- ans have, for them, an extremely positive feeling toward the "moon," while the Japanese feel similarly about "tree." Just why such affective investments should exist, I do not know, but I suspect they are reflections of uniquenesses

TABLE 3. CONCEPTS HAVING FAVORABLE, NEUTRAL, AND UNFAVORABLE
SD-ATTITUDE-SCORES AMONG STANDARD 100 CONCEPTS

Concepts	Language/Culture Communities						
Favorable	American	Dutch	Flemish	French	Finnish	Japanese	Kannada
Girl	2.1	2.0	2.3	1.9	1.4	1.1	1.1
Love	2.2	2.1	2.2	2.0	1.8	1.3	1.4
Marriage	2.3	1.9	2.0	2.0	1.7	1.4	1.1
Mother	2.1	2.1	2.1	2.3	1.1	1.9	1.7
Pleasure	1.8	1.9	2.3	2.2	1.3	2.0	1.1
Friend	1.8	1.4	2.0	1.5	1.1	1.5	1.8
Freedom	2.3	2.0	2.1	1.9	1.9	2.2	1.6
Sympathy	1.3	1.3	2.1	2.1	1.4	0.8	1.0
Music	1.6	1.7	1.9	1.3	1.2	1.4	1.9
Sleep	1.8	1.2	1.7	1.2	1.4	1.6	0.4
Sun	1.6	1.8	1.7	2.1	1.2	1.7	0.9
Success	1.5	2.1	2.1	1.7	0.5	2.2	1.0
Neutral							
Wind	0.6	−0.3	−1.0	0.6	0.1	0.4	0.3
Heat	0.4	0.5	0.3	0.8	0.0	0.3	0.4
Stone	0.0	−0.6	0.2	0.2	−0.4	0.4	−0.8
Cloud	1.3	0.5	0.1	−0.5	0.2	0.5	0.7
Root	0.6	0.0	−0.1	0.1	−0.4	0.5	0.9
Rope	0.2	0.3	0.5	−0.1	−0.7	0.6	0.7
Knot	0.2	0.0	0.0	0.8	0.0	0.0	0.5
Unfavorable							
Pain	−1.4	−1.8	−2.3	−1.0	−1.2	−1.9	−0.7
Anger	−1.9	−1.1	−2.2	−1.3	−1.3	−1.5	−1.3
Guilt	−1.2	−1.3	−2.2	−1.3	−0.9	−2.1	−0.5
Fear	−1.4	−1.4	−2.0	−1.4	−1.4	−1.5	−0.3
Danger	−1.6	−1.8	−2.1	−0.9	−1.1	−2.0	−0.8
Punishment	−0.9	−1.1	−2.3	−1.6	−1.7	−1.1	−1.1
Crime	−1.9	−1.8	−1.9	−1.9	−1.5	−2.5	−0.6
Thief	−1.9	−2.0	−2.2	−1.4	−1.4	−2.5	−1.3
Snake	−0.5	−1.1	−1.6	−1.4	−0.4	−2.0	−0.5
Poison	−1.7	−1.6	−2.3	−1.6	−1.4	−2.2	−0.9
Battle	−1.8	−1.4	−1.7	−1.7	−1.8	−2.1	−0.5
Defeat	−1.5	−1.5	−1.7	−1.5	−1.4	−1.3	−0.4
Death	−0.9	−1.6	−2.0	−0.3	−1.3	−1.2	−0.9

TABLE 4. ATTITUDINAL BITS TO CONJURE WITH

Concept	Language/Culture Community						
	American	Dutch	Flemish	French	Finnish	Japanese	Kannada
Wednesday	0.6	1.4	1.5	0.6	0.3	0.8	0.4
Chair	1.2	1.4	1.6	1.4	0.3	0.9	0.8
Moon	1.2	1.1	1.0	1.1	0.6	1.3	2.0
Tree	0.8	0.9	1.1	1.4	0.1	2.0	0.8
Husband	1.2	1.7	2.0	1.4	0.2	1.5	1.3
Father	1.9	1.2	1.4	2.2	1.0	1.9	1.4
Man	1.1	1.1	1.4	1.8	0.5	1.3	0.8
Woman	1.9	1.9	1.8	2.4	1.1	1.2	1.1
Mother	2.1	2.1	2.1	2.3	1.1	1.9	1.7
Girl	2.1	2.0	2.3	1.9	1.4	1.1	1.1
Hope	1.9	0.7	0.6	1.3	0.7	1.3	0.3
Future	1.4	0.7	0.5	1.2	0.3	1.1	0.5
Purpose	1.1	0.6	0.6	1.1	0.3	1.0	0.5
Hunger	−1.5	−1.3	−1.9	−0.3	−1.0	−1.2	0.5
Need	0.5	0.4	−2.7	0.0	0.1	0.9	0.7
Meat	1.6	0.7	1.5	0.7	−0.1	0.8	0.2
Bread	1.6	1.0	1.5	1.4	0.4	1.4	0.7
Fruit	1.5	1.4	2.2	1.5	0.7	1.7	1.5
Food	1.8	1.6	1.4	1.5	0.6	1.6	0.9
Laughter	1.9	1.2	1.9	1.6	1.1	1.2	0.2

in subjective culture and should be of interest to cultural anthropologists.

Other comparisons in this table—which I have titled "Attitudinal Bits to Conjure With"—may have similar interest. The second set of concepts, all referring to human and kin classifications, display close similarities among the Indo-European language groups, who, I believe, also share the same kinship system. We also note that attitudes toward "women" are higher than toward "men" everywhere except in Japan—however, keep in mind that our subjects were boys between 14 and 16 years of age. The set of future-oriented concepts, "hope," "future," and "purpose," dis-

play an interesting pattern—they are all positively evaluated by Americans, French and Japanese, but are essentially neutral attitudinally for the Dutch, Flemings, Finns, and Indians. Does this necessarily imply that Americans, French and Japanese are more hopeful about the future and more purposefully striving toward it?

The next set of concepts suggests a paradoxical kind of denial mechanism: The Indians in Mysore rate "hunger" and "need" relatively positively, and yet (with the exception of "fruit") have relatively neutral attitudes toward the food concepts; on the other hand, the well-off Americans, Flemings, and

Dutch have the most negative attitudes toward "hunger" (and the Flemings particularly toward "need"), yet display consistently positive attitudes toward the food concepts. It is as if those that have are most gratified with having and most concerned about being deprived! But, in the end, there is "laughter"; Americans and Flemings hold this form of social commentary in the highest esteem—Indians the least.

REFERENCE

Osgood, C. E., Suci, G. J., & Tannen-baum, P. H. *The Measurement of Meaning*. Urbana: University of Illinois, 1957.

12. A CONSIDERATION OF BELIEFS, ATTITUDES, AND THEIR RELATIONSHIP *

Martin Fishbein

Two persons who are equally opposed to segregation may have quite different conceptions of its nature, causes, and consequences and may hold different views concerning the actions that should be taken to eliminate segregation. In the language of this paper, these two persons are said to have the *same attitudes* toward segregation but to hold *different beliefs* about it. Attitudes are learned predispositions to respond to an object or class of objects in a favorable or unfavorable way. Beliefs, on the other hand, are hypotheses concerning the the nature of these objects and the types of actions that should be taken with respect to them.

Many writers do not maintain this distinction between attitudes and beliefs. Both notions are commonly subsumed under the single term "attitude," which is said to have affective (evaluative), cognitive, and conative (action) components. According to this view, an "attitude" toward segregation would include not only a person's negative feelings toward segregation, but also his ideas about its causes and implications, and this conviction that it should be attacked through mass demonstrations and legislation. There is, of course, no overwhelming reason why the word "attitude" should not mean all of these things. Words are created by man for his own convenience, and they may be used in any manner that man finds appropriate. But certain considerations lead us to believe that "attitude" is a more useful scientific word when it is given restricted meaning.

It is obvious that affect, cognition, and action are not always highly correlated. Different people like the same thing for very different reasons,, and a thin man who likes pastries may eat them because he believes they contain many calories while a fat man may spurn them for exactly the same reason. Consequently, a multicomponent conception of attitude turns out to be a

* This article was written specifically for this volume.

multidimensional conception, and the "attitude" of any one person toward an object or concept may fall at three very different positions on three different dimensions. But the operations by which attitudes are measured almost invariably yield a single score that is unlikely to reflect these three different components in any very precise fashion. As a matter of fact, people who construct "attitude scales" rarely maintain that their instruments are measuring three components; instead, they usually contend that their scales indicate people's evaluations (pro-con) of objects or concepts. Thus, although "attitudes" are often said to include all three components, it is usually only evaluation or "the affective component" that is measured and treated by researchers as the essence of attitude.

It is the contention of this paper that increased precision and understanding can be gained by bringing our definition of attitude into closer harmony with the techniques by which attitudes are measured. Multidimensional concepts are notoriously difficult to employ in rigorous theory, and they create almost unmanageable problems when theory is translated into research. A conceptual system in which only the affective component is treated as attitudinal, and the other two components are linked to beliefs, should permit a more productive approach to the study of attitudes.

ATTITUDE

Elsewhere in this volume (see Chapter 11), C. E. Osgood has described techniques for measuring the meanings that objects or concepts have for people.

Subjects rate the object or concept on a series of seven-step bipolar scales, the ends of which are identified by adjectives such as *good-bad*, *clean-dirty*, *strong-weak*, or *fast-slow*. Ratings obtained on a very large number of these scales have been subjected to a procedure called factor analysis that reveals the underlying dimensions of meaning along which people see various objects as falling. It is significant that Osgood has invariably found that one of the most critical aspects of meaning is an evaluative dimension. A very large share of the meaning of objects or concepts appears to be determined by the position that the object or concept is seen to occupy on a good-bad or pro-con continuum.

After reviewing many of the earlier definitions of attitude, Osgood and his associates (Osgood and Tannenbaum, 1955; Osgood, Suci, and Tannenbaum, 1957) concluded that:

It seems reasonable to identify attitude, as it is ordinarily conceived in both lay and scientific language, with the evaluative dimension of the total semantic space, . . . The meaning of a concept is its location in a space defined by some number of factors or dimensions, and attitude toward a concept is its projection onto one of these dimensions defined as "evaluative."

Osgood's definition of attitude has many advantages. First, it has the virtue of treating attitude as a unidimensional concept. It equates attitude with the evaluative meaning of an object or concept, that is, attitude refers only to the "evaluation" of a concept—its "favorableness" or "unfavorableness," its "goodness" or "badness." Other types of meaning that the object may have for a person (for example, its size, shape, speed, and so forth) are excluded from the notion of attitude except insofar as they may influence the placement that the person gives the object on the evaluative dimension. Second, as Osgood *et al.* (1957) point out, "every point in semantic space has an evaluative component (even though the component may be of zero magnitude when the evaluative judgments are neutral)." Thus, this definition makes it clear that with respect to any object or concept, an individual has a positive, negative, or neutral attitude. Third, it is consistent with the description of attitude as a learned predisposition to respond to a stimulus in a favorable or unfavorable way. According to Osgood, this definition characterizes attitude as a mediating evaluative response, that is, a learned implicit response that varies in intensity and tends to "mediate" or guide the individual's more overt evaluative responses to an object or concept.

Considerable evidence supporting the reliability and validity of Osgood's instrument for measuring attitudes (called the semantic differential) has been presented by Osgood *et al.* (1957) and Fishbein and Raven (1962). Although the semantic differential is not the only technique by which unidimensional attitude scores may be obtained, it provides a clear operational definition of the term "attitude" as it will be used in this paper.

BELIEF

In a recent paper, Fishbein and Raven (1962) suggested a definition of belief that is analogous to the definition of attitude. According to these investigators, an individual may not only evaluate a concept (that is, view it as *good* or bad, clean* or *dirty*, and so forth) but also he may believe or disbelieve in the existence of the concept (that is, view it as *existent* or *nonexistent, probable* or *improbable,* and so forth). As we have seen above, the first type of judgment has been viewed as a measure of the evaluative dimension of a concept, or more specifically, as an "attitude." The latter type of judgment may be viewed as a measure of the *probability* dimension of a concept, or more specifically, as a "belief." Just as Osgood and his associates demonstrated that valid and reliable measures of attitude could be obtained by having the subject judge the concept on a series of bipolar evaluative scales. Fishbein and Raven demonstrated that valid and reliable measures of belief could be obtained by having the subject judge the concept on a series of bipolar *probabilistic* scales (for example, probable-improbable, likely unlikely, possible-impossible, and so forth). It is this definition of belief—the position of the object or concept on the probability dimension—that will be used throughout this paper.

At first glance, however, it may appear that this conception of belief is a highly specialized one. That is, this definition of belief appears to be concerned only with the probability of the existence of an object—it does not appear to deal with the type of belief that most psychologists have considered. Particularly in the area of attitude research, almost all psychologists have been concerned with beliefs about the object. As was pointed out above, both the "cognitive" and "action" components of attitude can be viewed as beliefs about the object. The cognitive component refers to beliefs about the nature of the object and its relations to other "objects," while the action component refers to behavioral intentions, that is, beliefs about what should be done with respect to the object.

Fishbein and Raven recognized this problem, and suggested a distinction between *belief in* an object and *belief about* an object. "Thus far, we have defined *belief in,* or more completely, *belief in the existence of,* an object. One could also consider *belief in the existence of a relationship* between that object and some other object or some quality." Thus, just as an individual may believe or disbelieve in the existence of "God," so too might he believe or disbelieve in the existence of relationships involving "God," for example, "God is omnipotent," "God is omniscient," "God is vengeful," "God had a son," and so forth. Any of these statements could be placed above the probability scales, and the belief in the existence of that particular relationship could be measured. "The various *beliefs in the relationships* between an object and other objects or qualities would then be defined as *beliefs about* that object. While *belief in* refers to the existence of an object, *belief about* deals with the nature of that object, the manner in which it exists."

Thus, like *beliefs in, beliefs about* an object are also equated with the probability dimension of a concept. However, in the latter case, the "concept" is a relational statement—a statement associating the object of belief with some other object, concept, value, or goal. In general, then, a belief about an object may be defined as the probability or improbability that a particular relationship exists between the object of belief and some other object, concept, value, or goal.

This definition of beliefs about an object is consistent with the descriptions of beliefs that most investigators have suggested. That is, most investigators have reached implicit or explicit agreement that a belief about an object may be described as a relationship between the object (of belief) and some other object, value, goal, or concept. Indeed, most investigators are agreed that any belief about an object may be diagrammed as (X) _____ (Y), where (X) refers to the object of belief, (Y) refers to some other object or concept, and the line, _____, represents the relationship or assertion linking (X) and (Y). Thus, a belief about an object can, in part, be described as any statement that relates the object of belief to some other object, value, concept, or goal. This description, however, is really a definition of a belief statement; the belief *per se* is the position that an individual ascribes to the statement on the probability dimension—the probability or improbability that the particular relationship expressed in the statement does exist.

This conception of beliefs about objects appropriately represents the many different types of beliefs that an individual may hold. For example, consider the following different types of beliefs that have been referred to in the literature:

1. Beliefs about the component parts of the object;
2. Beliefs about the characteristics, qualities, or attributes of the object;
3. Beliefs about the object's relations with other objects or concepts;
4. Beliefs about whether the object

will lead to or block the attainment of various goals or "valued states";

5. Beliefs about what should be done with respect to the object;
6. Beliefs about what the object should, or should not, be allowed to do.

With respect to the "object" Negro, these six types of beliefs may be illustrated as follows:

1. (Negroes) *have* (dark skin);
2. (Negroes) *are* (athletic);
3. (Negroes) *are equal to* (White men);
4. (Negroes) *inhibit* (free expression of ideas);
5. (Negroes) *should be* (respected);
6. (Negroes) *should not be allowed to hold* (government jobs).

It should be noted that these six types of beliefs are the kinds of beliefs that have typically been considered as comprising the "cognitive" and "action" components of attitude. That is, when most investigators are talking about an individual's "cognitive structure" or the "cognitive component," they are referring to beliefs of Type 1, 2, 3, or 4. Similarly, when they are talking about an individual's "behavioral intentions" or the "action component," they are usually referring to beliefs of Type 5 or 6. In the present paper, however, rather than viewing "belief" as a part of "attitude," these concepts have been described and defined independently. "Attitude" has been characterized as a learned, implicit response that mediates evaluative behavior, and has been operationally defined as "a concept's position

on the evaluative dimension." Similarly, "belief" was operationally defined as "a concept's position on the probability dimension," and a distinction between *beliefs in* and *beliefs about* an object has been made. Specifically, *belief in* refers to the probability that a particular object or concept exists, and *belief about* refers to the probability that a particular relationship involving the object or concept exists. Thus, like attitude, belief is defined as a unidimensional concept, that is, the term belief refers only to the "probability" or "improbability" that a particular object (belief in) or a particular relationship (belief about) exists. In addition, we have seen that beliefs about objects may be described as relationships between the object of belief and any other object, concept, value, or goal. In the following section we shall consider some of the implications of this definition and description of beliefs about an object.

BELIEFS ABOUT OBJECTS

In the discussion of attitude, it was pointed out that every concept contains an evaluative component. That is, we have attitudes toward all concepts or objects. Thus, in considering a belief statement, an individual not only has an attitude toward the object of belief, but he also has an attitude toward the "related object." For example, with respect to the statement that "Negroes are athletic," an individual has an attitude toward "athletic" as well as toward "Negroes." Similarly, in the statement, "Negroes should not be allowed to hold government jobs," an individual has an attitude toward "government jobs." The attitude associated with the related concept shall henceforth be referred to as the *evaluative aspect of a belief about an object*. Thus, every belief about an object contains a positive, negative, or neutral evaluative aspect. In other words, every belief statement relates the object of belief to some other concept that is positively, negatively, or neutrally evaluated by an individual.

Further, the relation or assertion between the object of belief and the related object may be either positive or negative, "associative" or "dissociative." "Examples of associative [positive] relations are: is, has, includes, likes, produces, implies. Examples of dissociative [negative] relationships are: avoids, hates, hinders, defeats, destroys, is incompatible with." (Abelson, 1959, p. 345).

Thus, there are six basic types of belief statements:

1. The attitude object is positively associated with a positively evaluated concept;
2. The attitude object is positively associated with a neutrally evaluated concept;
3. The attitude object is positively associated with a negatively evaluated concept;
4. The attitude object is negatively associated with a positively evaluated concept;
5. The attitude object is negatively associated with a neutrally evaluated concept;
6. The attitude object is negatively associated with a negatively evaluated concept.

Each of these statements implies a favorable, neutral, or unfavorable attitude toward the attitude object. Specifi-

cally, statements of Type 1 and Type 6 indicate favorableness toward the attitude object. Thus, if an individual holds beliefs of Type 1 or Type 6, this would suggest that he has a positive attitude toward the object. Similarly, statements of Type 2 and Type 5 imply neutral evaluations of the attitude object, while statements of Type 3 and Type 4 indicate negative evaluations. The more favorable or unfavorable the evaluative aspect of the belief statement, the more favorable or unfavorable is the attitude indicated. It is important to note, however, that if one is to judge whether a given statement suggests a favorable or unfavorable attitude, it is necessary to know how the person making the statement (that is, holding the belief) evaluates the related concept. For example, most people would agree that if an individual believed that "Negroes are equal to White men," this would suggest that he had a positive attitude toward Negroes. This judgment, however, is based on an implicit assumption that all individuals evaluate "White men" positively. Yet, it is possible to argue that for some individuals, holding this belief, that is, agreeing with this statement, actually indicates a negative attitude toward Negroes. Consider the case of an Oriental respondent who has a strong negative attitude toward "White men." If this person believed that "Negroes are equal to White men," this belief would suggest that he had a negative attitude toward Negroes. That is, from his point of view, he is agreeing with a statement that associates Negroes with a negatively evaluated concept (a Type 3 statement). Thus, although two people may hold the same belief, this belief may mean quite different things to the people, and therefore, it may suggest that they hold quite different attitudes.

It is for this reason that careful attention is paid to item selection when one is attempting to construct an attitude scale. An attempt is made to select only those items that will have the same meaning for all respondents. For example, Thurstone Scales are usually constructed through the use of the methods of successive categories and equal-appearing intervals. That is, the experimenter selects a large number of statements involving the attitude object. These statements are then presented to judges who are asked to sort the statements into eleven categories ranging from (1) the statement indicates extreme unfavorableness toward the attitude object, through (6) the statement indicates neither favorableness nor unfavorableness toward the attitude object, to (11) the statement indicates extreme favorableness toward the attitude object. Essentially then, the judge is presented with a large number of belief statements, and he is asked to judge whether each of these statements indicates an unfavorable, favorable, or neutral attitude toward the attitude object. Since the major determinants of the degree of favorableness or unfavorableness indicated by a statement are (1) the nature of the association (positive or negative), and (2) its evaluative aspect (favorable, neutral, or unfavorable), and since the nature of the association is specified, one of the major variables determining where a judge will place a statement is his evaluation of the related concept. Only those statements that result in a consistent sorting by the judges are retained. Wherever there is much disagreement among the judges' ratings, the item is eliminated. Each statement that is retained is given a value equal to the mean or median of the category placements it has received from the judges. The experimenter then selects a final set of items that range all along the favorable-unfavorable continuum—items that link the attitude object with other objects that represent varying positions on the evaluative dimension.

It is important to note, however, that the discarded items are *not* eliminated because they don't indicate favorableness or unfavorableness toward the attitude object. Indeed, it is because different judges see them as indicating different attitudes that they are eliminated. Thus, discarded items are not ordinarily irrelevant to the attitude that one wishes his instrument to measure. But items that have different attitudinal significance for different judges are likely to have uncertain attitudinal significance for other people as well. For example, a statement such as "Negroes are happy-go-lucky," is likely to be eliminated from the sample. This is because some judges will evaluate being "happy-go-lucky" as good, others will evaluate it negatively, and still others will consider it neutral. Because the statement has different evaluative aspects for different judges, it will be placed in quite different categories. On the other hand, a statement such as "Negroes are intelligent" is likely to be retained. That is, almost all judges will be in agreement that being "intelligent" is good, and thus, almost all judges will view the statement as indicating a favorable attitude. If one knew how a given individual evaluated being "happy-go-lucky," his agreement or disagreement with the statement "Negroes are happy-go-lucky" would be just as good an indication of *his* attitude as would his agreement or disagreement with the statement "Negroes are intelligent." It should be noted, however, that no one belief is likely to be a very reliable or valid "indicator" of attitude. As we shall see below, it is only when many beliefs are considered collectively that reliable estimates of attitude can be obtained.

Consideration of the types of statements that are retained or eliminated from attitude scales also points out another important aspect of attitude research. Many investigators have attempted to distinguish between belief and attitude on the basis of "affect." Krech and Crutchfield (1948), for example, have stated that "beliefs, as such, are motivationally and emotionally neutral . . . attitude can be defined as either 'pro' or 'anti' while beliefs are conceived as neutral." Similary, Katz and Stotland (1959) have asserted that a belief is not an attitude "unless there is an attribution of good or bad qualities accompanying the specific belief." As was pointed out above, however, all belief statements may be viewed as indicating some degree of favorableness or unfavorableness toward the attitude object. Further, a statement that may contain an implicit or explicit *neutral* evaluation of the attitude object for one person, may contain an implicit or explicit *positive* or *negative* evaluation for another person. For example, consider the following statements:

1. (Negroes) *are* (good);
2. (Negroes) *are* (dirty);
3. (Negroes) *are* (musical);
4. (Negroes) *are* (superstitious);
5. (Negroes) *are* (tall);
6. (Negroes) *are* (dark-skinned).

Many investigators would say that statement 1 and probably statement 2

express an "attitude." Similarly, there would be general agreement that statements 5 and 6 express "beliefs." With respect to statements 3 and 4, however, little agreement would be reached. Some investigators would say these statements reveal "beliefs" while others would associate them with "attitudes."

From the point of view presented in this paper, all of the statements are belief statements—all of the statements consist of an associative relationship between "Negro" and some other "concept." Further, there is an attitude, an evaluative response, associated with each of these concepts; each of these statements contains an evaluative aspect. As Green (1954) has pointed out, the concept of "attitude" is a hypothetical variable, abstracted from the *many* statements and actions that an individual makes with respect to a given object. Thus, none of the above statements may be viewed as an attitude. All, however, serve as indicators of attitude. If an individual positively evaluates a "concept," and if he believes that there is an *associative* relationship between "Negro" and that "concept," his holding of this belief suggests that he has a positive attitude toward Negroes. Similarly, if an individual negatively evaluates a "concept," his belief that there is an associative relationship between "Negro" and that "concept" suggests he has a negative attitude toward Negroes. Although each belief suggests an attitude, the attitude *per se* can only be reliably abstracted by considering the many beliefs an individual holds.

The problem is that most investigators have overlooked the fact that, for a given individual, all concepts have an evaluative component. Generally speaking, they have tended to label agreement with a statement or the statement *per se* as an "attitude" when the concept related to the attitude object appeared to be universally favored or unfavored. When it could not be assumed that all individuals would evaluate the concept related to the attitude object in the same manner, most investigators have tended to label the statement as a "belief." The statements, however, are neither beliefs nor attitudes. They are all belief statements; the belief is the position an individual ascribes to the statement on the probability dimension. All belief statements do contain an evaluative aspect; all beliefs about an object carry some implicit or explicit evaluation of the attitude object. Thus, it would seem that the attempt to distinguish between "attitudinal" and "nonattitudinal" beliefs on the basis of "affect" is inappropriate.

One further point concerning beliefs about objects should be considered. In this section we have seen that a Thurstone Scale consists of a series of carefully selected belief statements. Each of the statements has previously been assigned some evaluative weight between 1 and 11. Further, this evaluative weight is primarily determined by the judges' attitudes toward the concepts related to the attitude object. Thus, the respondent is confronted with a series of belief statements with *different evaluative aspects*. The respondent's task is simply to indicate by a check mark those statements "which come closest to his own feelings." His attitude is then considered to be indexed by the mean or median value of the statements with which he agrees. Thus, the *single score* that represents the respondent's degree of favorableness or unfavorableness toward the attitude object is ob-

tained through a consideration of some of his beliefs about the object.

Likert Scales also consist of a series of carefully selected belief statements. However, rather than differentially weighting each of the statements, each statement is simply considered as indicating favorableness or unfavorableness toward the attitude object.[1] Instead of checking only those statements with which he fully agrees, the respondent is asked to indicate how strongly he agrees with (that is, believes) or disagrees with (disbelieves) each statement, usually by checking a five-step scale ranging from "strong agreement" to "strong disagreement." For statements judged as indicating favorableness toward the attitude object, "strong agreement" is given a value of 5 and "strong disagreement" is given a value of 1. The scoring is reversed for those statements indicating unfavorableness toward the attitude object; the value of 5 is assigned to "strong disagreement." The sum of the values is taken as the index of the respondent's attitude.. The higher the sum, the more favorable the attitude. Thus, once again, it can be seen that the single score that represents the respondent's attitude is obtained through a consideration of some of his beliefs about the object.

Similar descriptions could be made for most other types of "attitude scales," for example, Guttman Scales, Bogardus Scales, and so forth. Clearly, there are many differences among the various types of attitude scales. For example, Thurstone and Likert Scales

[1] Those statements that imply a neutral evaluation of the attitude object are usually eliminated from Likert Scales as a consequence of the correlational technique of item selection utilized in constructing Likert Scales.

place different emphasis on the relative importance of belief strength and the evaluative aspect of beliefs in obtaining attitude scores. That is, in Thurstone's system an individual either agrees with (1) or does not agree with (0) each statement, and the evaluative aspects of the statements vary from 1 to 11. In Likert's system, the degree of agreement varies from 1 to 5, and each statement is simply considered as indicating favorableness (+1) or unfavorableness (−1). The essential point, however, is that most attitude scales obtain attitude scores through a consideration of the respondent's beliefs about the object—through an examination of his "cognitive" or "action" components. Thus, rather than viewing these "components" as parts of attitude, beliefs are considered as separate phenomena that are related to, and serve as indicants of, an individual's attitude. Let us now turn to a more explicit consideration of the relationships between beliefs about an object and the attitude toward that object.

THE RELATIONSHIPS BETWEEN BELIEF AND ATTITUDE

So far, we have been primarily concerned with describing and defining a single belief about an object. However, an individual has many beliefs about any aspect of his "world." That is, an individual associates or relates many different concepts with a given attitude object. The totality of an individual's beliefs about an object can be considered to be a belief system. If the attitude object is viewed as a "stimulus," and if the various concepts or objects related to the attitude object are viewed as "responses," then belief statements may be viewed as associations between stimuli and responses. Similarly, beliefs about an object may be seen as being highly related to the probability that the stimulus elicits the response, that is, the probability that there is an association between the stimulus (attitude object) and the response (any other concept). Thus, a belief system can be viewed as a habit-family-hierarchy of responses (Hull, 1943). The higher the response in the hierarchy, the greater is the probability that the response is associated with the stimulus, that is, the stronger is the belief.[2] Once again, it should be noted that this conception of a belief system is entirely consistent with what other investigators have called an individual's "cognitive structure" or his "behavioral intentions"—the "cognitive" and/or "action" components of attitude. However, the placement of the concept of belief within the framework of behavior theory, along with our previous description of attitude (as a learned, mediating evaluative response), readily suggests a theory of the relationships between beliefs about an object and the attitude toward that object. That is, a theory of belief and attitude may be derived directly from a consideration of the principles of behavior theory, and in particular, the principle of mediated (secondary or conditioned) generalization.

[2] It should be noted that from this point of view, the assertion (associative or dissociative) is likely to be elicited along with the "response." For example, if a prejudiced person were presented with the stimulus "Negro," he might make the following responses: "not white," "not clean," "not intelligent," and so on.

Essentially, the theory may be stated as follows: (1) an individual holds many beliefs about any given object, that is, many different characteristics, attributes, values, goals, and concepts are positively or negatively associated with any given object; (2) associated with each of these "related objects" is a mediating evaluative response—an attitude; (3) these evaluative responses summate; (4) through the mediation process, the summated evaluative response is associated with the attitude object; and thus (5) on future occasions the attitude object will elicit this summated evaluative response—this attitude. One additional point should be mentioned, however. The amount of the evaluative mediating response that is available for summation is a function of the strength of the belief. The stronger the belief, the more the evaluative aspect of that belief becomes associated with the attitude object.[3]

According to the theory then, an individual's attitude toward any object is a function of (1) the strength of his beliefs about the object and (2) the evaluative aspect of those beliefs. Algebraically, it may be predicted that an individual's attitude toward any object

$= \sum_{i=1}^{N} B_i a_i$, where $B_i =$ the strength of belief "i" about the object, that is, the "probability" or "improbability" that the attitude object is related to some other object "x_i"; $a_i =$ the evaluative aspect of B_i, that is, the evaluation of "x_i"—its "goodness" or "badness"; and $N =$ the number of beliefs.

Although this hypothesis is similar to hypotheses proposed by other investigators (Rosenberg, 1953, 1956, 1960; Zajonc, 1954; Peak, 1955), several theoretical and methodological differences have been noted elsewhere (Fishbein, 1961). It is interesting, however, that these other investigators arrived at their hypotheses from completely different theoretical viewpoints. For example, Rosenberg's hypothesis was derived from a consideration of a consistency principle, while Zajonc developed his hypothesis within the framework of a theory of "cognitive set." Although there are several important differences between the theories, all of them lead to the hypothesis that an individual's attitude toward any object is a function of his beliefs about the object and the evaluative aspects of those beliefs.

Before turning to a consideration of some of the evidence supporting this hypothesis, one additional point should be made. A review of the literature on attitude organization and change clearly indicates that there is some question about the types of beliefs that are related to, and/or function as determinants of, attitudes. For example, as we saw earlier, many investigators (for example, Krech and Crutchfield, 1948; Katz and Stotland, 1959; Abelson and Rosenberg, 1960) have attempted to distinguish between beliefs that are

---

[3] It should be noted that the assumption of "summation" is not explicit in behavior theory. Thus, for example, a postulation of "averaging" would also have been consistent with behavior theory. Some of the differences between "summation" and "averaging" have been discussed by Fishbein and Hunter (1964a, 1964b); Triandis and Fishbein (1963); and Anderson and Fishbein (1965). For a more complete description of the theory, as well as its derivation within the framework of behavior theory, see Fishbein (1961). It should also be noted that from the point of view of behavior theory, it is unnecessary to postulate a need for consistency in order to explain the relationships between beliefs and attitude.

attitudinal in nature (those that contain an implicit or explicit evaluation of the attitude object) and beliefs that are unrelated to attitude (so-called "descriptive or reportorial" beliefs). Indeed, with very few exceptions (for example, Campbell, 1950; Zajonc, 1954; Fishbein, 1963), investigators have tended to ignore these "descriptive or reportorial" beliefs in their investigations of attitude. However, as we saw above, all beliefs about an object contain an evaluative aspect, and thus, from the point of view of the theory presented here, all of an individual's beliefs about an object (for example, descriptive beliefs, instrumental beliefs, beliefs about what should be done with respect to the object, and so forth) are related to his attitude toward that object.

Since most investigators of attitude have tended to ignore "descriptive beliefs," it was felt that this type of belief would provide the most severe test of the hypothesis. Thus, in the initial test of the theory, an attempt was made to predict Ss attitudes toward Negroes from their descriptive beliefs about Negroes (their beliefs about the characteristics and components of Negroes), and from the evaluative aspect of these beliefs. Specifically, following a procedure developed by Maltzman, Bogartz, and Breger (1953), 125 Ss listed what they believed to be five characteristics that described Negroes. The ten characteristics representing the most frequent responses of the subjects (dark skin, curly hair, athletic, musical, friendly, tall, and so forth) were then selected for further consideration. A belief statement about Negroes was constructed from each of the ten characteristics (for example, Negroes have

dark skin; Negroes are athletic; Negroes are tall). Although it is clear that not all the beliefs considered are "pure descriptive beliefs," many of them (Negroes have dark skin; Negroes have curly hair; and so forth) would have been considered as "nonevaluative" and/or unrelated to attitude by most investigators. Two weeks later, fifty of the Ss returned for a second session of the experiment. Using Fishbein and Raven's (1962) evaluative (A) and probability (B) scales to measure attitude and belief respectively, each S rated each of the characteristics on the A Scale and each of the belief statements on the B Scale. Both the A and B scales are forms of the semantic differential, with the A Scale containing five, empirically determined, evaluative bipolar scales, and the B Scale containing five, empirically determined, probabilistic bipolar scales. In addition, all Ss rated the concept "Negro" on the A Scale. Using the formula presented above, estimated attitude scores were computed for each S, using his ratings of the characteristics (a_i) and the belief statements (B_i). In support of the theory, the Spearman Rank-order correlation between the estimated attitude and the obtained attitude (that is, the direct evaluation of the concept "Negro" on the A Scale) $= .801$ $(N = 50, p < .001)$.

In other studies, it has been found that a leader's attitudes toward the members of his group could be predicted from a knowledge of his beliefs about the members' behaviors (that is, his rating of the "probability" or "improbability" that the member "listened attentively to others," "expressed his opinions tactfully," and so forth) and the evaluation of those behaviors (Fishbein, 1964). Similarly, Fishbein and Feldman (1963) have obtained evidence that a voter's attitude toward a political candidate is a function of his beliefs about the candidate's stand on various issues (the "probability" or "improbability" that the candidate "is in favor of Medicare," "is in favor of an immediate end to atmospheric nuclear testing," and so forth) and his (the voter's) evaluations of these issues.

These findings along with the previous findings of Rosenberg (1956, 1960), Zajonc (1954), and others, provide strong support for the general hypothesis that an individual's attitude toward any object is a function of his beliefs about the object and the evaluative aspect of those beliefs. Further, the wide range of beliefs that have been considered in the various studies, provides some support for the notion that all of an individual's beliefs about an object are important determinants of his attitude toward the object. Additional support for this latter position, as well as for the general hypothesis, may be found in the many studies (Carlson, 1956; Rosenberg and Abelson, 1960; Anderson and Fishbein, 1965; Fishbein and Hunter, 1964a, 1964b) that have demonstrated that an individual's attitude can be changed by changing his beliefs about the object. Further, not only may beliefs be viewed as determinants of attitude, but as Rosenberg (see Chapter 13) has shown, beliefs may also be viewed as consequences of attitude. That is, changes in attitude will produce changes in belief. Thus, beliefs and attitudes are in a dynamic relationship with one another. A change in any one part of the system will produce a change in the other part.

To summarize briefly, this paper has attempted to provide a definition of belief and attitude, and to indicate some of the relations between these phenomena. Beliefs have been operationally defined as a concept's position on the probability dimension, and attitudes have been operationally defined as a concept's position on the evaluative dimension. Further, a distinction between beliefs in the existence of an object and beliefs about an object was made, with *belief in* referring to the "probability" or "improbability" that a specific object exists and *belief about* referring to the "probability" or "improbability" that a specific relationship exists between the object of belief and some other object. Thus, rather than viewing beliefs as a part of attitude, beliefs and attitudes have been defined as separate phenomena. However, an attempt was made to demonstrate that an individual's beliefs about an object are related to his attitude toward the object. More specifically, an attempt was made to show that an individual's beliefs about an object may be viewed as determinants, indicants, and/or consequences of his attitude toward the object. Finally, a theory of the relationships between beliefs and attitude was presented, and support was provided for the hypothesis that an individual's attitude toward any object is a function of his beliefs about the object and the evaluative aspect of those beliefs.

REFERENCES

ABELSON, R. P. Modes of resolution of belief dilemmas. *Conflict Resolution,* 1959, 3, 343–352.

ABELSON, R. P., & ROSENBERG, M. J.   Symbolic psychologic: a model of attitudinal connation. *Behavioral Science,* 1958, **3,** 1–13.

ANDERSON, L. R., & FISHBEIN, M.   Prediction of attitude from the number, strength, and evaluative aspect of beliefs about the attitude object: a comparison of summation and congruity theories. *J. abnorm. soc. Psychol.,* 1965 (in press).

CAMPBELL, D. T.   The indirect assessment of social attitudes. *Psychol. Bull.,* 1950, **47,** 15–38.

CARLSON, E. R.   Attitude change through modification of attitude structure. *J. abnorm. soc. Psychol.,* 1956, **52,** 256–261.

FISHBEIN, M.   A theoretical and empirical investigation of the relationships between beliefs about an object and the attitude toward that object. Unpublished doctoral dissertation, U.C.L.A., 1961. Also appears as Technical Report No. 6, Contract Nonr 233 (54), U.C.L.A., 1961.

FISHBEIN, M.   An investigation of the relationships between beliefs about an object and the attitude toward that object. *Hum. Relat.,* 1963, **16,** 233–239.

FISHBEIN, M.   The prediction of interpersonal preferences and group member satisfaction from estimated attitudes. *J. abnorm. soc. Psychol.,* 1964 (in press).

FISHBEIN, M., & FELDMAN, S.   Social Psychological Studies in Voting Behavior: I. Theoretical and methodological considerations. Paper presented at American Psychological Association, September, 1963.

FISHBEIN, M., & HUNTER, RONDA.   Summation vs. balance in attitude organization and change. *J. abnorm. soc. Psychol.,* 1964a (in press).

FISHBEIN, M., & HUNTER, RONDA.   Summation vs. balance: a replication and extension. Paper presented at Western Psychological Association. April, 1964b.

FISHBEIN, M., & RAVEN, B. H.   The AB scales: an operational definition of belief and attitude. *Hum. Relat.,* 1962, **15,** 35–44.

GREEN, B. F.   Attitude measurement. In G. Lindzey (Ed.), *Handbook of Social Psychology.* Cambridge: Addison-Wesley, 1954.

HULL, C. L.   *Principles of Behavior.* New York: Appleton-Century, 1943.

KATZ, D., & STOTLAND, E.   A preliminary statement to a theory of attitude structure and change. In S. Koch (Ed.), *Psychology: A Study of a Science.* Vol. 3, *Formulations of the Person and the Social Context.* New York: McGraw-Hill, 1959.

KRECH, D., & CRUTCHFIELD, R. S.   *Theory and Problems of Social Psychology.* New York: McGraw-Hill, 1948.

MALTZMAN, I., BOGARTZ, W., & BREGER, L.   A procedure for increasing word association originality and its transfer effects. *J. exp. Psychol.,* 1958, **56,** 392–398.

OSGOOD, C. E., SUCI, G. J., & TANNENBAUM, P. H.   *The Measurement of Meaning.* Urbana: University of Illinois Press, 1957.

OSGOOD, C. E., & TANNENBAUM, P. H.   The principle of congruity in the prediction of attitude change. *Psychol. Rev.,* 1955, **62,** 42–55.

PEAK, H.   Attitude and motivation. In M. Jones (Ed.), *Nebraska Symposium on Motivation,* 1955. Lincoln: University of Nebraska Press, 1955.

ROSENBERG, M. J.   The experimental investigation of a value theory of attitude structure. Unpublished doctor's dissertation, University of Michigan, 1953.

ROSENBERG, M. J.   Cognitive structure and attitudinal affect. *J. abnorm. soc. Psychol.,* 1956, **53,** 367–372.

ROSENBERG, M. J.   A structural theory of attitude dynamics. *Pub. Opin. Quart.,* 1960, **24,** 319–340.

ROSENBERG, M. J., & ABELSON, R. P.   An analysis of cognitive balancing. In Rosenberg et al., *Attitude Organization and Change.* New Haven: Yale University Press, 1960.

TRIANDIS, H. C., & FISHBEIN, M.   Cognitive interaction in person perception. *J. abnorm. soc. Psychol.,* 1963, **67,** 446–453.

ZAJONC, R. B.   Structure of the cognitive field. Unpublished doctor's dissertation, University of Michigan, 1954.

13. INCONSISTENCY AROUSAL AND REDUCTION IN ATTITUDE CHANGE *

Milton J. Rosenberg

I do not love thee Dr. Fell.
The reason why I cannot tell;
But this I know and know full well,
I do not love thee Dr. Fell.

This well known bit of contemptuous doggerel in which Thomas Brown, in the late seventeenth century, examined his antipathy toward the Dean of Christ Church, Oxford, poses a psychological issue of large consequence. Is it in fact true that strong habits of emotional orientation can be so autonomous, so isolated from other psychological processes, that they can be neither justified nor explained by those who hold them?

Occasionally people do indeed seem to experience persisting emotions that appear to them both inexplicable and ungrounded; but when "depth exploration" is undertaken, either through free association or through hypnotic or narcosynthetic probing, both the meaning of the emotional pattern and its relationships to other psychological processes are readily uncovered. Good examples of such seemingly, but not actually, isolated emotional orientations are to be found among the classic "phobias" delineated in psychopathology. However when it comes to our feelings toward people, including feelings toward the Dr. Fells in our lives, our emotions rarely even *seem* that isolated.

There is reason then to doubt the absolute accuracy of Brown's report of this aspect of his psychological life.

However we are limited to mere conjecture in this instance because he is beyond investigation. We cannot determine whether he did actually hold any percepts about Dr. Fell; whether there were any attributes of the ill-judged Dean that stood out as "figural" for him; whether he had any thoughts about how Dr. Fell had behaved toward him or about Fell's opinions, appearance, manners and style of expression.

At any rate when we *are* able to question people about their likes and dislikes toward others (or for that matter when we question a Bircher about his antagonism toward "liberalism" or a liberal about his enthusiasm for the United Nations) we find, in contrast to the self-report of the disgruntled Oxonian, that people typically do "have reasons" for their persisting preferences and aversions. These "reasons" usually take the form of what psychological parlance designates as "cognitions": that is they are *beliefs* about how the liked or disliked object is related to still other liked or disliked "objects" such as positively or negatively judged attributes, qualities, goals and values.

Thus a student will usually view a disliked professor as possessing some of the following unfavorable characteristics: he will think that he is a bad lecturer; or he will think him unfair, cold, punitive, uninformed, prejudiced, boring, or uninterested in his students.

* Written specifically for this volume. Some portions of this article are adapted from one originally published in *The Public Opinion Quarterly*, 1960, 24: 319–340.

Similarly, a respondent in a public opinion interview who has expressed general approval of continued efforts toward nuclear disarmament will be likely to avow one or more of the following cognitions as his own: nuclear disarmament will decrease the danger of accidental war; it will increase trust and communication between east and west; it will return optimism and hope to the world; it is a moral necessity.[1]

In sum, the fact that we are endeavoring to clarify here is that stable evaluative orientations are regularly accompanied by beliefs that support and "justify" them. Not only is this evidenced by such impressionistic illustrations as we have so far offered, but equally pertinent are a number of research studies that have been directly concerned with important details of this relationship. Among these are studies by Campbell (1947), Cartwright (1949), Rosenberg (1956),[2] Scott (1959), Smith (1949), and Woodruff and DiVesta (1948). The work of these investigators

seems to have clearly confirmed the general observations we have already presented: that stable evaluative orientations toward social "objects" are integrated with consistent cognitions about those objects. More precisely, these studies have shown that liked objects are seen as positively related to other positive objects and as negatively related to negative ones; and that disliked objects are seen as negatively related to positive objects and as positively related to negative ones.

Some of these studies have also shown that stronger, or more extreme, evaluative orientations are associated with more univalent and one sided patterns of related cognitions. Another important finding is that the stronger, or the more extreme, the evaluative orientation, the "stronger" are the supporting cognitions. Two persons who favor the United Nations, one moderately and one quite intensely, are both likely to believe that "the U.N. fosters world peace"; but the latter person is likely to be more certain of this relationship or, for that matter, is likely to place a higher positive value upon the very goal of "world peace."

These studies are essentially correlative and static but they tend to suggest a new way of approaching the problem of attitude dynamics. Indeed they have served as the basis for the theory of attitude change that is the main concern of this article.

ATTITUDE AS AN INTEGRATED AFFECTIVE–COGNITIVE STRUCTURE

Because of a certain lack of agreement among social psychologists as to just what that term "attitude" ought

---

[1] As these examples suggest, the "objects" to which attitude objects are linked in relevant cognitions tend to be of different classes depending upon the type to which the attitude object itself belongs. Thus, attitudinal cognitions about liked or disliked persons and groups are usually concerned with their positive and negative attributes and "defining characteristics." On the other hand, cognitions about the actions of a person or about favored or disfavored social actions, proposed policy changes, legislative developments, and so on, are usually concerned with positive or negative goals or with general values whose attainment is seen as fostered or hampered through the agency of the attitude object.

[2] This study is reprinted in the first volume of this work. It may be consulted both for its presentation of data demonstrating the extent of affective-cognitive consistency in attitudes and also for its detailed description of the method of cognitive measurement used both in that study and in the later studies by the author that are reported in this article.

to encompass, we have not yet either defined or much employed it here. When social psychologists first began to use the term, they meant by it simply a comparatively stable affective (that is, emotional) set or disposition toward some "object"; or speaking operationally, attitude meant to them an habitual way of evaluating some aspect of the person's social world. It was acknowledged that beliefs about, and ways of behaving toward, the object of the attitude might be related to the attitude but these were viewed as external to it.

In recent years many social psychologists have accepted the idea that it would be more useful to include cognitions about the attitude object (and perhaps also habits of overt action toward the object) within the denotative scope of the attitude concept. To this expansion of the attitude concept has been added the notion, probably based in part upon the research studies mentioned above, that the various components of an attitude are organized together in an integrated, balanced structure, that is, that attitudes possess a considerable degree of internal consistency.[3]

[3] Among current writers on attitude theory, Fishbein (see Chapter 12 in this volume) favors a conceptual definition of attitude in solely affective terms. However, though he is mainly interested in how beliefs generate or change "attitudes," his contribution to this volume does acknowledge that "beliefs and attitudes are in a dynamic relationship with one another" and that "a change in any one part of the system will produce a change in the other part." The definitional issue might then appear to be moot; but the author is now more persuaded than he was earlier (see Rosenberg, 1956) that defining an attitude as an affective-cognitive structure is in closer accord with the meaning of available data and that it does open the way to certain quite useful directions in theory development.

Of a number of different theoretical approaches to attitude dynamics that have developed out of this new conceptualization, only one will be presented in this article. We shall state its basic propositions, explicate them and describe some experiments designed to test a particularly interesting prediction drawn from them. It should be understood that this theory, first presented by the author a few years ago (Rosenberg, 1956, 1960a, 1960b) and still in the process of development, is not offered as necessarily superior to other "consistency" models such as those of Heider (1958), Newcomb (1953), Festinger (1957), and Osgood and Tannenbaum (1955) or, for that matter, the closely related model developed by Abelson and Rosenberg (1958). A number of these other approaches are discussed elsewhere in this volume (see Chapter 4); and it is likely that the next stage in this area of social psychology will see the successful integration of at least some of them. The only distinctive virtue that is claimed for the theoretical approach presented here is its comparative simplicity and thus its utility as a framework into which may be fitted a number of important observations and questions about the attitude change process.

Before we turn directly to this theoretical approach, it will be useful to deal with certain important background matters. We have already characterized a group of earlier studies as demonstrating that the affective and cognitive components of attitudes show considerable consistency with one another. But we suggested that in these findings there is also a more dynamic implication: *that humans have a need to achieve and maintain affective-cognitive consist-*

ency and also that they have a related set of abilities by which they are capable of screening and organizing aspects of available "reality" so as to achieve and maintain such consistency.

The concept of some such need and of skills related to it is becoming more and more widely accepted. However, we should note that it raises certain important and difficult psychological questions. We shall briefly touch upon two of these: How might men come to develop this need? What kind of psychological utility is afforded by the achievement and maintenance of affective-cognitive consistency within attitudes?

From the perspective that stresses the role of social learning in shaping human needs we would stress the fact that the holding of internally-inconsistent orientations toward social objects makes it difficult to simply "approach or avoid" them in ways that bring tension reduction and psychological satisfaction. In such dilemmas (and we begin to encounter them in early childhood) humans tend to avail themselves of their rather unique capacity for symbol manipulation: they are capable of altering their representations to themselves of what they feel, believe and intend toward those objects in their worlds that demand some kind of overt response. As they do this, they reduce inconsistency in a way that makes it possible for them to develop stable, action-directing (and effort-saving) orientations toward those objects.

Take, for an example of this kind of sequence, a hypothetical five-year-old who is entering kindergarten. Although his affect may be basically positive, he develops these percepts during the first day: in kindergarten there are many exciting new toys; the cookies they give him taste good; the teacher reads interesting stories to the children but, on the other hand, she looks "mean"; he begins to wonder whether mother might forget to come and take him home. The latter two cognitions are inconsistent with the original positive affect and also with the other cognitions. Consequently, the child experiences some unpleasant conflict as he prepares for his second day at kindergarten. From his own need to reduce the resulting tension, and also guided by promptings and reassurances from his parents, he re-examines the kindergarten situation during and after the second day and manages to persuade himself that the teacher does *not* look mean and that mother will not forget to come for him. In altering these cognitions, he is achieving greater affective-cognitive consistency and in so doing he finds it easier to approach kindergarten on succeeding days; and consequently he also finds it more fun to be there. The reduction of intra-attitudinal inconsistency has brought him significant psychological gain.

This instrumental sequence in which inconsistency reduction is followed by some kind of "reinforcement" is repeated probably thousands of times in any life history. It occurs in relation to many situations, persons, institutions, events, and so forth, with which we must deal. A basic consequence of this frequently repeated experience is to render intra-attitudinal consistency desirable in and of itself; it becomes in effect what the learning theorist sometimes calls a "secondary learned incentive." To put this in different terms, it is probably because inconsistency reduction facilitates the reduction of other needs that we learn the need for coordinating the feelings and beliefs that are cued by a particular social object; and it is on these grounds then that we learn the need for consistency as such.

However, since individuals probably differ both in the extent to which they have encountered inconsistency dilemmas in the past and also in the extent to which they have received secondary social training in techniques of avoiding and reducing inconsistency, we cannot assume that all persons will be equally motivated by given magnitudes of inconsistency when they encounter them. On the other hand, we are entitled to assume that for any person, as regards any area of attitudinal focus, there is some degree of inconsistency that he will not accept and which, when it is reached, will set him striving toward inconsistency reduction.

INTRA–ATTITUDINAL INCONSISTENCY AND ATTITUDE CHANGE

In the foregoing discussion we have attempted, though only in loose, nonrigorous form, to provide the background of assumptions and general propositions from which there follows a particular way of theorizing about the attitude-change process. Now using a somewhat more rigorous form of discourse we shall present and explicate the propositions, hypotheses, and predictions which, when taken together, make up the core of one attempt to formulate a consistency theory of attitude dynamics.

PROPOSITION 1. When the affective and cognitive components of an attitude are mutually consistent, the attitude is in a stable state; barring disruption of that pattern of internal consistency, the attitude will persist over time.

PROPOSITION 2. When, through the effects of persuasive communications or other kinds of experiences, some portion of the total attitude is altered in a way that produces a degree of affective-cognitive inconsistency that exceeds the individual's "tolerance limit," the attitude is in an unstable state; under these circumstances the attitude will undergo reorganizing activity.

PROPOSITION 3. This reorganizing activity will persist until the affective-cognitive inconsistency has been eliminated or reduced to a tolerable level. Such a "homeostatic" effect will be achieved through one of three alternatives: (a) rejection of the communications, or other forces, that engendered the original inconsistency between affect and cognition and thus rendered the attitude unstable—restoration of the original consistent attitude; (b) "fragmentation" of the attitude through the isolation of each of the mutually inconsistent affective and cognitive components; (c) accommodation to the original inconsistency-producing change so that a new attitude, consistent with that change, is now stabilized—attitude change.

In broad terms it is possible to specify some of the conditions under which each of these three outcomes is most likely to occur. Thus, on the assumption that an individual's attitudes (defined as his consistent and persisting affective-cognitive structures) usually enable effective regulation of his adaptive behavior and are thus of value to him, it would be predicted that he will attempt to preserve them intact. It follows that, *if possible*, an individual will ultimately reject influences that have caused a temporary alteration in either the affective or cognitive component of one of his attitudes.

Frequently, however, the potency of the force leading to the alteration of one of the major components of an attitude is so great, or so persistent, as to make it *impossible* of rejection. When this is the case, fragmentation of the attitude (often facilitated by the defensive attempt to avoid "thinking about it") is likely to result if, by virtue of the needs or "objective realities" that maintain the attitude, the component persisting from the original attitude structure is unalterable. However, when this component is capable of alteration, it would be expected to give way, and general reorganization leading to the erection of a new attitude (that is, attitude change) will result.

We shall restrict our concern here to the case in which attitude change does occur. To do this, we shall elaborate the main attitude change hypothesis that it resident in the set of basic theoretical propositions. In its simplest form that hypothesis is: *The production of inconsistency between the affective and cognitive portions of an attitude will culminate in a general attitude reorganization (through which the affective-cognitive inconsistency is reduced or eliminated) when (1) the inconsistency exceeds the individual's present tolerance limit, and (2) the force producing it cannot be ignored or avoided.* In what follows, these two qualifying

conditions are assumed, although not necessarily restated, whenever this hypothesis or data bearing upon it are discussed.

Two different prediction can be derived from this hypothesis. The first is: *If a person somehow undergoes an "irreversible" change in his beliefs about an attitude object, his affect toward that object will show corresponding change.* The second prediction is the converse: *If a person somehow undergoes an "irreversible" change in his affect toward an object, his beliefs about that object will show corresponding change.*

Until recently there was much clearer and stronger evidence available for the former prediction than for the latter one. Some of this evidence is based upon the impression of applied workers in the persuasion professions that if an audience member's beliefs about the attributes and value-serving powers of an object (such as a consumer product, a social policy, or a political candidate) can be reorganized, his feelings toward that object, and ultimately his behavior toward it, will undergo corresponding change. In addition, there are scores of experimental studies in which communications designed to change cognitions about attitude objects are directed at subjects and do produce further changes in their affective responses.

A failing of many of these studies is that they do not provide for a direct check of whether, and to what extent, the communications designed to alter cognitions actually do so. Recently, however, a number of methods for the measurement of the cognitive aspects of attitude structures have become available. The test of cognitive structure developed and used in the author's earlier (1956) correlational study is one of these. It has since been employed in attitude change studies by Carlson (1956), Peak (1959), Nowlis (1960), and Scott (1959). All of these studies, and also a recent one by Fishbein and Hunter (1964), have shown that the alteration, usually through persuasive communications, of cognitions about an attitude object tends to generate consistency-restoring change in the affective orientation toward that object. Thus, these studies serve to confirm the first of our two major predictions.

However, to demonstrate, as our basic hypothesis asserts, that affective-cognitive inconsistency (rather than mere cognitive reorganization) leads to attitude change, the reverse prediction must also be confirmed: *It must be shown that the production of an irreversible change in an attitude's affective component will generate corresponding change in its cognitive component.* This prediction, unlike its opposite, does not receive unequivocal confirmation in the available experimental literature although the findings of certain experiments designed for other purposes do seem to support it.

A specific aim in two studies by the author was to directly test this prediction by investigating the effects of a "pure" experimental manipulation of attitudinal affect (one of which did not directly act upon the cognitive content of the attitude being modified). The manipulation used in these studies involved a posthypnotic suggestion of affect change. These studies will be described both for their bearing upon the main hypothesis and also because in discussing them we will be able to delineate certain further implications of the present theory.

EXPERIMENTS ON DIRECT ALTERATION OF ATTITUDINAL AFFECT

In the first study, eleven experimental subjects and eleven control subjects were individually tested on two separate occasions for their affective and cognitive responses toward various attitude objects, all of which were proposed social changes (limiting labor's right to strike, the provision of comprehensive federal medical insurance, Negroes moving into white neighborhoods, and so on). Between the two testing sessions, the experimental subjects (all of whom were capable of achieving deep hypnosis) were placed in hypnotic trances and then given the suggestion that upon awakening their affective reactions toward two separate attitude objects would be changed (from positive to negative, or vice versa) and that they would have no memory of the suggestion having been made until the presentation of an amnesia-removing signal. It was assumed that such a posthypnotic suggestion would foster strong and irreversible affect change for as long as posthypnotic amnesia was maintained.

In a control group that received no affect manipulation, the affective and cognitive responses toward attitude objects remained stable from the first to the second test administrations. In the experimental group, significant change occurred not only in the subjects' affects toward the attitude objects but also in their *beliefs* about the relationships between each of those objects and various "values" deemed important by the subjects. Additional control data ruled out the possibility that these changes could have been due to any general tendency toward response instability rather than to the effects of the affect manipulation.

By using a second control procedure in which subjects "role-played" the occurrence of affect change, and by interviewing conducted both before and after removal of the experimental subjects' posthypnotic amnesias, it was found that the affect and belief changes achieved by the experimental subjects were experienced by them as legitimate and veridical: the subjects really felt and *believed* differently about the attitude objects on which they had received the posthypnotic suggestions of affect change. Aspects of this study have been reported in other publications (Rosenberg and Gardner, 1956; Rosenberg, 1960a) and it will not be further described or discussed here except to note that its replication and extension were the main purposes of the second study.

In this second study, the hypnotic manipulation of attitudinal affect was kept in force for a full week rather than for a period of one or two hours as was the case in the earlier study. Eight new experimental subjects were used and they were tested for both their affective and cognitive responses to three different attitude objects on six different occasions. The first of these occasions came three days before the delivery of a posthypnotic suggestion of affect change with regard to one of the three attitude objects. In all cases, the subject's original affect toward this object (the abandonment of the United States policy of giving economic aid to foreign nations) was negative and was hypnotically manipulated in the positive direction in a way that involved no reference to any of the subjects' beliefs

about the attitude object's relationships with any of his values. Specifically, each subject was told in hypnosis:

After you awake, and continuing until our next meeting, you will feel very strongly opposed to the United States policy of giving economic aid to foreign nations. The mere idea of the United States giving economic aid to foreign nations will make you feel very displeased and disgusted. Until your next meeting with me you will continue to feel very strong and thorough opposition to the United States policy of economic aid to foreign nations. You will have no memory whatsoever of this suggestion having been made . . . until the amnesia is removed by my giving you the signal at our next session.

Following the delivery of the posthypnotic suggestion, the subject was awakened from hypnosis and the measures of affect and cognition were readministered. Two days later and two days after that, these tests were again administered. Exactly one week after the hypnotic session, the subject's amnesia for that session was removed and the experiment fully explained to him. Up to this point in the sequence, all subjects had been led to believe that the hypnotic session and the testing sessions (the former conducted by the author and the latter by an associate) had no connection with each other, and that they represented different and unrelated experiments.

Three days after amnesia removal, and seven days after that, the measures of affect and cognition were again administered to all subjects. Before presenting the data that bear on the prediction that the production of strong affect change generates corresponding change in associated cognitions, it will be necessary to describe the separate measures of affect and cognition by which these data were obtained. These measures were similar to those used in the author's earlier studies on attitude structure (1956) and dynamics (1960a).

The measure of affect consisted of three scales covering a 16-point range from "extremely in favor" to "extremely opposed." One of these scales dealt with the issue on which the subjects received the hypnotic affect manipulation. The other two scales dealt with issues that were not subjected to any manipulation and thus served as control areas against which changes on the manipulated issue could be compared.

The measure of the cognitive component involved thirty-two so-called "value cards." Sample value items are "all human beings having equal rights," "people being well educated," "making one's own decisions," "attaining economic security." In taking this test, the subject first judges each of the thirty-two values in terms of its importance to him, using a scale with a range of 21 points. The scale runs from -10 (which stands for "gives me maximum dissatisfaction") to $+10$ (which stands for "gives me maximum satisfaction"). He then judges each of these same values in terms of whether, and to what extent, he thinks it will be attained or blocked as a consequence of the attitude object (for example, the policy change of "abandoning foreign aid"). For this task he uses an 11-point scale running from -5 (which stands for "extreme blocking") through 0 (which stands for "neither blocked nor attained") to $+5$ (which stands for "extreme attainment"). Thus, at the end of the testing procedure there are available for each value term the subject's judgment of its importance as a positive or negative state, and his judgment of how that value's realization will be affected by the attitude object. These two judgments

are algebraically multiplied for each value term, respectively. In turn the thirty-two products are algebraically summed. The resulting quantity is taken as an index of the over-all import of the cognitive structure associated with the attitude object. In effect this index expresses, in a single number, the extent to which the subject sees the attitude object as serving the attainment or blocking of his values. This index was separately obtained for each of the three attitude objects (the one subjected to affect manipulation and the two not subjected to such manipulation) from the data collected during each of the six separate testing sessions.

To test the prediction that the production of a large and irreversible affect change will generate comparable and consistency-restoring changes in beliefs about the attitude object, affect-change scores and cognition-change scores were computed for the three separate attitude objects. These scores referred to the differences between the index obtained from the subject's premanipulation test performances and each of the five postmanipulation test performances, respectively. By application of the Randomization Test for Matched Pairs (see Siegel, 1956) it was possible to determine whether the subjects' affect-change and cognition-change scores for the manipulated attitude object were significantly greater than the means of their change scores for the two nonmanipulated attitude objects.

As shown in the accompanying Table 1, until the amnesia removal, the subjects showed significant change not only in their affective responses toward "abandoning the United States policy of economic aid to foreign nations" but also in their beliefs about how such abandonment will affect the reali-

TABLE 1. PROBABILITIES OF THE DIFFERENCES BETWEEN THE CHANGE SCORES FOR THE MANIPULATED AND NONMANIPULATED ATTITUDES [a]

Testing Sessions from Which Change Scores Are Computed [b]	Affect Change	Cognitive Change
Session 1–Session 2	.008	.024
Session 1–Session 3	.008	.024
Session 1–Session 4	.008	.008
Session 1–Session 5	N.S.[c]	.056
Session 1–Session 6	N.S.	.064

[a] All probabilities are two-tailed and are obtained through application of the Randomization Test for Matched Pairs. All significant differences are in the direction: manipulated attitude > mean of nonmanipulated attitudes.

[b] The first testing session occurred three days before hypnotic manipulation of affect toward "foreign aid"; the second testing session came immediately after the manipulation; and the third and fourth sessions came three and five days, respectively, after the manipulation. The fifth and sixth sessions came ten days and seventeen days after the manipulation (that is, three days and ten days after "amnesia removal"). The same tests were used in each of the six sessions—the affective scales dealing with the foreign aid issue and with the two unmanipulated issues, and the cognitive structure measures for each of those issues.

[c] N.S. = not significant.

zation of their values. When the test records are examined it is found that these statistically significant differences are based upon large-scale shifts in both affect and cognitions. Thus a typical subject changes his affective evaluation from extreme opposition to abandonment of foreign aid to extreme approval. At the same time he changes many of his related beliefs. For example, whereas before the affect manipulation he believes that abandoning foreign aid would defeat such positive goals (for him) as "the avoidance of economic depression" and would serve such negative goals as "the open expression of disagreement between people" he now sees the abandonment of foreign aid as *fostering* the former goal and *defeating* the latter.

Another kind of cognitive change that is widely employed is illustrated by the following: whereas before the affect manipulation the subject sees no relationship between abandoning foreign aid and the positive goal of "people making their own decisions" he now sees that goal as *fostered* by abandon-ment of foreign aid. Also certain others of the subject's original beliefs (for example, "abandoning foreign aid will decrease American prestige in foreign countries") which were consistent with his original affect and are inconsistent with the altered affect are simply eliminated from the cognitive component of the new attitude. (For example, after the hypnotic manipulation, the subject maintains that there is no instrumental connection between foreign aid and the maintenance of America's international prestige.)

In general, the subjects show rather pervasive patterns of change in their cognitions about the attitude object. However, it should not be concluded that *all* the beliefs expressed by them are consistent with the altered attitudinal affect. Usually a few of their original beliefs persist within the new structure and are inconsistent with its over-all import, although typically the intensity with which these beliefs are held is reduced after the affect manipulation. But in the light of the theoretical propositions advanced above, it is not assumed that total and perfect consistency need obtain in a stable attitude structure; all that is assumed is that in such a stable structure affective-cognitive inconsistency, if present at all, is at a level below the individual's tolerance limit. At any rate, as we have noted, the examination of the postmanipulation attitude structures of the subjects reveals an impressive degree of cognitive reorganization in the direction consistent with the altered affect.

As in the first study involving affect manipulation, interview procedures in the second revealed that the subjects' changes in affect and cognition were *experienced* by them rather than merely "role-played." Indeed, the findings reported in the last two rows of Table 1 provide a special kind of evidence to this effect in connection with the subjects' cognitive changes. These findings refer to data obtained after the posthypnotic amnesia was removed and the nature of the experiment was fully explained. While the removal of amnesia for the affect manipulation is followed by a return to the initial affective position, enough of the cognitive changes persist to make for a significant difference between the cognition-change scores on the manipulated issue and the mean of the cognition-change scores on the two nonmanipulated issues.

Since after amnesia removal the subjects' affective responses reverted to their original scale positions, it might be contended that the significant persistence of some of the cognitive changes calls into question our conception of attitude as an internally consistent affective-cognitive structure. Examination of the subjects' test performances reveals, however, that while a number of altered beliefs do persist, a still larger number are changed back to their original form. Thus, after amnesia removal, in seven out of the eight cases the overall index of cognitive structure has a negative sign and is thus consistent with the restored negative affect.

Many other aspects of this study, including data drawn from a group of unhypnotized control subjects, have not been covered in this account. But the data that have been reported or reviewed here seem to provide strong confirmation for the general hypothesis that the production of affective-cognitive inconsistency within a previously stable attitude makes for attitude change. The confirmation of this hypothesis argues for the validity of the more general set of theoretical propositions from which it was derived. It cannot of course be demonstrated that *all* attitude change occurs on the basis delineated by the theoretical approach that has been presented here: such universal assertions can never be finally validated. However, the author, together with many other workers in this area, has become increasingly convinced that the process of inconsistency arousal and reduction (whether conceived in the terms of the present theory or in terms of one of the other consistency formulations) is crucially involved in the mediation and consolidation of all those types of attitude change that have so far been examined.

SOME FURTHER ISSUES AND SPECULATIONS

It is in the nature of strongly stated attempts at theorizing that they often raise as many questions as they answer. Examination of such questions often helps not only to test the general applicability of the theoretical approach but also to further clarify its meaning. Thus we shall consider a few such incidental questions.

One such question is whether the type of attitude change sequence demonstrated in the affect-manipulation experiments is not after all an uncommon, and thus, an unimportant case. In this connection, it should be recalled that hypnotic suggestion was employed as an experimental analogue of a broad class of nonhypnotic experiences that seem to produce affect modification in everyday settings. It seems likely that whenever the expression of an old affective response is followed by negative reinforcement, or whenever the imitative or trial-and-error "rehearsal" of a new affective response is followed by positive reinforcement, affect change similar to that observed in the present experiment is fostered.

Such reinforcement need not come only from external agencies such as individuals and groups who respond to the person's expression of established attitudinal affects or to his tentative avowal of new ones. As the individual's inner needs and conflicts are altered through the vicissitudes of experience or of growth, the expression of old affects may come to heighten frustration and tension while the avowal of new ones may operate to reduce needs and resolve conflicts. By this point, much of the present analysis may be tied to the kind of psychodynamic or "functional" approach to attitudes that is exemplified in the contributions of Katz, Sarnoff, and McClintock (1956) and Smith, Bruner, and White (1956).

Whether common or uncommon, the kind of attitude change demonstrated in the present experiments is important for yet another reason. Some writer who have been interested in the relation between attitudinal affect and cognition have tended to represent the former as mainly a function of, or as generated by, the latter. In the author's opinion, this stress upon one type of attitude dynamic process tends to obscure the pertinence of the view that attitudes are structures or "fields" of related psychological responses and that their reorganization is mediated by their prior internal disruption, *however* that disruption is achieved. The availability of evidence that attitude change can be initiated not only through modification of cognition but also through modification of affect serves then as a corrective to the possibility that it will be viewed in a way that is too simple and one-sided.

Another matter that deserves comment is the implication in this article that most or all instances of attitude change might be reduced to either of two underlying sequences. It must be acknowledged that in many instances attitude change does not begin with the manipulation of either the cognitive or the affective component but, rather, that both may undergo manipulation at the same time. It should be clear, however, that from the present point of view the production of change in either major component will increase the likelihood of change in the other component. Furthermore, close analyis of attitude-change techniques and communications will probably indicate that they usually are specifically directed more toward one than toward the other of the two major components.

A further issue requiring some comment is that the present conceptualization of attitude as a stable and consistent structure of affective and cognitive components may seem to be contradicted by the fact that subjects tested for their affects and beliefs toward an "attitude object" sometimes reveal an apparently large degree of inconsistency. On this basis one might question the generality of formulations such as the present one. However, the kinds of data on which this objection would be based are usually collected without regard for the obvious fact that just because a subject chooses a nonneutral point on an attitudinal affect scale it cannot be assumed that he actually *holds* that attitude. Frequently his scale choice or, for that matter, his response to an evaluation-eliciting interview question does not reflect a real attitudinal affect but, rather, is due to loose and unreliable reference to an associated object toward which he may have some affect. Even more often such invalid self-reports may be forced by the wording of the questions or by the subject's anticipations of the experimenter's or interviewer's own affective preferences. In the light of these considerations it might be argued that the presence of gross and extreme inconsistency between a subject's affective and cognitive responses to a given "attitude object" (except when he has just been exposed to potent inducements to change) is presumptive evidence that he does not really *have* an attitude toward that object. In such a case it would be expected that retesting at a later date would yield evidence of significant instabilty on measures of both affect and cognition. Recent research by the author has suggested that this may indeed be the case and has indicated that in either experimental or field research more valid attitude measurement can be achieved when both the affective and cognitive components are assessed.

In conclusion, we shall briefly touch upon one other quite different, and quite important, concern. The study of the attitude-change process inevitably brings to mind certain ethical issues; issues that are rendered all the more salient by the development in the modern era of the professional role of the propagandist and of techniques and media through which large-scale persuasion is attempted.

The theoretical approach that has been presented in this paper may be useful in clarifying some of these ethical issues. For example, to the author it seems axiomatic that an ethical use of persuasion techniques requires a respect for the cognitive processes and achievements of those to whom persuasive communications are directed. Attempts by propagandists to change attitudinal affects by direct manipulation are often subordinated to cognitive appeals. But just as often this seems not to be the case. Procedures intended to produce affect alteration by methods that evade any significant recourse to the evidence and data bearing upon attitudinal beliefs may violate, or at least bypass, that which is most admirable in man—his potential for informed thought and independent analysis. The proper sphere of such methods is only in the *experimental study* of attitude dynamics, and only when, as in the case of the present studies involving hypnosis, considerable effort is applied after the data have been collected to clarifying for the subjects the nature of the phenomena that they have experienced.

Perhaps the ultimate utility of such experiments, apart from their contributions to theory development, is that they will better equip us to defend ourselves against some of the demeaning techniques by which persuasion is achieved through suppression of the claims of reason.

REFERENCES

ABELSON, R. P., & ROSENBERG, M. J.   Symbolic psycho-logic: a model of attitudinal cognition. *Behav. Science*, 1958, **3**, 1–13.

CAMPBELL, D. T.   *The generality of a social attitude*. Unpublished doctoral dissertation, Univer. of California, Berkeley, 1947.

CARLSON, E. R.   Attitude change and attitude structure. *J. abnorm. soc. Psychol.*, 1956, **52**, 256–261.

CARTWRIGHT, D.   Some principles of mass persuasion. *Hum. Relat.*, 1949, **2**, 253–268.

FESTINGER, L.   *A theory of cognitive dissonance*. New York: Harper & Row, 1957.

FISHBEIN, M., & HUNTER, R.   Summation vs. balance in attitude organization and change. *J. abnorm. soc. Psychol.*, 1964 (in press).

HEIDER, F.   *The psychology of interpersonal relations*. New York: John Wiley & Sons, 1958.

KATZ, D., SARNOFF, I., & McCLINTOCK, C.   Ego defense and attitude change. *Hum. Relat.*, 1956, **9**, 27–46.

NEWCOMB, T. M.   An approach to the study of communicative acts. *Psychol. Rev.*, 1953, **60**, 393–404.

NOWLIS, V.   *Some studies of the influence of films on mood and attitude*. O.N.R. technical report, mimeo., 1960.

OSGOOD, C. E., & TANNENBAUM, P. H.   The principle of congruity in the prediction of attitude change. *Psychol. Rev.*, 1955, **62**, 42–55.

PEAK, H.   *The effects of aroused motivation on attitudes*. O.N.R. technical report, mimeo, 1959.

ROSENBERG, M. J.   Cognitive structure and attitudinal affect. *J. abnorm. soc. Psychol.*, 1956, **53**, 367–372.

ROSENBERG, M. J.   Cognitive reorganization in response to the hypnotic reversal of attitudinal affect. *J. Pers.*, 1960a, **28**, 39–63.

ROSENBERG, M. J.   An analysis of affective-cognitive consistency. In Rosenberg, M. J., Hovland, C. I., *et al. Attitude organization and change*. New Haven: Yale University Press, 1960b.

ROSENBERG, M. J., & GARDNER, C. W.   Some dynamic aspects of posthypnotic compliance. *J. abnorm. soc. Psychol.*, 1958, **57**, 351–366.

SCOTT, W. A.   Cognitive consistency, response reinforcement, and attitude change. *Sociometry*, 1959, **22**, 219–229.

SIEGEL, S.   *Non-parametric statistics for the behavioral sciences*. New York: McGraw-Hill, 1956.

SMITH, M. B.   Personal values as determinants of a political attitude. *J. Psychol.*, 1949, **28**, 477–486.

SMITH, M. B., BRUNER, J. S., & WHITE, R. W.   *Opinions and personality*, New York: John Wiley & Sons, 1956.

WOODRUFF, A. D., & DiVESTA, F. J.   The relationship between values, concepts, and attitudes. *Educ. psychol. Measmt.*, 1948, 8, 645–660.

14.   FAUBUS AND SEGREGATION: AN ANALYSIS OF ARKANSAS VOTING *

Thomas F. Pettigrew and Ernest Q. Campbell

In the summer of 1954 a little-known young man from the mountains named Orval E. Faubus entered a four-man Democratic primary for Governor of Arkansas. His prospects were not bright. The incumbent, Francis Cherry, was a

* Reprinted from the *Public Opinion Quarterly*, 1960, 24: 436–447, with permission of the senior author and Princeton University Press.

heavy favorite to win re-election; after all, every Arkansas Governor in a generation had been returned for a second two-year term by the electorate.

Faubus ran a distant second, receiving a third of the votes; but Cherry missed accumulating the necessary majority by 7,500 votes (2.3 percent). In the August run-off, Faubus won with a scant 50.9 percent of the votes cast. In 1956, Faubus won the gubernatorial nomination with a convincing 58.1 percent of the votes cast in a five-man field. But it was his sweeping 68.9 percent first primary victory in July of 1958 that received wide attention from a world alerted to his career by his efforts on behalf of Little Rock segregation.

The present paper analyzes this "march of Faubus" in geographic and demographic terms. Particular attention is paid to the relationship between Faubus's four primary victories [1] and prosegregation sentiment. For this purpose three special segregation issues voted on by Arkansans in November of 1956 are particularly useful. Votes in these referenda for assigning public school pupils on factors other than race, for "interposition," and for "nullification" of the Supreme Court's integration rulings were widely interpreted as supporting racial segregation; thus they provide us with a convenient county-by-county index of anti-integration attitudes of the voters with which to compare the elections of Faubus.[2]

[1] In Arkansas, as in other one-party states, a primary victory is tantamount to election.

[2] Indication that the three referenda were seen as a single program is provided by the high correlations across counties between the three votes; each of these correlations is .90 or above. Therefore, throughout this paper we have combined the three votes into a single index of segregation sentiment for purposes of analysis.

THE RELATIONSHIPS BETWEEN THE FAUBUS AND SEGREGATION VOTES

Table 1 presents the ten product-moment correlations among the Faubus votes in four gubernatorial primaries and the 1956 segregation referenda vote.[3] Using the seventy-five Arkansas counties as the units of analysis, we note that the Faubus voting patterns in the 1954 and 1956 primaries are quite similar; these three votes correlate positively with each other and negatively with the segregation vote. In other words, the same Arkansas counties that tended to support Faubus throughout his initial three primary campaigns also oppose segregation relatively more than the rest of the state.

But the smashing primary victory of 1958 offers a radically different picture. Only small, insignificant correla-

[3] From the perspective of studying *white* Arkansas voting, some systematic error is introduced by our inability to remove the Negro vote from these analyses. But this error cannot be large, for a number of reasons. Official 1957 registration data indicate that Negroes, who comprise over one-fifth of the state's population, constitute only one-ninth of the registered voters. And over half these Negro registrants are concentrated in just eight counties. (See Margaret Price, *The Negro and the Ballot*, Atlanta, Ga., Southern Regional Council, pp. 78–79.) Furthermore, unofficial calculations indicate that, save for Little Rock, a smaller percentage of Negro registrants actually vote than white registrants. Thus, later in this paper it will be shown that the segregation vote of 1956 is highly and positively related to Negro ratio —an almost impossible result had there been a large and distributed Negro vote. Ogburn and Grigg, in their analysis of Virginian voting on segregation, noted the same phenomenon; they found the white vote by counties correlated +.92 with the total vote. (See W. F. Ogburn and C. M. Grigg, "Factors Related to the Virginia Vote on Segregation," *Social Forces*, Vol. 34, 1954, pp. 301–308.)

TABLE 1. INTERCORRELATIONS [a] OF THE PRO-FAUBUS AND PROSEGREGATION VOTES

Election	Faubus, Aug. 1954	Faubus, 1956	Faubus, 1958 [b]	Segregation 1956
Faubus, July 1954	+.84	+.54	−.09(−.32)	−.50
Faubus, Aug. 1954		+.56	.00(−.17)	−.68
Faubus, 1956			+.12(+.04)	−.49
Faubus, 1958				+.35

[a] These are product-moment correlations using the seventy-five Arkansas counties as the units of analysis. Correlations above .30 are significantly higher than zero correlation at the .01 level of confidence.

[b] The correlations in parentheses apply when the adjoining mountain counties, Newton and Madison, are removed from the analysis. These two counties, of which the latter is the home county of Faubus, were the only ones to run up large majorities for Faubus in all four of his elections.

tions exist between this fourth Faubus vote and the previous Faubus votes. Indeed, if two counties—one the home county of Faubus—are removed from the analysis, a significant negative association is found between the voting patterns of the first and fourth Faubus primaries. And, unlike his previous nominations, Faubus's 1958 primary vote relates positively and significantly with the 1956 segregation vote. Clearly, a new grouping of Arkansas counties

more favorable toward segregation emerged in 1958 as the base of Faubus's political power.

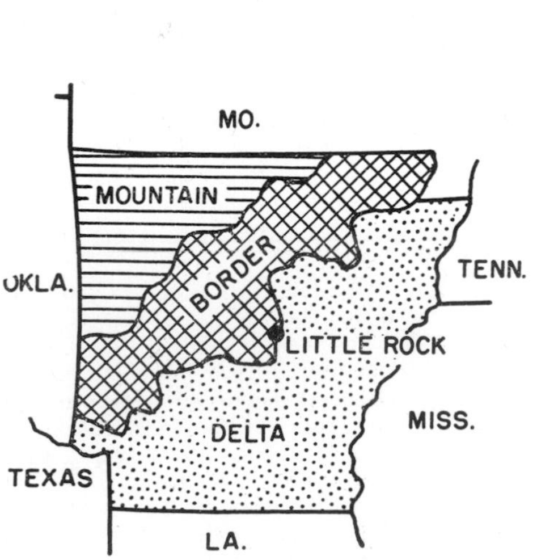

THE GEOGRAPHY OF THE SHIFTING VOTING PATTERNS

Three rough divisions of Arkansas can be made on the basis of both geography and current voting patterns: the mountains, the border area, and the delta, as shown in Figure 1. Arkansas political interests have frequently cut across these regions in the past,[4] but this division is helpful in highlighting the geographic shift in Faubus's political strength.

Figure 2 provides bar graphs indicating the total and regional percentages in the primaries and referenda. We observe first that Faubus's native mountain area was the backbone of his support in the early campaigns; in fact, neither the border nor the delta gave him a majority in the two 1954 pri-

Figure 1. Three geographic areas of Arkansas

[4] See V. O. Key, *Southern Politics*, New York, Knopf, 1949, Chap. 9.

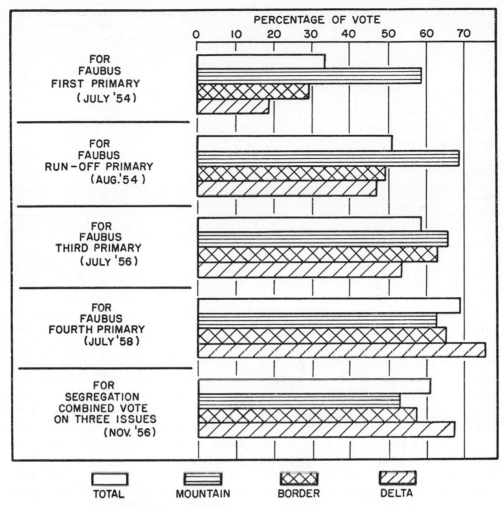

Figure 2. Comparison of four Faubus primaries for governor of Arkansas and combined vote for segregation by region of state

maries. In the 1956 primary all three geographic areas gave Faubus a majority, though the mountain percentage remained the largest. But the areas reversed this pattern in 1958. While both the border and delta areas strikingly increased their support, the mountains actually decreased their support as compared to 1956 and became the least pro-Faubus of all—a point overlooked at the time of Faubus's overwhelming triumph.[5] This new Faubus pattern resembles the 1956 segregation vote, as shown at the bottom of Figure 2.

[5] This mountain shift cannot be accounted for in terms of Faubus's opponents. Though he faced another mountain candidate in the July primary of 1956, neither of his 1958 opponents was from the mountains; hence, they were not in a position to cut into his mountain vote as "local boys."

TABLE 2. DEMOGRAPHIC CHARACTERISTICS OF THREE AREAS [a] OF ARKANSAS

| | Geographic Areas | | | |
Characteristic	Mountain	Border	Delta	Total State
Percentage of urban population, 1950	31.5	42.3	27.8	33.0
Percentage of rural-farm population, 1950	42.9	34.1	46.4	42.0
Percentage employed engaged in manufacturing, 1950	12.2	14.1	14.2	13.8
Percentage of white women in the labor force, 1950	20.5	21.6	17.9	19.8
Percentage of nonwhites, 1950	2.1	12.6	35.3	22.4
Median nonwhite family income, 1949	$978	$916	$683	$726
Median white family income, 1949	$1,330	$1,595	$1,709	$1,571

[a] As defined in the text.

SOURCE: *United States Census of Population, 1950,* Bureau of the Census, Vol. II, Part 4, Chap. B.

The principal demographic characteristics of these geographic areas are given in Table 2. The sixteen-county Ozark mountain area, bordering on southern Missouri and eastern Oklahoma, is predominantly rural and has only about one-sixth of the state's population. It has the smallest percentage of people employed in manufacturing and has the smallest nonwhite ratio, 1 per 48.[6] Its Negroes are concentrated in the two cities of the region, Fort Smith and Fayetteville; they earned in 1949 the highest median family income for nonwhites of the three areas. Mountain whites, by contrast, earned the smallest white median family income in 1949. Thus, the part of Arkansas that is least in favor of racial segregation consists of the relatively nonindustrial Ozarks, populated largely by poor, rural whites.

Separating the Ozarks from the delta in a narrow, diagonal strip running from southeast Missouri to the Ouachita mountain region of Oklahoma, the twenty-four-county border area comprises about one-third of the state's

population. Its voting percentages tend to be midway between the other areas (Figure 2), and it stands midway in terms of nonwhite percentage (1 per 8) and median family incomes of both nonwhites and whites. Little Rock, North Little Rock, and Hot Springs, three of the state's five largest cities in 1950, make this border region the most urban of the three and the least traditional as measured by the percentage of the white women in the labor force.[7]

The thirty-five-county delta region of Arkansas extends from Memphis-dominated southwest Tennessee to northern Louisiana and northeast Texas; it is indistinguishable from the better-known flat, rural, and densely Negro deltaland of Mississippi. Here lies the bulwark of segregation sentiment in the state and the new center of Faubus's strength. The Arkansas delta contains approximately half the state's population and furnished from 45 to 49 percent of the votes in the five contests

[6] Negroes constituted 99.7 percent of the nonwhites of Arkansas in 1950.

[7] Percentage of white women in the labor force, in addition to being an economic variable, is assumed to be an index of traditionalism because of the South's traditional sanctions against white women formally working.

under discussion. The 1860 census reveals that 7 out of every 9 slaves (78.5 percent) in Arkansas were in this delta area. Nonwhites are today still concentrated there,[8] where they receive the lowest median family income of any part of the state. Delta whites, however, have the highest median family income. Thus, the delta has the widest disparity between white and Negro income of the Arkansas regions,[9] a situation of economic discrimination consistent with a high segregation vote. Though the most rural area, the delta had a seventh of its 1950 employed labor force in manufacturing—a good figure by the modest standards of agricultural Arkansas. Relatively few white women in the delta, however, enter the labor force, probably a result of the area's traditionalism, its relatively higher income for whites, and the availability of a large and cheap Negro labor supply.

THE DEMOGRAPHY OF THE SHIFTING VOTING PATTERNS

The varying characteristics of the mountain, border, and delta areas of Arkansas suggest that demographic fac-

tors are importantly related to the Faubus and segregation votes. Analyzing the state as a whole, the correlations of Table 3 pinpoint these demographic relationships more precisely.[10]

We have already seen that a sharp shift in the voting patterns for Faubus occurred between his first and fourth primary races (Table 1 and Figure 2); now we note in Table 3 both similarities and differences in the demography of these patterns. In both contests, significantly negative relationships exist between the amount of support for Faubus, on the one hand, and the 1950 urban population percentage and population increase from 1940 to 1950, on the other hand. But the two primaries relate differently to four other variables. In 1958, the Faubus vote by counties was at significant levels positively associated with the 1950 percentage of rural-farm residents and negatively associated with the 1950 percentage of white women in the labor force and the Negro educational level; in July 1954, these factors did not significantly relate to the Faubus vote. Moreover, the best single predictor of the first Faubus vote, nonwhite percentage, reverses sign and becomes a small and positive correlate of the fourth Faubus vote. In brief, pro-Faubus counties in both the July 1954 and 1958 primaries tended to be rural and poor;[11] yet 1958 pro-Faubus counties were likely to be more agricultural, more traditional, and more populated by poorly educated Negroes.

We noted earlier that the fourth

---

[8] The twenty-seven counties with the largest nonwhite percentages in 1950 are all in the delta. Though these counties have been steadily losing Negroes by out-migration, the consistency of this relative pattern over time is attested to by the +.97 product-moment relationship between the 1900 and 1950 nonwhite percentages of counties.

[9] Blalock has found this condition to be generally true of Southern counties with high nonwhite percentages. He noted that housing and educational, as well as income, discrimination correlated positively and highly with the nonwhite percentages of counties. (See H. M. Blalock, Jr., "Per Cent Nonwhite and Discrimination in the South," *American Sociological Review*, Vol. 22, 1957, pp. 677–682.)

[10] Some error is introduced, particularly for the 1956 and 1958 votes, by the population changes that have occurred since 1950.

[11] The poverty of these counties is indicated by their loss of population from 1940 to 1950, a factor that is related to such economic indices as family income and percentage of dwellings with refrigerators.

TABLE 3. CORRELATIONS OF VOTING AND DEMOGRAPHIC FACTORS [a]

Variable	Faubus, July 1954	Faubus, 1958	Segregation, 1956
Percentage of urban population, 1950	−.31	−.35	+.18
Percentage of rural-farm population, 1950	+.17	+.40	−.17
Percentage of population increase, 1940–1950	−.26	−.31	+.15
Percentage of white women in the labor force, 1950	−.06	−.38	+.05
Median years of education for nonwhites over 24, 1950	+.14[b]	−.53[b]	−.57[b]
Percentage of nonwhites, 1950	[−.40][c]	[+.19][c]	[+.64][c]

[a] Save for the nonwhite education and nonwhite percentage results, these are product-moment correlations using the seventy-five Arkansas counties as the units of analysis. These twelve product-moment correlations are significantly greater than zero at the .05 level of confidence when they are larger than .23, at the .01 level when they are larger than .30. All demographic data are taken from the *United States Census of Population, 1950*, Vol. II, Part 4, Chap. B.

[b] These nonwhite education product-moment correlations apply only for the forty-three counties in Arkansas that had enough Negroes over twenty-four years old in 1950 for the census to establish a reliable educational median. With this size of sample, correlations above .39 are significantly greater than zero at the .01 level of confidence.

[c] Since in thirty-two Arkansas counties Negroes constituted less than 5 percent of the population, the distribution is too skewed to justify the use of product-moment correlations. The coefficients given are Kendall rank correlations. (See S. Siegel, *Nonparametric Statistics*, New York, McGraw-Hill, 1956, pp. 213–223.)

primary victory of Faubus correlated positively with the 1956 segregation vote (Table 1) and resembled its geographic pattern (Figure 2). But Table 3 reveals that there are important demographic differences between the two votes. Though they both relate negatively to Negro education (for a restricted sample), only the segregation vote is highly associated with the 1950 nonwhite percentage.[12] And, as we have noted, the 1958 Faubus vote relates more closely to the other four factors. To obtain a reasonably high relationship with this fourth primary vote, a combination of three variables is required: the segregation vote (Table 1), the rural-farm percentage, and the white women

in the labor force percentage. The resulting multiple correlation is .62, with the three predictors independently accounting for approximately equal amounts of the 1958 county variance. Thus the 1958 primary triumph of Faubus was not just an expression of racial segregation sentiment; it also had an agricultural and traditional cast that was independent of segregation voting.

These data are similar to the voting for segregation in two other Southern states. Heer has offered evidence for interpreting the 1948 South Carolina vote for the "Dixiecrat" candidate for President, J. Strom Thurmond, as a direct measure of "white supremacy sentiment."[13] Like the present segregation data, Thurmond's support in South

[12] Key noted a similarly high relationship between nonwhite percentage and the Arkansas county vote pattern in 1948 for the prosegregation "Dixiecrat" ticket (Key, *op. cit.*, p. 343).

[13] D. M. Heer, "The Sentiment of White Supremacy: An Ecological Study," *American Journal of Sociology*, Vol. 64, 1959, pp. 592–598.

Carolina was concentrated in the counties with large Negro ratios (+.67), particularly those with poorly educated Negroes (−.59).[14] And Thurmond's strength tended to be greatest in the type of rural, agricultural county that in 1958 gave Faubus his strongest backing; the "Dixiecrat" vote in South Carolina related positively to the percentage of rural-farm whites (+.37) and negatively with the percentage of nonfarm whites in manufacturing (−.53).[15]

The Ogburn and Grigg study of the 1956 Virginia referendum on public aid to private education provides another segregation vote for comparison.[16] This Virginia vote was most highly associated, too, with the percentage of Negroes (+.67) and the median years of Negro education (−.77).[17] It also had a poor, rural cast; it related negatively to Negro (−.45) and white (−.45) income and to population increase from 1940 to 1950 (−.47) and positively to the percentage of rural-farm population (+.29). Again, this poor, agricultural trend resembles the fourth Faubus primary but not the Arkansas segregation results. Indeed, from a cursory inspection of Table 3 one might conclude that segregation voting in Arkansas was slightly stronger in the more prosperous urban counties. Actually, this is an illusion. In Arkansas, unlike South Carolina and Virginia, many counties with a large Negro population are prosperous and urban by the meager standards of the state. Thus, when the percentage of Negroes is controlled, the urban, rural-farm, population change, and white women in the labor force correlations with the segregation vote reverse their signs but remain statistically insignificant.[18]

The status of Negroes, then, proves to be the most reliable index of voting on racial issues; the ratio of Negroes to whites and the level of Negro education prove important in all three Southern states. Economic and agricultural variables appear somewhat less important, though only in Arkansas do they fail to relate significantly with segregation sentiment.

DISCUSSION AND CONCLUSIONS

These crude geographic and demographic analyses do not, of course, allow us to determine the motivations and ideologies of individual voters.[19] But the findings do suggest three interesting trends.

1. THE MARCH OF FAUBUS   The four gubernatorial primaries of Faubus have

---

[14] The Negro education-Thurmond vote relationship was calculated from the 1950 census data by the present authors.

[15] It is important to note, too, that actual school desegregation, as opposed to voting, in the border states of Missouri and Kentucky came earliest to the prosperous rural and urban counties. T. F. Pettigrew, "Demographic Correlates of Border-state Desegregation," *American Sociological Review*, Vol. 22, 1957, pp. 683–689.

[16] Ogburn and Grigg, *op. cit.* Their correlations are based on restricted samples of Virginia counties, since not all the relevant data were available in the 100 Virginia counties.

[17] Even after the Negro ratio factor is partialed out, the level of Negro education significantly relates to segregation voting for restricted samples in Virginia (−.60) and Arkansas (−.45), though not in South Carolina (−.21).

[18] These Kendall partial rank correlations (S. Siegel, *Nonparametric Statistics*, New York, McGraw-Hill, 1956, pp. 223–229) varied in magnitude from .10 to .01.

[19] Another difficulty of such analyses is that they exaggerate the importance of the thinly populated counties by treating each county as an equal unit.

involved a drastic realignment in Arkansas politics. The "poor mountain boy" slipped into the Governor's mansion in 1954 largely on the basis of the overwhelming support he received from the Ozark counties. Though he gained in border and delta favor in 1956, he was still a mountain candidate. But after his role in the 1957 Little Rock school integration crisis, Faubus in 1958 had obviously become the delta favorite, and his native mountain area began to withdraw its support of him. Faubus maintained his "common man appeal," however; rural counties that lost residents from 1940 to 1950 tended to support him heavily in his fourth as well as his first primary.

These events are actually just the most recent reenactment of a long-time Southern political pattern. From Bacon's Rebellion to the Farmer's Alliance, the hill country of the South has traditionally opposed plantation interests. Though this breach in the "solid South" has frequently been obscured by the impotence of the upcountry in many states, a fundamental conflict of interests remains. It is not surprising, then, that the hills have provided the South with a large share of its deviantly liberal leaders—from Nathaniel Bacon and Thomas Jefferson of the past to Hugo Black and Ralph McGill of the present.[20] But the hills have also produced their share of opportunists, men who began as if in opposition to the conservative planters and ended up the planters' servants. South Carolina, for instance, has had a succession of such upcountrymen: John Calhoun of the early nineteenth century, "Pitchfork Ben" Tillman at the turn of the century, and J. Strom Thurmond of today.[21]

The march of Faubus, with differences only in detail, fits this broad outline. Faubus was the liberal alternative in the 1954 and 1956 primaries and consequently received his backing largely from the hills and his principal opposition from the delta. In 1957, by defending the segregation interests of the delta, Faubus joined the long line of opportunistic hillmen. And, like his predecessors, his political strength promptly shifted to the planter country.

2. FAUBUS AND SEGREGATION   The immediate press interpretation of Faubus's sweeping 1958 primary triumph was simply that the whole state had approved his prosegregation stand in Little Rock. The present results qualify this appraisal in two ways. First of all, one part of the state, the Ozarks, actually *decreased* its support of Faubus in 1958 (Figure 2).

Second, the voting patterns for Faubus in 1958 and for segregation in 1956, though moderately correlated (Table 1) and geographically similar (Figure 2), were demographically different (Table 3). The counties that ran up the largest majorities for Faubus in his fourth primary tended to be poor, traditional, and agricultural. None of these characteristics was associated with the segregation vote. Instead, only two

---

[20] This is not to imply that the upcountry people are particularly tolerant of the Negro. Rather, the point is that they have not allowed concern over the Negro to shape their thinking like those in the Black Belt. Moreover, the poor uneducated hillsmen of the South have frequently noted that measures ostensibly aimed at the Negro also discriminate against them (e.g. the poll tax).

[21] Tillman and Thurmond even came from the same Piedmont county, Edgefield. (See Key, *op. cit.*, Chap. 7.)

Negro variables—nonwhite percentage and nonwhite education—predicted the segregation vote.

These differences suggest that the prosegregation areas responded differently to Faubus in 1958. More specifically, the less prosperous, more rural counties that favored segregation in 1956 responded most strongly for Faubus in 1958; other counties that favored segregation tended to increase their support of Faubus in 1958 but not as much. Two possible explanations can be offered for this finding. As mentioned previously, the "common man appeal" of Faubus demonstrated in earlier primaries probably made him more acceptable in the rustic regions. Furthermore, these poor farm counties had the least to lose from Faubus's actions in Little Rock. The damage done to the state's industrial expansion by Faubus was already apparent by the summer of 1958 and was most sharply felt by the more urban, nonagricultural counties.[22] It appears, then, that a consideration of economics as well as segregation sentiment is necessary to understand fully the voting pattern of Faubus's fourth primary.

3. SOUTHERN VOTING ON SEGREGATION   Counties with a large percentage of Negroes and a low level of Negro education tend to vote heaviest for segregation in South Carolina, Virginia, and Arkansas. The importance of the Negro ratio variable is widely recognized. Not only is a large concentration of Negroes frequently seen by Southern whites as threatening, but such a concentration usually corresponds with an entrenched tradition of prejudice [23] and discrimination [24]—a tradition that may linger on even after the Negro percentage has been considerably reduced by out-migration.[25] And it is this entrenched tradition of discrimination that is being measured by Negro education. As an alternative explanation, Ogburn and Grigg have mentioned that whites might logically vote more in favor of school segregation when Negroes in their locality are unusually poorly educated.[26] Though this cause and effect interpretation may hold true for some white parents, it seems more likely that prosegregation voting and a long-time denial of full educational opportunities to Negroes in a county are two manifestations of the same thing: historically rooted cultural norms of racial discrimination.

[22] According to the official figures of the Arkansas Industrial Development Commission, 9,471 new manufacturing jobs were created in Arkansas in 1956, 11,424 in 1957, but only 5,780 in 1958 (*Arkansas Gazette*, Sept. 27, 1959, p. 2). This is too big a drop-off to be attributed to the 1958 recession alone.

[23] T. F. Pettigrew, "Desegration and Its Chances for Success: Northern and Southern Views," *Social Forces*, Vol. 35, 1957, pp. 339–344; and "Regional Differences in Anti-Negro Prejudice," *Journal of Abnormal and Social Psychology*, Vol. 59, 1959, pp. 28–36.

[24] Blalock, *op. cit.*

[25] H. D. Price, *The Negro and Southern Politics*, New York, New York University Press, 1957, pp. 35–54.

[26] Ogburn and Grigg, *op. cit.*

4

Communication
and Persuasion

15. COMMUNICATOR CREDIBILITY AND COMMUNICATION DISCREPANCY AS DETERMINANTS OF OPINION CHANGE *

Elliot Aronson, Judith A. Turner, and J. Merrill Carlsmith

Recent experiments in the area of communication and persuasion have shown that a number of variables affect the success of an influence attempt. One such variable is the credibility of the communicator. Experimental results have shown unequivocally that there is a positive relationship between the credibility of the communicator and the extent of opinion change (Arnet, Davidson, & Lewis, 1931; Haiman, 1949; Hovland & Weiss, 1952; Kelman & Hovland, 1953; Kulp, 1934). Another variable of obvious importance is the extent of the discrepancy between the opinion advocated by the communicator and the precommunication opinion of the recipient. However, experiments dealing with

this variable have yielded contradictory results. Several investigators have found that the degree of induced opinion change varies as a positive function of the degree of discrepancy (Cohen, 1959; Goldberg, 1954; Hovland & Pritzker, 1957; Zimbardo, 1960). However, other investigators have found evidence for resistance to change when the discrepancy is extreme (Cohen, 1959; Fisher & Lubin, 1958; Hovland, Harvey, & Sherif, 1957).

Some attempts have been made to explain these inconsistent findings. Hovland et al. (1957), for example, have suggested that there is a linear relationship between discrepancy and opinion change only when the audience is not

* Reprinted from *Journal of Abnormal and Social Psychology*, 1963, 67: 31–36, with permission of the senior author and the American Psychological Association. This research was supported by a grant (NSF-G-16838) from the National Science Foundation.

145

highly involved with the topic of the communication. They assert that when involvement is high, the function is curvilinear—that with great discrepancies there is little opinion change.

A different explanation, based upon the theory of cognitive dissonance (Festinger, 1957), was proposed by Festinger and Aronson (1960). They suggested that the apparently inconsistent findings could be explained by an interaction between discrepancy and credibility. According to Festinger and Aronson, when an individual finds that an opinion advocated by a credible communicator is discrepant from his own opinion he experiences dissonance. His cognition that he holds a particular opinion is dissonant with his cognition that a credible communicator holds a somewhat different opinion. The greater the discrepancy between his own opinion and the opinion advocated by the communicator, the greater the dissonance. Generally, a person might reduce this dissonance in at least four ways: He could change his own opinion to bring it closer to that of the communicator; change the communicator's opinion to bring it closer to his own opinion; seek support for his opinion by finding other people who hold similar opinions; derogate the communicator—that is, make the opinion of the communicator nonapplicable to his own by discounting the ability of the communicator to have a valuable opinion on the topic. However, in most experimental influence situations, a communication is delivered either by a noninteracting speaker or in the form of a written message. Hence, it is impossible for the recipient to influence the communicator's opinion. In addition, the recipient is usually a member of a noninteracting audience. Hence, he is unable to seek immediate social support. Therefore, in this type of situation, the recipient may reduce dissonance by changing his own opinion or by derogating the communicator.

The magnitude of dissonance increases as a function of the discrepancy. Thus, if dissonance were reduced by opinion change alone, then the degree of opinion change would increase as a direct function of the extent of discrepancy. But dissonance can also be reduced by derogating the communicator; as with opinion change, the tendency to derogate the communicator should likewise increase as a direct function of the extent of the discrepancy. Moreover, it seems reasonable to assume that at the extremes, opinion changes and derogation of the communicator are clear alternatives. A person is not likely to change his opinion in the direction of a communicator whom he has sharply derogated; similarly, he is not likely to derogate a communicator who had induced a major change in his opinion.[1]

What conditions will maximize dissonance reduction through opinion change rather than derogation? Credibility seems to be crucial. If a communicator has perfect credibility, he cannot be derogated (by definition). Here, dissonance can be reduced only by opinion change. In this situation, dissonance theory would predict that degree of opinion change would vary as a direct function of the extent of discrepancy. This prediction received support from

[1] This is true *only* at the extremes. Theoretically if neither opinion change nor derogation is extreme, dissonance may be reduced by a combination of both processes.

an experiment by Zimbardo (1960). In this experiment, if the communicator was the best friend of the recipient, she was able to induce the greatest opinion change when the discrepancy was the greatest; this was true even when the advocated position was described previously by the recipient as unreasonable and indefensible.

At the other extreme, if a communicator has no credibility, he can be derogated completely (by definition). In this case, there would be no opinion change regardless of the degree of discrepancy, since a discrepant statement would not arouse dissonance.

Consider a communicator of mild credibility. Here, both opinion change and derogation can be used to reduce dissonance. If a communication is relatively close to the opinion of the recipient, the existing dissonance can be reduced easily by a slight shift in opinion. On the other hand, if the discrepancy is great, a person can reduce dissonance much more easily by derogating the communicator. That is, if the position advocated by a mildly credible communicator is extreme, it may appear quite unrealistic to the recipient. If this were the case, it is unlikely that he would change his attitude very much. Instead, he might reduce dissonance by deciding that the communicator is unrealistic—or stupid, naive, untruthful, etc.

This experiment was designed to investigate the conditions under which changing one's opinion and derogating the communicator are chosen as alternative methods of reducing the dissonance which is created when an individual is exposed to an opinion which is discrepant from his own. Suppose subjects are exposed to persuasive communications at various distances from their original positions, and for some subjects the communicator is presented as highly credible (virtually indisparageable), while for other subjects the communicator is presented as mildly credible (easily disparageable). For each level of communicator credibility, we may predict a different function relating discrepancy to opinion change. Thus, it should be possible to construct a family of curves reflecting opinion change as a function of communicator credibility and degree of discrepancy. In the ideal case—the case of a communicator who is perfectly indisparageable—opinion change should be a linear function of discrepancy. The larger the degree of opinion change advocated, the greater the dissonance, and hence, the greater the opinion change. As the communicator becomes less credible, and derogation becomes a possible avenue of dissonance reduction, we predict that the curve will decline near the extreme end. As the discrepancy becomes large, derogation will be an easier method of dissonance reduction than opinion change, and consequently, there would be little or no opinion change and great derogation of the communicator. As the communicator becomes even less credible, the curve representing opinion change will begin to decline at a point closer to the origin (zero discrepancy). Finally, in the ideal case of zero credibility, the curve should be completely flat. Moreover, the curve for a highly credible communicator should be higher at all points of discrepancy. This follows because a highly credible communicator can arouse greater dissonance and hence induce greater opinion change; dissonance introduced by a communicator of low credibility can be more easily reduced by disparaging the communicator than by changing opinions. (See Figure 1 for theoretical and actual curves.)

PROCEDURE

In order to test these hypotheses, an experiment was designed which had the following characteristics:

1. The subjects were exposed to a persuasive communication which was identical for all groups except for the extent of the discrepancy and the credibility of the communicator.

2. The task was such that the original opinions of the subjects fell at the same position on some continuum so that the amount of change advocated could be determined independently of the initial position of the subject.

3. The subsequent opinions of the subjects as well as the amount of derogation of the communicator were measured.

The subjects were 112 female college students [2] who were paid volunteers for "an experiment in esthetics." They met in small groups, ranging in size from two to seven. The subjects were told that the experimenter was interested in studying how people evaluate poetry. They were first asked to rank order nine stanzas from obscure modern poems, all of which contained alliteration. The criterion for ranking was stated ambigu-

[2] Actually, 115 subjects participated in the experiment. The data from 3 were discarded because the experimental sanction against intercommunication was not observed; one of the subjects announced loudly (within earshot of the others) that she disagreed with the author of the essay.

ously: "the way the poet uses form to aid in expressing his meaning." Next, each subject was asked to read a two-page essay entitled "The Use of Alliteration in Poetry." This communication consisted mostly of general statements about the uses and abuses of alliteration in poetic writing. The final half page consisted of an illustration of the points made in the essay; that is, the ideas stated in the essay were applied in the evaluation of a particular stanza. For each subject, the stanza that was used as an illustration was the one that she had originally ranked as the eighth-best stanza.

For approximately one-third of the subjects there was a small discrepancy between her opinion of the stanza and the communicator's opinion; for approximately one-third of the subjects there was a moderate discrepancy; and for approximately one-third of the subjects there was an extreme discrepancy. The discrepancy was created by having the communication state that the poem was better than the subject had indicated in her first ranking. The slight discrepancy was established by introducing the stanza as average; the communication asserted that half of the stanzas were better, half worse. The medium discrepancy was established by introducing the stanza as one of the better examples; it was stated that two of the others were superior. The large discrepancy was established by introducing the stanza as the best example of the use of alliteration in the sample. In summary, the subjects were faced with a discrepancy of either three, five, or seven rank-order positions between their ranking of the crucial stanza and that of the communicator.

In each of these three conditions,

We have predicted a different curve for each degree of communicator credibility. The 45-degree line is a theoretical curve representing the "perfectly credible" communicator, perhaps unattainable experimentally. In response to such a communicator, disparagement is impossible, so that opinion change is the only means of reducing dissonance. The horizontal line is a theoretical curve representing the "perfectly incredible" communicator. In this case, the recipient would experience no dissonance regardless of the extent of the discrepancy between his opinion and that advocated by the communicator. The other two curves show intermediate degrees of credibility. These curves are empirical, representing the opinion change of the subjects in this experiment. As the communicator is made less credible, the curve is lowered at all points (since more disparagement takes place at all points, reducing some of the dissonance). Similarly, as the communicator is made less credible, the curve reaches its maximum sooner (as disparagement replaces opinion change as the major method of reducing dissonance).

To some extent, the results involving the derogation of the communicator lend support to this analysis. The results pertinent to derogation are presented in Table 2. It is clear that subjects derogated the mildly credible communicator to a greater extent than the highly credible communicator. This was the case irrespective of the degree of the discrepancy; for each condition of discrepancy, the difference between the derogation of the highly credible and mildly credible communicators is highly significant. These results are not unequivocal, however. As can be seen from inspection of Table 2, there was no difference in derogation among the various conditions of discrepancy in the Mildly Credible condition. These data do not support our theoretical analysis. That is, although we have demonstrated that credibility and discrepancy do interact to produce opinion change as predicted, our analysis suggests systematic differences in the derogation of the communicator within the Mildly Credible condition. Specifically, it was predicted that in the Mildly Credible condition, with high discrepancy, derogation would be used in lieu of opinion change as a means of reducing dissonance. Thus, if our analysis is correct, subjects in this condition appear to have ended the experiment carrying a barrel full of dissonance. This is an unenviable circumstance—for the theorists as well as the subjects. There appears to be no easy theoretical explanation for this datum. Methodologically, it is possible that our measure of derogation was not a very good one. It may have been sensitive enough to induce the subjects to playback the instructions, leaving

TABLE 2. DEROGATION OF THE COMMUNICATOR

Communicator	Discrepancy		
	Small	Medium	Large
Highly credible	31.75	29.31	32.43
Mildly credible	60.10	58.04	56.00

those in the Mildly Credible condition more derogatory than those in the Highly Credible condition. But our measure may not have been sensitive enough to reflect fine distinctions within the Mildly Credible condition. Similarly, it is well known that college students are often reluctant to make extremely negative statements about a fellow student. That is, in the Mildly Credible condition, there may have been a ceiling effect in the disparagement scale; the degree of derogation may have been maximal even when the communicator's position was not discrepant. Thus, subjects in this condition may have privately derogated the communicator without expressing it in writing. Although these methodological explanations are convenient from our point of view, they are hardly conclusive. Further research may suggest alternative explanations for these particular results.

Reconciliation of Results with Previous Findings

The main body of results supports the theoretical analysis and suggests a reconciliation of previous contradictory findings. It is a reasonable assumption that each of the previous experiments examined only one of the family of theoretical functions outlined above. We may at least tentatively support such an assumption by a brief analysis of the disparageability of the communicators used in these studies.

Let us first examine some studies which found a linear relationship between opinion change and degree of discrepancy. As previously mentioned Zimbardo (1960) used as a communicator a person who was not only a close friend of the subject, but one who was

also a proven expert in the area of the communication. Clearly, this communicator was highly credible. Hovland and Pritzker (1957) described their communicator as "respected by the recipient, and hence an authoritative source of opinion." Goldberg (1954) used, as an expert, the combined previous judgments of the subject himself and one or more peers. It seems reasonable that such a combined judgment (of from two to four people, *including* the subject himself) would be difficult to disparage.

In contrast, Hovland et al. (1957), who found decreasing opinion change with an extreme discrepancy, used a communicator without describing him to the subject. To quote the authors, there was "ambiguity about the credibility of the communicator." Fisher and Lubin (1958), who found a similar effect, used a single unexpert peer as a communicator. It seems apparent that such a communicator was relatively easy to disparage.

In Cohen's (1959) experiment the communicator was defined only by a description of the communication. When the communication was described as "difficult and subtle," "arguments . . . related in a complex fashion," Cohen found increasing opinion change with increasing discrepancy. However, when the communication was described as "easy to grasp," he found less opinion change with high discrepancy. It may be assumed that a communicator who has been able to compose a complex, difficult, and subtle argument is perceived as more intelligent and, hence, more credible than a communicator whose argument is simple and easy to grasp. Moreover, it is difficult to disparage a communicator after one has been told that one might not be able to understand the communication, since disliking the communication may be tantamount to failing to understand it.

REFERENCES

ARNET, C. C., DAVIDSON, HELEN H., & LEWIS, H. N. Prestige as a factor in attitude change. *Sociol. soc. Res.*, 1931, 16, 49–55.

COHEN, A. R. Communication discrepancy and attitude change, *J. Pers.*, 1959, 27, 386–396.

FESTINGER, L. *A theory of cognitive dissonance.* New York: Harper & Row, 1957.

FESTINGER, L., & ARONSON, E. The arousal and reduction of dissonance in social contexts. In D. Cartwright & A. Zander (Eds.), *Group dynamics: Research and theory.* (2nd ed.) New York: Harper & Row, 1960. Pp. 214–231.

FISHER, S., & LUBIN, A. Distance as a determinant of influence in a two-person serial interaction situation. *J. abnorm. soc. Psychol.*, 1958, 56, 230–238.

GOLDBERG, S. C. Three situational determinants of conformity to social norms.

J. abnorm. soc. Psychol., 1954, 49, 325–329.

HAIMAN, F. S. An experimental study of the effects of ethos in public speaking. *Speech Monogr.*, 1949, 16, 190–202.

HOVLAND, C. I., HARVEY, O. J., & SHERIF, M. Assimilation and contrast effects in reactions to communication and attitude change. *J. abnorm. soc. Psychol.*, 1957, 55, 244–252.

HOVLAND, C. I., & PRITZKER, H. A. Extent of opinion change as a function of change advocated. *J. abnorm. soc. Psychol.*, 1957, 54, 257–261.

HOVLAND, C. I., & WEISS, W. The influence of source credibility on communication effectiveness. *Publ. Opin. Quart.*, 1952, 15, 635–650.

KELMAN, H. C., & HOVLAND, C. I. "Reinstatement" of the communicator in delayed measurement of opinion change. *J. abnorm. soc. Psychol.*, 1953, 48, 327–335.

KULP, D. H. Prestige as measured by single-experience changes and their permanency. *J. educ. Res.*, 1934, 27, 663–672.

ZIMBARDO, P. G. Involvement and communication discrepancy as determinants of opinion conformity. *J. abnorm. soc. Psychol.*, 1960, 60, 86–94.

16. RECENCY AND PRIMACY IN PERSUASION AS A FUNCTION OF THE TIMING OF SPEECHES AND MEASUREMENTS *

Norman Miller and Donald T. Campbell

In a recent volume, Hovland, Campbell, Brock, Luchins, Cohen, McGuire, Janis, Feierabend, and Anderson (1957) have summarized and added to the perplexing literature on the conditions under which the first or the second of two opposing arguments have an advantage due to position per se. Their findings seem to have ruled out any completely general principle of primacy in persuasion, but have specified several sets of conditions under which a primacy effect may be expected. In adding to this growing literature, the present paper pays rela-

* Reprinted from the *Journal of Abnormal and Social Psychology*, 1959, 59: 1–9, with permission of the senior author and the American Psychological Association.

tively less attention to primacy, although we do find a primacy effect. Instead, attention is called to a pervasive and probably universal psychological principle generating recency effects, a principle about which psychology already knows enough to predict confidently the temporal conditions of presentation and measurement under which recency should appear most strongly. As a complement, the principle also predicts the temporal conditions under which a primacy effect appears most strongly, if indeed one is present.

Our judgments, our responses, our social perceptions, are a function of some net resultant of the past experiences both recent and remote. To the net resultant of the moment not all past experiences contribute equally: the casual experiences of this morning weigh more heavily than the comparably casual experiences of any single morning one year ago, one month ago, or even yesterday, all other things being equal. Were it not so, unlearning and new learning could hardly take place. But the advantage that this morning's experience now has will dissipate rapidly. By next month, its advantage over yesterday's contribution will be scarcely noticeable. The momentary advantage of the very recent may allow trivial events of this morning to overweigh momentarily more significant learnings of the past, but this momentary advantage will dissipate rapidly, allowing the relative influence of the older learnings to recover spontaneously tomorrow or the next day, if events like this morning's prove to be untypical and do not recur.

These homely truisms are economically summarized in the oldest dependable achievement of the scientific study of learning, the negatively accelerated forgetting curve of Ebbinghaus (1913), and in its implications for the relative strength of competing associations of different ages and strengths. From it, Jost's (1897) second law can be derived—of two associations equally strong at the moment, the older will decay less rapidly. These same considerations also predict spontaneous recovery (Miller & Stevenson, 1936). Hovland, Janis, and Kelley (1953, p. 126), although not making explicit use of the forgetting curve, have provided a parallel analysis of the effect of delays in measurement upon the relative strength of a first and second message:

Yet another important factor to consider is the time interval between the learning of the second communication and the occasion when remembering is required. In experimental results on simple verbal material one would predict recency effects when the time interval is short. But the passage of time would tend to decrease this recency effect and permit the other factors making for primacy to become relatively stronger. Underwood [1948] has shown that for verbal learning the relative superiority of the second list with respect to retention decreases as the time between learning and testing becomes greater. If the same factors operate in social communication one would expect to find that when the issue is raised quite a while after the communication, recency would be less likely to be operative. Striking data are offered on this point in an experiment by Bateman and Remmers [1941]. . . . The results show that immediately after the two communications the attitudes changed in the direction of the second communication. This is the predicted recency effect. Two months later however, the attitudes had changed in the direction of the first communication. Thus primacy effects occurred with time. While the data are consistent with the analysis suggested here, the experiment cannot be considered as presenting conclusive evidence because it did not include a control group and the order of presentation was not rotated.

The present study examines with better controls this effect of delay in measurement, and in addition considers the still stronger factor of the time interval between the first and second communication.

Figure 1 presents the implications of the Ebbinghaus curve as it applies to the relative weighting of two competing communications presented and measured at varying intervals, assuming no interaction of one with the other. In this diagram, the solid line (Line A) represents the contribution of a communication presented first, its strength decaying as time elapses. The two dashed lines (B and B′) represent the contributions of a second opposing communication. In one instance this second communication is presented immediately after the first (Line B), in the other instance, one week after the first (Line B′). Net effects of the two communications in combination are re-flected by the vertical distance between Line A and Line B or B′ at any given point in time. The numbered vertical slicings in the diagram represent four possible schedulings of a measure of net effect, designated as Conditions 1–4. Five predictions emerge, stated in terms of the relative magnitude of the recency effect, i.e., the dominance of the second communication in the composite under the four conditions: $3 > 4, 3 > 1, 3 > 2,$ $1 > 2,$ and $4 > 2$. The relative magnitudes of Conditions 1 and 4 cannot be predicted without specific knowledge of the parameters of the curve. The others follow from the simple assumption of similar negatively accelerated decrements for the three curves involved.

Figure 1 has been drawn assuming equal initial strength for the first and the second messages at the time of their delivery. But the ordering of the test conditions as to their *relative* favorableness to the second message is independent of this assumption of initial equality. These general decremental processes occur no matter how strong any given

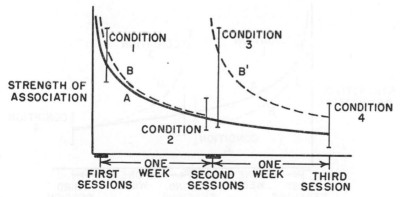

Figure 1. Hypothetical forgetting curves for a first and a second competing persuasive communication when both are presented during a single session (curves A and B) or when the two are presented one week apart (curves A and B′); the four conditions, appearing as vertical slicings, represent the timing of measurements

message happens to be. As can be seen from Figure 1, by assuming this initial equality in the strength of the two communications, though the magnitude of the effects varies, *only* recency effects can be generated. However, in persuasion studies there frequently appears an advantage to the first message, a primacy or prior entry effect, strong enough to show up even under conditions of testing such as Condition 1 in which a weak primacy effect would be covered over by a recency effect. Figure 2 has been drawn to indicate some degree of primacy effect, interpreted as an initially higher level for the first message at its onset than for the second message at its highest and, correspondingly, a higher eventual asymptotic level of strength for the first message than for the second. Under this assumption, a manifest or net primacy can occur, as in Condition 2. Note that such a primacy effect does *not* occur *instead of* a recency effect but, rather, *in addition* to a recency effect. Thus, attention is drawn to a conceptual distinction between recency effects which are a function of the general rates of decrement with the passage of time, and primacy effects which appear as a function of the higher asymptote eventually resulting from the advantage of prior entry. To predict whether primacy or recency will appear at any single point in time, knowledge of the specific parameters of the curves would of course be essential. But even without specification of parameters, solely upon the basis of assuming similar negatively accelerated decrements, the rank order of the four testing situations in terms of the relative advantage to recency can be specified, and are the same for Figure 2 as for Figure 1. However, the absolute magnitudes have been shifted, so that under Condition 2, which is the least advantageous condition for recency in both figures, a strong net primacy effect is predicted in Figure 2. In general, the more delayed the test period relative to the time gap between the two presentations, the more favorable are conditions for the appearance of a primacy effect.

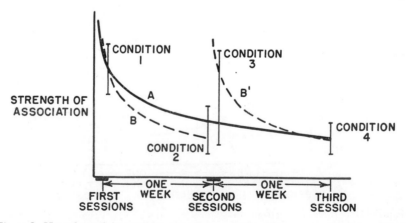

Figure 2. Hypothetical forgetting curves for two competing communications with an added primacy effect; the primacy effect is represented by the higher initial starting point and final asymptote of line A in comparison with lines B or B′

METHOD

Subjects

A total of 144 Northwestern freshman and sophomore students from introductory psychology and social science courses served as Ss. All Ss were volunteers. Some of the Ss were acquainted with the experimenter, but these were distributed in approximately equal numbers among the groups serving under different experimental conditions.

Communications

A desirable consideration that has not been met in most two-sided communication studies is that the subject matter or theme of the communications be one about which Ss have not already formed opinions or attitudes prior to the experiment. Learning prior to the experiment can eliminate the possibility of controlling or determining the effect of order of learning (Hovland et al., 1953; Lund, 1925). With such the case, primacy of the communication that is experimentally presented first may be a misnomer if the communication is considered in the context of all the communications received by the individual on the particular issue in question. It was therefore considered advantageous to experimentally create attitudes rather than arouse previously learned attitudes. As Weld and Roff (1938), we used a modified courtroom procedure to introduce experimentally pro and con statements about a topic with which Ss had no prior experience. A transcript of an actual trial involving a suit for damages supposedly incurred as a result of a defective vaporizer was edited for the purposes of the present experiment. Repetitious sections of the testimony were condensed and the names of the principals were changed. The sequence of the proceedings was rearranged so that all material for the plaintiff appeared in one consecutive block, and all material for the defendant appeared in another block. The testimony of witnesses for the plaintiff, the cross-examination by the plaintiff's lawyer of the witnesses for the defense, and the opening and closing speeches of the plaintiff's lawyer, will be called the "Pro" communication, the testimony of witnesses for the defense, and so on the "Con." These two communications were approximately equal, both in length and in the number of points to their arguments. Slight differences in persuasive strength of the two communications were present but are unimportant because of the counter-balanced design employed. The experimental communications were recorded, with different persons reading the parts of the different characters, lawyers, witnesses, etc. Each took approximately 45 minutes to run.

Response Measures

Four response measures were used. A graphic scale with nine described points (e.g., defendant is somewhat more responsible) enabled each S to express the degree to which he thought either the plaintiff or the defendant was responsible for the accident, the midpoint of 5 representing equal responsibility. Higher values indicated plaintiff's responsibility, that is, persuasion to the "Con" point of view. This scale served as the direct attitude measure. It was accompanied by a scale on which the S estimated how certain he was of his response, with possible values ranging from zero to 100 percent.

A multiple choice test was constructed to determine the amount of factual information that could be recalled from the two communications. The test contained a total of 28 four-choice items, 14 based on the material from the Pro communication and 14 based on the material from the Con communication.

The one other response measure used was included in an effort to get at differences in acceptance. Ss were requested to list those parts of the two communications that they could not · believe or accept. This response measure was preceded by a statement to the effect that no person believes everything he is told even if it is supposedly factual. Then, a list of the names of the persons who testified at the trial (a brief identifying description following each name) was supplied to each S in order to facilitate recall and identification of unacceptable statements. The response measures collectively took approximately 30 minutes.

Procedure

The two spacings of the first and second communication (immediate and one week apart), and, for each, the two spacings of the measurement efforts (immediately after the second and one week after the second) generate the four experimental conditions indicated in Figs. 1 and 2. Replicating these four conditions with the Pro-Con order and the Con-Pro order generates the eight basic experimental groups. Each of these groups contained 18 Ss, all presented the communications and tested together. All groups met in the same classroom at about the same time of day. Ss sat one seat apart from each other, and adjacent Ss had booklets in which the test materials were assembled in different orders. Through these precautions it was hoped to minimize the "neighbor effect" or "social diffusion," well-known reducers of the variability of the test scores of college students. Each group was measured but once in a Posttest Only Design (Campbell, 1957). For Condition 1, the single session took approximately 2½ hrs. with 5-minute breaks following both communications.

To make the findings on the various measures independent of the order in which the students filled them out, the three instruments (attitude and certainty being treated as one) were stapled together in the six possible orders, and three of each of these assemblies employed in each group of 18. Extra Ss were run in each group to allow for the inevitable loss through failure to keep appointments one week apart. Surplus Ss were discarded to leave 3 Ss each in the 48 cells of the total design. Since the order of the response measures turned out to have no effect in any of several analyses (Miller, 1957) it has been omitted in this report.

RESULTS

Attitude

In Table 1 are presented the mean attitude scores for each of the eight groups. Using Table 1 as a reference, two types of comparisons can be designated. The vertical comparisons within each of the two columns are appropriate to testing the predictions about the relative strength of the second message.

For this purpose, each column represents an independent experiment of four groups. It is for these comparisons that the Ebbinghaus curve predictions are made. Table 2 and the discussion of it below treat these results. The predictions in Table 2, and the columns of means of Table 1 taken individually, are silent on whether or not for any given condition the manifest effect found is one of primacy or recency. The predictions merely indicate under which condition a primacy effect, if present, should appear most strongly (that is, Condition 2) and under which a recency effect, if present, should appear most strongly (that is, Condition 3), and so on. For any one mean to be directly interpretable in terms of primacy and recency, one would need proof that the Pro and Con messages were exactly equal in persuasive power and that the assigned midpoint of 5 was the effective neutral point of judgment in absence of persuasive communications. But if one makes use of the comparison of the Pro-Con and the Con-Pro orders, that is, makes the horizontal comparisons of Table 1, the presence of manifest net primacy or recency effects can be examined, because the groups being compared have heard identical materials under identical spacings, and differ only in the order with which these have been heard. In Table 1 (and Tables 4 and 7), the higher the scores the more the Con material has been effective. Thus a comparison of the two Condition 2 groups shows that the Con material was weakest when occurring second, strongest when coming first, indicating a primacy effect, significant at the .01 level (using a two-tailed test, since direction was not predicted). Condition 3 shows a recency effect, significant at the .02 level. The results conform to the pattern predicted by Figure 2, in which a general primacy and recency effect coexist, the recency effect dominating under Condition 3, the condition predicted as most favorable to recency; the primacy effect dominates under Condition 2, predicted as least favorable to recency, and therefore as the place where a primacy effect would appear most strongly, if present. The two effects cancel each other in the two conditions of predicted intermediacy.

While the t tests reported in Table 1 and Table 2 provide more specific information, a double classification analysis of variance offers a more general

TABLE 1. MEAN ATTITUDE SCORES

Condition	Pro-Con Presentation	Con-Pro Presentation	Diff.	t	p [b]	Direction
1 (X_1X_2O) [a]	5.94	5.88	.06			
2 (X_1X_2—O)	4.50	6.61	−2.11	2.81	.01	Primacy
3 (X_1—X_2O)	6.00	4.33	1.67	2.46	.02	Recency
4 (X_1—X_2—O)	5.47	5.58	−.11			

[a] The shorthand characterization of the conditions employs a standardized symbolization of experimental treatments (Campbell, 1957), in which X_1 and X_2 represent the experimental stimuli, O the process of observation and measurement, and spacing from left to right the time dimension.

[b] Two-tailed, inasmuch as direction of difference not predicted.

TABLE 2. COMPARISON OF MEANS FOR ATTITUDE SCORES [a]

Prediction for Conditions	Pro-Con Presentation			Con-Pro Presentation			Combined
	Diff.	t	p	Diff.	t	p	p
1 > 2	+1.44	1.79	.04	+.73	1.00	.16	< .05
3 > 1	+.06	.08	.47	+1.55	2.03	.025	< .07
3 > 2	+1.50	2.14	.02	+2.28	3.12	.005	< .001
3 > 4	+.53	.78	.22	+1.25	1.56	.06	< .08
4 > 2	+.97	1.21	.11	+1.03	1.35	.09	< .06
(1, 4)	.47	.59	.56	.30	.38	.70	

[a] The *Diff.* column values are differences between the group means presented in Table 1, with positive signs applied to indicate differences in the predicted direction as favoring recency, thus reversing the natural subtraction signs for the Con-Pro groups for which favoring recency implies lower scores. No prediction was made for Conditions 1 vs. 4, and two-tailed *p* values are therefore presented for this comparison, while one-tailed values are used for the others.

test of the main hypothesis that the temporal spacing of communications and measurements determines the relative effectiveness of the communications in the composite. However, with a counterbalanced design, this hypothesis must be stated as an interaction rather than a main effect; the shifts in attitude occurring over conditions with the Pro-Con presentation should be analogous, but reciprocal or in opposite direction to those occurring with the Con-Pro order. In a 2×4 analysis of variance of the attitude scores, the F ratio for the interaction between Conditions and Order of Presentation is the only one that obtains significance. With 1 and 3 degrees of freedom, this F ratio of 4.06 is significant beyond the .01 level.

Table 2 presents, separately, for the Pro-Con and Con-Pro orders, the comparisons between conditions in terms of their predicted relative favorableness to recency. The positive signs indicate that the direction of difference was as predicted. (Note that for the Con-Pro groups, greater recency effects are indicated by lower scores.) All differences

are in the direction predicted. This score of 10 correct out of 10 predictions looks highly significant by a simple sign test, although since the same values have been re-used, independence of sampling error from comparison to comparison cannot be claimed. Table 2 also presents the t ratios and p values for the predicted comparisons of means and a compound p value (Baker, 1952) for the Pro-Con and the Con-Pro groups treated jointly. The most clearly significant difference occurs for the comparison for which the largest contrast was expected, that is, between Conditions 3 and 2. The other differences approach significance in the predicted directions. All in all, results seem strongly confirmatory of the predictions.

Recall of Information

Table 3 presents the recall data in terms of the mean number of Pro and Con items correctly answered in each condition. To state recall in terms of a net weighting, each S was given a score of Con items right minus Pro items

TABLE 3. MEAN NUMBER OF ITEMS CORRECT ON RECALL

	Pro-Con Presentation		Con-Pro Presentation	
Condition	Pro	Con	Pro	Con
$1(X_1X_2O)$	10.00	9.44	10.72	9.83
$2(X_1X_2—O)$	9.28	9.06	8.94	8.33
$3(X_1—X_2O)$	7.31	9.69	9.94	6.67
$3(X_1—X_2—O)$	7.50	8.50	7.78	6.89

right. The means of these net recall scores are presented in Table 4. The comparisons made in Table 4 parallel those in Table 1. In an analysis of variance of the net recall scores, a significant interaction obtains between Conditions and Order of Presentation. With 1 and 3 degrees of freedom, the F ration of 21.46 for the interaction is significant well beyond the .001 level. All horizontal comparisons show a net recency effect (conforming more to the model of Figure 1 than Figure 2), with the recency effect most highly significant for Condition 3, as expected.

Table 5 is constructed parallel to

TABLE 4. MEAN NET RECALL SCORES

Condition	Pro-Con Presentation	Con-Pro Presentation	Diff.	t	p [a]	Direction
$1(X_1X_2O)$	−.56	−.89	+.33	.39		
$2(X_1X_2—O)$	−.22	−.61	+.39	.55		
$3(X_1—X_2O)$	2.38	−3.27	+5.65	7.90	.001	Recency
$4(X_1—X_2—O)$	1.00	−.89	+1.89	2.62	.02	Recency

[a] Two-tailed.

TABLE 5. COMPARISON OF MEAN RECALL DIFFERENCE SCORES

Prediction for Conditions	Pro-Con Presentation			Con-Pro Presentation			Combined
	Diff. [a]	t	p	Diff.	t	p	p
$1 > 2$	−.34	.39	.64	+.28	.40	.36	$> .20$
$3 > 1$	+2.94	3.42	.0004	+2.39	3.21	.001	$< .0001$
$3 > 2$	+2.60	3.80	.0001	+2.67	3.54	.0002	$< .0001$
$3 > 4$	+1.38	1.76	.04	+2.39	3.52	.0003	$< .0001$
$4 > 2$	+1.22	1.54	.065	+.28	.45	.34	$< .10$
$(1, 4)$	1.56	1.67	.10	.00	.00	.50	

[a] See the footnote to Table 2.

Table 2. Of the ten predicted differences, nine are confirmed for sign. The three predictions involving Condition 3 are all very highly significant. The comparison between Conditions 1 and 2 fails of significance in either the Pro-Con or Con-Pro order. Considering the small number of items in the test, and their employment as a difference score (which should further increase their random variability), the results seem in general as confirmatory as one could expect. In both columns, two independent replications, the gap between Condition 3 and any other is most dramatically confirmed, as would be expected from Figure 2.

Nonacceptance

The mean number of Pro and Con arguments recalled as unbelieved under the eight conditions is shown in Table 6. As a net effect score, the number of unacceptable Con items was subtracted from the number of unacceptable Pro items. The means of these net scores for each group are presented in Table 7. For this measure, the interaction F ratio for Order $\times$ Conditions was insignificant. The Pro-Con vs. Con-Pro differences are predominantly in the primacy direction, although not of clear statistical significance. The most significant difference is in the primacy direction under Condition 2, predicted most favorable to primacy. The only difference in the recency direction is in Condition 3, predicted most favorable to recency. Table 8 presents the differences among the Pro-Con conditions, and among the Con-Pro conditions, arranged in terms of the predictions, although it is not clear that the predictions are appropriate to this measure. For the Pro-Con groups, all differences are trivial, and the

TABLE 6. MEAN NUMBER OF STATEMENTS FOUND UNACCEPTABLE

Condition	Pro-Con Presentation		Con-Pro Presentation	
	Pro	Con	Pro	Con
$1(X_1X_2O)$	1.28	.56	2.27	.33
$2(X_1X_2\text{—}O)$	1.39	.78	2.27	.44
$3(X_1\text{—}X_2O)$	1.31	.81	1.39	.95
$4(X_1\text{—}X_2\text{—}O)$	1.33	.39	1.33	.39

TABLE 7. MEAN NET NONACCEPTANCE SCORES

Conditions	Pro-Con Presentation	Con-Pro Presentation	Diff.	t	p [a]
$1(X_1X_2O)$	.72	1.94	−1.22	1.66	.10
$2(X_1X_2\text{—}O)$	.61	1.83	−1.22	1.91	.06
$3(X_1\text{—}X_2O)$	.50	.44	.06	.10	.92
$4(X_1\text{—}X_2\text{—}O)$	.94	.94	.00	.00	.50

[a] Two-tailed.

TABLE 8. COMPARISON OF MEAN NET NONACCEPTABLE SCORES [a]

| | Pro-Con Presentation | | | Con-Pro Presentation | | | Combined |
Comparison	Diff.	t	p	Diff.	t	p	p
1 > 2	+.11	.15	.44	−.11	.17	.57	> .20
3 > 1	−.22	.31	.64	+1.50	2.27	.012	< .05
3 > 2	−.11	.17	.57	+1.39	2.21	.014	< .05
3 > 4	−.44	.98	.84	+.50	.83	.21	> .20
4 > 2	+.33	.64	.26	+.89	1.53	.06	< .10
(1, 4)	.22	.38	.65	1.00	1.63	.10	

[a] See footnote for Table 2.

predicted direction of difference is found in only two of the five pairs. The Con-Pro groups offer four out of five confirmations, all those that approach significance being in the predicted direction.

In retrospect, it can be seen that our particular measure of nonacceptance is far from ideal. A more interpretable procedure would have asked for recall of testimony found particularly convincing in addition to testimony disbelieved. With only the recall of unacceptable material, the influence of credibility is mixed with the influence of greater readiness of recall, with opposing effects. For an item to be mentioned as unbelievable it has to be remembered. But mention of second message material as disbelieved is scored as a credibility advantage to the first. If, for the reason of greater recency, second message material is more easily remembered and therefore mentioned more often, the net effect gets scored as a primacy advantage for acceptance and credibility purposes.

Other Analyses

To assist in the interpretation of the processes that would allow a primacy effect for the attitude measure without a primacy effect for recall, cor-relation coefficients were computed among the three main variables, separately for each of the eight groups. The average of these values are: Attitude and Recall −.10, Attitude and Nonacceptance .43 ($p < .01$), Recall and Nonacceptance −.04. For the last two, the correlations for the individual groups are adequately represented by these averages. However, as a provocative item for contemplation if confirmed in future research, it can be noted that the correlations between Attitude and Recall seem to show systematic variance from substantial positive correlation under Condition 1 (.49 and .27) to substantial negative correlation under Condition 4 (−.51 and −.40).

As reported more fully elsewhere (Miller, 1957), certainty scores proved unrelated to the experimental conditions. Similarly, certainty of attitude did not correlate with amount of recalled information, nor did the usual curvilinear correlation between certainty and attitude-extremity appear. While the information test was not deliberately designed for the purpose, it was possible to order the wrong alternatives in the degree to which they implied conclusions favorable to the Pro or the Con argument, and to give each S a score indicating the preponderant directionality of his errors. This indirect attitude test (Campbell, 1950) correlated but .08 with the direct attitude score and showed no systematic relationship to the experimental conditions.

DISCUSSION

Recency

The clear-cut results for the attitude and recall measures clearly support the application of the Ebbinghaus curves to the field of persuasion. Nor would there seem to be any rival theory that could so economically predict the complex set of results. The ubiquity of the negatively accelerated forgetting curve in learning studies further supports the possibility of a thoroughly general recency principle, with the strength of recency being maximal for a long delay between first and second communication coupled with immediate measurement after the second communication, the strength of recency being minimal when the two presentations are contiguous and the testing delayed. One study does not make a general principle, and the area of persuasion has been particularly frustrating to such attempts, but the antecedent probabilities plus this clear-cut experimental confirmation give promise. The recognition that a recency effect (such as the Ebbinghaus curves predict) can be a concomitant of, rather than an excluding alternative to, a primacy effect makes the postulation of this general principle not in the least incompatible with any of the previous literature on order effects. Indeed, the only other study containing both a question of order of arguments and measurement at various removes in time confirms some of the predictions of this principle,

although that study is by today's standards so lacking in controls as to be uninterpretable (Bateman & Remmers, 1941).

Ebbinghaus' curve is simple and perhaps obvious, yet, as indicated, the simultaneous application of several such curves generates the nonobvious Jost (1897) law number 2, and even spontaneous recovery (Miller & Stevenson, 1936). Considering the length of time that the principle has been with us and its potential fertility, it is surprising that it has been so little used. One of the historical reasons is that with the observations of lack of forgetting during sleep and more rapid forgetting with similar materials during the interposed period, forgetting became something to be explained, and therefore attention was distracted from its use as an explanation. But even accepting an interference theory of forgetting, and even employing a psychological time scale (perhaps average interference rate during waking hours) the negatively accelerated curve has explanatory power and can be accepted at a molar level as a given for social psychology.

One of the most general findings in persuasion studies, involving repeated measurements over a long period of time, is that the change induced by persuasion dissipates with time. Similarly in everyday observations, successful remedial efforts and conversions are often followed by recidivism and backsliding. Usually such phenomena are interpreted as due to the competing effects of other communications occurring subsequent to the persuasive message, but under the aegis of Ebbinghaus' curves, one can interpret this decrement as a literal backsliding, due to the increasingly effective competition of the great bulk of pre-persuasion communications, as time since the persuasive effort increases. On the other hand, when one considers the volumes of communications that Ss have received prior to an experimental session, it becomes far from obvious that a 10-minute speech on a familiar topic could have any appreciable effect. Yet the most general finding in both published studies and in unpublished ones is that almost any speech will have an effect in its intended direction if the effect is measured immediately. If this fact needs explanation, as we think it does, it is found in the Ebbinghaus curves, which predict an extreme recency advantage under this condition. By the same token, the advantage rapidly dissipates. And if the speech is on a familiar topic, then even if no further communications were to be received, by next year the ten-minute speech will indeed be but a drop in the bucket.

Primacy Effects upon Attitude Measures

Paradoxically enough, the postulation of this general recency principle improves the case for a general primacy principle. The experimental arena employed in primacy-recency studies so far has been most similar to our Condition 1, immediate testing after contiguous presentations. This is a condition that is not optimal to the manifestation of either primacy or recency. In the present study they cancel each other out under this condition. The inconsistent evidence obtained at this point by the half-dozen studies which Hovland et al. (1957) review and report thus could be interpreted, if one wished, as consistent with an always present primacy effect. The strength of this primacy effect would

necessarily vary with the experimental conditions particular to each of the different studies and would frequently be masked by the recency effects also present. Testing this assumption would involve, in part, studies with sufficiently long delayed measurements to explore that end of the dimension represented by our Condition 2. It is not the purpose of this paper to argue the case for a general primacy effect but merely to point out that the evidence to date does not rule one out.

Would such a general primacy effect include learning phenomena as well as attitude phenomena? Here, again, test conditions such as Condition 2 are very rare. The trends in the available long delay studies favor primacy (Underwood, 1948), significantly so in one instance (Briggs, 1954). But in these studies, the first list learned was presented for more trials than the second, and none have employed as long a delay as one week. In our own recall data, no slightest hint of a net manifest or phenotypic primacy effect occurs. It seems clear that in the present study the primacy effect in the attitude measure is at very least much stronger than whatever hidden primacy effect might be latent in the recall data. The primacy effect for attitudes is thus not to be explained in terms of a primacy effect upon learning or memory of evidence or argument. Similarly, it cannot be explained in terms of such factors as set, attention, or reinforcement (Hovland et al., 1957), which assume that the second communication is less well listened to, less well assimilated content-wise, or subjected to stronger interference effects and, as a result, less well remembered. Our recall data are contrary to any such assumption. The primacy effect in attitude change seems related in the present instance to acceptance factors, as Hovland anticipated it might be (Hovland et al., 1953, p. 126). In this interpretation, the evidence on nonacceptance, rough though it is, mediates between the attitude and recall data. Coming first gives a statement no greater probability of being remembered, but does give it greater probability of being believed. We have a general tendency to find one side of an argument persuasive, providing we have not heard the other. Hearing it after we have heard the other, we are apt to be more critical and skeptical.

SUMMARY

The order in which opposing arguments were presented (Pro-Con and Con-Pro), the time interval between them (none and one week), and the time of testing (immediately after the second argument or one week after) were varied for eight groups, each tested once. For the attitude measure, a significant recency effect was found under the conditions most favorable to recency as predicted from the application of Ebbinghaus decay curves. A significant primacy effect was found under the conditions predicted to be least favorable to recency. For recall of information, only recency effects were found, these being strongest under conditions predicted to be most favorable.

REFERENCES

BAKER, P. C.   Combining tests of significance in cross validation. *Educ. psychol. Measmt.*, 1952, **12**, 300–306.

BATEMAN, R. M., & REMMERS, H. H.   A study of the shifting attitude of high school students when subjected to favor-

able and unfavorable propaganda, *J. soc. Psychol.*, 1941, **13**, 395–406.

BRIGGS, G. E.   Acquisition, extinction, and recovery functions in retroactive inhibition. *J. exp. Psychol.*, 1954, **47**, 285–293.

CAMPBELL, D. T.   The indirect assessment of social attitudes. *Psychol. Bull.*, 1950, **47**, 15–38.

CAMPBELL, D. T.   Factors relevant to the validity of experiments in social settings. *Psychol. Bull.*, 1957, **54**, 297–312.

EBBINGHAUS, H.   *Memory*. H. A. ROGER & C. E. BUSSENIUS (Trans.). New York: Teachers College Columbia Univer., 1913. (Original, *Über das Gedächtnis*, Leipzig, 1885.)

HOVLAND, C. I., JANIS, I. L., & KELLEY, H. H.   *Communication and persuasion*. New Haven: Yale Univer. Press, 1953.

HOVLAND, C. I., MANDELL, W., CAMPBELL, ENID H., BROCK, T., LUCHINS, A. S., COHEN, A. R., McGUIRE, W. J., JANIS, I. L., FEIERABEND, ROSALIND L., & ANDERSON, N. H.   *The order of presentation in persuasion*. New Haven: Yale Univer. Press, 1957.

JOST, A.   Die Assoziationsfestigkeit in ihrer Abhängigkeit von der Verteilung der Wiederholungen. *Zeitschrift für Psychologie und Physiologie der Sinnesorgane*, 1897, **14**, 436–472.

LUND, F. H.   The psychology of belief: IV. The law of primacy in persuasion. *J. abnorm. soc. Psychol.*, 1925, **20**, 183–191.

MILLER, N. E., & STEVENSON, S. S.   Agitated behavior of rats during experimental extinction and a curve of spontaneous recovery. *J. comp. Psychol.*, 1936, **21**, 205–231.

MILLER, N.   Primacy versus recency: The changing relative effectiveness of two opposing communications with the passage of time. Unpublished master's thesis, Northwestern Univer., 1957.

UNDERWOOD, B. J.   Retroactive and proactive inhibition after five and forty-eight hours. *J. exp. Psychol.*, 1948, **38**, 29–38.

WELD, H. P., & ROFF, M.   A study in the formation of opinion based upon legal evidence. *Amer. J. Psychol.*, 1938, **51**, 609–628.

17. THE EFFECTS OF PRIOR INFORMATION ON SUSCEPTIBILITY TO AN EMOTIONAL APPEAL *

Paul C. Lewan and Ezra Stotland

Considerable research has been done on the order of presentation of persuasive communications. A central problem of the research has been whether the earlier communication has any effect in reducing the effectiveness of the later communcation (Hovland, 1957). In these studies, the communications have typically consisted of a list of arguments to support a given point of view of some object or issue. The present study is addressed to the corollary issue of whether a communication of neutral material about an object can influence the effectiveness of subsequent communications. In the present study, the second communication is primarily emotional in its appeal. In other words, the problem is, "Can the prior acquisition of neutral information concerning some object influence susceptibility to a subsequent appeal regarding that object?"

Studies such as Hartman's (1936) and Janis and Feshbach (1953) have shown at least partially contradictory results. Hartman found that emotional appeals are more effective, while Janis found that extremely emotional appeals are not effective. One possible explanation for the somewhat inconsistent results may lie in the lack of prior information that the subjects had about the object of the appeal. The students of the Janis and Feshbach study may have been better informed about dental hygiene than the voters in Hartman's study

were about public issues. The importance of prior information is also suggested by Cantril's (1940) finding that better educated persons, who were probably better informed, were less influenced by emotionally tinged communications. However, it remains unclear as to whether the lowered susceptibility to influence is a result of a greater fund of information or of greater critical ability. The present study is aimed at showing that regardless of the subject's critical ability, his possession of more information does in fact reduce the affectiveness of an emotional appeal. The following hypothesis was tested:

Persons who have received neutral information regarding a given object lower their evaluation of the object to a lesser extent after hearing an emotional appeal against it than persons who have not received such neutral information.

METHOD

Subjects

Ninety-seven pupils in four twelfth grade social studies classes were used as subjects for this experiment. Approximately 52 percent of the subjects were male. The pupils in each of the four classes were seated in alphabetical order. No ability grouping by class

* Reprinted from *Journal of Abnormal and Social Psychology*, 1961, 62: 450–453, with permission of the senior author and the American Psychological Association.

was apparent to the experimenter; teachers described the classes in each case as "about average."

Experimental Conditions

The experimental groups received an information sheet on the same subject matter area as the emotional appeal; the control group received information on a nonrelevant subject. The possession of relevant prior information by the experimental subjects was the only condition in the design which distinguished the experimental groups from the control groups.

Each class was divided into an experimental and a control group of approximately equal size. Since all classes used alphabetical seating arrangements, subjects were assigned alternately to the experimental or control group by alphabetical order.

Procedure

The experiment can be divided into four major steps: the presentation of the fact sheets, administration of the first attitude scale, presentation of the emotional appeal, administration of the second attitude scale. The experiment was given four times on the same day, once in each of the four twelfth grade social studies classes.

First, the teacher in charge of each class introduced the experiment by informing the students that they were to study a little-known area of Europe in a way somewhat different from the usual classroom routine. The pupils were told that there were to be some tests administered after they had an opportunity to look at some information sheets. The teacher, with the experimenter acting

as an observer, handed out the "fact sheets" to the experimental and control groups. The experimental group received only information on Andorra (described below). The control group received only information of a similar nature about Etruria. The fact sheets consisted of items of information designed to be of a "neutral nature" on a subject matter area with which the students would not ordinarily be acquainted. From the time of the handing out of the information until the end of the experiment, inter-communication between pupils was not permitted. The subjects were instructed to read the fact sheets; when the teacher had observed that all subjects had finished, the sheets were recalled.

Immediately after the reading of the fact sheets the teacher passed out scales exploring the attitude of both groups in the relevant subject matter area (the scales and their construction will be discussed more fully later). Half of each group received Scale A, the other half received Scale B on the initial attitude exploration. The scales in every case were identified by number only, the person responding remaining anonymous.

After the completion and handing back of the first attitude scales, the experimenter was introduced by the teacher as a guest speaker from the University of Washington who would like to present a few remarks about Andorra. The experimenter immediately presented the emotional appeal, which consisted largely of name-calling generalities presenting an unfavorable picture of Andorra and had been edited to present a minimum of factual information.

After the appeal, the speaker retired once more to the role of observer and the teacher gave out the alternate attitude scales to both groups. Those students who had been given Scale A before the emotional appeal were now given Scale B and vice versa.

A comparison of the "change scores" (the difference between scores on the first and second attitude scales) for the experimental and control groups was used to test the hypothesis.

The Attitude Scales

In order to detect the expected changes of attitude in both the experimental and control groups, two "Likert type" attitude scales were constructed, using items similar to the sample shown below:

If an Andorrese (a citizen of Andorra) was coming to your school and you were asked if you would be a "buddy" until this student becomes better acquainted would you.

1. approve
2. disapprove
3. strongly disapprove
4. strongly approve

The Andorrese is basically an honest, hard-working person. Do you:
1. strongly disagree
2. disagree
3. agree
4. strongly agree

Each of the possible four responses for the 22 items on each scale was assigned a value of from one to four with the most unfavorable response (towards Andorra) being assigned the lowest value, the next most unfavorable responses being assigned the second lowest value, etc. The response categories in the scales were randomized in their order for each item to minimize the ef-

fects of position responses by the subjects.

The two forms, designed to be used as alternate scales, had been previously administered to a group of 26 eleventh graders (different from the experimental group) in a social studies class after the students had read the information sheet on Andorra. This class was characterized as an average class by several teachers and was composed of an equal number of boys and girls at the time of the testing, which was 5 weeks previous to the running of the experiment. The students were informed by their teacher, immediately before the passing out of the fact sheets, that this was to be a study of a little-known country of Europe and that some tests were to be administered after the reading. After the reading of the fact sheet, about half the class received the scales in the order AB; the other half received scales in the order BA. After completion of the scales the experimenter answered a few general questions about the subject matter area. The students were not informed as to the intended use of the attitude scales in the later experiment.

The mean score on Scale A was 63.08, the mean score on Scale B was 62.73. A product-moment correlation of .91 (without correction for attenuation) was found to exist between scores on the two forms.

Fact Sheets

The information sheet on Andorra received by the experimental groups was abstracted from *Collier's Encyclopedia* and carefully edited so that the items would be of a "neutral nature," that is, unlikely to form marked attitudes towards or against the subject. The neutral information consisted of the following: a description of the geography, the agriculture, the industry and mining, the language and the use of the flag, the political system and the French representation in foreign affairs, the fiscal system, and the country's origin. The paragraphs on the political system and the fiscal system are cited here as examples:

> The internal affairs are handled by a General Council of Notables, four from each of the country's six parishes, elected by the heads of the landowning families. France usually represents Andorra in foreign affairs and has the right to maintain law and order in emergencies within the country.
>
> The country has a small and balanced budget and uses both French and Spanish currencies since there is no such thing as Andorran coinage or money. Postal service is free within the country, being financed by the sale of Andorran stamps to stamp collectors. The Andorrese have almost no taxes but pay a small tribute every two years to the Bishop of Urgel (Spain) and the President of France, a traditional tribute which has been paid for almost 700 years.

The control group received information of a similar "neutral nature," on Etruria which was condensed from another work in the same source. The two fact sheets can be read in approximately the same length of time (about 8 minutes).

Emotional Appeal

The second "communication," the emotional appeal, was presented orally by the experimenter. It consisted largely of name-calling generalities and was designed to present a minimum of factual information while presenting an unfavorable opinion of the relevant subject

matter area (Andorra). The emotional appeal consisted of an attack on the Andorrese people as being ignorant, amoral, unworthy of membership in the United Nations or of American economic aid, undemocratic, weak, puny, potential dupes of the Communists in the United Nations, and dangerous to world peace. A typical section follows:

> We cannot, today, gamble nor compromise with our principles. The so-called "citizens" of Andorra are known throughout Europe as backward, ignorant, unprincipled, provincial, undemocratic people. They are notorious for being poverty-stricken ne'er-do-wells, uncaring of what happens outside their principality, unchanging, feudal, cold and remote to strangers. The Arkansas hillbilly would be a sophisticated "man of the world" compared to the average Andorrese. It is revealing that the national economy is based upon immorality, is based upon smuggling, blackmarket, and theft to a large extent. In fact, if you were to ask a well-informed person what is the one thing for which Andorra is noted, the answer would probably be "the absence of morality." In these times, when the world appears to be teetering on the brink of disaster, can we afford to give power to people of this sort? The answer must be no, we cannot and must not give to this degenerate country and its immoral people the power to manipulate our lives and destroy our freedom.

RESULTS

The hypothesis of the study is based on the assumption that the information provided to the subjects prior to the initial appeal was neutral with respect to the object of the appeal, Andorra. This assumption does not, however, require that every bit of information given be neutral; rather the total effect of the information should not cause the re-

TABLE 1. MEAN BEFORE-AFTER CHANGES IN ATTITUDES [a] TO ANDORRA
($N = 10$ in each cell [b])

Condition	Favorableness of Attitude Prior to Appeal		
	High	Medium	Low
Experimental	−12.7	−9.5	−8.8
Control	−17.5	−18.1	−12.5

[a] Negative changes mean changes to more unfavorable attitudes.
[b] Some Ns were dropped to equalize the Ns in the cells. The Ns to be dropped were those closest to the mean in each cell before equalization, thereby increasing the variance.

cipients as a group to be more or less favorable to Andorra. The assumption can be tested by comparing the experimental and control groups in their attitudes toward Andorra as measured immediately after they received information about Andorra and Etruria and before hearing the emotional appeal. The mean attitude scale score was 60.54 ($N = 47$) for the experimental groups and 59.22 ($N = 50$) for the control groups, the difference not being significant by a t test. (The higher figure indicates more favorable attitudes.) Thus, the assumption about the neutrality of the information is supported.

The hypothesis was tested by first dividing the sample into three equal groups according to degree of favorableness of attitude toward Andorra prior to the emotional appeal, to control for the differential possibility of change from different positions of favorableness of attitude, and to check on any interaction effects between the experimental treatments and original degree of favorableness. The mean change scores were then computed for each of the three groups in each of the experimental conditions. These data are presented in Table 1. They show that for each degree of original favorableness, the subjects in the experimental condition changed less after the negative emotional appeal than subjects in the control condition toward being more unfavorable to Andorra. The analysis of variance shown in Table 2 indicates that this difference is significant at the .05 level. The analysis of variance also shows no significant interaction, indicating that the experimental effect was the same for

TABLE 2. ANALYSIS OF VARIANCE OF CHANGES OF ATTITUDE

Source of Variation	SS	df	MS	F
Experimental condition	478.3	1	478.3	5.49[a]
Original attitude position	209.4	2	104.7	ns
Interaction	66.1	2	33.1	ns
Within cells	4793.1	54	88.8	ns

[a] $p < .05$.

subjects at all levels of original attitude. The hypothesis is therefore supported. The acquisition of neutral information about Andorra did serve as a deterrent to susceptibility to an emotional appeal against Andorra.

DISCUSSION

One interpretation of these results would hold that the prior information creates a cognitive structure with regard to the object of the attitude, which then serves as a source of attitudinal constancy, since any change in the evaluation of the object tends to require support from the cognitive structure regarding the object. To the extent that such a cognitive structure contains elements inconsistent with the changed evaluation of the object, the person should resist changing his evaluation of the object of the attitude. This interpretation is consistent with the approach of Krech and Crutchfield (1948).

The results of this study concerned resistance to changes in a negative direction. The obvious question arises as to whether such information would also act as a deterrent to changes in a positive direction. If the process underlying the presently observed effect is simply, as just suggested, that information provides an anchor or a basis of constancy of attitude, then the information should prevent positive changes as well. However, other processes may underlie the effect. For example, as a result of their familiarity with Andorra, the subjects may have identified with it, and, thus, become resistant to any negative appeal about Andorra. If this interpretation is valid, it might be expected that the better informed subjects would then be more susceptible to a positive emotional appeal than the less well informed ones. The importance of the factor of familiarity with, and consequent identification with, the object of the attitude can be tested by a study in which familiarity is systematically varied without varying the amount of information given about the object. In any case, it is possible that the present results can be generalized only to resistance to negative appeals and not to resistance to positive appeals.

Another possible limitation to the generalizability of the findings derives from the fact that it is impossible to make an emotional appeal without at the same time communicating some "information," even if it is minimal and/or false. In some cases, this "information" may be contrary to the originally imparted, neutral information. In this case, the results would be the same as in the present study, the original information presumably having the greater effect, as in Luchin's (1957) study. In other cases, the emotionally communicated "information" may be consistent with the prior, neutral information, or may give the neutral information an additional context in which the prior information is no longer neutral but supports an extreme pro or con attitude. In these cases, the outcome would probably be the opposite of the present study, the prior information increasing the likelihood of later susceptibility to an emotional appeal.

SUMMARY

The hypothesis of this study was that persons who have received neutral information with respect to an object lower their evaluation of the object to a lesser extent after hearing an emotional appeal against it than persons who have not received such neutral information. The hypothesis was tested in an experiment done in high school classes, using an object with which the subjects had little or no prior acquaintance. The results confirmed the hypothesis.

REFERENCES

CANTRIL, H. *The invasion from Mars.* Princeton: Princeton Univer. Press, 1940.

HARTMAN, G. W. A field experiment on the comparative effectiveness of "emotional" and "rational" political leaflets in determining election results. *J. abnorm. soc. Psychol.*, 1936, **31**, 99–114.

HOVLAND, C. (Ed.) *The order of presentation in persuasion.* New Haven: Yale Univer. Press, 1957.

JANIS, I., & FESHBACH, S. Effects of fear-arousing communications, *J. abnorm. soc. Psychol.*, 1953, **48**, 78–92.

KRECH, D., & CRUTCHFIELD, R. *Theory and problems of social psychology.* New York: McGraw-Hill, 1948.

LUCHINS, A. S. Primacy—recency in impression formation. In C. Hovland (Ed.), *The order of presentation in persuasion.* New Haven: Yale Univer. Press, 1957.

18. RECONCILING CONFLICTING RESULTS DERIVED FROM EXPERIMENTAL AND SURVEY STUDIES OF ATTITUDE CHANGE *

Carl I. Hovland

Two quite different types of research design are characteristically used to study the modification of attitudes through communication. In the first type, the *experiment*, individuals are given a controlled exposure to a communication and the effects evaluated in terms of the amount of change in attitude or opinion produced. A base line is provided by means of a control group not exposed to the communication. The study of Gosnell (1927) on the influence of leaflets designed to get voters to the polls is a classic example of the controlled experiment.

In the alternative research design, the *sample survey*, information is secured through interviews or questionnaires both concerning the respondent's exposure to various communications and his attitudes and opinions on various issues. Generalizations are then derived from the correlations obtained between reports of exposure and measurements of attitude. In a variant of this method, measurements of attitude and of exposure to communication are obtained during repeated interviews with the same individual over a period of weeks or months. This is the "panel method" extensively utilized in studying the impact of various mass media on

* Slightly abridged, from the *American Psychologist*, 1959, 14: 8–17, with permission of the American Psychological Association.

political attitudes and on voting behavior (cf., for example, Kendall & Lazarsfeld, 1950).

Generalizations derived from experimental and from correlational studies of communication effects are usually both reported in chapters on the effects of mass media and in other summaries of research on attitude, typically without much stress on the type of study from which the conclusion was derived. Close scrutiny of the results obtained from the two methods, however, suggests a marked difference in the picture of communcation effects obtained from each. The object of my paper is to consider the conclusions derived from these two types of design, to suggest some of the factors responsible for the frequent divergence in results, and then to formulate principles aimed at reconciling some of the apparent conflicts.

DIVERGENCE

The picture of mass communcation effects which emerges from correlational studies is one in which few individuals are seen as being affected by communications. One of the most thorough correlational studies of the effects of mass media on attitudes is that of Lazarsfeld, Berelson, and Gaudet published in *The People's Choice* (1944). In this report there is an extensive chapter devoted to the effects of various media, particularly radio, newspapers, and magazines. The authors conclude that few changes in attitudes were produced. They estimate that the political positions of only about 5 percent of their respondents were changed by the election campaign, and they are inclined to attribute even this small amount of change more to per-

sonal influence than to the mass media. A similar evaluation of mass media is made in the recent chapter in the *Handbook of Social Psychology* by Lipset and his collaborators (1954).

Research using experimental procedures, on the other hand, indicates the possibility of considerable modifiability of attitudes through exposure to communication. In both Klapper's survey (1949) and in my chapter in the *Handbook of Social Psychology* (Hovland, 1954) a number of experimental studies are discussed in which the opinions of a third to a half or more of the audience are changed.

The discrepancy between the results derived from these two methodologies raises some fascinating problems for analysis. This divergence in outcome appears to me to be largely attributable to two kinds of factors: one, the difference in research design itself; and, two, the historical and traditional differences in general approach to evaluation characteristic of researchers using the experimental as contrasted with the correlational or survey method. I would like to discuss, first, the influence these factors have on the estimation of overall effects of communications and, then, turn to other divergences in outcome characteristically found by the use of the experimental and survey methodology.

Undoubtedly the most critical and interesting variation in the research *design* involved in the two procedures is that resulting from differences in definition of exposure. In an experiment the audience on whom the effects are being evaluated is one which is fully exposed to the communication. On the other hand, in naturalistic situations with which surveys are typically concerned, the outstanding phenomenon is the limitation of the audience to those who *expose themselves* to the communication. Some of the individuals in a captive audience experiment would, of course, expose themselves in the course of natural events to a communication of the type studied; but many others would not. The group which does expose itself is usually a highly biased one, since most individuals "expose themselves most of the time to the kind of material with which they agree to begin with" (Lipset et al., 1954, p. 1158). Thus one reason for the difference in results between experiments and correlational studies is that experiments describe the effects of exposure on the whole range of individuals studied, some of whom are initially in favor of the position being advocated and some who are opposed, whereas surveys primarily describe the effects produced on those already in favor of the point of view advocated in the communication. The amount of change is thus, of course, much smaller in surveys. Lipset and his collaborators make this same evaluation, stating that:

As long as we test a program in the laboratory we always find that it has great effect on the attitudes and interests of the experimental subjects. But when we put the program on as a regular broadcast, we then note that the people who are most influenced in the laboratory tests are those who, in a realistic situation, do not listen to the program. The controlled experiment always greatly overrates effects, as compared with those that really occur, because of the self-selection of audiences (Lipset et al., 1954, p. 1158).

Differences in the second category are not inherent in the design of the two alternatives, but are characteristic of the way researchers using the two methods typically proceed.

The first difference within this class is in the size of the communication unit typically studied. In the majority of survey studies the unit evaluated is an entire program of communication. For example, in studies of political behavior an attempt is made to assess the effects of all newspaper reading and television viewing on attitudes toward the major parties. In the typical experiment, on the other hand, the interest is usually in some particular variation in the content of the communications, and experimental evaluations much more frequently involve single communications. On this point results are thus not directly comparable.

Another characteristic difference between the two methods is in the time interval used in evaluation. In the typical experiment the time at which the effect is observed is usually rather soon after exposure to the communication. In the survey study, on the other hand, the time perspective is such that much more remote effects are usually evaluated. When effects decline with the passage of time, the net outcome will, of course, be that of accentuating the effect obtained in experimental studies as compared with those obtained in survey researches. Again it must be stressed that the difference is not inherent in the designs as such. Several experiments, including our own on the effects of motion pictures (Hovland, Lumsdaine, & Sheffield, 1949) and later studies on the "sleeper effect" (Hovland & Weiss, 1951; Kelman & Hovland, 1953), have studied retention over considerable periods of time.

Some of the difference in outcome may be attributable to the types of communicators characteristically used and to the motive-incentive conditions operative in the two situations. In experimental studies communications are frequently presented in a classroom situation. This may involve quite different types of factors from those operative in the more naturalistic communication situation with which the survey researchers are concerned. In the classroom there may be some implicit sponsorship of the communication by the teacher and the school administration. In the survey studies the communicators may often be remote individuals either unfamiliar to the recipients, or outgroupers clearly known to espouse a point of view opposed to that held by many members of the audience. Thus there may be real differences in communicator credibility in laboratory and survey researches. The net effect of the differences will typically be in the direction of increasing the likelihood of change in the experimental as compared with the survey study.

There is sometimes an additional situational difference. Communications of the type studied by survey researchers usually involve reaching the individual in his natural habitat, with consequent supplementary effects produced by discussion with friends and family. In the laboratory studies a classroom situation with low postcommunication interaction is more typically involved. Several studies, including one by Harold Kelley reported in our volume on *Communication and Persuasion* (Hovland, Janis, & Kelley, 1953), indicate that, when a communication is presented in a situation which makes group membership salient, the individual is typically more resistant to counternorm influence than when the communication is presented

under conditions of low salience of group membership (cf. also, Katz & Lazarsfeld, 1955, pp. 48–133).

A difference which is almost wholly adventitious is in the types of populations utilized. In the survey design there is, typically, considerable emphasis on a random sample of the entire population. In the typical experiment, on the other hand, there is a consistent over-representation of high school students and college sophomores, primarily on the basis of their greater accessibility. But as Tolman has said: "college sophomores may not be people." Whether differences in the type of audience studied contribute to the differences in effect obtained with the two methods is not known.

Finally, there is an extremely important difference in the studies of the experimental and correlational variety with respect to the type of issue discussed in the communications. In the typical experiment we are interested in studying a set of factors or conditions which are expected on the basis of theory to influence the extent of effect of the communication. We usually deliberately try to find types of issues involving attitudes which are susceptible to modification through communication. Otherwise, we run the risk of no measurable effects, particularly with small-scale experiments. In the survey procedures, on the other hand, socially significant attitudes which are deeply rooted in prior experience and involve much personal commitment are typically involved. This is especially true in voting studies which have provided us with so many of our present results on social influence. I shall have considerably more to say about this problem a little later.

The differences so far discussed have primarily concerned the extent of overall effectiveness indicated by the two methods: why survey results typically show little modification of attitudes by communication while experiments indicate marked changes. Let me now turn to some of the other differences in generalizations derived from the two alternative designs. Let me take as the second main area of disparate results the research on the effect of varying distances between the position taken by the communicator and that held by the recipient of the communication. Here it is a matter of comparing changes for persons who at the outset closely agree with the communicator with those for others who are mildly or strongly in disagreement with him. In the naturalistic situation studied in surveys the typical procedure is to determine changes in opinion following reported exposure to communication for individuals differing from the communicator by varying amounts. This gives rise to two possible artifacts. When the communication is at one end of a continuum, there is little room for improvement for those who differ from the communication by small amounts, but a great deal of room for movement among those with large discrepancies. This gives rise to a spurious degree of positive relationship between the degree of discrepancy and the amount of change. Regression effects will also operate in the direction of increasing the correlation. What is needed is a situation in which the distance factor can be manipulated independently of the subject's initial position. An attempt to set up these conditions experimentally was made in a study by Pritzker and the writer (1957). The method involved preparing individual communications presented in booklet form so that the position of the communicator could be set at any desired distance from the subject's initial position. Communicators highly acceptable to the subjects were used. A number of different topics were employed, including the likelihood of a cure for cancer within five years, the desirability of compulsory voting, and the adequacy of five hours of sleep per night.

It was found that the greater the amount of change advocated, the greater the average amount of opinion change produced. Similar results have been reported by Goldberg (1954) and by French (1956).

But these results are not in line with our hunches as to what would happen in a naturalistic situation with important social issues. We felt that here other types of response than change in attitude would occur. So Muzafer Sherif, O. J. Harvey, and the writer (1957) set up a situation to simulate as closely as possible the conditions typically involved when individuals are exposed to major social issue communications at differing distances from their own position. The issue used was the desirability of prohibition. The study was done in two states (Oklahoma and Texas) where there is prohibition or local option, so that the wet-dry issue is hotly debated. We concentrated on three aspects of the problem: How favorably will the communicator be received when his position is at varying distances from that of the recipient? How will what the communicator says be perceived and interpreted by individuals at varying distances from his position? What will be the amount of opinion change produced when small and large deviations in position of

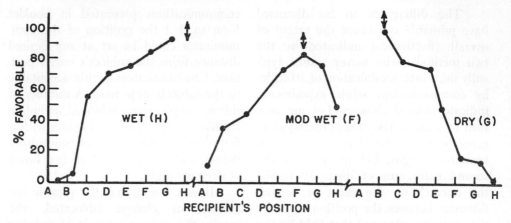

Figure 1. Percentage of favorable evaluations ("fair," "unbiased," etc.) of wet (H), moderately wet (F), and dry (B) communications for subjects holding various positions on prohibition. Recipients position range from A (very dry) to H (very wet). Position of communications indicated by arrow. [From Hovland, Harvey, & Sherif, 1957]

communication and recipient are involved?

Three communications, one strongly wet, one strongly dry, and one moderately wet, were employed. The results bearing on the first problem, of *reception*, are presented in Figure 1. The positions of the subjects are indicated on the abscissa in letters from A (extreme dry) to H (strongly wet). The positions of the communication are also indicated in the same letters, B indicating a strongly dry communication, H a strongly wet, and F a moderately wet. Along the ordinate there is plotted the percentage of subjects with each position on the issue who described the communication as "fair" and "unbiased." It will be seen that the degree of distance between the recipient and the communicator greatly influences the evaluation of the fairness of the communication. When a communication is directed at the pro-dry position, nearly all of the dry subjects consider it fair and impartial, but only a few percent

of the wet subjects consider the identical communication fair. The reverse is true at the other end of the scale. When an intermediate position is adopted, the percentages fall off sharply on each side. Thus under the present conditions with a relatively ambiguous communicator one of the ways of dealing with strongly discrepant positions is to *discredit* the communicator, considering him unfair and biased.

A second way in which an individual can deal with discrepancy is by distortion of what is said by the communicator. Thus is a phenomenon extensively studied by Cooper and Jahoda (1947). In the present study, subjects were asked to state what position they thought was taken by the communicator on the prohibition question. Their evaluation of his position could then be analyzed in relation to their own position. These results are shown in Figure 2 for the moderately wet communication. It will be observed that there is a tendency for individuals whose position is close to that of the communicator to report on the communicator's position quite accurately, for individuals a little bit removed to report his position to be substantially more like their own (which we call an "assimilation effect"), and for those with more discrepant positions to report the communicator's position as more extreme than it really was. This we refer to as a "contrast effect."

Now to our primary results on opinion change. It was found that individuals whose position was only slightly discrepant from the communicator's were influenced to a greater extent than those whose positions deviated to a larger extent. When a wet position was espoused, 28 percent of the middle-of-the-road subjects were changed in the direction of the communicator, as compared with only 4 percent of the drys. With the dry communication 14 percent of the middle-of-the-roaders were changed, while only 4 percent of the wets were changed. Thus, more of the subjects with small discrepancies were changed then were those with large discrepancies.

These results appear to indicate that, under conditions when there is some ambiguity about the credibility of the communicator and when the subject is deeply involved with the issue, the greater the attempt at change the higher the resistance. On the other hand, with highly respected communicators, as in the previous study with Pritzker using issues of lower involvement, the greater the discrepancy the greater the effect.

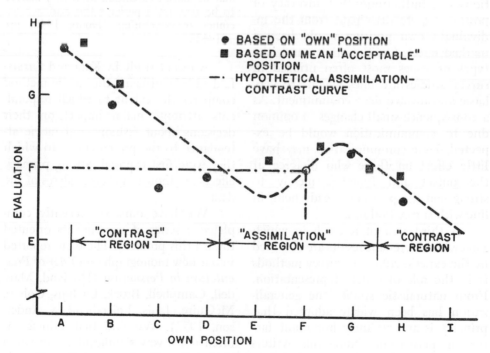

Figure 2. Average placement of position of moderately wet communication (*F*) by subjects holding various positions on the issue, plotted against hypothetical assimilation-contrast curve. [From Hovland, Harvey, & Sherif, 1957]

A study related to ours has just been completed by Zimbardo (1959) which indicates that, when an influence attempt is made by a strongly positive communicator (i.e., a close personal friend), the greater the discrepancy the greater the opinion change, even when the experimenter made a point of stressing the great importance of the subject's opinion.

The implication of these results for our primary problem of conflicting results is clear. The types of issues with which most experiments deal are relatively uninvolving and are often of the variety where expert opinion is highly relevant, as for example, on topics of health, science, and the like. Here we should expect that opinion would be considerably affected by communications and furthermore that advocacy of positions quite discrepant from the individual's own position would have a marked effect. On the other hand, the types of issues most often utilized in survey studies are ones which are very basic and involve deep commitment. As a consequence small changes in opinion due to communication would be expected. Here communication may have little effect on those who disagree at the outset and function merely to strengthen the position already held, in line with survey findings.

A third area of research in which somewhat discrepant results are obtained by the experimental and survey methods is in the role of order of presentation. From naturalistic studies the generalization has been widely adopted that primacy is an extremely important factor in persuasion. Numerous writers have reported that what we experience first has a critical role in what we believe. This is particularly stressed in studies of propaganda effects in various countries when the nation getting across its message first is alleged to have a great advantage and in commercial advertising where "getting a beat on the field" is stressed. The importance of primacy in political propaganda is indicated in the following quotation from Doob:

The propagandist scores an initial advantage whenever his propaganda reaches people before that of his rivals. Readers or listeners are then biased to comprehend, forever after, the event as it has been initially portrayed to them. If they are told in a headline or a flash that the battle has been won, the criminal has been caught, or the bill is certain to pass the legislature, they will usually expect subsequent information to substantiate this first impression. When later facts prove otherwise, they may be loath to abandon what they believe to be true until perhaps the evidence becomes overwhelming (Doob, 1948, pp. 421–422).

A recent study by Katz and Lazarsfeld (1955) utilizing the survey method compares the extent to which respondents attribute major impact on their decisions about fashions and movie attendance to the presentations to which they were first exposed. Strong primacy effects are shown in their analyses of the data.

We have ourselves recently completed a series of experiments oriented toward this problem. These are reported in our new monograph on *Order of Presentation in Persuasion* (Hovland, Mandell, Campbell, Brock, Luchins, Cohen, McGuire, Janis, Feierabend, & Anderson, 1957). We find that primacy is often *not* a very significant factor when the relative effectiveness of the first side of an issue is compared experimentally with that of the second. The research suggests that differences in design may account for much of the discrepancy. A key variable is whether there is exposure to both sides or whether only one side is actually received. In naturalistic studies the advantage of the first side is often not only that it is first but that it is often then the only side of the issue to which the individual is exposed. Having once been influenced, many individuals make up their mind and are no longer interested in other communications on the issue. In most experiments on order of presentation, on the other hand, the audience is systematically exposed to both sides. Thus under survey conditions, self-exposure tends to increase the impact of primacy.

Two other factors to which I have already alluded appear significant in determining the amount of primacy effect. One is the nature of the communicator, the other the setting in which the communication is received. In our volume Luchins presents results indicating that, when the same communicator presents contradictory material, the point of view read first has more influence. On the other hand, Mandell and I show that, when two different communicators present opposing views successively, little primacy effect is obtained. The communications setting factor operates similarly. When the issue and the conditions of presentation make clear that the points of view are controversial, little primacy is obtained.

Thus in many of the situations with which there had been great concern as to undesirable effects of primacy, such as in legal trials, election campaigns, and political debate, the role of primacy appears to have been exaggerated, since the conditions there are those least conducive to primacy effects: the issue is clearly defined as controversial, the partisanship of the communicator is usually established, and different communicators present the opposing sides.

Time does not permit me to discuss other divergences in results obtained in survey and experimental studies, such as those concerned with the effects of repetition of presentation, the relationship between level of intelligence and susceptibility to attitude change, or the relative impact of mass media and personal influence. Again, however, I am sure that detailed analysis will reveal differential factors at work which can account for the apparent disparity in the generalizations derived.

INTEGRATION

On the basis of the foregoing survey of results, I reach the conclusion that no contradiction has been established between the data provided by experimental and correlational studies. Instead it appears that the seeming divergence can be satisfactorily accounted for on the basis of a different definition of the communication situation (including the phenomenon of self-selection) and differences in the type of communicator, audience, and kind of issue utilized.

But there remains the task of better integrating the findings associated with the two methodologies. This is a problem closely akin to that considered by the members of the recent Social Science Research Council summer seminar on *Narrowing the Gap Between Field Studies and Laboratory Studies in Social Psychology* (Riecken, 1954). Many of their recommendations are pertinent to our present problem.

What seems to me quite apparent

is that a genuine understanding of the effects of communications on attitudes requires both the survey and the experimental methodologies. At the same time there appear to be certain inherent limitations of each method which must be understood by the researcher if he is not to be blinded by his preoccupation with one or the other type of design. Integration of the two methodologies will require on the part of the experimentalist an awareness of the narrowness of the laboratory in interpreting the larger and more comprehensive effects of communication. It will require on the part of the survey researcher a greater awareness of the limitations of the correlational method as a basis for establishing causal relationships.

The framework within which survey research operates is most adequately and explicitly dealt with by Berelson, Lazarsfeld, and McPhee in their book on Voting (1954). The model used by the survey researcher, particularly when he employs the "panel" method, stresses the large number of simultaneous and interacting influences affecting attitudes and opinions. Even more significant is its provision for a variety of "feedback" phenomena in which consequences wrought by previous influences affect processes normally considered as occurring earlier in the sequence. In contrast, the experimentalist frequently tends to view the communication process as one in which some single manipulative variable is the primary determinant of the subsequent attitude change. He is, of course, aware in a general way of the importance of context, and he frequently studies interaction effects as well as main effects; but he still is less attentive than he might be to the complexity of the influence situation and the numerous

possibilities for feedback loops. Undoubtedly the real life communication situation is better described in terms of the survey type of model. We are all familiar, for example, with the interactions in which attitudes predispose one to acquire certain types of information, that this often leads to changes in attitude which may result in further acquisition of knowledge, which in turn produces more attitude change, and so on. Certainly the narrow question sometimes posed by experiments as to the effect of knowledge on attitudes greatly underestimates these interactive effects.

But while the conceptualization of the survey researcher is often very valuable, his correlational research design leaves much to be desired. Advocates of correlational analysis often cite the example of a science built on observation exclusively without experiment: astronomy. But here a very limited number of space-time concepts are involved and the number of competing theoretical formulations is relatively small so that it is possible to limit alternative theories rather drastically through correlational evidence. But in the area of communication effects and social psychology generally the variables are so numerous and so intertwined that the correlational methodology is primarily useful to suggest hypotheses and not to establish casual relationships (Hovland et al., 1949, pp. 329–340; Maccoby, 1956). Even with the much simpler relationships involved in biological systems there are grave difficulties of which we are all aware these days when we realize how difficult it is to establish through correlation whether eating of fats is or is not a cause of heart disease or whether or not smoking is a cause of lung cancer. In communications research the complexity of the problem makes it inherently difficult to derive causal relationships from correlational analysis where experimental control of exposure is not possible. And I do not agree with my friends the Lazarsfelds (Kendall & Lazarsfeld, 1950) concerning the effectiveness of the panel method in circumventing this problem since parallel difficulties are raised when the relationships occur over a time span.

These difficulties constitute a challenge to the experimentalist in this area of research to utilize the broad framework for studying communication effects suggested by the survey researcher, but to employ well controlled experimental design to work on those aspects of the field which are amenable to experimental manipulation and control. It is, of course, apparent that there are important communication problems which cannot be attacked directly by experimental methods. It is not, for example, feasible to modify voting behavior by manipulation of the issues discussed by the opposed parties during a particular campaign. It is not feasible to assess the effects of communications over a very long span of time. For example, one cannot visualize experimental procedures for answering the question of what has been the impact of the reading of *Das Kapital* or *Uncle Tom's Cabin*. These are questions which can be illuminated by historical and sociological study but cannot be evaluated in any rigorous experimental fashion.

But the scope of problems which do lend themselves to experimental attack is very broad. Even complex interactions can be fruitfully attacked by experiment. The possibilities are clearly shown in studies like that of Sherif and Sherif (1953) on factors influencing cooperative and competitive behavior in a camp for adolescent boys. They were able to bring under manipulative control many of the types of interpersonal relationships ordinarily considered impossible to modify experimentally, and to develop motivations of an intensity characteristic of real-life situations. It should be possible to do similar studies in the communication area with a number of the variables heretofore only investigated in uncontrolled naturalistic settings by survey procedures.

In any case it appears eminently practical to minimize many of the differences which were discussed above as being not inherent in design but more or less adventitiously linked with one or the other method. Thus there is no reason why more complex and deeply-involving social issues cannot be employed in experiments rather than the more superficial ones more commonly used. The resistance to change of socially important issues may be a handicap in studying certain types of attitude change; but, on the other hand, it is important to understand the lack of modifiability of opinion with highly involving issues. Greater representation of the diverse types of communicators found in naturalistic situations can also be achieved. In addition, it should be possible to do experiments with a wider range of populations to reduce the possibility that many of our present generalizations from experiments are unduly affected by their heavy weighting of college student characteristics, including high literacy, alertness, and rationality.

A more difficult task is that of experimentally evaluating communications under conditions of self-selection of exposure. But this is not at all impossible in theory. It should be possible to assess what demographic and personality factors predispose one to expose oneself to particular communications and then to utilize experimental and control groups having these characteristics. Under some circumstances the evaluation could be made on only those who select themselves, with both experimental and control groups coming from the self-selected audience.

Undoubtedly many of the types of experiments which could be set up involving or simulating naturalistic conditions will be too ambitious and costly to be feasible even if possible in principle. This suggests the continued use of small-scale experiments which seek to isolate some of the key variables operative in complex situations. From synthesis of component factors, prediction of complex outcomes may be practicable. It is to this analytic procedure for narrowing the gap between laboratory and field research that we have devoted major attention in our research program. I will merely indicate briefly here some of the ties between our past work and the present problem.

We have attempted to assess the influence of the communicator by varying his expertness and attractiveness, as in the studies by Kelman, Weiss, and the writer (Hovland & Weiss, 1951; Kelman & Hovland, 1953). Further data on this topic were presented earlier in this paper.

We have also been concerned with evaluating social interaction effects. Some of the experiments on group affiliation as a factor affecting resistance to counternorm communication and the role of salience of group membership by Hal Kelley and others are reported in *Communication and Persuasion* (Hovland et al., 1953).

Starting with the studies carried out during the war on orientation films by Art Lumsdaine, Fred Sheffield, and the writer (1949), we have had a strong interest in the duration of communication effects. Investigation of effects at various time intervals has helped to bridge the gap between assessment of immediate changes with those of longer duration like those involved in survey studies. More recent extensions of this work have indicated the close relationship between the credibility of the communicator and the extent of postcommunication increments, or "sleeper effects" (Hovland & Weiss, 1951; Kelman & Hovland, 1953).

The nature of individual differences in susceptibility to persuasion via communication has been the subject of a number of our recent studies. The generality of persuasibility has been investigated by Janis and collaborators and the development of persuasibility in children has been studied by Abelson and Lesser. A volume concerned with these audience factors to which Janis, Abelson, Lesser, Field, Rife, King, Cohen, Linton, Graham, and the writer have contributed will appear under the title *Personality and Persuasibility* (1959).

Lastly, there remains the question of how the nature of the issues used in the communication affects the extent of change in attitude. We have only made a small beginning on these problems. In the research reported in *Experiments on Mass Communication*, we showed that the magnitude of effects was directly related to the type of attitude involved: film communications had a significant effect on opinions related to straightforward interpretations of policies and events, but had little or no effect on more deeply intrenched attitudes and motivations. Further work on the nature of issues is represented in the study by Sherif, Harvey, and the writer (1957) which was discussed above. There we found a marked contrast between susceptibility to influence and the amount of ego-involvement in the issue. But the whole concept of ego-involvement is a fuzzy one, and here is an excellent area for further work seeking to determine the theoretical factors involved in different types of issues.

With this brief survey of possible ways to bridge the gap between experiment and survey I must close. I should like to stress in summary the mutual importance of the two approaches to the problem of communication effectiveness. Neither is a royal road to wisdom, but each represents an important emphasis. The challenge of future work is one of fruitfully combining their virtues so that we may develop a social psychology of communication with the conceptual breadth provided by correlational study of process and with the rigorous but more delimited methodology of the experiment.

REFERENCES

BERELSON, B. R., LAZARSFELD, P. F., & McPHEE, W. N. *Voting: A study of opinion formation in a presidential campaign.* Chicago: Univer. Chicago Press, 1954.

COOPER, EUNICE, & JAHODA, MARIE. The evasion of propaganda: How prejudiced people respond to antiprejudice propaganda. *J. Psychol.,* 1947, 23, 15–25.

DOOB, L. W. *Public opinion and propaganda.* New York: Holt, 1948.

FRENCH, J. R. P., JR. A formal theory of social power. *Psychol. Rev.,* 1956, 63, 181–194.

GOLDBERG, S. C. Three situational determinants of conformity to social norms.

J. abnorm. soc. Psychol., 1954, 49, 325–329.

GOSNELL, H. F. *Getting out the vote: An experiment in the stimulation of voting.* Chicago: Univer. Chicago Press, 1927.

HOVLAND, C. I. Effects of the mass media of communication. In G. Lindzey (Ed.), *Handbook of social psychology.* Vol. II. *Special fields and applications.* Cambridge, Mass.: Addison-Wesley, 1954. Pp. 1062–1103.

HOVLAND, C. I., HARVEY, O. J., & SHERIF, M. Assimilation and contrast effects in reactions to communication and attitude change. *J. abnorm. soc. Psychol.,* 1957, 55, 244–252.

HOVLAND, C. I., JANIS, I. L., & KELLEY, H. H. *Communication and persuasion.* New Haven: Yale Univer. Press, 1953.

HOVLAND, C. I., LUMSDAINE, A. A., & SHEFFIELD, F. D. *Experiments on mass communication.* Princeton: Princeton Univer. Press, 1949.

HOVLAND, C. I., MANDELL, W., CAMPBELL, ENID H., BROCK, T., LUCHINS, A. S., COHEN, A. R., McGUIRE, W. J., JANIS, I. L., FEIERABEND, ROSALIND, L., & ANDERSON, N. H. *The order of presentation in persuasion.* New Haven: Yale Univer. Press, 1957.

HOVLAND, C. I., & PRITZKER, H. A. Extent of opinion change as a function of amount of change advocated. *J. abnorm. soc. Psychol.,* 1957, 54, 257–261.

HOVLAND, C. I., & WEISS, W. The influence of source credibility on communication effectiveness. *Publ. opin. Quart.,* 1951, 15, 635–650.

JANIS, I. L., HOVLAND, C. I., FIELD, P. B., LINTON, HARRIETT, GRAHAM, ELAINE, COHEN, A. R., RIFE, D., ABELSON, R. P., LESSER, G. S., & KING, B. T. *Personality and persuasibility.* New Haven: Yale Univer. Press, 1959.

KATZ, E., & LAZARSFELD, P. F. *Personal influence.* New York: Free Press, 1955.

KELMAN, H. C., & HOVLAND, C. I. "Reinstatement" of the communicator in delayed measurement of opinion change. *J. abnorm. soc. Psychol.,* 1953, 48, 327–335.

KENDALL, PATRICIA L., & LAZARSFELD, P. F. Problems of survey analysis. In

R. K. Merton & P. F. Lazarsfeld (Eds.), *Continuities in social research: Studies in the scope and method of "The American Soldier."* New York: Free Press, 1950. Pp. 133–196.

KLAPPER, J. T. *The effects of mass media.* New York: Columbia Univer. Bureau of Applied Social Research, 1949. (Mimeo.)

LAZARSFELD, P. F., BERELSON, B., & GAUDET, HAZEL. *The people's choice.* New York: Duell, Sloan, & Pearce, 1944.

LIPSET, S. M., LAZARSFELD, P. F., BARTON, A. H., & LINZ, J. The psychology of voting: An analysis of political behavior. In G. Lindzey (Ed.), *Handbook of social psychology.* Vol. II. *Special fields and applications.* Cambridge, Mass.: Addison-Wesley, 1954. Pp. 1124–1175.

MACCOBY, ELEANOR E. Pitfalls in the analysis of panel data: A research note on some technical aspects of voting. *Amer. J. Sociol.,* 1956, **59,** 359–362.

RIECKEN, H. W. (Chairman) Narrowing the gap between field studies and laboratory experiments in social psychology: A statement by the summer seminar. *Items Soc. Sci. Res. Council,* 1954, **8,** 37–42.

SHERIF, M., & SHERIF, CAROLYN W. *Groups in harmony and tension: An integration of studies on intergroup relations.* New York: Harper & Row, 1953.

ZIMBARDO, P. G. Involvement and communication discrepancy as determinants of opinion change. Unpublished doctoral dissertation, Yale University, 1959.

19.   PERSISTENCE OF THE RESISTANCE TO PERSUASION INDUCED BY VARIOUS TYPES OF PRIOR BELIEF DEFENSES *

William J. McGuire

A number of previous studies have tested the relative efficacy of various types of prior defenses in making a person's belief resistant to change when he is later confronted with massive counterarguments against the belief. None of these previous studies were designed to measure the effect on resistance of varying the time interval between the defense and the attack. By systematically varying this interval, the present experiment investigates the relative persistence of the immunity of persuasion conferred by the different types of prior defenses. It is of some interest to know for each type of defense the rate at which its conferred immunity decays over time. Of even greater theoretical interest are comparisons among the decay rates for the different types of defense.

The predictions regarding these differential decay rates derive from the same postulates as gave rise to the earlier predictions, tested and confirmed in previous experiments, regarding the relative immunizing effectiveness of various defenses *without* regard to the time interval between defense and attack. Hence, it is useful to mention several of the relevant previous findings and their theoretical bases. The previous studies, and the present one as well,

* Reprinted from the *Journal of Abnormal and Social Psychology,* 1962, 64: 241–248, with permission of the author and the American Psychological Association. This study was supported, in part, by a grant from the National Science Foundation, Division of Social Sciences.

used cultural truisms as the beliefs being defended and attacked—for example, the belief that "We should brush our teeth after every meal if at all possible." It had been postulated that there is little belief-dissonant information available regarding such cultural truisms in the person's normal ideological environment. This unavailability, combined with the characteristic tendency to avoid even such belief-dissonant material as is available, would have left the person underestimating the vulnerability of his belief and, hence, unmotivated to acquire bolstering material and unprepared to deal with strong counterarguments when he is forced to expose himself to them.

From this theoretical analysis follow several of the previously confirmed hypotheses regarding immunization against persuasion which are relevant to the hypotheses being tested in the present experiment. One of these previous findings (McGuire & Papageorgis, 1961) is that prior refutational defenses are superior to prior supportive defenses in making cultural truisms resistant to subsequent persuasion. Refutational defenses involve mention and refutation of possible counterarguments against the belief, while ignoring arguments positively supporting the belief. Supportive defenses do mention and elaborate arguments positively supporting the belief, while ignoring possible counterarguments against it. This superiority of the refutational defense would follow from the above theoretical assumptions, since the refutational defense contains a threatening element—mention of the counterarguments to whose existence the subject has probably given little, if any thought—which stimulates him to bolster his belief. The supportive defense

of the truism, on the other hand, seems to labor the obvious, so that the subject is little motivated to assimilate the positive arguments and is left, if anything, even less motivated to bolster further the belief he regards as obvious.

It was also demonstrated (Papageorgis & McGuire, 1961) that the refutational defense confers resistance to subsequent attacks even by novel counterarguments, different from those explicitly refuted in the defense. This conferral of generalized immunity by the refutational defense also follows from the theoretical assumptions. The immunizing efficacy derives not only from weakening the credibility of the specific counterarguments refuted, but also from the threat induced stimulation to bolster one's defense. Hence, the refutational defense increases resistance even to attacks by counterarguments other than those refuted.

The foregoing theoretical interpretation of the previous findings gives rise to three predictions regarding the temporal persistence of the resistance conferred by the different types of prior defense. First, it is hypothesized that the supportive defense will not only be initially inferior to the refutational in the amount of resistance it confers, but in addition that such resistance as it does confer will decay more rapidly than that conferred by the refutational defense. This prediction follows from the above interpretation that the immunizing efficacy of the supportive defense derives solely from the acquaintance with the positive arguments which it contains and which tend to be forgotten over time; the efficacy of the refutational defenses, on the other hand, derives in part from the threat induced motivation to bolster one's defenses.

Since for some time the subject will continue to act on the motivation, the forgetting of the refutational material will be partly offset by this continued acquisition of bolstering material.

The second hypothesis is that the temporal decay of conferred immunity occurs more rapidly against attacks by the same counterarguments as had been explicitly refuted than against attacks by novel counterarguments. The theoretical basis for this prediction is quite similar to that yielding the first hypothesis. The immunity to attacks by the very counterarguments refuted derives from both recall of the specific refutations, which decays over time, and the amount of bolstering material the subject has acquired on the basis of his induced motivation, which increases over time. The immunity to attacks by novel counterarguments derives solely from the latter mechanism. Hence, conferred resistance to novel counterarguments should tend to catch up over time with resistance to the very counterarguments refuted.

The third hypothesis, which follows as a corollary of the second, is that the refutational defense has a delayed-action effect in conferring resistance to attacks by novel counterarguments. The refutations per se should not confer any resistance in this case, at least, not in so far as the counterarguments used in the attack are indeed novel. Hence, any resistance conferred derives from the second mechanism, the motivation to bolster one's belief induced by exposure to the threatening counterarguments during the defense. Acting on this motivation requires time, particularly in the monolithic ideological environment that tends to surround cultural truisms. Hence, the resistance to attack by novel arguments will continue to grow for

some time after the threatening pre-exposure. As time passes, the induced motivation will, of course, itself decay so that the total time function will be nonmonotonic. But for a time at least the conferred immunity will grow.

To test these temporal-trend predictions adequately it is important that we have some idea of the time parameters involved. It was in part to explore these parameters that the time interval between defense and attack was deliberately varied, from experiment to experiment, in the previous studies in this series. For example, in McGuire (1961a), the attack came immediately after the defense; in McGuire and Papageorgis (1961), 2 days intervened; and in Papageorgis and McGuire (1961), the interval was 1 week. Hence, it is possible to make a crude test of the three temporal-trend hypotheses by cross-experimental comparisons. The results based on such cross-experimental comparisons are depicted in Figure 1a and can be seen to be in accord with each of the three hypotheses. This confirmation of the predictions cannot be regarded as definitive since extraneous conditions varied somewhat from experiment to experiment. For example, the issues, defensive and attacking messages, and types of subjects all differed somewhat among the experiments. The confirmations are sufficiently clear, however, that we were encouraged to vary systematically the time intervals within the present experimental design over comparable magnitudes.

METHOD

Procedure

The study was represented to the subjects as an investigation of personality correlates of verbal skills, a deception that was bolstered by several tasks the subjects were called upon to perform during the experimental sessions. Each of the 160 subjects took part in two experimental sessions. During the first they received 600-word mimeographed messages defending their initial beliefs on medical truisms such as "Everyone should visit his doctor at least once a year for a routine physical check up." The subject was told that he would be scored on his ability to analyze such technical passages and he was given 4 minutes to read and, in each paragraph, underline the shortest clause that summarized the main point being made in the paragraph. This underlining task was introduced to encourage careful reading and to disguise the persuasive purpose of the messages. He was then given various personality tests, not relevant to the hypotheses under discussion, to disguise further the persuasive intent of the study.

The second session came either 2 days (for 80 subjects) or 7 days (for the other 80) later. In the second session, each subject received further defensive messages on additional medical truisms and then, within the same booklet, additional messages attacking the previously defended truisms and, in control conditions described under Design, previously undefended truisms as well. As in the first session, the subject was given 4 minutes to read and underline the crucial clauses in each of these defensive and attacking messages. Another personality questionnaire was then administered and then the subject was asked to fill out an opinion questionnaire indicating his own beliefs on the medical issues dealt with in the messages, on the pretext that we wished to check on whether the subject's personal opinions on the topics discussed in the passages

affected his ability to read these passages analytically. The subjects then filled out a questionnaire designed to ascertain the extent to which the desired experimental conditions obtained,[1] after which the true nature of the experiment and the nature of and reasons for the deceptions were explained to the subject.

Defensive and Attacking Messages

Two types of defensive messages were employed. The "supportive" defense had an introductory paragraph mentioning that the truism in question was obviouly valid but that it was wise to consider some of the reasons why it was indeed valid. Two arguments in support of the belief were then mentioned. There followed two paragraphs each developing in a calm, factual way one of the two supportive arguments. These supportive messages avoided any mention of possible counterarguments against the truism.

The "refutational" defenses began

[1] This Critique of the Experiment final questionnaire was designed to measure the adequacy of the time allowances, how much the subject had heard of the experiment in advance and whether he suspected its persuasive intent. About 20 percent of the subjects complained that some section of the test had been given either a too long or a too short time allowance; more than half the complaints were that the time allowed for the noncrucial personality test was too short. The subjects were indeed rushed through this section to keep the session down to 50 minutes. A surprising number admitted having heard something about the experiment in advance, despite our request to the subjects that they refrain from discussing it with anyone until the end of the experimental period. Hearing that the test involved a reading comprehension test or that it dealt with medical topics was admitted by 31 out of the 160 subjects. In addition, 4 heard that one's opinions were measured. When called upon to suggest what else—besides verbal skills—the experiment could have measured, only 5 suggested any purpose having to do with opinion change, persuasion, or propaganda.

with a similar introductory paragraph mentioning that the truism was obviously valid but that, since occasionally one heard misguided counterarguments attacking it, it was wise to consider some of these counterarguments and show wherein they erred. Two counterarguments against the truism were then mentioned. The following two paragraphs each refuted in a calm, factual way one of these counterarguments. These refutational messages avoided mention of arguments directly supporting the truism—they merely refuted counterarguments against it.

The attacking messages were similar in format to the defensive, each being about six hundred words in length and divided into three paragraphs. The introductory paragraph stated that most laymen would be surprised to learn that advanced medical and scientific work was beginning to cast some doubt on the validity of the truism in question and, hence, it would be wise to ponder some of these recently discovered counterarguments against the belief, two of which were then mentioned. Each of the following two paragraphs expounded in a calm, factual manner the validity of one of these counterarguments. When the attacking message followed a refutation defense, one of two alternatives was used. Half of the subjects received attacks employing the very counterarguments refuted; the other half of the subjects received attacks employing novel counterarguments, different from those previously refuted.

Since· the experimental design called for each subject's serving in four different defensive conditions, it was necessary to prepare supportive defense, refutational defense, and attacking messages on four different truisms. Further-

more, since half the refutational defenses had to be followed by attacks employing the same counterarguments as refuted and half by novel counterarguments, it was necessary to prepare two alternative forms of the refutational defense message and of the attacking messages on each issue, each dealing with a different pair of counterarguments. For symmetry of design, we prepared alternative forms of the supportive defense on each issue, each form using a different pair of supportive arguments. Hence, 24 messages in all were employed in the present study, 6 on each of four issues.[2]

Opinion Questionnaire

Beliefs on the four issues were measured by a 17-item opinion questionnaire. Each item consisted of an assertion on one of the issues (e.g., "Everyone should brush his teeth after every meal if at all possible.") followed by a graphic scale containing 15 numbered categories with Definitely False at one end and Definitely True at the other. The subject was told to make an "X" in whichever of the categories best indicated his own agreement with the statement. There were four items on each issue.[3] The scores cited in the Results section and in Table 19.1 are based

[2] All 24 of the defensive and attacking messages used in this study have been deposited with the American Documentation Institute. Order Document No. 7058 from ADI Auxiliary Publications Project, Photoduplication Service, Library of Congress; Washington 25, D. C., remitting in advance $2.25 for microfilm or $5.00 for photocopies. Make checks payable to: Chief, Photoduplication Service, Library of Congress.

[3] This opinion questionnaire has been deposited with ADI and can be obtained by writing for the document mentioned in Footnote 2.

on the mean of the four items on each issue, with the possible range going from 1.00, for complete rejection of the truism, to 15.00 for complete agreement therewith. One of the 17 items was a repeat to serve as a reliability check. The two responses to this repeated item yielded an intrasubject correlation of .82.

Experimental Design

The design included four blocks of subjects. The subjects in the first block received refutational defenses on all four issues. They received such defenses on two issues in a first session 2 days previous to the attack; and the defenses on the other two issues at the second session immediately before the attack. In each session the defense on one issue involved refutations of the same counterarguments as would be used in the attack, and on the other issue, the refutation of alternative counterarguments to those that would be used in the attack. The subjects in the second block received the same treatments as those in the first block, except that for them the first session preceded the attacks by 1 week rather than 2 days.

The subjects in the third block received defenses on only two issues. Both of these were supportive defenses, one coming in the first session 2 days before the attack and one in the second session just before the attack. As regards the other two undefended issues, one was attacked in the second session to ascertain the impact of the attacks in the absence of any prior defense and one was not attacked to obtain an estimate of the initial belief levels in the absence of both defense and attack. The subjects in the fourth block received the same treatments as those in the

third, except that for them the first session preceded the attacks by 1 week rather than 2 days.

Since there were four issues and two alternative sets of materials on each issue, eight subconditions were necessary in each block to allow the materials to be systematically rotated around the four treatment conditions. Five subjects served in each of these eight "materials" subconditions, so that 40 subjects served in each of the four blocks.[4]

The purpose of this rather complex design was to allow more sensitive tests of the theoretically relevant and likely-to-be-small treatment effects. Thus, all comparisons between refutational defenses, for example, those predicted in the second and third hypotheses, involve intrasubject analyses. Likewise, comparisons between the supportive defense (which usually has the smallest effect—see for example, McGuire & Papageorgis, 1961) and no defense conditions also involve sensitive intrasubject analyses. It is true that comparisons between the refutation defenses on the one hand and the supportive defense, or the no defense control conditions involve across-subject comparisons, but such variations have been demonstrated in previous studies to produce sizable differentials.

The complexity of the design did necessitate the computation of several different error terms to evaluate the differential effects presented in the Results section below. In general, the error terms are based on the residual variance in the conditions being compared. The individual differences variance was removed when the comparison involved repeated measures on the same subject,

[4] The design of the present study is described in detail in Table A of the ADI document mentioned in Footnote 2.

for example, the effects of refutation of same vs. alternative counterarguments; or an interaction effect between type of defense and time of attack; or the effect of a supportive defense vs. no defense. When the comparison was between a refutational defense and a supportive or a no defense condition, the large between-subject residual variance, including individual differences among the subjects, was used as the error term.

Subjects

All 160 subjects were selected from a pool of students enrolled in the introductory psychology course at the University of Illinois. Among those who indicated at the beginning of the semester that they were regularly available on the days and hours chosen for running the experiment, the selection was random. About 75 percent of the 220 subjects requested to appear actually participated in the experiment and the data reported below are based on the first 160 of those who appeared for both sessions. The majority were sophomores and about 55 percent were females.

RESULTS AND DISCUSSION

General Effects

The two control conditions set the probable limits within which the differential immunization effects can take place. The mean belief level in the neither-attack-nor-defense control condition is 11.74 on the 15-point scale, and can be taken as an estimate of the initial belief level on the four truisms. Actually the estimate is probably conservative, since it is based on the indicated belief on an issue unmentioned in the mes-

sages, but taken after the receipt of messages strongly attacking three other truisms and, hence, may reflect a general wariness on the part of the subject (see McGuire & Papageorgis, 1961, and Papageorgis & McGuire, 1961, for data on the accuracy with which such postcommunication beliefs on control, unmentioned issues estimate the initial level of the beliefs). The mean belief level in the other control condition (attack-only) is 8.49, indicating that in the absence of any defense, the attacks were effective in reducing the beliefs 3.25 points on the 15-point scale ($p < .001$). The overall belief level in all three defense-and-attack conditions at all three time intervals is 10.17, which is almost exactly midway between the neither-attack-nor-defense and the attack-only means and significantly ($p < .01$) different from either. Furthermore, the means in all nine defense-and-attack conditions (see Table 1) do lie between the two means of the neither-attack-nor-defense and attack-only conditions.

Relative Persistence after Supportive and Refutational Defenses

The supportive defenses conferred less resistance to the attack than did the refutational defenses regardless of whether the attack came immediately, 2 days, or 1 week after the attack. When the attack followed immediately, the superiority of the combined refutational defense conditions to the supportive was significant at the .01 level, but this superiority was primarily due to the conditions in which the very counterarguments used in the attack were refuted: the superiority over the supportive reached only the .20 level of

TABLE 1. PERSISTENCE OF THE RESISTANCE TO PERSUASION CONFERRED
BY THREE TYPES OF PRIOR BELIEF DEFENSE

Interval Between Defense and Attack	Type of Defense That Preceded the Attack			Attack Without Prior Defense	Neither Attack nor Defense
	Supportive Arguments	Refutation of Counter-arguments Used in the Attacks	Refutation of Alternative Counterarguments		
Immediate	9.71 (80)[a]	11.36 (80)	10.41 (80)		
Two days	8.51 (40)	11.08 (40)	11.45 (40)	8.49 (80)	11.74 (80)
Seven days	8.82 (40)	9.49 (40)	9.68 (40)		

Note.—Scores in the cells are final belief levels on the Truisms as measured on a 15-point scale.

[a] Numbers in parentheses indicate the number of individual scores on which the cell mean is based.

significance when counterarguments alternative to those used in the immediate attack were refuted.

Where 2 days intervened between the attack and defense, this superiority of the combined refutational to the supportive defense became even more pronounced $(p < .001)$. Whereas the immediate resistance conferred by the supportive defense had decayed $(p < .05)$ almost completely after the 2-day interval, that conferred by the refutational defense actually showed a trivial gain from the immediate to the 2-day interval. As can be seen in Table 19.2, this gain yielded an F of only 1.05. This interaction effect between the supportive vs. refutation type-of-defense variable and the immediate vs. 2-day interval variable is significant at the .01 level and confirms the first hypothesis. It will be noted that this interaction effect is in the opposite direction to that to be expected on the basis of a simple regression effect: the resistance conferred by the supportive defense is not only

less to immediate attacks, but such as it is, it also decays more rapidly than the greater immediate resistance conferred by the refutation.

There is an alternative theoretical interpretation of this superior persistence of the immunity conferred by the refutational defense, an explanation related to the "sleeper effect" described by Hovland and his colleagues (Hovland, Lumsdaine, & Sheffield, 1949, Ch. 7; Hovland & Weiss, 1951; Kelman & Hovland, 1953). According to these theorists, if a persuasive message is initially accompanied by a discounting cue, its opinion change impact might actually increase with time passage, or at least decline relatively slowly (Weiss, 1953) as compared with a message not so accompanied. The recall of the persuasive content does, of course, decay over time but so does the recall of the discounting cue, thus, reducing or even reversing the net decay of induced opinion change. In the present situation the refutational defense could be inter-

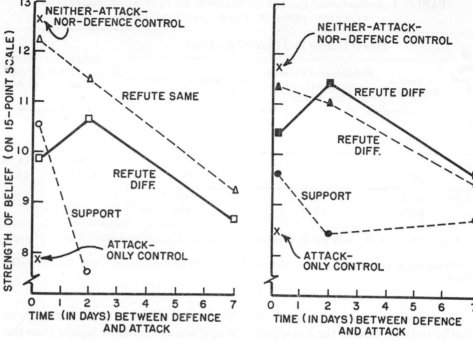

1a. Based on data from previous experiments. (Zero interval points are based on data from McGuire, 1961a; 2-day interval points, on McGuire and Papageorgis, 1961, and McGuire, 1961b; and 7-day points, on Papageorgis and McGuire, 1961)

1b. Based on data from the present experiment as shown in Table I

Figure 1. Persistence of the resistance to persuasion conferred by three types of prior defense: supportive, refutation of the same counterarguments as used in the attack, and refutation of counterarguments different from those used in the attack

preted as containing a discounting cue, namely, mention of the refuted counterarguments, the forgetting of which dampens the decay of the initially induced opinion change. The supportive defense contains no such incidental discounting cue, so that its greatest impact should be felt immediately and decay thereafter without any mitigating effect of a simultaneously decaying discounting factor. Some credence is given to this interpretation by the results of an earlier study (McGuire & Papageorgis, 1961) indicating that the direct strengthening effect prior to any attack was somewhat

greater ($.05 < p < .10$) with the supportive than the refutational defense, even though the latter conferred more resistance ($p < .01$) to an attack 2 days later.

Relative Resistance after Refutation of Same and of Alternate Counterarguments

As can be seen in Figure 1b, the resistance conferred by the refutational-same defense, that is, the defense involving prior refutation of the very counterarguments to be used in the attack, declines monotonically as the interval between defense and attack increases. The decline from the immediate to the 2-day interval is not significant but that from 2 days to 1 week is significant on the .01 level. A quite different, nonmonotonic time trend can be seen with the refutational-different defense, i.e., the defense involving prior refutation of counterarguments different from the ones that are actually to be used in the attack on the given belief. Although this type of defense was inferior ($p <$ .05) to the refutation-same defense in conferring resistance to the immediate attack, it has become trivially superior when the attacks do not come until 2 days later (see Table 2). The interaction effect between the same vs. different refutational-defense variable and the immediate vs. 2-day interval variable appears on all four issues individually, and the effect combined over issues is significant above the .05 level. Hence, the second hypothesis—that the decay of the resistance conferred against attacks by different counterarguments will be slower than that to attacks by the same counterarguments as had been refuted—is confirmed. As can be seen in

TABLE 2. MEAN BELIEF SCORES (ON A 15-POINT SCALE) AND ANALYSIS OF VARIANCE IN THE CONDITIONS INVOLVING ATTACKS BY THE SAME OR BY NOVEL COUNTERARGUMENTS IMMEDIATELY AFTER AND TWO DAYS AFTER THE REFUTATION DEFENSES, WITH ISSUE-BY-ISSUE SUBMEANS

Issues	Refutational-Same Defense		Refutational-Different Defense		All Treatments
	Immediate Attack	Attack after 2 Days	Immediate Attack	Attack after 2 Days	
Chest X ray	10.10	8.50	8.96	9.92	9.42
Penicillin	12.59	12.95	11.92	12.48	12.41
Toothbrushing	10.35	9.92	9.84	10.78	10.18
Annual physical	12.41	12.92	10.92	12.62	12.04
All issues	11.36	11.08	10.41	11.45	11.01

Source	SS	df	MS	F
Type defense (refutational-same vs. refutational-different)	248	1	248	2.19
Time (immediate attack vs. 2 days)	119	1	119	1.05
Type × Time	552	1	552	4.88[a]
Issues	5,965	3	1988	17.59[b]
Issues × Treatments	517	9	57	0.50
Subject	17,755	79	225	1.99
Residual	16,425	145	113	
Total	41,581	239		

[a] $p < .05$.
[b] $p < .001$.

Figure 1*b*, there is actually greater resistance in the "different" refutation condition than in the "same" at both the 2- and 7-day intervals, which is embarrassingly more than the theory demands but this differential is trivial in magnitude.

The results also corroborate the third hypothesis, regarding a delayed-action effect in the resistance conferred by refutation of counterarguments different from those used in the attack. As can be seen in Table 2, the resistance conferred by this type of defense is greater against an attack 2 days later than against an immediate attack on all four issues individually, as well as in the combined results ($p < .05$).

In general, the results from this experiment agree closely with the cross-experimental comparisons from the previous studies in the introductory section. As can be seen from a comparison of Figures 1*a* and 1*b*, the two sets of curves are quite similar in shape and even as regards absolute parameters, except that in the present experiment, the refutational-different defense tends to be somewhat more effective than in the previous experiments. The general implication of the study, particularly when considered in the context of the previous studies in this series, is to corroborate further the initial postulate: that the supportive defense confers resistance to persuasion only in so far as the material presented is assimilated and retained— an activity that the subject is little motivated to carry out in the case of a "truism." The resistance conferred by the refutational defense, on the other hand, derives not only from the assimilation and retention of the bolstering material actually presented but also from the motivational effect of the pre-exposure to threatening material, the mention of the counterarguments, contained in the refutational defense. If this interpretation is correct, then the temporal differentials found among the defenses in this study should be reduced as we move from the truisms used in this study, with respect to which the defense stimulating threat is particularly necessary and possible, to beliefs on more controversial issues. The results do seem fairly general as regards truisms, as can be seen in the trivial magnitude of the Issues × Treatments interaction effects (see Table 2).

SUMMARY

Theoretical considerations like those which led to the predictions tested in the previous studies of this series on immunizing beliefs against persuasion yielded several hypotheses regarding differential persistence of the immunity conferred by various types of prior belief-defenses. First, it was predicted that the immunity conferred by refutational defenses would decay less rapidly than that conferred by the supportive defenses. Secondly, within the refutational-defense conditions, it was predicted that the conferred resistance to attacks by counterarguments other than the explicitly refuted ones would decay less rapidly than resistance to attacks by the very counterarguments refuted. A related third prediction was that there would be a delayed action effect in the immunity to attacks by novel counterarguments conferred by the refutational defense.

Each of the 160 college students subjects served in two experimental sessions. The first involved reading defensive articles on medical truisms. The defenses involved either arguments supporting the truism, or refutations of counterarguments against the truism, either the very counterarguments to be used in the later attack or alternative counterarguments. The second session came either 2 days (for 80 subjects) or 7 days (for the other 80) after the first, and involved a second defensive treatment on another truism and then attacks on the previously defended and undefended truisms. The subjects' beliefs on all the truisms were then measured. All three hypotheses received substantial confirmation.

REFERENCES

Hovland, C. I., Lumsdaine, A. A., & Sheffield, F. *Experiments on mass communication*. Princeton: Princeton Univer. Press, 1949.

Hovland, C. I., & Weiss, W. The influence of source credibility on communication effectiveness. *Publ. opin. Quart.*, 1951, **15**, 635–650.

Kelman, H., & Hovland, C. I. "Reinstatement" of the communicator in delayed measurement of opinion change. *J. abnorm. soc. Psychol.*, 1953, **48**, 327–335.

McGuire, W. J. The effectiveness of supportive and refutational defenses in immunizing and restoring beliefs against persuasion. *Sociometry*, 1961, **24**, 184–197. (a)

McGuire, W. J. Resistance to persuasion conferred by active and passive prior refutation of the same and alternative counterarguments. *J. abnorm. soc. Psychol.*, 1961, **63**, 326–332. (b)

McGuire, W. J., & Papageorgis, D. The relative efficacy of various types of prior belief-defense in producing immunity against persuasion. *J. abnorm. soc. Psychol.*, 1961, **62**, 327–337.

Papageorgis, D., & McGuire, W. J. The generality of immunity to persuasion produced by pre-exposure to weakened counterarguments. *J. abnorm. soc. Psychol.*, 1961, **62**, 475–481.

Weiss, W. A "sleeper" effect in opinion change. *J. abnorm. soc. Psychol.*, 1953, **48**, 173–180.

5

Interpersonal Perception
and Attraction

———◆·◆———

20.   COGNITIVE TUNING AS A FACTOR AFFECTING
IMPRESSION FORMATION *

Arthur R. Cohen

Zajonc (1960) has differentiated two sets or "readinesses" to deal with information and has explored the effects of these sets on cognitive structure. One set he calls "Transmission Tuning," the other "Reception Tuning." In the former, the individual expects to communicate his cognitions to others; in the latter he expects to receive additional material or the other person's cognitions. When the individual is tuned for transmission, cognitive structure is more rigid and polarized; when tuned for reception, his cognitive structure is less rigid, les polarized and more flexible. Thus, according to Zajonc, when information is available under transmission tuning, it is transformed into more rigid cognitive sets whose subsets act as

potential units of transmittable information.

Zajonc's distinctions become relevant for the problem of impression-formation when we consider that the situational demands placed upon the person can be thought of as guiding the way he organizes conflicting impression material (Jones & Thibaut, 1958). When set to transmit his impression to others, the person should tend to *polarize*, that is he should tend to exclude or suppress or minimize one polarity of the contradiction and order the relevant cognitions around the other extreme. When set to receive others' impressions, the person should tend to *suspend*, that is he should bring together or see as related —or explain away—the contradictions

* Excerpted from the *Journal of Personality*, 1961, 29: 235–245, with permission of the Duke University Press.

between cognitions by entertaining the opposing cognitive elements and minimizing their contradictions. It is expected that under transmission tuning, where the S has to deal with information which he is required to pass on to others, polarization in the interests of a clear, transmittable picture should occur: the Ss should discard contradictory strands with the resulting achievement of an unambiguous cognition. However, under reception tuning, where the S is set to receive more information, where he has to retain it and deal with it within himself, he should be more accepting of diverse strands. Here, suspension should occur and the contradictory strands entertained together. These expectations regarding the mode of organization of contradictory impression material grow directly out of Zajonc's data on general cognitive processes.

(The present discussion is somewhat similar to Gollin's [1954] discussion of alternative modes of impression formation. He speaks of unified impression as having been achieved either through the recognition and retention of contradictory behavioral themes organized by means of an inferential statement, or through the elimination of one major character theme which is deemed incomprehensible in the face of a contradictory theme [polarization here]. He also describes the residual mode of "aggregation," where themes may be seen as contradictory, though they are not necessarily organized through an inferential statement. In the present report, this latter mode, along with polarization, is given major emphasis. Here the aggregation mode is called suspension. The concern here is not so much with the actual inferences by which organization is achieved as with the degree to which contradictory ele-

ments are contained and considered in the cognitive structure.)

Differences consistent with the effects of the tuning sets might also be expected in the degree to which persons desire information concerning the stimulus person, as well as the kind of information desired. Transmission tuning should discourage the search for more information, and if such information is desired, it should be expected to represent one or another polarity of the contradiction. These expectations are consistent with the view that people exposed to transmission tuning want a simpler cognitive picture which is easier to pass on to others.

Finally, we might also assume that the nature of the impression material presented would have an important bearing on the suspension-polarization tendencies of the Ss. Material which is highly contradictory should exaggerate the impact of different tuning sets whereas material which is only moderately contradictory should minimize this difference.

METHOD

General Design

Ss were asked to take part in a study concerned with peoples' impressions about one another. Half of the Ss were exposed to an experimental induction designed to create the set of transmitting their impressions to others; the other half of the Ss were given a set to receive others' impressions. Within each of these groups, half of the Ss were given trait lists in which the material was highly contradictory; half were given moderately contradictory trait lists. Ss were then asked to write a sketch giving their impressions about the person whose traits they received. This was followed by a postexperimental questionnaire.

Subjects

One hundred and twenty Yale undergraduates make up the sample employed in the present study. They were approached in their dormitories and run through the experiment singly or in groups of two or three.

Procedure

The E introduced himself as someone working on the problem of peoples' impressions of one another, of how people form and communicate first impressions. The importance of the problem was stressed and the usefulness of data on the issue was brought to the Ss' attention. It was emphasized to the Ss that first impressions are extremely pervasive determinants of success, achievement, and propriety of behavior. These inductions, it is assumed, helped to provide the Ss with high motivation for the experiment.

THE MANIPULATION OF TUNING All Ss were told by E, "I'm going to give you a list of character traits referring to a Yale student. What I want you to do is look over these traits and get a good idea of what kind of person Jim is." In the *transmission* condition, Ss were told: "After you have read over these traits, your job will be to communicate to other fellows who are taking part in this experiment all you can about Jim. In other words, I want to see if you can transmit your impressions of Jim to these other fellows." (There were, of course, no "other fellows" with whom S actually interacted. In this way,

however, S was made to feel that there were people to whom he had to communicate or who would communicate to him.)

In the *reception* condition Ss were told: "After you have read over these traits you will receive the impressions about Jim of other fellows who are taking part in this experiment. I want you to receive other people's impressions of Jim."

Both groups were then told: "This is not a test of memory or intelligence, and so forth, so don't memorize the list of characteristics. Try to get a general picture of what sort of individual Jim is so that: [a, transmission] the other fellow will be able to understand fully your impressions of Jim, [b, reception] you will be able to understand fully the impressions about Jim of the other fellows."

THE MANIPULATION OF CONTRADICTION The Ss were then given the adjective trait lists. Half of the Ss in each tuning condition were placed in the *high-contradiction* group, half in the *low-contradiction* group. The former were given a list of ten traits with positive and negative characteristics intermingled. Five of the traits were extremely positive and five extremely negative. The low-contradiction group was given a matched list where the traits were defined as more moderate in their positive or negative quality. The trait lists were defined as moderate or high contradiction on an a priori basis. The trait lists are given below:

high contradiction

Very friendly
Extremely generous
Ruthless
Extremely dependable

Overly conceited
Very kind
Scheming
Very cold
Highly loyal
Insincere

low contradiction

Fairly friendly
Generous
Somewhat ruthless
Fairly dependable
Conceited
Kind
Slightly scheming
A bit cold
Loyal
A little insincere

The S was given about five minutes to peruse the list and it was then collected. He was then handed a sheet on which to record his impression of Jim with the following instructions: "On this sheet, I want you to write out as fully as you can what sort of individual you think Jim is. Be sure to write your complete impression of Jim."

POSTEXPERIMENTAL QUESTIONNAIRE After the impressions had been written and the sheets collected, Ss were then asked: "Now I'd like to get some of your reactions to this before we go any further. Fill out the questionnaire rapidly; don't spend too much time on any one item." This questionnaire was designed to check on the experimental manipulations, to get at the S's desire for more information, and to explore his perceptions of contradictions and his handling of them.

The experiment was then terminated and the S told about it in as much

detail as feasible. This completed the experimental session.

Measures

Two response measures derived from the written impressions were used to obtain suspension–polarization tendencies:

1. Each complete thought was scored as being positive, neutral, or negative with regard to Jim. The more the character traits mentioned in the impression represent an extreme positive or an extreme negative view of Jim, the more the S is assumed to be organizing his impression around one extreme or another. The more the positive and negative traits are in balance, the more he is assumed to be entertaining the diverse strands. The coding of these items was a straightforward procedure: they were merely counted. Therefore no measure of intercoder reliability was taken. From these items a 10-point scale was generated; the low end of the scale indicates more suspension, the high end more polarization.

2. In this measure, a more impressionistic coding scheme similar to Dittes' (1959) was used. The data were coded into two categories: (a) a story in which the S mentions both sides equally, or achieves some superficial integration by stressing the essential compatibility of both kinds of traits; or (b) a story on one side or the other where the S organizes the material by distorting traits on one side to support the other side, or else simply ignores incompatible traits which do not fit the dominant impression. Here Ss were placed in one or the other category; the written impressions were coded as indicating either suspension or polarization. Interjudge coding

reliability on this meausre was 86 percent agreement.

Data were also gathered from the postexperimental questionnaire:

1. *Check on the tuning manipulation.* Ss were asked whether "in studying the list of characteristics given, were you thinking in terms of: (*a*) transmitting your impression to others, or (*b*) receiving others' impressions."

2. *Check on the contradiction manipulation.* Ss were asked "to what extent did there appear to be contradictions or inconsistencies among the characteristics you were given." They responded to this by means of an a priori eight-point scale varying from "Extremely contradictory" to "Not contradictory at all."

3. *Desire for information.* Ss were asked to check "yes" or "no" in response to the question, "Did you feel that you needed more information about Jim?" If they answered "yes," then they were asked, "What kind of information?" They checked one of the following three categories: (*a*) information mostly concerning his good qualities, (*b*) information mostly concerning his bad qualities, (*c*) information on both his good and bad qualities. The first two responses are assumed to indicate a desire for information consistent with a polarizing tendency. The last category is assumed to represent tendencies toward suspension, that is, a desire for information on both sides.

RESULTS

Evidence on the Effectiveness of the Experimental Manipulations

The data show that the tuning and contradiction manipulations were ex-

tremely successful in creating different orientations toward the information and different degrees of perceived contradiction. In all cases, appropriate statistical comparisons (by *t* test) show differences significant beyond the .001 level.[1]

Perception of Contradiction

The data were examined to see whether or not any tendency existed for the Ss to deny contradictions in the material where they were assumed to exist. On the measure of perceived contradiction taken in the questionnaire, only two Ss out of 120 said they perceived no contradictions at all in the trait lists they were given. Both Ss were in the low-contradiction condition. Only six persons in the entire population indicated less than "slight contradiction" on the scale. We may thus conclude that in these data Ss perceived the traits they were given as being, at the very least, in some degree of conflict with one another.

When the same data were examined for the tuning groups, no differences were found: within each contradiction condition, Ss in the different tuning conditions were almost identical in their perception of degree of contradiction.

Suspension and Polarization in the Written Impressions

The first data from the written impressions concern the specific traits mentioned by the Ss. Here we are concerned with the degree to which the S balanced mention of Jim's good traits with mention of his negative traits, or conversely, the degree to which he over-

[1] All statistical tests in this report are two-tailed tests.

TABLE 1. MEAN EFFECTS OF COGNITIVE TUNING ON ORGANIZATION
OF THE WRITTEN IMPRESSIONS $(N = 120)$

Cognitive Tuning	Degree of Contradiction		
	High	Low	Combined
Transmission	3.30	2.48	2.90
Reception	2.10	1.96	2.03
Combined	2.70	2.22	

whelmingly mentioned traits on either one side or the other. The former tendency is assumed to represent suspension, the latter, attempts at polarization around one extreme or another. In these data, the lower the mean, the more the balance, that is, the more the suspension. The means for each experimental conditions are given in Table 1. The N for each cell is 30.

An analysis of variance reveals that the difference between the tuning conditions is reliable at beyond the .01 level $(F = 7.92)$ while the difference between the contradiction conditions only approaches significance at the .10 $(F = 2.15)$. Within the high-contradiction condition, the difference between the tuning groups is significant by t test at beyond the .001 level and within the low-contradiction group, the tuning conditions differ at the .05 level by t test. However, though the effect of the tuning manipulations appears to be somewhat stronger within the high-contradiction condition than the low, the interaction effect does not approach statistical significance $(F < 1)$.

The second kind of data bearing on suspension and polarization are derived from a more impressionistic coding of the written impressions in order to explore the Ss' attempts to write a story either indicating (a) predominant sus-

pension or (b) partiality on one side or the other where opposite traits are distorted and used to support the dominant impression.

These data are highly consistent with the data given in Table 1. The over-all difference between the transmission and reception conditions indicating that the latter suspend, the former polarize, is significant by chi-square test at beyond the .01 level. In addition, whereas the tuning conditions do not differ significantly within the low-contradiction group, within the high-contradiction group they are different in the expected direction at beyond the .05 level by chi-square.

The data, then, indicate that when actually writing their impressions, Ss respond differently to different cognitive sets. In general Ss differ widely in whether they tend to polarize or suspend depending upon whether they are set to transmit or to receive impressions. There is also a tendency for highly contradictory material to trigger off differences between tuning variations more than moderately contradictory material.

Desire for Information

In Table 2 are presented the percentages of Ss in each experimental condition who said that they needed more information about Jim for their impressions. It was expected that those exposed to transmission tuning, faced with the necessity of communicating a clear and unambiguous concept, would want new information less than those exposed to reception tuning. Also, it was expected that among the Ss who want more information, those exposed to transmission tuning would tend to want more about either Jim's good or bad qualities, whereas those exposed to reception tuning would tend more to want information about both aspects of Jim. The latter trend is assumed to indicate a tendency toward suspension, the former a tendency toward polarization. These data are also in Table 2; significance levels are derived from chi-square tests.

Table 2 shows that both in their desires for new information and in their desires for information on both sides, people set to receive others' impressions have greater desires than people set to transmit their own impressions. Though there are strong differences between the tuning conditions within low contradiction for desire for information, the overall trend is consistent with the hypotheses. Thus, those people faced with the necessity of communication to others tended to indicate a desire for a more restricted and partial cog-

nitive structure than those who were only set to receive others' impressions.

DISCUSSION

In general, the data confirm the notion that reception tuning is more facilitative of suspension and the entertainment of contradictory cognitions in a person's impression than transmission tuning, and that this trend may be somewhat stronger when the cognitions constituting the impression are highly contradictory than when they are moderately contradictory.

It is curious that people who have to transmit information concerning a complex impression to others do, in fact, want less additional information than those who are to receive others' complex impressions. Furthermore, the information they do want tends to be one-sided and narrowly defined, whereas those exposed to reception tuning desire material more on both sides of the issue. However, these results, as well as the results on the written impressions, become plausible once it is understood that transmission requires a tight and well-bound cognitive "package" which can be communicated to others. Additional and contradictory information

TABLE 2. PERCENTAGE OF Ss DESIRING MORE INFORMATION AND KIND OF INFORMATION DESIRED

Cognitive Tuning	Desire for New Information		Desire for Information on Both Sides (Suspension)	
	Hi. Contrad.	Low Contrad.	Hi. Contrad.	Low Contrad.
Transmission	.46	.35	.50	.80
Reception	.70	.84	.81	.74
p value of diff.	< .05	< .01	< .05	n.s.

about the person makes it more difficult to order a clear and unambiguous cognitive structure which can be passed on. When set to receive others' impressions, the person can entertain a more flexible and ambiguous picture, and may forestall the quick polarization demanded by the instrumental requirements.

In the present experiment all Ss appeared to be aware that there were at least some contradictions inherent in the material they were given. In addition, they did not differ in the degree to which they were aware of these contradictions as a function of cognitive tuning. When it comes to actually writing their impressions, however, quite different trends emerge from those described above. In this case the cognitive set becomes pervasive in its effects and when set to transmit, all Ss actually do polarize their impressions around one extreme or another more than they do when they are set to receive. Thus, the instrumental demands given by the tuning manipulation do not affect simple awareness of contradictions: all the S has to do is receive the stimulus requirements without any necessity for action. However, when the S must actually produce the impression that is to be transmitted or to which other impressions are to be assimilated, responsiveness to the tuning inductions is very strong.

It should be noted that under transmission tuning the difference in organization between the contradiction conditions is sizeable ($p < .01$ by t test), whereas under reception tuning it is negligible. It seems plausible that the suspension tendencies engendered by reception tuning are equally potent for both contradiction conditions. Under conditions where the S expects additional information, he keeps his cognitive structure open and flexible, no matter how contradictory are the items he is initially given. However, when the S is set to transmit, the sharper the contradictions among the cognitions, the greater the tendency to exclude items on one or another extreme; the more moderate the contradiction the more easily can items on both extremes be transmitted within the framework of a coherent impression.

These results demonstrate the influence of set on the organization of impressions, but there is at least one important qualification that should be mentioned concerning generalization from these results. The proposition that transmission tuning leads to greater polarization might not hold true if it involved the expectation that the individual would have to transmit information to respected, well-informed persons who are neutral or opposed to the individual on an issue. Before such an audience, a tendency for suspension and even integration might be fostered. On the other hand, transmission to people who are relatively uninformed, or who are interested in finding out only the gist of something with no regard for evaluating it, might show the predicted effects. The present experiment did not attempt to study this question.

REFERENCES

DITTES, J. E.   Effects of changes in self-esteem on impulsiveness and deliberation in making judgments. *J. abnorm. soc. Psychol.*, 1959, **58**, 348–356.

GOLLIN, E. S.   Forming impressions of personality. *J. Pers.*, 1954, **23**, 65–76.

JONES, E. E., & THIBAUT, J. W.   Interaction goals as bases of influence in interpersonal perception. In R. Taguiri and L. Petrullo (Eds.), *Person Perception and Interpersonal Behavior.* Stanford: Stanford Univer. Press, 1958. Pp. 151–178.

ZAJONC, R. B. The process of cognitive tuning in communication. *J. abnorm. soc. Psychol.*, 1960, **61**, 159–167.

21. SOME STUDIES OF SOCIAL DISTANCE *

Harry C. Triandis and Leigh M. Triandis

INTRODUCTION

In all societies there are norms specifying the "correct" or "appropriate" behaviors for members when they encounter other people. For instance, some societies have what is known as a "mother-in-law taboo," a norm which states that "when you are in the presence of your mother-in-law, you hide or avoid getting close to her." Here the "person" is identified by the kin relationship, and the behavior is one of keeping physical distance.

In our society, certain kinds of people have norms of avoidance of persons who are different from themselves with respect to such characteristics as physical type (race), belief system (religion or political philosophy,) occupation, nationality, and so forth. Avoidance may involve exclusion of persons with such "undesirable" characteristics from the "friendship circle," the neighborhood, the occupational group, the place of work, and sometimes from the country. The degree to which individuals are willing to accept people who differ from themselves into their own social group may be considered a measure of their "social distance" from these outgroup persons. Research shows that a number of factors influence social distance judgments. The most important of these factors will be considered in this article. They include both characteristics of the persons being judged— their race, religion, nationality, occupation, and sex; and characteristics of the judges—their culture, social class, educational level, and personality traits.

THE MEASUREMENT OF SOCIAL DISTANCE

It is possible to find out what kinds of people are avoided, and how much they are avoided, by asking a person to indicate whether he would accept a particular kind of person (for example, a Negro) as an intimate friend, as a neighbor, as a fellow employee, and so on, or whether he would exclude him from such relationships. The sociologist Bogardus established a scale of social distance by employing the following items, which are listed below in the order of increasing social distance: (1) would admit to close kin by marriage; (2) would admit to my club as personal chum; (3) would admit to my street as neighbor; (4) would admit to employment in my occupation; (5) would admit to citizenship in my country; (6)

* This article was written specifically for this volume.

TABLE 1. SCALE VALUES OF STATEMENTS USED IN TWO CULTURES

Statement	American Scale Value	Greek Scale Value
I would marry this person	0.00	0.00
I would accept this person as an intimate friend	11.1	13.5
I would accept this person as a close kin by marriage	21.5	28.5
I would accept this person as a roommate	29.5	—
I would accept this person as a member of my intimate social group (in Greek, *parea*)	—	31.1
I would accept this person as a personal chum in my club	31.1	—
I would accept this person as my family's friend	40.9	24.0
I would accept this person as a neighbor	38.7	—
I am going to invite this person to dinner	—	33.3
I would live in the same apartment house with this person	49.4	—
I would rent a room from this person	57.5	42.8
I would be willing to participate in the lynching of this person (in Greece: I would kill this person if I had the chance)	100.0	100.0

would admit as a visitor only to my country; (7) would exclude from my country. Bogardus (1928) found that American white subjects maintained little social distance toward Englishmen, Canadians, and Northern Europeans, and more social distance toward Southern Europeans such as Italians and Greeks. The greatest amount of social distance was found for people who differed from the subjects with respect to racial characteristics (such as, Orientals and Negroes).

However, these results are ambiguous. When an Amereican white subject indicates much social distance toward Negroes, it is difficult to know whether he rejects them because of their physical type or their probable lower-class background. Or, to take another example, when an American shows social distance toward Irishmen, does he object to their nationality or to their probable religion (Roman Catholic)? Triandis and Triandis (1960) avoided this ambiguity by

asking their white American subjects to react to hypothetical persons who were described in greater detail than is customary in studies of social distance. Thus subjects were asked to indicate their acceptance of a Negro who is a physician, Portuguese, and a Roman Catholic. By a statistical technique called analysis of variance it was possible to find out whether the race, the occupation, the nationality, or the religion of the stimulus persons determined the social distance.

Let us clarify this procedure. The first step requires a standardization of the social distance scale. A large number of statements, such as those used by Bogardus, are presented to a group of judges. The judges are asked to indicate, on an 11-point scale, how much social distance is implied by agreement with each of the statements. Typically the statement, "I would marry this person," is given as an anchor, and defines the zero social distance point; the statement,

"I would kill this person," is used as the anchor for the other end of the scale. When that is done, a judge may decide that agreement with the statement, "would exclude from the neighborhood," implies considerable social distance— say, six points on an eleven-point scale. A group of judges typically provides a distribution of such judgments for each statement. The distribution of judgments for each statement is analyzed by a technique developed by the psychologist Thurstone, and a single scale value is derived for each statement.

Table 1 shows some social distance statements and some values obtained from such a standardization process. Suppose that an American subject is asked whether he would or would not do the various things listed in Table 1 with a "Negro Physician." Let us say that a subject indicates that he would *not* accept the Negro Physician as an intimate friend, as a close kin by marriage, as a roommate, or as a personal chum, but would accept him as a neighbor, as a family friend, in the same apartment, and so on; and would not do any of the negative things that are listed. Then the social distance of this subject toward "Negro Physicians" is 38.7.

Let us assume that a subject obtains the following social distance scores when he evaluates four types of persons: Negro physicians, Negro laborers, white physicians, and white laborers.

It is intuitively clear that this sub-ject pays more attention to the "race" of the stimulus than to the "occupation," because the difference between the "Negro" and "White" stimuli is about 75 points, while the difference between the "Physician" and "Unskilled Laborer" stimuli is only about 40.

When the analysis of variance technique is used, it is possible to learn several things.

(A) Whether the subject "pays attention" to a particular characteristic. For instance, a subject might obtain the following scores:

	Negro	White
Physician	11.1	11.1
Unskilled laborer	68.7	68.7

This pattern of scores would indicate that "race" is of no relevance whatever in the determination of his social distance scores. In the analysis of variance, the characteristic "race" would be found to control no "significant amount of variance." It is desirable to compute the statistical significance of the variance of the social distance scores that is controlled by each of the characteristics of the stimulus persons so that one may disregard apparent effects that are probably accidental or undependable. The level of significance tells us whether the obtained difference in social distance scores, when shifting from the "preferred" to the "nonpreferred" value of the characteristic, is likely to have been

	Negro	White	Total
Physician	38.7	11.1	49.8 } Difference = 40.4
Unskilled laborer	68.7	21.5	90.2
Total	107.4	32.6	

Difference = 74.8

observed by chance, or not likely to have been observed by chance. In the latter case, we may infer that the subject has been "paying attention" to the characteristic.

(B) It is possible to learn the relative importance of the characteristics for the particular subject. The statistical procedure indicates how much variability in social distance scores is controlled by each of the characteristics, and also how much total variability there is in the social distance scores obtained by a particular subject. The percentage of the total variability which is controlled by a specific characteristic serves as an index of the weight of that characteristic for the subject. For example, if the total variability were 100, race might control 60 percent, occupation 30 percent, and "error" 10 percent of the total variability. We would say that the weights for race and occupation are 60 and 30. This means that race controls twice as much variability (or makes twice as much difference) as does occupation in the determination of the subject's social distance scores.[1]

(C) Finally, we can learn whether there are so-called "interactions" be-

tween the characteristics. In the first example shown above, there is an interaction between race and occupation. The subject shows some social distance toward Negroes, and some toward unskilled laborers; but he shows a particularly large amount of social distance toward the stimulus that has *both* the "nonpreferred" characteristics. The statistical technique also permits checks of the statistical significance of this interaction.

Thus, the use of this procedure permits us to learn at least three things: (A) whether the subject really pays attention to a particular stimulus characteristic, (B) whether he pays attention to combinations of characteristics, and (C) how much importance he attaches to each of the characteristics and their combinations.

THE RELATIVE IMPORTANCE OF THE CHARACTERISTICS OF THE STIMULUS PERSONS

The first study that used this technique showed that American white subjects paid some attention to all four of the characteristics used in the study and attached the following weights to them: race 77, occupation 17, religion 5, and nationality 1. (Note: these weights add to 100.) When the responses of the subjects were averaged out before the analysis, there was no evidence of any interactions but for individual subjects there were many interactions. In other words, one subject might have shown particularly large social distance toward "unskilled Negroes," and another toward "unskilled Jews."

Weidemann and Triandis (in preparation) did a study in which the char-

---

[1] To be completely correct, this procedure requires the subtraction of the error variance from the variance due to a particular source. The "correction" formula typically leads to ratios or weights that differ by less than 10 percent from the ratios obtained without the correction. In the example in the text this correction would result in weights of 45.5 and 18.2, which are still in the ratio of *about* 2 to 1. In all the work reported in this article, this correction has not been used because the "weights" obtained by the more elaborate procedure are extremely similar to the uncorrected weights. As long as one is interested in the question, "what is the order of importance of the weights," it is unnecessary to make the correction, since the corrected and uncorrected weights give the same answer.

acteristics being considered were the sex, race, religion and status of the stimulus persons. Since many of the social distance items that are appropriate for other groups (such as, admit to my street as neighbor, admit to close kin by marriage, exclude from my country) are not very appropriate for measuring attitudes toward women, the authors used a series of questions which involved placing the stimulus persons in positions of varying status. In order to control for the context in which the status differential occurred, five triads of superior, equal and subordinate status positions were used. One such triad, for example, was as follows:

Superior Status: a director of a play in which you are acting

Equal Status: another actor or actress with you

Subordinate Status: a stage hand in a play in which you are acting.

The subjects of this study were white and predominantly Christian students at the University of Illinois. The weights obtained for the male subjects were: race (white-Negro), 46; religion (Christian-Jewish), 25; sex (male-female), 28; status (superior-equal-subordinate), 1. The weights for the women were: race 60, religion 26, sex 13, and status 1. Thus the women placed more emphasis upon race and less on sex than did the men. Whites were preferred to Negroes, Christians to Jews, and men to women by both male and female subjects. Status was unimportant in determining social distance, when considered for all stimulus persons. However, interaction effects showed that both Negroes and women were rejected in positions of superior status by both male and female subjects. Although the overall social distance toward women is con-

siderably less than that expressed toward Negroes, women were rejected more strongly than were Negroes in superior positions; that is, subjects preferred a Negro man to a white or Negro woman for superior status positions. This preference occured for both male and female subjects but was much stronger for women (race x status = 26, sex x status = 74) than for men (race x status = 42, sex x staus = 58).

SUBJECT CHARACTERISTICS: FIRST STUDY

Some subjects showed much more social distance than other subjects. Thus, social distance appears to be determined not only by societal norms, but also by the demographic and personality characteristics of the subjects.

Demographic Characteristics

Triandis and Triandis (1960) found that upper class subjects tend to show less social distance than lower class subjects; that Jewish subjects tend to show less social distance than Christian subjects; and that subjects with a Southern or Eastern European national background tend to show less social distance than subjects with a Northern or Western European background. These differences probably reflect, in part, the norms of these various societal groups and, in part, the historic factors that are related to immigration to this country.

Personality Characteristics

Some subjects, regardless of ethnic or national background, show more distance than other subjects. In the study described above, subjects who scored high on the California Fascism Scale tended to show more social distance than did subjects who scored low on that scale. The California F scale is an instrument that reflects (inversely) the social sophistication or breadth of perspective of the subject (Kelman and Barclay, 1963).

A good deal of previous research employing the F-scale, and other scales designed to measure different aspects of the subject's personality, suggested that a person may show more social distance if he is insecure about his own merit. A secure person is capable of facing people different from himself, who may challenge his values and assumptions much more comfortably than is an insecure person. People hold many kinds of beliefs about which there can be no objective proof. The only way for them to feel sure that their beliefs are correct is to talk with other people who hold the same views. Thus, people who hold different beliefs pose a real threat to an insecure individual and he is likely to avoid them. If an individual has a narrow, unsophisticated perspective, he is likely to have a very simple system of beliefs, and "strange" people can be particularly threatening to this system (Rokeach, 1960).

To summarize, then, a person's social distance from other people is in part determined by the norms of his social group and in part by his own personality. Norms are learned from talking to his parents, friends, and valued associates; personality is determined by both genetic predisposing factors and the childhood training experiences to which he was subjected by his parents. His general education and level of sophistication are additional fac-

tors that may broaden his perspective and make other people, who are different from himself, less threatening.

SUBJECT CHARACTERISTICS: SECOND STUDY

From these considerations, Triandis and Triandis (1962) derived two hypotheses: (1) different cultures have different norms about social distance, and (2) within a culture, the more insecure and anxious an individual is, the higher the amount of social distance he will feel towards people who are not like himself.

To test these hypotheses, Triandis and Triandis administered a questionnaire to 100 university students at the University of Athens, Greece, and to 100 students at the University of Illinois. The questionnaire presented complex stimuli varying in all possible combinations of the following characteristics: Race: White-Negro; Occupation: Bank Manager-Coal Miner; Religion: Same-Different from that of the subject; and Nationality: French-Portuguese. The "same-different" religion was explained to the subjects by asking them to think of their own religion when seeing the words "same religion"; and of that religion, out of a set that included different Christian and Jewish denominations, which they considered most different from their own when seeing the words "different religion." In other words, an American Jewish subject who saw the stimulus: "Portuguese, Negro, Bank Manager, Different Religion" may have responded to "Portuguese, Negro, Bank Manager, Roman Catholic"; and a Greek Orthodox subject, looking at the *same* stimulus may have responded to a

"Portuguese, Negro, Bank Manager, Conservative Jew."

The first step in the study involved separate standardizations of the social distance scales in the two cultures. The scale statements were standardized by the Thurstone successive intervals technique, described above, using a population of 100 Greek high school students.

Table 1 presents some of the statements used in the study and shows the scale values of the statements that were obtained from the American and Greek judges.

The 16 stimuli generated by the characteristics mentioned above (race, religion, occupation, and nationality) and the social distance statements were presented to a new sample of 100 Greek and 100 Illinois students. The patterns of responses obtained from the two cultures had numerous similarities. In both cultures the preferred stimulus was the "French, Bank Manager, White, Same Religion." In both cultures the "Portuguese Miner, Negro, Different Religion" stimulus was the least preferred. The average distance toward the latter stimulus was 37.1 and 33.4 for the American and the Greek subjects respectively. The average American subject would accept a "Portuguese Miner, Negro, Different Religion" person as a neighbor and the average Greek would invite him to dinner. But, it must be remembered that these average social distance scores are greatly depressed by the large number of both Illinois and Greek students who would accept *all* of the stimuli under all circumstances. Actually, although none of the subjects indicated that they would be willing to kill any of the stimulus persons, there were some who would exclude Negro or Jewish stimuli from

their country and *many* who would exclude them from their neighborhoods.

The similarities between the American and Greek scores suggest that there is about the same variability in the social distance scores in the two cultures. The next question is this: Are the social distance scores determined by the same characteristics in the two cultures? The answer is no, particularly if we pay attention to the relative weights of the characteristics.

The Culture of the Subjects

The American subjects in this study gave a large weight to race; the Greeks gave a large weight to religion. The American weights were as follows: race 86; occupation 3; religion 8; and nationality ½. The Greek weights were: race 24; occupation 5; religion 56; and nationality 0. Thus, the Americans gave large weights to race as they had done in the previous study (Triandis and Triandis, 1960), and small weights to religion (anti-Semitism) and occupation, while the Greeks gave religion the biggest weight and race and occupation smaller weights.

This finding supports the hypothesis that different cultures have different norms about social distance. The average American subject apparently focuses more on *race*, and the average Greek subject more on *religion*. This hypothesis is further strengthened by Triandis, Davis and Takezawa (in preparation). These researchers repeated the Triandis and Triandis (1962) study with German high school students and Japanese university students. For the German study they used stimuli formed from different combinations of race (Negro-white), occupation (physician-unskilled laborer), religion (Protestant-Catholic-Jewish), and nationality (German-American-Italian). The Japanese stimuli were also formed with the characteristics of race (Negroid-Caucasoid-Mongoloid), occupation (physician-unskilled laborer), religion (Protestant-Catholic), and nationality (Japanese-American-Portuguese). The same stimuli were also presented to two samples of Illinois students.

First, we might ask, what kind of results were obtained from the American students who responded to the "German study stimuli" and those who responded to the "Japanese study stimuli." Since the stimuli were a little different from those used in the previous studies, we should expect some differences. The weights obtained with the German stimuli and white American Protestant subjects were as follows: race 60; occupation 22; religion 6; and nationality 1. For the Japanese stimuli the weights were: race 57; occupation 35; religion 1; and nationality 4. Table 2 summarizes these findings. The stars indicate the level of significance of the results. When there are four stars it means that there is one chance in 10,000 that the subjects in the particular culture did *not* pay attention to the corresponding characteristic.

The results of Table 2 are fairly consistent with the previous results. The major difference occurs on the weight given to occupation. This is probably due to the fact that the difference between Bank Manager and Coal Miner employed in the Greek study is smaller than that between Physician and Unskilled Laborer employed in the German and Japanese studies. The other difference is on religion and nationality between the Greek and the Japanese studies. But here again the stimuli account for the difference. The Japanese

stimuli did not include the characteristic "Jewish," hence the drop in the size of the weights from 8 to 1, and they did include the nationality "Japanese," while in the Greek study the nationalities were French and Portuguese. These results suggest that the weights depend on the extent to which one uses extreme characteristics to describe a particular dimension. Thus, weights must be considered in conjunction with the kinds of stimuli used in a particular study. However, when samples from two different cultures are given the same stimuli, differences in the weights will reflect differences in emphases that are due to the cultures of the subjects.

The German subjects provided the following weights: race 6; occupation 70; religion 12; and nationality 2. There is a spectacular difference between the American and German subjects in the weights given to race and occupation, with the American subjects giving more weight to race and less weight to occupation than do the Germans. The Germans also give more weight to religion and nationality than do the Americans. In the case of the Japanese, the weights were: race 38; occupation 50; religion 0; and nationality 3. Again the Americans give more weight to race and less weight to occupation than do the Japanese.

To sum up, there is little doubt that different cultures employ different weights in the determination of the social distance. The typical American weights are much larger for the characteristic race than for other characteristics. The typical Greek weights are larger for the characteristic religion. The typical German weights are very high for occupational status, moderately high for religion, and relatively low for race. The typical Japanese weights are very

TABLE 2. RELATIVE WEIGHTS OBTAINED IN THREE STUDIES OF SOCIAL DISTANCE
(Each study employed a different set of stimulus persons)

Characteristics	Greeks	Americans With Greek Stimuli	Germans	Americans With German Stimuli	Japanese	American With Japanese Stimuli
Race	24**	86***	6***	60*****	38*****	57*****
Occupation	5*	3***	70*****	22****	50*****	35*****
Religion	56****	8***	12**	6****	0	1***
Nationality	0	0.5	2*	1***	3****	4***

Stimuli used for:

Race:	Negro–White	Negro–White	Negro–White–Mongoloid
Occupation:	Bank Manager-Coal Miner	Physician-Unskilled Laborer	Physician-Unskilled Laborer
Religion:	Same-Different from subject	Protestant-Catholic-Jewish	Protestant-Catholic
Nationality:	French-Portuguese	German-American-Italian	Japanese-American-Portuguese

* $p < .05$
** $p < .01$
*** $p < .001$
**** $p < .0001$

high for occupation and race, and small for nationality. It must *not* be assumed, however, that these results characterize every subject in each of these cultures. There is a great deal of variability within cultures that is attributable to the religion and social class of the subjects. For example, Triandis, Davis and Takezawa found that the weights given by different subsamples of American subjects were quite different. The American Jewish male subjects showed little social distance, and the amount they did show was mostly determined by the occupation of the stimulus persons. The American Jewish female subjects showed a similar pattern, though they did give substantially larger weights to "religion" than did the male subjects.

The Personality of the Subjects

In both their American and their Greek samples, Triandis and Triandis (1962) found that subjects who obtained high social distance scores tended to answer "yes" to a wide variety of attitude questions, including items from the California F scale and statements that were intended to be the obverse of those items. Persons who obtained high social distance scores also showed a tendency to check the most extreme positions on graphic rating scales, thus indicating either very strong agreement or very strong disagreement with attitude statements. Psychologists are not agreed concerning the meaning of "acquiescent" and "extreme" styles of response to attitude questionnaires, but such reactions are commonly believed to reflect personality factors. Through the use of analysis of variance, Triandis and Triandis were able to show that the cultural backgrounds (American or Greek) of their subjects controlled almost twice as much

variance in social distance scores as did the two response styles.

In a later study (Triandis, Davis and Takezawa), several personality measures were obtained and correlated with social distance scores. American subjects who scored high on social distance tended to be low on independence of judgment (measured by a scale developed by Barron) and on tolerance for ambiguity (measured by a scale developed by Budner). German subjects who were high on social distance also showed low tolerance for ambiguity (measured by a scale developed by Brengelmann). Thus, there is a cross-cultural replication of this result, with two different kinds of scales measuring tolerance for ambiguity. This characteristic is related to the ability of the subject to "suspend judgment" until he has considerable information. Subjects who have low tolerance for ambiguity tend to "prejudge" other people on the basis of obvious group characteristics such as their race or religion. From the Weidemann and Triandis (in preparation) study, it is worth noting that "prejudice toward women," as measured by the Nadler-Morrow (1959) Scale, correlates .30 (p < .01) with the authoritarian content of the F-Scale, corrected for response acquiescence. This suggests that the correlates of antifeminine prejudice are similar to those of anti-Negro and anti-Semitic prejudice.

The attitudes of the high social distance subjects are also of some interest. Such subjects are very likely to agree *strongly* with attitude statements such as "What youth needs most is strict discipline, rugged determination and the will to work and fight for family and country," or "In my opinion patriotism and loyalty are the first requirements of a good citizen." These statements are similar in content to some of the propaganda messages disseminated by Fascists and Nazis before the Second World War. It is interesting that the postwar young German subjects (born in 1944) tested in the Triandis, Davis and Takezawa study rejected such statements more strenuously than did the Illinois subjects tested in the same study. The attitudes of the latter subjects toward a large variety of social and political issues were measured by Triandis *et al.* and related to the degree of social distance shown by the subjects. It was found that high social distance subjects indicated much more conformity to existing social institutions and prevailing points of view about political behavior, and were more conservative and uncritical of these values, than did the low social distance subjects.

SUMMARY

For normal populations, such as those tested in the studies described above, social distance is greatly influenced by cultural norms concerning what is appropriate behavior towards persons who are "different." Individuals who are particularly sensitive to these norms, and who tend to conform and accept uncritically the values imparted to them by their culture, are particularly likely to show large amounts of social distance.

REFERENCES

BOGARDUS, E. S. *Immigration and race attitudes.* Boston: Heath, 1928.

KELMAN, H. C., & BARCLAY, JANET The F Scale as a measure of breadth of perspective. *J. abnorm. soc. Psychol.,* 1963, **67,** 608–615.

NADLER, E. B., & MORROW, W. R. Authoritarian attitudes toward women and their correlates. *J. soc. Psychol.,* 1959, **49,** 113–123.

ROKEACH, M. *The open and closed mind.* New York: Basic Books, 1960.

TRIANDIS, H. C., & TRIANDIS, LEIGH MINTURN. Race, social class, religion and nationality as determinants of social distance. *J. abnorm. soc. Psychol.,* 1960, **61,** 110–118.

TRIANDIS, H. C., & TRIANDIS, LEIGH MINTURN. A cross-cultural study of social distance. *Psychol. monogr.,* 1962, **76,** No. 540.

TRIANDIS, H. C., DAVIS, E. E., & TAKEZAWA, S. I. Some determinants of social distance among American, German and Japanese students. Submitted for publication, 1964.

WEIDEMANN, SUE ROWAND & TRIANDIS, LEIGH MINTURN. A study of discrimination with respect to race, religion, and sex. Unpublished Senior Honors Thesis, University of Illinois, 1963. Submitted for publication, 1964.

22. STABILITIES UNDERLYING CHANGES IN INTERPERSONAL ATTRACTION *

Theodore M. Newcomb

It is a safe prediction that individuals who are initially strangers to one another will, under conditions assuring that they will become well acquainted, experience many changes in the degree of their attraction toward one another. Such changes, like any others that scientists investigate, presumably occur in

* Excerpted from the *Journal of Abnormal and Social Psychology,* 1963, 66: 376–386, with permission of the author and the American Psychological Association.

orderly ways, and the principles governing both change and nonchange correspond to constancies. Lewin (1947), paraphrasing Cassirer (1923), notes that "throughout the history of mathematics and physics, problems of constancy of relations rather than of constancy of elements have gained importance and have gradually changed the picture of what is essential" (p. 5). The present report points to a few such constancies of relations that have been observed on the part of two populations of initial strangers over a 4-month period, while their attitudes (elements involved in the relations) toward one another were characterized by a good deal of inconstancy.

As reported more fully elsewhere (Newcomb, 1961), two sets of 17 male students served in two successive years as subjects in an investigation of the phenomena of getting acquainted. They had been successfully selected as total strangers to one another, and lived and took their meals together in a house reserved for them. During each of 16 weeks they responded to a selected set of questionnaires, attitude scales, or other instruments, many of which were repeated from time to time. In particular, they rated or ranked each other as to favorability of interpersonal attitudes (henceforth referred to as *attraction*) during almost every week. In addition, they frequently estimated one anothers' attitudes of various kinds. The present paper partially summarizes and also supplements findings reported in the original monograph, for the specific purpose of noting constancies that underlie inconstancies.[1]

The theoretical considerations from which the investigation stemmed were direct descendants from Heider's (1958) theory of "balanced states." For the purposes of this study, the elements among which a balanced relationship may exist for an individual are: his degree of attraction, positive or negative, toward another individual; his attitude, favorable or unfavorable, toward some object (in the inclusive sense, referring to persons, issues, and abstractions like general values); and the second individual's attitude, as preceived by the first individual, toward the same object. A balanced state exists among these elements insofar as attraction is positive and the individual perceives that his own and the others' attitudes are similar. Perceived dissimilarity together with positive attraction represents an imbalanced state; negative attraction (with which this paper does not specifically deal) together with perceived similarity of attitudes may be either imbalanced or merely nonbalanced (a matter of indifference); together with perceived dissimilarity, negative attraction may be either balanced or merely nonbalanced.[2] These rules of balanced relationships include the specification of certain conditions, most important of which are that the attitude objects be of relatively high importance and be considered to have common impact

---

[1] There were, of course, individual instances of nonchange, but as population variables most of the attitudes here considered were highly inconstant.

[2] This description of balance as associated with negative attraction differs from Heider's position, according to which negative attraction together with dissimilarity is balanced, and imbalanced together with perceived similarity. Theoretical considerations suggest that the former combination need not be rewarding nor the latter distressing; and empirical findings from the investigation here reported indicate that the former combination often does not have the stability that is characteristic of balanced relationships, while the latter does not necessarily have the instability characteristic of imbalanced relationships.

upon self and others, in similar ways.[3]

The significant feature, for present purposes, of balanced and imbalanced states is, in Heider's (1958) words, that "if a balanced state does not exist, then forces toward this state will arise. If a change is not possible, the state of imbalance will produce tension" (p. 201). Thus balanced states tend to be stable and imbalanced ones unstable. In either case we are dealing with relations, in Lewin's terms, and not merely with elements attitudes.

INDIVIDUALS' ATTITUDES

It is to be expected that individuals' attraction to the remaining group members will at first be unstable, because initial attraction responses (made on the third day) are necessarily based upon first impressions only; and that week-to-week changes should be in the direction of increased stability—that is, that the rate of change will be a declining one, because in successive weeks the amount of "new" information that individuals receive about one another will decline. The kinds of information about another person that are relevant to attraction toward him are, in general, those that result in the attribution to him of properties that are regarded as rewarding. These are not necessarily persistent or "inherent" personal properties; they may equally well include properties that are elicited only in interaction with specific other persons and they may, of course, be idiosyncratically attributed. Changes in attraction result not only from new discoveries of what characteristics another person already has, but also from

[3] For a fuller statement concerning this theoretical approach see Newcomb 1953, 1959.)

TABLE 1. MEANS OF 17 INDIVIDUAL CORRELATIONS (rho's) FOR PAIRS OF ADJACENT WEEKS

Weekly Interval [a]	Year I	Year II
0–1	.51	.65
1–2 through 4–5 [b]	.82	.84
5–6 through 9–10 [b]	.86	.91
10–11 through 14–15 [b]	.88	.90

Note.—In rank ordering attraction toward other 16 subjects.

[a] Week numbers refer to the number of preceding weeks of acquaintance.

[b] Variations within these sets of adjacent weeks are so slight that values for the pairs of weeks have been averaged, rather than presenting each one.

observing qualities that, whether one knows it or not, one has oneself helped to elicit in him.[4]

Table 1 presents means of week-to-week "reliability coefficients"; each subject's rank ordering of the other 16 subjects in attraction at each week was correlated with his rank ordering for the following week. Table 2 shows similar coefficients, computed over longer intervals. The two tables together provide

TABLE 2. MEANS OF 17 INDIVIDUAL CORRELATIONS (rho's) OVER VARYING INTERVALS OF TIME

Weekly Interval	Year I	Year II
0–15	.29	.31
0–10	.32	.35
0–5	.38	.43
5–15	.66	.70
5–10	.82	.84
10–15	.83	.85

Note.—In rank ordering attraction toward other 16 subjects.

[4] Certain distinguishable sources of interpersonal reward, and thus of attraction, have been elsewhere described by Newcomb (1960).

TABLE 3. RELATIONSHIP BETWEEN GIVING HIGH ATTRACTION AND PERCEPTION
OF RECEIVING HIGH ATTRACTION FROM SAME PERSONS
(Year I)

Estimated Rank of Reciprocated Attraction	Number of Subjects Estimating Reciprocation From Their Rank I Choices at Level Indicated		
	Week 1	Week 5	Week 15
1–2 (very high)	14	14	12
3–4 (high)	3	2	2
5–8 (second quarter)	0	1	3
9–16 (lower half)	0	0	0
Total	17	17	17

strong support for both predictions: initial responses have little predictive value even for so short a period as 5 weeks, whereas Week 5 responses predict almost as well to Week 15 as to Week 10 ($p < .001$ in either case). Change continues throughout the entire period, but the rate of change declines hardly at all after the first 5 or 6 weeks. Except for very unpopular subjects, whose high attraction choices are not reciprocated and continue to be relatively erratic, attraction choices show comparatively little change after the first 6 weeks.

Such changes should occur, hypothetically, in spite of the individual's tendency to maintain a constant relationship between degree of perceived agreement and attraction to others concerning objects of importance to himself. If it may be assumed that the self is such an object, and in general a positively valued one, then it is to be expected that high attraction toward others will be associated with the perception of reciprocation of high attraction toward oneself. Table 3 supports this prediction for Year I, and results for

Year II are almost identical. All estimates of reciprocation by Rank 1 choices are at all times in the upper half of the distribution, and most of them in the upper eighth. There is a very strong tendency (not necessarily warranted) to assume that one's highest ranked associates return the compliment.

It is to be expected, on similar grounds, that attraction to other individuals will be paralleled by perceived agreement with them as to the relative attractiveness of the remaining House members. As shown in Table 4, which summarizes relationships between level of attraction to others and degree of perceived agreement with them about the relative attractiveness of other House members, there is in both populations, at all stages of acquaintance, a significant relationship between these two variables.

A special instance of this tendency is to be found in the almost universal tendency to assume that one's two most preferred sociometric choices are highly attracted toward each other. (In view of the fact that reciprocated attraction from Rank 1 and Rank 2 choices is also

TABLE 4. SUMMARY OF RELATIONSHIPS FOUND BETWEEN LEVEL OF ATTRACTION TO OTHER SUBJECTS AND PERCEIVED AGREEMENT WITH THEM ABOUT ATTRACTIVENESS OF REMAINING SUBJECTS

Time of Response	x^2	df
Year I, week 1	55.81***	2
Year I, week 5	31.13***	2
Year I, week 14	38.94***	2
Year II, week 2 [a]	17.54***	1
Year II, week 5 [a]	6.73*	1
Year II, week 12 [a]	9.95**	1

[a] In Year II only 5 percent of all possible estimates, based on a randomly drawn sample, were made. The somewhat lower significance levels in Year II result, in part at least, from the smaller Ns in that year.
* $p < .01$.
** $p < .005$.
*** $p < .001$.

perceived as very high, this set of phenomena may be labeled "the perception of perfect triads.") According to the Year I data, which for this purpose are more complete than in Year II but which are well supported by the latter, the relationships shown in Table 5 are typical of all stages of acquaintance. It seemed to be almost unthinkable to

these subjects that their two most preferred choices should be hostile to each other, and almost so that they should be merely "neutral." Early estimates to this effect were in several cases quite inaccurate; lack of information invites autistic judgments. Later ones were highly accurate; as earlier perceptions of perfect triads were discovered to be erroneous, preferences shifted in such manner as to justify the perception of perfect triads.

Balance inducing forces should also result, at all times, in the perception of closest agreement with most attractive others with respect to objects other than the self and House members. The data most suitable for testing this prediction are subjects' rankings of the six Spranger values in Year II, together with their estimates of how each other subject would rank them. Both at Week 2 and at Week 14 the relationships between attraction toward other subjects and estimates of agreement with them were highly significant; x^2 values are 17.19 and 11.63, respectively, corresponding p values being $< .001$ and $< .005$, $df = 2$. The slight decline in this relation, from Week 2 to Week 14, is also found in other tests of the same prediction; it reflects in part the countereffects of

TABLE 5. SUMMARY OF SIGNIFICANCE LEVELS AT WHICH TWO HIGHEST RANKING CHOICES BY ALL SUBJECTS ARE JUDGED TO BE HIGHLY ATTRACTED TO EACH OTHER
(Year I, Week 5)

Category of Estimated Attraction	Number of Estimates		x^2	df
	Obtained	Expected		
Highest quarter	22	8.5	26.51*	1
Upper half	33	17.0	28.30*	1
"Favorable"	34	23.6	13.68*	1

* $p < .001$.

greater accuracy with increasing acquaintance.

Thus the data show a continuing increase, though at a rapidly declining rate, in the stability of attraction toward others. They also show that at all times, to about the same degree, attraction toward others is related to perceived agreement with them concerning a variety of things.

DYAD RELATIONSHIPS: MUTUAL ATTRACTION AND ACTUAL AGREEMENT

Insofar as subjects were alert to increments of information about one another with continued interaction among them, it is predictable that estimates of others' attitudes will become increasingly accurate with continued acquaintance; and that actual relationships between mutual attraction and agreement will increasingly approach the perceived relationships. The latter prediction presumes that, with increasing accuracy, subjects will discover that some of their assumptions about agreement with attractive others are not justified, and will tend either to modify their own attitudes or to shift their attraction preferences to individuals with whom they are in fact more closely in agreement.

With respect to the self as an object, the data do not support the first prediction: estimates of others' attraction toward oneself do not become more accurate with increasing acquaintance, and this is true at all levels of expressed attraction. Frequencies and magnitudes of inaccuracies are quite constant, although they are at all times predominantly in the direction of overestimating

the true level of reciprocated attraction. Estimates are in general fairly accurate, especially at the extremes of expressed attraction. Most subjects, apparently, are rather sensitive to others' indications of attraction toward themselves, at all times, and at all times there is a constant tendency to exaggerate the degree to which one's own attraction toward another person is reciprocated at about the same level.

The accuracy with which subjects estimate each others' attraction preferences toward other House members does increase. During the early period (Weeks 0–5) this increase is significant only for the estimator's highest attraction ranks, representing individuals with whom he is likely to have associated frequently enough after 5 weeks to estimate their preferences reasonably well. By Week 15 the trend is unmistakable at all attraction ranks: in Year I (the population in which these data are most nearly complete) 15 of 17 subjects were more accurate than at Week 1—the binomial probability of which is beyond .001.

Subjects' accuracy in estimating others' rank ordering of Spranger values increases at a high level of significance, as shown in Table 6, in which the indices of accuracy represent rank-order correlations between each subject's estimated rank ordering of each other subject's responses and the latter responses as actually made. The mean accuracy of 272 estimates, according to this index, is .25 at Week 2 and .49 at Week 14.

Turning now to actual dyadic relationships, it is to be expected that sensitivity to others' responses to oneself will increasingly result in similar levels of attraction on the part of dyad members, whatever that level may be. Insofar as

TABLE 6. RELATIVE ACCURACY OF ESTIMATING OTHERS' RANK ORDERING OF SPRANGER VALUES, EARLY AND LATE

Accuracy Level [a]	Number of Estimates at Indicated Levels of Accuracy		
	Week 2	Week 14	Total
≥ .60	66	110	176
< .60, > .14	103	95	198
< .14	103	67	170
Total	272	272	544

Note.—$\chi^2 = 17.92$, $p = .001$, $df = 2$.
[a] Rho between each estimated rank with actual rank.

forces toward balance with regard to the self are tempered with considerations of reality, dyad members should come to assign about the same degree of attraction to one another. Table 7 shows that this is indeed the case. A large proportion of the dyads whose members accord very different levels of attraction to each other include a very popular or a very unpopular individual, or both. Apart from this consideration, the tendency toward increasing reciprocation of attraction by dyad members at closely similar levels is almost universal. This fact about objective dyadic relationships, combined with the unchanging tendency to perceive favorably reciprocated attraction, reflects shifts in actual attraction preferences: changes are such that increasingly accurate judgments of others' attraction toward oneself result in increasingly close reciprocation.

With respect to Spranger values, also, the effects of increased accuracy in judging others, together with constant forces toward balance, are that actual agreement is increasingly associated with high mutual attraction. At Week 2, when these responses were first obtained, there was no relationship between pair agreement and mutual pair attraction ($\chi^2 = 1.17$, $p < .50$, $df = 1$). At Week 14, however (when responses were last obtained), the relationship had

TABLE 7. NS OF DYADS WHOSE MEMBERS' ATTRACTION TO EACH OTHER DIFFER BY 3 (of 16) RANKS OR LESS

Time of Response	Obtained	Expected	χ^2	df
Year I, week 0	51	50	.00	1
Year II, week 0	59	53	.61	1
Year I, week 15	77	53	10.61**	1
Year II, week 15	72	53	6.46*	1

* $p < .02$.
** $p < .002$.

become highly significant, as shown in Table 8. The χ^2 value of this distribution, with both variables equally dichotomized, is 9.52, $df = 1$, and $p < .001$ by a one-tailed test.

It happened that there were almost no changes in subjects' ranking of the six Spranger values between early and late acquaintance; it was therefore possible to predict later dyad attraction from initial agreement nearly as well from early as from late agreement; early agreement did not, however, predict to early attraction. Similar results were obtained with two other sets of attitude items, each quite wide-ranging in content, from which indices of dyad agreement were computed.

In view of the general increase in accuracy of estimating others' attitudes and in view of the constant tendency to prefer balanced to unbalanced states, it follows that with increasing acquaintance there should be an increasing tendency toward relationships that are balanced not merely phenomenologically but also in fact. This means that, except in the case of attitudes that show little or no change, change in mutual attraction between dyad members should be accompanied by change in their actual agreement. This prediction is best tested with respect to agreement about the relative attractiveness of House members. The early relationship between mutual dyad attraction and agreement about House members approached zero in both populations, and increased to a significant level in the later weeks. Typically, there was a good deal of shifting about during the earlier weeks, both with respect to mutual attraction and to preferences among other House members, with the result that the relationship between attraction and actual agreement becomes a highly significant one. It can also be shown, by more detailed analysis, that among dyads at a high level of mutual attraction in early weeks there is significantly higher agreement 3 months later on the part of dyads whose mutual attraction remains at the same high level than on the part of dyads whose mutual attraction has de-

TABLE 8. RELATIONSHIP BETWEEN DEGREE OF AGREEMENT ABOUT SPRANGER
VALUES AND MUTUAL PAIR ATTRACTION
(Week 14, Year II)

| Level of Agreement | Number of Dyads at Attraction Level Indicated | | | | Total |
	Highest Quarter [a]	Second Quarter [a]	Third Quarter [a]	Lowest Quarter [a]	
Highest quarter	12	6	9	6	33
Second quarter	10	16	6	4	36
Third quarter	9	4	8	11	32
Lowest quarter	7	4	10	14	35
Total	38	30	33	35	136

[a] For reasons described in the full report, dyad scores are routinely categorized according to proportions of *expected*, not obtained, frequencies, which typically show slight differences.

creased. Change or non-change in these two respects proceeds together and interdependently.

INDIVIDUAL CHARACTERISTICS OF SUBJECTS

Several theoretically derived expectations have been shown to be supported by empirical findings. Our tests, however, have been statistical ones, pertaining to populations or subpopulations and not to individuals. There are two relevant questions concerning the manner in which individuals' characteristics contribute to the findings.

First, it is possible that a comparatively few individuals contribute all or most of the variances that account for the statistically significant findings; if so, the generalizability of the findings is severely limited. The findings depend rather heavily on assumptions concerning two kinds of individual tendencies: to prefer balanced to imbalanced relationships; and at the same time to take account of "reality" in the form of accretions of information that may disturb existing states of balance. Individual indices of both of these tendencies (sensitivity to balance, and accuracy in judging others) were therefore constructed. Results of intensive analyses of all 34 subjects may be summarized as follows:

1. Individual differences are clearly apparent, with respect to both balance and accuracy.

2. In estimating others' attitudes toward varying kinds of objects there are in each population typically one or two individuals who show little or no sensitivity to balance, or no greater than chance accuracy in making estimates.

3. The subjects who are deviant in these ways with respect to one attitude object at a particular stage of acquaintance are not necessarily deviant with respect to other attitude objects, or at other times.

In sum, the tendencies to be sensitive to balanced relationships and to judge others' attitudes more accurately with increasing acquaintance, which underlie our theoretically derived predictions, appear to be present, at least in some degree, in all of our subjects.

As to measured individual characteristics, authoritarianism (as measured by the F Scale) seemed most likely to be relevant to the problems of this investigation. Our expectations concerning authoritarianism stem from several studies suggesting that F Scale scores (Adorno, Frenkel-Brunswik, Levinson, & Sanford, 1950) are related to "perceptiveness of others" (Christie & Cook, 1958, in a review of the relevant evidence on this point, pp. 180–183). Such evidence leads to the expectation that low F scorers should be relatively accurate in estimating others' attitudes. With one exception (estimates of others' ordering of attraction toward House members in Year I), the prediction is supported with respect to various attitude objects, and according to different indices of accuracy, in both populations. The data that best lend themselves to detailed analysis of accuracy consist of estimates of others' rank ordering of Spranger values, made in identical manner at Weeks 2 and 14 of Year II. These data show that on the rather difficult task of ranking other subjects according to agreement with the estimator, the nonauthoritarians excel the authoritarians in accuracy on late but not on early acquaintance; the correlation of .56 between F score and accuracy at the later time is significant at $< .01$.

Inaccurate estimates of others' attitudes may represent distortions either in the balance promoting direction or in the opposite direction; the former may be considered autistic, and if we assume that imbalanced relationships represent a form of ambiguity, of which authoritarians are relatively intolerant (cf. Adorno et al., 1950), then it is to be expected that high F scorers' inaccuracies will be in the autistic direction, relative to low F scorers. No difference in this respect appears at Week 2, when autistic errors are relatively frequent at all F score levels; but the prediction is well supported at Week 14: comparisons of autistic, accurate, and contra-autistic estimates for low, intermediate, and high F scorers yield a χ^2 of 13.02 in the predicted direction, significant at $< .01$, $df = 4$, by a one-tailed test.[5]

These and other findings are consistent with the following interpretation. The greater sensitivity of the very low F scorers enables them to select as most attractive those with whom they are in fact most closely in agreement about a rather wide range of values. The nonauthoritarians' characteristic solution to imbalance is nonautistic: they tend to achieve balance not by exaggerating actual agreement with those to whom they are attracted (on other grounds), but by judging rather accurately who is in agreement with them and letting their highest attractions be determined accordingly. The characteristic solution of the more authoritarian subjects tends to

[5] If the "accurate" estimates are ignored, in order to compare autistic and contra-autistic responses only, the inverse relationship between autism and authoritarianism is still significant at the .05 level.

be just the reverse: instead of letting their personal preferences be determined by accurate perceptions of agreement, they tend to perceive more agreement than actually exists with those toward whom they are already attracted.

NATURE OF CONSTANT RELATIONS

Three kinds of elements, in Lewin's (1947) sense, have been considered: an individual's attraction toward another person; his attitude toward some object other than that person; and that person's attitude, as he perceives it, toward the same object. Under the conditions of the investigation here reported, the stability curves of these three kinds of elements were quite different: attitudes toward nonperson objects (especially toward general values) showed little change from first to last acquaintance; attraction toward other House members, on the part of most subjects, became relatively stable by the end of the first 6 weeks or so; and estimates of others' attitudes were relatively slow in stabilizing, though with individual differences. If the study had been concerned only with subjects' own attitudes and attractions, it might well have been terminated after 6 rather than 16 weeks. But in view of the crucial place, in the present formulation, of perceptions of others' attitudes, and in view of the relatively slow and continuing changes in estimates of others' attitudes, it might be argued that the study should have been continued for another several weeks.

What does remain relatively constant, in spite of these differential rates of stability and change, is the second-order relationship between the relationship of two of them (own and other's perceived attitude) and attraction. With regard to such diverse attitude objects as the individual subject himself, other group members, and a range of non-person objects, such a relationship, described as a balanced one, is found at all stages of acquaintance. This constant relationship is maintained despite the fact that all of the related elements are changing, or some of them are changing while others are not. Eventually, the single elements tend to become stable, but the level at which they do so is governed by the same constancy of relationships that prevailed throughout the earlier periods of change.

The psychological processes by which intrapersonal states of balance are maintained may be described as follows. As group members interact with one another, each of them selects and processes information—about objects of common interest, about one another as sources of attitudes toward those objects, and about one another as objects of attraction—in such ways that the inconsistencies and conflicts involved in imbalanced relationships tend to be avoided. Both autistic processes ("balance at all costs") and realistic ones ("the truth, whatever it costs") are involved, their respective weightings being determined both by individual differences and by the strength of the attitudes involved. When interaction begins with total strangership, increments of information are inevitable; attitude change results from the necessity to adapt simultaneously to increments of information and to constant preferences for balanced relationships.

Interacting members of dyads and larger groups necessarily make such adaptations to one another simultane-ously. Insofar as they do so realistically, the consequence of reciprocal adaptation is a mutual relationship that is in fact maximally satisfying to both or all of them—that is, maximally within the limits of what is possible. Realism tends to increase with acquaintance and, combined with constant tendencies toward balance, the inevitable trend is toward mutuality of attraction. Stable relationships tend to persist, and relationships that are in fact balanced tend to be stable because they are mutually rewarding and not likely to be disturbed by increments of information with continued interaction.

Viewed intrapersonally, the generalizable constancies underlying changes in interpersonal attraction that apply to all individuals—regardless of their differences in preferring some personal properties to others and regardless of the personal traits that others present—are preferences for balanced relationships, and tendencies to adapt to information regarded as valid. Viewed interpersonally, the generalizable constancies are the necessities (which may become internalized as preferences) confronting each of a set of interacting persons to make successive adaptations to one another, simultaneously and reciprocally, in the direction of establishing relationships that are both realistic and balance promoting for each. It is relationships that are simultaneously rewarding to each and realistically apprehended by each that tend to be stable. Such relationships are both psychologically (intrapersonally) balanced and objectively (interpersonally) balanced.

Attitude changes that are governed by these constancies stem from a triple confrontation that is characteristic of *la condition humaine*. Each of us must somehow come to terms, simultaneously, with the other individuals and groups of which our interpersonal environment is constituted; with the world that we have in common with those persons and groups; and with our own, intrapersonal demands, including the preference for balanced states. Insofar as the individual's confrontation is characterized by changing input of information, the elements that correspond to his attitudes are subject to inconstancy, but the lawfulness with which they change corresponds to certain constancies in relationships among the elements. It is such constancies that make possible viable adaptations, simultaneously, to multiple confrontations.

REFERENCES

ADORNO, T. W., FRENKEL-BRUNSWICK, ELSE, LEVENSON, D. J., & SANFORD, R. N. *The authoritarian personality.* New York: Harper & Row, 1950.

CASSIRER, E. *Substance and function.* Chicago: Open Court, 1923.

CHRISTIE, R., & COOK, PEG. A guide to published literature relating to the authoritarian personality through 1956. *J. Psychol.*, 1958, **45**, 171–199.

HEIDER, F. *The psychology of interpersonal relations.* New York: Wiley, 1958.

LEWIN, K. Frontiers in group dynamics: Concept, method and reality in social science; social equilibria and social change. *Hum. Relat.*, 1947, **1**, 5–41.

NEWCOMB, T. M. An approach to the study of communicative acts. *Psychol. Rev.*, 1953, **60**, 393–404.

NEWCOMB, T. M. Individual systems of orientation. In S. Koch (Ed.), *Psychology: A study of a science.* Vol. 3. New York: McGraw-Hill, 1959. Pp. 384–422.

NEWCOMB, T. M. Varieties of interpersonal attraction. In D. Cartwright & A. Zander (Eds.), *Group dynamics: Research and theory.* (2nd ed.) New York: Harper & Row, 1960. Pp. 104–119.

NEWCOMB, T. M. *The acquaintance process.* New York: Holt, Rinehart and Winston, 1961.

23. INTERPERSONAL CHOICE AS A FUNCTION OF ASCRIBED SIMILARITY AND DEFINITION OF THE SITUATION *

Melvin J. Lerner and Selwyn Becker

Among the general theoretical propositions that have wide acceptance in social psychology are those which focus on the observed correlations among "feelings of positive affect," "social acts of agreement," and the "perception of similarity" between persons. A cognitive or interpersonal system is considered to be "in balance" (Heider, 1946), or "symmetrical" (Newcomb, 1953), or "consonant" (Festinger, 1957) if, for example, people who are perceived to be similar to us agree with us. We also tend to like people who agree with us (Newcomb, 1953), agree with people who are similar to us (Homans, 1950; Riecken

* Reprinted from *Human Relations*, 1962, 15: 27–34, with permission of the senior author and the Tavistock Institute of Human Relations. This research was conducted while the senior author was a Russell Sage Resident. It was supported by the National Institute of Mental Health, United States Public Health Service, Post Doctoral Research Grant MF-6846-C.

& Homans, 1954), and consider similar to us people we like (Fiedler, 1954). We are comfortable if people who are perceived to be similar to us agree with us in social judgments (Festinger, 1954). Elaborations such as these can be extended to include a large body of accepted evidence.

There are data to suggest that when there is a contradiction in these elements the individual will act in such a manner as to reduce the contradiction (Festinger & Thibaut, 1951; Newcomb, 1953; Schachter, 1951). The expression of a deviant opinion by a member of a group (that is, someone who is perceived as being similar) results in a group pressure toward uniformity (Back, 1951; Schachter, 1951). If the deviance persists, the members of the group may resolve the contradiction by redefining the intractable deviant as "different," not a member of the group. At this point the system is in balance and pressure to communicate to the deviant to gain agreement ends. The members have ascribed the contradictory judgement to a "dissimilar" person. It would appear, then, that communication enters into the interpersonal system both as a natural outgrowth of the perception of similarity (Homans, 1950) and in the process of overcoming dissonance or imbalance.

The two experiments reported here are concerned with some of the social-psychological processes which determine an individual's choice of a similar or dissimilar other with whom to interact. In the first experiment hypotheses derived from balance theory are used to predict the individual's choice of a similar or dissimilar other when the outcome of the interaction is clear and limited. Similarity and difference are ascribed by

the identification of the general values and temperament of the participants.

In the second experiment the choice of whether to communicate with the similar or dissimilar other occurs following contradictory behavior on the part of the others. The relevance of balance theory in predicting choice is tested under conditions of low and high motivation to change the position taken by the other. In this experiment similarity is ascribed by the noting of common experiences relevant to the subject-matter of the interaction.

EXPERIMENT I

If we assume that there is some value to the individual in maintaining symmetry or balance in his cognitive elements, then we can suggest that, when given the opportunity, the individual will strive to match the anticipated outcome of an interaction with the kinds of others with whom he interacts. The individual will be most comfortable if a situation ends with a similar outcome for himself and a similar other, and/or a different outcome for himself and a differing other. These effects will be enhanced if there is also a differential value to the outcomes in the second case, and if the outcome with the similar other is of positive value. We tested these assertions concerning balance by enabling the individual to select or design his situation by choosing as a co-participant a similar or different other when the possible outcomes of the interaction were clear and delimited.

The hypotheses were:

1. *An individual will prefer to interact with someone who is perceived as*

similar rather than different if the situation of interaction is such that it allows mutual gain (approximately similar gain is expected for both participants);

2. An individual will prefer to interact with someone who is perceived as different rather than similar if the situation of interaction is such that it will result in gain for one at the expense of loss for the other (differing gains for the participants are expected).

Method

SUBJECTS   Thirty-two high-school students from five high schools were obtained through the U.S. Employment Service. Each S was paid $1.25 for participating in the experiment.

PROCEDURE: ASCRIBED SIMILARITY AND DIFFERENCE   As each S arrived for his appointment he was given the identifying letter B. He filled out the "Mood Adjective Check List" (Nowlis, 1953) and a paired-comparison scale of values adapted from Morris and Jones (1955) [1] in preparation for the second part of the

[1] Seven statements from Morris's paragraphs describing various value systems were presented in forced-choice paired-comparison form. The statements used were: (a) One should avoid dependence upon persons or things—the center of life should be found within oneself; (b) One should live outwardly with gusto, enjoying the good things of life, working with others to secure the things which make possible a pleasant and energetic social life; (c) Man's future depends primarily on what he does, not on what he feels or on his speculations; (d) Life is more a festival than a workshop or a school for moral discipline; (e) The rich internal world of ideas, of sensitive feelings, of reverie, of self-knowledge is man's true home; (f) The good things of life come of their own accord and come unsought; (g) Life is to have clarity, balance, refinement, and control.

experiment. E ostensibly scored the tests and gave each S his scores, along with the score sheets for two other persons (A and C). The excuse employed for making the protocols of the other two fictitious Ss available to the real S was that S was the last one scored in the group and was to carry all the score sheets to the E conducting the next part of the study.

The score sheets were designed to be easily readable and in each case S's score sheet was obviously like one of the others and different from the second. Also, it was intended that the scores should convey the impression of "difference" and "similarity" while making it difficult for the S to interpret these scores in terms of some dimension of better or worse. Therefore, for half the Ss the "similar" scores were shown as "above average" on both tests, with the "different" scores as "much above average" on the check list and "below average" on the scale of values. For the other half of the sample this was reversed. It was found that there were no systematic differences in preference associated with the different identifying letters or profiles.

After the protocols had been given to S he was told about the second part of the experiment. In one condition (mutual gain) S was told that he was going to play a game with one other person in which both of them could win some more money. In the other condition (gain for one, loss for the other), E stated that the two players would play a game with the money that they were paid for participating until one of them won it all. In both conditions the instructions concluded with S choosing either A or C as a partner for the game. From the hypotheses it was predicted

ATTITUDE SCALE SCORE SHEET

Subject				
Adjective Check list	Much below average	Below average	Above average	Much above average
Scale of values	Much below average	Below average	Above average	Much above average

that under condition one (mutual gain) the S would choose to play the game with the similar other and that under condition two (gain for one and loss for the other) S would choose to play with the different other.

Results and Discussion

The results are summarized in Table 1. Both hypotheses were confirmed. In the first condition, mutual gain, the subjects tended to choose the similar other. In the second condition, gain for one and loss for the other, the subjects tended to choose the different other.

In this experiment the choice of the similar and dissimilar other may have been determined not only by the attempt of the individual to match the similarity of the other with the outcome, as we suggested initially, but by the individual's preference for a similar other when a desirable outcome was more likely (Cond. 1) and a dissimilar other when the situation was more likely to arouse aggressive or combative

TABLE 1. RELATIONSHIP BETWEEN CHOICE OF OTHER WITH WHOM TO INTERACT AND DEFINITION OF INTERACTION SITUATION

Definition of the Situation	Choice of Other		χ^2	p [a]
	Similar Other Chosen	Different Other Chosen		
Hypothesis 1 Condition 1 mutual gain	15	1	10.56	< .001
Hypothesis 2 Condition 2 gain for one, loss for the other	4	12	3.06	< .05
		Over-all	12.95	< .001

[a] Significance levels are based on one-tailed tests.

acts (Cond. 2).[2] Although further research should more carefully distinguish among these factors, all of these possibilities are within the scope of the "balance" explanation proposed here.

EXPERIMENT II

In general, according to a balance hypothesis, a contradictory act from an other who is perceived initially as similar will be more likely to arouse the individual to communicate than if the contradiction came from an other who is perceived as different. The contradictory act from a "similar" other is less expected and arouses more efforts to communicate with the other to achieve some kind of agreement and thereby restore balance. On the other hand, when the interaction occurs in a situation in which other motivational systems become salient, the efforts of the individual to achieve balance may be forestalled or eliminated to all intents and purposes. If the individual is compelled to gain agreement from the other with a particular position, then efforts to achieve cognitive balance may become comparatively irrelevant if not danger-

ous to his strategy of persuasion. A strategy of persuasion will be best served by the individual's choosing to communicate with the "different" other, assuming that there are favorable implications of differing power or status, or that the individual feels he can design a persuasive communication based on the relative comprehensibility of the contradiction from a different other.

Given acts of contradiction from both an other who was identified as similar and an other who was identified as different, the hypotheses were:

1. *An individual will choose to communicate with the similar other if the situation does not compel the individual to persuade the other.*

2. *An individual will choose to communicate with the different other if the situation does compel the individual to persuade the other to agree.*

Method

SUBJECTS   The *Ss* were 29 freshman and sophomore students, 12 males and 17 females, enrolled in the same introductory psychology class.

PROCEDURE   The experimental procedure was designed to accomplish two purposes: (i) to create the impression of "similar" and "dissimilar" positions among the *Ss*, and (ii) to induce a feeling in half the *Ss* of the great importance of the consequences of their joint decisions, so that after contradictory behavior on the part of the other they would feel compelled to persuade and gain agreement; and in the remaining half to induce a feeling of the low relevance of the consequences of their decisions so that even after contradictory behavior the *Ss* would remain in a relatively com-

---

[2] A short informal interview was conducted with each subject following his choice of a partner. It was apparent that for almost all the subjects their choices were not well integrated into a cognitive system. The typical initial response was a smile and a shrug of dismay. If pressed further, the subjects showed an apparent increase in discomfort and then possibly made some statement to the effect that they merely preferred that letter which indicated the chosen other. (Of course, the letters were alternated and there was no systematic difference associated with preference for letters A or C.) Because of the subjects' general discomfort, presumably aroused by the difficulty in making a "sensible" response, when questioned, there was no serious attempt to press for post-choice reports.

fortable situation, less compelled to persuade.

The three Ss for each session entered the experimental room in such a manner that they were unable to see one another, and at no time during the experiment did they speak to or see one another. They were seated next to one another facing E and a blackboard, and were close enough together for noises from the adjoining cubicles to give ample evidence that there were others actually present. In one experimental condition (important consequences—persuasion salient) E presented an elaborate statement to the effect that the decisions which they were going to make would be actually used by an "experimentally-minded" judge in determining the sentence of a 17-year-old boy convicted of a crime. In the second condition (persuasion not salient) they were given the same instructions with the added statement that the judge had already sentenced the boy, but that they would go through with the procedure so that the Ss could still receive class credit for having participated in an experi-

ment. Later interviews confirmed the effectiveness of the instructions.

To create the initial impression of "similarity" and "dissimilarity" the Ss were told that two of them were members of the same psychology class and the other was not from a psychology class. An experimental ruse was employed to give the impression that they were each Juror B, and alternately Juror A or C was identified as a psychology student and a non-psychology student.

Following the initial instructions and identification, E read the Ss a case history adapted from Evans (1948) and distributed a seven-point rating scale upon which each S could indicate the degree to which he felt the boy was at fault or the environment was to blame.

The sheets indicating the Ss' attitudes were then collected. Since the story read to them was slanted, their attitudes were almost all at the "environmental" end of the scale. E then returned to each S his own score sheet with an indication of the choices of the other two Ss in the room. In all cases both the similar (psychology student)

_____1. Johnny had many decent influences of which he could have taken advantage. The blame for the crime must be placed entirely upon his shoulders.

_____2.

_____3.

_____4. Johnny had both helpful and disturbing influences. The blame for his crime must be placed equally both on Johnny and on conditions in which he lived.

_____5.

_____6.

_____7. Considering the terrible conditions under which Johnny lived, it would seem almost a miracle that he didn't come out worse than he did. Not he but his environment is entirely to blame for his misdeeds.

Directions: Place a check next to the number which most accurately reflects your best judgment. If you feel, for example, that No. 7 is too strong but that No. 4 is too weak then check either No. 5 or No. 6. If you feel closer to No. 7 than to No. 4 in the above example, check No. 6, etc.

Figure 1. Sample of seven-point scale on which Ss expressed their opinions

TABLE 2. CHOICES OF SIMILAR AND DIFFERENT OTHERS UNDER
CONDITIONS OF DIFFERING CONSEQUENCES

Condition	Choice of Other		χ^2	p^a
	Similar other chosen	Different other chosen		
Consequences significant	4	11	2.4	< .10
Consequences irrelevant	11	3	3.5	< .05
		Over-all	5.8	< .01

a Significance levels are based on one-tailed tests.

and dissimilar (nonpsychology student) jurors were shown to have made judgements four points away from the S towards the "personal responsibility" end of the seven-point scale. The Ss were then allowed to choose only one of the two others (ostensibly because of time limitations) with whom to discuss the case before the final judgements were to be balloted.

At the completion of the procedure, each S should have felt that he was in the room with a similar other (psychology student) and a different other (nonpsychology student) and that his opinions on the case-material presented by E were markedly different from them both. Because of the difficulty encountered with post-choice verbal responses in the first experiment, the subjects were interviewed in their experimental groupings in a rather informal manner and only with reference to their acceptance of the experimental ruse. There was almost total acceptance of the ruse, and where there was some doubt, it was negligible.

Results and Discussion

It was predicted that under the important consequences-compel agreement condition Ss would more fre-

quently choose to interact with the different other; and under the neutral consequences—not compel agreement condition Ss would more frequently choose to interact with the similar other. From the data, summarized in Table 2, it is concluded that both hypotheses were supported.

The post-experimental interviews did little to clarify the thought processes underlying the choices of the dissimilar other when persuasion was important. It is not clear whether the Ss chose the differing others because of the consideration that the "psychology" status was of higher prestige in the persuasion context or whether they felt more able to impart relevant information to the student who had not had psychology and thereby gain agreement. In either case the "dissimilar" other would be preferable in a persuasion context.

CONCLUSIONS

The most general conclusion of these studies is that the perception of others in terms of similarity and difference is relevant to a person's choice of an other with whom to interact. It also appears that this choice will be determined by the person's motivation to maintain or achieve cognitive or interpersonal balance among situational factors such as the kind of social acts required, the outcome of the interaction, and the "similarity" of the other. For example, if a situation is likely to arouse supportive acts and result in a similar desired outcome for both participants, the individual will prefer to interact with a "similar" other.

Further, it appears that, given a situation in which the individual is engaged in some meaningful interaction, he will be more motivated to maintain or gain agreement in social judgements with a "similar" person than with a "dissimilar" one; however, the achievement of this kind of balance may be delayed or eliminated as other motivational systems of the individual become dominant, and the individual's choice will reflect a strategy of goal achievement.

Although these studies demonstrate the relevance of balance theory and point to a number of situational variables, unfortunately they offer little clarification of the relative importance of these variables. For example, would a person prefer a similar or dissimilar other if strongly competitive or pain-inflicting acts were required, even though the outcome would definitely be comparatively valuable to the participants? Further research emphasizing more careful exploration of the cognitive processes should prove fruitful in this area.

SUMMARY

In two experiments the individual's choice of a "similar" or "dissimilar" other was examined in relation to his attempt to maintain or achieve cognitive "balance" in various situations.

In the first experiment high-school students preferred others who were similar as partners for a game in which both could win to a certain extent. When the Ss were confronted with a game in which the outcome required that one partner should win everything at the other's expense, the Ss preferred the "dissimilar" person as a partner.

In the second experiment college students were offered the opportunity to communicate with either a "similar" (psychology student) or a "dissimilar" (non-psychology student) other after the others had made a social judgement radically different from S. A "balance" hypothesis—choice of similar other—held when the consequences of the interaction were comparatively irrelevant, and did not hold—choice of the dissimilar other—when the S was compelled to gain agreement from the other.

REFERENCES

BACK, K. W. (1951). Influence through social communication. *J. abnorm. soc. Psychol.* **46**, 9–23.

EVANS, J. (1948). Johnny Rocco. *J. abnorm. soc. Psychol.* **43**, 357–83.

FESTINGER, L. (1954). A theory of social comparison process. *Hum. Relat.* **7**, 117–140.

FESTINGER, L. (1957). A *Theory of Cognitive Dissonance*. New York: Harper & Row.

FESTINGER, L., & THIBAUT, J. (1951). Interpersonal communication in small groups. *J. abnorm. soc. Psychol.* **46**, 92–100.

FIEDLER, F. E. (1954). Assumed similarity measures as predictors of team effectiveness. *J. abnorm. soc. Psychol.* **49**, 381–8.

HEIDER, F. (1946). Attitudes and cognitive organization. *J. Psychol.* **21,** 107–112.

HOMANS, G. C. (1950). *The human group.* New York: Harcourt, Brace & World.

MORRIS, G., & JONES, L. V. (1955). Values, scales, and dimensions. *J. abnorm. soc. Psychol.* **51,** 523–36.

NEWCOMB, T. (1953). An approach to the study of communicative acts. *Psychol. Rev.* **60,** 393–404.

NOWLIS, V. (1953). The development and modification of motivational systems in personality. In M. R. Jones (Ed.), *Nebraska symposium on motivation.* Lincoln: Univ. Nebr. Press. Pp. 114–39.

RIECKEN, H. W., & HOMANS, G. C. (1954). Psychological aspects of social structure. In G. Lindzey (Ed.), *Handbook of social psychology.* Cambridge: Addison-Wesley. Pp. 786–833.

SCHACHTER, S. (1951). Deviation, rejection and communication. *J. abnorm. soc. Psychol.* **46,** 190–208.

6

Interpersonal Influence

24. THE EFFECT OF INCREASED SALIENCE OF A MEMBERSHIP GROUP ON PAIN TOLERANCE *

Wallace E. Lambert, Eva Libman, and Ernest G. Poser

Membership in a group requires a certain amount of behavioral conformity to the rules, either explicit or implicit, which have been established by all members of that group. The concept of "group" itself signifies that there is some distinctive pattern of behaviors which characterizes members of a particular group and differentiates them from others. The fact that people are always members of more than one group indicates that their patterns of behavior should vary as they take on particular roles in one group and temporarily shed the roles of another. While this generalization is verified in the every day experiences of most human beings, few experimental demonstrations are available of behavioral variations attributable to changes in one's roles or his feelings of identification with certain groups. Newcomb (1950, p. 275 ff.) has dis-

cussed the significance of this phenomenon and Charters and Newcomb (1958) have demonstrated how social attitudes vary when individuals' awareness of being members of religious groups is experimentally modified. In their reseach plan, some Ss were made aware that they were expressing attitudes as Catholics (or Jews, or Protestants, depending on their actual religious affiliation) while other Ss gave their attitudes as they assumed the role of university students. Those Catholic Ss whose religious affiliation was made salient manifested a pattern of attitudes much more similar to the orthodox Catholic position than did control Ss for whom religious affiliation was not made salient. The results for Jews and Protestants were less clear, suggesting that the two roles required of Catholic students (as Catholics and as students) are com-

* Reprinted from the *Journal of Personality*, 1960, 28: 350–357, with permission of the senior author and the Duke University Press.

paratively more dissimilar, at least in terms of the attitudes given consideration in the study.

The purpose of the present studies was to extend our understanding of the effect of group membership by paying attention to aspects of behavior other than social attitudes. We attempted to vary experimentally the salience of religious-group membership and to observe changes in Ss' responses to pain. Responses to pain have been related to religious affiliation by Chapman (1944) and Zborowski (1952). Chapman showed that samples of Jewish Ss exhibited both lower pain perception and pain-tolerance thresholds than non-Jewish Ss with North European ethnic backgrounds. Zborowski found that Jewish Americans tended to exaggerate their reactions and sensitivity to pain more than Americans of other religious or ethnic backgrounds. Social psychologists have become interested in the matter of pain tolerance since Moede (see Murphy & Murphy, 1931) demonstrated that thresholds for intolerable pain were increased when onlookers were present or when competition existed between Ss.

In the two studies presented here, Ss' pain-tolerance thresholds were measured, first when they were asked to assume the role of university students volunteering to assist in a scientific investigation, and then, after certain information was given them, as potential contributors to their own religious group's comparative standing in ability to tolerate pain. Between the two measurements for pain tolerance, Ss were told that members of their religious groups had been found, on the average, to have a lower (in Experiment II, either lower or higher) pain-tolerance threshold when compared to other re-

ligious groups and that the objective of the experiment was to test the reliability of the evidence. We predicted that this procedure would prompt the experimental Ss to compete against the hypothetical "other groups," as though we were manipulating an ethnocentric prestige motive, somewhat analogous to rivalry in Moede's study.

EXPERIMENT I

Method

The sample consisted of 40 Jewish and 40 Protestant Ss, all women students ranging in age from 18 to 23 years. Ss were selected from the McGill University library and other parts of the campus in the following manner: each individual was approached by E (E.L.) and asked if she would be willing to participate in a short research project. Attention was paid to physical characteristics in order to estimate the religion of each S. At the time of testing, religious affiliation was verified and only the data from Jewish and Protestant Ss are considered here. Ss were alternately placed in experimental and control groups.

The instrument used for testing pain tolerance consisted of a clinical sphygmomanometer with sharp, hard rubber projections sewn into the pressure cuff. The cuff was adjusted with the hard rubber projections resting against the medial surface of the S's upper arm, and the pressure was gradually increased at the rate of approximately 10 mm. Hg per sec. A pressure reading was taken at the moment when S first felt pain (this measure is not considered here) and then when the S pronounced the pain intolerable, the index of pain-tolerance level, measured as mm. of Hg on a standard sphygmomanometer gauge. Pressure was then released. This method has high reliability and correlates well with the usual methods for producing superficial pain (see Clark & Bindra, 1956). After the pain-tolerance level had been determined each S was told that she would be given a retest approximately five minutes later "for purposes of establishing reliability." During this period of time, the experimental Ss were told in a casual manner (usually they asked about the purpose of the study at this time) that there was experimental evidence that Jews (Protestants) have a lower pain-tolerance level (take less pain) that non-Jews (other groups), and that the object of the experiment was to test the reliability of the evidence. Control Ss simply waited for five minutes between their first and second measures of pain tolerance.

Results and Discussion

From Table 1, it is clear that Jewish experimental Ss significantly increased their pain-tolerance scores on retest while Jewish control Ss showed an insignificant decerease. No difference was found between Protestant experimental and control Ss: both groups showed hardly any change in pain-tolerance scores on retest. We conclude that the Jewish Ss were clearly influenced by the interpolated statement which alluded to Jewish "inferiority" with regard to withstanding pain. The fact that an equivalent provoking statement had no apparent effect on Protestants can be interpreted as meaning that Protestantism does not function as a reference group in the same sense that Judaism does. It may well be, however, that the reference to own-group inferiority in comparison to non-Jews was more provocative for Jews in the sense that they very likely compared themselves with Christians and thought about the issue of Jewish-Christian prejudice. Protestants, on the other hand, were directed to compare their group's performance with other groups and they need not have interpreted this in terms of a Protestant-Jewish issue nor made any other comparison which would be emotionally involving. Following this reasoning, we predicted that an explicit com-

TABLE 1. PAIN-TOLERANCE SCORES FOR JEWISH AND PROTESTANT Ss, EXPERIMENT I

	Jewish				Protestant			
	Experimental (N = 20)		Control (N = 20)		Experimental (N = 20)		Control (N = 20)	
	Test 1	Test 2	Test 1	Test 2	Test 1	Test 2	Test 1	Test 2
Mean [a]	86	103	83	77	115	114	92	90
Mean Differences	+17		−6		−1		−2	
t	2.78*		n.s.		n.s.		n.s.	

[a] Units are in mm. Hg; the higher the score the greater the pain tolerance.
* $p < .01$, 2-tailed test for correlated data.

parison of Jews and Christians would be more equally provocative for members of both religious groups and that Christians receiving this information would display an increased pain-tolerance threshold.

The change in the pain-tolerance threshold for the Jewish Ss indicates that they were motivated to reduce the discrepancy between their group's purported pain sensitivity and that of non-Jews, but it is not clear whether they were interested in (*a*) surpassing non-Jews (thereby making their own group distinctive) or (*b*) merely closing the gap (thereby making their own group indistinguishable from non-Jews). If Jewish Ss were told that their religious group reportedly could tolerate more pain that Christians, we could then determine the nature of their motivation: if motivated to surpass the Christians, their pain-tolerance thresholds should still increase, but if they reduced their pain-tolerance thresholds we could conclude that they were oriented to close the gap. The second experiment was carried out to investigate these extensions of the findings reported above.

EXPERIMENT II

Method

The Ss were 160 women undergraduate students of McGill University; 80 were Jewish and 80 were Protestant. The same general procedure used in Experiment I was repeated with several modifications. A different sphygmomanometer and different (but supposedly identical) hard rubber projections were used in the second study. Two Es, one recognizably Jewish and the other recog-

nizably not Jewish, were both present at each testing, either one applying the pressure cuff and giving the interpolated information, the other recording the results which were read out to her in code.[1]

Between the first and second measures of pain tolerance, 30 Jewish Ss were told that it had been reported in the literature that Jews as a group take less pain than Christians, and 30 were told that Jews take more pain than Christians. Two groups of 30 Christian Ss were given the same information— for one group that Christians take less pain than Jews and for the other that Christians take more pain that Jews. Two control groups (one Jewish and one Christian) of 20 Ss each were given no information between their two tests.

Results and Discussion

The results are presented in Table 2. There is a clear replication of the findings of the first experiment in that the Jewish Ss reliably increased their tolerance threshold upon being informed that Jews as a group take less pain than Christians. The Jewish control Ss, who were given no interpolated information, show an insignificant decrease in their threshold, a finding that supports the

[1] As will be seen by comparing Tables 1 and 2, the means of the pain tolerance measures are markedly higher in the second study. We are unable to account fully for these differences. A different apparatus and different Es were used; furthermore, in the second study measurements were always taken with one E as an onlooker while the other conducted the study. Whatever the reason(s), the measures were higher in the second study, and in three or four cases Ss were dropped because their pain perception thresholds were so high that the Es felt that there would be too little opportunity for change to be recorded after the experimental treatment.

TABLE 2. PAIN-TOLERANCE SCORES FOR JEWISH AND PROTESTANT Ss, EXPERIMENT II

	Jewish						Christian					
Condition	Take Less		Take More		Control		Take Less		Take More		Control	
Test	1	2	1	2	1	2	1	2	1	2	1	2
Mean[a]	160	179	163	172	139	133	187	202	158	180	156	150
Mean Difference	+19		+ 9		− 6		+15		+22		− 6	
N	30		30		20		30		30		20	
t	2.74[b]		1.21		.68		2.34		2.76		.88	
p	.02		n.s.		n.s.		.03		.01		n.s.	

[a] Units are in mm. Hg; the higher the score the greater the pain tolerance.
[b] Two-tailed tests of significance for correlated data are used throughout.

conclusion that the change in threshold for the Jewish experimental Ss is not due to taking the test twice nor to the unreliability of the measure. When Jewish Ss are informed that Jews typically take more pain than Christians they tend to "hold the line" rather than reducing their thresholds ("closing the gap") or increasing their thresholds ("extending the differences"). Although this group does increase its mean tolerance threshold (from 163 to 172 units) this is not a reliable change. When the difference scores (subtracting the first from the second tolerance scores) for this group are compared with the difference scores for the Jewish control Ss, again there is no reliable increase for that group, $t = 1.29$ with 48 df.

The Christian Ss also are clearly affected by the interpolated information. There are significant increases in tolerance thresholds when they are informed that Christians typically take less pain or take more pain than Jews, We have evidence here that Christianity (which more clearly calls to mind the Christian-Jewish comparison) is a more effective reference group than Protestantism as used in the first experiment. We also have evidence that the Christian Ss are motivated to extend the difference between Christians and Jews on pain tolerance in that they increase their threshold when informed that their religious group typically takes more pain than Jews.

In summary, the over-all findings suggest that Ss do change their patterns of behavior in meaningful ways when they alternately refer themselves to different membership groups, in this case first as university students contributing to a scientific investigation and then as members of a particular religious group. Samples of Jewish Ss appear to be interested in both reducing any differences between their religious group and Christians with respect to ability to withstand pain as well as maintaining any superiority they may have in this regard (although the latter point is not clear from our data). Christian Ss (but not "Protestants") appear ready to eliminate any inferiority their group may have in regard to pain tolerance when compared to Jews and to extend the difference between groups when they are led to believe their group is superior in withstanding pain.

Others working with pain sensitivity have reported differences attributable to religious affiliation (for example, Chapman, 1944). We were able to compare our Jewish and Christian Ss on their pain-tolerance thresholds (first test) since no experimental treatment was given to any S until after the first measure of pain tolerance. For the Ss in Experiment I, the mean threshold for Jews was not reliably different from that of the Protestants, $t = 1.63$, $df = 78$, corrected for heterogeneous variances. For Ss in Experiment II, the Jewish mean was again not reliably different from that of Protestants, $t = 1.08$, $df = 158$. We therefore offer no evidence for differences in pain sensitivity attributable to religious affiliation for Jewish and Protestant women. In both studies, however, we do find significantly less variance of pain-tolerance scores for Jewish in contrast to Christians Ss, in Experiment I, $F = 3.15$ ($p = .01$) and Experiment II, $F = 1.56$ ($p < .05$). One explanation for this reliable finding comes from Zborowski's (1952) interpretation of the social and cultural significance of pain. He finds that Jewish patients typically search for the symptomatic meaning of pain and communicate their concern about their health and their family's welfare to family members and associates. Zborowski feels that this reaction pattern is acquired "by the individual members of the society from the earliest childhood along with other cultural attitudes and values which are learned from parents . . ." (p. 28). He argues that each culture develops an ideal pattern of attitudes and reactions to pain which are passed on during socialization. Our findings of more homogeneous reactions to pain among Jews would suggest that something like an ideal pattern of reactions to pain is either more standardized and/or more effectively communicated among Jews than Christians.

SUMMARY

Jewish and Protestant female Ss were tested for their tolerance of pain first when they were asked as students to participate in a scientific study and then, after their religious membership group was made salient to them by having them believe that scientific evidence indicated that their religious group characteristically is less able to withstand pain than others. The Jewish, but not the Protestant, Ss showed a reliable increase in their mean pain-tolerance threshold after this information was given them.

In a second experiment subgroups of Jewish and Protestant Ss were told either that their religious group typically takes less or more pain than other religious groups but in this case an explicit comparison was made between Jews and Christians. Both Jewish and "Christian" Ss increased their pain tolerance when told their groups were typically inferior in regard to this variable. The Christian Ss who were informed that their group was superior in pain tolerance further increased their tolerance while Jewish Ss, similarly treated, showed no reliable change in their tolerance levels. The findings are conceptualized in terms of a theory of membership groups.

No evidence was found for the differences in normal pain-tolerance thresholds attributable to religious differences, although Jewish Ss showed reliably less variability of pain-tolerance scores than did Protestant Ss in both studies.

REFERENCES

CHAPMAN, W. P. Measurements of pain sensitivity in normal control subjects and in psychoneurotic patients. *Psychosom. med.*, 1944, 6, 252–257.

CHARTERS, W. W., & NEWCOMB, T. M. Some attitudinal effects of experimentally increased salience of a membership group. In Maccoby, Eleanor E., Newcomb, T. M., & Hartley, E. L. (Eds.), *Readings in social psychology*. New York: Holt, Rinehart and Winston, 1958.

CLARK, J. W., & BINDRA, D. Individual differences in pain thresholds. *Canad. J. Psychol.*, 1956, 10, 69–76.

NEWCOMB, T. M. *Social psychology*. New York: Holt, Rinehart and Winston, 1950.

MURPHY, G., & MURPHY, L. B. *Experimental social psychology*. New York: Harper & Row, 1931.

ZBOROWSKI, M. Cultural components in response to pain. *J. soc. Issues*, 1952, 8, 16–30.

25. SOME CONDITIONS OF OBEDIENCE AND DISOBEDIENCE TO AUTHORITY *

Stanley Milgram

The situation in which one agent commands another to hurt a third turns up time and again as a significant theme in human relations. It is powerfully expressed in the story of Abraham, who is commanded by God to kill his son. It is no accident that Kierkegaard, seeking to orient his thought to the central themes of human experience, chose Abraham's conflict as the springboard to his philosophy.

War, too, moves forward on the triad of an authority who commands a person to destroy the enemy, and perhaps all organized hostility may be viewed as a theme and variation on the three elements of authority, executant, and victim. We describe an experimental program, recently concluded at Yale University, in which a particular expression of this conflict is studied by experimental means.

In its most general form, the problem may be defined thus: If x tells y to hurt z, under what conditions will y carry out the command of x and under what conditions will he refuse? In the more limited form possible in laboratory research, the question becomes: If an experimenter tells a subject to hurt another person, under what conditions will the subject go along with this instruction, and under what conditions will he refuse to obey? The laboratory

* Slightly abridged from *Human Relations*, 1965, 18 (in press), with the permission of the author and publisher. This research was supported by two grants from the National Science Foundation: NSF G-17916 and NSF G-24152. Exploratory studies carried out in 1960 were financed by a grant from the Higgins Funds of Yale University. For a more detailed account of some of the earlier work in this program see Milgram (1963).

problem is not so much a dilution of the general statement, as it is one concrete expression of the many particular forms this question may asume.

One aim of the research was to study behavior in a strong situation of deep consequence to the participants, for the psychological forces operative in powerful and lifelike forms of the conflict may not be brought into play under diluted conditions.

This approach meant, first, that we had a special obligation to protect the welfare and dignity of the persons who took part in the study; subjects were, of necessity, placed in a difficult predicament, and steps had to be taken to assure their well being before they were discharged from the laboratory. Toward this end, a careful, postexperimental treatment was devised and has been carried through for subjects in all conditions.[1]

[1] It consisted of an extended discussion with the experimenter and, of equal importance, a friendly reconciliation with the victim. It is made clear that the victim did not receive painful electric shocks. After the completion of the experimental series, subjects were sent a detailed report of the results and full purposes of the experimental program. A formal assessment of this procedure points to its over-all effectiveness: 83.7 percent of the subjects indicated that they were glad to have taken part in the study; 15.1 percent reported neutral feelings; and 1.3 percent stated that they were sorry to have participated. A large number of subjects spontaneously requested that they be used in further experimentation. Four-fifths of the subjects felt that more experiments of this sort should be carried out, and 74 percent indicated that they had learned something of personal importance as a result of being in the study. Furthermore, a University psychiatrist, experienced in outpatient treatment, interviewed a sample of experimental subjects with the aim of uncovering possible injurious effects resulting from participation. No such effects were in evidence. Indeed, subjects typically felt that their participation was instructive and enriching.

TERMINOLOGY

If y follows the command of x, we shall say that he has obeyed x; if he fails to carry out the command of x, we shall say that he has disobeyed x. The terms to obey and disobey, as used in this study, refer to the subject's overt action only, and carry no implication for the motive or experiential states accompanying the action.

To be sure, the everyday use of the word *obedience* is not entirely free from complexities. It refers to action within widely varying situations and connotes diverse motives within those situations: there is a difference in meaning of a child's *obedience* and a soldier's *obedience* and the love, honor, and *obey* of the marriage vow. However, a consistent behavioral relationship is indicated in most uses of the terms: in the act of obeying, a person does what another person tells him to do. Y obeys x if he carries out the prescription for action that x has addressed to him; the term suggests, moreover, that some form of dominance-subordination, or hierarchical element is part of the situation in which the transaction between x and y occurs.

A subject who complies with the entire series of experimental commands will be termed an *obedient* subject; one who at any point in the command series defies the experimenter will be called a *disobedient* or *defiant* subject. As used in this report, the terms refer only to the subject's performance in the experiment and do not necessarily imply a general personality disposition to submit to or reject authority.

SUBJECT POPULATION

The subjects used in all experimental conditions were male adults, residing in the greater New Haven and Bridgeport areas, aged 20 to 50 years, and engaged in a wide variety of occupations. Each experimental condition described in this report employed 40 fresh subjects and was carefully balanced for age and occupational types. The occupational composition for each experiment was: workers, skilled and unskilled: 40 percent; white collar, sales, business: 40 percent; professionals: 20 percent. The occupations were intersected with three age categories (subjects in 20's, 30's and 40's, assigned to each condition in the proportion of 20 percent, 40 percent, and 40 percent respectively).

THE GENERAL LABORATORY PROCEDURE

The focus of the study concerns the amount of electric shock a subject is willing to administer to another person when ordered by an experimenter to give the "victim" increasingly severe punishment. The act of administering shock is set in the context of a learning experiment, ostensibly designed to study the effect of punishment on memory. Aside from the experimenter, one naive subject and one accomplice perform in each session. On arrival each subject is paid $4.50. After a general talk by the experimenter telling how little scientists know about the effect of punishment on memory, subjects are informed that one member of the pair will serve as teacher and one as learner. A rigged drawing is held so that the naive subject is always the "teacher," and the accomplice becomes the "learner." The learner is taken to an adjacent room and strapped into an "electric chair."

The naive subject is told that it is his task to teach the learner a list of paired associates, to test him on the list, and to administer punishment whenever the learner errs in the test. Punishment takes the form of electric shock, delivered to the learner by means of a shock generator controlled by the naive subject. The teacher is instructed to increase the intensity of electric shock one step on the generator for each error. The learner, according to plan, provides many wrong answers, so that before long the naive subject must give him the strongest shock on the generator. Increases in shock level are met by increasingly insistent demands from the learner that the experiment be stopped because of the growing discomfort to him. However, in clear terms the experimenter orders the teacher to continue with the procedure in disregard of the learner's protests. *Thus, the naive subject must resolve a conflict between two mutually incompatible demands from the social field. He may continue to follow the orders of the experimenter and shock the learner with increasing severity, or he may refuse to follow the orders of the experimenter, and heed the learner's pleas. The experimenter's authority operates not in a free field, but against ever mounting countervailing pressure from the person being punished.*

A few technical points need to be considered before describing the findings of the study. For the purpose of delivering shock, a simulated shock generator is used, with 30 clearly marked voltage levels that range from 15 to 450 volts (and each activated by one of 30 individual lever switches set in a horizontal line). The naive subject is given a sample shock of 45 volts to convince him of the authenticity of the instrument. The generator bears verbal designations that range from "Slight Shock" to "Danger: Severe Shock."

The responses of the victim are standardized on tape, and each protest is coordinated to a particular voltage level on the shock generator. Starting with 75 volts the learner begins to grunt and moan. At 150 volts he demands to be let out of the experiment. At 180 volts he cries out that he can no longer stand the pain. At 300 volts he refuses to provide any more answers to the memory test, insisting that he is no longer a participant in the experiment and must be freed. In response to this last tactic, the experimenter instructs the naive subject to treat the absence of an answer as equivalent to a wrong answer, and to follow the usual shock procedure. The experimenter reinforces his demand with the statement: "You have no other choice, you must go on!" (This imperative is used whenever the naive subject tries to break off the experiment.) If the subject refuses to give the next higher level of shock the experiment is considered at an end. A quantitative value is assigned to the subject's performance based on the maximum intensity shock he administered before breaking off. Thus any subject's score may range from zero (for a subject unwilling to administer the first shock level) to 30 (for a subject who proceeds to the highest voltage level on the board). For any particular subject and for any particular experimental condition, the degree to which

participants have followed the experimenter's orders may be specified with a numerical value corresponding to the metric on the shock generator.

This laboratory situation gives us a framework in which to study the subject's reactions to the principal conflict of the experiment. Again, this conflict is between the experimenter's demands that he continue to administer the electric shock, and the learner's demands, which become increasingly more insistent, that the experiment be stopped. The crux of the study is to vary systematically the factors believed to alter the degree of obedience to the experimental commands, to learn under what conditions submission to authority is most probable and under what conditions defiance is brought to the fore.

PILOT STUDIES

Pilot studies for the present research were completed in the Winter of 1960; they differed from the regular experiments in a few details. For one, the victim was placed behind a silvered glass with the light balance on the glass such that the victim could be dimly perceived by the subject (Milgram, 1961).

Though essentially qualitative in treatment, these studies pointed to several significant features of the experimental situation. At first, no vocal feedback was used from the victim. It was thought that the verbal and voltage designations on the control panel would create sufficient pressure to curtail the subject's obedience. However, this was not the case. In the absence of protests from the learner, virtually all subjects, once commanded, went blithely to the end of the board, seemingly indifferent to the verbal designations ("Extreme Shock" and "Danger: Severe Shock"). This deprived us of an adequate basis for scaling obedient tendencies. A force had to be introduced that would strengthen the subject's resistance to the experimenter's commands, and reveal individual differences in terms of a distribution of break-off points.

This force took the form of protests from the victim. Initially, mild protests were used, but proved inadequate. Subsequently, more vehement protests were inserted into the experimental procedure. To our consternation, even the strongest protests from the victim did not prevent all subjects from administering the harshest punishment ordered by the experimenter; but the protests did lower the mean maximum shock somewhat and created some spread in the subjects' performance; therefore, the victim's cries were standardized on tape and incorporated into the regular experimental procedure.

The situation did more than highlight the technical difficulties of finding a workable experimental procedure: it indicated that subjects would obey authority to a greater extent than we had supposed. It also pointed to the importance of feedback from the victim in controlling the subject's behavior.

One further aspect of the pilot study was that subjects frequently averted their eyes from the person they were shocking, often turning their heads in an awkward and conspicuous manner. One subject explained: "I didn't want to see the consequences of what I had done." Observers wrote:

. . . subjects showed a reluctance to look at the victim, whom they could see through the glass in front of them. When this fact was brought to their attention they indicated that it caused them discomfort to see the victim in agony. We note, however, that although the subject refuses to look at the victim, he continues to administer shocks.

This suggested that the salience of the victim may have, in some degree, regulated the subjects' performance. If, in obeying the experimenter, the subjects found it necessary to avoid scrutiny of the victim, would the converse be true? If the victim were rendered increasingly more salient to the subject, would obedience diminish? The first set of regular experiments was designed to answer this question.

IMMEDIACY OF THE VICTIM

This series consisted of four experimental conditions. In each condition the victim was brought "psychologically" closer to the subject giving him shocks.

In the first condition (Remote Feedback) the victim was placed in another room and could not be heard or seen by the subject, except that at 300 volts, he pounded on the wall in protest. After 300 volts he no longer answered or was heard from.

The second condition (Voice Feedback) was identical to the first except that voice protests were introduced. As in the first condition, the victim was placed in an adjacent room but his complaints could be heard clearly through a door left slightly ajar and through the walls of the laboratory.

The third experimental condition (Proximity) was similar to the second, except that the victim was now placed in the same room as the subject and 1½ feet from him. Thus visible as well as audible cues were provided.

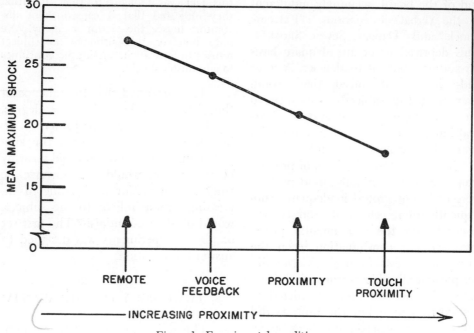

Figure 1. Experimental conditions

The fourth, and final condition of this series (Touch-Proximity) was identical to the third, with this exception: the victim only received a shock when his hand rested on a shockplate. At the 150 volt level the victim again demanded to be let free and, in this condition, refused to place his hand on the shockplate. The experimenter ordered the naive subject to force the victim's hand onto the plate. Thus, obedience in this condition required that the subject have physical contact with the victim in order to give him punishment beyond the 150 volt level.

Forty adult subjects were studied in each condition. The data revealed that obedience was significantly reduced as the victim was rendered more immediate to the subject. The mean maximum shock for the conditions is shown in Table 1. Expressed in terms of the proportion of obedient to defiant subjects, we find that 34 percent of the subjects defied the experimenter under the Remote Feedback condition, 37.5 percent in Voice Feedback, 60 percent in Proximity, and 70 percent in Touch-Proximity.

How are we to account for this effect? A first conjecture might be that as the victim was brought closer, the subject became more aware of the intensity of his suffering and regulated his behavior accordingly. This makes sense but our evidence does not support the interpretation. There are no consistent differences in the attributed level of pain across the four conditions (that is, the amount of pain experienced by the victim as estimated by the subject and expressed on a 14 point scale). But it is easy to speculate about alternative mechanisms.

Empathic Cues

In the Remote and to a lesser extent the Voice Feedback condition, the victim's suffering possesses an abstract, remote quality for the subject. He is aware, but only in a conceptual sense, that his actions cause pain to another person; the fact is apprehended, but not felt. The phenomenon is common enough. The bombardier can reasonably suppose that his weapons will inflict suffering and death, yet this knowledge is divested of affect and does not move him to a felt, emotional response to the suffering resulting from his actions. Other, similar observations have been made in wartime. It is possible that the visual cues associated with the victim's suffering trigger empathic responses in the subject and provide him with a more complete grasp of the victim's experience. Or it is possible that the empathic responses are themselves unpleasant, possessing drive properties that cause the subject to terminate the arousal situation. Diminishing obedience, then, would be explained by the enrichment of empathic cues in the successive experimental conditions.

Denial and Narrowing of the Cognitive Field

The remote condition allows a narrowing of the cognitive field so that the victim is put out of mind. The subject no longer considers the act of depressing a lever relevant to moral judgment, for it is no longer associated with the victim's suffering. When the victim is close, it is more difficult to exclude him phenomenologically. He necessarily intrudes on the subject's awareness because he (the victim) is continuously visible. In the remote conditions, his existence and reactions are made known only after the shock has been administered. The auditory feedback is sporadic and discontinuous. In the proximal condition the victim's inclusion in the immediate visual field renders him a continuously salient element for the subject. The mechanism of denial can no longer be brought into play. One subject in the remote condition said: "It's funny how you really begin to forget that there's a guy out there, even though you can hear him. For a long time I just concentrated on pressing the switches and reading the words."

Reciprocal Fields

If in the Proximity condition, the subject is in an improved position to observe the victim, the reverse is also true. The actions of the subject now come under proximal scrutiny by the victim. Possibly, it is easier to harm a person when he is unable to observe our actions than when he can see what we are doing. His surveillance of the actions directed against him may give rise to shame, or guilt, which may then serve to curtail the action. Many expressions of language refer to the discomfort or inhibitions that arise in face-to-face confrontation. It is often said that it is easier to criticize a man "behind his back" than to "attack him to his face." If we are in the process of lying to a person, it is reputedly difficult to "stare him in the eye." We "turn away from others in shame" or in "embarrassment" and this action serves to reduce our discomfort. The manifest function of allowing the victim of a firing squad to be blindfolded is to make the occasion less stressful for him, but it may also serve a latent function of reducing the stress of the executioner. In short, in the proximal conditions, the subject may sense that he has become more salient in the victim's field of awareness. Possibly he becomes more self-conscious, embarrassed, and inhibited in his punishment of the victim.

Phenomenal Unity of Act

In the remote conditions, it is more difficult for the subject to gain a sense of *relatedness* between his own actions and the consequences of these actions for the victim. There is a physical and spatial separation of the act and its consequences. The subject depresses a lever in one room, and protests and cries are heard from another. The two events are in correlation, yet they lack a compelling phenomenological unity. The structure of a meaningful act—*I am hurting a man*—breaks down because of the spatial arrangements in a manner somewhat analogous to the disappearance of phi phenomena when the blinking lights are spaced too far apart. The unity is more fully achieved in the proximal conditions as the victim is brought closer to the action that causes him pain. It is rendered complete in Touch-Proximity.

Incipient Group Formation

Placing the victim in another room not only takes him further from the subject but also draws the subject and the experimenter relatively closer. There is incipient group formation between the experimenter and the subject from which the victim is excluded. The wall between the victim and the others deprives him of an intimacy that the experimenter and subject feel. In the remote condition, the victim is truly an outsider who stands alone physically and psychologically.

When the victim is placed close to the subject, it becomes easier to form an alliance with him against the experimenter. Subjects no longer have to face the experimenter alone. They have an ally who is close at hand and eager to collaborate in a revolt against the experimenter. Thus, the changing set of spatial relations leads to a potentially shifting set of alliances across the several experimental conditions.

Acquired Behavior Dispositions

It is commonly observed that laboratory mice will rarely fight with their litter mates. Scott (1958) explains this in terms of passive inhibition. He writes: "By doing nothing under circumstances (the animal) learns to do nothing, and this may be spoken of as passive inhibition . . . this principle has great importance in teaching an individual to be peaceful, for it means that he can learn not to fight simply by not fighting." Similarly, we may learn not to harm others simply by not harming them in everyday life. Yet this learning occurs in a context of proximal relations with others and may not be generalized to that situation in which the person is physically removed from us. Or possibly in the past, aggressive actions against others who were physically close resulted in retaliatory punishment that extinguished the original form of response. In contrast, aggression against others at a distance may have only sporadically led to retaliation. Thus, the organism learns that it is safer to be aggressive toward others at a distance and precarious to be so when the parties are within "arm's reach." Through a pattern of rewards and punishments, he acquires a disposition to avoid aggression at close quarters, a disposition that does not extend to harming others at a distance. And this may account for experimental findings in the remote and proximal experiments.

Proximity as a variable in psychological research has received far less attention than it deserves. If men were sessile it would be easy to understand this neglect. But we move about; our spatial relations shift from one situation to the next, and whether we are near or remote may have a powerful affect on the psychological processes that mediate our behavior toward others. In the present situation as the victim is brought closer to the man ordered to give him shocks, increasing numbers of subjects break off the experiment, refusing to obey. The concrete, visible, and proximal presence of the victim acts in an important way to counteract the experimenter's power and to generate disobedience.[2]

CLOSENESS OF AUTHORITY

If the spatial relationship of the subject and victim are relevant to the degree of obedience, would not the relationship of subject to experimenter also play a part?

There are reasons to feel that, on arrival, the subject is oriented primarily to the experimenter rather than to the victim. He has come to the laboratory to fit into the structure that the experimenter—not the victim—provides. He has come less to understand his behavior, than to *reveal* that behavior to a competent scientist, and he is willing to display himself as the scientist's purposes require. Most subjects seem quite concerned about the appearance they are making before the experimenter and one could argue that this preoccupation, in a relatively new and strange setting, makes the subject somewhat insensitive to the triadic nature of the social situation. In other words, the subject is so concerned about the show he is putting on for the experimenter, that influences from other parts of the social field do not receive as much weight as they ordinarily would. This strong orientation

---

[2] It is difficult to convey on the printed page the full tenor of the victim's responses, for we have no adequate notation for vocal intensity, timing, and general qualities of delivery. Yet these features are crucial to producing the effect of an increasingly severe reaction to mounting voltage levels. In general terms, however, the victim indicates no discomfort until the 75 volt shock is administered, at which time there is a light grunt in response to the punishment. Similar reactions follow the 90 and 105 volt shocks, and at 120 volts the victim shouts to the experimenter that the shocks are becoming painful. Painful groans are heard on administration of the 135 volt shock and at 150 volts the victim cries out, "Experimenter, get me out of here! I won't be in the experiment any more! I refuse to go on!" Cries of this type continue with generally rising intensity, so that at 180 volts the victim cries out, "I can't stand the pain," and by 270 volts his response to the shock is definitely an agonized scream. Throughout, he insists that he be let out of the experiment. At 300 volts the victim shouts in desperation that he will no longer provide answers to the memory test; and at 315 volts, after a violent scream, he reaffirms with vehemence that he is no longer a participant. From this point on, he provides no answers but shrieks in agony whenever a shock is administered. This continues through 450 volts. Of course, many subjects will have broken off before this point.

to the experimenter would account for the relative insensitivity of the subject to the victim, and would also lead us to believe that alterations in the relationship between subject and experimenter would have important consequences for obedience.

In a series of experiments, we varied the physical closeness and degree of surveillance of the experimenter. In one condition the experimenter sat just a few feet away from the subject. In a second condition, after giving initial instructions, the experimenter left the laboratory and gave his orders by telephone; in still a third condition, the experimenter was never seen, providing instructions by means of a tape recording activated when the subjects entered the laboratory.

Obedience dropped sharply as the experimenter was physically removed from the laboratory. The number of obedient subjects in the first condition (Experimenter Present) was almost three times as great as in the second, where the experimenter gave his orders by telephone. Twenty-six subjects were fully obedient in the first condition and only 9 in the second. (Chi Square, obedient vs. defiant in the two conditions, 1 d.f. = 14.7; $p < .001$). Subjects seemed able to take a far stronger stand against the experimenter when they did not have to encounter him face to face, and the experimenter's power over the subject was severely curtailed.

Moreover, when the experimenter was absent, subjects displayed an interesting form of behavior that had not occurred under his surveillance. Though continuing with the experiment, several subjects administered lower shocks than were required and never informed the experimenter of their deviation from the correct procedure. (Unknown to the subjects, shock levels were automatically recorded by an Esterline-Angus event recorder wired directly into the shock generator; this provided us with an objective record of the subjects' performance.) Indeed, in telephone conversations, some subjects specifically assured the experimenter that they were raising the shock level according to instruction while, in fact, they were repeatedly using the lowest shock on the board. This form of behavioir is particularly interesting; although these subjects acted in a way that clearly undermined the avowed purposes of the experiment, they found it easier to handle the conflict in this manner than to precipitate an open break with authority.

Other conditions were completed in which the experimenter was absent during the first segment of the experiment, but reappeared at the point the subject definitely refused to give higher shocks when commanded by telephone. Although he had exhausted his power via telephone, the experimenter could frequently force further obedience when he reappeared in the laboratory.

Experiments in this series show that the physical *presence* of an authority is an important force contributing to the subject's obedience or defiance. Taken together with the first experimental series on the proximity of the victim, it would appear that something akin to fields of force, diminishing in effectiveness with increasing psychological distance from their source, has a controlling effect on the subject's performance. As the victim is brought closer, the subject finds it harder to administer shocks to him. When the victim's position is held constant relative to the subject and the authority is made more remote, the subject finds it easier to break off the experiment. This effect is substantial in both cases, but manipulation of the experimenter's position yielded the more powerful results. Obedience to destructive commands is highly dependent on the proximal relations between authority and subject.

TENSION

The description of final scores does not fully convey the character of the subject's performance, and it would be useful to interrupt our reporting of quantitative relationships to remark on the subject's general reaction to the situation.

One might suppose that a subject would simply break off or continue as his conscience and temperament dictate. Yet this is very far from what actually happened. There were powerful reactions of tension and emotional strain in a substantial proportion of the participants. Persons were observed to sweat, tremble, stutter, bite their lips, and groan as they found themselves increasingly implicated in the experimental conflict. Some sense of the subject's mood can be gotten from a transcript of their remarks at break-off point. Here are the remarks of two defiant subjects:

Is he banging? . . . Is he hurt out there? Well I don't want to be responsible for anything that happens to him. No I can't go on with it. I don't know whether he's all right or not. I mean he may have a heart condition or something; I wouldn't feel right doing it. He's banging for help. He's evidently in trouble or he wouldn't bang. . . . I don't see any sense to this—to knocking him out or something. I just can't see it. (Subject refuses to administer shocks) [Subject 0108]

This man is banging. He wants to get out. . . . I'm sorry. If the man wants to get out I'd just as soon stop. . . . I don't want to administer any more. [Extremely excited] . . . I will gladly refund the check, but I will not harm this man . . . I'm sorry, I will not give him any more if he obviously wants to get out. There is no money in the world that will make me hurt another individual.

[Subject 010X]

And here is a transcript from an obedient subject. He began the experiment calmly, but became increasingly tense as the experiment proceeded. After administering the 150 volt shock, he began to address the experimenter in agitated tones:

150 Volts Delivered. You want me to keep going?

165 Volts Delivered. That guy is hollering in there. There's a lot of them here. He's liable to have heart condition. You want me to go?

180 Volts Delivered. He can't stand it! I'm not going to kill that man in there! You hear him hollering? He's hollering. He can't stand it. What if something happens to him? . . . I'm not going to get that man sick in there. He's hollering in there. You know what I mean? I mean I refuse to take responsibility. He's getting hurt in there. He's in there hollering. Too many left here. Geez, if he gets them wrong. There's too many of them left. I mean who is going to take responsibility if anything happens to that gentleman? [The experimenter accepts responsibility.] All right.

195 Volts Delivered. You see he's hollering. Hear that. Gee, I don't know. [The experimenter says: "The experiment requires that you go on."] I know it does, sir, but I mean—huh—he don't know what he's in for. He's up to 195 volts.

210 Volts Delivered.

225 Volts Delivered.

240 Volts Delivered. Aw, no. You mean I've got to keep going up with the scale? No sir. I'm not going to kill that man! I'm not going to give him 450 volts! [The experimenter says: "The experiment requires that you go on."] I know it does but that man is hollering in there, sir.

. . .

Despite his numerous, agitated objections, which were constant accompaniments to his actions, the subject unfailingly obeyed the experimenter, proceeding to the highest shock level on the generator. He displayed a pronounced dissociation between word and action. Although at the verbal level he had resolved not to go on, his actions were fully in accord with the experimenter's commands. Although this subject did not want to shock the victim and found it an extremely disagreeable task, he was unable to invent a response that would free him from the experimenter's authority. Many subjects could not find the specific verbal formula that would enable them to reject the role assigned to them. Perhaps our culture does not provide adequate models for disobedience.

One puzzling sign of tension was the regular occurrence of nervous laughing fits. In the first four conditions, 71 of the 160 subjects showed definite signs of nervous laughter and smiling. The laughter seemed entirely out of place, even bizarre. Full blown, uncontrollable seizures were observed for 15 of these subjects. On one occasion, we observed a seizure so violently convulsive that it was necessary to call a halt to the experiment. In the postexperimental interviews, subjects took pains to point out that they were not sadistic types and that the laughter did not mean they enjoyed shocking the victim.

In the interview following the experiment, subjects were asked to indicate on a 14 point scale just how nervous or tense they felt at the point of maximum tension.

The scale ranged from "Not at all tense and nervous" to "Extremely tense and nervous." Self reports of this sort are of limited precision, and at best provide only a rough indication of the subject's emotional response. Still, taking the reports for what they are worth, it can be seen that the distribution of responses spans the entire range of the scale, with the majority of subjects concentrated at the center and upper extreme. A further breakdown showed that obedient subjects report themselves as having been slightly more tense and nervous than the defiant subjects at the point of maximum tension.

How is the occurrence of tension to be interpreted? First, it points to the presence of conflict. If a tendency to comply with authority were the only psychological force operating in the situation, all subjects would have continued to the end and there would have been no tension. Tension, it is assumed, results from the simultaneous presence of two or more incompatible response tendencies (Miller, 1944). If sympathetic concern for the victim were the exclusive force, all subjects would have calmly defied the experimenter. Instead, there were both obedient and defiant

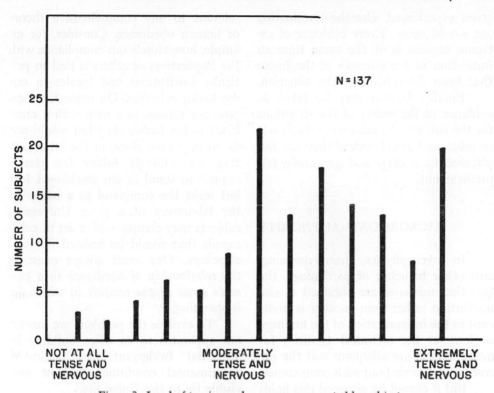

Figure 2. Level of tension and nervousness reported by subject

Figure 2 shows the self-reports on "tension and nervousness" for 137 subjects in the Proximity experiments. Subjects were given a scale with 14 values ranging from "Not at all tense and nervous" to "Extremely tense and nervous." They were instructed: "Thinking back to that point in the experiment when you felt the most tense and nervous, indicate just how you felt by placing an X at the appropriate point on the scale." The results are shown in terms of mid-point values.

outcomes, frequently accompanied by extreme tension. A conflict develops between the deeply ingrained disposition not to harm others and the equally compelling tendency to obey those who are in authority. The subject is quickly drawn into a dilemma of a deeply dynamic character and the presence of high tension points to the considerable strength of each of the antagonistic vectors.

Moreover, tension defines the strength of the aversive state from which the subject is unable to escape through disobedience. When a person is uncomfortable, tense, or stressed, he tries to take some action that will allow him to terminate this unpleasant state. Thus, tension may serve as a drive that leads to escape behavior. But in the present situation, even where tension is extreme, many subjects are unable to perform the response that will bring about relief. Thus, there must be a competing drive, tendency, or inhibition that precludes activation of the disobedient response. The strength of this inhibiting factor must be of greater magnitude than the stress experienced, else the terminating act would occur. Every evidence of extreme tension is at the same time an indication of the strength of the forces that keep the subject in the situation.

Finally, tension may be taken as evidence of the reality of the situations for the subjects. Normal subjects do not tremble and sweat unless they are implicated in a deep and genuinely felt predicament.

BACKGROUND AUTHORITY

In psychophysics, animal learning, and other branches of psychology, the fact that measures are obtained at one institution rather than another is irrelevant to the interpretation of the findings, as long as the technical facilities for measurement are adequate and the operations are carried out with competence.

But it cannot be assumed this holds true for the present study. The effectiveness of the experimenter's commands may depend in an important way on the larger institutional context in which they are issued. The experiments described thus far were conducted at Yale University, an organization that most subjects regarded with respect and sometimes awe. In postexperimental interviews, several participants remarked that the locale and sponsorship of the study gave them confidence in the integrity, competence, and benign purposes of the personnel; many indicated that they would not have shocked the learner if the experiments had been done elsewhere.

This issue of background authority seemed important to us for an interpretation of the results that had been obtained thus far; moreover, it is highly relevant to any comprehensive theory of human obedience. Consider, for example, how closely our compliance with the imperatives of others is tied to particular institutions and locales in our day-to-day activities. On request, we expose our throats to a man with a razor blade in the barber shop but would not do so in a shoe store; in the latter setting, we willingly follow the clerk's request to stand in our stockinged feet but resist the command in a bank. In the laboratory of a great University, subjects may comply with a set of commands that would be resisted if given elsewhere. One must always question the relationship of obedience to a person's sense of the context in which he is operating.

To explore the problem, we moved our apparatus to an office building in industrial Bridgeport and replicated experimental conditions without any visible tie to the University.

Bridgeport subjects were invited to the experiment through a mail circular similar to the one used in the Yale study, with appropriate changes in the letterhead, and the like. As in the earlier study, subjects were paid $4.50 for coming to the laboratory. The same age and occupational distributions used at Yale, and the identical personnel, were employed.

The purpose in relocating in Bridgeport was to assure a complete dissociation from Yale and, in this regard, we were fully successful. On the surface, the study appeared to be conducted by *Research Associates of Bridgeport*, an organization of unknown character. (The title had been concocted exclusively for use in this study.)

The experiments were conducted in a three room office suite in a somewhat run-down commercial building located in the downtown shopping area. The laboratory was sparsely furnished, though clean, and marginally respectable in appearance. When subjects inquired about professional affiliations, they were informed only that we were a private firm conducting research for industry.

Some subjects displayed skepticism concerning the motives of the Bridgeport experimenter. One gentleman gave us a written account of the thought he experienced at the control board:

. . . Should I quit this damn test? Maybe he passed out? What dopes we were not to check up on this deal. How do we know that these guys are legit? No furniture, bare walls, no telephone. We could've called the police up or the Better Business Bureau. I learned a lesson tonight. How do I know that Mr. William [the experimenter] is telling the truth. . . . I wish I knew how many volts a person could take before lapsing into unconsciousness. . . .   [Subject 2414]

Another subject stated:

I questioned, on my arrival, my own judgment [about coming]. I had doubts as to the legitimacy of the operation and the consequences of participation. I felt it was a heartless way to conduct memory or learning processes on human beings and certainly dangerous without the presence of a medical doctor.   [Subject 2440 V]

There was no noticeable reduction in tension for the Bridgeport subjects. And the subjects' estimation of the amount of pain felt by the victim was slightly, though not significantly, higher than in the Yale study.

A failure to obtain complete obedience in Bridgeport would indicate that the extreme compliance found in the New Haven subjects was tied closely to the background authority of Yale University; if a large proportion of the subjects remained fully obedient, very different conclusions would be called for.

As it turned out, the level of obedience in Bridgeport, although somewhat reduced, was not significantly lower than that obtained at Yale. A large proportion of the Bridgeport subjects were fully obedient to the experimenter's commands (48 percent of the Bridgeport subjects delivered the maximum shock vs. 65 percent in the corresponding condition at Yale.)

How are these findings to be interpreted? It is possible that if commands of a potentially harmful or destructive sort are to be perceived as legitimate, they must occur within some sort of institutional structure. But it is clear from the study that it need not be a particularly reputable or distinguished institution. The Bridgeport experiments were conducted by an unimpressive firm lacking any credentials; the laboratory was set up in a respectable office building with its title listed in the building directory. Beyond that, there was no evidence of benevolence or competence. It is possible that the *category* of institution, judged according to its professed function rather than its qualitative position within that category, wins our compliance. Persons deposit money in elegant, but also seedy-looking, banks without giving much thought to the differences in the security they offer. Similarly, our subjects may treat one laboratory as equally competent as another, so long as it *is* a scientific laboratory.

It would be valuable to study the subjects' performance in other contexts that go even further than the Bridgeport study in denying institutional support to the experimenter. It is possible that beyond a certain point, obedience disappears completely. But that point had not been reached in the Bridgeport office: almost half the subjects obeyed the experimenter fully.

FURTHER EXPERIMENTS

We may mention briefly some additional experiments undertaken in the Yale series. A considerable amount of obedience and defiance in everyday life occurs in connection with groups. And we had reason to feel, in the light of many group studies already done in psychology, that group forces would have a profound effect on reactions to authority. A series of experiments was run to examine these effects. In all cases only one naive subject was studied per hour, but he performed in the midst of actors who, unknown to him, were employed by the experimenter. In one experiment (Groups for Disobedience) two actors broke off in the middle of the experiment. When this happened 90 percent of the subjects followed suit and defied the experimenter. In another condition the actors followed the orders obediently; this strengthened the experimenter's power only slightly. In still a third experiment, the job of pushing the switch to shock the learner was given to one of the actors, while the naive subject performed a subsidiary act. We wanted to see how the teacher would respond if he were involved in the situation but did not actually give the shocks. In this situation, only three subjects out of 40 broke off. In a final group experiment, the subjects themselves determined the shock level they were going to use. Two actors suggested higher and higher shock levels; some subjects insisted, despite group pressure, that the shock level be kept low; others followed along with the group.

Further experiments were completed using women as subjects. Another set dealt with the effects of dual, unsanctioned, and conflicting authority. A final experiment concerned the personal relationship between victim and subject. These will have to be described elsewhere, lest the present report be extended to monographic length.

It goes without saying that future research can proceed in many different directions. What kind of responses from the victim are most effective in causing disobedience in the subject? Perhaps passive resistance is more effective than vehement protest. What conditions of entry into an authority system lead to greater or lesser obedience? What is the effect of anonymity and masking on the subject's behavior? What conditions lead to the subject's perception of responsibility for his own actions? Each of these could be a major research topic in itself, and can readily be incorporated into the general experimental procedure described here.

LEVELS OF OBEDIENCE AND DEFIANCE

One general finding that merits attention is the high level of obedience manifested in the experimental situation. Subjects often expressed deep disapproval of shocking a man in the face of his objections, and others denounced it as senseless and stupid. Yet many subjects complied even while they protested.

The proportion of obedient subjects greatly exceeded the expectations of the experimenter and his colleagues. At the outset, we had conjectured that subjects would not, in general, go above the level of "Strong Shock." In practice, many subjects were willing to administer the most extreme shocks available when commanded by the experimenter. For some subjects, the experiment provides an occasion for aggressive release. And for others, it demonstrates the extent to which obedient dispositions are deeply ingrained and are engaged irrespective of their consequences for others. Yet this is not the whole story. Somehow, the subject becomes implicated in a situation from which he cannot disengage himself.

The departure of the experimental results from intelligent expectation, to some extent, has been formalized. The procedure was to describe the experimental situation in concrete detail to a group of competent persons, and to ask them to predict the performance of 100 hypothetical subjects. For purposes of indicating the distribution of break-off points, judges were provided with a diagram of the shock generator, and recorded their predictions before being informed of the actual results. Judges typically underestimated the amount of obedience demonstrated by subjects.

In Figure 3, we compare the predictions of 40 psychiatrists at a leading medical school with the actual performance of subjects in the experiment. The psychiatrists predicted that most subjects would not go beyond the tenth shock level (150 volts; at this point the victim makes his first explicit demand to be freed). They further predicted that by the twentieth shock level (300 volts; the victim refuses to answer) 3.73 percent of the subjects would still be obedient, and that only a little more than one tenth of one percent of the subjects would administer the highest shock on the board. But, as the graph indicates, the obtained behavior was very different. Sixty-two percent of the subjects obeyed the experimenter's commands fully. Between expectation and occurrence there is a significant discrepancy.

Why did the psychiatrists underestimate the level of obedience? Possibly, because their predictions were based on an inadequate conception of the determinants of human action, a conception that focuses on motives *in vacuo*. This orientation may be entirely adequate for the repair of bruised impulses as revealed on the psychiatrist's couch, but as soon as our interest turns to action in larger settings, attention must be paid to the situations in which motives are expressed. A situation exerts an important press on the individual. It exercises constraints and may provide push. Under certain circumstances, it is not so much the kind of person a man is as it is the kind of situation in which he is placed that determines his actions.

Many people, not knowing much about the experiment, claim that subjects who go to the end of the board are sadistic. Nothing could be more foolish as an over-all characterization of these persons. It is like saying that a person thrown into a swift flowing stream is necessarily a fast swimmer or that he has great stamina because he moves so rapidly relative to the bank. The context of action must always be considered. The individual, upon entering the laboratory, becomes integrated into a situation that carries its own momentum.

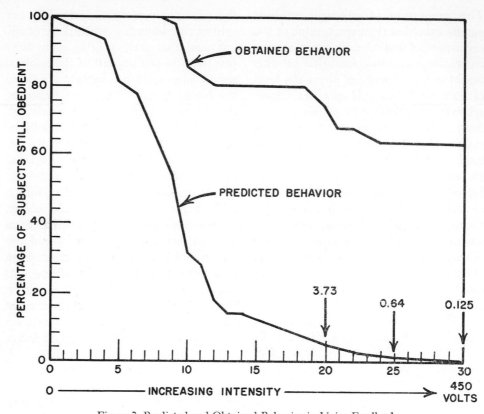

Figure 3. Predicted and Obtained Behavior in Voice Feedback

The subject's problem, then, is how to become disengaged from a situation that is moving in an altogether unpleasant direction.

The fact that disengagement is so difficult testifies to the potency of the forces that keep the subject at the control board. Are these forces to be conceptualized as individual motives and expressed in the language of personality dynamics, or are they to be seen as the effects of social structure and pressures arising from the situational field?

A full understanding of the subject's action will, I feel, require that both perspectives be adopted. The person brings to the laboratory enduring dispo-sitions toward authority and aggression, and at the same time he becomes en-meshed in a social structure that is no less an objective fact of the case. From the standpoint of personality theory one may ask: What mechanisms of person-ality enable a person to transfer respon-sibility to authority? What are the motives underlying obedient and dis-obedient performance? Does orientation to authority lead to a short-circuiting of the shame-guilt system? What cog-nitive and emotional defenses are brought into play in the case of obedi-ent and defiant subjects?

The present experiments are not, however, directed toward an exploration of the motives that are engaged when the subject obeys the experimenter's commands. Instead, they examine the situational variables responsible for the elicitation of obedience. Elsewhere, we have attempted to spell out some of the structural properties of the experimental situation that account for high obedience, and this analysis need not be repeated here (Milgram, 1963). The experimental variations, themselves, represent our attempt to probe that structure by systematically changing it and noting the consequences for behavior. It is clear that some situations produce greater compliance with the experimenter's commands than others. However, this does not necessarily imply an increase or decrease in the strength of any single definable motive. Situations producing the greatest obedience could do so by triggering the most powerful, yet perhaps the most idiosyncratic of motives in each subject confronted by the setting. Or they may simply recruit a greater number and variety of motives in their service. But whatever the motives involved—and it is far from certain that they can ever be known—action may be studied as a direct function of the situation in which it occurs. This has been the approach of the present study, where we sought to plot behavioral regularities against manipulated properties of the social field. Ultimately, social psychology would like to have a compelling *theory of situations* that will first present a language in terms of which situations can be defined, then proceed to a typology of situations, and then point to the manner in which definable properties of situations are transformed into psychological forces in the individual.

POSTSCRIPT

Almost a thousand adults were individually studied in the obedience research, and there were many specific conclusions regarding the variables that control obedience and disobedience to authority. Some of these have been discussed briefly in the preceding sections, and more detailed reports will be released subsequently.

There are now some other generalizations I should like to make that do not derive in any strictly logical fashion from the experiments as carried out, but which, I feel, ought to be made. They are formulations of an intuitive sort that have been forced on me by observation of many subjects responding to the pressures of authority. The assertions represent a painful alteration in my own thinking; and since they were acquired only under the repeated impact of direct observation, I have no illusion that they will be generally accepted by persons who have not had the same experience.

With numbing regularity, good people were seen to knuckle under the demands of authority and perform actions that were callous and severe. Men who are in everyday life responsible and decent were seduced by the trappings of authority, by the control of their perceptions, and by the uncritical acceptance of the experimenter's definition of the situation into performing harsh acts.

What is the limit of such obedience? At many points we attempted to establish a boundary. Cries from the victim were inserted; they were not effective enough. The victim claimed heart trouble; subjects still shocked him on command. The victim pleaded that he be let free and his answers no longer registered on the signal box: subjects continued to shock him. At the outset, we had not conceived that such drastic procedures would be needed to generate disobedience, and each step was added only as the ineffectiveness of the earlier techniques became clear. The final effort to establish a limit was the Touch-Proximity condition. But the very first subject in this condition subdued the victim on command, and proceeded to the highest shock level. A quarter of the subjects in this condition performed similarly.

The results, as seen and felt in the laboratory, are to this author disturbing. They raise the possibility that human nature, or more specifically the kind of character produced in American democratic society, cannot be counted on to insulate its citizens from brutality and inhumane treatment at the direction of malevolent authority. A substantial proportion of people do what they are told to do, irrespective of the content of the act and without limitations of conscience, so long as they perceive that the command comes from a legitimate authority. If, in this study, an anonymous experimenter could successfully command adults to subdue a 50-year-old man and force on him painful electric shocks against his protests, one can only wonder what government, with its vastly greater authority and prestige, can command of its citizenry. (There is, of course, the extremely important and separate question of whether malevolent institutions could or would arise in American society. The present research contributes nothing to this issue.)

In an article titled "The Dangers of Obedience," Harold J. Laski (1929) wrote:

. . . civilization means, above all, an unwillingness to inflict unnecessary pain. Within the ambit of that definition, those of us who heedlessly accept the commands of authority cannot yet claim to be civilized men.

. . . Our business, if we desire to live a life not utterly devoid of meaning and significance, is to accept nothing which contradicts our basic experience merely because it comes to us from tradition or convention or authority. It may well be that we shall be wrong; but our self-expression is thwarted at the root unless the certainties we are asked to accept coincide with the certainties we experience. That is why the condition of freedom in any state is always a widespread and consistent skepticism of the canons upon which power insists.

REFERENCES

LASKI, HAROLD J. The dangers of obedience. *Harper's Monthly Magazine*, 1929, 159: 1–10.

MILGRAM, S. Dynamics of obedience: Experiments in social psychology. Mimeographed report. *National Science Foundation*, January 25, 1961.

MILGRAM, S. Behavioral study of obedience. *J. abnorm. soc. Psychol.*, 1963, 67: 371–378.

MILLER, N. E. Experimental studies of conflict. In J. McV. Hunt (ed.), *Personality and the Behavior Disorders*, New York: Ronald Press, 1944.

SCOTT, J. P. *Aggression.* Chicago: University of Chicago Press, 1958.

26. DEVIATION, CONFORMITY, AND COMMITMENT *

Harold B. Gerard

The now classic conformity experiments of Asch (1956) confronted the subject with unanimous disagreement from a group of peers on a series of unambiguous visual judgments. This paper will consider certain of Asch's findings as well as data from subsequent research in an attempt to shed some light on the role of commitment in these experiments and in social influence processes in general.

The stimuli used by Asch consisted of two oblong white cards placed one meter apart. The one on the left contained a single black line and the one on the right contained three lines of different length, with one being equal in length to the single line on the left-hand card. The subject's task was to decide, and to announce publicly, which one of the comparison lines was equal in length to the single standard line. The standard and accompanying comparison lines differed from trial to trial. The experimental groups ranged in size from eight to ten members, all but one of these members being preinstructed confederates of the experimenter. They were seated in full view of each other, announcing their judgments publicly on each trial, with the lone, naive subject responding next to last. According to a prearranged sequence, in 12 of the 18 trials the confederates, who were always unanimous, chose one of the two incor-

rect lines, the choice usually being blatantly incorrect. Approximately one-third of the naive subjects' announced judgments conformed to the bogus consensus, a finding that is startling because the lines themselves provided an unambiguous judgmental stimulus. This is attested to by the fact that in the absence of the bogus consensus virtually no errors were made.

What accounts for this "group effect"? In his own past, the subject has learned to lean heavily on the two sources of evidence he is forced to confront in this experiment: the direct data from his eyes, and the reports of how others see things. In the present case he would certainly not expect these two sources of information to be discrepant. Yet they are. The fact that the situation is removed from his everyday experience does not render his problem any the less real; it is anything but trivial for him. The conflict produced by the discrepancy is experienced by all subjects, the majority of whom eventually resolve it one way or the other, by reporting the line they themselves see as correct or by reporting the incorrect group choice. The subject's behavior, yielding or not, follows in a consistent way from his own resolution of the problems and issues embodied in the conflict that confronts him, and he will presumably act on the basis of what he himself con-

* This paper was written specifically for this volume while the author was a U. S. Public Health Service Fellow in residence at The Center for Advanced Study in the Behavioral Sciences. Support from the Center as well as from the USPHS is gratefully acknowledged. For detailed information about the studies discussed in this paper, the reader is referred to the original published reports.

siders important. Once having made a decision, and having acted on the basis of it, any change or reversal by the subject during subsequent trials would be inconsistent with his initial decision, and perforce with the considerations that generated that decision in the first place, since the basic conditions from trial to trial remain relatively unchanged. A change in behavior would also necessarily rearouse the original conflict, forcing the subject to again work through the same doubts and misgivings. The initial decision, then, commits the subject, although not irrevocably, to yield to the group or to be independent whenever the same two alternatives present themselves on succeeding trials.

Any decision has the consequence of freezing or fixing the behavior it generates because of constraints, however minimal, which operate against undoing the behavior. The constraints may involve, as in our case, the resistance the person may have to working through the various considerations involved in the original conflict. For other types of decisions, commitment may derive from different kinds of constraints. For example, once a person has made a purchase, he may be unable to reverse his decision. The store may be unwilling to take it back, or the prospect of having to face the sales clerk or the store manager may be too unpleasant. Similarly, once a person has left one job for another, it is usually very difficult for him to reinstate the original situation. Many such actions lead to a sequence of subsequent actions, all of which have to be reversed in order to recreate the original conditions that existed before the initial choice. Other actions produce commitment by virtue of sheer physical constraints. Entering a Los Angeles freeway

during the five o'clock rush hour is an action that cannot easily be undone. A decision to leap off the Golden Gate Bridge cannot be reversed once the person has begun his fall. In general, then, any constraints that operate against changing behavior serve to commit the person to that behavior. Some decisions are easily revokable whereas others may be impossible to revoke because of physical constraints or psychological resistance to reinstating the original conditions.

Now let us consider some specific results of the Asch conformity situation from the point of view of behavioral commitment. A relevant finding in Asch's original experiment was that when a subject started out being independent, by making correct judgments on the critical trials, he tended to remain independent till the end of the series. Thus, either a subject made yielding responses very early in the series or not at all. Evidently processes were generated that served to sustain independence.

Keeping this finding in mind, let us examine the results produced by a variant of Asch's basic procedure. In this experiment, he ran a number of subjects through the same situation except for one slight difference. Instead of having three comparison lines to choose from on each trial, the subject had only two. On the twelve critical trials, the choice was between the correct line and the line chosen by the group—the same incorrect line chosen by the group in the original three-comparison-line condition. In the original experiment, the other incorrect line was chosen relatively rarely and then only when its length was between the correct line and the group choice. A striking difference occurred between the subject's behavior using this procedure and his behavior when there were three comparison lines to choose from. In the original experiment, there were a large number of completely independent subjects, many who yielded on all or nearly all of the critical trials, and many who vacillated, yielding on some trials and being independent on others. The two-comparison-line variation, on the other hand, produced a dramatic bimodal reaction with subjects tending to go along with the group on every trial or not at all. There were virtually no subjects in the intermediate error categories. The subject was thus forced, at the outset, to resolve the basic conflict one way or the other: either to go by his own sensory information or to go with the group, with no third possibility (which had been rarely chosen when there was one). Subjects in the intermediate categories in the original experiment are, after all, those who were presumably still in conflict about what to do as each trial came up. They made and then revoked decisions from trial to trial, which is presumably a painful process and apparently occurred because the third alternative was available; it was not completely an either-or choice. This interpretation is bolstered by the results of the sequel to the two-comparison-line procedure in which Asch substituted the original three-comparison-line card for a second series of judgments after the subjects had been through the series with two comparison lines. The results did not show the error distribution of the original three-comparison-line experiment; the subject's behavior was markedly consistent with his earlier behavior during the two-comparison-line series. If he had been a yielder on the first series, he continued to yield completely on the second;

whereas, if he had been independent on the first series, he remained completely independent on the second. Evidently once the subject was forced into a commitment to go with the group or with reality by the two-comparison-line procedure, his subsequent behavior when a third alternative was available was influenced by his earlier commitment.

SOME EFFECTS OF SELF-COMMITMENT AND PUBLIC COMMITMENT

We may discover the factors responsible for maintaining a commitment to yielding or to independence by varying features of the experimental situation that we suspect may remove or impose constraints upon behavior change. One feature that was uncontrolled in the experiment was the extent to which the subject committed himself to his judgment initially, upon seeing the stimulus cards and before hearing the others' judgments. Also, constraints may have been induced by the fact that the subject was forced to announce his judgment publicly on each trial.

In a subsequent experiment, Deutsch and Gerard (1955), using groups of four subjects each, manipulated initial commitment and public confrontation in order to study their contribution to the effects observed by Asch. Public confrontation was manipulated by comparing results using Asch's original public announcement procedure with one in which the subject made his judgments anonymously. In the anonymous procedure, four naive subjects were seated side by side and were separated visually from one another by partitions. Each subject had a display panel on his table that consisted of twelve red signal lamps arranged in four rows and three columns. The rows were labeled by subject number, "1," "2," "3," and "4"; and the columns were labeled "a," "b," and "c' for the comparison lines. The experimenter displayed the same sequence of standard and three-comparison-line judgment cards used by Asch. On the subject's table was a small box with three push-buttons labeled "a," "b," and "c." He indicated his choice of comparison line, when his number was called, by pressing one of these buttons. He was told that the subject numbers were assigned to the cubicles at random so that no one could be identified personally with his judgments. A ruse was resorted to here. Each subject was privately informed that he was 3 and assumed that the others were 1, 2, and 4. They were told that the judgments of each subject would appear, as they were made, on each display panel in the row corresponding to that subject's number. Thus, the judgments of subject 1 would appear, as they were made, in row 1 on each subject's panel; 2's judgments would appear in the second row of each panel, and so on. In actuality, the panels were so wired that each subject's own response appeared only in the third row of his own panel and also on a monitor panel from which they could be recorded by an unseen accomplice of the experimenter. This accomplice also fed in false information to each of the four subjects as to what the judgments of subjects 1, 2, and 4 were on each of the eighteen trials, using the same sequence of judgments as those announced by the three paid participants in the face-to-face procedure when the one naive subject was always the third one to announce his judgment.

Two sequences of the eighteen trials were run.

The effect of initial commitment was determined by comparing three treatments that were run under both the anonymous and face-to-face procedures. In one treatment, the subject had a sheet of paper on which he circled the letter corresponding to his choice before he heard (in the face-to-face treatment) or saw (in the anonymous treatment) the judgments of 1, 2, and 4. In a second treatment he was asked to note his choice down on a "magic writing pad" (consisting of a sheet of thin, clear celluloid, another of a thin onion skin, and a third of carbon paper) with which most people are familiar from their childhood. Anything written on it with a stylus can be erased by lifting the two top sheets. Since the subject was asked to erase his choice after each trial, his commitment was only tentative. In the third treatment, no written commitment was made before the subject was exposed to the others' judgments.

Comparing first the face-to-face and anonymous treatments, we find a somewhat greater yielding in the face-to-face treatment, but of immediate concern to us here is the tendency for an initially independent subject to remain so in the face-to-face treatment but not in the anonymous treatment. Thus, only the data in the face-to-face treatment are similar to those of Asch. Subjects who yielded also tended to do so with greater frequency in the face-to-face treatment. The error distribution was bimodal in the face-to-face treatment but not nearly as markedly so as in Asch's two-comparison-line variation. Evidently we can account for the continued independence of some subjects in Asch's original experiment by suggesting that public confrontation results in a greater tendency to resolve the conformity conflict one way or the other. Further corroboration is found in an experiment by Thibaut and Strickland (1956) in which subjects who committed themselves publicly to an unpopular stand and did not yield to the majority became more adamant with succeeding trials.

The initial self-commitment variations in the Deutsch and Gerard experiment also showed clear effects. The written commitment produced the greatest independence and the tentative "magic pad" commitment somewhat less independence. Subjects showed the least independence where there was no initial written commitment. Thus, reaching a definite commitment prior to finding out what the group consensus is fixes the behavior.

The initial commitment and public confrontation procedures served to confront the subject with negative consequences for changing his decision. In the strong initial commitment treatment, when the subject wrote down his choice before hearing or seeing the others' judgments, conforming would violate the image the person had of himself of being true to his conviction, which was "staring" up at him from his sheet and could not be erased. With the tentative commitment, achieved with the magic writing pad technique, constraints against conforming were lowered because, in effect, the evidence of the initial decision was "destroyed" after each trial. Finally, constraints were lowered even further when there was no decisional commitment whatsoever. The public commitment, produced in the face-to-face condition, had a similar effect which acted through time in the presence of the others to whom the subject had verbally committed himself. He assumed, of course, that they would remember what he had done on previous trials, knowledge which he, therefore, could not "erase." He knew what they presumably knew. Once the subject had openly conformed or deviated, constraints were created against changing the behavior since this would have been a public avowal, as well as an avowal to himself, of inconstancy. This probably acted in much the same manner as writing the judgment down, thus sustaining the behavior from trial to trial.

COGNITIVE SUPPORT FOR BEHAVIOR

What are the cognitive accompaniments of a behavioral commitment of this kind? Somehow the person has to come to terms with difficulties induced by his having to suffer the negative consequences of the action and having to forego the positive consequences of reversing himself. In line with the theory of cognitive dissonance (Festinger, 1957), he will attempt to justify his action by supplying cognitive support for the chosen action and by negating the nonchosen action alternative; a kind of "sour grapes, sweet lemon" reaction. Cognitive work does not occur in the abstract, divorced from behavior, but is generated by the person's need to establish and maintain an unequivocal behavioral orientation toward his environment.

In the judgmental situation used in these experiments, one way of justifying behavior *vis à vis* the group is to attribute characteristics to the self and to the others that would be consistent with the person's decision to conform or deviate. This cognitive "bolstering" makes the chosen behavior even more likely the next time a decision is required. Under ordinary life circumstances, where strong commitments are usually operating, the influence process tends, due to cognitive bolstering, to be circular and cumulative making conformity more likely with each subsequent instance of conformity and making deviation more likely with each subsequent instance of deviation.

EXPERIMENTAL EVIDENCE FOR COGNITIVE BOLSTERING

An experiment by Gerard and Rotter (1961) contains evidence that cognitive bolstering does accompany a behavioral commitment. Four naive subjects per group were used in the Deutsch and Gerard cubicle situation. They responded to four series of line judgments composed of nine trials each. In each series there were six critical trials (in which the bogus consensus was wrong) and three neutral trials (in which "the others" chose the correct line). After each series of judgments, a questionnaire was administered, which asked the subject to evaluate his own performance, the performance of the others, and to guess how they evaluated him. Each of these evaluations used the same six-point rating scale going from very satisfactory (scored $+ 3$) to very unsatisfactory (scored $- 3$) with no zero or indifference point available. The judgmental discrepancy arouses a consideration of these three evaluations since, as the interviews revealed, relative ability is one of the important factors at issue here. We would expect the sub-

ject's evaluations to be brought into alignment, that is, to be internally consistent, to the extent that his behavior shows evidence of commitment to either conformity or deviation. Evaluational consistency should be a correlate of behavioral consistency. This follows from the hypothesis that the subject will bolster his behavior cognitively to the extent that he is committed to that behavior. Each evaluation, being either positive or negative, yields the eight possible evaluation triads shown in Table 1. We assume that the subject anticipates a negative evaluation from the others for deviating from them and a positive evaluation from them for conforming. There is a great deal of anecdotal support for this assumption in Asch's interview data. The table also offers systematic supporting evidence as indicated by the fact that 19 of the 25 subjects making one error or none guessed, on the final questionnaire, that the others would evaluate them negatively. On the other hand, 17 out of the 24 subjects making eleven errors or more guessed that the others would rate them positively. The assumption eliminates consideration of triads I, II, V, and VI for a deviate and configurations III, IV, VII, and VIII for a conformer. Triads III and VIII are also inconsistent for a deviate. The subject would tend not to have deviated had he evaluated the others positively as in III. Nor would he evaluate both himself and the others negatively as in VIII; surely someone is correct. For the deviate, then, this leaves IV as the behaviorally consistent triad containing a positive self-evaluation and VII as the consistent triad containing a negative self-evaluation. Using the same sort of reasoning, configurations I and VI are the consistent

TABLE 1. INITIAL (FIRST QUESTIONNAIRE) AND FINAL (LAST QUESTIONNAIRE)
DISTRIBUTION OF TRIAD TYPES BY TOTAL JUDGMENT ERRORS

Total Errors	I (+++)		II (++−)		III (+−+)		IV (+−−)		V (−++)		VI (−+−)		VII (−−+)		VIII (−−−)	
	Init.	Fin.	Init.	Fin.	Init.	Fin.	Init.	Fin.	Init.	Fin.	Init.	Fin.	Init.	Fin.	Init.	Fin.
0–1	7	6	**		9	4	7	15					2	3		
2–4	4	7			9	5	6	7	1				2	2		
5–10	12	11	1	1	7	5	2	6					2	3	1	1
11–24	12	17	1	1	5	4	1		1				4			
Total	35	41	2	2	30	18	16	28	2				10	8	1	1

* The first of the three signs indicates a positive or negative self evaluation, the second sign indicates the evaluation the second subject guessed the others made of him, and the last sign indicates the evaluation the subject made of the others.

** An empty cell indicates no cases.

triads for the conformer. It follows from the above that triads II, III, V, and VIII are internally inconsistent irrespective of whether the subject conforms or deviates.

The triad data in Table 1 show trends that reflect the reasoning of the previous paragraph. The error classification shown was designed to apportion the subjects into four approximately equal groupings. First, it will be noted in the table that, irrespective of the number of times he yields, there is an overwhelming tendency for the subject to evaluate himself positively. This is indicated by the preponderance of subjects having evaluation triads I through IV, all of which have a positive self-evaluation component; and only 9 out of the 96 subjects have a negative final self-evaluation. In line with our reasoning, then, we would expect conformers to support their behavior with a type I triad and deviates to support their behavior with a type IV triad. The data in the table show that this is clearly the case. Examining the initial distribution, we see that there is a greater likelihood for a subject to have a type I triad the more he yields and for a subject to have a type IV triad the greater his independence. These initial tendencies become more marked over time as indicated by the final distribution of subjects for those triad types. Within each error category the same subjects are redistributed among the triad types from the initial to the final triad determination. It is therefore apparent, by comparing the initial with the final distributions within each row of the table, what has been happening over time. A number of subjects have been changing from a type III triad, which as we indicated is unstable, to either a

type I (if they tend to conform) or a type IV (if they tend to deviate). The other changes in the distribution are also in the direction of greater consistency or "balance" that is, in turn, more consistent with behavior. Triad III is evidently a transitional state, and it is likely that if the judgments continued, more subjects would have changed out of that state to an evaluation triad that was consistent with their behavior. Examination of the marginal column totals shows what has been happening on an over-all basis. There is an increase in the number of subjects with type I and IV triads from 51 to 69, which is associated with a decrease in the other triad types.

Undoubtedly our assumptions do not account for all of the data. Other factors must have been operating in the situation to account for the fact that one subject maintained a type VIII triad, that three subjects who conformed a great deal maintained a type VII triad, and so on through the table. By adding assumptions, we could account for these discrepant cases but our theory would then become quite cumbersome and inelegant.

Our theory as it stands is quite simple. It states that a discrepancy in judgment will call into question the person's estimate of his ability to make the judgment. Since other people have seen his judgment, the person will assume an evaluation by the others of himself that is based upon how he behaved toward them. He will then support that behavior by bringing his evaluation of the others into alignment with his self-evaluation and the evaluation he assumes they have of him.

Obviously we cannot make as strong a case as we would like for the contention that a behavioral commitment of conforming or deviating engages a process of evaluational consistency attainment. The initial distribution of triads in Table 1 shows either that the process was well underway after the first nine judgments or that a certain amount of evaluational consistency existed before the very first discrepancy confrontation. It is likely that both processes do in fact operate—a person behaves in a manner that is consistent with the relevant evaluations he holds and, once having committed himself to behave in a particular way, he further adjusts his evaluations so they become more consistent with his behavior. We suggested earlier that the process is circular and cumulative. There is much evidence in the social influence literature supporting the evaluation-leading-to-behavior link in this circular chain but no evidence beyond the type of correlational relationship we have just examined for the other, equally important and ubiquitous one of behavior-leading-to-changed-evaluations. The awesome and dramatic example of "brainwashing" comes to mind as an instance of this other link in operation. Evidently the technique involves getting the person to commit himself just once to a behavior that would not ordinarily follow from his beliefs and values. Once having committed himself to a very mildly reprehensible act, which is dissonant with his values, the person must then engage in cognitive work in order to develop support for the behavior. The new alignment of values makes him "ripe" for another confrontation in which he may be induced, with relative ease, to perform some act that would have been reprehensible earlier but is now consistent with his new value alignment.

Once the new alignment is consolidated, the person may be ready for a more extreme behavior commitment, and so on. This kind of circular process is not restricted to the brainwashing situation but pervades everyday life. Another example that may fit our paradigm is teenage "necking" in which a commitment to a kiss may lead in a circular fashion to more intimate acts. An investigation of other kinds of behavior such as drinking, smoking, and drag racing might also show evidence of the same underlying process. The process is not confined to morally nonsanctioned behavior but may also account for the development of moral values themselves as, for example, when a child is induced by his parents to behave in socially acceptable ways.

At this point we would like to say that the data in Table I offer unequivocal support for our hypothesis that behavioral consistency leads to evaluational consistency, but we cannot infer the causal direction from the data as they stand. Inferences concerning cause-effect relationships should be based on evidence obtained from more carefully controlled experiments.

THE EXPERIMENTAL MANIPULATION OF CONFORMITY AND DEVIATION

An attempt was made to overcome the limitations of the previous study by producing conformity and deviation experimentally. We are still assuming that when the subject conforms he will expect the others to evaluate him positively and that when he deviates they will evaluate him negatively. In the previous experiment, we observed a

Figure 1. A typical stimulus

strong tendency for the subject to evaluate himself positively, which limited the consistent or "balanced" evaluation triads to types I (+++) and IV (+−−). If we were able to induce a negative as well as a positive evaluation, triads VI (−+−) and VII (−−+) would also be possible balanced end states. Thus, if we were able to produce conformity and deviation and also induce either a positive or a negative self evaluation, two of the evaluations in a given triad would have been fixed experimentally and tendencies toward cognitive bolstering of behavior could be determined by measuring the third component, namely the subject's evaluation of the others. From our theory we would predict an evaluation that will yield a balanced triad.

Forty-eight subjects were run three at a time in the cubicle situation described in the previous experiments. Each subject was first exposed to one of two ability treatments. The task through which these ability manipulations were effected consisted of having the subject select, from a pair of multipointed stars that were briefly flashed on a projection screen, the one having the greater number of points. A typical stimulus is shown in Figure 1. As we proceed, the reasons for using a two alternative task will become clear. The subject pressed a button with his left index finger if he chose the left-hand star or another

button with his right index finger if he guessed that the right-hand one had a greater number of points. Only he and the experimenter knew what his responses were during this first series. After each judgment, he indicated his confidence and then a lamp on his display panel lit up if he was correct. Half of the subjects were arbitrarily informed, irrespective of whether or not they were actually correct, that they were correct on 14 out of the 15 judgments, whereas the other half were told that they were correct on only 5 of the 15. There is little question that the subjects were affected by the ability manipulation. Subjects in the former, *high ability*, treatment showed a steady increase in confidence, whereas subjects in the latter, *low ability*, treatment showed a steady decrease.

After the ability induction, dummy electrocardiograph (EKG) electrodes were strapped to the subject's forearms and the instructions continued:

You now have an idea of how good you are at this type of judgment. We have found thus far that nine correct judgments is about average. Thirteen or more correct is exceptionally good, whereas six or fewer correct is well below average. You know how many correct judgments you made by the number of times the green "correct" light went on after each judgment that you made.

We are interested not only in your considered decisions but also in your first impulses. We suspect that there are some unusual phenomena that are linked to one's first impulses in a judgmental situation of this type. During this next phase of the experiment, each of you will have both of your forearms connected to some electromyographic equipment that will amplify the electrical potentials generated by certain muscle groups in your forearms. These muscles are among those you have just used in making your judgments. The nerve pathways to your forearm muscles are now set to trigger these muscles when you are simply asked to make a choice. The potentials will be used to operate the lamp panel in front of you. Instead of actually making your choice when your green light comes on, your immediate impulse at that moment will register on your panel and on the panels of the other two people in the other booths. During this part of the experiment you will be given an opportunity to see the others' first impulses. These will appear in the corresponding rows on your panel and will be displayed in numerical sequence. We are going to ask you some questions about the others' judgments after the series is over.

First, subject 1's green light will go on and his immediate impulse will be displayed on all three panels. Then subject 2's green light will go on and his immediate impulse will be displayed. Finally, subject 3's green light will go on and his immediate impulse will be displayed. Keep both arms perfectly still while the judgments are being displayed. There is nothing you need do except look at the stimulus on each trial. Since we are going to ask you about the others' judgments, you must also look at their judgments as they are displayed on your panel. Up until your green "respond" light goes on, your impulse may have changed back and forth from one forearm to the other. However, the electromyograph recorder will register the impulse that occurs immediately after your green light flashes on. This may not necessarily be the same impulse you had upon first seeing the stars on that trial.

During this "dummy electrode" series, the subject was exposed to one of two preprogrammed sequences of lamp displays. One sequence gave him the impression that his first impulse was to deny his own senses and conform to the group, whereas the other sequence gave him the impression that his first impulse was to make the correct judgment and thus deviate from the others. By the same ruse used in the previous experiments, all three subjects were informed that they were 3. The judgments of 1 and 2 and their own presumed first impulses were displayed in what appeared to be a naturally paced sequence. The same series of 18 star-pairs were presented to subjects in both the "deviate" and "conformer" conditions.

The details of the conformer-deviate induction were as follows. On the first 3 trials, 1, 2, and 3 (the subject himself, of course) all chose the correct star. On the fourth trial, 1 chose the incorrect star whereas 2 and 3 chose the correct one. On trial 5 they all agreed with reality again. On the sixth and seventh trials, 1 and 2 both chose the incorrect star, whereas 3 chose the correct one. Up to this point, everything was the same for both the conformer and deviate. On trial 8 the separation occured: the conformer found that his first impulse was to go along with 1 and 2, who both chose the incorrect star, whereas the deviate found that his first impulse was to choose the correct star and thus not to go along with the other two. From this point until the end of the series the conformer found that he always agreed with 1 and 2 regardless of whether or not they were actually correct, whereas the deviate found that his first impulse was always to choose the physically correct star, which had the effect of placing him in disagreement with 1 and 2 for most of the remaining trials.

After the conformer-deviate induction, the subject was given a projective test devised by Libo (1953). This test has been shown to measure a person's evaluation of others in his present social situation. In consists of four stylized drawings of an individual in different group situations. In taking the Group Picture Impressions (GPI) test, the subject is asked to write a story about each one of the pictures describing what led up to the scene depicted, what is happening now, and what is going to happen in the future. The subject's stories are later coded for content, which indicates approach or avoidance reactions to the others by the main character in each of the pictures; an approach statement is scored plus, and an avoidance statement, minus.

After taking the GPI test, the subject answered a questionnaire that was designed to provide an additional measure of his evaluation of the others, and also to provide a check on the experimental manipulations of ability and conformity-deviation. He was asked to estimate how many correct judgments he and the others had made on the first series and how many times there was complete agreement during the second series. This last question was the check on the conformity-deviation induction and showed a marked difference between the two treatments: the conformers estimated

approximately 14 out of 18 trials of complete agreement, and the deviates estimated approximately eight out of eighteen, which accurately reflects what happened.

The GPI data as well as the self and other ability attributions are shown in Table 2. Examining first the ability attributions, we see that the low ability conformer rates the others low, whereas his high ability counterpart rates them high. The deviate, on the other hand, rates the others high, relative to himself, if he was low in ability and low, relative to himself, if he was high in ability. The fact that both the high and low ability deviate give the others virtually the same estimate is probably an effect of convergence resulting from the attempt of each type of deviate to contrast the others with himself. Assuming, as we have, that a conformer estimates that the others will evaluate him positively and that a deviate will anticipate a negative evaluation, the data confirm our predictions. The high ability conformer's evaluations show a type I $(+++)$ triad and those of the low ability conformer a type VI $(-+-)$ triad. The evaluations of the high ability deviate show a type IV $(+--)$ triad and those of the low ability deviate a type VII $(--+)$ triad.

All four cells show positive GPI scores, which indicates a general positive evaluation of the others. The questionnaire data showed a similar effect as indicated by the tendency to estimate that the others had turned in a better than average performance (an average score was 9 correct). When, however, we compare the degree of positive evaluation among the four cells, we find the same trends as in the questionnaire data. These findings are, there-

TABLE 2. SELF AND OTHER EVALUATIONS AND GROUP PICTURE IMPRESSIONS SCORES FOR CONFORMERS AND DEVIATES OF HIGH AND LOW ABILITY

	Conformer			Deviate		
	Number of Own Judgments Correct on First Series	Number of Others' Judgments Correct on First Series	GPI Score	Number of Own Judgments Correct on First Series	Number of Others' Judgments Correct on First Series	GPI Score
Hi ability	14.07^{*}_a	12.10_b	5.12_m	13.67_a	10.32_d	1.67_n
Lo ability	6.47_c	9.54_d	2.67_n	6.00_c	10.60_d	6.00_m

* Figures with the same subscript are not significantly different from one another at the .05 level by a t-test. The correct judgments and GPI scores are, of course, not comparable so that their subscripts are not to be compared.

for the ability manipulation upon self-estimate of correct judgments and a significant interaction between the two experimental variables upon the estimate of the number of correct judgments made by the others. There is also a significant interaction of the GPI scores.

fore, in line with the predicted evaluation triads. The data, then, lead us to conclude that evaluational consistency follows a behavioral commitment to conform or deviate.

SUMMARY AND CONCLUSIONS

We chose to regard conformity that can be produced experimentally not as a time-bound curiosity but as a phenomenon that might reveal a relationship between cognitive processes and action. Evidence was examined that suggested that commitment plays a fundamental role in producing the behavioral consistency observed in the typical conformity experiment where the subject tends to yield very early in a series of judgments or does not yield at all. We hypothesized that the relationship between commitment and behavioral consistency is mediated by cognitive work.

Data from two experiments confirmed the hypothesis. The first of these experiments related cognitive bolstering to the actual decision made by the subject to conform or deviate, whereas the second related the bolstering to conformity and deviation that was experimentally induced. However, certain difficulties remain. The last experiment does not pin down exactly how cognitive consistency is achieved, given a behavioral commitment. We have suggested a process, namely that the evaluation the subject makes of the others follows from our having fixed the other two evaluations in the triad. In this proposed sequence, the evaluation he guessed the others had made of him was assumed to be fixed by the subject's behavior (of conforming or deviating) toward them. It may very well be, how-

ever, that his behavior first fixes the subject's evaluation of the others and the evaluation he guesses they have of him (as measured in the earlier experiment) may then follow in a consistent way from his evaluations of them and himself. Let us see how that might work. The conformer may assume that since the others are similar to him in their judgments, they are also similar to him in ability, whereas the deviate might assume that since his judgments differ from theirs, he and the others are different in ability. The data in Table 2 are perfectly consistent with these assumptions. Additional research is needed to determine the immediate evaluational effect of conformity or deviation; that is, whether it produces the evaluation of the others based upon what the subject knows about himself or whether the behavior, conformity, or deviation produces an assumed "reflected" evaluation of himself by the others. The two processes are quite different; the former being a relatively passive one of social comparison, based upon an immediate evaluative reaction of the others by the subject when he finds out that he just happens to agree or disagree with them; whereas the latter process is both more active and more complex. It assumes that the person can "take the role of the other" and evaluate himself "in their eyes" as he would evaluate them were the situation reversed. The similarity-contrast, social-comparison hypothesis is appealing because of its simplicity, but the interaction hypothesis is supported by the anecdotal evidence in Asch's work and in the statements volunteered by the subjects in these experiments. Both processes form the core of the social-psychological behavior of man, one depending upon comparative information and the other upon interaction and reciprocal perceptions. Both probably operate simultaneously in everyday confrontations.

REFERENCES

Asch, S. E. Studies of independence and conformity. *Psychol. Monogr.*, 1956, 70, No. 9 (whole No. 416).

Deutsch, M., & Gerard, H. B. A study of normative and informational social influence upon individual judgment. *J. abnorm. soc. Psychol.*, 1955, 51, 629–636.

Festinger, L. A *Theory of Cognitive Dissonance*. Evanston, Ill.: Harper & Row, 1957.

Gerard, H. B., & Rotter, G. S. Time perspective, consistency of attitude, and social influence. *J. abnorm. soc. Psychol.*, 1961, 62, 565–572.

Libo, L. *The Cohesiveness of Groups*. Ann Arbor: The Research Center for Group Dynamics, 1953.

Thibaut, J. W., & Strickland, L. H. Psychological set and conformity. *J. Pers.*, 1956, 25, 115–129.

27. CONFORMITY AND NEED–ACHIEVEMENT UNDER CROSS–CULTURAL NORM CONFLICT *

Robert B. Zajonc and N. Kishor Wahi

Experimental studies of conformity, such as those of Asch (1956) for instance, represent a paradigm of conflict. The subject is generally under the influence of two opposing forces—the stimulus and his preception thereof on the one hand, and the pressures of the group majority on the other. It might be well to note that this experimental paradigm is not especially representative of conformity problems in everyday life. Conflict in conformity is more of an exception than a general case. An individual in learning a set of norms in his own society is more often subject to congruent rather than to incongruent sources of conformity pressures. For an indigenous population conflict in conformity arises when groups, such as parents, teachers, or peers, exercising conformity pressures, represent different norms or values—an

instance relatively infrequent—or when the norms of the given society demand from the individual the inhibition of his impulses, drives, or desires.

The experimental paradigm of conformity, and especially its conflict aspect, is perhaps more valid for foreign students. Foreign students maintain some degree of membership in two countries. As members of their home country they are subject to one set of conformity pressures, and by virtue of their temporary membership in the host country, to another. Often the two norms stand in clear conflict with one another (Zajonc, 1952; Smith, 1956; French & Zajonc, 1957). Studies on foreign students show that there exist different ways of resolving this conflict. Scandinavian students, for instance, have been found to accept some American norms and reject

* Reprinted from *Human Relations*, 1961, 14: 241–250, with permission of the senior author and the Tavistock Institute of Human Relations.

others, a pattern labelled the 'Smörgasbord approach' (Smith, 1955). Some foreign students have been observed to maintain their original norms by refraining from entering into close contact with American students, others seem to assimilate very rapidly (Passin & Bennett, 1954; Sewell, Morris, & Davidsen, 1954). The resolution of normative conflict depends above all on the strength of the conflict, and on conformity patterns developed during early training. In terms of the latter aspect, conformity behavior has been found to be highly related to independence training, which in turn determines the development of the achievement motive (McClelland, Atkinson, Clark, & Lowell, 1953). However, studies relating conformity to the achievement motive often obtained conflicting results. For instance, McClelland *et al.* (1953) analysed in terms of the achievement motive data collected by Asch in his conformity studies. These authors report that of the subjects with n-achievement scores above the group median 13 percent were 'yielders', while 87 percent of those with scores below the median were found to yield to conformity pressures. However, Samelson (1958) found a positive relation between conformity and the achievement motive. In a visual recognition task subjects were confronted with wrong majority judgments. When the subjects were told that they were 'better than others in recognizing words', those with high n-achievement scores showed a significantly stronger tendency to conform than those with low n-achievement scores.

If n-achievement is viewed in terms of its relation to independence training, then among foreign students those characterized by high n-achievement should find it easy both to abandon their original norms and to reject the norms of the host country. On the other hand, as Burdick (1955) suggested, conformity may in many cases be instrumental to achievement, and consequently, in cases of norm conflict, we might expect foreign students with high n-achievement scores to resolve the conformity conflict by accepting the new norms. For individuals who are characterized by weak achievement motives, whether conformity is or is not instrumental to achievement is immaterial, and they should therefore respond in terms of the relative strengths of the opposing conformity pressures.

The purpose of this study is to examine the following set of predictions relating conformity of Indian students to American norms to n-achievement, when the instrumental value of conformity is manipulated. First, we would expect on the basis of past research that, when conformity has no particular value for achievement and when the norms of the two countries are congruent, subjects with low n-achievement will show higher conformity than subjects high on n-achievement scores. Secondly, when the instrumental value of conformity is increased and when the two norms are congruent, the tendency to conform for subjects with high n-achievement scores will increase. When the norms of the two countries are in conflict and conformity to American norms has instrumental value for achievement, the relation between conformity to American norms and n-achievement will be reversed. That is, we would expect higher conformity from individuals with high than from those with low n-achievement scores. This difference will again tend to decrease when conformity is perceived as having no particular instrumental value for achievement. In general, variations in conformity for individuals with high n-achievement will depend more on whether or not conformity is instrumental to achievement than on whether the American and Indian norms are congruent or incongruent. On the other hand, conformity to American norms for individuals with low n-achievement scores will depend to a larger extent on whether or not norms are in conflict, and instrumentality will be of minor importance.

METHOD

Subjects

The Ss were thirty male students from India, enrolled in the University of Michigan during the spring of 1960. Most of them were juniors or seniors in engineering. They had resided in the United States for periods of four months to three years. The median age of the Ss was twenty-four. Six of these Ss refused to take part in the second experimental session, thus leaving a total of twenty-four Ss.

Procedure

ASSESSMENT OF N-ACHIEVEMENT The Ss were given the n-achievement test in groups of ten. Out of the four pictures shown, one was an original TAT picture (Father-Son, Card 7 BM from TAT), and the remaining three pictures used were developed by Atkinson (1958) for the purposes of measuring n-achievement. The four pictures, according to Atkinson's identifying number scheme (Atkinson, 1958, pp. 832–5), were Nos. 1, 2, 59, and 100.

Both inter-rater and the so-called 'expert coding' reliability measures were obtained. Using the rank correlation method, a coefficient of .80 was obtained on the first, and .73 on the second.

The Ss were divided at the median into 'high' and 'low' n-achievement groups, each including twelve Ss. The range of scores for the high n-achievement group was between 14 and 28, and for the low n-achievement group between 1 and 12. The mean n-achievement scores of the two groups were 18.3 and 8.3 respectively.

STIMULI For the purposes of measuring conformity a set of seventy-two statements concerning behavior relevant to American and Indian norms was selected. The procedure of selection employed three Indian judges who judged a large set of such statements in terms of whether or not they involved conflict situations for Indian students. Out of the large set of statements, seventy-two items on which the judges' agreement was high were selected. One-half of the items pertained to congruent and one-half to incongruent norms. The agreement of the judges on the statements selected was 76.4 percent. The following are some examples of items involving incongruent norms: 'Women should not be kissed in public'; 'We should be informal with our teachers'; 'Men should help their wives in preparing meals'. Items involving congruent norms were, for instance, 'One should not sleep in the nude'; 'One may smoke in the presence of his father'; or 'We should follow the current fashions in clothing'.

INSTRUMENTALITY ASSESSMENT The seventy-two statements were given to ten Indian students who were not Ss in the present experiment to rate on a four-point scale as to whether conformity by an Indian student to the particular American norm involved in the statement was 'important in getting ahead'. Each statement was then given a mean instrumentality score and the statements involving congruent and incongruent norms were each broken at the median into 'low instrumentality' and 'high instrumentality' items.

EXPERIMENTAL   PROCEDURE   One and one-half months after the n-achievement test was administered, conformity to American norms was observed. For this purpose each S was brought individually to an experimental cubicle, believing that besides him there were three other Ss in the cubicles. The S was told that his task would be to respond to a set of questions which he would hear through an intercommunication system, and that he would also hear the responses of the three Ss. Actually the responses of these individuals were prerecorded by a set of three paid participants, who by virtue of their accents appeared as S's compatriots. Each S was assigned the letter D, being previously told that the letters of the three other participants were A, B, and C. However, he would not have the opportunity to see them or communicate with them. The Ss were instructed to respond in alphabetical order. Thus, each S was last to respond, being previously exposed to the responses of the three paid participants. All Ss were exposed to the same tape recording. The entire session was conducted in English.

After the initial instructions were issued Ss heard E read the seventy-two statements in intervals of approximately 30 seconds. These statements as well as the responses of the paid participants were pre-recorded. Following each statement the Ss were asked to indicate whether they "agreed" or "disagreed" with the given statement. The responses of the paid participants to twenty-five of the statements were unanimous, and in the remainder a majority of two was employed. The items were assigned positions on the list on a random basis. Likewise, the responses of the paid participants were randomized in terms of unanimity, as well as in terms of whether they agreed or disagreed with the statements. Furthermore, to eliminate any possible effects deriving from response sets, half of the items were phrased in a positive and half in a negative manner.

Conformity was scored in the following way. It should be noted that the focus of this study is on conformity to American norms. It will be further noted that the paid participants could show either conformity or non-conformity to the American norm, thus creating additional pressures on the Ss towards or away from conformity to the American norm. We might therefore distinguish between what may be called *normative* and *situational* conformity. Normative conformity deals with behavior viewed with reference to established cultural norms. Situational conformity denotes yielding to the group pressures immediately given. Thus, the Ss in the present experiment were under both normative and situational conformity pressures, and four progressively more intense degrees of conformity could be distinguished. When a subject rejects a given American norm which his immediately present compatriots accept, he seems to show a greater degree of independence than when his compatriots also reject it. Conversely, the endorsement of an American norm which is not complied

TABLE 1. CONFORMITY SCORES

Conformity of the Paid Participants to the American Norm

		Yes	No
Conformity of the subjects to the American norm	Yes	3	4
	No	1	2

with by an immediately present refer-ence group involves overcoming restrain-ing forces, and thus it might be thought of as stronger than endorsement made with social support. The four conform-ity scores which thus emerged were arbi-trarily designated as ranging from 1 to 4 (see Table 1).

On the basis of this scoring system, for each S four conformity scores were obtained: one based on the mean con-formity to congruent-high instrumental-ity items, one to congruent-low instru-mentality items, one to incongruent-high instrumentality items, and one to incon-gruent-low instrumentality items.

RESULTS

1. *The Effects of Instrumentality and Congruence of Norms on Conformity*

The results are presented in Table 2, and the analysis of variance in Table 3.

It is at first apparent that there is a somewhat higher conformity on the part of subjects with high n-achievement scores than on the part of subjects with low n-achievement scores, the former showing a mean of 2.63 and the latter 2.51. The main effect of achievement

TABLE 2. MEAN CONFORMITY SCORES

Type of Item	High n-Achievement			Low n-Achievement		
	Congruent Items	Incongruent Items	Both	Congruent Items	Incongruent Items	Both
High instrumentality	2.80	2.80	2.80	2.88	2.33	2.61
Low instrumentality	2.22	2.69	2.46	2.40	2.41	2.40
Both combined	2.51	2.75	2.63	2.64	2.37	2.51

TABLE 3. ANALYSIS OF VARIANCE FOR DATA IN TABLE 2

Source	df	MS	F	p
n-Achievement (A)	1	.350	6.03	.05
Error (between)	22	.058		
Congruence (C)	1	.006	< 1.00	—
Instrumentality (I)	1	1.814	20.38	.001
C × I	1	1.602	18.00	.001
C × A	1	1.550	17.42	.001
I × A	1	.122	1.37	—
C × I × A	1	.011	< 1.00	—
Error (within)	66	.089		

is significant at the .05 level. It is also clear that instrumentality has a very important consequence for conformity. Mean overall conformity to items of high instrumentality was 2.70 and to items of low instrumentality 2.43. This main effect was significant at the .001 level ($F = 20.38$). Congruence of norms in itself did not generate significant differences. It is of interest to note, however, that individuals with high n-achievement show higher conformity to incongruent items, and those with low n-achievement to congruent items. The $C \times A$ interaction was significant at the .001 level ($F = 17.42$). The analysis of variance also indicates that instrumentality in itself does not differentiate between subjects with high and low n-achievement scores, the $I \times A$ interaction not being significant.

On the whole therefore the data give a fairly clear support to the predictions. Some questions of interest which are suggested by the results must however be examined. Contrary to previous results, the overall effects of n-achievement on conformity are positive. A scrutiny of the cell means shows that this effect is due to the fact that under conditions of high instrumentality there is a high degree of conformity on the part of subjects with high n-achievement scores, regardless of whether the norms are congruent or not. The two means are both equal to 2.80. Moreover, with respect to items of low instrumentality, the subjects with high n-achievement scores seem to conform to a larger extent when the norms are incongruent. The means here are 2.69 for incongruent and 2.22 for congruent items, this difference being significant at the .001 level by *t*-test. Individuals with low n-achievement scores, however, respond negatively to incongruent items, that is they conform to a lesser extent, regardless of whether instrumentality is involved or not, the means being 2.33 and 2.41 respectively. This difference is not significant. When the items are congruent, however, the low n-achievement subjects are affected by instrumentality although not to such an extent as the high n-achievement subjects. The mean conformity scores for high n-achievement subjects on congruent items were 2.80 for high and 2.22 for low instrumentality. This difference is highly significant ($t = 6.6$, $p < .001$). The corresponding means for the low n-achievement group was 2.88 and 2.40, this difference also being significant ($t = 5.5$, $p < .001$). The question arises then, why should individuals with low n-achievement tendencies respond in terms of instrumentality for achievement. Of course, the data in the present experiment do not permit a definite solution. However, it might be argued that we are not dealing here with individuals characterized by the absence of achievement motivation, or even a low level of achievement motivation. The mean n-achievement score of the low n-achievement group was, it will be recalled, 8.3; seven of these twelve Ss earned scores of 10 or more. The means generally obtained for a comparable American population are below 8.0 (Atkinson, 1958). It seems, therefore, that Indian students who undertake to study in the United States are relatively high in n-achievement.

One might also inquire why subjects with high n-achievement scores should show a fairly high level of conformity to incongruent items which are not instrumental to achievement, but rather low conformity to congruent items. For items of low instrumentality, the means of the high n-achievement group were 2.69 for incongruent and 2.22 for congruent items, this difference, it will be recalled, being significant at the .001 level ($t = 5.4$). In the context of this study conformity refers to the acceptance of the American norms. For congruent items, then, conformity implies the acceptance of both the American and the Indian norms. When the norms are in conflict, however, conformity (that is, acceptance of the American norm) necessarily implies the rejection of the Indian norm. It might be argued on the basis of the relation between n-achievement and independence training, therefore, that the high n-achievement subjects are better able to reject their original norms. Perhaps, it might be conjectured, the American norms which are in conflict with the corresponding Indian norms are in general more compatible with achievement striving than Indian norms. For instance, the statement that "students should not defer to their elders," which was rated as having relatively low instrumentality, was endorsed more often by subjects with high n-achievement scores. Apparently lack of independence of elders, while not in itself instrumental, is perceived by high n-achievement subjects as capable of hindering achievement. For the congruent items of low instrumentality, conformity to the American norm simultaneously implies acceptance of the original Indian norm, and it is here that least conformity is observed.

It was also predicted that the conformity of the high n-achievement group will be subject to variation primarily on the basis of instrumentality, and that of the low n-achievement group primarily on the basis of norm congruence. There are some indications in the results that this may be the case. For the high n-achievement subjects the mean difference between high and now instrumentality is .34 and the mean difference between conformity to incongruent and congruent items, .24. For the low n-achievement group these mean differences are respectively .21 and −.27. In addition, the high n-achievement group conforms more under incongruence, and the low n-achievement group under congruence. More confidence in these results is gained when separate analyses of variance are performed for the two n-achievement groups. These are summarized in Table 4. It is clear from the analyses that for the high n-achievement

TABLE 4. SEPARATE ANALYSES OF VARIANCE ON THE EFFECTS OF INSTRUMENTALITY AND CONGRUENCE FOR THE HIGH AND LOW N-ACHIEVEMENT GROUPS

Source	df	High n-Achievement			Low n-Achievement		
		MS	F	P	MS	F	P
Congruence (C)	1	.677	19.34	.01	.880	5.91	.05
Instrumentality (I)	1	1.435	41.00	.001	.500	3.36	—
Subjects (Ss)	11	.059	1.69	—	.056	< 1.00	—
C × I	1	.677	19.34	.01	.992	6.67	.05
C × Ss	11	.085	2.43	—	.125	< 1.00	—
I × Ss	11	.060	1.71	—	.077	< 1.00	—
C × I × Ss	11	.035			.149		

TABLE 5. MEAN TRANSFORMED SITUATIONAL CONFORMITY SCORES

| | Situational Pressure With Respect to American Norms | |
	Towards Acceptance	Towards Rejection
Incongruent items		
High n-ach group	58.57*	48.33
Low n-ach group	55.50	50.58
Congruent items		
High n-ach group	46.47	53.80
Low n-ach group	53.90	50.54

* arc sin $\sqrt{50\%}$ = 45.00

group instrumentality is considerably more important than congruence. The main effect of congruence is significant at the .01 level ($F = 19.34$), and the main effect of instrumentality at the .001 level ($F = 41.00$). The main effect of instrumentality does not reach the acceptable level of significance for subjects with low n-achievement, but the effects of congruence are significant at the .05 level ($F = 5.91$).

2. The Effects of Situational Pressures on Conformity

The above data dealt with conformity to presumably well established cultural norms. The experimental design employed in this study also allows the analysis of the effects deriving from immediately present situational pressures, and we may inquire whether n-achievement is a factor in yielding to a group majority, when the group supports and when the group rejects the subjects' own norms. Thus two kinds of conformity were distinguished in the present study, *normative* and *situational*. The first part of the experiment focused on normative and the second on situational conformity.

For the purposes of the analysis of situational conformity, subjects were assigned percentage scores based on the number of times they agreed with the paid participants.[1] Since situational conformity scores were based on relatively small numbers the angular transformation was performed. Mean transformed situational conformity scores for the high and low n-achievement groups are shown in Table 5 and the analysis of variance in Table 6.

The results indicate that the overall effects of n-achievement as well as those deriving from direction of situational pressure are not significant. The extent of conformity is somewhat higher for incongruent than congruent items, and this overall difference is significant at the .05 level. Among the first-order interactions only situational pressure × n-achievement is significant. Data in Table 5 reveal that on incongruent items with situational pressure directed towards the rejection of American norms, and therefore towards the acceptance of Indian norms, the level of conformity of the

[1] Since the effects of instrumentality have already been demonstrated and since a breakdown in terms of instrumentality would reduce the stability of the individual conformity scores, being based only on nine responses, the data were pooled for both instrumentality levels.

low n-achievement group is higher than that of the high n-achievement group. When the situational pressure is directed towards the acceptance of the American and the rejection of the Indian norms, the high n-achievement group shows greater conformity. It should be noted that these results are reversed for congruent items. We would, therefore, expect a sizeable second-order interaction. In fact, the situation × congruence × n-achievement interaction shows an F-ratio of 40.99, significant well beyond the .001 level. It is quite clear from the results that the high n-achievement group is relatively more free of cultural influences than the low n-achievement group. When the norms are congruent, and when the group majority endorses both norms, the high n-achievement group shows a relatively lower level of agreement with the group majority (46.47) than the low n-achievement group (53.90). However, when the immediate group rejects both norms, individuals with high n-achievement scores manifest higher situational conformity than those with low n-achievement scores.

It is also well to note that with respect to congruent items the high n-achievement group shows somewhat less overall situational conformity than the low n-achievement group (50.14 and 52.22 respectively). For incongruent items this result is reversed, but the difference is negligible. These findings are of course consistent with the previous result. It appears thus that the direction of situational pressures and normative pressures plays a very important role in mediating the relation between n-achievement and situational conformity. When the situational pressures support American norms, and the American and Indian norms are congruent, then the low n-achievement group shows higher conformity. When the norms are incongruent then the high n-achievement group shows higher conformity. When the situational pressures are directed against the acceptance of American norms and when the norms are congruent the high n-achievement group conforms to a larger extent. But when the norms are incongruent, faced with a situational force against the American (and therefore in favor of the

TABLE 6. SUMMARY OF ANALYSIS OF VARIANCE FOR DATA IN TABLE 5

Source	df	MS	F
n-Ach (A)	1	11.95	< 1.00
Error (b)	22	111.90	
Situational pressure (S)	1	7.82	< 1.00
Congruence (C)	1	104.98	4.15*
S × A	1	128.74	5.10*
C × A	1	30.30	1.20
S × C	1	30.34	1.20
S × C × A	1	1034.49	40.99**
Error (w)	66	25.24	

* Significant at the .05 level
** Significant at the .001 level

Indian) norms, the high n-achievement group shows less conformity.

SUMMARY

An experiment on the relation between conformity and n-achievement was conducted using Indian students as subjects, and Indian and American norms as objects of conformity. It was argued that the relation between conformity and n-achievement is mediated by the instrumental value of conforming behavior. In particular it was predicted that when conformity is perceived as instrumental to achievement a positive rather than a negative relation between conformity and n-achievement will be obtained. The results substantiate the prediction.

The experiment also analysed conformity in the presence of normative conflict. It was found that when there exists conflict between cultural norms, individuals with high n-achievement scores tend to resolve it in favor of the American and those with low n-achievement scores in favor of the Indian norms. Moreover, the results show that the high n-achievement group is more sensitive to the instrumental value of conformity than to the fact of whether or not the two norms are congruent. For the low n-achievement group the opposite seems to be the case.

Analysis was also made of the effects of situational pressures on conformity of high and now n-achievement groups. On the whole, the groups were found not to differ in susceptibility to situational pressures. However, differences were observed depending on whether the situational pressures were directed at the acceptance or rejection of the American norms.

REFERENCES

ASCH, S. E. (1956). Studies in independence and submission to group pressure: I. A minority of one against a unanimous majority. *Psychol. Monogr.*, No. 416.

ATKINSON, J. W. (Ed.) (1958). *Motives in fantasy, action, and society.* Princeton, New Jersey: Van Nostrand Co.

BURDICK, H. A. (1955). The relationship of attraction, need achievement and certainty to conformity under conditions of a simulated group atmosphere. Unpublished doctoral dissertation, Univer. of Michigan.

FRENCH, J. R. P., JR. & ZAJONC, R. B. (1957). An experimental study of cross-cultural norm conflict. *J. abnorm. soc. Psychol.* 54, 218–24.

McCLELLAND, D. C., ATKINSON, J. W., CLARK, R. A. & LOWELL, E. L. (1953). *The achievement motive.* New York: Appleton-Century-Crofts.

PASSIN, H. & BENNETT, J. W. (1954). The American-educated Japanese. *Ann. Amer. Acad. pol. soc. Science,* 295, 83–96.

SAMELSON, F. (1958). The relation of achievement and affiliation motives to conforming behavior in two conditions of conflict with a majority. In J. W. Atkinson (Ed.), *Motives in fantasy, action, and society.* Princeton, New Jersey: Van Nostrand Co. Pp. 421–33.

SEWELL, W. H., MORRIS, R. T. & DAVIDSEN, O. M. (1954). Scandinavian students' images of the United States: a study in cross cultural education. *Ann. Amer. Acad. pol. soc. Science,* 295, 126–35.

SMITH, M. (1955). Some features of foreign student adjustment. *J. higher Educ.* 26.

SMITH, M. B. (1956). Cross-cultural education as a research area. *J. soc. Issues,* 12, 3–8.

ZAJONC, R. B. (1952). Aggressive attitudes of the "stranger" as a function of conformity pressures. *Hum. Relat.* 5, 205–16.

28. COMPETENCE AND CONFORMITY IN THE ACCEPTANCE OF INFLUENCE *

E. P. Hollander

When one member influences others in his group it is often because he is competent in a focal group activity. A member may show such competence by individual actions that further the attainment of group goals (cf. Carter, 1954); more specific situational demands may variously favor the ascent of the expediter, advocate, or what Bales and Slater (1955) have termed the task specialist. An additional condition for the acceptance of influence involves the member's perceived adherence to the normative behaviors and attitudes of his group. His record of conformity to these expectancies serves to sustain eligibility of the sort Brown (1936) calls "membership character."

A person who exhibits both competence and conformity should eventually reach a threshold at which it becomes appropriate in the eyes of others for him to assert influence; and insofar as these assertions are accepted he emerges as a leader. But it is still necessary to account for the "nonconformity" that leaders display as they innovate and alter group norms. Certain shifts must therefore occur in the expectancies applicable to an individual as he proceeds from gaining status to maintaining it.

This process has been considered recently in a theoretical model of status emergence (Hollander, 1958). It features the prospect that behavior perceived to be nonconformity for one

member may not be so perceived for another. Such differentiations are seen to be made as a function of status, conceived as an accumulation of positively disposed impressions termed "idiosyncrasy credits." A person gains credits, that is, rises in status, by showing competence and by conforming to the expectancies applicable to him at the time. Eventually his credits allow him to nonconform with greater impunity.[1] Moreover, he is then subject to a new set of expectancies which direct the assertion of influence. Thus, whether for lack of motivation or misperception, his failure to take innovative action may cause him to lose status.[2]

It is readily predictable that in task oriented groups a member giving evidence of competence on the group task should with time gain in influence. If he simply nonconforms to the procedures agreed upon, the opposite effect should be observed. But the sequential relationship of nonconformity to competence is especially critical.

From the model, it should follow that, with a relatively constant level of

[1] This is a newer formulation of an observation long since made regarding the latitude provided leaders (e.g., Homans, 1950, p. 416). It is further elaborated in Hollander (1959).

[2] This proposition is consistent with various findings suggestive of the greater social perceptiveness of leaders (for example, Chowdhry & Newcomb, 1952).

* Reprinted from *Journal of Abnormal and Social Psychology*, 1960, 61: 365–369, with permission of the author and the American Psychological Association. This paper is based upon a study completed under ONR Contract 1849.

manifest competence, the influence of a person who nonconforms *early* in the course of group interaction should be more drastically curtailed than in the case of a person who nonconforms *later*. Indeed, a reversal of effect would be predicted in the latter instance. Once a member has accumulated credits, his nonconformity to general procedure should serve as a confirming or signalizing feature of his status, thereby enhancing his influence. Accordingly, it may be hypothesized that given equivalent degrees of task competence, a member should achieve greater acceptance of his influence when he has conformed in the past and is now nonconforming than he should when nonconformity precedes conformity.

METHOD

Design

Twelve groups, each composed of four male subjects, were engaged in a task involving a sequence of 15 trials. A group choice was required for each trial from among the row alternatives in a 7×7 payoff matrix (see Figure 1). In every group, a fifth member was a confederate whose prearranged response was contrived to be correct on all but four trials, i.e., 2, 3, 6, and 12, thus reflecting considerable competence on the task. All interactions among participants took

place through a system of microphones and headsets from partitioned booths. Subjects were assigned numbers from 1 to 5 for communicating with one another. The central manipulation was the confederate's nonconformity to procedures agreed upon by each group in a pretrial discussion. In terms of a division of the 15 trials into three zones—early, middle, and late—of 5 trials each, six treatments were applied: nonconformity throughout, nonconformity for the first two zones, for the first zone alone, for the last two zones, for the last zone alone, and a control with no nonconformity. In one set of treatments the confederate was designated number 5, and in the other number 4, to test possible position effects. Acceptance of the confederate's influence was measured by the number of trials by zone in which his recommended response was accepted as the group's. This was supplemented by post-interaction assessments.

Subjects

The 48 subjects were all juniors in the College of Engineering and Science at the Carnegie Institute of Technology. All had volunteered from introductory psychology sections after being told only that they would be taking part in a study of problem solving in groups. Care was taken in composing the 12 groups so as

	Green	Red	Blue	Yellow	Brown	Orange	Black
Able	−1	−12	+5	−1	−2	+15	−4
Baker	+10	−1	−2	−7	+4	−3	−1
Charlie	−5	+5	−3	+3	−11	−1	+12
Dog	+5	−7	+10	−2	−5	+1	−2
Easy	−4	−1	−1	+1	+13	−10	+2
Fox	−6	+15	−5	−1	−3	−1	+1
George	−1	−1	−2	+10	+4	−2	−8

Figure 1. Matrix used in group task.

to avoid either placing acquaintances together or having membership known in advance. Thus, no two subjects from the same class section were used in the same group, and subjects reported at staggered times to different rooms. By the time a subject reached the laboratory room where the experiment was actually conducted, he had been kept apart from the others and was not aware of their identity. The subjects never saw one another during the entire procedure, nor were their names ever used among them.

Instructions and Set

Once seated and assigned a number, every subject was given a sheet of instructions and the matrix used for the task. These instructions fell into two parts, both of which were reviewed aloud with each subject individually, and then with the entire group over the communication network. The first part cautioned the subjects to always identify themselves by number (for example, "This is Station 3. . . .") before speaking and not to use names or other self-identifying references. The second part acquainted them with the procedures to be used, emphasized the aspect of competition against a "system," and established the basis for evident procedural norms. It read as follows:

1. You will be working with others on a problem involving a matrix of plus and minus values. Everyone has the same matrix before him. The goal is to amass as many plus units as possible, and to avoid minus units. Units are worth 1 cent each to the group; the group begins with a credit of 200 units. You cannot lose your own money, therefore. There will be fifteen trials in all.

2. In any one trial, the task in-

volved is for the group to agree on just *one* row—identified by Able, Baker, Charlie, and so on—which seems to have strategic value. Once the group has determined a row, the experimenter will announce the column color which comes up on that trial. The intersecting cells indicate the payoff. Following this announcement, there will be thirty seconds of silence during which group members can think individually about the best strategy for the next trial, in terms of their notion about the system; note please that there are several approximations to the system, although the equation underlying it is quite complex. But work at it.

3. At the beginning of each trial the group members must report, one at a time, in some order, as to what they think would be the best row choice on the upcoming trial. Members may "pass" until the third time around, but must announce a choice then. Following this, groups will have three minutes on each trial to discuss choices and reach some agreement; this can be a simple majority, or unanimous decision; it is up to the group to decide. If a decision is not reached in three minutes, the group loses 5 units.

4. Before beginning the trials, the group will have five minutes to discuss these points: (*a*) The order of reporting; (*b*) How to determine the group choice for a given trial; (*c*) How to divide up the money at the end. These decisions are always subject to change, if the group has time and can agree. After the 15th trial, group members may have as much as five minutes to settle any outstanding decisions. Then headsets are to be removed, but group members remain seated for further instructions, and the individual payment of funds.

Instruments and Procedure

The matrix was specially constructed for this study to present an ambiguous but plausible task in which alternatives were only marginally discrete from one another.[3] The number of columns and rows was selected to enlarge the range of possibilities beyond the number of group members, while still retaining comprehensibility. The fact that the rows are unequal in algebraic sum appears to be less important as a feature in choice than the number and magnitude of positive and negative values in each; there is moreover the complicating feature of processing the outcome of the last trials in evaluating the choice for the next. All considered, the matrix was admirably suited to the requirements for ambiguity, challenge, conflict, immediate reinforcement, and ready manipulation by the experimenter.

The confederate, operating as either 4 or 5 in the groups, suggested a choice that differed trial by trial from those offered by other members; this was prearranged but subject to modification as required. Since subjects rather typically perceived alternatives differently, his behavior was not unusual, especially during the early trials. For the 11 trials in which the confederate's row choice was "correct," the color that "came up" was contrived to yield a high plus value without at the same time providing a similar value for intersection with another person's row choice. Had his recommendation been followed by the group on these trials, high payoffs would have accrued.

The device of a 5-minute pretrial discussion had special utility for establishing common group expectancies, in the form of procedures, from which the confederate could deviate when called for in the design. Predictable decisions on these matters were reached unfailingly. But their importance lay in having a *public affirmation* of member intent. Thus, on order of reporting, it was quickly agreed to follow the order of the numbers assigned members. Each group, despite minor variants suggested, decided on simple majority rule. Regarding division of funds, equal sharing prevailed, sometimes with the proviso that the issue be taken up again at the end.

In the zones calling for nonconformity, the confederate violated these procedures by speaking out of prescribed turn, by questioning the utility of majority rule, and by unsupported—but not harsh—challenges to the recommendations made by others. He manifested such behaviors on an approximate frequency of at least one of these per trial with a mean of two per trial considered optimum. Thus, he would break in with his choice immediately after an earlier respondent had spoken and before the next in sequence could do so; when there were periods of silence during a trial he would observe aloud that maybe majority rule did not work so well; and he would show a lack of enthusiasm for the choice offered by various others on the matter of basis. Lest he lose credibility and become a caricature, in all instances he chose his moments with care and retained an evident spontaneity of expression.[4]

---

[3] The matrix is an adaptation, at least in spirit, of a smaller one used with success by Moore and Berkowitz (1956).

[4] The same person, H. E. Titus, was the confederate throughout.

RESULTS AND DISCUSSION

The task gave quite satisfactory signs of engrossing the subjects. There was much talk about the "system" and a good deal of delving into its basis, possibly made the more so by the subjects' academic background; the returned matrices were littered with diagrams, notations, and calculations. Though quite meaningless in fact, the confederate's tentative accounts of his "reasoning" were evidently treated with seriousness, perhaps as much because of the contrived time constraint, which prevented probing, as of his jargon regarding "rotations" and "block shifts." In any case, the confederate at no time claimed to have the system completely in hand. He delayed his response from the sixth trial onward to suggest calculation of an optimum choice in the face of conflicting alternatives; and the four trials on which he was "wrong" were spaced to signify progressive improvement, but not total perfection.

Most pertinent, however, is the fact that there were no manifestations of suspicion concerning the confederate's authenticity. The others seemed to believe that he was one of them and that he was "cracking" the system; the post-interaction data were in full agreement.

Since all of the interactions were available on tape, it was possible to derive a number of indices of acceptance of influence. The most broadly revealing of these appeared to be the frequency of trials on which the confederate's recommended solution was followed.

In Table 1 this index is employed to discern the effects of three major variables. The analysis is arranged by zones (Z) of trials, and in terms of the confederate's nonconformity (NC) in the *current* zone and immediate *past* zone.[5] The means given in each cell indicate the number of trials, out of five per zone, on which the confederate's choice was also the group's. In a chi square test, the effect of position upon this measure was found to be nonsignificant, and is therefore omitted as a distinction in the analysis of variance.

The significant F secured from Zones is in accord with prediction. It reveals the ongoing effect of task competence in increasing the acceptance of the confederate's choice, to be seen in the rising means across zones. While current nonconformity does not yield a significant effect, past nonconformity does. Viewing the table horizontally, one finds that the means for "without" *past* NC exceed the means for "with" *past* NC in all instances but one. Regarding the significant interaction of *current* and *past* NC, the combination "without-without" has a sequence (2.00, 3.75, 4.75) of persistently higher value than has "with-with" (1.67, 3.25, 4.00); this, too, is in line with prediction. Finally, the maximum value of 5.00 in Zone II for the combination "'without' *past* NC but 'with' *current* NC con-firms the key prediction from the model, at least within the context of the relative magnitudes there; the same value is also seen in Zone III for the identical combination; still another reading of 5.00 holds there, however, for the inverse

[5] For Zone I, the "past zone" refers to the discussion period. If he was to nonconform there, the confederate would question majority rule and suggest that the division of funds be left until the end rather than agree then on equal shares.

TABLE 1. MEAN NUMBER OF TRIALS ON WHICH A GROUP ACCEPTS
CONFEDERATE'S RECOMMENDED SOLUTION

Confederate's Previous Conformity	Zone I (Trials 1–5)		Zone II (Trials 6–10)		Zone III (Trials 11–15)	
	Non-conforming [a]	Con-forming	Non-conforming	Con-forming	Non-conforming	Con-forming
With procedural nonconformity in immediate *past* zone	1.67 6[b]	—	3.25 4	3.00 2	4.00 4	5.00 2
Without procedural nonconformity in immediate *past* zone	—	2.00 6	5.00 2	3.75 4	5.00 2	4.75 4

ANALYSIS OF VARIANCE

Source	SS	df	MS	F
Current nonconformity	.20	1	.200	—
Zones	47.05	2	23.525	35.01**
Past nonconformity	3.36	1	3.360	5.00*
Int: current NC × Z	1.22	2	.610	—
Int: current NC × Past NC	13.52	1	13.520	20.12**
Int: Z × Past NC	.72	2	.360	—
Int: Current NC × Z × Past NC	4.11	2	2.055	3.06
Residual	16.12	24	.672	
Total	86.30	35		

[a] Confederate showed procedural nonconformity on the trials in this zone.
[b] Indicates number of groups upon which cell is based.
* $p < .05$
** $p < .001$.

combination, but in a tight range of values quite beyond separation of effects for interpretation.

Considerable consistency was found too in the post-interaction data. On the item "over-all contribution to the group activity," 44 of the 48 subjects ranked the confederate first; on the item "influence over the group's decisions," 45 of the 48 ranked him first. Two things bear emphasis in this regard: subjects had to individually write in the numbers of group members next to rank, hence demanding recall; and their polarity of response cut across all six treatments, despite significant differences among these in the actual *acceptance of influence*. That the confederate therefore made an impact is clear; but that it had selective consequences depending upon the timing of his nonconformity is equally clear.

In detail, then, the findings are in keeping with the predictions made from the model. The operational variable for measuring acceptance of influence was confined to the task itself, but nontask elements are touched as well. In that respect, the findings corroborate the subtle development of differential impressions as a function of even limited interpersonal behavior.

Some unquantified but clearly suggestive data are worth mentioning in this regard. Where, for example, the confederate began nonconforming *after* the first zone, his behavior was accepted with minimal challenge; by the third zone, his suggestion that majority rule was faulty yielded a rubber stamping of his choice. Again, if he had already accrued credit, his pattern of interrupting people out of turn not only went unhindered but was taken up by some others. Quite different effects were elicited if the confederate exhibited nonconformity from *the outset*, notably such comments of censure as "That's not the way we agreed to do it, five."

The findings are especially indicative of the stochastic element of social interaction and its consequence for changing perception. Especially interesting is the fact that these effects are produced even in a relatively brief span of time.

SUMMARY

A study was conducted to test the relationship between competence on a group task and conformity or nonconformity to procedural norms in determining a person's ability to influence other group members. Data were gathered from 12 groups engaged in a problem solving task under controlled conditions. Each was made up of five members one of whom was a confederate who evidenced a high degree of competence during the 15 trials. His nonconformity to the procedural norms

agreed upon by the group was introduced at various times, early, middle, or late, in the sequence of trials. Influence was measured by the number of trials (per segment of the entire sequence) in which the confederate's recommended solution was accepted as the group's choice. As a broad effect, it was found that a significant increase in his influence occurred as the trials progressed, presumably as a function of the successive evidences of competence. Past conformity by the confederate was also found to be positively and significantly related to the acceptance of his influence; finally, there was a statistically significant interaction between past and current nonconformity reflected in high influence in the groups in which the confederate had conformed earlier in the sequence of trials but was presently nonconforming. These results were all thoroughly consistent with predictions made from the "idiosyncrasy credit" model of conformity and status.

REFERENCES

BALES, R. F., & SLATER, P. E.   Role differentiation in small decision-making groups. In T. Parsons, R. F. Bales et al. (Eds.), *Family, socialization, and interaction process.* New York: Free Press, 1955.

BROWN, J. F.   *Psychology and the social order.* New York: McGraw-Hill, 1936.

CARTER, L. F.   Recording and evaluating the performance of individuals as members of small groups. *Personnel Psychol.,* 1954, 7, 477–484.

CHOWDHRY, KAMLA, & NEWCOMB, T. M.   The relative abilities of leaders and nonleaders to estimate opinions of their own groups. *J. abnorm. soc. Psychol.,* 1952, 47, 51–57.

HOLLANDER, E. P.   Conformity, status, and idiosyncrasy credit. *Psychol. Rev.,* 1958, 65, 117–127.

HOLLANDER, E. P. Some points of rein-
terpretation regarding social conformity.
Soc. Rev., 1959, 7, 159–168.
HOMANS, G. C. *The human group.* New
York: Harcourt, Brace & World, 1950.

MOORE, O. K., & BERKOWITZ, M. I. Problem solving and social interaction. *ONR
tech. Rep.*, 1956, No. 1 (Contract
Nonr-609(16), Yale University Department of Sociology)

29. THE EFFECTS OF INFORMATION SOURCE STATUS AND DOGMATISM UPON CONFORMITY BEHAVIOR *

Robert N. Vidulich and Ivan P. Kaiman

The present investigation attempted to provide a partial answer to the question: are highly authoritarian persons uniformly conforming to all directive-producing sources, or are they differentially influenced by information sources that are high or low in status? Previous research has indicated that both variables, source status and authoritarianism are related to conformity behavior (for example, Crutchfield, 1955; Lefkowitz, Blake, & Mouton, 1955).

Rokeach (1960) in his theory of general authoritarianism or "dogmatism" differentiates between persons who are relatively *open* (low dogmatic or low authoritarian) or *closed* (high dogmatic or high authoritarian) with respect to their belief-disbelief systems about reality. A person's belief-disbelief system is relatively open or closed depending on his ability to "receive, evaluate and act on relevant information received from the outside on its own intrinsic merits ... the more closed the belief-system, the more difficult should it be to distinguish between information received about the world and information re-

ceived about the source [of this information] ..." (pp. 57–58).

Rokeach's (1960) theory would predict that relatively closed persons should confuse what an external authority had to say about a situation with who the authority was, leading to increased conformity to the authority if he were high in status, and decreased conformity to, or even rejection of, the authority were he seen as being low in status. Relatively open individuals should be capable of discriminating source from message, and should show little difference in their reactions to varying source figures.

METHOD

Apparatus

The experimental situation used the autokinetic effect and the general procedure of Sherif (1935). Subjects in the present study were asked to report the *direction* rather than the distance of autokinetic movement.

The stimulus light box was mounted

* Reprinted from the *Journal of Abnormal and Social Psychology*, 1961, 63: 639–642, with permission of the senior author and the American Psychological Association.

on a table 32 inches above the floor at one end of a lightproof and semisound-proof room. A point of light was exposed through a hole 1 millimeter in diameter in one end of a lightproof wooden box, 9 inches long, 3 inches wide, and 3 inches high, painted flat black inside and out. The light source was a small radio bulb at the far end of the box. The bulb was connected to a transformer to receive a constant electrical input of 2.5 volts. Two thicknesses of tissue paper diffused the light. Exposure time was automatically controlled by two Hunter timers so that the light was alternately activated and shut off for 10 second intervals. This sequence was repeated for the total experimental period. The light was visible at all times except when the experimenter switched off the power supply between the two phases of the experiment.

The subjects and the experimenter were seated at the opposite end of the experimental room from the light source, the subject being 197 inches (5 meters) from the light aperture. The experimental room was in complete darkness at all times.

Subjects

From a pool of 307 undergraduates in introductory psychology courses at Louisiana State University who had taken the 40-item Dogmatism scale, Form E (Rokeach, 1960), 30 high and 30 low scorers were selected as subjects. All 60 subjects were in the upper or lower quartiles of Dogmatism scale scores, all were females between the ages of 18 and 23 years, and all but 4 were sophomores. None had previous knowledge about the autokinetic phenomenon. The mean Dogmatism scale score for

the 30 open subjects was 126.75 ($\sigma =$ 11.66); for the 30 closed subjects, the mean Dogmatism score was 181.37 ($\sigma =$ 11.87).

Each subject was in the experimental situation with a confederate of the experimenter throughout the experiment. The 60 subjects were divided into four groups: Group I consisted of 15 subjects who had scored high on the Dogmatism scale (closed), for whom the confederate was identified as a high status person; Group II consisted of 15 closed subjects for whom the confederate was identified as a low status person. Groups III and IV each consisted of 15 subjects who had scored low on the Dogmatism scale (open), for whom the confederate was identified as being high or low in status, respectively.

Procedure

During Phase A of the experiment, the subject observed 30 exposures of the light, judging the direction of the light's "movement," either left or right, and privately recording these judgments on one or another of two 3×5 pads in front of him. During Phase B, the subject observed 30 additional exposures of the light, now making his responses verbally, with the experimenter recording these responses. The confederate reported his "judgments" prior to those of the subject during Phase B.

Eighty percent of the confederate's responses during Phase B were randomly given in the direction least frequently reported by the subject in Phase A. Upon determining the subject's least predominant directional choice of Phase A, the experimenter informed the confederate of the response pattern to be reported by tapping him on the right or left shoulder. The confederate used a string of beads and knots to determine the direction of each response to be given.

The subject entered the already darkened room in which the confederate was seated, and was guided to his seat by the experimenter. The meeting of the subject and the confederate took place in complete darkness. For Groups I and III (high status source), the confederate was presented as "Dr. John Wilson, who has been doing a good deal of research at LSU. He will be observing the same thing as you and we are interested in comparing your reactions with his." For Groups II and IV (low status source), the confederate was presented as "John Wilson, who is a high school student at Baton Rouge High. He will be observing the same thing as you and we are interested in comparing your reactions with his." These introductory statements were made to the subject while the experimenter was escorting him to the experimental room.

Task instructions were given as follows:

When I give the signal "Ready" a light will go on. After a short time, the light will start to move. Then the light will go off. When the light goes off you are to mark the direction of the light's movement on one of the two pads directly in front of you. There is a pencil between the two pads. If the light moved to the left, make a mark on the left pad; if the light moved to the right, make a mark on the right pad. Sometimes the light will move a great distance, at other times it will move only slightly. Be sure you make a mark for each trial, and *only one* mark to indicate the

direction in which the light moved on each trial. When I give the signal there will be *no* talking. Ready.

The 30 trials of Phase A were then administered. After the thirtieth exposure, the experimenter said:

Please hand me your pads. In order to speed this up a little bit, the next time the light goes on, I want you to tell me which way the light moved, and I'll record your answers myself. This should take less time. You can tell me your answers after the light goes off. And out of courtesy to the faculty [visiting student], Dr. Wilson [John] you can go first.

At the termination of Phase B, the subject was asked not to discuss the procedures of the experiment with anyone. The experimenter then escorted the subject out of the room, asking the confederate to remain "to talk to you for a few minutes." Thus the subject never saw the confederate.

RESULTS

The first response measure defining conformity was calculated by subtracting the number of the least dominant directional responses of Phase A from the number of same direction responses during Phase B for each subject (*difference score*). The second response measure was calculated by tabulating the number of responses of each subject which agreed with those of the confederate during Phase B (agreement score). For both measures, the higher the score, the greater the presumed conformity to the confederate's responses.

From the upper portion of Table 1, it is evident that neither dogmatism nor status source is significantly related to the shift in directional judgments from Phase A to Phase B (difference score). The major source of variance is attributable to the interaction of these two variable ($F = 21.74$, $p < .01$). The lower portion of Table 1 indicates that the closed group exposed to a high status source shifted most toward the confederate's responses from Phase A to Phase B (difference = 5.93), while the closed-low status group shifted *away* from the "judgments" of the confederate (difference = −0.53). The open groups displayed dissimilar behavior, agreeing significantly more with the directional responses of the low status than the high status source. That these results are not due to differential responsiveness during Phase A is indicated by the following: the mean number of least dominant directional responses during Phase A are 11.40, 10.80, 10.87, and 10.93 for Groups I through IV, respectively.

The analyses of agreement scores generally corroborate the foregoing results. Analysis of variance (upper portion of Table 2) indicates that both source status and dogmatism are highly significant sources of variation when considered alone, a finding which differs from the difference score analysis, but that the interaction of these two variables again produces the greatest effect ($F = 50.96$, $p < .01$).

Again, the closed subjects agreed

TABLE 1. TREATMENT OF DIFFERENCE SCORES

Analysis of Variance

Source	SS	df	F	p
Source status	56.06	1	3.95	ns
Dogmatism	19.26	1	1.36	ns
Interaction (S × D)	308.29	1	21.74	< .01
Within	794.12	56		
Total	1177.73			

Comparison of Subgroup Means

	Source Status					
	High		Low		t	p
Dogmatism	M[a]	SD	M[a]	SD		
Closed group	5.93	4.45	−0.53	4.53	3.29	< .01[b]
Open group	2.53	2.69	5.13	3.02	2.48	< .05
t	2.52		4.02			
p	< .01[b]		< .01[b]			

[a] $N = 15$ for each group.
[b] One-tailed test of significance used for these comparisons.

TABLE 2. TREATMENT OF AGREEMENT SCORES

Analysis of Variance

Source	SS	df	F	p
Source status	355.26	1	30.73	< .01
Dogmatism	96.26	1	8.33	< .01
Interaction (S × D)	589.09	1	50.96	< .01
Within	647.32	56		
Total	1687.93	59		

Comparison of Subgroup Means

	Source Status					
Dogmatism	High		Low		t	p
	M[a]	SD	M[a]	SD		
Closed group	18.27	3.89	7.13	2.45	9.36	< .01[b]
Open group	14.53	3.88	15.93	3.15	1.09	ns
t	2.62		8.80			
p	< .01[b]		< .01[b]			

[a] N = 15 for each group.
[b] One-tailed test of significance used for these comparisons.

more with the high than with the low status source (lower portion of Table 2). Out of 30 possible agreements during Phase B, the closed groups averaged 18.27 agreements under the high status condition and only 7.13 agreements when responding following the low status source (t = 9.36, p < .01). The open groups did not differ significantly in mean agreement responses under the two source status conditions.

DISCUSSION

The results of this experiment generally support the contention that conformity is a function of both the status of the source of information to which the person is exposed, and the authori-

tarian tendencies of the person being influenced. Analyses of both conformity measures used indicate that a highly important interaction exists between the variables of general authoritarianism (cognitive closedness) and information source status, which is more influential in the determination of conformity behavior than either variable taken alone. These data amply illustrate the importance of jointly considering field conditions and person characteristics in examining conformity/influence behavior.

That these results cannot be attributed to intelligence and/or cognizance of the "rigged" nature of the situation is supported by two ancillary findings. No differences were found between open and closed subjects in gross intellectual ability (as estimated by academic grade point average). Previous studies with the Dogmatism scale also indicate that it is unrelated to intelligence for this population (Rokeach, 1960). With regard to the second possibility, no subject reported having suspected that the auto-kinetic movement of the light was not real, or that the confederate was anything but what he was introduced as.

With regard to the postulated inability of the closed person to discriminate a message from its source, the present findings are seen as suggestive rather than definitive. What is required in future studies of this hypothesis is the use of an experimental situation in which it is possible for the subject to evaluate independently the information received about reality from a source and the source itself. A modified Asch-type procedure, such as that used by Crutchfield (1955), would appear to be appropriate.

Two weaknesses of the present study are readily apparent. The control conditions of having the subjects alone in Phase B, and having the subjects in the presence of the confederate without having the confederate make responses during Phase B, would be helpful in determining the reasons for the presently-puzzling behavior of the open groups which tended to conform more to low than to high status sources. Also, the reliability of the two response measures used in this study has not been established. A third experimental phase in which the subject's judgments are not preceded by those of the confederate is required to determine if it is the *judgment* of the subject or his *announcement* of his judgment that is altered in the present situation. Similar attempts to determine the temporal duration of "conformity" are notably lacking in previously-reported studies in this area also.

SUMMARY

This study tested the prediction that cognitively open (high authoritarian) and closed (low authoritarian) persons should be influenced differentially by high and low status information sources.

Groups of 30 open and closed subjects, selected on the basis of extreme scores on Rokeach's Dogmatism scale, were placed in an autokinetic situation. Each subject privately judged the directional movement of the light for 30 exposures and then made an additional 30 judgments following reports of a confederate of the experimenter. For one-half of each group, the confederate was presented as a college professor (high status); he was introduced as a high school student for the low status groups. During the second experimental phase, the confederate made responses which were 80 percent in the least-judged direction of the subject during the private judging experimental phase.

Data analyses for two response measures of conformity fully support the prediction of an interaction between cognitive closedness (authoritarianism) and information source status. The closed groups agreed significantly more with the high status than with the low status source. Open groups tended to agree more with low than with high status sources.

REFERENCES

CRUTCHFIELD, R. S. Conformity and character. *Amer. Psychologist,* 1955, 10, 191–198.

LEFKOWITZ, M., BLAKE, R. R., & MOUTON, JANE S. Status factors in pedestrian violation of traffic signals. *J. abnorm. soc. Psychol.*, 1955, **51,** 704–706.

ROKEACH, M.   *The open and closed mind.* New York: Basic Books, 1960.

SHERIF, M.   A study of some social factors in perception. *Arch. Psychol.*, 1935, No. 187.

7

Social Stratification, Social Norms, and Roles

---

30. STRUCTURAL CHARACTERISTICS OF NORMS *

Jay Jackson

In the absence of some scheme for representing the structure of a *norm*, much of the potential of this conceptual tool for analysis of social phenomena fails to be realized. In this paper, a model that attempts to embrace the essential properties of the idea is introduced. A number of characteristics of norms will be examined and related to observable phenomena and to the results of available studies that have utilized this approach. The construction of the model is an attempt to think about norms and their properties in a differentiated and systematic way and to suggest methods of measuring these properties with relative precision.[1]

[1] A more complete discussion of some of the problems described in this paper can be found in *The Dynamics of Instructional Groups*, Fifty-ninth Yearbook of the National Society for the Study of Education, Part II, pp. 136–163, Nelson B. Henry (Ed.). Illinois: The University of Chicago Press, 1960.

* This article was written specifically for this volume.

A MODEL FOR ANALYSIS AND MEASUREMENT OF NORMS

A Dimension of Behavior

A norm is always about something; it has an object. Ordinarily, its object is some act of behavior that is considered to be appropriate or inappropriate. A person is expected to *wear* certain articles of clothing and not others on particular occasions. There are norms about *discussing* certain topics, about *disagreeing* with a superior—in fact, about most aspects of behavior in social situations. One essential element of a model for describing a norm is, therefore, a *behavior dimension*.

Norms also exist for attitudes or tendencies to behave. Some norms, too, have as their object an activity of the group itself, for example, one defining

301

the appropriateness of meeting without the chairman. Ultimately, however, norms about attitudes or group activities concern the behavior of individual members, since attitudes are inferred from behavior, and activities consist of patterned behavior of group members.

Intrinsic to a norm is the specification of the amount or quality of behavior expected of the actor by relevant others. A supervisor may be expected to control the activities of a work group. How much control is appropriate? Either too much or too little may be disapproved. A student may be frowned upon for over- or under-participation. Some behaviors are so taboo in certain situations, however, that it does not seem necessary to specify the amount expected—for example, overt sexual behavior in the classroom. Yet the norm might be described using a qualitative behavior dimension, from "highly overt" to "completely covert." Thus, the model assumes that any act of behavior can be located upon a dimension either of quantity or quality.

A Dimension of Evaluation

In almost every conception of a norm, the idea of evaluation is either explicit or implicit. Even when we refer to an individual's "norms" for perceiving or judging the objects in his environment, we imply that he has expectations about what he will consider to be appropriate or inappropriate. A group's norm involves shared tendencies to approve or disapprove the acts along a particular behavior dimension. In medical school, according to Merton and his colleagues, "If he acts presumptuous about his knowledge, a student will be reproached

by his classmates, whereas an admission of ignorance on his part may evoke their approval." [2] The evaluation of an act of behavior can vary from strong approval to strong disapproval through some middle point of indifference. An *evaluation dimension* is thus an essential element of any scheme for describing norms.

The behavior dimension and the evaluation dimension are the two main components of the model represented in Figure 1. The following section describes how they are put together to derive a number of structural characteristics of norms.

Distribution of Approval-Disapproval

On any given behavior dimension, the amount of approval or disapproval felt by members of a group toward a particular act may in principle fall anywhere along the evaluation dimension. It is possible, therefore, to plot a curve to describe the feelings of the group's members. Suppose that in Figure 1 the behavior dimension represents the number of times a member could speak in an hour's session of a discussion group. The scale varies from "no participation" to "speaking eight times," an arbitrary maximum. Instead of referring to approval-disapproval we have adopted the neutral term, "return," for the evaluation dimension. If a person behaves in an approved manner, he potentially could receive some positive return; if he behaves in a disapproved manner, he potentially could receive some negative return. If group members feel indifferent

[2] Merton, R. K. Reader, G. G. and Kendall, P. L. (Eds.) *The Student-Physician.* Cambridge, Mass.: Harvard University Press, 1957.

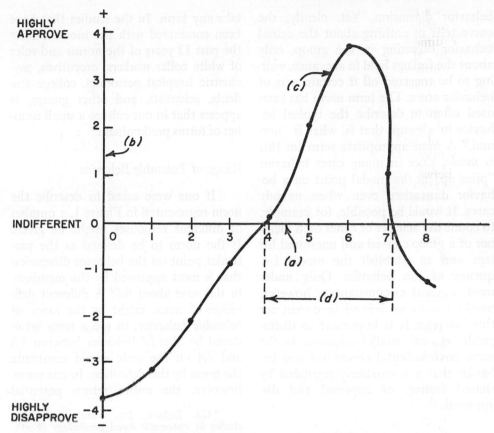

Figure 1. Schematic diagram showing the *Return Potential Model* for representing norms. (*a*) A *behavior dimension*; (*b*) an *evaluation dimension*; (*c*) a *return potential curve*, showing the distribution of approval-disapproval among the members of a group over the whole range of behavior; (*d*) the range of tolerable or approved behavior. This figure is reproduced from the *Fifty-Ninth Yearbook* of the National Society for the Study of Education, with permission of the Society.

to his behavior, the person could receive a neutral return.

The *return potential curve* is plotted through the means of group members' feelings about each scale position on the behavior dimension. In the example in Figure 1, group members highly disapprove nonparticipation in the discussion. In fact, unless a member participates at least four times his behavior is disapproved. There is a tendency to decrease approval of a person's participation

when it exceeds six times, but disapproval is not felt unless a member participates more than seven times. The curve does not specify how much return the actor *will* receive but how much he potentially *could* receive if all members of the group were to express their feelings toward his behavior.

The return potential curve describes the distribution of feelings of approval and disapproval by a particular set of Others for a given Actor, situation, and behavior dimension. Yet, clearly, the curve tells us nothing about the actual behavior occurring in the group; only about the feelings held in abeyance, waiting to be triggered off if certain acts of behavior occur. The term *norm* has been used often to describe the typical behavior in a group, that is, what is "normal." A more appropriate term for this is *mode*, since in many cases behavior "piles up" at the modal point on a behavior dimension, even when nobody cares. It would be possible, for example, to count the number of times each member of a group crossed and uncrossed his legs and to establish the modal frequency of this behavior. Only under most unusual circumstances, however, would a norm as defined here exist for this behavior. It is important to distinguish between parallel responses to the same environmental conditions and behavior that is normatively regulated by shared feelings of approval and disapproval.

CHARACTERISTICS OF A NORM

In the situation illustrated by Figure 1, the norm for participation is very restrictive for members of the group; it places a premium upon active participation; strong feelings exist about conformity and deviation; and over the entire behavior dimension there is a greater probability of a member being disapproved than approved. Each of these statements about the return potential curve describes a property of the norm. In some groups, the shape of the curve might be entirely different. Perhaps failure to participate would be quite acceptable behavior or even highly approved. In principle, a return potential curve can

take any form. In the studies that have been conducted with the model during the past 12 years of the norms and roles of white collar workers, executives, psychiatric hospital personnel, college students, scientists, and other groups, it appears that in our culture a small number of forms predominate.[3]

Range of Tolerable Behavior

If one were asked to describe the norm represented in Figure 1, a number of different responses might be given. Is the norm to be defined as the particular point on the behavior dimension that is most approved by the members, in this case about 6.5? A different definition of norm might be the *range of tolerable behavior*, to use a term introduced by Sherif.[4] Behavior between 3.8 and 7.4 on the scale would constitute the norm by this definition. In one sense, however, the entire return potential

[3] C.f. Jackson, Jay. *Norms and roles: studies in systematic social psychology* (Forthcoming). Also: Jackson, J. M. and Butman, J. W. "The effect of organizational factors on the social sensitivity of affective and effective leaders." Paper read at the Annual Meetings of the American Sociological Society, Washington, D. C., 1956; Glick, Oren W. "The effect of behavioral norms on the selection of associates." Unpublished Master's thesis, The University of Kansas, 1962; Glick, Oren W. "An investigation of changes in the normative system of students in a small liberal arts college." Unpublished Doctor's dissertation, The University of Kansas, 1963; Jackson, Jay. "The normative regulation of authoritative behavior." A chapter in *The Making of Decisions: A Reader in Administrative Behavior*. W. J. Gore and J. W. Dyson (Eds.) New York: The Free Press, 1964; Jackson, Jay. "A conceptual and measurement model for norms and roles." Comparative Studies of Mental Hospital Organization. The University of Kansas, 1963 (mimeographed).
[4] Sherif, M. and C. W. Sherif. *An outline of social psychology*. New York: Harper & Row, 1956 (revised).

curve defines the norm, since it describes how behavior is evaluated over the entire range.

The *range of tolerable behavior*, (*d*) in Figure 1, is that part of a behavior dimension that members of a group approve. It has been suggested [5] that the greater the consequence behavior has for a group, the narrower will be the range of tolerable behavior. Sherif also states that in important matters the range of tolerable behavior will be narrower for a leader than for members. Others have pointed to the lack of adequate studies in this area but have suggested that some deviation from particular norms may be permitted to leaders.[6]

Intensity of a Norm

In certain areas of behavior, a transgression is punished severely; in others there seems to be little concern by members of a group regardless of how individuals behave. Sometimes "ideal" behavior is accorded tremendous approval and reward, for example, when it is called heroism or self-sacrifice. Norms differ greatly with respect to the intensity of approval or disapproval evoked by appropriate or inappropriate behavior.

The *intensity* of a norm is indicated by the height of the return potential curve, both above and below the point of indifference. A convenient index is developed by summing the ordinates at each scale position on the behavior

dimension. This measure describes the over-all intensity of feeling in the group, whether of approval or disapproval. regarding the dimension of behavior.

Norms about matters of personal taste, such as style of speaking, walking, or dress, usually have low intensity. When the members of a group are indifferent, the curves for such norms will be relatively flat. In contrast, in the area of school or family "discipline" of children, for example, one typically finds both concern and disagreement. Norms for behavior here should have high intensity, depending upon the amount of consensus. One needs to identify carefully the properties of norms involved in this problem, however. Does a "strict" discipline imply a narrow range of tolerable behavior and high intensity of both approval and disapproval, or just the latter? Does it perhaps refer to the proportion of all behavior that is regulated by norms in the situation, defined elsewhere as the *scope* of the norms? [7] Answers to such questions would make more meaningful findings such as the one reported by Kent and Davis,[8] that the children of more "demanding" parents develop intellectually more rapidly than do those whose parents are somewhat "unconcerned."

Potential Return Difference

When the range of tolerable behavior for a particular norm is narrow, there is more potential disapproval than

---

[5] *Ibid.*

[6] Riecken, H. W. and Homans, G. C. "Psychological aspects of social structure." In *Handbook of social psychology*, Vol. II. Edited by G. Lindzey. Cambridge, Mass.: Addison-Wesley, 1954.

[7] C.f. the original chapter in *The Dynamics of Instructional Groups, op. cit.*, pp. 149–151.

[8] Kent, H. and Davis, D. R. "Discipline in the home and intellectual development." *British Journal of Medical Psychology*, 1957, XXX, 27–33.

approval awaiting a person's behavior. If many norms were characterized by similar narrow tolerances, life in the group would be essentially threatening rather than promising. One might predict a low level of initiative and creativity among members, a high level of anxiety, and high concern for the opinions of others, especially of those possessing high status. Thus, in terms of its implications for the feelings and behavior of group members, the *potential return difference* appears to be a meaningful property of a norm. It is computed for each behavior dimension by subtracting the negative intensity from the positive intensity—it is the algebraic sum of the ordinates. When the PRD is negative, the atmosphere for the particular area of behavior is threatening; to the degree that the index is positive, the atmosphere is correspondingly supportive.

An experiment by Schachter and Hall illustrates the importance of threatening and nonthreatening atmospheres for members' behavior.[9] They found that more students were willing to volunteer to participate in an experiment when the "group restraints" were reduced. But when the atmosphere was more threatening, a higher proportion of those who had volunteered to participate actually appeared for their appointments. Thus, depending upon whether we want to encourage spontaneity and initiative or compliant behavior, we should strive to increase or decrease the potential return differences of behavioral norms.

[9] Schachter, S., and R. Hall. "Group-derived restraints and audience persuasion." *Hum. Relat.*, 1952, 5, 397–406.

Point of Maximum Return

Another important characteristic of a norm is the point on a behavior dimension that is maximally approved by the relevant set of Others. This *point of maximum return* is the modal point of a return potential curve and can be seen to represent "ideal" behavior. It is likely that this point varies for different members of a social system depending upon their status. On certain behavior dimensions, it clearly would be located differently for male and female members. Discovering the point of maximum return would be another way of determining whether, as Sherif proposes,[10] norms are more exacting for leaders than for ordinary members. This property lends itself, too, to comparisons of a group's norms over a period of time, or of the norms of different groups on particular behavior dimensions.

Crystallization of a Norm

One of the important questions regarding any particular area of behavior is whether a norm "exists" in a group or social system. The question is quite ambiguous in this simple form. The return potential model provides a more precise formulation. When the intensity is very low, for example, it might be said that there is no norm for that type of behavior. Another condition that might signify the absence of a norm is when there is little agreement among the members of a group in regard to a given area of behavior. In such a situation the return potential curve would be quite flat, indicating low intensity. But since

[10] Sherif & Sherif, *op. cit.*

the curve is plotted through the return potential means for all members of the group, its flatness might be concealing intense feelings of approval-disapproval by members who are in disagreement.

A measure called the crystallization of a norm can be derived from the return potential model by computing the variance for each scale position on the behavior dimension, and then calculating $100 - D^2$.[11] When the dispersion is great and crystallization is therefore low, members' ideas of appropriate or inappropriate behavior do not coincide.

Although both low intensity and low crystallization could signify that a norm does not exist, they represent different conditions in the group. Gibb maintains, for example, that the experiences in a T-group can be understood in terms of the development of a number of norms critical for effective group functioning.[12] Initially these norms are missing, and members typically suffer confusion and strain before the requisite norms emerge from the interaction. In the early stages of such a group, crystallization of norms would be low in spite of high intensity of individual feelings. Even in its final hour, however, there might be certain norms whose intensity would be relatively low in spite of high crystallization. To say that no norm exists in a group for a particular behavior dimension might, thus, have different implications for predicting interaction among members, depending upon whether it signified low crystallization of the norm with high intensity, or low in-tensity in spite of high crystalliza-tion.[13]

When crystallization is high and intensity low, members of a group do not consider the behavior dimension to be very important. When crystallization is low, a number of interpretations are possible, depending upon other factors. As Gibb has pointed out, this condition might point simply to the relative "immaturity" of the group.[14] If the group is well established, however, some writers would take low crystallization of norms to be a sign of disintegration.[15] A study by Georgopoulos of an industrial organization found that agreement concerning norms, or high crystallization, was positively related to organizational effectiveness.[16] He selected behavior dimensions that were judged to be of central importance. There may be many areas of behavior in a group or organization, however, in which the degree of crystallization may not be so significant. In Merton's study of medical education, for example, a faculty member points to low crystallization without exhibiting great concern, saying that "there just aren't many 'ground rules' in this area."[17]

APPLICATION OF THE MODEL IN RESEARCH

In a continuing program of research, the Return Potential Model has

---

[11] Cronbach, L. & G. C. Gleser. "Assessing similarity between profiles." *Psychol. Bull.*, 1953, 50, 456–473.

[12] Gibb, J. R. "Trustformation." In *T-group Theory and Laboratory Method*, by Bradford, L. P., Gibb, J. R., & Benne, K. (Eds.), New York: Wiley, 1964, pp. 279–310.

[13] The two properties are not completely independent, since both maximum and minimum intensity require maximum crystallization.

[14] Gibb, *op cit.*

[15] Sherif & Sherif, *op. cit.*

[16] Georgopoulos, B. S. "The normative structure of social systems: a study of organizational effectiveness." Unpublished Doctor's dissertation, University of Michigan, 1956.

[17] Merton *et al. op. cit.*

provided conceptual tools for the investigation of a variety of problems. It has been possible to measure the characteristics of norms described in this paper and a number of additional properties of the normative structure of groups and organizations.[18] Since most of these studies are not yet published, a brief summary of some of the research will conclude this report.[19]

The norms of 36 oil refinery executives were studied in a management training workshop setting. Crystallization of the norms of men with specialized or professional training, based on higher education, was greater than for nontechnical executives of similar status. The norms of "technical" men also were more exacting, as measured by the mean range of tolerable behavior and the mean potential return difference. Ideal behavior in relating to one's superior, indicated by the point of maximum return, also was markedly different for these two groups.

Two studies have been conducted on the problem of authority conceived in terms of norms for authoritative behavior.[20] One explored the norms for 20 management interdepartmental coordinating committees in a large organization at two levels in the hierarchy. Both within committees and among levels, crystallization was high for problems that flowed readily along the line organization; but when interdepartmental relations were involved, there was little consensus within the committees or among them and superior committees regarding appropriate allocation of authority.

A second study involved the authority structure in a state system of mental hospitals. A number of findings in this project point to the complexity of authority structures. The norms for authoritative behavior vary significantly among different institutions, for different positions, among functional areas of behavior, and as defined by different role groups—as measured by crystallization, intensity, point of maximum return, and potential return difference. These indices also relate in meaningful ways to characteristics of the treatment environment.

An instrument has been developed to measure the roles of mental patients in hospitals and "normal" persons living in the community. In an exploratory study with 60 psychiatric nurses, it was found that their norms were more exacting for "patients" than for "neighbors". In a different state hospital system, however, this finding has been reversed, suggesting possibilities for comparative research on the relative supportiveness or punitiveness of treatment environments.

A longitudinal study of the norms for behaviors such as dancing, drinking, smoking, swearing, and church attendance of the students in a Mennonite liberal arts college [21] has provided some insight into the changes that occur in the normative system and in the differences between students who remain in college and those who drop out during the first three years. It was also found

---

[18] Many of these additional characteristics are discussed in the original chapter from which this paper is condensed.

[19] The studies summarized here have been conducted by the author and his students. They will be included in Jackson, Jay. *Norms and roles: studies in systematic social psychology* (Forthcoming), where appropriate credit will be given.

[20] Jackson, Jay. "The normative regulation of authoritative behavior," *op. cit.*

[21] Glick, Oren, 1962, *op. cit.*, 1963, *op. cit.*

that one basis for the formation of leisure-time friendship groups was similarity between norms for these and other "moral" behaviors.

In addition to the research mentioned, the model has been utilized by other investigators in studies of juvenile deliquency, human relations training groups, decision-making norms, and the role definitions of management personnel. As the results of research in different areas accumulate, based upon a common conceptual model and standard operations, it is hoped that findings will be comparable and thus will reinforce and enhance one another, as well as raising systematic issues for further investigation.

31. THE PERPETUATION OF AN ARBITRARY TRADITION THROUGH SEVERAL GENERATIONS OF A LABORATORY MICROCULTURE *

Robert C. Jacobs and Donald T. Campbell

According to Sumner (1906) "the mores can make anything right," and he went on to illustrate with a chapter on sacral harlotry and child sacrifice. According to Tarde (1903) "imitation is the key to the social mystery," "society is imitation," "social man is a veritable somnambulist." Such quotations indicate the late 19th century awareness of the power of culture to perpetuate arbitrary beliefs. Less drastically expressed, some such perspective permeates present day social science, although tempered somewhat by functionalism in anthropology and sociology. In social psychology, for example, cultural tradition tends to be invoked primarily as an "explanation" for social evils, prejudice, resistance to ameliorative social change, and the like. The current emphasis upon conformity reinforces this view, in spite of Asch's (1952) demurrer. Yet there are, no doubt, restraints upon a complete arbi-

trariness to culture, particularly with regard to beliefs that lie within people's direct range of observation. Thus arbitrary and erroneous superstitions about the shape of fishhooks probably would not long survive the systematic drift pressures resulting from continual minor variations some of which are in the direction of noticeably more effective form. Here lies the problem in the theory of culture for which a laboratory analogue was sought.

Since Sherif's (1936) classic studies on the formation of "social norms" in laboratory groups, there have been sporadic efforts to bring the process of cultural transmission into the laboratory. While much small group research might be so interpreted, the present study was in particular inspired by Sherif's studies, by Rose and Felton's (1955) "experimental histories of culture," and by the preliminary report of experiments on

* Reprinted from *Journal of Abnormal and Social Psychology*, 1961, 62: 649–658, with permission of the senior author and the American Psychological Association.

the evolution of "microcultures" by Gerard, Kluckhohn, and Rapoport (1956). In the latter two studies and in the present one, there is an effort to demonstrate a perpetuation of "cultural" characteristics that transcends the replacement of individual persons. In the present study confederates have been employed to establish an extreme cultural norm, the inculcation and survival of which is then studied as the confederates are one by one taken out of the group, naive new members gradually introduced, who then unwittingly become the further transmitters of the belief to still newer entrants.

The specific culture trait and the ecology of the group relative to such traits should obviously affect the success in the indoctrination of each new generation, and the rate of erosion of the tradition by innovation. In the Rose and Felton (1955) study, group interpretations of Rorschach cards were employed, a material offering considerable latitude for cultural arbitrariness and idiosyncrasy. In the Gerard, Kluckhohn, and Rapoport (1956) study, the groups were continually faced with new instances of a very difficult puzzle series, and were continually confronted with evidences of the lack of perfection of their traditional solutions, a situation encouraging the evolution of more adaptive norms, and unfavorable to the perpetuation of pure superstition. For the present study, a task was sought which would allow as much latitude for cultural arbitrariness as the Rose and Felton situation, and which would, in addition, make possible the ready quantification of effects. The original Sherif (1936) autokinetic movement situation was judged to provide this: if a person views a pinpoint of light in an otherwise totally blacked-out room,

the light soon appears to move. The illusion is a strong one for most persons, and is apparent even to those who know the light to be stationary. As Sherif has shown, naive respondents are very suggestible as to the degree of movement seen, and laboratory group norms on the amount of movement are rapidly established without the respondents being aware of the fictitiousness of their judgments.

So labile is the autokinetic experience or at least the translation of it into judgments of linear extent, that one reading the reports of studies employing it might expect that an arbitrary group norm once established would be passed on indefinitely without diminution; that once well indoctrinated, the naive group members would become as rigid and reliable spokesmen for the norm as were the confederates who preceded them; that each new generation would unwittingly become a part of a self-perpetuating cultural conspiracy propagating superstition and falsehood.

But the autokinetic experience is not completely labile. The very fact that sophisticated observers under strong "suggestion" to see the light remain fixed still perceive movement, shows this. Haggard and Rose (1944), in attempting to condition perceived movement on a right-left dimension, found for most respondents a strong rightward bias. In preliminaries to the present experiment, we learned that for our setting, respondents reporting alone produced mean individual judgments over 30 trials of from .64 to 6.67 inches, and with individual judgments rarely if ever approaching the arbitrary cultural norm of 15 to 16 inches which the confederates in our study provide. It is the presence of this potential natural norm that makes our inculcated cultural norm truly "arbitrary," and provides a counterpressure to the cultural tradition in its transmission across the experimental generations.

METHOD

Respondents

The 175 respondents who took part in this experiment were students, enrolled in introductory social sciences courses. They were unsophisticated concerning the autokinetic phenomenon and were unadvised as to the nature of the experiment previous to the time of serving in it. The respondents were assigned randomly to the six conditions involved. The number of respondents participating per group is shown in Table 1.

Materials, Apparatus, and Common Procedure

The experiment took place in a completely darkened, windowless, fan-ventilated room. The respondents were seated in a row 8 feet from a box designed to emit a small pinpoint of light. A 1 rpm induction motor was attached in series with the lamp, and a single switch controlled both. The motor was used solely as an auditory effect supporting the illusion of movement.

All respondents were blindfolded when brought into the experimental situation and were asked to put their blindfolds on whenever the door was opened to allow old respondents to leave and new ones to enter. This gave the respondents little if any knowledge of the size and arrangement of the experi-

mental room. The individual respondents received the following instructions:

This is a movement experiment. It is designed to test the students' visual perceptions with respect to space. In the next room is an apparatus that will project a small light. A few seconds after we begin, the light will move. It may move in a wavy motion or pattern or it may follow a recognizable course. However, your specific task will pertain merely to judging the distance that the light moves from the time that it appears until it is turned off. All judgments should be made in inches along a straight line connecting the starting point and the ending point on each trial.

Respondents going into group conditions received these additional instructions:

You are going to join a student (or number of students) who are already serving in this experiment. . . . You will be seated in the seat on the far left. To simplify recording procedure I will ask you to report your judgments beginning with the person on the far right and ending with you on the far left. When I stop you the person on the far right will leave, each of you inside will move right one seat, and a new person will be brought in.

Each trial was 5 seconds in length and after each block of 30 trials a ventilation fan was turned on by the experimenter. During this time in the group conditions, the "oldest" member of the group was taken out, other members moved to the right one seat, and a new member introduced. In the solitary conditions, respondents were told that ventilation took place as a health requirement. The ventilation period was timed to take approximately the same amount of time that was necessary to give instructions to a new respondent and bring him in in the other conditions.

Experimental Conditions

Table 1 shows the main feature of the six treatment conditions. (These have been given designations summarizing the group's construction. C and X stand for control and experimental. The first digit indicates the size of the group, while the second digit indicates the number of confederates present in the first generation.) There are two control conditions. In C-1-0 each respondent judged the movement of the light in solitude for four periods (called generations for the group conditions) of 30 judgments each. In C-3-0 respondents were run in groups of three, replacing one each generation (or 30 trials), for a total of nine generations.

A major dimension of experimental variation was the number of "culture-bearing" confederates with which the first naive respondent found himself placed. In experimental groups X-2-1, X-3-2, and X-4-3, the initial generation consisted of a solitary naive respondent sitting to the left of one, two, or three confederates who gave their judgments before he did, and who had been instructed to give judgments between 15 and 16 inches. The experimental variation in number of confederates was expected to produce cultural traditions of increasing strength. Confederates were recruited from the same subject pool as were the naive respondents. All were pledged to secrecy, with apparent success.

Another mode of manipulating cultural strength was explored by adding X-3-1, a group of two naive respondents led by one confederate. Thus C-3-0, X-3-1, and X-3-2 provide a set of three-person groups of 0, 1, and 2 confederates in the first generation.

The confederates who were present in the starting condition were removed one at a time, after each round of 30 judgments. Thus the groups with more confederates present in the first generation likewise had some stooging present for more generations. The shifting of members one chair to the right each generation, plus the rule of responding in turn from right to left, insured that

TABLE 1. EXPERIMENTAL PARADIGM

Condi- tion	Size of Group	Number of Con- federates	Trials per Generation	Number of Gener- ations	Genera- tions per Respond- ent	Number of Replica- tions	Number of Naive Respond- ents
C-1-0	1	0	30	—	4	24	24
C-3-0	3	0	30	10	3	3	30
X-2-1	2	1	30	9	2	3	27
X-3-2	3	2	30	10	3	3	30
X-4-3	4	3	30	11	4	3	33
X-3-1	3	1	30	9	3	3	29

on each trial a confederate or the eldest member of the group spoke first.

Each of the groups was replicated three times, while 24 respondents were run in the solitary control condition. The conditions were given in a counter-balanced order insuring that the differences in respondent selection from one part of the term to the other were kept independent of treatments.

RESULTS

Control Treatments

Figure 1 shows the results for the two control conditions. It will be noted that for C-1-0 the mean of the 24 respondents starts at 3.80 and decreases steadily generation by generation to a value of 2.90. This decrease is highly significant statistically, being found in the individual records of 21 of the 24 respondents, for which, by a two-tailed sign test, $p <$ .0002.

The three-person group control, C-3-0, shows very comparable mean levels, and likewise a general decline. The effect is not so clearly significant and is beclouded by the mutual influence that the group situation introduces. In the three replications, two groups declined, while one started abnormally low and increased. Comparing Generation 1 with the last generation with three persons present, Number 8, average judgment changes were 3.93–2.90, 6.72–2.03, and 1.72–2.49. Notice that in spite of the idiosyncratic norms of Generation 1, the three replications became more similar as the process of

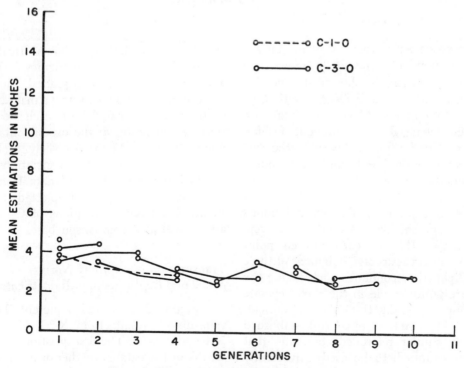

Figure 1. Mean judgments of the control groups.

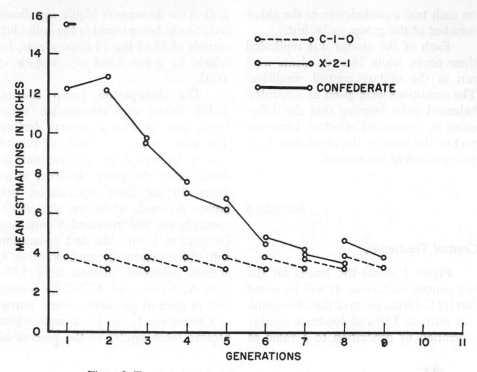

Figure 2. Transmission of arbitrary norm in two-person groups.

successive replacement went on. Of the 27 respondents present in more than one generation, 16 showed declines between their first and last generation.

In graphing C-3-0, the data have been averaged in a different fashion from the foregoing. To show the successive replacement and overlapping generational character, the careers of each successive replacement have been plotted separately. The plotted points represent the average of the three replications; that is, each plotted point represents the average judgment of three individual respondents, each taking the corresponding role in the three separate groups replicating this control treatment.

The two types of control established such similar reference standards that they cannot both be used conveniently as visual base lines in the graphing of

the results of the experimental treatments. For this reason, in Figures 2, 3, and 4, only C-1-0 has been plotted. This plotting has been done in such a manner as to provide a parallel for each new starting generation in the experimental group. Thus in Figure 2, where each respondent stays only two generations, the first two generations of data from C-1-0 have been repeatedly plotted. In Figure 4, all four generations of C-1-0 are needed as a comparison base.

Transmission of Arbitrary Norms over Total Replacement of Indoctrinator

Figures 2, 3, 4, and 5 present the transmission results from X-2-1, X-3-2, X-4-3, and X-3-1. The first question that we ask of the data is whether or not the naive respondents, once indoctrinated by the confederates, have themselves transmitted any vestiges of the arbitrary cultural norm once the original indoctrinators have passed on. To test this, one can examine the judgments of the first generation of respondents to judge without any confederates present. For X-2-1, X-3-2, and X-4-3 these values are 12.07, 9.79, and 9.82. Each of these differs significantly ($p < .01$) from the C-1-0 control group by t test, when the mean of the 3 experimental respondents is compared with the mean of the 24 control respondents. For X-3-1, the mean is 5.34, not significantly different from the C-1-0 value of 3.80.

By pooling groups X-2-1, X-3-2, and X-4-3, we can compare to the 24 C-1-0 respondents 9 experimental respondents newly introduced at each of several generations beyond the final confederate.

For the first such generation, $M = 10.57$, $t = 7.25$, $p < .0001$; for the second, $M = 7.80$, $t = 3.74$, $p < .0001$; for the third, $M = 6.06$, $t = 4.02$, $p < .0001$; for the fourth, $M = 5.08$, $t = 2.04$, $p < .03$; for the fifth, $M = 4.37$, $t = 1.31$, $p < .10$. Thus the arbitrary norm is transmitted in some degree up through the fourth and perhaps the fifth generation beyond the last confederate. By the sixth it has entirely disappeared, the mean of 3.60 being slightly below the control value of 3.80.

Differences in Strength of Induced Traditions

The experimental comparisons were introduced in the expectation that induced cultures of differing strengths and persistence would be produced. In fact,

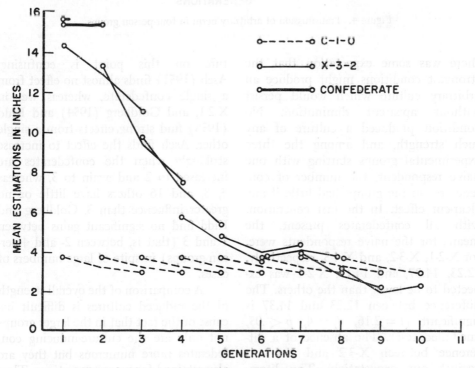

Figure 3. Transmission of arbitrary norm in three-person groups.

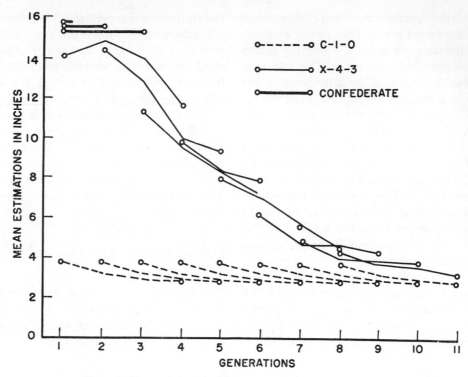

Figure 4. Transmission of arbitrary norm in four-person groups.

there was some expectation that the strongest conditions might produce an arbitrary culture which would persist without apparent diminution. No condition produced a culture of any such strength, and among the three experimental groups starting with one naive respondent, the number of confederates in the groups had little if any clear-cut effect. In the first generation, with all confederates present, the means for the naive respondents were, for X-2-1, X-3-2, and X-4-3, respectively, 12.23, 14.37, and 14.13. X-2-1 was expected to be lower than the others. The difference between 12.23 and 14.37 is significant $(t = 2.16, df = 4, p < .05,$ one-tailed test). The absence of a difference between X-3-2 and X-4-3 is against our expectation. The litera-

ture on this point is confusing. Asch (1951) finds almost no effect from a single confederate, whereas we, in X-2-1, and Goldberg (1954) and Kidd (1958) find strong effects from a single other. Asch finds the effect to increase strikingly when the confederates are increased to 2 and again to 3, whereas 4, 8, and 16 others have little or no greater influence than 3. Goldberg and Kidd find no significant gains between 1 and 3 (that is, between 2- and 4-person groups) in spite of large numbers of cases.

A comparison of the overall strength of the induced cultures is difficult because of the fact that in the larger groups not only are the culture-inducing confederates more numerous but they are also retained for more generations. Thus it would seem unfair to compare all groups at the fourth generation from the beginning, since X-4-3 would have had a confederate in the immediately preceding generation, while X-2-1 would have been without a confederate for three generations. Perhaps more appropriate is a comparison of strength in the first generation subsequent to the removal of the last confederate. The values are, respectively, 12.09, 9.79, and 9.82. The smallest group, X 2 1, seems strongest at this stage although the differences do not approach significance. But this comparison is not exactly fair, either, because for X-2-1 the confederate, when present, dominated the culture, while for X-4-3 the final confederate had his influence diluted by the vocal presence of two not completely loyal naive re-spondents. By the fifth postconfederate generation, these three values are 4.69, 3.90, and 4.55. Lacking both striking differences and an optimal comparison, it seems fair to conclude that no differences in effective cultural strength have been achieved by thus manipulating group size.

One manipulation did indeed provide indoctrinations of varying magnitude. The naive respondents of X-3-1 were significantly different from C-1-0 only in the first generation, that is, with the confederate present ($t = 3.88$, $p <$ .01). But even at this stage the naive respondents of X-3-1 were significantly less indoctrinated than those of X-3-2 at Generation 2, when it likewise consisted of but one confederate and two naive persons ($t = 4.69$, $p < .001$, 10 df).

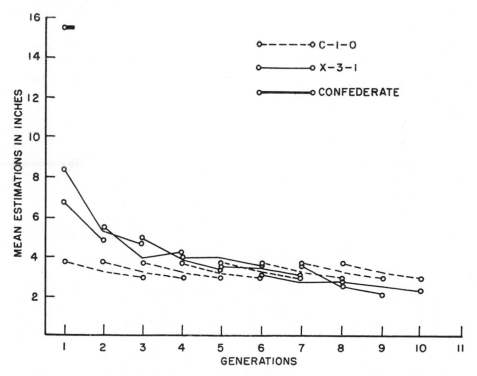

Figure 5. Transmission of arbitrary norm in a three-person group initiated by one confederate and two naive respondents.

Thus manipulating the ratio of confederates to naive judges has little effect when achieved through adding more confederates, but has great effect when achieved through manipulating the number of naive respondents. As Asch (1951) has noted, this adding of a "true partner" seems to have an effect disproportionally greater than would be expected from the simple fact of diluting the majority. This dimension has not been systematically explored, however. In the present setting it would be interesting to compare groups of varying size in which the naive-to-confederate ratio was held constant, as through a group consisting of two confederates and two naive respondents, to be compared with X-2-1, etc.

Judgments as a Compromise between Own and Other's Observations

The deterioration of the cultural norm occurs, in part, because each naive respondent makes judgments somewhat lower, somewhat closer to the natural norm, than do the confederates or elder citizens serving as his mentors. Of 36 naive respondents serving for the first time in X-2-1, X-3-2, and X-4-3 during the first four generations (where some significant strength to the cultural norm was still present) 34 made mean judgments lower than the average of their mentors (for which, $p < .0000001$). This clear-cut fact we take as supporting the interpretation that each judgment represents a pooling of the person's own observations (the value for which we infer from the control group) with the reported observations of others. In the resulting compromise the person's own observations are not given much weight, but they are given some.

In the first generation of the experimental groups, the conditions are simple enough so that we can make some estimates of this relative weighting of own observations and other's reports. For the first naive respondent in X-2-1, the other's (confederate's) report averages 15.52. The own observation is inferred from C-1 to be 3.80. If the naive respondent weighted his own observation equally with the report of the confederate, his judgment would fall halfway between these values, at 9.66. Instead, the judgment is 12.23, much closer to the confederate's. Rather than regarding the confederate as an equally good observer as himself, the respondent has weighted the confederate's opinion 2.6 times as heavily as his own. The formula for the weighting ratio is $(12.23-3.80)/(15.52-12.23)$. Assuming each confederate to be equally weighted, and solving for the weight given a single confederate's opinion, we get values of 4.6 for X-3-2 and 2.5 for X-4-3. Since these ratios are based upon the performances of but three naive respondents each, they are quite unstable, and are provided here primarily for illustrative purposes. Similar computations for the later generations have been omitted because of the difficulty of taking into account the reciprocal effect of new respondents upon the older naive respondents acting as indoctrinators. The first generation situation is computable just because the confederates were unresponsive to the judgments of their fellows.

Whatever the weighting ratio, as long as some weight is given own observations, and as long as own observations deviate in a consistent direction from the cultural norm, the arbitrary culture is doomed to deterioration eventually, at least in the limited sanction system of this laboratory. While the question has not been stated in this form, the relative respect for own observations over the reports of others is much higher in less ambiguous situations, as Asch (1951) has shown. It is easy to understand how the ambiguities of the autokinetic situation lead to lack of confidence in own opinion, but it is perhaps an indication of human trust that this same ambiguity does not lead to a proportional lack of confidence in the reports of others.

Forgetting and Reciprocal Influence

If the previous factor of compromise weighting were all that was involved, the deterioration in culture as graphed in Figures 2, 3, and 4 might have been of a stair-step fashion, with each new inductee starting lower than his indoctrinator, but once started, holding to his initial level through the several generations of his life in the group. As can be seen from the graphs, this is not the case. Instead, the respondent is less loyal to the old culture the longer he stays in the group. Of the 36 naive respondents introduced in the first four generations of X-2-1, X-3-2, and X-4-3, 31 made lower mean judgments on their last session than on their first (for which, $p < .00001$).

In the present design, three factors are confounded in generating this effect. While we have not extricated them, it seems well to mention them. The first factor is the autonomous decline noted previously in the control groups. In terms of absolute magnitude, this would seem to account for little of the total effect.

A second factor is forgetting. Were a respondent to judge with the leadership of a culture-bearing confederate, and then to judge in isolation for several sessions, he would in these later sessions be pooling his immediate visual impression of the stimulus with the remembered reports of the other in a previous session. As these memories dimmed, their weighting could be expected to diminish, and the relative weighting of own observation could be expected to increase. No doubt in the present situation forgetting of indoctrination provides some of the decline within the judgment series of a single respondent.

A third possible source of this within-respondents decline in loyalty to the arbitrary culture is the effect of the new group member upon his elders. Since judging was always from eldest to youngest on any given stimulus presentation, this would have to involve an influence carrying over from one turn to the next. We feel sure that some such influence was present, but its demonstration would require a separate experiment placing confederates in the final answering position.

DISCUSSION

In presenting these materials to our colleagues, we have found them most fascinated by the fact of the cultural transmission surviving total replacement of specific individuals, and by the fact of naive respondents becoming unwitting conspirators in perpetuating a cultural fraud. This demonstration was of course our main intent, and this outcome was inevitable if the conformity research upon which we built had any transfer validity. But while these results are highly significant statistically, they fall short of our expectations. The inculcated arbitrary norms turn out to be eroded by innovation at a much more rapid rate than we had expected. We have hardly provided a laboratory paradigm for the examples of tenacious adherence to incredible superstition with which anthropologists and students of comparative religion provide us.

Of course, a relative weakness in strength is to be expected in a laboratory example. Mature individuals are undergoing transient indoctrination by unknown age-mates, as opposed to the natural setting of the teaching of the very young by tribal adults over a period of years. Fewer confederates are involved than in the tribal situation, although the effect of number upon degree of conformity is unclear in the laboratory. More important, there are no sanctions rewarding conformity nor punishing innovation. Furthermore, it is even possible that the subject of judgment in our experiment is less ambiguous than the subject material of religious belief, for example. There is, after all, a fairly clear consensus among our naive solitary observers. In our situation, the spontaneous deviations from orthodoxy were all in the same direction, whereas for many arbitrary items of culture the deviations may lack such concerted direction.

Nonetheless, the outcome may well warn us against the assumption that a purely arbitrary cultural norm could be perpetuated indefinitely without other sources of support. Even if people weigh the opinions of their elders many times that of their own direct observations, the collective effect of their own observations probably soon erodes a *functionless* arbitrary belief. Where we observed tenacious bizarre cultural belief we must look to more than mere tradition, suggestibility, or conformity, to explain its

retention. Latent functions (for example, Merton, 1949) at the personal or societal level must be present to counteract the pressures from continuous spontaneous innovation in a more natural direction. For example, Moore (1957) and Aubert (1959) have recently suggested such latent functions to superstitious magical lotteries used in the selection of hunting and fishing sites. As our understanding of the requisites of individual and social life further increases, we may expect to discover such latent functions for many if not all of those "meaningless" superstitions which stubbornly persist.

SUMMARY

In an autokinetic judgment situation in which solitary judgments of movement averaged 3.8 inches, confederates were used to establish arbitrary "cultural norms" of 15.5 inches. The transmission of this norm was studied as one at a time confederates and old members were removed from the group while new members were added. Significant remnants or the culture persisted for four or five generations beyond the last confederate. Gradually in each of the 12 experimental groups the arbitrary norm decayed and the group judgments drifted away from it back to the natural norm found in the control groups. The size of group had no clear effect upon the endurance of the norm established, although a group beginning with one confederate and two naive respondents was markedly weaker than the others and transmitted no culture beyond one generation.

Major effects are interpreted in terms of a judgment process in which each respondent weighs the reports of others and his own observations, achieving a compromise between them. Even with the respondents giving the reports of others from 2.5 to 4 times the weight of their own observations, slight "innovations" result which rapidly cumulate to erode the original arbitrary cultural norm. Details of the process and analogues to the cultural transmission of bizarre beliefs are discussed.

REFERENCES

Asch, S. E. Effects of group pressure upon the modification and distortion of judgments. In H. Guetzkow (Ed.), *Groups, leadership, and men.* Pittsburgh: Carnegie Press, 1951. Pp. 177–190.

Asch, S. E. *Social psychology.* Englewood Cliffs, N. J.: Prentice-Hall, 1952.

Aubert, V. Chance in social affairs. *Inquiry*, 1959, 2, 1–24.

Cerard, R. W., Kluckhohn, C., & Rapoport, A. Biological and cultural evolution: Some analogies and explorations. *Behav. Sci.*, 1956, 1, 6–34,

Goldberg, S. C. Three situational determinants of conformity to social norms. *J. abnorm. soc. Psychol.*, 1954, 49, 325–329.

Haggard, E. A., & Rose, E. Some effects of mental set and active participation in the conditioning of the autokinetic phenomenon. *J. exp. Psychol.*, 1944, 34, 45–59.

Kidd, J. S. Social influence phenomena in a task-oriented group. *J. abnorm. soc. Psychol.*, 1958, 56, 13–17.

Merton, R. K. *Social theory and social structure.* New York: Free Press, 1949.

Moore, O. K. Divination, a new perspective. *Amer. Anthropologist*, 1957, 59, 72.

Rose, E., & Felton, W. Experimental histories of culture. *Amer. sociol. Rev.*, 1955, 20, 383–392.

Sherif, M. *The psychology of social norms.* New York: Harper & Row, 1936.

Sumner, W. G. *Folkways.* Boston: Ginn, 1906.

Tarde, G. *The laws of imitation.* (Paris ed., 1890) New York: Holt, Rinehart and Winston, 1903.

32. TASK ROLES AND SOCIAL ROLES IN PROBLEM-SOLVING GROUPS *

Robert F. Bales

During the last ten years, a number of laboratories for the study of social interaction within small groups and organizations have been started in university research centers, hospitals, clinics, and military installations. The studies and experiments I shall describe were conducted in one of these laboratories, which was established in 1947 at Harvard University.

The laboratory consists of a large, well-lighted room for the group under study and an adjoining room for observers who listen and watch from behind windows with one-way vision. The subjects are told at the beginning that

* Reprinted from *Readings in Social Psychology* by E. Maccoby, T. Newcomb, and E. Hartley (Editors), New York: Holt, Rinehart and Winston, 1958, pp. 437–447, with permission of the author and publisher.

the room has been constructed for the special purpose of studying group discussion, that a complete sound recording will be made, and that there are observers behind the one-way mirrors. The purpose of the separation is not to deceive the subjects but to minimize interaction between them and the observing team.

Over a number of years we have evolved a more or less standard type of group and task which has formed the setting for a number of studies. The data I shall report came from several studies, all done under essentially the same conditions, so that a description of the most recent investigation will serve in substance for the others.

PROCEDURES

The sample which provided data for the most recent investigation consisted of 30 five-man experimental groups. Subjects were 150 Harvard freshmen who were recruited by letters sent to a random sample of the entering class which briefly described the experiment as one concerned with group problem-solving and decision-making. Volunteers were offered a dollar an hour. The groups were randomly composed. Typically the members of a group did not know each other, nor were they introduced to each other. In effect, they were faced with the problem of getting organized as well as with the more obvious problem that was issued to them. The more obvious problem, which we call the standard task, involved the discussion of a human-relations case, a five-page presentation of facts about a problem facing an administrator in his organization. Members were given sep-

arate identical copies of the case to read ahead of time and were told that, although each was given accurate information, we intended to leave them uncertain as to whether they each had exactly the same range of facts. The cases were collected after they had been read by the members individually, to prevent direct comparison of typed copies, although members were allowed to take notes. The task defined for each group was to assemble the information, to discuss why the people involved were behaving as they did, and to decide what should be recommended as action for the solution to the problem presented. The groups were asked to time themselves for 40 minutes and to dictate the group solution for the sound record in the final one or two minutes of the meeting.

While the group members began to organize themselves and to solve the case problem, the observers got to work in the observation room. They systematically recorded every step of the interaction, including such items as nods and frowns. Each observer had a small machine with a moving paper tape on which he wrote in code a description of every act—an act being defined essentially as a single statement, question, or gesture. Acts ordinarily occurred at the rate of 15 to 20 per minute. The recorded information on each act included identification of the person speaking and the person spoken to and classification of the act according to predetermined categories. The categories included attempts to solve either the organizational problems of the group or the task problems by the offering of information, opinions, and suggestions. Questions and several types of positive and negative reactions completed

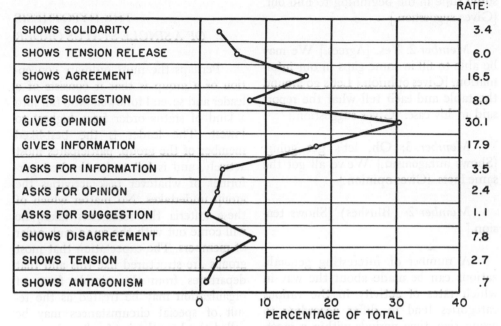

RATE:

					RATE:
SHOWS SOLIDARITY					3.4
SHOWS TENSION RELEASE					6.0
SHOWS AGREEMENT					16.5
GIVES SUGGESTION					8.0
GIVES OPINION					30.1
GIVES INFORMATION					17.9
ASKS FOR INFORMATION					3.5
ASKS FOR OPINION					2.4
ASKS FOR SUGGESTION					1.1
SHOWS DISAGREEMENT					7.8
SHOWS TENSION					2.7
SHOWS ANTAGONISM					.7

0   10   20   30   40
PERCENTAGE OF TOTAL

Figure 1. Types of interaction and their relative frequencies. This profile of rates is the average obtained on the standard task from 24 different groups, four of each size from two to size seven, each group meeting four times, making a total of 96 sessions. The raw number of scores is 71,838. (From Robert F. Bales, "How People Interact in Conferences," *Scientific American*, Vol. 192 [March, 1955].)

the set of 12 categories (see Figure 1). This method is called "interaction-process analysis."[1] The categories are meant to have a general-purpose usefulness for group research and their use is not confined in any way to the laboratory conditions described here, although the best norms exist for the standard task and the group type described here.[2]

[1] Robert F. Bales, *Interaction Process Analysis: A Method for the Study of Small Groups* (Cambridge, Mass.: Addison-Wesley Co., Inc., 1950).

[2] For norms, see Robert F. Bales and Edgar F. Borgatta, "Size of Group as a Factor in the Interaction Profile," in A. Paul Hare, Edgar F. Borgatta, and Robert F. Bales, *Small Groups, Studies in Social Interaction* (New York: Alfred A. Knopf, Inc. 1955), pp. 396–413.

As Figure 1 shows, on the average about half (56 percent) of the acts during a group session on the standard task fall into the categories of problem-solving attempts; the remaining 44 percent are distributed among positive reactions, negative reactions, and questions. In other words, the process tends to be two-sided, with the reactions serving as a more or less constant feedback on the acceptability of the problem-solving attempts. The following example will illustrate the pattern of interchange.

Member 1: I wonder if we have the same facts about the problem? [Asks for opinion.] Perhaps we should take some time in the beginning to find out. [Gives suggestion.]

Member 2: Yes. [Agrees.] We may be able to fill in some gaps in our information. [Gives opinion.] Let's go around the table and each tell what the report said in his case. [Gives suggestion.]

Member 3: Oh, let's get going. [Shows antagonism.] We've all got the same facts. [Gives opinion.]

Member 2: (Blushes) [Shows tension.]

A number of interesting generalizations can be made about the way in which rates of activity in the various categories tend to differ according to group size, time periods within a meeting, development of a group over a series of meetings, pre-established status characteristics of members, and the like.[3] The present article, however, will be concerned with a particular set of problems in which the interaction data have played an important part—whether there are tendencies for persons to develop different roles during interaction, even though there are no pre-established status differences, and if so, what kind, and why? There are several plausible views about this set of problems. The following account presents four distinguishable views and shows how research led from one view to another in the course of several studies.

THE HYPOTHESIS OF A SINGLE-STATUS ORDER

Perhaps the most ordinary conception of a group is that it consists of a leader and several followers who fall into a kind of status order from highest to lowest. The leader is the best-liked member of the group, participates most actively, and is felt to be the best performer of whatever task activities the group undertakes. No matter which of these criteria the researcher takes, he will come out with the same rank order of members. The expectation that most groups are structured like this and that departures from this simple form of organization may be treated as the result of special circumstances may be called the hypothesis of a "single-status order."

This is a plausible hypothesis. It underlies much research on leadership. It is congruent with the ideological position that for good leadership it is very important that a good leader should be an all-around "great man," and it assumes that there are such men, at least relative to the other members in a given group.[4] This hypothesis assumes role differentiation but essentially only along a single quantitative dimension, leadership status.

Early in the research we began to ask group members about their likes and dislikes for each other, their opinions of who had the best ideas and who showed the most leadership, and other

[3] For a short review, see Robert F. Bales "Some Uniformities of Behavior in Small Group," in Guy E. Swanson, Theodore M. Newcomb, and Eugene L. Hartley (eds.), *Readings in Social Psychology* (New York: Holt, Rinehart and Winston, Inc., 1952), rev. ed., pp. 146–159.

[4] For some evidence that there are some such men, in relative terms, see Edgar F. Borgatta, Arthur S. Couch, and Robert F. Bales, "Some Findings Relevant to the Great Man Theory of Leadership," *Am. Sociol. Rev.*, 1954, XIX, 755–759.

similar questions. We wanted to know how these questions related to each other and to our observations of interaction. The question as to whether or not there is role differentiation within a group can be reduced in part to whether group members show some consensus that certain members stand higher than others on a given criterion and whether different criteria give different status orders rather than a single-status order.

When I first began to examine data from our experimental groups. I worked under the assumption that there might be some such thing as a "simply organized group," that is, one in which the rank order of members on activity, task ability, and likeability would coincide, and that these groups would in some sense or other be the most successful or best satisfied.[5]

Figure 2 shows the results which raised a most interesting set of questions. The total interaction initiated by one man in the course of a meeting establishes the basis for ranking him relative to the others on activity. If there is a strong tendency toward a single-status order, top men on activity should also rank highest in group-member responses to such questions as "who has the best ideas," and should also receive the highest number of "liking" votes and lowest of "disliking."[6] The second man on activity should, on the average, be second highest on the other criteria

of excellence, and so on. The rank order on each criterion should be highly correlated to the rank order on the other criteria.

What does Figure 2 suggest? First, there seems to be a positive correlation between activity rank and idea rank, although the second man seems a little low. But on liking-received rank, there is a marked discrepancy. The top man on activity appears considerably lower than expected on liking received. Both the second and the third men are higher on

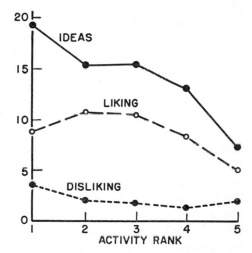

Figure 2. Average ratings * received on ideas, liking, and disliking by men of each activity rank. (From Robert F. Bales, "The Equilibrium Problem in Small Groups," Ch. IV in Talcott Parsons, Robert F. Bales, and Edward A. Shils [eds.], *Working Papers in the Theory of Action* [New York: Free Press, 1953], p. 146.)

* Each entry at a given activity rank is a mean over 12 sessions for the persons who occupied that rank as of each meeting. (Four separate five-man groups were involved.) The idea index is not actually a rating but an index obtained by adding rankings received (including self-rankings) and subtracting the total from the highest possible, 25. The like and dislike indexes are average ratings received, with the highest possible, 28.

[5] Robert F. Bales, "The Equilibrium Problem in Small Groups," Ch. IV in Talcott Parsons, Robert F. Bales, and Edward A. Shils (eds.), *Working Papers in the Theory of Action* (New York: Free Press, 1953).

[6] The actual questions used are presented in the source indicated at the foot of Figure 3. They are omitted in the present paper for the sake of brevity.

the average than he. Is the top man doing something to lose likes and provoke dislikes? Here one notes the dislike curve. The differences are small and probably not significant but they suggest that the top man is possibly the highest on dislikes received. Liking seems to be centering on the second and third man in activity, and they both seem to be lower than expected on idea ranking. Can it be that these men are tending to avoid too heavy an emphasis on the task area for fear of being disliked?

On further investigation of this problem it turned out that something happened in groups over a series of four sessions that was equally thought-provoking. In the first sessions, if a given man held top position on the idea ranking by his fellow members, the probability was about 50–50 that he would *also* hold a top position on a likeability ranking. But in the second meeting the probability dropped markedly, and by the fourth meeting was only about one in ten. The percentage of cases in which the same man held the top position on liking and idea rankings at the same time, divided by session, may be charted as follows:

Sessions

1	2	3	4
56.5	12.0	20.0	8.5

Could it be that there was something about arriving in a top-status position, owing to technical contribution to the task problems of the group, that tended to "lose friends and alienate people"? If so, was another man likely to rise who paid more attention to the social-emotional problems of the group

and so tended to collect more liking? The idea that this happens with sufficient frequency that it can be viewed as typical may be called "the hypothesis of two complementary leaders."

THE HYPOTHESIS OF TWO COMPLEMENTARY LEADERS

Why, if at all, should groups tend to have two complementary leaders, one a task specialist, the other a social-emotional specialist?[7] Perhaps it would be helpful to look at the interaction of men highest on idea ranking received but not highest on liking received, and vice versa. It may be that men of these two types behave differently and the differences in behavior may give us some clues as to the reasons for the differences.

Table 1 shows the composite profiles of 44 matched session-pairs[8] of idea men (who were not best liked in their group) and best-liked men (who were not top in idea ranking). Slater, from whose paper the table is taken, comments: "The most salient general difference in Table 1 is the tendency for the Idea man to initiate interaction more heavily in Area B (Problem-Solving Attempts) and the Best-liked man in Area A (Positive Reactions). The Idea man also seems to disagree somewhat more, and show a little more antagonism, while

[7] A theory is advanced in Robert F. Bales and Philip E. Slater, "Role Differentiation in Small Decision-making Groups," Ch. V in Talcott Parsons *et al.* (eds.), *Family, Socialization, and Interaction Process* (New York: Free Press, 1955).

[8] Although the number of *sessions* was 44, the number of separate individuals involved was not 88, since each group ran over four sessions, and some individuals were in the same position more than once.

TABLE 1. COMPOSITE PROFILES IN PERCENTAGES OF 44 TOP MEN ON IDEA RANKING AND 44 TOP MEN ON LIKE RANKING FOR THE SAME SESSIONS *

| | | Initiated | | Received | |
	Interaction Category	Idea Men	Best-Liked Men	Idea Men	Best-Liked Men
Area A:	Shows solidarity	3.68	4.41	2.57	3.15
Positive	Shows tension release	5.15	6.98	7.95	9.20
reactions	Shows agreement	14.42	16.83	23.29	18.27
Area B:	Gives suggestion	8.97	6.81	7.01	7.22
Problem-solving	Gives opinion	32.74	28.69	25.52	31.09
attempts	Gives orientation	18.54	17.91	14.06	14.54
Area C:	Asks orientation	3.04	3.71	3.62	2.80
Questions	Asks opinion	1.84	2.94	1.94	1.74
	Asks suggestion	.93	1.33	.85	.84
Area D:	Shows disagreement	8.04	7.60	10.65	9.35
Negative	Shows tension increase	1.92	2.16	1.59	1.35
reactions	Shows antagonism	.73	.63	.95	.45

* From Philip E. Slater, "Role Differentiation in Small Groups," *Am. Sociol. Rev.*, 1955; XX, 305.

the Best-liked man asks more questions and shows more tension." [9]

On the receiving end, the situation is largely reversed, with the idea man receiving more agreement, questions, and negative reactions, while the best-liked man receives more problem-solving attempts, and more solidarity and tension release. The general picture is thus one of specialization and complementarity, with the idea man concentrating on the task and playing a more aggressive role, while the best-liked man concentrates more on social-emotional problems, giving rewards and playing a more passive role.

The kind of complementarity that

[9] Slater, *op. cit.* in footnote to Table 1. It is not possible to state that all of the detailed differences indicated are significant, because rates in the various categories are interdependent. However, Slater shows that the two types are in general significantly different from each other.

shows in the behavior, then, is a kind that occurs in short interchanges in conversations where a problem-solving attempt by one person is followed by an agreement or disagreement from some other, or where a pleasant remark or a joke by one is followed by a smile or a laugh from the other. Such a division of labor by type of act is very common and easily recognized. There may or may not be a specialization so that one person continues to produce more of one form of behavior than the other.

But now consider an important fact. Almost exactly the same sort of difference in interaction profile tends to be found between high participators and low participators,[10] even if one ignores the idea and like ratings. High partici-

[10] See Edgar F. Borgatta and Robert F. Bales, "Interaction of Individuals in Reconstituted Groups," *Sociometry*, 1953, XVI, 302–320.

pators tend to specialize in problem-solving attempts, low participators tend to specialize in positive or negative reactions or questions. Moreover, the proportion of problem-solving attempts increases when a man is placed with lower participators and decreases when he is working with higher participators.[11] What do these facts suggest?

For one thing, these facts seem to imply that the qualitative differences in the type of act attributed to a given person may be more or less forced by the tendency of others in the group to talk a little or a great deal, thus giving him an opportunity to make the problem-solving attempts or leaving him only in a position to respond to the quicker or more valuable proposals of others.

Insofar as the ratings a man receives are based on the way he behaves, the ratings others give him will surely be dependent on how much he talks. Let us suppose that a man can receive a high rating on ideas only if he makes many problem-solving attempts. He can do this only by talking a good deal. Then, to receive a high rating on ideas he will have to talk a lot. Or, conversely, let us suppose that a man can receive a high rating on liking only if he rewards others by positive reactions. He can do this only if he permits them to make many problem-solving attempts, which in turn requires that he let the other(s) talk a lot. Then, to receive a high rating on liking he will have to talk less.

This line of reasoning seems to fit with the facts so far presented and, moreover, has a certain plausibility in terms of common organizational arrangements. The husband and wife in many families seem to play comple-

mentary roles of the sort described. Many administrators find cases from their experience where organizations in fact have two leaders, one who specializes on the task side, one on the social-emotional side. It is a kind of political maxim that it is almost impossible to elect the person who is technically best suited for an office—he is generally not popular enough. Surely there must be many persons in leadership positions who welcome any theory that explains to them that their lack of popularity is no fault of their own but a result of a specialization that is in the nature of things.

The problem now is that it might be inferred from this ideological version of the theory that there is no essential distinction between sheer activity and ratings received on goodness of ideas and, moreover, that there is a negative correlation between these two and liking received. Is it true that leaders must choose between task effectiveness and popularity?

THE HYPOTHESIS OF THREE ORTHOGONAL FACTORS

Fortunately, a number of studies in the literature bear on this question and the results of a number of researchers tend to converge on an answer. When members of small groups are asked to rate and choose each other on a wide variety of descriptive criteria or are assessed by observers, three factors or distinct dimensions generally tend to appear.

Carter [12] indicates the frequency

[11] *Op. cit.*

[12] Launor F. Carter, "Recording and Evaluating the Performance of Individuals as Members of Small Groups," *Personn. Psychol.*, 1954, VII, 477–484.

with which these factors are found in reviewing a series of factor analytic studies, such as those of Couch and himself, Sakoda, Wherry, and Clark.[13] A recent study by Wispe [14] may be added to the list.

Carter describes the factors as follows:

Factor I. *Individual prominence and achievement:* behaviors of the individual related to his efforts to stand out from others and individually achieve various personal goals.

Factor II. *Aiding attainment by the group:* behaviors of the individual related to his efforts to assist the group in achieving goals toward which the group is oriented.

Factor III. *Sociability:* behaviors of the individual related to his efforts to establish and maintain cordial and socially satisfying relations with other group members.

These factors seem to represent underlying dimensions in the evaluations persons make of each other, whether as observers or as fellow group members. It may be that the best way of looking at these factors is not as personality traits but as frameworks in which the perceiver responds to personality traits of others.

[13] Arthur S. Couch and Launor F. Carter, "A Factorial Study of the Rated Behavior of Group Members," Paper read at Eastern Psychological Association, March 1952; J. M. Sakoda, "Factor Analysis of OSS Situational Tests," *J. Abnorm. & Soc. Psychol.*, 1952, XLVII, 843–852; R. J. Wherry, *Factor Analysis of Officer Qualification Form QCL-2B* (Columbus: Ohio State University Research Foundation, 1950); R. A. Clark, "Analyzing the Group Structure of Combat Rifle Squads," *Am. Psychologist*, 1953, VIII, 333.
[14] Lauren G. Wispe, "A Sociometric Analysis of Conflicting Role-Expectations," *Am. J. Sociol.*, 1955, LXI, 134–137.

But the important thing to note is that in these studies the three factors, which I shall call "activity," "task ability," and "likeability," are not, in general, mutually exclusive: a high standing on one does not preclude or interfere with a high standing on the other. Nor are they mutually supportive in general but, rather, they tend to be uncorrelated.

The fact that they are uncorrelated in general does not necessarily mean, of course, that there are no dynamic relationships between the phenomena represented by the factors. It means that there is no simple linear relationship that tends to be found over all populations, so that knowing where a man stands on one does not allow for a prediction of his standing on either or both of the others. If there are dynamic relationships between the factors they must be more complicated, nonlinear, or circumstantial. What suggestions of relationship are there left?

THE HYPOTHESIS OF INDIVIDUAL DIFFERENCES IN OVERTALKING

Although it is not true that simply by talking a great deal does one guarantee a high rating on the quality of his ideas, it is still probably true that in groups of the sort we were studying it is very difficult to make a substantial contribution to the task without talking a great deal, especially in the first meeting, and overtalking may be resented by other members as a threat to their own status and a frustration of their own desire to talk. Results of other experimenters provided some findings that are congruent with this line of thought. Let

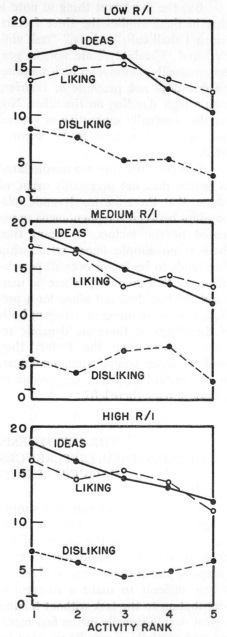

LOW R/I
20
IDEAS
15
LIKING
10
DISLIKING
5
0

MEDIUM R/I
20
IDEAS
15
LIKING
10
5
DISLIKING
0

HIGH R/I
20
IDEAS
15
LIKING
10
DISLIKING
5
0
1   2   3   4   5
ACTIVITY RANK

Figure 3. Average ratings * received on ideas, liking, and disliking by men of each activity rank, according to their feedback ratio (R/I). (Condensed from Robert F. Bales, "Task Status and Likeability as a Function of Talking and Listening in Decision-making

us look for a moment at some of these results.

Leavitt and Mueller [15] explored the effect of one-way communication in a restricted communication situation where the receiver of the information is given no opportunity to "feed back" acknowledgements, questions, or negative reactions to the sender. They find that an initial reaction of hostility toward the sender tends to appear.

Thibaut and Coules [16] find that receivers who are not permitted to communicate to a person who has sent them an act of hostility show less post experimental friendliness to the sender than those permitted to reply.

A peripheral position in a restricted network approximates in some ways the position of a receiver with no opportunity for feedback. In an experiment where members were allowed to communicate only in written form through set channels on a task of assembling information, Leavitt [17] finds that members in peripheral positions are less well satis-

[15] H. J. Leavitt and R. A. H. Mueller, "Some Effects of Feedback on Communication," *Hum. Relat.*, 1951, IV, 401–410.
[16] J. W. Thibaut and J. Coules, "The Role of Communication in the Reduction of Interpersonal Hostility," *J. Abnorm. & Soc. Psychol.*, 1952, XLVII, 770–777.
[17] H. J. Leavitt, "Some Effects of Certain Communication Patterns on Group Performance," *J. Abnorm. and Soc. Psychol.*, 1951, XLVI, 38–50.

Groups," in Leonard D. White [ed.], *The State of the Social Sciences* (Chicago: University of Chicago Press, 1956, pp. 148–161).

* Each entry at a given activity rank is the mean for ten persons. The idea index is not actually a rating, but an index obtained by adding rankings received (including self-rankings) and subtracting the total from the highest possible, 25. The like and dislike indexes are average ratings, with the highest possible, 28.

fied with their jobs than those in central positions.

These results suggested to us that the relatively low average of likeability preferences received by top participators might be due to the presence of some men in the total population of top men who overtalk, in the sense that they do not allow an appropriate amount of feedback of objections, qualifications, questions, and countersuggestions to occur. Our method of observation allowed us to examine the amount of interaction a given man received in relation to the amount he initiated. We thus arrived at the hypothesis that the ratio of interaction received to that initiated might help distinguish between those top interactors who were proportionately well liked and those who were not.

In general, as has been indicated, activity, task-ability ratings, and liking ratings appear in many studies as orthogonal factors, uncorrelated with each other over the total population assessed. It is important to recognize, however, that subparts of a population, or a different population, may show the variables related in a different way. It is the possibility that subparts of our population may show different relationships of these variables that we now explore.

We first make a basic division of the population according to the rank of each person within his own group on the gross amount of participation he initiated and call this his activity. Five ranks are thus recognized, since the groups were five-man groups.

The second division of the population is made within each rank. All the men of each rank are divided into three subpopulations according to their own ratio of amount of participation received from others to the amount of participation they initiate. This ratio is known as the R/I, or the feedback ratio. Within each rank, then, there are three subpopulations of ten men each, low, medium, and high on the feedback ratio.

Figure 3 shows the average values of ratings or ranking received for each of the subpopulations of ten men on liking, disliking, and ideas. The ratings or rankings were given to each man by his four fellow group members and have been converted for plotting in such a way that high numbers mean high average rankings received.

The point of greatest interest is the difference in the relations of liking to activity when the feedback ratio is taken into account. Figure 3 indicates that among the third of the population with a low feedback ratio, the top two men seem definitely lower than would be expected if liking received increased linearly in proportion to activity. The correlation between activity and liking received is near zero.

However, both the medium R/I and the high R/I thirds show a positive correlation. From these data it is still plausible to suppose that the top man even in the high R/I third shows a little less liking received than one would expect. But the effect is slight.

The data obtained by asking about dislikes present essentially the same picture. The highest participators among the third of the population with the lowest feedback ratio not only are less well liked but are more disliked than their less active colleagues in the same subpopulation. In this third of the population, the more the person talks, the more he is disliked. But in the opposite third of the population, those who have a high feedback ratio, there is no relation between how much a man talks and how much he is disliked.

With regard to idea rankings received, there is a definite indication that the highest participators in the third of the population with the low feedback ratio tend to suffer on idea rankings received, as they do on liking received, although the effect is not so marked. This effect seems to disappear completely in the medium R/I and high R/I groups.

It is plain, however, that there is an appreciable linear correlation between activity and idea rankings received over the total of the three subpopulations. This finding thus differs from other studies which find these two variables to be generally orthogonal. We attribute the correlation in our groups at least partly to the fact that we are dealing in this study with data from first meetings entirely. Data on groups running over four sessions indicate that this correlation tends to fall over time, especially in groups where the initial consensus as to who has the best ideas is low.[18] The correlation between ideas and liking also tends to fall as indicated above in Table 1. In short, the three factors tend to separate out as independent more clearly in later meetings than in the first.

To summarize briefly: In the groups in this total sample there is only a weak correlation between liking received and activity, providing one makes no breakdown into subpopulations. But for about one third of the population there is a positive and linear correlation between how much a man talks and how well he is liked. This is the third, who receive

[18] Philip E. Slater, "Role Differentiation in Small Groups," *Am. Sociol. Rev.*, 1955, XX, 300–310.

more interaction in proportion to the amount they initiate, that is, who have a high feedback ratio. The falling-off of liking received among the individuals who talk the most in total population is attributable especially to the other extreme third of the population, who talk proportionately most above the amount they receive. The same may be said for their rankings.

CONCLUSION

It appears that activity, task-ability ratings, and likeability ratings should be treated as three distinct factors, since over a large population of members, meetings, and groups they tend to be uncorrelated with each other. If one accepts this assumption a simple and very useful classification of role types in small groups suggests itself.

1. A member who is high on all three of the factors corresponds to the traditional conception of the good leader, or the "great man." Such men are found, but, if the factors are uncorrelated, are rare.

2. A member who is high on activity and task-ability ratings but less high on likeability is a familiar type who may be called the "task specialist." This type is not so rare as the first type and may operate effectively in cooperation with the third.

3. A member who is high on likeability but less high on activity and task ability may be called the "social specialist." This type is much less rare than the first type and groups which operate under the dual leadership of a man of this type and of the second type are common.

4. A member who is high on activ-

ity but relatively low on task ability and likeability ratings may be called an "overactive deviant." This type is not rare. This is the person who, in the leadership literature, is said to show "domination" rather than "leadership."

5. A member who is low on all three may be called an "underactive deviant" and may indeed be a kind of scapegoat. On the assumption that the factors are uncorrelated this type should be as rare as the first type, but since the lack of correlation traces mainly to discrepancies at the upper end of the scales, this type is not actually so rare as the first type and is, in fact, probably very common.

Logically, of course, one can distinguish many additional types. Those mentioned, however, have a certain intuitive distinctness and for present purposes serve to summarize and harmonize the various views on role differentiation that have been examined in this paper.

33. SOCIAL STATUS IN JURY DELIBERATIONS *

Fred L. Strodtbeck, Rita James Simon, and Charles Hawkins

Occupational specialization has two distinguishable effects. First, it increases productivity and, second, it provides the basis for a status hierarchy. Perhaps it is less commonplace to think that role differentiation in face-to-face groups arises from a similar economic process and results in similar status differences. For groups to define and achieve their goals, however, they must control the use of their primary-group resource—their common time together. Only one or, at most, a few persons can talk at any given instant and be understood. Who talks and how much he talks is, within limits, determined by the reactions of the group to the speaker. Acts that are perceived as relevant to the solution of the group's problems are generally favorably received and the responsible speaker is encouraged to continue. In the long run participation tends to become differentiated, and a small fraction of the group's members will account for most of the participation.

For the purposes of the present study which inquires into the relationships between occupation and selected aspects of role differentiation, it is desirable that the focus of the small-group discussion is not too narrowly circumscribed by status prerogatives. For example, a group of officers and enlisted men discussing military problems or a group of doctors and nurses discussing a medical problem would not provide the circumstance we require. A greater presumption of equality is desired.

In the jury situation not only does the widespread norm assume that group members should act toward one another as equals, but the presumption of equal-

* Revised from a version prepared especially for *Readings in Social Psychology* by E. E. Maccoby, T. M. Newcomb, and E. L. Hartley (Eds.), New York: Holt, Rinehart and Winston, 1958. This article reports one phase of experimental jury investigations conducted under the sponsorship of the Ford Foundation.

ity is reinforced by the requirement that the verdict be unanimous. Equal and responsible participation in the deliberation, therefore, is an institutionalized expectation. If evidence indicates that the status differences of the larger community become manifest during the deliberation, then it may be expected that a similar generalization of status will be found in other situations of interaction where hierarchical considerations are more prominent.

It is essential for our study that wide background differences be present within the juror population. This is assured in metropolitan areas such as Chicago, St. Louis, and Minneapolis where our experimental jury research has been conducted since jurors are selected here by a random process from voting-resistration lists. The resultant jury-pool population compares closely with the expected population computed from census reports, although the professions and very low education and occupation groups are slightly underrepresented.

Occupations are classified in four groups: proprietor, clerical, skilled, and labor. "Proprietor" includes the census category [1] of proprietors, managers and officials as well as professionals such as architects, accountants, and engineers who are not excluded from service. "Clerical" and "skilled" categories correspond to the census categories and "labor" subsumes the census categories of semiskilled workers, nonfarm laborers, and servants. Farm owners and laborers are absent from our populations, and

retired persons have been classified by their occupations prior to retirement. Women are classified by their stated occupations, except that housewives are classified by their husbands' occupations.

Previous studies indicate that power and participation in face-to-face situations are related to status. Caudill [2] observed the daily exchange of information at administrative conferences among the staff of a small psychiatric hopsital and found that the relative participation by the director of the service, the residents, the head nurse, the nurses, and the occupational therapist were ordered by their statuses in the hospital, even though the lower-status persons ordinarily spend more time with the patients. Torrance [3] used nonmilitary problems but found that pilots, navigators, and gunners recognized a power hierarchy in the contrived situation which paralleled that ordinarily in effect in airship operation. Strodtbeck [4] demonstrated that the greater economic and religious power of Navaho in contrast with Mormon women was reflected in their greater power in husband-wife decision-making. More pertinent, perhaps, is a study [5] relating to the continuation in jury deliberations of a strong emphasis by women on expressive and integrative

---

[1] Alba M. Edwards, *Bureau of the Census Alphabetical Index of Occupations by Industries and Social-Economic Groups* (Washington, D.C.: Department of Commerce, 1937).

[2] William Caudill, *The Psychiatric Hospital as a Small Society* (Cambridge, Mass.: Harvard University Press, 1957).

[3] E. P. Torrance, *Some Consequences of Power Differences on Decision Making in Permanent and Temporary Three-Man Groups,* "Research Studies," XXII (Pullman: State College of Washington, 1954), pp. 130–140.

[4] F. L. Strodtbeck, "Husband-Wife Interaction over Revealed Differences," *Am. Sociol. Rev.,* 1951, XVI, 141–145.

[5] F. L. Strodtbeck and R. D. Mann, "Sex Role Differentiation in Jury Deliberations," *Sociometry,* 1956, XIX, 3–11.

acts. The components that had been found descriptive of women's roles in family-interaction situations were found to characterize women's roles in jury deliberations.

It is important to stress that while the related studies are consistent insofar as they suggest a parallel between generalized status and status in face-to-face systems, they do not provide a firm basis for generalizing to the situation at hand, at least in terms of the measure of correspondence. In Torrance's experiment the pilots probably dominated to a lesser degree in the experimental situation than they would have when the airship was in operation. While the ordering was preserved, it was undoubtedly attenuated. In the present case, what differences are to be expected? The relation between roles like pilot and gunner or clerical worker and laborer is not equally clear in the interaction differences they imply. There is no compelling reason to believe that clerical workers and laborers will have had sufficient experience together to evolve a stable pecking order. Furthermore, once the jurors have completed their deliberations, they do not expect a continued relationship that would provide an opportunity for external status differences to become manifest. If status differences are present in the jury room, it is almost certain that they arise in part because the varied requirements of the deliberation re-create within the jury the need for the differential experiences associated with status. Whether or not the differences which stem from the external system are great enough to become apparent in a one- to two-hour deliberation is the empirical question we seek to answer.

SOURCE OF DATA

Mock jury deliberations were conducted in which the participants were jurors drawn by lot from the regular jury pools. The jurors listened to a recorded trial, deliberated, and returned their verdict—all under the customary discipline of bailiffs of the court. The jury deliberations were recorded, fully transcribed, and scored in terms of interaction-process categories.

This paper is based primarily upon 49 deliberations for which interaction-process analysis has been carried out. Two civil trials were used as the basis for the deliberations. In the first (29 deliberations) the plaintiff, a secretary, sought compensation for injuries incurred in a two-car collision. In the second (20 deliberations) a young child sought compensation for facial disfigurement incurred in a fire alleged to have been caused by a defective vaporizer. A total of 49 by 12, or 588, different jurors were involved. Data on 14 additional vaporizer cases and 28 recent experimental trials are utilized in other portions of the paper. In total data from 91 juries are used in the examination of different status effects.

PROCEDURES

Selecting a Foreman

After the jury listened to the case, they were told to select their foreman and begin their deliberation. In more than half of the deliberations, the foreman was nominated by one member and then quickly accepted by the remainder of the group. In about a third

TABLE 1. OCCUPATIONAL STATUS
OF 49 JURY FOREMEN

Occupation	Expected *	Observed	Index
Proprietor	9.73	18	185
Clerical	15.03	15	100
Skilled	9.56	8	84
Labor	14.68	8	54

* Computed under assumption that foremen will be proportional to portion of sample in the given occupation.

of the deliberations the man who opened the discussion and sought either to nominate another, or to focus the group's attention on their responsibity in selecting a foreman, was himself selected foreman. However, in all instances the selection of a foreman was quickly and apparently casually accomplished. There was no instance in which mention of any socioeconomic criteria was made, but this is not to say that socioeconomic criteria were not involved. For example, Table 1 shows that some foremen were selected from all strata, but the incidence was three and a half times as great among proprietors as among laborers. In addition, although the details are not given in the table, tabulations show that only one fifth as many women were chosen foreman as would be expected by chance.

Relative Participation

The deliberations were recorded with two microphones to facilitate binaural identification of individual participants. The protocols were fully transcribed, and from the protocol each speaker's contributions were separated into units of discrete action, each of which is roughly the equivalent of a simple declarative sentence. Identification of the speaker was checked with the original observer's notes, and an assistant tabulated the scores with the aid of the recording plus indications of nonverbal gestures made by the original observer.

Since there were 12 persons in the jury, one twelfth of the total acts is the pro-rata percentage for each juror's acts. This provides the base line against which the effects of external status may be appraised. The higher the average participation of an occupational group, the greater their relative share of the common resource of time. It may be seen in Table 2 that in all occupations males talked more than females and the amount of participation was sharply differentiated between higher than expected values for proprietors and clerical workers, and lower than expected values for skilled and unskilled laborers.

While the moderately differing values in Table 2 are averages based upon the scores of more than 500 persons, within any particular deliberation there was a very steep differentiation between the most- and least-verbal jurors. For example, in 82 percent of the juries the top three participators accounted for one half or more of the total acts, while the remaining acts were distributed among the other nine members. It is to be emphasized that the averages of Table 2 describe the relative participation of occupation and sex groups; they do not reflect the wide variation within any one jury.

One source of differences in participation within a jury may be attributed to the election of one member to play the role of foreman. The foreman was responsible for approximately one fourth of the total acts and as shown in Table 1

TABLE 2. PERCENTAGE RATES OF PARTICIPATION IN JURY DELIBERATION
BY OCCUPATION AND SEX OF JUROR

Sex	Occupation				
	Proprietor	Clerical	Skilled	Laborer	Combined
Male	12.9	10.8	7.9	7.5	9.6
	(N = 81)[a]	(N = 81)	(N = 80)	(N = 107)	(N = 349)
Female	9.1	7.8	4.8	4.6	6.6
	(N = 31)	(N = 92)	(N = 28)	(N = 62)	(N = 213)
Combined	11.8	9.2	7.1	6.4	8.5
	(N = 112)	(N = 173)	(N = 108)	(N = 169)	(N = 562)[b]

[a] Numbers of jurors are shown in parentheses.
[b] Twenty-six of 588 jurors from the 49 juries used were not satisfactorily classified by occupation and are omitted.

was more frequently selected from the higher-status groups. When foreman scores were eliminated the average-participation values were:

proprietor	8.9
clerical	7.0
skilled	6.3
labor	5.9

The gap between clerical and skilled workers is narrower but the rank order is unchanged.[6]

The latent premise in the study of participation is that high participation indicates greater ability to influence others. Earlier research supports such an interpretation for *ad hoc* problem-solving groups and for families. Further evidence is available from the present research. Jurors were asked before the deliberation what, if anything, they would award the plaintiff. In general,

the higher the socio-economic status of the juror, the lower the award. The relative magnitude of the awards in terms of an index number with the mean equal 100 is proprietor, 83; clerical, 92; skilled, 97; and laborer, 122. A detailed examination of individual pre-deliberation decisions with the subsequent group awards in 29 deliberations reveals that the more active jurors shifted their predeliberation position less often than less active jurors in the process of reaching a unanimous group verdict.[7] The relation between participation and influence by status level may be documented by comparing the average predeliberation award (listed according to occupational group) with the jury verdict. The correlations are:

proprietor	.50 ($p < .05$)
clerical	.11
skilled	.29
labor	.02

Members from the same occupational group sometimes initially favored differ-

[6] A further check was made on the effects of jury participation when another person of one's own occupation group was also present. For juries in which at least two of each occupational group are present, the values are quite similar to Table 2, and while there is some tendency for higher-status persons to talk more when they are alone, or in a marked minority, further corrections have minor effects.

[7] Allen Barton, *Persuasion and Compromise in Damage Awards*, December, 1956, unpublished manuscript.

TABLE 3. AVERAGE VOTES RECEIVED AS HELPFUL JUROR BY OCCUPATION AND SEX

Sex	Occupation				
	Proprietor	Clerical	Skilled	Laborer	Combined
Male	6.8	4.2	3.9	2.7	4.3
	(N = 113)	(N = 108)	(N = 115)	(N = 143)	(N = 479)
Female	3.2	2.7	2.0	1.5	2.3
	(N = 34)	(N = 116)	(N = 36)	(N = 76)	(N = 262)
Combined	6.0	3.4	3.5	2.3	3.6
	(N = 147)	(N = 224)	(N = 151)	(N = 219)	(N = 741)*

* This number includes 14 additional juries for which interaction process scores are not available.

ent verdicts, and in this case not all the members of this group achieved their desired outcome. Nonetheless, the correlation between the proprietors' average and the jury verdicts is significant. This result corresponds to the participation values after they have been corrected by eliminating the foreman. Since our content analyses clearly show that foremen were more neutral than other actively participating jurors during the discussion of monetary awards, the corrected participation values are probably a more satisfactory measure of influence in the damage-award deliberation.

The meaning of participation levels may be viewed from still another perspective. After the deliberation, the jurors were asked to answer a battery of questions concerning their personal satisfaction with the quality of the deliberation and the tone of interpersonal relations. The level of an individual's satisfaction was positively correlated with the level of his own participation $(r = .52, \ p < .05)$. The involvement that high participation represented in the jury is not unlike the involvement of higher-status people in the affairs of the larger community; both are instruments for group-derived satisfactions.

In addition, responses to the post-deliberation question, "Who do you believe contributed most to helping your group reach its decision?" were tabulated by occupation of the target person. The average number of helpfulness votes received by occupation groups (see Table 3) closely parallels the participation by occupation groups (see Table 2). The correlation between votes received and participation is about .69 when sets of individual values are correlated. Male clerical workers get slightly fewer votes than their participation would appear to warrant and male skilled workers get slightly more, but the overwhelming impression is that the number of such votes received, like participation, influence, and satisfaction, parallels status differentiation in society at large.

Perceived Fitness as Jurors

The Courts Martial reform, which permitted enlisted men to request other enlisted men for their trial panels, was largely nullified by their preference to leave their cases in the hands of officers. How do jurors react? A departure from random selection might have two possible effects. Given a choice, jurors might tend to overselect people in the higher occupations just as they had in distributing their helpfulness ballots. Or, taking the class theory as the basis of our prediction, we might assume that the chooser might select more jurors from his own occupation group. How these counter tendencies might be balanced is a question for which we have no theoretical answer and, therefore, must investigate empirically.

In an effort to probe deeper for evidence of class identifications, the following question was asked of 28 juries.

The jury pool is made up of people from all walks of life. However, if a member of your family were on trial and you had your choice, which of the following kinds of people would you prefer to make up the majority of the jurors who would hear your case?

———— business and professional people
———— clerical and white collar workers
———— skilled workers
———— unskilled workers

The expected values, determined by assuming that equal preference will be shown for each status group, have

been divided into the observed values, and the resultant ratio was multiplied by 100 to give the index numbers shown in Table 4. All groups, except laborers, would prefer to have a member of their family tried before a jury the majority of whose members were proprietors. Like other groups, laborers were also upwardly oriented in their preferences but their first choice was skilled workers, then proprietors. Clerical and skilled workers chose persons from their own occupation group as their second choice. All groups except laborers ranked laborers last. Laborers placed themselves third and clerks last. It is to be stressed that Table 4 represents the choice of jurors in terms of occupational stereotypes. It is what a member of one occupational group perceives in terms of his generalized conception of his own and other occupational groups.

We also asked jurors to choose "four of your fellow jurors whom you would best like to have serve on a jury if you were on trial." This question asks jurors not for generalized conceptions of other occupational groups but for evaluations of particular persons. We wished to know if the selections made on the basis of face-to-face contact were similar or different from stereotype

TABLE 4. CHOICE OF JUROR IF MEMBER OF RESPONDENT'S FAMILY WERE ON TRIAL, BASED UPON OCCUPATION STEREOTYPES
(Pro rata expected is 100) *

Respondent's Occupation		Preferred Occupation			
		Proprietor	Clerical	Skilled	Laborer
Proprietor	(N = 63)	241	95	51	13
Clerical	(N = 107)	206	112	71	11
Skilled	(N = 72)	172	55	139	33
Laborer	(N = 76)	126	42	147	84

* These data were collected from jurors in our 28 most recent experimental juries.

TABLE 5. CHOICE OF JUROR IF RESPONDENT WERE ON TRIAL,
BASED UPON DELIBERATION EXPERIENCE
(Pro rata expected is 100)*

Respondent's Occupation		Preferred Occupation			
		Proprietor	Clerical	Skilled	Laborer
Proprietor	(N = 78)	169	110	119	39
Clerical	(N = 129)	145	100	101	75
Skilled	(N = 74)	147	104	84	73
Laborer	(N = 130)	162	100	112	74

* The expected values used to form the index numbers have been determined by assuming that each person distributes his four choices simultaneously under conditions that give an equal chance of each of the 11 fellow jurors' being chosen.

choices.[8] If a prototype of a social system had grown during deliberation, jurors might come to regard one another more in terms of performance in the task at hand than in terms of general social status. It was also possible for the deliberation to reveal status-based ideologies that would open latent schisms. The data suggest that differences were ordinarily not magnified by the deliberation and the jurors came to be convinced that a just job had been done. The special thrust of the question "if a member of your family were on trial" could have sensitized jurors to think in terms of personal interests rather than abstract principles such as competence or justice. Possibly these respondents became so sensitive to their personal interests that they turned away from those jurors who had been the arbiters of consensus in their own deliberations.

Table 5 shows a preference for proprietors but at a somewhat lower level.

[8] The stereotype-juror preference question was not asked of the juries in Table 5. The 28 juries of Table 4 are an entirely different set, so that the possible bias of face-to-face choices by the prior administration of the stereotype choices is avoided.

More detailed effects of the face-to-face experience in contrast with the response to occupational categories may best be illustrated by subtracting Table 4 from Table 5. It is to be noted that while Tables 4 and 5 are based on different populations, the respondents in both cases are random samples from the population available in successive weeks in the jury pool. When Table 4 is subtracted from Table 5 (see Table 6) a positive value in the matrix represents an increase in index value associated with the face-to-face experience.

The main diagonal shows that "own group" choices were lower at each occupation level, particularly among proprietors and skilled laborers. That is, choices after the deliberation experience are not determined by a narrow "interest group." In addition, all values above the main diagonal are positive. That is, face-to-face experience caused lower-status persons to be evaluated more highly! As shown below the main diagonal, proprietors were reduced in the evaluation of clerical and skilled workers and increased in the evaluation of laborers; clerical workers were rated more highly by both skilled workers and laborers; and laborers decreased their former preference for skilled workers. The lower range of index values in the face-to-face situation arose in part from the effects of forcing the distribution of four votes among the 11 jurors who were members of the respondent's particular jury. Notwithstanding this flattening effect, it still appears that the face-to-face experience (1) results in fewer proprietor and skilled worker "own group" choices; and (2) brings the choice gradients into smoother conformity with the observed contribution of each status group to the deliberation.

DISCUSSION

Jury deliberations have been used to examine the intersection of occupational status and sex with the typically small-group measures of participation, influence, satisfaction, and perceived competence. The assumption that there is no relation between these modes of classification can be safely rejected. Men, in contrast with women, and persons of higher-status, in contrast with lower-status, occupations have higher participation, influence, satisfaction, and perceived competence for the jury task.

The present study does little to explain the cause of this differentiation.

Insofar as selection of the foreman may be taken as a guide to more general expectations concerning desirable attributes for the jury task, it appears that the foreman is expected to be a male, preferably a male of higher occupational status. Although we know of no empirical studies, we assume that the business discipline and related experiences of higher-status occupations involve both substantive knowledge and interactional skills that may be used during the deliberation. Hence, in the competition for the available deliberation time, higher-status males may rise to prominence because their comments are perceived to have greater value. On the other hand, since the cues of status—dress, speech, and casual references to experiences—are easily read, the differentiation may in part be explained by these expectations instead of actual performance.

Jurors who spoke at greater length were perceived by respondents to be the jurors desired if they were on trial. This finding suggests that whatever the criteria used by the groups to regulate the contributions of their members, these criteria were broadly held. The different distribution of speaking time was achieved without serious violation of developing group norms. Further, choices made after face-to-face experience, in

TABLE 6. CHANGE IN INDEX VALUE ASSOCIATED WITH DELIBERATION EXPERIENCE
(Value of Table 4 subtracted from Table 5)

Respondent's Occupation	Preferred Occupation			
	Proprietor	Clerical	Skilled	Laborer
Proprietor	−72	15	68	26
Clerical	−61	−12	30	64
Skilled	−35	49	−55	40
Laborer	36	58	−35	−10

contrast with those based on occupational stereotypes, tended to smooth into a gradient which paralleled both activity rates and status. These findings and others reported above constitute a preliminary clarification of the small-group process during a jury deliberation.

While our data do little to illuminate *how* differentiation arises, they show that status gradients emerge clearly in as brief a time as the one- or two-hour discussions under study. Although careful study will be required to determine the degree to which one may generalize from status in the larger social system to a particular interaction context, this demonstration of status continuity should be noted in any theory concerned with describing the process of status affirmation and maintenance.

34. THE MEANINGS OF OCCUPATIONAL PRESTIGE *

Joseph R. Gusfield and Michael Schwartz

Many studies have attempted to measure, describe or gauge the relative rankings of different occupations. Specialists in stratification have tried to find the various rungs of the occupational ladder in order to ascertain social mobility patterns. They have sought to understand the bases of occupational choice, exit, and self-respect. Of the many studies labelled "occupational prestige" or "occupational evaluation" the one conducted in 1947 by the National Opinion Research Center has remained the most influential. But what is being asserted when respondents rate occupations?

WHAT DO PRESTIGE SCALES SCALE?

Ratings scales, such as the NORC scale, can be focused upon at least four different dimensions of "occupational prestige." It is the major point of this paper (and the data that we will report) that rating scales have confounded these and have led to conclusions which assume that only one of the following dimensions has been used by the respondent.

1. The respondent's perception of social differentiation: Here the respondent is telling the investigator that some jobs are perceived as "better" than others, as he sees it. Lawyers get more than filling station attendants and the respondent recognizes this factual order of things.
2. The respondent's perception of others: This is the posture of the natural sociologist. Here the respondent reports on the system of his society. He tells us that whatever his own views or judgments, this is how jobs are ranked in his society. He displaces the professional sociologist.

In both of the above cases the emphasis is on the perception of the factual

* Excerpted from *American Sociological Review*, 1963, 28: 265–271, with permission of the senior author and the American Sociological Association.

order—this is how things happen here. It is by no means normative. It tells us little about his evaluation of jobs. The respondent may admit that doctors earn more money or command more prestige than do janitors but he need not evaluate this as acceptable, good or just. Veblen certainly saw that lawyers, clergymen and businessmen occupied honorific positions in American life. His irony was a way of saying that he thought honor was unjustly bestowed on occupations not worthy of it.

3. The prestige dimension *per se:* Here we attempt to find out what relative amounts of honor or respect are bestowed by the respondent on occupations. The normative aspect of prestige attribution suggests that some jobs, though they bring money and power, are degrading; others dignifying. Here we would try to see if the respondent does indeed follow such a process with respect to specific occupations.
4. The attribution of justice: Here we look at the normative order in its clearest form. This would represent the evaluation the respondent has of the rightness of the factual order and his conception of the just system. It would tell us whether or not respondents think doctors and lawyers *should* get more than machinists and salesmen.

It is worth noting that Centers found that approximately 45 percent of the urban working class and of both rural middle and working classes felt that doctors and lawyers made too much money. These occupations, which ranked very high in "occupational standing" were the highest in being judged as instances of overenrichment.[1]

[1] Richard Centers, *The Psychology of Social Classes: A Study of Class Consciousness*, Princeton: Princeton University Press, 1949, p. 142.

THE RELATION BETWEEN NORC SCALE RANKINGS AND SEMANTIC DIFFERENTIAL PATTERNS FOR FIFTEEN OCCUPATIONS

The above considerations set the stage for the study reported here. We wanted to find the imagery of the occupations and their relation to the NORC ratings. Specifically, we wished to determine whether occupations with high NORC ranks also received high ranks on (a) an evaluation scale, or (b) on a factual-normative, that is, descriptive, scale, or (c) on both scales or (d) on neither scale. The Semantic Differential[2] was selected as the most appropriate instrument, since it eliminates verbal fluency of the respondents as an intervening variable while it measures connotative meanings that respondents attribute to word concepts. In general, it is the connotative meanings attributed to occupations that remain uncontrolled. The Semantic Differential permits the measurement of that aspect of meaning. We wanted to know whether the meanings attributed to occupations of varying ranks are evaluative meanings in the "good-bad," "base-honorific" sense, or whether they are essentially factual-normative, reality-based, descriptive meanings. The Semantic Differential is composed of scales of polar-adjectives with seven points interposed between the adjectives, such as

Good: —: —: —: —: —: —: —: Bad

Respondents are asked to rate a word concept on each of these scales. Osgood

[2] Charles E. Osgood, George J. Suci and Percy H. Tannenbaum, *The Measurement of Meaning*, Urbana: University of Illinois Press, 1957.

has shown that different pairs of polarities are highly intercorrelated and that some of these pairs represent an evaluation dimension of meaning, other pairs, an activity dimension, and others a potency, or strength, dimension. We selected six items that have high factor loadings on the evaluation dimension from Osgood's thesaurus study: honest-dishonest, useful-useless, successful-unsuccessful, dirty-clean, sweet-sour, secure-insecure. From the remaining factors, we selected scales that are primarily reality-based descriptive ones. We have also constructed some new scale items for this purpose. These scales are: Middle class-Working class, Sober-Drunk, Democrat-Republican, Rural-Urban, Poor-Rich, Negro-White, Unemotional-Emotional, Young-Old, and Things oriented-People oriented. Finally, we selected some items that are rather ambiguous in that they have both evaluative and descriptive aspects. We refer to these as "mixed items." They are: Passive-Active, Religious-Irreligious, Masculine-Feminine, Foreign-American, Strong-Weak, Light-Heavy, and Tough-Tender.

The question with which we are concerned is the extent to which the rank of each mean scale value for each occupation is related to the rank of the occupation on the NORC scale, for example, is the highest ranked occupation also highest on each of the 22 scales, on some of them (and if so, which ones), or on none of them. If respondents rank occupations in terms of prestige in the evaluative sense, we would expect only the evaluative items to be related to the occupational ordering. On the other hand, if the respondents are in fact assuming the posture of the natural sociologist and are ordering occupations in

terms of the way others see it or are describing the factual order of things, then we would expect the group of descriptive items to be highly related to the occupational ordering. Finally, respondents may indicate that both sets of items, as well as the mixed type, are related to the occupational orderings, in which case we may speculate that "prestige" or "general standing" may be determined by more than one component.

An occupational rating questionnaire was administered to 337 students in sociology and architecture classes. The questionnaire was identical to the one used in the NORC study, but it included 34 of the 90 occupations. Three weeks later a Semantic Differential was administered to the same groups, using 15 of the 34 occupations as concepts to be judged on the 22 seven-point scales. The composition of the group of respondents is unimportant for our purposes here, since our sole interest is in the consistency between rank order of the 15 occupations on the NORC scale and rank order on the 22 scales. The 15 occupations, in the order of their rank in the sample on the NORC scale, is as follows: Scientist, lawyer, mayor, civil engineer, banker, building contractor, school teacher, radio announcer, farm owner, store manager, policeman, traveling salesman, locomotive engineer, plumber, and machine operator.

As we can see from this order, the results were similar to those reported in 1947 by North and Hatt. Professionals and people in authority ranked higher than farmers, salesmen and manual laborers. Each of the 22 scales yielded a rank order for the 15 occupations which varied to some degree from the rankings on the administered NORC scale. For

TABLE 1. TOTAL SAMPLE SEMANTIC DIFFERENTIAL RANKS (LOW TO HIGH)

Semantic Differential Scales *

Occupation	NORC Rank	D-C	P-A	Y-O	R-I	Usf-Usl	F-M	F-A	To-Te	So-Sw	W-S	S-Un	Un-EM	H-D	T-Pe	Mc-Wc	L-H	R-U	D-R	P-R	N-W	So-Dr	In-Se
Scientist	1	11	9	12	15	1	4	1	13	5	5	5	1	2	2	5	3	9	11	7	8	1	11
Lawyer	2	14	15	8	11	5	8	14	8	10	3	2	9	6	14	1	6	14	14	14	13	6	14
Mayor	3	12	12	14	3	10	9	15	9	11	7	3	12	14	13	3	8	15	8	13	15	4	10
Civil engr.	4	7	14	4	10	3	11	8	7	6	10	4	3	5	1	4	9	6	13	12	7	9	13
Banker	5	15	5	15	7	8	6	12	10	8	6	1	2	4	9	2	7	13	15	15	14	3	15
Bldg. contr.	6	5	13	6	12	6	13	6	4	4	12	6	8	9	7	6	10	7	12	11	11	10	9
School tchr.	7	13	7	5	2	2	1	10	15	15	1	8	15	1	15	8	1	3	7	11	4	2	12
Radio anncr.	8	10	6	1	13	14	3	13	14	14	4	9	14	8	11	7	4	11	9	9	9	12	3
Farm owner	9	4	11	10	1	4	14	7	3	9	15	7	10	3	5	11	14	1	5	6	6	5	8
Mgr. of store	10	8	3	9	8	13	2	4	12	12	3	10	11	11	9	9	5	10	10	5	10	8	5
Policeman	11	6	8	3	5	7	10	9	2	13	13	11	4	13	8	12	13	12	4	1	2	7	6
Trav. slsmn.	12	9	10	2	14	15	5	11	11	7	2	14	13	15	12	10	2	5	6	3	12	13	1
Loco. eng.	13	2	4	13	4	11	15	5	1	1	14	13	3	7	6	14	15	2	2	8	3	11	7
Plumber	14	3	2	11	9	9	12	3	6	2	11	12	6	10	3	13	11	4	3	2	5	14	4
Mach. opr.	15	1	1	7	6	12	7	2	5	3	9	15	7	12	4	15	12	8	1	4	1	15	2

* The scale abbreviations and meaning are listed below:

D-C = Dirty-Clean	To-Te = Tough-Tender	Mc-Wc = Middle class-Working class
P-A = Passive-Active	So-Sw = Sour-Sweet	L-H = Light-Heavy
Y-O = Young-Old	W-S = Weak-Strong	R-U = Rural-Urban
R-I = Religious-Irreligious	S-Un = Successful-Unsuccessful	D-R = Democrat-Republican
Usf-Usl = Useful-Useless	Un-Em = Unemotional-Emotional	P-R = Poor-Rich
F-M = Feminine-Masculine	H-D = Honest-Dishonest	N-W = Negro-White
F-A = Foreign-American	T-Pe = Things oriented-People oriented	So-Dr = Sober-Drunk
		In-Se = Insecure-Secure

TABLE 2. SPEARMAN RANK ORDER COEFFICIENTS BETWEEN OCCUPATIONAL RANKS
AND SEMANTIC DIFFERENTIAL RANKS

Scale No.	Description	Coefficient	Probability	Rank of rho
1	D-C	−.74	.005	6
2	P-A	−.70	.005	8
3	Y-O	−.20	.10	19
4	R-I	−.23	.10	17.5
5	Usf-Usl	+.60	.01	10
6	F-M	+.19	.10	20
7	F-A	−.40	.10	14.5
8	To-Te	−.40	.10	14.5
9	So-Sw	−.23	.10	17.5
10	W-S	+.24	.10	16
11	S-Un	+.92	.0005	2
12	Un-Em	+.13	.10	22
13	H-D	+.47	.05	12
14	T-Pe	−.18	.10	20
15	Mc-Wc	+.93	.0005	1
16	L-H	+.41	.10	13
17	R-U	−.48	.05	11
18	D-R	−.83	.0005	3
19	P-R	−.74	.005	6
20	N-W	−.62	.01	9
21	So-Dr	+.74	.005	6
22	In-Se	−.80	.0005	4

Twelve Scales Significant at .05 or Beyond

Group I high	Group II moderate
±.93 to ±.70	±.69 to ±.48

D-C (dirty-clean)	So-Dr (sober-drunk)
P-A (passive-active)	In-Sec (insecure-secure)
S-Un (successful-unsuccessful)	Use-Usl (useful-useless)
Mc-Wc (middle class-working class)	H-D (honest-dishonest)
D-R (Democrat-Republican)	R-U (rural-urban)
P-R (poor-rich)	N-W (Negro-white)

example, "manager of a store" ranked tenth among these 15 occupations in "general standing." It ranked eighth on the Dirty-Clean scale, third on the Passive-Active scale, and ninth on the Middle class-Working class scale. (Read left hand as the first rank. Thus, on the Passive-Active scale, the machine operator ranked first. This means he had the highest score for passivity of the 15 occu-

pations. The entire rank order for each occupation and for each scale is reproduced in Table 1.) Spearman rank order coefficients were computed between the rank order on each scale and the rank order on the NORC modified scale. Twelve of these were statistically significant at the .05 level or less. These were also the 12 with the highest correlations, ranging between .47 (Honest-Dishonest) to .93 (Middle class-Working class). The entire table of coefficients is reproduced in Table 2. Among these 12, six are from the factual-normative scales, five are evaluative scales and one is a mixed type. The high correlations of the Successful-Unsuccessful and Secure-Insecure evaluative scales on the one hand and the Middle class-Working class and Poor-Rich descriptive scales on the other hand, suggest circular reasoning may be at work. It is as if the respondent said, "In American society, lawyers, bankers and scientists are successful people and in the middle class. Therefore, they have a high general standing or *vice-versa*." This leads us to believe that the NORC scale did not reflect only a set of values applied to occupations but rather a set of perceptions about the social status which the occupations receive in the society (factual-normative) as well as a set of values. In short, they may reflect a justified factual-normative order of stratification. This interpretation is not unqualified. The moral designations do appear related to occupational rating. Honesty and usefulness are imputed to highly ranked occupations with more intensity than they are to the lower ranked occupations, although these scales showed only the tenth and eleventh highest correlations (.69 for Useful-Useless and .47 for Honest-Dishonest).

EVALUATION OF SPECIFIC OCCUPATIONS

Analysis of some specific occupations indicates the "mix" of different patterns tapped by the scaling instrument. Examining the scientist and the lawyer we can see some important dif-ferences between the occupations ranked first and second on our NORC scale. They both ranked among the top five in usefulness. The lawyer was identified as urban while the scientist was somewhere in the middle. Both were viewed as among the five least religious occupations, the scientist being the most irreligious. The scientist was clearly things-oriented and the lawyer clearly people-oriented. The scientist was seen as the least emotional and the lawyer as ninth least emotional. While both were among the five most secure (lawyer second and scientist fifth) the lawyer was viewed second richest (the banker was first) and the scientist as seventh. There is very little that we can designate as a common evaluative framework for these two occupations. The lawyer ranks fifth most useful while the scientist is seen as the most useful. The lawyer appears as a rich, powerful figure while the scientist is much less so but is highly useful.

The fact that a high-ranking occupation can be comparatively disesteemed is certainly seen when we look at the banker as well as the lawyer. The lawyer is viewed as sixth most honest. The banker ranks fifth on the NORC rating but is only the eighth most useful. Similarly traveling salesmen and plumbers rank 12 and 14 respectively, but the salesman has the lowest score for honesty and usefulness while the plumber's rating for honesty and for usefulness are above his NORC rank (10 and 9). The difference between descriptive and evaluative patterns is perhaps best seen in the case of the public school teacher. Here there is the sharpest contrast between elements of esteem and status, on the one hand, and those of power and income on the other. The teacher ranks as the second most useful occupation, the weakest, the most honest. He ranks seventh on the scale of general standing, a ranking close to his position on scales reflecting distribution of power and income—eighth most middle class and sixth richest.

CONCLUSIONS

The recent work of Reiss, *et al.*,[3] and of Kreisberg[4] also indicates the tenuousness of using NORC and other occupational rating scales in use as evidence of prestige or of the value accorded occupations. Using published and unpublished data from the original NORC study, Reiss found that considerations of "prestige" were seldom called into play in choosing an occupation, although respondents did report lack of prestige as one significant variable in deciding they might leave an occupation in the near future. They concluded, as Kreisberg also did, that "it is not clear that a 'prestige' component is consciously perceived as a reward attached to occupations." Respondents reported a number of criteria almost equally used as the "one main thing about such jobs that gives this standing." (Our results suggest there is far from one main thing.) In common with other studies, lower economic strata were more likely to emphasize the factual order and used

income and security. Higher strata were more likely to focus on self-expression and "prestige" in the Weberian sense of a separate dimension. Kreisberg's evidence bolsters our suggestion that respondents often act like natural sociologists. In keeping with our findings of a general set of terms used in ranking (Middle-Working class and Successful-Unsuccessful) Kreisberg found that the variable of prestige accorded professionals was the most significant variable in explaining rating of dentists. Other perceived characteristics of the occupation, such as degree of skill or the utility of dentists, were not as crucial as knowledge of a hierarchy in which professionals had a high rating. As Kreisberg wrote, "It may be that a person accords an occupation high prestige because he knows *as a matter of fact* that most persons accord members of that occupation high prestige."

Both these findings and ours suggest there is a distinct possibility that in the study of occupational prestige we are not getting only the system of evaluations which respondents may use in judging occupations. Either we obtain the descriptions of a factual order, in which the existent fact that A is a "better" job than B is recognized, or we may be confronted with a "pluralistic ignorance" in which each respondent assumes that the factual order is a reflection of the normative order which others, not himself, possesses. In either case the ratings emerge as descriptive rather than evaluative or ambiguously both. Kriesberg's suggestion that people learn prestige ratings apart from imputation of any qualities or moral judgments of specific occupations is in line with our reasoning. Our data lead us to con-

[3] Albert J. Reiss, Jr., Otis Dudley Duncan, Paul K. Hatt and Cecil C. North, *Occupations and Social Status*, New York: The Free Press of Glencoe, 1961, p. 41.

[4] Louis Kriesberg, "The Bases of Occupational Prestige: The Case of Dentists," *American Sociological Review*, 27 (April, 1962), pp. 238–244.

clude that future studies that require judgments of prestige be designed in a manner that will permit the investigator to designate the amount of variance explained by each of the component elements of the judgment.

But the point is more than peripheral and methodological. It cuts to the heart of a major issue in sociology. Recent criticisms of functional theory have pointed out the conflict between perspectives which emphasize the individuals' adaptation to facts of power in institutional arrangements. If we assume that description is evaluation, we unwittingly approve or condemn rather than analyze. We find congruence where none has been displayed.

35. PRESTIGE VS. EXCELLENCE AS DETERMINANTS OF ROLE ATTRACTIVENESS *

Eugene Burnstein, Robert Moulton, and Paul Liberty, Jr.

Individuals high in need-achievement have a strong internal push to excel. When an activity permits the demonstration of excellence, they are likely to be more attracted to it and out-perform low need achievers. If the activity is irrelevant to personal competence, the differences as a function of need-achievement tend to disappear. In fact under the latter conditions, when high productivity leads to an early escape from work, performance seems to be negatively related to achievement motivation.[1] This suggests that getting out of work has more appeal as achievement motivation decreases. Thus, individuals high in need-achievement desire activities which provide an unambiguous test of competence, while those low in need-achievement seem to avoid such a test. These latter individuals may be forced into striving for a "successful" situation in life, but at the same time they hesitate to approach positions which afford a clear, realistic assessment of their competence. Under these conditions individuals low in need-achievement may be attracted to activities which do not require excellence but do give the external appearance of "success," for example, occupations which confer high prestige but demand relatively little competence. As a first approximation, low achievement motivation may imply an other-directed person, highly impressed by the

[1] Elizabeth G. French, "Some Characteristics of Achievement Motivation," *Journal of Experimental Psychology*, 50 (October, 1955), 232–236.

* Excerpted from *American Sociological Review*, 1963, 28: 212–219, with permission of the senior author and the American Sociological Association. This study was in part supported by the School of Labor and Industrial Relations, Michigan State University. During much of the work the third author held a Predoctoral Research Fellowship from the National Institute of Health, United States Public Health Service.

positive evaluations of others, who tends to avoid tests of his capacities.[2]

This relation between need-achievement and striving has been noted outside the laboratory as well as in it. Thus, achievement motivation has been shown to be positively associated with social status,[3] mobility,[4] entrepreneurial activity,[5] and role aspirations.[6] For example, individuals high in achievement motivation are less likely to be defensive about their occupational future; they tend to have a higher level of aspiration and are less willing to settle for relatively unsatisfying occupational roles if the struggle for success could be foregone.

Nevertheless, achievement motivation, in and of itself, may not be sufficient to produce a stable and widespread predilection for difficult occupational roles. It is unlikely to provide adequate direction for achievement motivated performance (for example, need-achievement may be expressed through such nonvocational activities as sports and hobbies) nor is it likely to support the onerous choices which accompany occupational striving (for example, deciding that familial ties are secondary concerns). In considering the consequences of achievement motivation for social mobility, Rosen[7] has noted that the need-achievement can be expressed through a wide range of behavior, some of which may not facilitate social mobility. Even when expressed through vocational activity, the achievement motive may be directed into deviant occupations (for example, the criminal) or into low status vocations (for example, the individual whose achievement motivation is expressed and satisfied through his desire to be the best welder among his peers). Whether the individual will decide to seek success in situations which facilitate mobility in our society will, in part, be determined by his *values*. In a factor analysis of value-achievement

---

[2] David C. McClelland, John W. Atkinson, Russell A. Clark, and Edgar L. Lowell, *The Achievement Motive*, New York: Appleton-Century-Crofts, 1953, hold that the high need achiever has strongly internalized standards of excellence and is comparable to Riesman's inner-directed type. They reasoned, therefore, that conformity to the judgments and suggestions of others will decrease as achievement motivation increases. Their analysis of stories written by subjects in Asch's classic conformity experiment substantiated this hypothesis. However, more recent findings suggest that the relationship between conformity and achievement motivation depends on whether or not the person perceives the former as instrumental to achievement. See Franz Samuelson, "The Relation of Achievement and Affiliation Motives to Conforming Behavior in Two Conditions of Conflict with a Majority," in J. W. Atkinson, editor, *Motives in Fantasy, Action and Society*, Princeton, N.J.: Van Nostrand, 1958, pp. 421–433; Robert B. Zajonc and N. Kishor Wahi, "Conformity and Need-Achievement under Cross-Cultural Norm Conflict," *Human Relations*, 14 (August, 1961), 241–250.

[3] Bernard C. Rosen, "The Achievement Syndrome: A Psychocultural Dimension of Social Stratification," *American Sociological Review*, 21 (April, 1956), 203–211.

[4] Harry J. Crockett, Jr., "The Achievement Motive and Differential Occupational Mobility in the United States," *American Sociological Review*, 27 (April, 1962), 191–204.

[5] David C. McClelland, "Some Social Consequences of Achievement Motivation," in Marshal R. Jones, *Nebraska Symposium on Motivation*, 1955, Lincoln: University of Nebraska Press, 1955; D. C. McClelland, *The Achieving Society*, Princeton, N.J.: Van Nostrand, 1961.

[6] Charles H. Mahone, "Fear of Failure and Unrealistic Vocational Aspirations," *Journal of Abnormal and Social Psychology*, 60 (March, 1960), 253–261; Eugene Burnstein,

"Fear of Failure, Achievement Motivation and Aspiring to Prestigeful Occupations," *Journal of Abnormal and Social Psychology* (in press).

[7] Bernard C. Rosen, *op. cit.*

items,[8] Strodtbeck found that beliefs which (a) stress the possibility of rational mastery of the situation, and (b) sanction independence of, or separation from the family are positively related to indices of achievement striving, academic success, socio-economic status, Since similar relationships exist between such indices and need-achievement, it is likely that achievement values and achievement motivation also act jointly as determinants of achievement striving in the selection of role activities.

Prestige is rewarding to most individuals independent of need-achievement and value-achievement. Yet in a society containing a sufficient number of members with high achievement motivation and strong achievement values, prestige may be a *relatively unimportant* incentive for choosing certain occupational activities. For these individuals the correlation between the amount of competence required by an occupational role and its attractiveness should be markedly greater than the correlation between occupational prestige and attractiveness. On the other hand, the correlation between prestige and attractiveness among individuals low in need-achievement and value-achievement should be appreciably greater than that between required competence and attractiveness. Thus, at any level of prestige, occupational roles requiring a relatively high level of competence will be more attractive to individuals high in achievement motivation and achievement values than roles requiring a relatively low level of competence. Further-

more, the attractiveness of occupations which require a high level of competence should be greater for these individuals than those low in achievement motivation and achievement values, who are not differentially attracted as a function of excellence. However, in order to test these hypotheses a representative sample of occupations is needed in which prestige is unrelated, or at least only weakly related to required competence. As the correlation between prestige and excellence increases, it becomes more difficult to separate their independent effects on role attractiveness. But, given a sample of occupations covering a broad range of prestige values, it is highly unrealistic to expect prestige and required competence to be independent of each other.

However, a small subset of occupations is likely to be present in which prestige is not commensurate with the degree of excellence required. When an appreciable discrepancy obtains between prestige and required competence, activities demanding a high degree of excellence relative to their prestige are likely to be more attractive to individuals high in achievement motivation and achievement values than activities which award a good deal of prestige relative to the excellence demanded. The reverse should be true for those weak in need-achievement and value-achievement.

RESEARCH PROCEDURE

The sample consisted of 116 undergraduate males in different sections of an introductory psychology course at the University of Texas. To measure achievement motivation, responses to

---

[8] Fred L. Strodtbeck, "Family Interaction, Values, and Achievement," in David C. McClelland, Alfred L. Baldwin, Urie Bronfenbrenner and Fred L. Strodtbeck, *Talent and Society*, Princeton, N.J.: Van Nostrand, 1958.

four Thematic Apperception Test type pictures were scored by a procedure that Atkinson and his associates have standardized,[9] in which the strength of achievement motivation is measured by the frequency of achievement imagery in the stories. Subjects with scores above the median were considered high in achievement motivation; those below the median were considered low. A month later a second experimenter administered a "Student Questionnaire." Subjects evaluated 17 occupations (see Table 1) and answered items relevant to achievement values.

The evaluations of occupations were made along three dimensions—occupational prestige, competence required by the occupation, and the attractiveness of the occupation. These evaluations were made in terms of the following questions: 1. "How pleased or disappointed would you be if you had the following occupations as an adult?" Six alternatives ranging from "highly pleased" to "highly disappointed" were given. 2. "All jobs have a certain amount of social standing or social prestige associated with them. Encircle the statement next to each job that indicates your own opinion of its social standing or prestige." Besides each occupation in this second listing, six alternatives were given ranging from "A job of the highest social standing" to "A job of poor social standing." 3. "All jobs differ in the amount of competence, that is, specialized training, ability, knowledge, and skill, they require. Encircle the statement that in-

dictates your own opinion of the amount of competence required by the particular job." Next to each occupation in this third listing were six alternatives ranging from "A job requiring an extremely high degree of competence" to "A job requiring almost no competence." In all three questions a score of "one" was given for the first alternative and a score of "six" for the last. No neutral categories were presented.

Two sets of items have been used in the past to assess achievement values. One set developed by deCharms [10] consists of nine items which must all be answered positively in order to be high in value-achievement. A second set used by Strodtbeck [11] consists of eight items, all but one of which must be answered negatively to be high in achievement values. A large body of research [12] has clearly shown that there is a general tendency based on stimulus properties of the item and on personality characteristics of the respondent to answer affirmatively or negatively *independent of the content of the item.*

This fact most likely accounts for

---

[9] See "Appendix I," in J. W. Atkinson, editor, *op. cit.*, pp. 685–734. The two independent scorers used in the present study had inter-judge reliability of .92 (product-moment correlation).

[10] Richard C. deCharms, H. William Morrison, Walter R. Reitman and David C. McClelland, "Behavioral Correlates of Directly and Indirectly Measured Achievement Motivation," in David C. McClelland, editor, *Studies in Motivation*, New York: Appleton-Century-Crofts, 1955.

[11] Fred L. Strodtbeck, *op. cit.*

[12] For example, see Charles Hanley, "Response to the Wording of Personality Test Items," *Journal of Consulting Psychology*, 23 (July, 1959), 261–265; Arthur Couch and Kenneth Keniston, "Yeasayers and Naysayers: Agreeing Response Set as a Personality Variable," *Journal of Abnormal and Social Psychology*, 60 (March, 1960), 151–174; Dean Peabody, "Attitude Content and Agreement Set in Scales of Authoritarianism, Dogmatism, Anti-Semitism, and Economic Conservatism," *Journal of Abnormal and Social Psychology*, 63 (July, 1961), 1–11.

TABLE 1. RANKING OF OCCUPATIONS IN TERMS OF THEIR REQUIRED COMPETENCE (C) AND THEIR PRESTIGE (P) BY INDIVIDUALS DIFFERING IN THEIR MOTIVATIONAL STRUCTURE (ACHIEVEMENT MOTIVATION AND ACHIEVEMENT VALUES) AND BY A NATIONAL SAMPLE (N.O.R.C.)

		Rank							
		High Achievement Motivation				Low Achievement Motivation			
		High Achievement Values		Low Achievement Values		High Achievement Values		Low Achievement Values	
Occupation	N.O.R.C. P	P	C	P	C	P	C	P	C
Physician	1	1	1	1	1	1	1	1.5	2
College professor	2	5.5	3	7.5	4	7	4	7	3
Banker	3	3	7	2.5	8.5	2.5	6	6	10
Minister	4	4	8.5	5	8.5	4	7.5	3	6
Chemist	6	7	4	6	3	6	3	8	4
Member of board of directors of large corporation	6	2	5	2.5	6	2.5	5	1.5	5
Nuclear physicist	6	5.5	2	5	2	5	2	5	1
Accountant	8	8	6	9	6	9	7.5	7	7
Novelist	9	9	10	7.5	6	8	9	9	8
Public school teacher	10	10	8.5	10	10	10	10	10	9
Undertaker	11	11	12	12	12	11	11.5	11	12
Mail carrier	12	14	13.5	14	16	13	14	14	14.5
Auto mechanic	13	13	11	13	11	14	11.5	13	11
Clerk	14	12	13.5	11	13	12	13	12	13
Taxi driver	15	16	15	16	15	15	15	15.5	16
Night watchman	16	15	16	15	14	16	16	15.5	14.5
Janitor	17	17	17	17	17	17	17	17	17

353

the positive correlation deCharms et al.,[13] obtained between their measure and the F-scale. It was decided to combine both the deCharms and the Strodtbeck items to form an approximately balanced scale of achievement values— ten items which must be answered positively and seven items requiring negative answers to be high in achievement values. Only those who were high (above the median) on *both* the deCharms and the Strodtbeck items were used as high value-achievement subjects while only those who scored low (below the median) on *both* sets of items were included as low value-achievement subjects. This provided a sample of 82 subjects who completed the occupational ratings and for whom adequate need-achievement and achievement value scores were available. For the purposes of analysis two subjects were discarded at random, so that the four subgroups, high achievement motivation-high achievement values, high achievement motivation-low achievement values, low achievement motivation-high achievement values, and low achievement motivation-low achievement values each contained 20 subjects.

RESULTS AND DISCUSSION

The representativeness of our sample may in part be determined by comparing their ratings of prestige with that made by a national sample. A rank order correlation of .96 obtains between our prestige ranking and that found by the National Opinion Research Center[14]

during the mid-1940's (see Table 1). In terms of their evaluation of occupational prestige our sample is in no sense deviant. The discrepancies that occur, for example, college professor, may be due to the sample's special familiarity with the occupation or to shifts in normative evaluations over time.

The rank order correlations between prestige and competence, .90, and between prestige and attractiveness, .92, suggest that (a) prestige inequalities correspond to differences in the level of excellence required by the roles, and (b) such inequalities may induce individuals to strive for the more prestigeful roles, that is, they increase the attractiveness of the more prestigeful roles. Given the strong association between prestige and competence, it is not possible to separate the independent effects of these factors on role attractiveness for the total sample of occupations. However, an examination can be made of the two sets of rankings to select a subset of occupations whose positions in regard to prestige are not commensurate with their positions in regard to competence. In selecting such occupations the following criteria were used: An occupation with high prestige relative to its required competence is one whose prestige rank is 2.5 or more positions higher than its competence rank *in all four conditions.* An occupation with high required competence relative to its prestige is one whose competence rank is at least 2.5 positions higher than its prestige rank *in all four conditions.*

[13] Richard C. deCharms, H. William Morrison, Walter R. Reitman and David C. McClelland in David C. McClelland, editor, *op. cit.*

[14] National Opinion Research Center, "Jobs and Occupations: A popular Evaluation," in Reinhard Bendix and Seymour M. Lipset, editors, *Class, Status and Power: A Reader in Social Stratification*, New York: The Free Press, 1953.

TABLE 2. MEAN ATTRACTIVENESS OF OCCUPATIONS LOW IN PRESTIGE RELATIVE
TO REQUIRED COMPETENCE AND HIGH IN PRESTIGE RELATIVE TO REQUIRED COMPETENCE
FOR INDIVIDUALS WITH DIFFERENT MOTIVATIONAL STRUCTURES

Motivational Structure of the Individual	Low Prestige-High Competence Occupations	High Prestige-Low Competence Occupations
High achievement motivation High achievement values	1.82* (a)	3.46 (b)
High achievement motivation Low achievement values	2.98 (c)	3.10 (d)
Low achievement motivation High achievement values	3.03 (e)	2.87 (f)
Low achievement motivation Low achievement values	3.68 (g)	2.03 (h)
Differences in attractiveness	(a) − (b) = − 1.64 (e) − (f) = 0.16 (c) − (d) = − 0.12 (g) − (h) = 1.65	

* 1 = a job of the highest attractiveness.
6 = a job of the lowest attractiveness.

Three occupations fall within each of these categories. Member of the board of directors of a large corporation (mean prestige rank of 2.1, and a mean competence rank of 4.9, across all four conditions), banker (mean prestige rank of 3.5 and mean competence rank of 7.9), and clergyman (mean prestige rank of 4.0 and mean competence rank of 7.6) were perceived in all four conditions as occupations with high prestige relative to the competence required. Nuclear physicist (mean prestige rank of 5.1 and mean competence rank of 1.8), chemist (mean prestige rank of 6.8 and mean competence rank of 3.5), and college professor (mean prestige rank of 6.8 and mean competence rank of 3.5) were perceived in all four conditions as requiring a good deal of competence relative to the prestige they confer.

The mean attractiveness ratings of these two sets of three occupations are presented in Table 2. It was hypothesized that individuals high in achievement motivation and achievement values are more attracted by the low prestige-high competence occupations than by the high prestige-low competence occupations while individuals low in need-achievement and value-achievement are more attracted by the latter than by the former. In terms of the scoring of attraction, that is, the higher the attraction, the lower the numerical value assigned, the difference in attractiveness between the sets of occupations (low prestige-high competence minus high prestige-low competence), should tend to be some negative value for individuals high in achievement motivation and achievement values and some positive value for individuals low in achievement motivation and

TABLE 3. ANALYSIS OF VARIANCE OF DIFFERENCES IN ATTRACTIVENESS OF HIGH PRESTIGE-LOW COMPETENCE AND LOW PRESTIGE-HIGH COMPETENCE OCCUPATIONS

Source of Variation	df	Mean Square	F
Achievement values (V)	1	110.59	16.12*
Achievement motivation (M)	1	27.83	4.06**
V × M	1	1.39	—
Within groups	76	6.86	—
Total	79		

* Significant at the .01 level of confidence.
** Significant at the .05 level of confidence.

achievement values (the mean differences are presented at the bottom of Table 2). An analysis of variance of the difference scores in the four conditions confirm this prediction. A summary of the analysis is presented in Table 3. The difference in attraction to the two sets of occupations is significant as a function of both achievement motivation and achievement values. In addition, t-tests of the attractiveness rating given to the low prestige-high competence set versus that given to the high prestige-low competence set within each condition indicates that high need achievers-high value achievers are more attracted to the low prestige-high competence occupations ($t = 2.56$, $p < .05$) while low need achievers-low value achievers are more attracted to the high prestige-low competence occupations ($t = 2.73$, $p < .05$). The differences within the other two subgroups did not approach significance. The shift in attraction as a function of our motivational antecedents can be easily seen if the proportions of individuals within each condition who rate the low prestige-high competence set as more attractive, equally attractive, or less attractive than the high prestige-low competence set are examined. Table 4 demonstrates that as achievement motivation and achievement values increase in strength, the preference for occupations demanding a high level of excellence increases.

The findings, thus, indicate that *both* the excellence demanded by a role and the prestige conferred by a role may act to increase role attractiveness and presumably, the striving for role attainment. However, the relative strength of these incentives depends on the motivational structure of the members of the role system. A system containing a sufficient number with high achievement motivation and strong achievement values may not have to rely on prestige inequalities to promote and guide role striving. The challenge of the role will in part perform these functions.

Of course, there are certain dysfunctional potentials. Roles that demand a high level of excellence tend to increase in importance and may also increase in prestige. They thereby become attractive both to individuals high in their need for achievement and those high in their need for prestige. Over time, as importance and prestige increases, concomitant innovations in technology and social organization may reduce the level

TABLE 4. PERCENT OF INDIVIDUALS WITH DIFFERENT MOTIVATIONAL STRUCTURES
WHO ARE MORE ATTRACTED BY A ROLE'S REQUIRED COMPETENCE THAN
BY ITS PRESTIGE (c > p), EQUALLY ATTRACTED BY BOTH (c = p),
AND MORE ATTRACTED BY ITS PRESTIGE THAN BY ITS
REQUIRED COMPETENCE (c < p)

Motivational Structure of the Individual	Attractiveness of Competence vs. Attractiveness of Prestige		
	$C > P$	$C = P$	$C < P$
High achievement motivation High achievement values	55%	25%	20%
High achievement motivation Low achievement values	30%	15%	55%
Low achievement motivation High achievement values	35%	30%	35%
Low achievement motivation Low achievement values	20%	5%	75%

of excellence required. The outcome of such a process would be a decrease in the attractiveness of important and formerly desirable roles for individuals with high achievement motivation and strong achievement values. Such a state of affairs could be quite disruptive for a social system containing a large number of such members. Nevertheless, in terms of the present analysis, whether or not prestige differences are necessary for an adequate allocation of members to roles depends on the prevalence of individuals who are high in achievement motivation and achievement values. With a sufficient number of such people, prestige distinctions become an unnecessary inequality.

36. ROLE PLAYING VARIATIONS AND THEIR INFORMATIONAL VALUE FOR PERSON PERCEPTION *

Edward E. Jones, Keith E. Davis, and Kenneth J. Gergen

Largely under the impetus of Heider's (1944, 1958) persistent concern with phenomenological analysis, much of the recent research in social perception has addressed itself to the naive psychology of the individual perceiver. How do in-

* Reprinted from *Journal of Abnormal and Social Psychology*, 1961, 63: 302–310, with permission of the senior author and the American Psychological Association. This research was conducted under Grant 8857 from the National Science Foundation.

dividuals use the behavior of others to infer the probable existence of more enduring personal characteristics? What are the bases for social evaluation that in turn color the impressions one forms of another? What information is ignored and what information is made central in the formation of an impression? A number of investigators have sought a partial answer to these questions by assuming that a basic feature of naive phenomenology is the assignment of observed behavior to psychological causes. It seems logical to propose, for example, that behavior whose locus of causation lies within the person is more relevant to inferences about his particular characteristics than behavior that is induced or constrained by external events. The present investigation was designed to demonstrate this proposition with specific reference to the adoption and performance of social roles.

The concept of role has had a lively and controversial history in the literature of social science. It is often treated as a crucial bridging concept since it concerns the relations between social requirements and normative expectations on the one hand, and individual perceptions and behavior on the other. Controversy has surrounded the many attempts to define role, as Levinson (1959) notes, because these attempts have vacillated between viewing role as an aspect of social structure and viewing it as a description of socially relevant individual behavior. In the present paper, the concept of role refers to role demands rather than actual behavior. Role is herein treated as a set of expected behaviors implicit in the instructions to a stimulus person. These instructions define the impression the stimulus person should attempt to create in presenting himself

to an interviewer, and variations in behavior given this role definition represent the major independent variable.

The present treatment of role is quite consistent with any other treatment that stresses the shaping of individual responses by social expectations or externally imposed norms. The point has often been made that general adherence to relevant sets of social norms is very important in facilitating social interaction. Particularly in organizational contexts, but by no means exclusively there, many social interactions can be effectively described in terms of the interplay of appropriate role behaviors. Jones and Thibaut (1958) have emphasized the economic significance of such interactions between roles as reducing the need for inferences about idiosyncratic personal characteristics. The complement of this point is that behavior appropriate to role expectations has little informational value in highlighting these individual characteristics.

To follow this line of reasoning a little further, roles facilitate interaction and the social cognitions that support it. The naive person has his own repertory of role constructs that help to anchor his perceptions of the social environment and to endow it with the necessary stability for planful action. On the other hand, the performance of social roles tends to mask information about individual characteristics because the person reveals only that he is responsive to normative requirements. If these requirements are unclear or conflicting, of course, he may reveal something about himself by the way in which he defines and displays appropriate behavior. The stronger and more unequivocal the role demands, however, the less information is provided by behavior appropriate to the role. Following our introductory comments, this conclusion may be derived from considering probable differences in the attribution of phenomenal causality. When a person's behavior is very much in line with clear and potent social expectations, we tend to treat it as externally caused and uninformative with regard to a wide range of personal characteristics. When it departs from normative expectations, on the other hand, we tend to locate the cause for the departure in motivational forces peculiar to the person. We may assume, of course, that he misperceived the expectations, but we would then wish to push on to determine the motivational sources of this perceptual distortion.

From the perceiver's point of view, the behavior of a stimulus person which departs from role expectations takes on special significance for appraising the latter's personal characteristics. In assessing the motives behind such a departure from role, the perceiver must view the sample of behavior available against the background of role specifications. In general, our inferences from behavior to personality must take into account the stimulus conditions eliciting the behavior. This is no less true when the stimulus conditions consist of clearly established role expectations.

In attempting to predict the nature and direction of inferences, given a sample of behavior that departs from role expectations, a number of factors must be considered. For one thing, there may be tendencies for the perceiver either to minimize or maximize the nature of the departure. In organizing his impression of the stimulus person, the perceiver may assimilate the latter's behavior sample to the role specifications governing the situation, thus, avoiding

the problem of inferring unique characteristics. Alternatively, there may be a contrast effect in that the behavior sample becomes cognitively salient and is recalled as departing even more from the role than was actually the case. We are not as yet in a position to choose between these alternative possibilities, or to specify the conditions favoring assimilation versus contrast. The present study does provide a measure of memory distortion, however.

Assuming that assimilation does not occur, or that it occurs incompletely, the perceiver's inferences about unique characteristics rest on his attempt to understand *why* the departure from role expectations took place. Undoubtedly, some departures are intended to achieve a humorous effect (the exchange of "friendly insults" between collaborators on a task); others are intended to play down role characteristics that might be offensive (the "soft-selling" salesman); still others stem from motives of rebellion and nonconformity. In the typical case, however, departure from role suggests a pattern of motivation and skill that is at variance with specific role requirements. The individual does not play the role because, somehow, he cannot or will not. In such cases, personality seems to override role expectations or to color role performance in a unique and significant way. The most probable inference from role departures of this type is that the person reveals something of his "true self" through his failure to perform the expected role.

The present investigation treats this last conjecture as a proposition. An experiment was designed in which stimulus persons were instructed in one of two patterns of role performance. The behavior of the stimulus person was arranged to be consistent with either the first or the second of these patterns, thus, creating two experimental treatments where the person's behavior was "in role" and two treatments where it was clearly "out of role." The general hypotheses prompting the study were:

1. Persons performing in line with role expectations reveal little of value for assessing their personal characteristics. When asked to describe such a person, subjects do so with little confidence and tend to avoid extreme statements.

2. Persons whose performance departs from role expectations reveal their personal characteristics through the direction and form of this departure. Their behavior is judged as internally caused and forms the basis for direct inferences about personal characteristics, characteristics that may be judged with confidence.

3. Roles do, however, serve as an organizing function in person perception. Because of its predictive value, in-role behavior is more accurately recalled than behavior that departs from role expectations.

Note that no specific hypothesis was formulated concerning the possibilities of assimilation and contrast, but data bearing on these possibilities are to be presented.

was made to assign approximately equal numbers of subjects to each condition. The actual cell frequencies varied from 31 to 37. As one attempt to control for individual differences in orientation to others, care was also taken to compose the treatment groups of approximately equal numbers of high, middle, and low scorers on Christie's Mach IV Scale. This scale was originally designed to measure differences in the tendency to endorse Machiavellian sentiments. A high score reflects a tough minded, cynical, and somewhat opportunistic attitude toward others; low scorers are more inclined to value affective involvement with others and to feel that social relations should be governed by strict ethical norms. A description of item content and some sampling comparison data may be found in Christie and Merton (1958). Studies by Jones and Daugherty (1959) and Jones, Gergen, and Davis (in press) provide data on the experimental validity of the scale. Though the present study was not designed to validate the Mach IV Scale, and the scale served mainly as a control variable, the Mach IV score was included as a potential source of variation in the analysis of data. It was felt that the highs and the lows might respond differently to the experimental conditions, though no specific hypotheses involving Machiavellianism were formulated.

METHOD

Subjects

One hundred and thirty-four male undergraduates participated as subjects in groups ranging in size from 5 to 20. Since the experimental design consisted of four treatment variations, an attempt

Procedure Overview

Each experimental session began with a brief introduction in which the experimenter described the study as a problem solving task involving judgments of another person. Subjects were instructed to listen carefully to a tape recorded interview between a psychologist and a student, in which the student would be instructed to play a particular role. The tape recording began with the psychologist giving explicit instructions to the stimulus person (SP) about the interview to follow. Although the recordings were actually based on carefully constructed scripts, an attempt was made to convince the subjects that the SP was given no information about the interview and his role that did not appear on the tape. Thus, the taped instructions emphasized that the SP was to present himself in the interview in such a way as to impress the interviewer that he was ideally suited for a particular job. In interviews played to different groups of subjects one of two jobs requiring radically different personal qualifications was described. In this way the content of the role was manipulated. The SP was told in the recording to "be as honest as you can unless you think another answer would help your chances better of getting the job." In the interview that followed, SP answered some standard questions about his background in a neutral fashion and then responded to a series of choice items some of which were clearly relevant to the job for which he was applying. In responding to these items, the SP either gave answers appropriate to the job description he had been given or answers which revealed markedly different preferences. Thus, the design involved presentation of four different stimulus patterns, two of which were "in-role" and two of which were "out-of-role."

After listening to the interview, each subject was asked to state his general impression of the SP and to fill out in succession the following dependent variable forms: given the same choice items to which the SP responded in the

interview, subjects were asked to reconstruct from memory SP's response to each item; after this choice test form was collected the subject was handed an identical form and instructed to indicate how the SP would have responded if he were being completely honest in describing himself; finally, each subject was given a 16-item trait-rating scale and instructed to rate the SP, and indicate his subjective confidence for each rating. The stimulus materials and dependent variable forms are more fully described below.

Stimulus Variations

As implied by the foregoing discussion, the experimental design called for the construction of four separate tapes to be played as the stimulus pattern for independent groups of subjects. These tapes varied along two cross-cutting dimensions: on half of the tapes the job described was that of a submariner, on the remaining half the job was that of an "astronaut" in training for space flights; on half of the tapes the job description was followed by a set of responses appropriate for the submariner job (other-directed pattern), on the remaining half the responses were more appropriate for the astronaut job (inner-directed pattern). The four tapes were actually constructed by separately recording these four segments, always with the same person reading the part of the SP, and splicing them into the following combinations: Submariner-Other, Submariner-Inner, Astronaut-Inner, and Astronaut-Other.

ROLE DESCRIPTIONS Presentation of the submariner's role was prefaced by a reference to the capacities of atomic submarines and the corresponding qualities necessary for adjusting to the social conditions of submarine life. The following excerpts give both the flavor and some of the content of the role description:

People at the submarine school are pretty sure they know quite a bit about the kind of person who adapts well to submarine life. . . . The main thing they look for is stability and good citizenship . . . constant cooperation with others is essential . . . willingness to tolerate routine . . . not supposed to think for himself . . . sticks to the rules. . . . Since submariners are in such constant contact with each other, it's important, of course, that the good submariner enjoys other people around, that he be relaxed and friendly and slow to irritate.

Presentation of the astronaut's role capitalized on the timely issue of sending a single man into space. The role description is suggested again by the following excerpts:

One of the most difficult requirements of space travel, at least in its early stages, is that it will most likely involve a man's being isolated from virtually all human contact for long periods of time . . . looking for men who don't need to have other people around . . . inner resources and the ability to maintain concentration without stimulation from others . . . alert, imaginative, resourceful . . .

These particular role descriptions were designed, of course, without regard to truth value, solely to emphasize plausibly two sets of qualities that might best be described as other- versus inner-directed.

BEHAVIOR SAMPLES SPs on each of the four tapes responded in an identical fashion until they were asked by the interviewer to take a "choice test which has recently been devised to indicate how well a person will fit into various

niches in life. . . ." The test that followed consisted of 22 items, each comprising a pair of statements. The SP was instructed to choose the member of each pair which was more characteristic of himself and to indicate his certainty on an 11-point scale. Half of the items were buffer items not specifically relevant to the difference between roles and always answered in the same manner by the SPs. The remaining 11 items were "critical" in reflecting the intended difference between inner- and other-directed response patterns. The following examples indicate some of the pair members endorsed by the SPs in the two behavior samples:

	Other-Directed	Inner-Directed
3.	I always like to support the majority.	I like to feel free to do what I want to do.
9.	I would like to be a door-to-door salesman.	I would like to be a forest ranger.
17.	When planning something I always seek suggestions from others.	When planning something I like to work on my own.
21.	I like to know how other people think I should behave.	I avoid situations where I am expected to behave in a conventional way.
22.	I like to settle arguments and disputes of others.	I like to attack points of view that are contrary to my own.

For each of these item pairs, the SP orally endorsed the statement appropriate to the condition and indicated the degree of his certainty. Degree of certainty was predetermined so that the same scale positions were endorsed the same number of times for each behavior sample. This was to equalize any tendency to regress toward or away from less certainty in the memory task.

Impression Rating Scale

The final task of the subjects was to record their impression of the SP in terms of a 16-item rating scale. Each item consisted of two polar adjectives separated by 10 scale points. To the right of each item was a 5-point confidence scale for that item. Thus, subjects were to indicate what they thought the SP was "really like" and how confident they were of each rating. Ten of the items were chosen to reflect five distinct clusters whose contents were relevant to the hypotheses being tested. Each cluster consisted of two items, each suggesting an aspect of cluster meaning but balanced for direction to inhibit tendencies toward response set. Thus the conformity cluster consisted of the pairs "conforming-independent" and "creative-unoriginal." Other clusters were affiliation, intelligence, motivation, and candor. The remaining six items were related to each other only in their strong evaluative tone: warm-cold, popular-unpopular, likable-irritating, and so forth.

In analyzing the results, cluster scores were derived simply by adding the scale placements for the two component items, naturally reversing the score of one item. Confidence scores were similarly derived by simple addition of scale values.

RESULTS

Predicted Differences in Perception

In line with the general hypotheses of the study, the first specific prediction was that SPs performing out-of-role (Astro-Others and Sub-Inners) would be perceived as revealing their true preferences in the simulated interview more than SPs performing in-role (Astro-Inners and Sub-Others). The most direct test of this hypothesis may be found in the data provided by the subjects in trying to indicate how the SP would have responded in the interview if he was being completely faithful to himself. These data are summarized in Figure 1*a* and in Table 1. It is clear that the prediction is confirmed. The Astro-Other and the Sub-Inner SPs are both seen as revealing their true preferences, though there is a slight and understandable regression toward the mean. Interestingly enough, and quite in line with predictions, the two in-role groups locate the true answers of the SPs almost exactly half-way between the other-directed and the inner-directed pattern. Since behavior appropriate to powerful role requirements generally masks the characteristics of the actor, the perceivers apparently feel that their best guess is a completely neutral one.

The next issue to be raised is the extent to which these results are restricted to the particular pattern of items covered in the recorded interview. That is, do the highly significant results summarized in Table 1 merely reflect rational manipulations of the specific response scale used by the SP, or do they generalize to related measures of

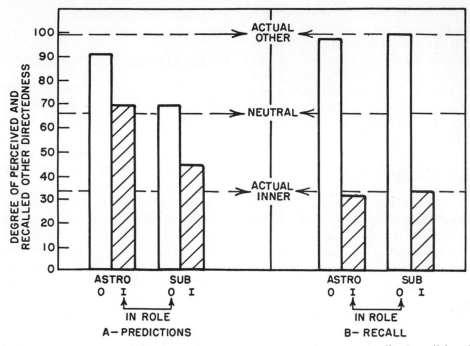

1*a*. Predictions of "true answer patterns" (Means).   1*b*. Recall of answers actually given (Means).

Figure 1. Degree of perceived and recalled other directedness.

perception and inference? Recall that the subjects also filled out a bipolar adjective rating scale, in an attempt to express their appraisal of the SP's true characteristics. The items of this scale were members of small clusters of re-

TABLE 1. PREDICTIONS OF SP'S TRUE RESPONSES
(Summary of Analysis of Variance [a] and *t* Test Results)

Source	df	MS	F	Group	N	$\bar{X}$	t
A. Astro-sub	1	1,554.73	63.56[b]	AO	33	91.12	
B. Inner-other	1	1,764.91	64.27[b]	SO	31	69.26	5.32[b]
C. Mach	2	18.81					
A × B	1	8.63		AI	33	69.15	
A × C	2	62.67		SI	37	43.92	5.98[b]
B × C	2	31.23					
A × B × C	2	22.84					
Error	122	27.46					
Total	133						

[a] Using the approximation technique for unequal cell frequencies (Snedecor, 1946).
[b] $p < .001$.

TABLE 2. PERCEPTIONS OF AFFILIATION AND CONFORMITY

N	Astro-Other 33	Astro-Inner 33	Sub-Other 31	Sub-Inner 37	Comparisons Direction	t
Affiliation						
$\overline{X}$	15.27	11.12	12.00	8.64	AO > SO	4.02**
SD	2.92	3.81	3.53	4.73	AI > SI	2.12*
Conformity						
$\overline{X}$	15.91	13.09	12.58	9.41	AO > SO	4.02**
SD	3.22	3.42	3.39	4.95	AI > SI	3.65**

Note.—The higher the mean value, the greater the perceivd affiliation or conformity. Comparisons between AO and SI are not tabled, but the differences between these conditions would of course be highly significant.

* $p < .05$.
** $p < .001$.

lated traits, varying in their relevance to the dimension of inner-other directedness. Two of the most relevant clusters, by a priori judgment, were attempts to measure perceptions of affiliation and conformity. It was predicted that the two out-of-role SPs would be perceived to differ markedly in both affiliation and conformity and that the two in-role SPs would not. The results, as summarized in Table 2, clearly confirm this prediction. The Astro-Other is seen as significantly more affiliative and conforming than the Sub-Inner, and each is seen as differing significantly from its in-role control. Analyses of variance indicate that Machiavellianism contributes to no significant effects and there are no significant interactions between role and behavior sample. This result seems to indicate that genuine perceptual decisions have been made that involve assessing the meaning of the behavior sample provided by the SP against the background of the role playing instructions imposed on him.

Since the predictions involving the direction and magnitude of perceptual rating differences have been borne out, the next relevant question concerns the confidence with which perceptual judgments were made. The general hypothesis, it will be recalled, predicted that in-role ratings would be less confidently made than ratings of out-of-role behavior. This prediction could be easily tested since the subject rendered a judgment of confidence with respect to each trait rated. The most precise test of the general prediction involves confidence ratings based on the two clusters most relevant to the differences between role: affiliation and conformity. When confidence ratings on these clusters are summed for each individual, the resulting pattern clearly confirms the hypothesis. As Table 3 shows, the interaction between role and behavior sample is highly significant. As for the individual mean comparison, in each case the subjects feel more confident about rating the SP who is behaving out of role than the SP who is behaving the same way *in* role.

TABLE 3. CONFIDENCE RATINGS
BY TREATMENTS
(Analysis of Variance [a] Summary)

Source	df	Affiliation and Conformity	
		MS	F
A. Astro-Sub	1	.07	
B. Inner-Other	1	1.62	3.29
C. Mach	2	.26	
A × B	1	8.58[b]	17.42[c]
A × C	2	.33	
B × C	2	.84	
A × B × C	2	.47	
Within	122	.49	
Total	133		

[a] Using the approximation technique for unequal cell frequencies (Snedecor, 1946).
[b] Results of tests of individual mean comparisons: AO > SO, $t = 3.30$, $p < .01$; SI > AI, $t = 2.55$, $p < .02$.
[c] $p < .001$.

Difference in Recall

As one of their tasks, all subjects were asked to reproduce the responses made by the SP in the simulated interview. The fidelity of these attempts at recall was treated in two ways. First, a recall score was computed for each subject involving the degree of discrepancy in scale points for each item, summed without regard to direction. For convenience we may call these absolute error scores. Subjects were expected to make fewer errors in recalling the behavior samples of the in-role treatments than those in the out-of-role treatments. The assumption was that roles, like all categories that summarize relevant information, facilitate cognitive organization and enhance one's ability to predict behavior that is appropriate to the role. In the present case, the behavior sample available in the in-role treatments tended to

confirm the expectations established by the role instructions. For subjects in the out-of-role treatments, the role instructions could not be used to organize and predict the behavior which occurred, except insofar as the subjects were led to adopt a clear negative expectation that the behavior was the opposite of that called for.

The results on this measure of absolute recall confirm the hypothesis. The responses of the in-role SPs (Astro-Inner and Sub-Other) are recalled with greater accuracy than the responses of the out-of-role SPs (Astro-Other and Sub-Inner). As Table 4 shows, the predicted interaction is significant ($p < .05$). Most of this interaction effect comes from the two cells in which the SP is other-directed (Sub-Other > Astro-Other, $t = 2.60$, $p < .01$; Astro-Inner > Sub-Inner, $t = .64$, $p < .50$). There is no obvious reason for this dif-

TABLE 4. ABSOLUTE RECALL ERRORS
BY TREATMENTS
(Analysis of Variance [a] Summary)

Source	df	MS	F
A. Astro-Sub	1	3.89	
B. Inner-Sub	1	1.36	
C. Mach	2	.30	
A × B [b]	1	9.59	6.23[c]
A × C	2	3.61	
B × C	2	.13	
A × B × C	2	1.40	
Within	122	1.54	
Total	133		

[a] Using the approximation technique for unequal cell frequencies (Snedecor, 1946).
[b] The means for the four cells represented by this interaction were: $\overline{X}$ (Astro-Other) = 12.42; $\overline{X}$(Sub-Other) = 9.52; $\overline{X}$(Astro-Inner) = 10.00; $\overline{X}$(Sub-Inner) = 10.56.
[c] $p < .05$.

ference unless the submariner role was more helpfully predictive in organizing information about the other-directed behavior sample than was the astronaut role in organizing information about the inner-directed sample.

The recall data were also scored to take account of the direction of deviation from accuracy. These data are relevant for answering any question dealing with the assimilation of recalled responses to categories implied by the roles. In fact, as Figure 1*b* shows, there was no evidence of either assimilation or contrast in directional recall of the SP's interview preferences. Those errors which the subjects did make (see the foregoing data on absolute errors) were quite evenly distributed on either side of the true scale position. As far as the mean directed error scores are concerned, then, the group recall accuracy was extremely high. Of course, we cannot state on the basis of these results that distortions from accurate recall of social behavior are always random distortions, but in the present case there is no evidence for directional errors

either toward or away from the role category implied by the instructions to the SP.

Perception of Additional Characteristics

In planning the experiment, it seemed at least conceivable that many subjects would attribute the SP's out-of-role performance in the Astro-Other and Sub-Inner conditions to poor motivation, lack of intelligence, or both. If such were the case, then it would not necessarily follow that the behavior sample provided would be taken as a "true" reflection of the SP's affiliative and conforming tendencies (or the lack thereof). We have seen that most subjects did consider the out-of-role performance to be reflections of these tendencies, but it is still of interest to note their ratings of the SP on trait clusters tapping perceived motivation and intelligence. As Table 5 shows, the Sub-Other SP was seen as more highly motivated and intelligent than the Astro-Other SP ($p < .01$), but this expected trend was slightly reversed in the case of the two inner-directed SPs. It

TABLE 5. SELECTED TRAIT AND CLUSTER MEANS BY TREATMENTS
WITH APPROPRIATE COMPARISONS

Clusters	Astro-Other $n = 33$	Sub-Other $n = 33$	Astro-Inner $n = 31$	Sub-Inner $n = 37$	Relevant Comparisons
Motivation					
$\overline{X}$	9.97	12.10	9.64	10.92	SO > AO, $p < .01$
SD	3.47	3.66	4.48	4.09	
Intelligence					
$\overline{X}$	8.00	11.13	9.39	9.84	SO > AO, $p < .01$
SD	3.35	4.15	3.72	3.94	
Candor					
$\overline{X}$	12.42	9.68	10.09	12.08	AO > SO, $p < .01$;
SD	4.09	3.61	3.68	3.77	SI > AI, $p < .05$

would appear, then, that the in-role SP is judged to have greater motivation and intelligence only when the role involves volunteering for the submarine service. There is no obvious reason for this difference in response to the two roles. Perhaps the inner-directed pattern seemed more artificial or obvious in the context of astronaut instructions, or perhaps the meaning of motivation and intelligence became less situation-bound when subjects were asked to appraise a truly inner-directed man.

Also of interest are the ratings of perceived candor. It might be expected that performing out-of-role would be construed as evidence of the SP's frankness and sincerity. The results in Table 5 do show a clear difference between in-role and out-of-role SPs with regard to the perception of candor. As expected, the in-role SPs are judged by the average subject to fall at or near the midpoint of the scale (10.00 for the cluster); the out-of-role SPs are seen as significantly more candid in each variation of role instructions.

Results on the remaining traits add little to the picture already presented. For the most part the means fall into a pattern similar to those reflecting perceived affiliation and conformity. That is, the two in-role SPs are perceived to be relatively neutral on most of the evaluative trait dimensions; the Astro-Others are seen as significantly more likable (versus irritating), warm (versus cold), popular (versus unpopular), and helpful (versus disinterested) than the Sub-Inners. This pattern of findings might suggest the operation of a strong "halo" or "generosity" effect favoring those who are perceived as other directed. However, it must be recalled that the Astro-Other SP is seen as less highly motivated and

less intelligent than the Sub-Other SP, personal attributes that are usually considered to be quite evaluative. Also, Astro-Other and Sub-Inner SPs are both seen as more candid than their in-role controls. It seems more likely, then, that evaluative traits like warm, popular, likable, and helpful are linked to other-directedness more by direct association than through an underlying decision that the Astro-Other SP is good and the Sub-Inner SP is bad. This conclusion is supported by two further results: to an extent that is nearly significant, the two out-of-role SPs are seen as more interesting (versus boring) than the two in-role SPs; also, the Astro-Inner SP is seen as significantly more conceited (versus self-effacing) than either the Astro-Other or the Sub-Inner SP. While these incidental findings are not all easy to rationalize, they do point up the complexity and subtlety of the cognitive impressions created by the experimental combinations of role and behavior sample.

Machiavellianism

While the study was designed without any consideration of the possible role of Machiavellianism as measured by Christie's Mach IV Scale, it did seem possible that high scorers on the Mach Scale might be generally more sensitive to variations in role instructions and more inclined toward negative evaluation of the SPs who were unable or unwilling to play the prescribed role.

In all of the major analyses, Mach level was included routinely as a potential source of variance. In no case did it contribute to significant main or interactive effects. Either the situational manipulations were simply too powerful for individual differences on this dimension to manifest themselves, or our knowledge of Mach Scale correlates is insufficient to make meaningful predictive statements. In view of the results of a recently completed study by Jones, Gergen, and Davis (in press), the latter alternative seems quite tenable. With respect to one meaningful comparison, however, Machiavellianism does make a significant contribution. The high scorers tend to attribute greater intelligence to the in-role than the out-of-role SPs whereas the low scorers show the reverse pattern in perceiving intelligence. This difference between highs and lows is significant $(t = 2.15, p < .05)$. A similar trend was noted with regard to perceived motivation, but this fell short of significance $(t = 1.62, p < .15)$. Though the differences in perceived intelligence are consistent with what little knowledge we do have about high and low Mach scorers, there is little else in the data to suggest that the variable is relevant to the perception of in-role and out-of-role SPs.

DISCUSSION

The results of the present study are unequivocal. Starting from the assumption that individual characteristics are obscured when a person is exposed to strong and demanding stimulus forces, we have reasoned that social stimuli embraced by the role concept may operate in this same way. Thus a person who conforms to salient social expectations reveals little about his basic and distinguishing characteristics. On the other hand, one who rejects or ignores pressures to play a defined role is considered to reflect his true disposition and is perceived with confidence.

It is undoubtedly true that this reasoning is ubiquitous in the psychologist's approach to personality assessment. In many programs of assessment, the patient or subject is exposed to a variety of situational pressures and task demands. Of his responses to these situations, his nonmodal reactions are clearly more informative and carry the most interpretive weight. To take another example, psychological screening for desirable jobs must cope with the problems raised by this study in order to be effective. Since the role constraints for the applicant are often obvious, the interviewer or employer must penetrate to more subtle cues or fall back on projective devices which, though unreliable at best, at least produce the response variety essential for individualized judgment.

It is probably true that short-term social interactions can perfectly well proceed in line with established expectations defining reciprocal roles. If the interaction is self-limiting (as, say, between a hotel guest and his bellhop) there is little need for personalized information to sustain the interaction. When a relationship is more permanent, however, and involves the prospect of interactions in varied situations, such information rapidly increases in value. It is to the perceiver's advantage, in such cases, to be especially attuned to out-of-role behaviors and to create situations in which out-of-role behaviors can be most clearly observed. The results of the present study show that such behaviors, rightly or wrongly, are perceived to be peculiarly diagnostic of individual characteristics. Judgments about these personal qualities are presumably most important in governing the perceiver's behavior as he ventures into new situations with the SP.

REFERENCES

CHRISTIE, R., & MERTON, R. K.   Procedures for the sociological study of the values climate of medical schools. *J. med. Educ.*, 1958, 33, 125–153.

HEIDER, F.   Social perception and phenomenal causality. *Psychol. Rev.*, 1944, 51, 358–374.

HEIDER, F.   *The psychology of interpersonal relations.* New York: Wiley, 1958.

JONES, E. E., & DAUGHERTY, B. N.   Political orientation and the perceptual effects of an anticipated interaction. *J. abnorm. soc. Psychol.*, 1959, 59, 340–349.

JONES, E. E., GERGEN, K. J., & DAVIS, K. E.   Some determinants of reactions to being approved or disapproved as a person. *Psychol. Monogr.*, in press.

JONES, E. E., & THIBAUT, J. W.   Interaction goals as bases of inference in interpersonal perception. In R. Tagiuri & L. Petrullo (Eds.), *Person perception and interpersonal behavior.* Stanford: Stanford Univer. Press, 1958. Pp. 151–179.

LEVINSON, D. J.   Role, personality, and social structure in the organizational setting. *J. abnorm. soc. Psychol.*, 1959, 58, 170–180.

SNEDECOR, G. W.   *Statistical methods.* (4th ed.) Ames, Iowa: Collegiate Press, 1946.

8

Power and Leadership

❧◆❧

37. SOCIAL INFLUENCE AND POWER *

Bertram H. Raven

Social influence is defined here as change in a person's cognition, attitude, or behavior, which has its origin in another person or group. We are interested in such phenomena as: the policeman influencing the motorist to move his car; the teacher influencing the student to use a specific method in solving a mathematics problem; the mother influencing her child to avoid playing in the street; the flying saucer fancier influencing his friend to "see" a flying saucer in a fuzzy cloud formation. Others have considered these situations in terms of "imitation," "suggestion," "persuasion," or "contagion." We will use the word "power" to mean *potential* influence— or, conversely, influence is *kinetic* power. This article will develop further an ap-

proach to the analysis of social influence and power that was first presented in a joint paper with J. R. P. French, Jr. (French & Raven, 1959). A number of studies, many of which grew out of other theoretical orientations, will be presented to illustrate the usefulness of the present conceptualization.

SOCIAL DEPENDENCE AND SOCIAL INFLUENCE

In many cases of social influence, the changes that result involve dependence upon the source of influence, the influencing agent. Doing thousands of simple addition problems would likely have no meaning for a subject in an

* This article is a revised version of Chapter 5 from *Interpersonal Relations and Behavior in Groups*, B. Raven (New York: Basic Books, Inc., 1965), a volume in the series entitled "Basic Topics in Psychology," edited by Edwin G. Boring. It includes research and theoretical developments supported by the Group Psychology Branch of the Office of Naval Research.

experiment, nor would he continue so boring a task if he did not relate his behavior to the experimenter, the experimenter's right to prescribe that behavior, or the implicit threat the experimenter could utilize if the subject were not to comply. We would, therefore, call this *socially dependent*, or merely dependent influence. If the experimenter had carefully explained to the student subject that, while he had no further obligation to the experimenter, doing these addition problems would aid the subject in an important mathematics examination, it is possible that the subject would do the work, but the source of the influence would no longer be relevant. The student's behavior would now be *socially independent* of the influencing agent. It would, however, be dependent upon a number of other cognitions in the subject's cognitive system—he would see his behavior as relevant to his studies. We will call this change *independent influence* even though it is an outgrowth of the communication from the experimenter. As an analogy, we might point to F. Heider's discussion of two classes of movements of a ball.

> In one case, a ball is pushed so that it rolls across a plane. In another case, the ball is guided by a hand and its movements are dependent at each moment on the movement of the hand . . . in the first case, an influence from the outside is active once . . . in the other case, when the ball is guided during the whole movement, the course of events is continuously influenced from the outside (Heider, 1959, pp. 4–5.)

The second case represents dependent influence, the hand being the influencing agent. In the first case, the movement of the pushed ball is inde-

pendent of the influencing agent once it has received its initial impetus, but it is, of course, dependent upon a number of other elements such as the surface of the plane below, the surface of the ball itself, gravity, air pressures and currents, and so on. In the same fashion, independent influence will occur as the result of an act on the part of the agent but will thenceforth be independent of the agent and be dependent, instead, on a number of other elements in the influencee's environment.

Independent Influence Stemming from Information

Independent influence is the result of a basic change in cognitive elements and its basis is *information* communicated by the agent. For this reason, it was earlier referred to as "informational influence" (French & Raven, 1959). It is the content of the communication that is important, not the nature of the influencing agent.

A vacuum cleaner salesman may convince the housewife to purchase a new carpet sweeper. He would do this by emphasizing the advantages of the machine that he offers for sale while stressing the disadvantages of the housewife's older model. If he is successful, he will have established new cognitive elements and new relationships for the housewife. The resulting *informational influence* would thus become independent of the influencing agent.

A great deal of the research on the effectiveness of different media of communication relates to informational influence. Informational influence will be more effective when the object of change is ambiguous and subject to cognitive reorganization.

Public-Dependent Influence
and Its Sources: Coercion and Reward

While it is the information or content of the communication that is the basis for independent influence, there are a number of sources of socially dependent influence. In some cases, the ability to observe by the influencing agent is necessary for influence to occur and continue, while in other cases this perception is not important. Thus a distinction has sometimes been made between *public-dependent* influence and *private-dependent* influence (French & Raven, 1959). In the latter instance, the influencee is unconcerned about the possibility that the influencing agent will know whether or not he has complied.

There are two sources of *public-dependent* influence—coercion and reward—both mediated by the influencing agent. *Coercive power* stems from the ability of the agent to mediate punishment for the influencee; *reward power* results from the ability of the agent to mediate rewards. In keeping with our general orientation, it is not the objective ability of the influencing agent to mediate such rewards and punishments that is important, but rather the potential rewards and punishments as perceived by the influencee. Examples of *reward power* might include (a) a supervisor's ability to increase a worker's pay for increasing production; (b) a mother's willingness to pay her child fifty cents for mowing the lawn; (c) the behavior of a member of a teen-age gang who commits a petty theft because he hopes thereby to win the approval of his companions. *Coercive power* would result from (a) the supervisor's capacity to dismiss a worker; (b) a sergeant's ability to assign an enlistee to kitchen duty; (c) a mother's threat to withhold her love from her child unless he tidies up his room. Note that, in each case, the first two examples are of an impersonal nature and the last is personal. Approval, love, acceptance, liking, and agreement may become commodities that represent potential reward; disapproval, dislike, hatred, rejection, and disagreement may become potential sources of coercive power that may be much more potent than an impersonal punishment, such as receiving a spanking for noncompliance. The potency of personal coercive or reward power is a function of the influencee's evaluation of the influencing agent.

Illustrations of the coercive and reward power of a supervisor over the worker seem quite obvious. There are also clear instances of the coercive power of the work group over the individual worker. A clothes presser, recently hired in a factory, rapidly learns her job and increases her rate of production to the point where it clearly exceeds the group average. Soon there are evidences of disapproval by fellow workers; she is subjected to ridicule and isolation until her production is lowered to the group average. The public-dependent nature of the influence is apparent when she is removed from her work-group and her production rate soars (Coch & French, 1948).

Private-Dependent Influence
and its Sources: Expertness, Reference, and Legitimacy

Three sources of social power—expertness, reference, and legitimacy—result in social influence that is dependent upon the influencing agent but wherein observability is unimportant. As compared to influence stemming from reward and coercion, the effects continue regardless of whether or not the influencee believes that his behavior will become apparent to the influencing agent.

EXPERT POWER   This source stems from the attribution of superior knowledge or ability to the influencing agent. A teacher tells the student to solve a mathematics problem by means of a specified formula, and the student follows his teacher's advice. If the student does so because he now understands why that particular formula will bring forth the solution, informational influence has taken place. Such influence is independent of the agent. However, if the student uses the formula without seeing its utility but on faith that the teacher, being more skilled in mathematics, must know that such is the road to a solution, expertness is the basis for influence, and the influence is socially dependent. Furthermore, given such faith, the influence is private—observability is unimportant. The student will show signs of influence even if the teacher is not able to see whether he has complied. Since expert influence is dependent, any later knowledge that raises questions about the teacher's expertise will reduce or eliminate the change that has occurred. This will not be true in the case of informational influence.

REFERENT INFLUENCE   This occurs when a person uses another person or group as a "frame of reference," as a background, or as a yardstick against which he evaluates some aspect of himself. We tend to adopt opinions, attitudes, and behaviors similar to those of people with whom we identify and opposite to those of people from whom we dissociate ourselves. Many of the studies of balance, congruence, or dissonance reduction in social relationships can be seen as instances of referent influence. If an individual finds that two persons whom he likes dislike one another, he may tend to reject one or both of them; if they are perceived as liking one another, he is more apt to continue his friendship with them (Festinger & Hutte, 1954). The same can be seen on a much larger scale in a study of the effects of nominating conventions and elections on the evaluation of political candidates. In 1960, students who had already indicated their political affiliation were asked on several occasions to evaluate potential presidential candidates on a semantic differential scale that allowed for measurement of perceived deviation from an "ideal president." As might be expected, respondents tended to favor potential candidates who were members of their own party, but polarization was very clear immediately after the nominating conventions —the Republican candidate became even more attractive to Republicans, the Democratic candidate looked even more like an "ideal president" to Democrats. There was also a rejection of Kennedy by the Republicans, although there was no comparable rejection of Nixon by Democrats. These polarizing effects occurred so soon after the conventions that it is unlikely that new information about the candidates was responsible for the changes. Nominating conventions and the campaign led to further salience of the political parties as reference groups such that by November referent influence was particularly great. The election, however, appears to have had the effect of suddenly reducing the referent influences of political parties, and very soon after the election the candidate of the opposing party was seen in a much more favorable light. This was particularly true for the president-elect as rated by members of the losing party—suggesting that "the nation as a whole" replaced the political party as a source of referent influence (Raven & Gallo, in press).

It is often the case that a person must evaluate his abilities in order to predict how well he will do on a task or to set some level of aspiration. If he has no prior experience with a task that could serve as a frame of reference, his judgment of himself will be uncertain and will fluctuate. In this event, knowledge of the abilities of others may serve as a frame of reference. In a class in introductory psychology, students who were asked to predict their scores on the first examination were very inaccurate. When students in a similar class were told that the average male premedical student had answered 50 items correctly, accuracy of prediction increased dramatically. The referent group offered a point on a yardstick against which students could predict their own position (Raven & Fishbein, in press).

LEGITIMATE INFLUENCE   There is considerable evidence to indicate that there are broad, general norms about the behaviors, beliefs, opinions, and attitudes that are appropriate or proper in a given situation. Whether such determinations come from tradition, from internalized values, or from present expectations of others, each person carries with him a set of prescriptions that have the nature of "oughtness." Each person

carries similar prescriptions that he applies to others. This dimension of evaluation could be called "legitimacy"— some behaviors are seen as legitimate, some as nonlegitimate. Legitimate behaviors may differ according to a person's position in a social structure. In the family, there are some behaviors that are appropriate for the father, some for the mother, and some for the older and younger children. Included in these "role prescriptions" is the expectation that a person in one position may legitimately determine behaviors or beliefs of one in another position and the requirement that the latter obey the former. Legitimate influence, then, is based on the influencee's acceptance of a relationship in the power structure such that the agent is permitted or obliged to prescribe behaviors for him and the influencee is legitimately required to accept such influence (cf. Weber, 1947; Goldhammer & Shils, 1939).

It has been demonstrated that members may accept a group as an agent that legitimizes the power of a supervisor (Raven & French, 1958). Other studies have indicated that a subject in an experiment accepts a structural relationship with the experimenter that gives the latter very great legitimate power over the subject—the ability to influence him to do a meaningless task for long hours (Orne, 1962) or to go counter to basic values of interpersonal behavior by giving supposedly painful or even harmful shocks to another subject (Milgram, 1963). It may be recalled that former officials of Nazi extermination camps insisted that they had to commit their cruel deeds because legitimate power figures ordered them to do so.

Negative Influence

Thus far, we have discussed influence mainly in terms of changes in the influencee that are in the direction of the wishes of the agent or that make the influencee more similar to the agent. However, some instances of influence are negative; changes occur that are opposed to the intentions of the agent or that increase the discrepancy between the influencee and the agent. We have already alluded to negative referent influence where the influencee does not see himself as a member of a social unit or tends to disassociate himself from the agent. The "beatniks" or "Bohemians" may claim to be unconcerned about the norms of society as a whole, desiring to be nonconformists. But they strive to behave, look, and dress differently because society serves as a very powerful *negative referent* for them. Parents may sometimes use other children as negative referents for their own: "Don't shout like that. Do you want to be like Johnny?" *Negative expert influence* might account for the "boomerang effect." A film designed to create a more favorable attitude toward Britain during World War II actually led many of its viewers to become more *negative*. Suspicion that the communicator was attempting to influence the viewers in a direction not necessarily in their own best interests led to negative expert influence that was greater than the positive informational influences (Hovland, Lumsdaine, & Sheffield, 1949). *Negative legitimacy* might also operate in certain rare cases, such as those involving prisoners of war who define the role structure as demanding that they do the opposite of whatever the captor

requests. *Negative informational* influences may occur when the agent inadvertently calls the attention of the influencee to factors that lead him to diverge from the agent. *Coercion* and *reward* may also produce negative effects but generally by affecting one of the other sources, as will be indicated later.

Secondary Influence

A little boy, seeing a bowl of porridge for the first time, which appears unappetizing, may take his first spoonful only because his mother threatens him with punishment if he does not do so. If the boy finds that the taste is indeed quite pleasing, behavior resulting from coercion has led to new cognitions, and the initially public-dependent change has become independent. Similar secondary changes have occurred in the case of restaurateurs who first served members of minority groups after the passage of a nondiscrimination law (coercion or legitimacy) and subsequently found that their anticipated loss of business did not materialize. College students, in an experiment, found themselves holding opinions with respect to a juvenile delinquency case that were sharply at variance with those of their fellow group members. Change was especially likely when students were asked to write descriptions of the case for other group members, even though there was no necessity for them to state their opinions. The change was particularly great when there was a possibility that the student might be rejected from the group for holding contrary opinions. The point of interest here is the evidence that students in writing about the case were likely to emphasize the information from the case that supported the group's point of view (coercive influence) and later to change their private opinions to bring them into line with the content that they had communicated (Raven, 1959).

Festinger suggests that results such as those obtained above might also occur as a consequence of dissonance reduction—one experiences dissonance if one behaves in a manner that is inconsistent with one's cognitions, and one can reduce dissonance by changing one's cognitions. This would occur, however, only when coercion and reward are not very great but great enough to produce public-dependent change. When rewards or coercion are very great they may provide sufficient justification for compliance without dissonance, and no secondary change will result (Festinger, 1957).

The exercise of one type of power may have a secondary influence upon another type of power. A supervisor who uses coercive power to influence his workers to change their rate of production will obtain public-dependent influence, but the workers will personally reject the supervisor, and negative referent influence may operate on their private opinions regarding rate of production. This negative change is likely to show itself when the supervisor is away and cannot ascertain the extent of conformity (Raven & French, 1958).

Finally, secondary influence can sometimes be obtained by changing the perceptions of the power source. During World War II, a series of studies were conducted on changing food habits. It was found that housewives could not be influenced to buy sweetbreads and other unpopular meats through the informational or expert influence of a lecturer. However, groups of house-wives, encouraged to discuss the problems of the meat shortage, and agreeing as a group to buy these meats, could influence the food habits of individual members—powerful referent influence was operative (Lewin, 1952). Similar results were obtained in studies of group decision in industrial settings (Coch & French, 1948).

Manipulation

The term manipulation is generally used to refer to social influence wherein the intentions of the agent are hidden from the influencee. In this sense, it might be considered a form of secondary influence. One may imagine a political campaign worker, probably apocryphal, who deliberately makes himself extremely obnoxious at a bar, then leaves, advising the others to "Vote for Blotz," the opposing candidate. This person has established himself as a negative referent, hoping thereby to influence others to behave in a manner opposite from that which they believe is his preference. Sometimes a cynical group leader may skillfully guide group discussion toward a decision that appears to come from the group, but which he has selected beforehand. The result is referent influence from the group on individual members, but this effect stems secondarily from the influence of the leader on the group. Manipulation runs counter to basic societal values; and when it is discovered by the influencee, it is likely to establish the manipulator as a person with very strong negative expert and negative referent power. Consequently, when manipulation is apparent it is likely to have an effect that is opposite to that intended by the manipulator.

COMPARISON OF SOURCES
OF SOCIAL INFLUENCE

Several investigations have examined two or more sources of power with the aim of comparing their stability, dependence upon observability, effect on perceptions of the influencing agent, or effects on other sources. We illustrate with three examples: reward-coercion, expertness, and reference.

These sources of social influence were compared in an ingenious experiment by Kelman (1958). The study grew out of a somewhat different theory of social influence, but the variables are clearly similar to those which have been discussed above. The subjects, freshmen in an all-Negro college, were presented with a tape-recorded communication that advocated a position at variance with their own. The communication asserted that some all-Negro colleges should remain segregated even after all other universities have been integrated. Different groups of subjects heard the same communication, but it was attributed to different communicators. In a condition that combined reward and coercive power, the communicator was identified as a very powerful president of a Foundation for Negro Colleges who could be expected to support the college and students who agreed with him and effectively to punish those who disagreed with him. In this condition, students' attitudes changed in the direction of the communicator, but only when the students were informed that their responses on the questionnaire would be seen by him—public dependent influence had resulted. Other students heard the same communication, this time attributed to a referent power—a Senior

and president of the student council in a leading Negro university who was also said to represent the opinions of most Negro college students. Referent influence led to change that was equally great regardless of whether or not questionnaire responses would be seen by the agent. However, the effects of the referent influence were unstable and did not appear on questionnaires administered several weeks later. In an expert power condition, the communicator was introduced as a professor of history who had considerable knowledge about minority groups and the Negro community. In that condition, influence was great regardless of whether or not observability was present, and it continued at a high level for several weeks thereafter.

Legitimacy and Coercion

Female subjects in this experiment were presented with the task of cutting patterns out of cardboard. Since they needed a supervisor, it was decided that they should elect one. The election served to give legitimate power to the supervisor, a fact which was clearly evidenced by responses to questionnaires. In some conditions, for reasons that were unclear to the subjects, the elected supervisor was replaced by one of the other subjects. In accordance with instructions communicated privately by the experimenter, the supervisor told all subjects to cut more slowly and more accurately, a change that would have the effect of reducing the workers' pay. For half the subjects this request involved a coercive influence attempt because it was accompanied by a threat of a fine for noncompliance. Both coercion and legitimacy led to increased conformity to the supervisor as evidenced by the number of pieces cut. However, legitimacy produced private as well as public compliance; coercion led to conformity only in behavior that was observable to the agent. With coercion, there was a discrepancy between what the "worker" did and what she felt she should do, accompanied by a show of hostility. There was also greater attraction to the legitimate supervisor than to the coercive supervision (Raven & French, 1958). Additional research indicates that coercion may not lead to personal rejection of the supervisor, provided the worker sees coercion as part of the legitimate role of the supervisor (French, Morrison, & Levinger, 1960).

Expertness and Reference

Subjects participating in groups of four attempted to "receive" extra-sensory images which, presumably, were being sent by a "sender" in another room. They were to indicate whether or not they had received the image by pressing an appropriate key. Subjects were more likely to report receiving ESP images when they had been led to believe that the other members in their group had reported reception, as compared to a control condition in which they were given no information about the responses of their coparticipants. Furthermore, in the former condition they were more likely to believe in the existence of extra-sensory perception, even to the extent of giving vivid postexperimental descriptions of the images that they had received (though, in fact, there was no "sender" involved at all). In a second study, all subjects were given the impression that their coparticipants had received images. However, the perceptual

ability attributed to the coparticipants was varied. Some subjects were told that their coparticipants had been tested and found to have very keen perceptual ability; some were led to believe that the other three were only slightly more perceptive than the average college student. It was expected that both referent and expert power would be related to attributed ability. Expert influence should have a strong effect on private beliefs and, as predicted, at the close of the experiment subjects were most likely to believe in ESP if the reported reception was made by coparticipants with high perceptual ability. However, referent influence should operate on *reported reception,* and subjects were most likely to use the "slightly above average" subjects as a basis for comparison. When coparticipants were expert perceivers, their reported reception led the subjects to believe more strongly in ESP, but the subjects were unconcerned about their inability to see what the coparticipants saw and they were not so likely to report reception. When the coparticipants were average students, the subjects were more inclined to report reception like that of their associates, but subjects were not so likely to increase their belief in ESP (Raven, Mansson, & Anthony, 1962).

WHICH TYPE OF SOCIAL INFLUENCE IS MOST EFFECTIVE?

In a typical influence situation, several different sources of power may be operating. Moreover, the influencing agent often may choose from among rival sources. The doctor may emphasize his legitimate role as doctor and stress the "fact" that a patient must obey his doctor; he may try to speak his patient's language and develop a friendly relationship with his patient that will give him referent power; he may emphasize his training and line his office with medical books, journals, and diplomas in order to establish his expert power; he may use approval and disapproval as personal reward and personal coercion or threaten the patient with loss of medical compensation; or he may carefully explain to the patient the nature of his illness and the reason for the prescribed exercises or medication (informational influence). The question arises as to which source of influence is most effective.

The agent will want to be certain that his chosen source of power is within his domain. The doctor will not attempt to exert expert influence if his patient happens to be another doctor whose training is equivalent to his own. In that event, he may rely upon legitimacy or informational power.

Private influence would seem to be less costly than public-dependent influence since it does not require continual surveillance or the resources that are necessary for the administration of reward and punishment. It is not surprising that prominent figures in history, having assumed political power by force, go to great lengths to establish their legitimacy by carefully tracing their regal lineage or by conducting rigged elections.

Informational influence appears to be the most stable, and it fits conveniently into our modern day value system regarding individual froodom of choice. For this reason it has received considerable stress in modern educational circles. However, informational influence may not be feasible until the influencee has acquired an appropriate body of knowledge. In the early stages of a calculus course it may be necessary for the teacher to use expert power, asking the students to memorize certain formulae on the basis of the teacher's superior knowledge. An understanding of the bases for these formulae may not come until much later. Military officers, realizing that the press of battle might lead to catastrophe if soldiers were to expect a complete explanation of every order, go to great lengths to establish an expectation of legitimate power over informational ("Ours is not to reason why. . . ."), and keep coercive power in the background just in case.

Coercive power and manipulation both run sharply counter to our value system, yet where change is crucial, as is probably the case with respect to civil rights, and where all other sources have proven ineffective, there may be no alternative. In these cases it is well to remember that if we also wish to obtain secondary independent change, we should utilize a degree of coercion that is just sufficient to bring about compliance. A "just sufficient" level of coercion is likely to create dissonance after compliance and to induce subsequent change in attitude (Festinger, 1957).

Personality and cultural factors also help to determine the effectiveness of the source of influence. For example, persons with a high need for affiliation are especially susceptible to referent influence and personal reward (Becker & Carroll, 1962). There is also evidence that the power preferences of parents are adopted by their children (Mussen & Kagan, 1958). A cross-cultural experiment has suggested that Norweigian college students are more susceptible to several forms of social influence than are their French contemporaries (Milgram, 1961).

In a study in a large public mental

hospital, members of the nursing service were presented with a problem regarding a patient who habitually slept during the day and disturbed the ward at night. They were asked to indicate the method they would employ to alter this habit. Most reported that they would use informational influence ("explain the reasons for changing the patient's sleeping habits"). The next most popular choice was "benevolent manipulation"—"Figure out some ways to keep him busy during the day so he will *want* to sleep at night." Few considered the use of legitimate power, reward power, or coercion. Coercion was considered to involve the most effort. Benevolent manipulation was considered most effective but was rated as involving too much work and trouble (Rosenberg & Pearlin, 1962).

Clearly more research is needed regarding power preference in varying situations and cultures and particularly on the conditions under which one type of power will be more effective than another.

SUMMARY

We have examined six types of social power, classified according to their sources. Informational influence, arising from the content of a communication, becomes independent of the influencing agent but depends upon cognitive changes in the influencee. Coercion and reward lead to influence that is continually dependent upon the agent and specifically dependent upon his ability to monitor the influencee's responses. Expertness, reference, and legitimacy result in influence that is also dependent upon the agent, but the agent need not exercise continuous surveillance over the influencee.

Power was defined as potential influence. Influence may be positive or negative, depending upon whether its effects are congruent or opposite to the intentions of the influencing agent. Secondary influences may occur when the exercise of one type of influence creates the conditions that permit another type of influence to operate. This is especially likely to happen when the first influence attempts lead the influencee to experience dissonance or to alter his perceptions. Manipulation may be viewed as a special case of secondary influence in which the agent's intentions are disguised and he achieves his end by creating perceptions or attitudes that give him a new basis for power.

Several sources of power may be operating simultaneously, or an agent may have a choice of sources. Existing evidence does not permit us to make very many confident statements about the relative effects of various sources, but the studies cited in this article indicate that this problem is one that can be subjected to careful research. Future investigations should reveal many relationships that are of importance to an understanding of social behavior.

REFERENCES

1. Becker, S., & Carroll, Jean. Ordinal position and conformity. *J. abnorm. soc. Psychol.*, 1962, **65,** 129–131.
2. Coch, L., & French, J. R. P., Jr. Overcoming resistance to change. *Hum. Relat.*, 1948, 1, 512–532.
3. Festinger, L. *A theory of cognitive dissonance.* New York: Harper & Row, 1957, pp. 291.
4. Festinger, L. & Hutte, H. A. An experimental investigation of the effect of unstable interpersonal relations in a group. *J. abnorm. soc. Psychol.*, 1954, **49,** 513–532.

5. French, J. R. P., Jr., Morrison, H. W., & Levinger, G. Coercive power and forces affecting conformity. *J. abnorm. soc. Psychol.,* 1960, **61,** 93–101.

6. French, J. R. P., Jr., & Raven, B. H. The bases of social power. In D. Cartwright (Ed.), *Studies in social power.* Ann Arbor: Univ. Mich. Press, 1959, pp. 150–167.

7. Goldhammer, H., & Shils, E. A. Types of power and status. *Amer. J. Sociol.,* 1939, **45,** 171–178.

8. Heider, F. Thing and medium. *Psychol. Issues,* 1959, **1,** 1–34.

9. Hovland, C. I., Lumsdaine, A. A., & Sheffield, F. D. *Experiments in mass communication.* Princeton: Princeton Univ. Press, 1949.

10. Kelman, H. C. Compliance, identification, and internalization: Three processes of attitude change. *Conflict Resolution,* 1958, **2,** 51–60.

11. Lewin, K. Group decision and social change. In G. E. Swanson, T. M. Newcomb, & E. L. Hartley (Eds.), *Readings in social psychology* (2nd Ed.), New York: Holt, Rinehart and Winston, 1952, 459–473.

12. Milgram, S. Behavioral study of obedience. *J. abnorm. soc. Psychol.,* 1963, **67,** 371–378.

13. Milgram, S. Nationality and conformity. *Scientific Amer.,* 1961, **205,** 45–51.

14. Mussen, P. H., & Kagan, J. Group conformity and perception of parents. *Child Developm.,* 1958, **29,** 57–60.

15. Orne, M. T. On the social psychology of the psychological experiment: With particular reference to demand characteristics and their implications. *Amer. Psychol.,* 1962, **17,** 776–783.

16. Raven, B. H. Social influence on opinions and the communication of related content. *J. abnorm. soc. Psychol.,* 1959, **58,** 119–128.

17. Raven, B. H., & Fishbein, M. Social referents and self-evaluations in examinations. *J. soc. Psychol.,* (in press).

18. Raven, B. H., & French, J. R. P., Jr. Legitimate power, coercive power, and observability in social influence. *Sociometry,* 1958, **21,** 83–97.

19. Raven, B. H., & Gallo, P. S. The effects of nominating conventions, elections, and reference group identification, upon the perception of political figures. *Hum. Relat.* (in press).

20. Raven, B. H., Mansson, H. H., & Anthony, E. The effects of attributed ability upon expert and referent influence. Los Angeles, Calif.: Univ. of Calif., 1962 (Tech. Rep. No. 10, Contract Nonr 233 [54]).

21. Rosenberg, M. & Pearlin, L. I. Power-orientation in the mental hospital. *Hum. Relat.,* 1962, **15,** 335–349.

22. Weber, M. *The theory of social and economic organization.* Oxford: Oxford Univ. Press, 1947.

38.   LEARNING A SOCIAL STRUCTURE *

Clinton B. De Soto

For some years social psychologists have shown increasing interest in mathematical properties of social structures, ranging from investigations of the extent to which sociometric choices are mutual to experimental manipulations of the

* Reprinted from the *Journal of Abnormal and Social Psychology,* 1960, 60: 417–421, with permission of the author and the American Psychological Association. This work was supported in part by Grant NSF-G4827 from the National Science Foundation.

centrality of communication networks. This interest has been accompanied, however, by a curious lack of concern with the subjects' (Ss') views of these properties. For example, in the studies of mutuality of sociometric choices, the Ss are not ordinarily asked if *they* expect the choices to be mutual. Only recently, in such work as Tagiuri's (1958) generalization of sociometry, relational analysis, and Heider's (1957) discussion of naive psychology, has there been serious concern with the Ss' perception of such properties.

Apparently psychologists have assumed that Ss cannot or do not appreciate these properties. Yet folklore is full of essentially mathematical statements about interpersonal relations: "The way to get someone to like you is to like him," "You can't serve two masters," "There's always a faster gun somewhere." And recent questionnaire studies (De Soto & Kuethe, 1958, 1959) have demonstrated that Ss ascribe such properties rather freely to interpersonal relations, sometimes accurately, sometimes inaccurately.

Historically social psychologists have repeatedly been compelled to recognize the importance of cognitive processes in man, to the need, for example, for crediting people with role expectations as well as role behaviors. This fact makes it appear unwise to ignore their readiness to assign mathematical properties to interpersonal relations. It makes it important to look for effects of such attributions of properties in activities besides answering questionnaries. There are in the literature many findings which are suggestive of such effects. For example, Kogan and Tagiuri (1958) found that people expect those they choose to choose one another, thus evidencing,

for a special case, their expectation that sociometric choices will be mutual.

One task in which Ss' tendencies to assign properties to interpersonal relations might be expected to have especially prominent effects is that of learning a social structure. Learning a social structure means learning the relations among a set of people. It is a task that usually faces a person when he enters a social group, and it can be quite difficult as indexed by the information he must assimilate. It is a reasonable prediction that his assignments of properties to the relations which form the structure, operating as expectancies or hypotheses, will facilitate or hinder his learning of the structure according to their validity. The present study was designed to verify this general prediction and also to examine in more detail some of the psychological processes involved.

The study was basically a verbal learning experiment in which Ss learned miniature social structures. The dependent variable was the number of trials required. There were two independent variables: the interpersonal relation that formed the structure, and the mathematical properties of the structure. In their questionnaire study of the properties assigned to various interpersonal relations, De Soto and Kuethe (1959) found that the relations fell into two main classes: those regarded as asymmetric, which were also regarded as transitive, and those regarded as symmetric, some of which were also regarded as transitive and some of which were not. For the present study, the relation "influences" was chosen to exemplify the relations people expect to be asymmetric and transitive, "likes" was chosen to exemplify those expected to be symmetric and transitive, and "confides

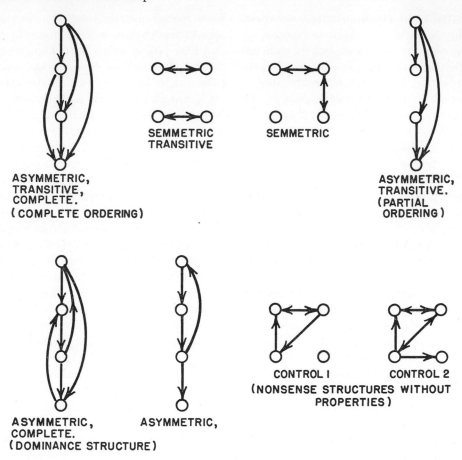

Figure 1. Structures used in the learning experiment

in" was chosen to exemplify those expected to be symmetric but not transitive.

Structures characterized by eight different sets of mathematical properties were used. Four-man structures were used because they were the largest Ss could learn with relative ease in pilot studies. The structures are depicted in Figure 1, with circles representing people and arrows a relation. An arrow going from one circle to another means the first person stands in the given relation to the second; if the relation is "influ-

ences," it means the first person influences the second. The requirements for the various properties may be defined informally as follows: For symmetry, the arrows must go in both directions, or not at all, between a pair of individuals. For asymmetry, the arrows must never go in both directions between a pair of individuals. The requirement for transitivity is more complex. If there is an arrow from Individual a to Individual b, and another from Individual b to Individual c, then, for the transitive property to hold, there must be one from a to c.

For the complete property to hold, there must be at least one arrow connecting the individuals in all possible pairs. More formal definitions of these and other properties are given by Coombs, Raiffa, and Thrall (1954) and Kershner and Wilcox (1950). The names given to some of the structures in Figure 1 are based on their properties.

The task given each S in the experiment was to learn one of the structures. He did not see a drawing of the structure, however, nor was the relation represented by abstract arrows. Instead, the arrows were replaced by one of the flesh-and-blood relations, "influences," "likes," or "confides in," and he had to learn, by repeated trial and error, whether or not Jim likes Ray, whether or not Ray likes Stan, and so on for the 12 ordered pairs of names which exist in a four-man structure. This arrangement of the task avoided unintended suggestions to the S about properties of the structure and approximated the real-life case where people learn a social structure by observing the pair-wise interactions among its members rather than from devices like organizational charts.

An experimental condition in this study was a combination of one of the abstract structures and one of the interpersonal relations. There were 19 experimental conditions. Each of the first three structures in Figure 1 was formed from each of the three relations, producing 9 conditions, and the remaining five structures were formed from the relations "influences" and "likes," producing 10 more conditions. The first 9 conditions were the basic experimental ones, since a crucial interaction was predicted for them. On the basis of the conclusion by De Soto and Kuethe (1959) that college students (used as Ss in that study and this) are alert to power based orderings, it was predicted that they would expect the relation "influences" to be asymmetric and transitive and, possibly, complete and would therefore learn a complete ordering based on "influences" more readily than one of the symmetric structures, while for "likes" and "confides in," which Ss expect to be symmetric, the converse would be true. The remaining conditions were included to provide further analytical possibilities.

METHOD

The experimental method resembled that of traditional paired-associates learning experiments. The Ss, male undergraduates at Johns Hopkins University, were assigned randomly, nine to each of the 19 experimental conditions, and were run individually.

Their task is described well by the instructions given them:

This experiment is on the learning of interpersonal relationships. There are four people involved, Bill, Jim, Ray, and Stan, and your job is to learn who likes who among these people.

On the upper side of each of these cards are printed the names of two of the four people. In each case, the first person either does or does not like the second. If he does, it says so on the other side of the card. If he doesn't, nothing is printed on the other side of the card.

When I tell you to begin, look at the names on the top card. If you think the first person likes the second, say so. If you don't think he does, say so. For example, if the first name were

Sam and the second were Charlie, you would say either "Sam likes Charlie" or "Sam doesn't like Charlie." Then, turn the card over and see whether or not he does, and place the card on a new pile.

Go through the rest of the cards the same way, and then I will shuffle them and you can go through them again. As we go through the cards again and again, you should learn better and better who likes who.

Take your time. Don't rush.

The above are the instructions given to all Ss who learned a social structure based on "likes." The instructions given to Ss who learned a social structure based on "influences" or "confides in" were identical in form except that the appropriate one of the following definitions was added: "To influence someone means to have some degree of control over what he does"; "To confide in someone means to have complete faith and confidence in him so that you trust him with secrets or rely on him for help."

Each S worked with a deck of 12 cards appropriate for his experimental condition.

RESULTS

The difficulty of learning the various social structures was measured by the mean number of trials required by the Ss to learn them to a criterion of two successive correct trials. These means are shown in Table 1. The standard errors of the means, highly correlated with their values, range from 1.06 to 4.27.

The hypothesized interaction between relations and structures is evident in Table 1. The Ss learned a complete ordering based on "influences" very readily, but had somewhat more difficulty with symmetric structures based on "influences." They had difficulty learning a complete ordering based on "likes" or "confides in," but learned symmetric structures based on these relations easily. An analysis of variance performed on the data for these nine conditions yielded an interaction mean square significant at the .01 level.

Examination of the remaining ten means shows that the partial ordering was learned relatively easily, at least when based on "influences," but the other conditions were all difficult, some

TABLE 1. MEAN TRIALS TO CRITERION

Structure	Relation		
	Influences	Likes	Confides in
Asymmetric, transitive, complete (complete ordering)	8.9	14.7	16.2
Symmetric, transitive	12.9	10.9	9.1
Symmetric	11.7	13.0	10.9
Asymmetric, transitive (partial ordering)	12.1	14.7	
Asymmetric, complete (dominance structure)	26.4	23.7	
Asymmetric	16.3	29.1	
Control 1	16.1	20.6	
Control 2	16.7	21.0	

of them exceedingly so. Particularly striking is the finding that the asymmetric and complete structure based on "influences" took substantially longer to learn than any of the nonsense structures, rather than showing facilitation from the fact that its properties were partly as expected by the Ss.

DISCUSSION

The experimental results clearly support the general hypothesis that people's assignments of mathematical properties to an interpersonal relation influence the ease with which they learn a social structure based on the relation, and they invite analysis of the psychological processes involved.

Perhaps the most remarkable finding is this: although the combination of the asymmetric, transitive, and complete properties (complete ordering) greatly facilitates the learning of a social structure based on "influences," the combination of only the asymmetric and complete properties (dominance structure) seems to make the learning task even more difficult than it is for structures without properties. The Ss failed completely to profit from the latter combination of properties, although in principle it too could be a valuable aid to learning a structure. Why?

It appears an inescapable conclusion that for the Ss these properties were not independent of one another, even though they are independent mathematically, and even though Ss are able to ascribe them separately to relations when questioned (De Soto & Kuethe, 1958, 1959). De Soto and Kuethe noted a tendency for Ss usually to ascribe the transitive property whenever they ascribed the asymmetric property to a relation. Evidently this tendency to couple the properties is so powerful that it prevents people from using the properties in isolation when learning a social structure. People expect mathematical properties in social structures, to be sure, but they expect them in bundles, and incomplete bundles are of no use to them.

It is as if the Ss had a theory about the social structure, a mathematical model for it which was very helpful when its properties corresponded with those of the social structure, but which had to be applied in an all-or-nothing manner in the sense that it was not readily abridged in the face of some lack of correspondence and became instead a hindrance. Such a theory, marked by certain essential properties but doubtlessly skeletal and sketchy in other respects, seems most aptly called a *schema*, roughly following Bartlett (1932) and Woodworth (1938).

The present data, then, might be interpreted to indicate that the Ss possessed an ordering schema which they automatically applied to a social structure based on the relation "influences," although not to one based on "likes" or "confides in." "Influences" might be said to tap or arouse people's ordering schema. This ordering schema, the residue perhaps of countless experiences with social and nonsocial orderings in the world, seems to be marked by the properties of asymmetry, transitivity, and, possibly, completeness. Thus the Ss expected these properties in a social structure based on "influences," but not as independent expectations; rather, as derivatives of the overriding expectation that the structure was an ordering. Perhaps the dominance structure was more difficult than the nonsense structures because it perpetually titillated and tantalized the Ss' ordering schema, preventing the suppression of it that occurred for the nonsense structures.

Evidence that more sophisticated students of social structures also possess and can be victims of an ordering schema is found in many writings about peck rights among birds. Birds establish peck rights on the basis of pair-wise encounters, a process which insures that the eventual social structure is asymmetric and complete, but not that it is transitive. The birds, being simple-minded creatures not possessed of an ordering schema, thus innocently build a social structure that puzzles and provokes more thoughtful creatures who write about the "pecking out of order," "curious exceptions," "irregularities," "imperfect orderings," "lack of a hierarchy," "polygonal dominance," "cyclic pecking," "triangular pecking," and "complex, triangular hierarchies" (Allee, 1931; Collias, 1944; Murchison, 1935; Murphy, Murphy, & Newcomb, 1937; Schjelderup-Ebbe, 1935). People consider this primitive and simple social structure surprising and complex because they expect an ordering. To turn the thing around, it may be that the expectation of an ordering tends to *produce* an ordering, that human social groups would show fewer orderings and more dominance structures and even property free structures if it were not for the shared expectation of orderings.

The finding that the partial ordering was learned quite readily when based on "influences," with the Ss' ordering schema presumably aroused, suggests that the property of completeness is a less integral part of the ordering schema than the properties of asymmetry and transitivity. However, any partial order-

ing can be mathematically treated as made up of two or more complete orderings (Coombs & Kao, 1955; Kershner & Wilcox, 1950), and it is possible that the Ss accomplished essentially this analysis of the partial ordering.

The property of symmetry seems to be fairly easy to detect and utilize even when it is not expected, as in the structures based on "influences." The results suggest that for "likes" and "confides in" a symmetric and transitive structure is learned easier than a merely symmetric one, but the differences are not large, and it should be noted that the so-called symmetric and transitive structure of Figure 1 is only *vacuously* transitive (Kershner & Wilcox, 1950), having too few members to be truly transitive. Thus, it is impossible to say more than that a lack of transitivity is not the severe handicap in learning symmetric structures that it is in learning asymmetric ones. This conclusion is consistent with the view expressed earlier (De Soto & Kuethe, 1959) that the primary property ascribed to these relations is symmetry, and that transitivity is ascribed secondarily, only after long experience which teaches that relations like "likes" are commonly transitive, dividing people into cliques or friendship groups. The grouping schema, as applied to interpersonal relations at least, is a higher development of the symmetry schema.

SUMMARY

By means of a learning experiment it was shown that a social structure is easiest to learn when it possesses the mathematical properties people expect in it. People attribute the properties of asymmetry, transitivity, and completeness (the properties of an ordering) to the relation "influences." If a social structure formed of the relation "influences" has these properties, they learn it readily. If it is symmetric, or if it has no mathematical properties, they have more difficulty; and if it is asymmetric and complete but not transitive (a dominance structure), they have great difficulty. Similarly, structures based on "likes" or "confides in" are learned most readily when they are symmetric, as people expect them to be. The findings were interpreted as reflecting the operation of schemas in the Ss.

REFERENCES

ALLEE, W. C. *Animal aggregations: A study in general sociology.* Chicago: Univer. Chicago Press, 1931.

BARTLETT, F. C. *Remembering.* Cambridge: Cambridge Univer. Press, 1932.

COLLIAS, N. E. Aggressive behavior among vertebrates. *Physiol. Zool.,* 1944, 17, 83–123.

COOMBS, C. H., & KAO, R. C. Non-metric factor analysis. *Engng. res. Bull.* No. 38. Ann Arbor: Univer. Michigan Press, 1955.

COOMBS, C. H., RAIFFA, H., & THRALL, R. M. Some views on mathematical models and measurement theory. *Psychol. Rev.,* 1954, 61, 132–144.

DE SOTO, C. B., & KUETHE, J. L. Perception of mathematical properties of interpersonal relations. *Percept. mot. Skills,* 1958, 8, 279–286.

DE SOTO, C. B., & KUETHE, J. L. Subjective probabilities of interpersonal relationships. *J. abnorm. soc. Psychol.,* 1959, 59, 290–294.

HEIDER, F. *The psychology of interpersonal relations.* New York: Wiley, 1958.

KERSHNER, R. B., & WILCOX, L. R. *The anatomy of mathematics.* New York: Ronald, 1950.

KOGAN, N., & TAGIURI, R. Interpersonal preference and cognitive organization. *J. abnorm. soc. Psychol.,* 1958, 56, 113–116.

MURCHISON, C. The experimental measurement of a social hierarchy in *gallus domesticus:* I. The direct identification and direct measurement of social reflex no. 1 and social reflex no. 2. *J. gen. Psychol.,* 1935, 12, 3–39.

MURPHY, G., MURPHY, L. B., & NEWCOMB, T. M. *Experimental social psychology.* (Rev. ed.) New York: Harper & Row, 1937.

SCHJELDERUP-EBBE, T. Social life of birds. In C. Murchison (Ed.), *Handbook of social psychology.* Worcester, Mass.: Clark Univer. Press, 1935.

TAGIURI, R. Social preference and its perception. In R. Tagiuri & L. Petrullo (Eds.), *Person perception and interpersonal behavior.* Stanford, Cal.: Stanford Univer. Press, 1958.

WOODWORTH, R. S. *Experimental psychology.* New York: Holt, Rinehart and Winston, 1938.

39. LEADER'S CONTRIBUTION TO TASK PERFORMANCE IN COHESIVE AND UNCOHESIVE GROUPS *

Fred E. Fiedler and W. A. T. Meuwese

Although a group or a team may be frequently less efficient than individuals working alone (Faust, 1959; McCurdy & Lambert, 1952; Shaw, 1932) when taken on a per man-hour basis, teamwork is essential where the task precludes

* Reprinted from *Journal of Abnormal and Social Psychology,* 1963, 67: 83–87, with permission of the senior author and the American Psychological Association. This study was conducted under Contract NR 177-472, Nonr-1834(36), "Group and Organization Factors Influencing Group Creativity," between the Office of Naval Research and the University of Illinois.

individuals from independent action. A single individual cannot operate a submarine or represent three widely divergent viewpoints. One of the leader's main functions is the effective use and coordination of his team members' skills and abilities.

Interestingly enough, practically no work has been published on the specific conditions under which efficient utilization of the leader's or his group members' abilities takes place. We have generally assumed that a good group simply consists of abler members than a poor group. Leaders tend to be chosen from among those most competent to perform the job they are to supervise. The present paper attempts to show that the leader's ability to contribute to the task depends to a considerable extent on the cohesiveness of his group.

The underlying hypothesis deriving from earlier work (Fiedler, 1958) can be described as follows: The leader's ability to contribute to the group's productivity requires that the group's structure enable him to communicate effectively with all members, and that the members be willing to follow the directions of the leader.

It is probably also necessary that the leader is free to devote his influence to the task rather than having to direct his efforts mainly toward group maintenance. From empirical evidence (Back, 1951; Fiedler, 1958) it may be inferred that these conditions are fulfilled if there is a certain degree of *cohesiveness* in the group. In this paper a group is defined to be cohesive if one or both of the following conditions are present in the group: the members feel attracted to the group, the members are adjusted to the group and free of interpersonal tension. Both of these conditions can be assessed by questionnaires administered to the group members.

We shall here examine data which were obtained in four different studies. The analyses were based on the assumption that a correlation between some person's ability or achievement score and some measure of his group's performance provides a measure of the individual's direct influence on the group's task performance.

The major operational hypothesis to be tested was that: The leader's ability score will correlate positively with a measure of group effectiveness in cohesive groups, but not in uncohesive groups.

METHOD AND RESULTS

Tank Crew Study

A study was conducted on 25 Army tank crews which participated in an experiment comparing tank equipment (Fiedler, 1955). Each crew consisted of five enlisted men, viz., a tank commander (TC) who was the formal leader of the group, a gunner (G), a driver (D), a loader (L), and a bow gunner (BG). All crews remained intact during the course of the study.

Each crew was assigned to work with five different models of tanks and each tank test entailed driving toward, recognizing, and hitting five different targets. A combined criterion was developed which estimated the probability that a tank performing in this manner would emerge victorious in a duel with a similar tank. This score was based on the number of seconds required for each of the three subtasks; time to travel to the target, time to recognize the target, and time to hit the target. Army General

TABLE 1. CORRELATION (rho) OF ARMY GENERAL CLASSIFICATION TEST (AGCT)
AND PROFICIENCY SCORES WITH TANK CREW CRITERIA
$(N = 8)$

Group	TC	G	D	L	BG
			AGCT Score		
Cohesive	26	05	52	76**	59
Uncohesive	−21	−29	20	23	−21
			Proficiency Score		
Cohesive	94***	38	94***	47	49
Uncohesive	−21	−38	−66*	43	−23

Note.—TC = Tank commander, G = Gunner, D = Driver, L = Loader, BG = Bow gunner.
* $p < .10$, two-tailed.
** $p < .05$, two-tailed.
*** $p < .01$, two-tailed.

Classification Test (AGCT) scores as well as individual proficiency scores were obtained for all crew members prior to the experiment.

The sample was divided into the eight most cohesive and the eight least cohesive groups on the basis of sociometric choices which were obtained from crew members at three points in the experiment. As can be seen from Table 1, Column 1, the contribution of the leader is greater in cohesive groups. This trend emerges most clearly when proficiency scores are utilized.

Although this was not hypothesized, it can also be seen from Table 1 that the ability of the other crew members generally correlated positively in cohesive teams while zero or negative relations were found in uncohesive teams.

B-29 Bomber Crews

A second set of crew performance and individual proficiency data were obtained in the course of a study on B-29 bomber crews (Fiedler, 1955). These crews, each consisting of five officers and six enlisted men, were in training at Randolph Air Force Base during the Korean war in 1951.

Ground School Grades (GSG) were available for several crew members. These grades reflect with reasonable accuracy the crew member's competence on his crew tasks. According to research of the Air Force Crew Research Laboratory at Randolph Field, one of the best objective measures of crew effectiveness was the "Radar Bomb Score circular error average" (RBS). The reliability of this score was estimated to be .45 (Knoell & Forgays, 1952).

Several measures were obtained which indicate the cohesiveness or attractiveness of the crew. These were the crew members' ratings of confidence in the aircraft commander, liking for the aircraft commander, liking for fellow crew members, and feeling of crew effectiveness. The median intercorrelation of these measures was .59 and the ratings were, therefore, combined.

On the basis of these combined

TABLE 2. CORRELATIONS (rho) OF INDIVIDUAL GROUND SCHOOL GRADES AND RADAR
BOMB SCORES UNDER DIFFERENT CONDITIONS OF ATTRACTION
TO GROUP (Cohesiveness)

Group	Cohesiveness					
	High		Low		Very Low	
	N	r	N	r	N	r
Officers						
Aircraft commander	6	67	7	85*	4	−40
Pilot	6	70	7	43	5	30
Bombardier	5	80	7	22	5	−30
Radar operator	5	48	6	41	5	30
$\bar{r}$		66		48		−02
Enlisted						
Radio operator	5	−20	7	47	5	−18
Left gunner	5	−30	7	−01	5	10
Right gunner	5	−78	7	−87**	5	−70
$\bar{r}$		−43		−14		−26

* $p < .05$, two-tailed.
** $p < .01$, two-tailed.

cohesiveness or attractiveness scores, the crews were divided into those having high, low, and very low attractiveness to crew members.[1] Table 2 presents the correlation of ground school scores with the radar bomb score criterion.

The officers' proficiency score correlated positively with radar bomb scores in high and low cohesiveness conditions, but not in very low cohesive groups. The proficiency of the enlisted men correlated zero or negatively with the criterion. In essence, therefore, these findings support those obtained on Army tank crews. This analysis also suggests the possibility that not only the leader's proficiency, but also the proficiency of the key members, in this case the officers, can influence group effectiveness only in cohesive teams.

[1] Data for "medium cohesive" crews were too incomplete to be of use.

Research on Antiaircraft Artillery Crews

A study was conducted by Hutchins and Fiedler (1960) on antiaircraft artillery crews, each of which consisted of 8–12 enlisted men. AGCT scores were gathered on all available personnel. As was the case in other studies, complete data could not be obtained from all crews in the sample because of sickness, temporary leaves, or duty assignments away from the site of testing.

Crew performance scores were based on crew rankings by officers in charge of companies and platoons. These rankings correlated with objective target acquisition and performance scores which were the accepted crew performance criteria indicating that the guns were accurately aimed on the targets.

The General Army Adjustment (GAA) scores which are indices of

TABLE 3. CORRELATION (rho) OF AGCT WITH EFFECTIVENESS IN GROUPS HIGH, MEDIUM, AND LOW ON LEADER'S AND MEMBER'S GENERAL ARMY ADJUSTMENT SCORE

	High	Medium	Low
	Leader's GAA Score		
	$(N = 6)$	$(N = 9)$	$(N = 9)$
AGCT leader	84*	−21	23
$\overline{AGCT}$ members	24	−37	−17
	Member's $\overline{GAA}$ Score		
	$(N = 8)$	$(N = 8)$	$(N = 8)$
$\overline{AGCT}$ leader	57	26	−05
$\overline{AGCT}$ members	−48	−01	−07

Note.—Seventeen groups were omitted from the analysis because of missing data.
* $p < .05$, two-tailed.

morale and crew attractiveness served to indicate the cohesiveness of the group. The groups were divided into crews high, medium, and low on these two criteria. The AGCT score of the leader and the average AGCT score of the members were correlated with the crew's effectiveness. The results are presented in Table 3.

Again, it can be seen that the leader's AGCT score correlates with performance in cohesive crews (high GAA) but not in uncohesive crews. Member AGCT, on the other hand, does not correlate with crew performance in either cohesive or uncohesive groups.

Research on Group Creativity

The last study to be described was intended to identify leader attitudes which are conducive to group creativity (Fiedler, Meuwese, & Oonk, 1961). This investigation was conducted in the Netherlands and utilized 32 Catholic and 32 Calvinist university students. Each sub-ject participated in two groups: once in a four-man team having homogeneous membership, and once in a team consisting of two men from each religion. In 16 of the groups the experimenters appointed a chairman, while the other 16 groups worked as "informal" teams.

The task consisted in devising three different stories from the same TAT card, either Card 11 or 19. The creativity expressed in these stories was judged by two raters on the basis of a manual. The correlation between the two judges' ratings was .81 for Card 11 and .88 for Card 19.

A 14-item Analogies test[2] was administered to all subjects and we are here concerned with the relation of performance on this short intelligence test and group creativity. The groups were divided into those which seemed tense and unpleasant and thus uncohesive, and those which were relaxed and at ease,

[2] Constructed by J. C. van Lennep, University of Utrecht. This test is similar in form and content to the Miller Analogies Test.

TABLE 4. CORRELATIONS (rho)
BETWEEN GROUP CREATIVITY
AND ANALOGIES SCORES

Analogies Score of	"Cohesive" No Destructive Critic (N = 14)	"Uncohesive" Destructive Critic (N = 17)
Informal leader	54*	24
Group members	−02	18

Note.—In one group it was impossible to determine the informal leader on the basis of the sociometric questions.

* $p < .05$, one-tailed.

hence cohesive. This was inferred from sociometric questions which asked the subjects to name individuals who were "destructively critical." The informal leader of the group was determined by means of sociometric questions, that is, "Which of the group members had most influence on the opinions of others?"

Correlations between creativity and informal leader's Analogies scores and member's average Analogies scores are presented in Table 4.

Here again, we find that the leader's intelligence influences the group performance most in cohesive, pleasant groups. The informal leader has little direct influence in groups which are relatively uncohesive. It can thus be concluded that this analysis also confirms the hypothesized relationship.

Significance of Results

To assess the combined probability that this series of results could have been obtained by chance, a set of four independent cases was formed, consisting of the *smallest* correlations for each separate sample from Table 5 in which the main results of this study are summarized. The combined probability for these four samples, computed according to Jones and Fiske (1953), was below the .01 level, one-tailed test.

DISCUSSION

The results clearly confirm the hypothesis that a leader directly influences the effectiveness of the group only if the group is cohesive. This relationship was found in four entirely different studies and it thus seems to be fairly general.

The results do *not* indicate that the leader does not have *power* in uncohesive groups. He may or may not have power; but if he does, he exerts it in a way that is not directly reflected in the group's product. Thus, the leader of an uncohesive group may be forced into a position in which it is necessary to exert influence mainly on the maintenance of the group. Cohesive groups probably do not require as much of the leader's effort to maintain the group as would be the case in uncohesive groups. The leader may, therefore, be able to influence the level of group task performance by contributing directly to the solution of the problem.

REFERENCES

BACK, K. Influence through social communication. *J. abnorm. soc. Psychol.,* 1951, 46, 9–23.

FAUST, W. L. Group versus individual problem-solving. *J. abnorm. soc. Psychol.,* 1959, 59, 68–72.

FIEDLER, F. E. The influence of leader-keyman relations on combat crew effectiveness. *J. abnorm. soc. Psychol.,* 1955, 51, 227–235.

FIEDLER, F. E. *Leader attitudes and group effectiveness.* Urbana: Univer. Illinois Press, 1958.

FIEDLER, F. E., MEUWESE, W. A. T., &

TABLE 5. CORRELATIONS OF LEADER'S ABILITY WITH GROUP EFFECTIVENESS

Study	Ability Score	Effectiveness Criterion	Cohesiveness Criterion	Correlation (rho)			
				Cohesive Groups	N	Uncohesive Groups	N
Army tank crews	AGCT	Probability of winning a battle	Sociometric	.26	8	−.21	8
Army tank crews	Proficiency rating	Probability of winning a battle	Sociometric	.94**	8	−.21	8
B-29 bomber crews	Ground School Grade	Radar bomb score	Liking for the group	.67	6	−.40	4
Antiaircraft artillery crews	AGCT	Ratings	Leader's Army Adjustment score	.84*	6	.23	9
Antiaircraft artillery crews	AGCT	Ratings	Member's Army Adjustment score	.57	8	−.05	8
Dutch creativity study	Analogies score	Creativity ratings	Presence of destructive critic	.54*	14	.24	17

* p < .05.
** p < .01.

Oonk, Sophie. An exploratory study of group creativity in laboratory tasks. *Acta psychol., Amsterdam*, 1961, **18**, 100–119.

Hutchins, E. B., & Fiedler, F. E. Task-oriented and quasi-therapeutic role functions of the leader in small military groups. *Sociometry*, 1960, **23**, 393–406.

Jones, L. V., & Fiske, D. W. Models for testing the significance of combined results. *Psychol. Bull.*, 1953, **50**, 375–382.

Knoell, Dorothy, & Forgays, D. G. Interrelationships of combat crew performance in the B-29. *USAF Hum. Resour. Res. Cent., Res. Note*, 1952, CCT 52–1.

McCurdy, H. G., & Lambert, W. E. The efficiency of small human groups in the solution of problems requiring genuine cooperation. *J. Pers.*, 1952, **20**, 478–494.

Shaw, Marjorie E. A comparison of individuals and small groups in the rational solution of complex problems. *Amer. J. Psychol.*, 1932, **44**, 491–504.

40. AN EXPERIMENTAL TEST OF A THEORY OF COALITION FORMATION *

William A. Gamson

Coalition formation is comparatively rare among sociological phenomena in its susceptibility to experimental study. A number of such studies have already explored coalitions in the three-person group.[1] In an earlier paper,[2] a theory was presented which attempted to generalize coalition formation beyond the triad while still handling existing results. Earlier results provided a post-hoc "test." This paper describes the results of an experiment designed to test the theory more directly.

The theory applies to situations which meet the following conditions: (1) There is a decision to be made and there are more than two social units attempting to maximize their share of the payoff; (2) No single alternative will maximize the payoff to all participants; (3) No participant has dictatorial powers, that is, no one has initial resources sufficient to control the decision by himself; (4) No participant has veto power, that is, no member *must* be included in every winning coalition.

To predict who will join with whom in any specific instance, information is needed on the following:

1. The initial distribution of resources. We must know what the rele-

[1] See especially W. E. Vinacke and A. Arkoff, "An Experimental Study of Coalitions in the Triad," *American Sociological Review*, 22 (August, 1957), pp. 406–415; T. M. Mills, "Coalition Pattern in Three-Person Groups," *American Sociological Review*, 19 (December, 1954), pp. 657–667; J. R. Bond and W. E. Vinacke, "Coalitions in Mixed-Sex Triads," *Sociometry*, 24 (March, 1961), pp. 61–75; W. E. Vinacke, "Sex Roles in a Three-Person Game," *Sociometry*, 22 (December, 1959), pp. 343–360; S. Stryker and G. Psathas, "Research on Coalitions in the Triad: Findings, Problems, and Strategy," *Sociometry*, 23 (September, 1960), pp. 217–230; and H. H. Kelley and A. J. Arrowhead, "Coalitions in the Triad: Critique and Experiment," *Sociometry*, 23 (September, 1960), pp. 231–244.

[2] William A. Gamson, "A Theory of Coalition Formation," *American Sociological Review*, 26 (June, 1961), pp. 373–382. See this paper for a fuller description of the theory and its relation to the sociological and mathematical literature.

* Reprinted from *American Sociological Review*, 1961, 26: 565–573, with permission of the author and the American Sociological Association. This research was conducted under a grant from the Social Science Research Council.

vant resources are for any given decision and, at some starting point, how much of these resources each participant controls.

2. The payoff for each coalition. The theory specifies that only one coalition wins and the payoff to all non-members is zero. Therefore, we need know only the payoff associated with each possible winning coalition.

3. Non-utilitarian strategy prefer-cnccs. We must have a rank ordering (with ties allowed) of each participant's inclination to join with every other player *exclusive of that player's control of the resources.*

4. The effective decision point. We must know the amount of resources necessary to determine the decision.

A minimal winning coalition is a winning coalition such that the defection of any member will make the coalition no longer winning. The cheapest winning coalition is that minimal winning coalition with total resources closest to the decision point. The general hypothesis of the theory states that *any participant will expect others to demand from a coalition a share of the payoff proportional to the amount of resources that they contribute to a coalition.*

Any participant, A, estimates the *payoff to himself* from a prospective coalition as a product of the *total payoff* to that coalition and A's expected share of that total. The total payoff is known to A and the general hypothesis specifies the share that A will expect to give to others. Thus, A can assign to any prospective coalition a personal payoff value —his proportion of the resources in the coalition multiplied by the total payoff for that coalition.

When a player must choose among alternative coalition strategies where the total payoff to a winning coalition is constant, he will maximize his payoff by maximizing his *share.* The theory states that he will do this by maximizing the ratio of his resources to the total resources of the coalition. Since his resources will be the same regardless of which coalition he joins, the lower the total resources, the greater will be his share. Thus, where the total payoff is held constant, he will favor the *cheapest winning coalition.*

Finally, a coalition will form if and only if there are *reciprocal strategy choices* between two participants. To illustrate, let us assume the X's desired coalition in some three-person game is XY, that Y's is XY or YZ, and that Z's favored coalition is XZ. Only X and Y have *reciprocal strategy choices,* i.e., require the other in their preferred coalition, and, thus, the coalition XY is predicted by the theory. The model envisions the process of coalition formation as a step-by-step process where the participants join two at a time. Once a coalition has been formed, the situation becomes a new one—that is, there is a fresh distribution of resources—and, in the new coalition situation, the original strategies may or may not be appropriate.

EXPERIMENTAL DESIGN

A total of 120 subjects were recruited from social fraternities at the University of Michigan. They were told that they would be participating in an experimental study of "how political conventions operate" and that each of them would be playing the role of delegation chairman at a series of political conventions. At the beginning of every convention, each subject was given a sheet with the number of votes he and each of the other delegation chairmen controlled. The experiment consisted of 24 five-man groups composed of three men from one fraternity house and two from another.

The object of the game, for each subject, was to "win" political patronage or "jobs." To do this, he had to put together a majority of the votes by combining with other chairmen in a prescribed fashion. To form a coalition, he had to decide with the other chairman or chairmen how to divide up the jobs to which their coalition was entitled.

The operationalizations of the variables of the theory are:

1. INITIAL DISTRIBUTION OF RESOURCES The number of votes or delegates controlled by each subject were the resources of the convention; the total number of votes was 101.

2. THE PAYOFF A certain number of jobs were associated with every winning coalition and the subjects were told to try to acquire as many of these jobs as possible over all the conventions.

3. NON-UTILITARIAN STRATEGY PREFERENCE The use of fraternity members as subjects was dictated by this variable. We assumed that every subject had a positive preference for the other subject or subjects who were members of the same fraternity as himself and that he was neutral between members within any one house.

Positions in the conventions were labeled by color and these colors were assigned in two different ways to vary non-utilitarian strategy preferences. In Condition RBW, the three-man contingent received the colors red, blue, and white randomly distributed among them while the two-man contingent received yellow and green. In Condition YGW, the three-man contingent received yellow, green, and white and the two-man group received red and blue. Assignments were made alternately, resulting in 12 groups under each condition of non-utilitarian strategy preference. An effort was made to keep the social status of the members the same *within* any house, that is, active or senior fraternity members were not placed with new initiates or "pledges."

4. DECISION POINT A simple majority of the 101 votes was necessary for a coalition to be awarded the designated number of jobs and thus end the convention.

Specific Procedures

For each convention,[3] the subjects had a list giving the initial distribution in votes and information from which they could calculate the payoff to any coalition. Table 1 reproduces these figures with the positions identified by color.

The subjects were seated behind partitions so that they were not visible to each other although they could all be seen by the experimenter. Each had a set of five invitation cards which had the color of each chairman including the subject's own color. At a given signal, the subjects held up the single card of the person with whom they wished to bargain or, if they did not wish to bar-

---

[3] Each group participated in four conventions altogether, with each convention adding an additional complexity. The final convention, while it had some interesting developments, was inconclusive as a test of the theory and will not be reported here.

TABLE 1. INITIAL DISTRIBUTION OF RESOURCES AND PAYOFF
FOR THREE EXPERIMENTAL SITUATIONS

Convention		Player				
		Red	Yellow	Blue	Green	White
One	Votes	20	20	20	20	20
	Jobs	100	100	100	100	100
Two	Votes	17	25	17	25	17
	Jobs	100	100	100	100	100
Three	Votes	15	35	35	6	10
	Jobs	90	100	0	90	0

gain at that time, their own card. The experimenter then announced whether or not reciprocal choices had occurred.

If and only if such reciprocal choices occurred, the two subjects left their partitions and entered the "smoke filled room" where they were allowed to discuss the terms of a deal for a period of three minutes. In order to form a coalition, they had to reach an agreement on some *division of the jobs* which would be their portion if they ended up in a winning coalition. They were not committed to reach an agreement simply because they had entered the bargaining room and they could meet again later by the procedure of reciprocal invitations.

At the end of each bargaining session, the experimenter announced to the rest of the group whether or not an agreement had been reached although he did not reveal the terms. If an agreement was reached and the chairmen involved possessed a majority of the votes, the convention was over and the experimenter distributed the job tokens in the manner specified by their agreement. If, as in most cases, their agreement left them short of a majority, they then returned to the "convention floor,"

where they were allowed to sit behind the same partition and communicate freely. For the duration of the convention, they played as a *unit*; the coalition acted in every way as if it were a single player with the combined resources of its members. Together the two members of a coalition held up only one card and any other player invited the whole coalition or other unattached players.

Subsequent bargaining sessions might involve three or even four people but they were essentially two-man sessions with one side of the table being represented by a two-member delegation in which one person acted as spokesman. These bargaining sessions were recorded on tape. Each convention continued by the procedure described until an agreement had been reached between chairmen who controlled a majority of the votes. The convention was then complete and the jobs were distributed.

To avoid the necessity of listing all coalitions, subjects were given the following rule by which they could calculate the payoff for any coalition: A winning coalition receives the highest number of jobs associated with any member; a losing coalition receives nothing. Thus, in Convention Three (see Table 1) a coalition between Red, Yellow, and Green would receive 100 jobs while one between Blue, Green, and White received 90 jobs.

A cash prize was given to the person with the highest job total at each position over all 24 groups. The experimenter pointed out to the subjects that this manner of awarding the prize meant that there was nothing to gain by "punishing" someone in the present group during the later conventions in the series because of his high total on earlier ones. We hoped by this means to forestall one possible interdependence between conventions. The results of each convention were not announced until the conclusion of all conventions and the subjects were prohibited from looking ahead or making any commitments beyond the duration of one convention.

An illustrative example from Convention Two might provide some feeling for the action of the experiment. On round one of the invitations, Red (with 17 votes) and Yellow (with 25 votes) hold up each other's cards and there is no reciprocity among the others. Red and Yellow enter the bargaining room and agree to divide their share, 40 percent for Red and 60 percent for Yellow. They return to the convention floor and there are no reciprocal invitations for a few rounds. Finally, on the fifth round, Red-Yellow and Blue hold up each other's cards.

They are unable to reach an agreement, and on round six, Red-Yellow and White hold up each other's cards and Blue and Green also choose each other. Red-Yellow and White meet in one room and Blue and Green also bargain in another. The former group reaches an agreement in which White receives 30 percent and Red-Yellow get 70 percent.

This coalition is now winning and is entitled to 100 jobs under the formula given earlier of which White receives 30, Red receives 28 (40 percent of 70 jobs) and Yellow gets 42 (60 percent of 70 jobs).

EXPERIMENTAL RESULTS

The assumption that subjects would prefer members of their own fraternity to those from a different group was simpler than the actual case. Occasionally, exactly the opposite effect was true. Some players preferred to take their chances with a starnger rather than to bargain with a "difficult" fraternity brother. In short, nonutilitarian strategy preferences were somewhat uncontrolled, with fraternity affiliation as perhaps the most important but still only one of several determinants.

Convention One

Convention One (see Table 1) actually tests the validity of the fraternity distinction rather than the theory. It indicates the extent to which individuals choose to join with their fraternity brothers where the "rational" parameters of the theory are held constant.

In Table 2 we can see that while there is a tendency present it is somewhat less than universal. The chance frequencies of choosing one's fraternity brothers are given in parentheses next to the actual frequencies. The choices are tabulated separately for those who had only one fraternity brother in the group and those who had two. Only when all rounds in which there were no reciprocal invitations previously are taken to-

TABLE 2. FREQUENCY OF CHOOSING FRATERNITY BROTHERS IN CONVENTION ONE

		Brother	*Other*	N [b]	P
First round	3-man-group	57% (50%)	43% (50%)	68	NS
	2-man group	36% (25%)	64% (75%)	45	≐.10
Other rounds [a]	3-man group	60% (50%)	40% (50%)	63	≐.10
	2-man group	28% (25%)	72% (75%)	46	NS
Total	3-man group	59% (50%)	41% (50%)	131	<.05
	2-man group	32% (25%)	68% (75%)	91	NS

[a] Where no reciprocal choices occurred on earlier rounds.

[b] The total number of first round choices is only 113 since seven subjects held up their own color on the first round.

gether is the tendency for subjects to choose their fraternity brother statistically significant; the magnitude remains slight.[4]

We must conclude that there is very little validity to fraternity membership as a measure of nonutilitarian strategy preference. Few of the results in the remainder of the experiment differed between the two methods of assigning colors. Consequently, the results for the two conditions will be combined with a few exceptions where the differences are still of interest.

The theory actually makes two kinds of predictions. One type concerns the individual invitations in each convention ("choice" hypotheses), while the other concerns the formation of coalitions through reciprocal choices ("combinatorial" hypotheses).

There is one genuine test of the theory contained in Convention One. When the two coalitions have formed without a majority being reached, the

situation is a Caplow Type 3 triad[5] in which two "players" have 40 votes and a third has 20 votes. This occurred in seven of the groups. The choice hypothesis in this situation is that the players with 40 votes will choose the player with 20 votes rather than each other.

This hypothesis is tested twice, independently, every time the situation occurs, and of the 14 independent tests, 13 were predicted correctly ($P < .001$). The combinatorial hypothesis would predict that the final coalition will *not* be between the two groups with 40 votes each. This was confirmed in six of the seven cases and the one exception occurred only after three earlier bargaining sessions had failed to produce a coalition which would have confirmed the hypothesis.

Convention Two

In this convention, the theory predicts that Red, Blue, and White will choose each other and that the cheapest coalition, Red-Blue-White, will be the final coalition.

[4] The null hypothesis in this and subsequent cases is calculated on the assumption that players are choosing at random. To test the significance of departures from chance frequencies, the binomial distribution was used with a small N (under 25) and Chi Square was used with a larger N.

[5] See Theodore Caplow, "A Theory of Coalitions in the Triad," *American Sociological Review,* 21 (August, 1956), pp. 489–493.

TABLE 3. INITIAL CHOICES FOR CONVENTION TWO

	Percentage Correctly Predicted	N	P
Red, blue, white	61 (50)[a]	67	<.10
Red, blue, white (revised) [b]	66 (50)	56	<.02
Yellow, green	33 (75)	48	(<.01)[c]

[a] The expected chance percentages are included next to the actual percentages in this and in subsequent tables.

[b] Excluding choices by White in Condition YGW.

[c] In opposite direction.

The case of Yellow and Green in Convention Two is an interesting one and raises a problem which is frequently encountered by "rational" theories. How much credit for foresight is assumed? The cheapest winning coalition for either Yellow or Green would be formed by joining with two of the players with 17 votes. Shouldn't Yellow and Green, therefore, choose among Red, Blue, and White according to the theory presented here?

Yellow and Green may reason that while *their* best interest lies with these players, Red, Blue, and White have no incentive to choose them. Therefore, the most "rational" strategy in the circumstances may be to play in a manner which will disrupt the game or, in other words, to play for an "error." If Yellow and Green combine quickly, for example, they may be able to woo one of the others before they can combine. Yet, there is no reason to expect that playing for an error in this way is preferable to playing for a "direct" error by assuming that Red, Blue, or White will fail to see their proper strategy from the outset. If all errors are equally possible, Yellow and Green should still estimate their expected payoff from a coalition in the manner predicated by the theory. Ac-

cordingly, we predicted that in Convention Two, Yellow and Green will choose either Red, Blue, or White.

Table 3 shows that Red, Blue, and White do have some tendency to choose each other as predicted. Under condition YGW where Red and Blue are from one fraternity and Yellow, Green, and White are from the other, White is in a position where he *must* choose a member of a rival fraternity if he is to choose Red or Blue as the theory predicts. Therefore, we have provided in Table 3 a revised initial choice tally which excludes those cases in which *all* of the predicted choices were in a different fraternity from the chooser. With the removal of these eleven cases, the significance level goes up sharply and the hypothesis is more substantially confirmed.

More striking than the confirmation of the hypothesis concerning Red, Blue, and White is the significant *reversal* of the hypothesis concerning Yellow and Green. Not only might Yellow and Green feel that the predicted choices would not reciprocate, but they are also from the same fraternity house in both conditions. Where they were the only members from that house, in condition RBW, the tendency to pick each other

TABLE 4. FINAL COALITIONS AND FIRST POTENTIALLY WINNING SESSION
FOR CONVENTION TWO

	Final Coalition	First Potentially Winning Session
RBW (predicted)	8 (p < .002)	10 (p < .001)
RYB	2	1
RBG	2	2
RGW	3	3
YBW	1	1
RYW	0	0
BGW	0	0
RYG	2	3
YBG	1	1
YGW	5	3
Total	24	24

is considerably greater. In this case, they pick each other 79 percent of the time with a chance expectancy of 25 percent, while in condition YGW, they choose each other only 54 percent of the time (.10 > p > .05). Apparently, Yellow and Green are eschewing the "lost cause" of inviting Red, White, or Blue and are instead turning to each other.

As we can see in Table 4, they are sometimes successful in luring one of the players with 17 votes into the coalition and for considerably less than ⅓ of the jobs. While the predicted coalition Red-Blue-White takes place significantly more often than chance, there are numerous "errors." Occasionally, Red, Blue, and White reached the bargaining room as the theory predicted but could not reach an agreement. Subsequently, they may have joined or some other winning coalition may have formed. To be able to predict who will reach the bargaining room in this situation is at least partial support for the theory, so we have examined this criterion as well. It reveals more impressive confirmation for the theory despite

the fact that where Red, Blue, and White *finally* joined they were not always the first potentially winning group to meet.

Since the theory frequently favors the initially weak against the initially strong, it is interesting to examine the following four-man situation which occurs fairly frequently in Convention Two: [6]

Red-Blue:	34 votes
Green:	25 votes
Yellow:	25 votes
White:	17 votes

Here, the cheapest winning coalition is between the strongest player, Red-Blue, and the weakest, White; those who are in between in resources are in the strategically weakest position according to the theory. This hypothesis is supported in 10 out of 12 instances (p < .001).

Many other situations develop in the step-by-step process of coalition for-

[6] For convenience, the coalition is called Red-Blue and the player with 17 votes, White.

mation that are in effect new situations. These, as in the four-man situations described above, confirm the theory, frequently with high levels of significance.[7]

Convention Three

This convention has two new elements. First, there are now *different payoffs* depending on the composition of the winning coalition and, second, it is possible for two player (Yellow and Blue) to form a winning coalition in a *single* round. There are seven minimal winning coalitions, but because of the sequential nature of the coalition formation process, non-minimal coalitions can, and occasionally do, occur. Nevertheless, a "null hypothesis" of one-seventh is the most conservative estimate we can use in evaluating the results.

Differences in the number of steps necessary to form a winning coalition add a new variable not considered in the theory. It was implicitly assumed that the formation of alternative coalitions would offer the *same* practical difficulties and involve equal risk. In the experimental design, getting into the bargaining room was not always easily accomplished and the "bird in hand" philosophy frequently prevailed. Subjects would accept an offer here and now despite a belief that a better deal was possible through additional bargaining sessions.

The result was an advantage in the final division of the jobs for those who had already formed a coalition as long as the other players were divided. In Conventions One and Two, the spokes-

man for a coalition frequently used the argument, with considerable effectiveness, that the coalition's alternatives were immediate while the other player's single alternative depended on himself and the remaining two players joining in a process which necessarily took two steps.

A similar effect was apparently working in Convention Three. Yellow and Blue could avoid the risks and additional bargaining by *immediately* agreeing in spite of the fact that their coalition was the least cheap of the minimal winning coalitions.

In this game, Yellow-Green-White is the cheapest coalition with the highest payoff. For Blue, the coalition Blue-Green-White is most desirable, but Green and White will prefer to join with Yellow where the coalition receives 100 instead of 90 jobs to divide. Similarly, Red-Yellow-Green will be Red's choice but not the first choice of the others. It is interesting to note that the "weakest" player, Green, is included in every player's preferred coalition strategy according to the theory.

Tables 5 and 6 indicate, as in Convention Two, a somewhat complicated pattern of support and rejection. Green and White follow the coalition strategy predicted but Yellow sharply deviates. More than 70 percent of Yellow's "incorrect" choices are his choice of Blue. Yellow apparently prefers to try the less risky and quicker coalition with Blue than the cheaper coalition with Green and White. Similarly, the reversal of correct predictions for Blue is accounted for by his choice of Yellow on 12 occasions. In fact, the theory leads to a rather impractical strategy for Blue since, as we shall see in discussing the final division of jobs, he can rarely do

---

[7] In one particularly noteworthy triadic situation where one party has 34 votes, one has 50, and one has 17, the predicted choices are made in 29 out of 32 cases (p < .001).

TABLE 5. INITIAL CHOICES FOR CONVENTION THREE

Chooser	Percentage Correctly Predicted	N	P
Green	59 (50)	22⎫	<.02
White	74 (50)	23⎬	
Yellow	25 (50)	24	(<.02)[a]
Red	43 (50)	23	NS
Blue	33 (50)	24	(<.10)[a]

[a] In wrong direction.

better than join with Yellow although this is *not* true of Yellow's joining with Blue.

Table 6 indicates that the distribution of final coalitions does not significantly support the theory. Yellow-Green-White, while it occurs more than average, is less frequent than Blue-Yellow. However, if we limit our attention to the 6 three-man minimal winning coalitions where *the number of steps necessary to form the coalition is held constant*, the results appear a little more favorable. The three most likely coalitions according to the theory occurred 10 out of 18 times (NS). However, using the criterion of the first potentially

winning bargaining session, the three predicted coalitions met 12 out of 17 times (p = .07).

As in Convention Two, intermediate four-man and three-man situations allow for additional tests of the theory. With virtually any start other than a coalition between Yellow and Blue, the action of Convention Three gives supporting evidence.

Test of the General Hypothesis

The experimental results *indirectly* test the general hypothesis of the theory since the specific predictions of choices and coalitions are largely based upon it.

TABLE 6. FINAL COALITIONS AND FIRST POTENTIALLY WINNING SESSION FOR CONVENTION THREE

	Final Coalition	First Potentially Winning Session
YGW (predicted)	5 (NS)	6 (NS)
RYG	4	2
BGW	1	4
RYW	2	2
RBG	3	2
RBW	1	1
YB	6 (NS)	7 (p = .07)
YBG	1	0
RYB	1	0
Total	24	24

TABLE 7. AVERAGE JOBS PER COALITION FOR EACH COLOR

Convention		R	Y	B	G	W
One	Votes	20	20	20	20	20
	j/c [a]	33.9	33.7	33.4	30.7	32.6
	N	19	15	13	16	10
Two	Votes	17	25	17	25	17
	j/c	27.9	38.8	32.4	37.0	33.1
	N	17	11	14	13	17
Three	Votes	15	35	35	6	10
	j/c	27.8	50.6	41.8	22.1	24.7
	N	11	19	13	14	9

[a] Average number of jobs received when a member of the winning coalition.

However, data on the actual division of the jobs shed further light on the process.

What is the relationship between the initial distribution of resources (votes) which a player has and his share of the payoff (jobs)? In Table 7, we consider the average number of jobs per winning coalition for each color. In Convention One, where all have equal votes, there are few differences. In Convention Two, although the two strong players are included in the winning coalition less frequently than the others, on those occasions in which they are included, they are able to demand a larger share of the jobs than the others. Yellow and Green together average 37.8 jobs against 31.1 jobs for Red, Blue, and White ($p < .001$). Similarly, job share follows resources in Convention Three. Yellow is able to fare better than Blue in Convention Three because his presence in a coalition will mean a higher total payoff.

It is interesting to compare Yellow's success with various coalition strategies in Convention Three. He is most successful when he follows the predicted strategy of joining with White and Green where he averages 55.4 jobs in five such coalitions. He does virtually as well by joining with Blue on six occasions for a 54.3 job average. However, when he is involved in any other coalition, as he was on eight occasions, he averages only 45.0 jobs. Blue, on the other hand, averages 45.7 jobs when joining with Yellow but only 38.5 when following any other strategy.

In general, the main hypothesis of the theory is supported. There are few equal divisions where the participants have unequal votes *despite equalities of strategic position.* Players are able to get more than their proportional share in some situations, but they are rarely able to achieve what they might hope to get if differences in resources were ignored.

To illustrate this, where two non-winning coalitions have formed, the fifth player might be expected to get up to 50 percent of the total jobs since the alternative to his inclusion is for the two coalitions to join. In practice, players in this situation rarely received anything close to 50 percent and, in fact, *rarely demanded that much.* Some subjects settled for as little as ⅓ or less and those who received as much as 40 percent were highly pleased. Despite the nature of their strategic position, subjects seemed to feel that any amount which they received above their proportional share was, as it were, sheer profit.

The Bargaining Process

The verbatim transcriptions of the bargaining sessions of the "smoke filled room" are a rich source of insight into the thinking processes of the subjects as they plotted and planned their future strategies and discussed the reasons for their past actions. There is much informal evidence in these dialogues for the validity of the general hypothesis. Space limitations unfortunately prevent the reproduction of verbatim excerpts.

When a two-man coalition was formed, the players generally used their additional time to discuss whom they would invite to join on the next round. Arguments which amounted to informal statements of the general hypothesis of the theory were given explicitly again and again and could be inferred from many other statements.

The argument that initial resources are irrelevant because any combination considered will be winning is also used, although less frequently, and it is used invariably by players with few resources. However, those who use it rarely demand what its logic would dictate. In fact, they appear to act as if there existed a "just price" described by their share of the votes even when they are demanding more. They are willing to benefit from the favorable position in which they find themselves, but the very words "benefit" and "favorable" imply a comparison with some standard or expectation.

CONCLUSIONS

To summarize the results, the theory was generally successful in predicting the *initial choices* of those players who were members of the predicted winning coalition. Thus, Red, Blue, and White's choices in Convention Two and Green and White's choices in Convention Three corroborated the hypotheses. However, Yellow, in Convention Three, chooses in direct opposition to the prediction.

The theory was not successful in predicting the initial choices of those players who were *not* members of the predicted winning coalition. Thus, we failed to predict successfully Yellow and Green's choices in Convention Two or Red and Blue's in Convention Three.

We were successful in predicting the final coalitions in Convention Two but not so in Convention Three. However, we were able to predict which among the three-man winning coalitions would occur in Convention Three and to predict choices and coalitions in later stages. In other words, the predictions were generally correct in those groups in which Yellow and Blue did not join initially.

Thus, the theory is generally supported with two important exceptions. First, there is an important variable involved which the theory neglects—the risk or difficulty involved in alternative coalition strategies. Subjects frequently preferred a strategy which took only one step for successful completion to one which required two steps.

A single player bargaining with a

coalition realized that, if he failed to reach an agreement, a successful alternative strategy would require two steps. If the other players had a coalition as well, his alternative required only one step and his previous disadvantage in bargaining vanished. Similarly, Yellow and Blue in Convention Three frequently joined in the only winning coalition which could be completed in a single step. One might speculate that this occurred *only* 25 percent of the time because it was the least *cheap* of the minimal winning coalitions.

The second exception to the general support of the theory was the failure to predict the choices of those whom the theory predicted would not be included in the final coalition. These people had an interesting duality of strategy, for if they followed the predicted strategy *and everyone else did also*, they would be excluded from the winning coalition. They might benefit the most by an error if they followed the predicted strategy. Still, by joining quickly themselves, they might hope to gain the advantage of the earlier coalition.

One method of formulating the regularities in a process as complex as coalition formation is to add variables to an incomplete formulation and, thus, successively to approximate a completely adequate theory. It is possible to include both of the exceptions mentioned in a more general variable which can be incorporated into the theory. Instead of assuming that all coalition strategies are equally difficult, it might be possible to assign probabilities of success to each alternative.

While considerable care would be required in the assignment of definitive probabilities of success for alternative strategies, an example might indicate the direction of such an attempt in this particular situation. Every bargaining session has a certain probability of success. While this is to some degree variable, for practical purposes it could be treated as a constant. Then, if this figure were, for example, $\frac{3}{4}$, a two step strategy would have only $\frac{9}{16}$ probability of success instead of the $\frac{3}{4}$ probability of a one step strategy.

Similarly, those not included in the predicted winning coalition might not assume that all other players are equally likely to choose them. It may be more reasonable to assume that the reciprocity of choice necessary for entrance into the bargaining room is more likely to come from others who are excluded from the predicted coalition. The assignment of precise probabilities offers difficulties but even rough approximations would help to explain the major deviations from the present theoretical predictions.

The estimated payoff to an individual from any prospective coalition would then be a product of three factors instead of two. The share and the total payoff would be considered as before, but now the probability of the prospective strategy being successfully executed would also be part of the product.

9

Group Processes, Structure, and Productivity

---

41. INDIVIDUAL ABILITY AS A DETERMINANT OF GROUP SUPERIORITY *

Jacob Tuckman and Irving Lorge

Shaw (1932) and others (Lorge, Fox, Davitz, Weltz, & Herrold, 1954) have argued from empirical evidence that groups are superior to individuals in their ability to solve problems. Lorge and Solomon (1955) have suggested two ability models that may account for group superiority on a non-interactional hypothesis. Their models, essentially, are based on the assumption that the superiority of the group is due to the greater probability of its containing at least one member who can solve the problem. As a matter of fact, the Lorge and Solomon models, when applied to the Shaw data, suggest the tenability of the conclusion that the ability of the members of the group rather than personal interaction accounts for the superiority of group solutions. Empirical verification of the models suggested by Lorge and Solomon is needed to supplement their proposed mathematical models.

One such empirical demonstration would require that individuals should solve as individuals, and then be brought together as a group to solve the same problem again. If, as a control, a group had been brought together to solve the problem without any prior experience with it as individuals, comparisons could be made to test whether the superiority of the group was a function of the ability of its best members or of interaction. For instance, performances of individuals could be compared with their performances as re-solving groups, and re-

* Reprinted from *Human Relations*, 1962, 15: 45–51, with permission of the senior author and the Tavistock Institute of Human Relations. This research was conducted under a contract [AF 18(600)341] with the Human Resources Research Institute, Maxwell Air Force Base.

solving groups could be contrasted with groups solving the problem initially. In general, if the solutions of groups solving for the first time are not different from those of re-solving groups, ability would seem to be the determinant. Such a design was the basis of this experiment.

SAMPLE AND PROCEDURE

The subjects were 420 cadets, randomly selected from the Air Force Reserve Officers Training Corps at Columbia College and at Manhattan College. In background and intelligence, these men were fairly homogeneous. Of the 420 cadets, 70 *ad hoc* groups of five men, also selected randomly, were required to solve a problem as a group and to write its solution without prior experience with it as individuals. These 70 groups, serving as a control, will be referred to hereafter as *groups initially*. Seventy individuals (hereafter referred to as *individuals initially*), again selected randomly from the same university, were required to solve the same problem as individuals and to write its solution. In the case of individuals, each of five cadets was tested independently of every other one on the same day. The following day, these five men were reassembled as an *ad hoc* group. Each member of this reassembled *ad hoc* group re-read his written solution, which had been returned to him. When he had done so, he returned it to the examiner. Then, the reassembled *ad hoc* group was required to re-solve the same problem as a group and write its solution. The 14 groups of five men reassembled to re-solve the problem after solving it as individuals initially will be referred to as *re-solving groups*.

The Mined Road Problem was adapted from the one developed by the Office of Strategic Services (1948). It requires the formulation of a plan of action for getting a cadre of five men across a road mined with supersensitive enemy mines which can be neither neutralized nor dug up. The road is twelve feet wide, bordered with trees about forty feet tall. Scattered about one side of the road is a variety of potentially usable material and debris, including beams, ropes, discarded auto tire, pulley, etc.[1]

The written solutions of the seventy groups initially, of the seventy individuals initially, and of the fourteen re-solving groups were evaluated by the Quality Point Score (QPS) method (Lorge *et al.*, 1955). Essentially, the QPS is a sum of the credits for significant elements in the solution. The weights had been estimated on the basis of important factors, such as safety, efficiency, workability, and quality of thinking. For the Mined Road Problem, the QPS was oriented around four major elements: (i) bridging the road, i.e. the use of beams or a combination of beams, swinging, broadjumping, throwing men or materials across, making an overhead bridge, etc., (ii) removing the bridging from the road, i.e. any procedure for removing the basic or secondary bridging, (iii) removing clues indicative of escape or escape route, that is, materials hidden or carried away, and (iv) time, —elapsed time from presentation of the problem to the formal written solution.

[1] The Mined Road Problem was prepared to be administered at seven levels of remoteness from reality: from a verbal description to the actual real field setting. The quality of the solutions at each of the seven levels was equivalent. In this paper, therefore, no reference is made to presentation differences.

In actual practice, as tested out by the research team, it was quite evident that certain methods of bridging the road or removing the bridging were superior to or more workable than others. For instance, it was found by tryout that solutions involving a man swinging by rope from a tree on the starting side would not work except under the joint specific conditions that the rope had to be suspended from a branch at least twenty feet high, and at the same time the man must begin the swing from an elevation of about six feet from someone else's shoulder or from a piece of lumber to get the necessary momentum. Or, it was found that a solution involving a man broadjumping across the road would not work at all, since the run-space was only fifteen feet long and on an upgrade. The Physical Education Department of Columbia College stated that it was highly improbable that anyone could broadjump the road under the actual conditions, especially if the groups were out of condition or if the broadjumper lacked necessary track equipment. On the other hand, solutions involving throwing a tire with attached rope across to the other side of the road would work, even though there was some danger that the rope or tire might hit the road.

After the workability of the solutions had been field-tested, values were assigned to various aspects of the written solutions. For example, in bridging the road with a beam or combination of beams, the fourteen-foot beam was given a weight of 25, whereas the fourteen-foot beam tied to the twelve-foot beam was given a weight of 20; or, to give another instance, the twelve-foot beam tied to the fourteen-foot beam about one foot from its end, spread into an X, was given a weight of 15. The suggested use of a beam without specifying its length was given a weight of 8; whereas the use of the twelve-foot beam (which could not bridge the road) was given a weight of 0. Similarly, removing or leaving clues indicative of the escape route were given differential credits: for example, leaving all materials on the original starting side and removing footprints was given a weight of 25; leaving some materials on the starting side and hiding some materials on the other side and removing footprints from both sides of the road was given a weight of 20; leaving some materials on the starting side of the road and some on the other side and removing footprints was given a weight of 15; no reference to removal of materials on either side of the road, yet implying removal, was given a weight of 7; leaving a rope suspended across the road between two trees was given a negative weight of −8; leaving a beam bridging the road as well as a rope suspended across the road between two trees was given a negative weight of −15.

RESULTS

Re-solving groups made significantly better solutions (at < .001 level) than their members had made as individuals initially. The average QPS is 53.4 for the resolving groups, and 24.9 for their members solving as individuals initially. The corresponding standard deviations are 28.6 and 23.6 respectively, for re-solving groups and individuals initially.

The superiority of solutions of re-solving groups over their members' solutions as individuals initially, moreover, is evident for elements reported in the solutions. The analysis of the ele-

TABLE 1. ELEMENTS IN THE SOLUTION FOR THE MINED ROAD PROBLEM: FOR INDIVIDUALS INITIALLY, FOR RE-SOLVING GROUPS, AND FOR GROUPS INITIALLY: PERCENTAGE SELECTING SPECIFIED ELEMENTS

Element	Individuals Initially N = 70 %	Re-Solving Groups N = 14 %	Groups Initially N = 70 %
* A. Use of beam	51	71	86
* B. Methods employed in bridging the road by beam	51	71	86
** C. Swinging as a method of bridging the road			
Total	11	21	20
In conjunction with Element A	1	7	9
As the only method	10	14	11
** D. Broadjumping	4	7	1
** E. Throwing materials or men as a preliminary step in bridging the road			
Total	26	36	23
In conjunction with Element A	10	21	20
As the only method	16	14	3
** F. Rope bridging as a method in crossing the road			
Total	30	29	21
In conjunction with Element A	7	7	13
As the only method	23	21	9
** G. Methods indicating no understanding of the problem	16	0	0
* K. Removing the bridging device from the road	39	71	87
* L. Removing clues of escape route	49	86	90
** M. Added aspects (throwing materials from far to near side in order to remove clues of escape route)	6	0	11
** Q. Exceeding time-limits	6	0	36

* Superior method.
** Inferior method.

ments used in the solutions made by individuals initially, made by groups initially, and made by re-solving groups is given in Table 1. A higher proportion of re-solving groups than of individuals initially employ superior methods, for example, use a beam to bridge the road, remove the bridging from the road, and leave fewer clues to their escape route. Nevertheless, a higher proportion of re-solving groups also employ some less adequate methods, for example, swing across the road, or throw materials or men as a first step to bridge the road. The re-solving groups, however, use such inferior methods in conjunction with a superior method not, as individuals initially do, as the only method. No re-solving group—as against 16 percent of individuals initially—reports a solution showing no understanding of the problem. Not only does a higher proportion of re-solving groups than of individuals initially employ superior methods, but the re-solving groups tend to employ these methods more adequately. In comparing re-solving groups with individuals initially who use a beam to bridge the road, the average score for the elements involved (Elements A and B) is 39.7 for the re-solving groups, and 28.8 for individuals initially. For removal of the bridging device from the road (Element K), the average score is 15.0 for re-solving groups, and 12.4 for individuals initially. For removal of clues of the escape route (Element L), the average score is 15.9 for re-solving groups, and 9.5 for individuals initially.

These results indicate the superiority of the solutions of re-solving groups over those of their members as individuals initially. The question must still be raised whether re-solving groups are superior because of the possibilities of practice effects or of interaction among their members. For this purpose, it is possible to compare the QPS of groups initially with that of re-solving groups. The average QPS was 53.4 for the re-solving groups, and 55.7 for the groups initially. The corresponding standard deviations are 28.6 and 25.1 respectively, for re-solving groups and groups initially. The differences are not statistically significant.

In general, there is little difference in the way the elements of the solutions are utilized by re-solving groups and by groups initially. Such differences as are observed are not consistent in their direction. A higher proportion of groups initially use superior methods to bridge the road than do re-solving groups; but more groups initially use some inferior methods in removing clues to their escape route, for example, throwing materials from one side to the other; and 36 percent of the groups initially com-

pared with none of the re-solving groups take so much time to reach a solution that they would fail to meet the guerilla truck, as would be necessary for the mission's success. In using a beam to bridge the road, the average score for Elements A and B is somewhat higher for groups initially than for re-solving groups. In removing the bridging device from the road (Element K), the average score is somewhat higher for groups initially than for re-solving groups. On the other hand, in removal of clues (Element L), groups initially are somewhat poorer than re-solving groups. None of these differences is statistically significant. The elements are basically the same for groups initially and for re-solving groups.

Research on problem-solving suggests that groups are superior to individuals in that the group is a more effective problem-solving unit. The group's greater effectiveness may stem from the opportunity for each member of the group to express his own ideas, interact with the other members, and be better motivated to work toward group goals. If the group is a more effective problem-solving unit, the re-solving group solution should be a product somewhat better than the best ideas of its individual members. Such an hypothesis could be tested by comparing the re-solving group solution with those written by its members, as individuals initially, the day before. From the five individual solutions, a composite was made that selected the best ideas from each of the five individual solutions about each element. For instance, if, for Element A, the 14' beam was specified as the means to bridge the road by one individual, the 12' beam by another, the 12' and 14' beams tied together by a third, broadjumping by a fourth, and swinging to the other side by a fifth, then the best idea, use of the 14' beam, was selected. Similar procedures were followed for all other elements. The average QPS of the 'concocted' composite solutions is 68.9, which is superior to the average of 53.4 for the re-solving groups. The group does not even incorporate or summate the best ideas of its members.

Observations tended to confirm the ineffectiveness of group processes of these *ad hoc* groups. Although in a few groups members worked effectively together, stimulating one another and taking into account their physical adequacies and limitations in utilizing suggested solutions, most groups operated less as a group of all five members. Rather, they tended to form cliques or sub-groups working independently, with one clique attempting to convince any other of the soundness of its thinking. In most groups at least one individual did not even participate in the deliberations. In some groups a single member dominated the discussion to the extent of coercing the acceptance of his solution, and, in one group, so much antagonism was engendered among its members that communication ceased.

Basically, the data confirm the suggestion by Lorge and Solomon [2] that the presence of ability in at least one member, rather than group process, is a more reasonable explanation for the superiority of solutions by re-solving groups over those by individuals initially. The QPSs for the re-solving group solutions and for the solutions of the five members solving as individuals initially, ranked in order

[2] Statistical tests suggested for the Lorge and Solomon models are based on percents passing or failing but not on quantitative scores representing range of goodness of solution.

of merit, given in Table 2, indicate that the re-solving group solution tends to be more like that of the best individual within the group. For the fourteen re-solving group solutions, the mean QPS is 53.4; for the solutions of the best individual initially within the group, 54.9. It is interesting to point out that not only is the average score of the next best member lower than that of the best, but that its variability also decreases. Apparently, inadequacy not only is evident, but the range of it is very small. Re-solving groups could have been expected to formulate a solution superior to that of their members as individuals initially, since each member had given the problem prior consideration and should have been concerned with demonstrating and utilizing his knowledge of it. The data, however, do not support this suggestion. On the contrary, ability and practice do not seem to be better than ability alone.

If the re-solving group solution is like that of its best member, the correlation between the best individual solution and the re-solving group solution should be positive. The Pearsonian correlation of .54 (since its direction is predicted) significantly different from zero at the .05 level. The correlation suggests the conclusion that the re-solving group solution is a function of the solution of its best member. It must be emphasized that the correlation is based on just fourteen re-solving groups.

A qualitative analysis of the elements utilized in the solutions of re-solving groups gives evidence of a clear tendency for such solutions to use those elements selected from the solutions of their best members. A point-for-point comparison has been made that clearly indicates that points are never selected

TABLE 2. QUALITY POINT SCORES FOR SOLUTIONS TO THE MINED ROAD PROBLEM: FOR FOURTEEN RE-SOLVING GROUPS AND THEIR FIVE MEMBERS SOLVING AS INDIVIDUALS INITIALLY, RANKED IN ORDER OF MERIT

QPS of Re-Solving Groups		QPS of Members as Individuals Initially				
Group No.		Best	Next Best	Middle	Fourth	Lowest
A	55	64	28	26	21	7
B	38	37	30	30	5	3
C	12	29	12	7	5	0
D	58	19	16	7	7	0
E	86	77	36	30	7	3
F	26	85	51	27	17	7
G	66	81	40	10	7	2
H	106	66	60	55	28	18
J	7	26	7	7	5	0
K	30	50	7	7	7	3
L	78	66	27	24	7	4
M	42	7	7	7	3	3
N	58	70	46	23	23	16
P	85	91	54	40	30	3
Mean	53.4	54.9	30.1	21.4	12.3	4.9
SD	28.2	25.9	17.8	14.3	9.1	5.4

from their poorest members. Selection of workable elements is always from the best, next-to-best, and middle members.

Qualitatively, of the fourteen re-solving group solutions, six are almost identical to the elements of the solution of their best member; three are like those of the next-to-best or middle members; and five have elements from the top three members, with some added.

The standard deviation of the re-solving groups is 28. Using half a standard deviation as a referent, it was assumed that if any QPS of members as individuals initially was within fourteen points of the re-solving group score, it would be considered indicative of the fact that that individual's score was highly contributory to the group. For instance, in Group A the score is 55. It was assumed that any score within plus or minus fourteen would be indica-tive of the acceptance of that individual's contribution. In this instance 64 is within the range; all other scores lie outside. On that basis, five re-solving group solutions are better than that of their best member, three are poorer, and six are as good.

CONCLUSIONS

Research literature indicates that groups are superior to individuals in problem-solving because learning is facilitated through interaction. The evidence in this study suggests that groups are superior to individuals, not so much on account of the greater effectiveness of groups in solving problems, but rather on account of the greater probability of getting a good solution from a group of five than from any one individual.

The groups had no tradition of working together in solving problems, which may be the reason that they functioned so ineffectively. Yet the generalization about group superiority is based on groups without tradition. Ultimately, evidence may be developed to indicate that solutions of groups with good dynamics are superior to those of groups with poor dynamics, but that evidence is not yet available. Even so, such superiority, if it were to be shown, may really mean that groups with good dynamics permit the solution of their best members to emerge, whereas groups with poor dynamics suppress it. The relationship of the adequacy of group process to the utilization of the best thinking of group members needs to be put to the test.

REFERENCES

LORGE, I., Fox, D., DAVITZ, J., WELTZ, P. & HERROLD, K. (1954). Research on the products of groups and of individuals. Unpublished MS.

LORGE, I. & SOLOMON, H. (1955). Two models of group behavior in the solution of Eureka-type problems. *Psychometrika* 20, 139–48.

LORGE, I., TUCKMAN, J., AIKMAN, L., SPIEGEL, J. & Moss, G. (1955). Solutions by teams and by individuals to a field problem at different levels of reality. *J. educ. Psychol.* 46, 17–24.

OSS Assessment Staff (1948). *Assessment of men.* New York: Holt, Rinehart and Winston.

SHAW, M. E. (1932). Comparison of individuals and small groups in the rational solution of complex problems. *Amer. J. Psychol.* 44, 491–504.

42.   CONTRASTING CORRELATES OF GROUP SIZE *

Philip E. Slater

Studies of group size have centered around two concerns, one practical and one theoretical. The practical concern has been to determine what size working group is optimum in terms of efficiency, productivity, stability or satisfaction, for a given type of task. The theoretical concern has been to determine what kinds of variables differentiate the smaller group from the larger, in terms of the nature of the interaction, the structure of relationships, and the types of stress that may arise.

Small group literature has little to say regarding optimum size, due largely to the fact that few studies have been carried out which attempt to cover a wide range of different sizes. In general experimenters have restricted themselves to showing the superiority of some one size over another. The paucity of studies is in sharp contrast to the complexity of the problem, however, since one must determine not only what is optimum in terms of each different criterion, but also what is optimum for different types of group task.

The problem of differentiating var-

* Excerpted from *Sociometry*, 1958, 21: 129–139, with permission of the author and the American Sociological Association. This research was supported by the Rand Corporation.

iables has fared somewhat better, although most of the studies have dealt with variables which permitted the experimenters to describe different sizes as "better" or "worse" in terms of some practical standard, and have been less concerned with differences of intrinsic interest. Comparative studies of the latter sort have been concerned primarily with showing differences in leadership structure by size (4, 7, 8, 16), although the study by Bales and Borgatta on interaction differences, and the recent one by Ziller on problem solving provide exceptions to this rule (3, 18).

Smaller groups have, in general, been very much favored over larger groups in the more evaluative studies. The larger groups have been shown to be less stable (9), to have more difficulties in communication and to inhibit individual participation (1, 4, 5, 6), to create more stress (6, 11), and although successful in some tasks because of the greater number of skills available (13, 15), to be less efficient or productive in many others (7, 10, 13, 14).

The present study is concerned with group size as it relates to member satisfaction, with particular emphasis on optimum size as perceived by the members themselves, and on contrasting sources of dissatisfaction in larger and smaller sizes. Specifically, it seeks the answers to four questions:

1. At what point do members of a group tend to feel it is too large to accomplish the task at hand?
2. At what point do members of a group tend to feel it is too small to accomplish the task at hand?
3. What makes a group "too" large?
4. What makes a group "too" small?

PROCEDURE

The sample, task, and procedure used in this study have been discussed in considerable detail elsewhere (3, 12), and will be described only briefly here. The sample consisted of 24 groups of from two to seven men each, with four groups of each size. Each group met four times, for a total of 96 meetings.

The groups were composed of paid male undergraduates with little or no prior acquaintance with one another. Each meeting consisted of a 40-minute discussion of one of four human relations problems. These problems were presented individually in the form of a five-page factual summary of a conflict situation confronting an administrator in an organization. Each case involved a central character guilty of some rule infraction, and thus presented a value dilemma as well as a diagnostic and action problem. The subjects discussed and analysed the problem and submitted a group decision regarding possible techniques toward its solution. The discussions were observed through a one-way mirror, and the interaction categorized using interaction process analysis.

Following each meeting the subjects filled out a questionnaire which consisted largely of sociometric choices and ratings and a 60-item check list. This check list was composed of statements about group meetings often made by subjects in the past. The subjects were asked to check as many or as few statements as they felt were applicable to their own meetings, so that a response presumably represented a real concern with the problem posed by the item.

TABLE 1. PERCENTAGE OF OCCASIONS ON WHICH SUBJECTS FELT GROUP WAS TOO SMALL OR TOO LARGE TO CARRY OUT ASSIGNED TASK, IN GROUPS OF VARYING SIZES (*Preliminary Sample*)

Size	Percent Too Small	Percent Too Large	Number of Opportunities
2	100	0	2
3	30	0	30
4	8	0	40
5	2	4	50
6	0	17	6

Among these statements were two which provide the basis for this study:

    5. This group is too small in number of members for best results on the job it is trying to do.

    6. This group is too large in number of members for best results on the job it is trying to do.

RESULTS

Preliminary Sample

Before the present series of groups had been completed, a tabulation was made of responses to these two check-list statements in a series of groups not included in the present sample, but studied with the same procedure. Among these groups were a single two-man group, ten meetings each of three-man, four-man, and five-man groups, and one six-man group.

Although the sample was somewhat inadequate, the results of this preliminary tabulation, which appear in Table 1, were encouraging. The proportion of "too small" responses decreases regularly as size increases, while the proportion of "too large" responses seems to vary directly with size. The optimum size seems to be five, which has the smallest proportion of total complaints.

Study Sample

The percentage of subject responses to each of the two check list questions in groups of each size for the present sample appears in Table 2. The trends essentially duplicate those in Table 1, with size five emerging as the only size

TABLE 2. PERCENTAGE OF OCCASIONS ON WHICH SUBJECTS FELT GROUP WAS TOO SMALL OR TOO LARGE TO CARRY OUT ASSIGNED TASK, IN GROUPS OF VARYING SIZES

Size	Percent Too Small	Percent Too Large	Number of Opportunities
2	34	0	32
3	17	0	48
4	11	0	64
5	0	0	80
6	0	14	96
7	0	13	112

group in which no complaints of either type appear. Although perhaps not surprising in view of the small number of total responses, it is of some interest that in no size did subjects make both types of complaints.

When chi-square tests are applied to these findings, they prove to be highly significant. Members of five-man groups make significantly fewer "too small" complaints than sizes two, three, and four (.001 level) and significantly fewer "too large" complaints than sizes six and seven (.01 level). They also have significantly fewer total complaints than either of the groups adjacent to them (that is, four and six), with $p < .01$ in both cases.

The Content of Dissatisfaction

Unfortunately, while these results indicate rather clearly than size five is the preferred one for this type of task, they give no hint of the reasons for this choice. Other items in the 60-item check list, however, deal with more specific comments and complaints, and were therefore examined individually in an attempt to remedy this deficiency.

There are two ways in which the trends in Tables 1 and 2 could arise. First, size five could constitute a kind of ideal, deviations from which might be identical in kind, regardless of direction. Second, it might represent a kind of compromise size, avoiding *two* types of difficulties, one of which increases with size while the other decreases. The first type of effect would involve a single set of interrelated variables orthogonal to size, while the second would involve two interrelated sets of variables, one correlated positively with size, the other negatively.

The hypothesis that the first type of effect is operating here may be tested by comparing, on all other check list items, those sizes closest to five with those farthest removed from five, regardless of direction. Differences between sizes four, five, and six on the one hand and two, three, and seven on the other, were therefore tested for all items, using a chi-square test.

Only three out of the 58 remaining check list items showed differences significant at the .05 level between these two classes of groups, a result which could be obtained by chance. This finding would seem to warrant the conclusion that preference for size five does not result from the influence of a single set of variables.

The hypothesis that preference for size five results from the fact that it provided maximal avoidance of two negatively related sets of evils may be tested by comparing, on all check list items, the smaller groups [2, 3, 4] with the larger [5, 6, 7]. We would expect to find certain complaints and satisfactions more frequent in the former and other complaints and satisfactions, of a different nature, more frequent in the latter.

When differences between small and large groups on check list items are tested in this way a number prove to be significant at the .05 level or better, and these appear in Tables 3 and 4.

Unfortunately, these differences seem merely to establish the superiority of the smaller sizes in the eyes of the members, and give very little hint of any counterforces which would lead to a "compromise" at size five.

None of the items preferred by smaller groups evidence dissatisfaction of any kind, while those preferred by

TABLE 3. CHECK LIST ITEMS WITH WHICH LARGE GROUPS AGREED SIGNIFICANTLY
MORE OFTEN THAN SMALL GROUPS

Item	P
4. The time available to solve the problem was not sufficient.	.01
9. This group doesn't make the best use of its time.	.001
16. There is a definite leader in this group and his leadership is well accepted.	.05
18. This group doesn't stay on the track so far as getting the job done is concerned.	.01
19. This group needs somebody to keep it on the track.	.001
20. This group needs a more definite leader.	.001
26. Some people in this group talk too much.	.001
27. Some people in this group are crowded out of the discussion.	.01
28. Some people in this group should participate more.	.001
33. There are considerable differences of ability and competence between members of this group.	.05
39. There is too much competition among members in this group.	.02
42. There is an "inner circle" and an "outer fringe" in this group, and it is an effective and satisfactory arrangement.	.05
56. This group is not accomplishing as much as it could.	.01

larger groups seem to consist almost entirely of complaints.

Members of larger groups feel that the group is disorderly and wastes time and that its members are too pushy, aggressive and competitive. Despite several items suggesting the existence of an established and accepted hierarchy, some of the complaints call for more central control over the discussion or deplore the lack of it, while others grumble over the highhandedness with which some group members dominate the discussion.

These findings tend to support those of other studies referred to briefly above, in which larger groups created more stress in individual members, produced more difficulties in communication, and inhibited individual participation. However, they fail utterly to explain why size five is viewed so favorably. If these difficulties are found in larger groups we have still to find some other type of deficiency inherent in the very small group—a problem made difficult by the fact that the small groups make no complaint other than that their groups are too small.

One might argue that this very absence of specific complaints, together

TABLE 4. CHECK LIST ITEMS WITH WHICH SMALL GROUPS AGREED SIGNIFICANTLY
MORE OFTEN THAN LARGE GROUPS

Item	P
14. There is no definite leader in this group and no need for one.	.02
32. All the members of this group are at about the same level of ability and competence.	.001
45. I am well satisfied with my position in this group.	.001
53. I predict this group will reach a satisfactory conclusion to its work.	.05

with the tendency of small group members to respond with greater frequency to somewhat rose-colored bromides, springs not from satisfaction but from inhibition and constraint—from an unwillingness to tolerate the thought that even normal conflicts and dissatisfactions might arise in the group. Such an hypothesis, however, demands corroborative data if it is to be more than a speculative reversal of the manifest sense of the evidence.

In this instance supporting evidence is available. Bales and Borgatta (3) studying the same sample, found that expressions of tension in groups decreased as size increased, despite the fact that disagreement and antagonism appeared, if anything, to show an increase with size. Tension release and giving suggestions also increased with size while agreement decreased. These findings suggest that members of smaller groups are unable to tolerate overt expressions of conflict, and not only avoid such expressions but also any moderately aggressive activity, such as giving suggestions, which might give rise to them. They further avoid such conflicts by frequent manifestations of agreement, acts which seem to be unnecessary in groups in which the members feel at home with one another.[1] As this process continues, unresolved tension tends to build up, with no apparent mechanism available for its release. Parenthetically it might be added that while this atmosphere of constraint aroused comment

---

[1] This notion is suggested by an as yet unpublished finding that in groups of all sizes overt expressions of agreement decrease over time. Since groups show no systematic tendency to deteriorate over time, one is led to the conclusion that as group members become better acquainted, such demonstrations of consensus become less necessary.

from casual observers of our smaller groups, they also remarked most particularly upon the relative superficiality of the content of their discussions. While no content analyses of these discussions were made, it was difficult to escape the impression that all potentially controversial subjects were being avoided.

These tendencies are most striking in two-man groups, and Bales and Borgatta explain this fact by pointing out a unique quality of this size, first noted by Simmel (17), namely that a majority is unanimity. There is no public opinion or mediator, and complete cooperation is essential if the destruction of the group is to be avoided. To a considerable extent, however, this reasoning may be generalized to apply to all of the smaller sizes. That is, as the size of the group increases, the consequences of alienating a single member become less and less severe.

One might summarize this hypothesis by saying that in the larger group physical freedom is restricted while psychological freedom is increased. The member has less time to talk, more points of view to integrate and adapt to, and a more elaborate structure into which he must fit. At the same time he is more free to ignore some of these viewpoints, to express his own feelings and ideas in a direct and forceful fashion, and even to withdraw from the fray without loss of face (cf. 3, p. 402–403).

Ordinarily, of course, one thinks of the smaller group in everyday life as characterized by an easy intimacy and greater rather than less behavioral freedom. That such a view is in part erroneous was argued with some force by Simmel (17, p. 45–46), but there are obvious limitations to the generality of this hypothesis. It is intended to apply only to those groups in which the participants are (a) engaged in an intellectual task which requires that differing opinions about ambiguous data be reconciled, and (b) strangers who have not chosen to work together and cannot easily withdraw from the situation. Under such conditions it would not be surprising to find a high premium placed on rather passive, nonaggressive modes of behavior. Unlike the larger group where the problem seems to be to avoid being trampled underfoot, in the smaller group one is, in a sense, walking on eggs.[2]

SUMMARY

At the outset of this study we posed several questions. We attempted first to determine the points at which group members tended to feel their group was too large or too small to accomplish the task set for it. It was found that groups larger than size four were never felt to be too small and groups smaller than six were never felt to be too large.

Size five emerged clearly, therefore, as the size group which from the subjects' viewpoint was most effective in dealing with an intellectual task involving the collection and exchange of information about a situation, the co-

ordination, analysis, and evaluation of this information, and a group decision regarding the appropriate administrative action to be taken in the situation. Such a task is the most common variety faced by groups in everyday life, save those engaged in some physical or manual operation. If, therefore, this finding can be replicated, its practical significance may be considerable.

Since it was determined that "too small" and "too large" meant quite different things in terms of the actual content of complaints made about these two types of circumstance, the second group of questions concerned the nature of the disadvantages inherent first in larger and then in smaller groups.

The disadvantages of the larger groups match those found by earlier studies, and are readily verbalized by the subject. Group members are seen as too aggressive, impulsive, competitive, and inconsiderate, and the group as too hierarchical, centralized, and disorganized.

The disadvantages of the smaller groups are not verbalized by members, but can only be inferred from their behavior. It appears that group members are too tense, passive, tactful, and constrained, to work together in a manner which is altogether satisfying to them. Their fear of alienating one another seems to prevent them from expressing their ideas freely. Their failure to verbalize this complaint may be due to the absence of anything resembling it in the check list from which the complaints of the larger groups were drawn. On the other hand, it may be merely another symptom of their apparent need to avoid any expression of negative affect. These accommodating tendencies are rarely viewed as culturally deviant by

---

[2] In his original report of this research Professor Slater presented detailed observational evidence in support of this interpretation. In the smaller groups, inhibited, passive, "safe" behaviors were observed to occur more frequently than they did in larger groups. Moreover, in small groups such behaviors occurred about equally often in each of the four experimental sessions, whereas in larger groups they occurred with decreasing frequency during the later sessions.

contemporary observers of the American scene, however, and it may be that *both* experimenters and subjects failed to conceive of the possibility that a culturally acceptable form of behavior could have unsatisfactory consequences.

These findings suggest that maximal group satisfaction is achieved when the group is large enough so that the members feel able to express positive and negative feelings freely, and to make aggressive efforts toward problem solving even at the risk of antagonizing each other, yet small enough so that some regard will be shown for the feelings and needs of others; large enough so that the loss of a member could be tolerated, but small enough so that such a loss could not be altogether ignored.

REFERENCES

1. BALES, R. F., F. L. STRODTBECK, T. M. MILLS, & M. E. ROSEBOROUGH. "Channels of Communication in Small Groups," *American Sociological Review*, 1951, **16**, 461–468.
2. BALES, R. F. "In Conference," *Harvard Business Review*, 1954, **32**, 44–50.
3. BALES, R. F., & E. F. BORGATTA. "A Study of Group Size: Size of Group as a Factor in the Interaction Profile," in A. P. Hare, E. F. Borgatta, and R. F. Bales, *Small Groups*, New York: Knopf, 1955.
4. CARTER, L. F., W. HAYTHORN, B. MEIROWITZ, & J. LANZETTA. "The Relation of Categorizations and Ratings in the Observation of Group Behavior," *Human Relations*, 1951, **4**, 239–254.
5. DAWE, H. C. "The Influence of the Size of Kindergarten Group upon Performance," *Child Development*, 1934, **5**, 295–303.
6. GIBB, J. R. "The Effects of Group Size and of Threat Reduction upon Creativity in a Problem-solving Situation," *American Psychologist*, 1951, **6**, 324.
7. HARE, A. P. "A Study of Interaction and Consensus in Different Sized Groups," *American Sociological Review*, 1952, **17**, 261–267.
8. HEMPHILL, J. K. "Relations between the Size of the Group and the Behavior of 'Superior' Leaders," *Journal of Social Psychology*, 1950, **32**, 11–22.
9. JAMES, J. "A Preliminary Study of the Size Determinant in Small Group Interaction," *American Sociological Review*, 1951, **16**, 474–477.
10. MARRIOT, R. "Size of Working Group and Output," *Occupational Psychology*, 1949, **23**, 47–57.
11. RICE, A. K. "The Use of Unrecognized Cultural Mechanisms in an Expanding Machine Shop," *Human Relations*, 1951, **4**, 143–160.
12. SLATER, P. E. "Role Differentiation in Small Groups," *American Sociological Review*, 1955, **20**, 300–310.
13. SOUTH, E. B. "Some Psychological Aspects of Committee Work," *Journal of Applied Psychology*, 1927, **11**, 437–464.
14. TAYLOR, D. W., & W. L. FAUST. "Twenty Questions: Efficiency in Problem Solving as a Function of Size of Group," *Journal of Experimental Psychology*, 1952, **44**, 360–368.
15. WATSON, G. B. "Do Groups Think More Efficiently Than Individuals?" *Journal of Abnormal and Social Psychology*, 1928, **23**, 328–336.
16. WHYTE, W. F. "The Social Structure of the Restaurant," *American Journal of Sociology*, 1949, **54**, 302–310.
17. WOLFF, K. H. *The Sociology of Georg Simmel*, New York: The Free Press, 1950.
18. ZILLER, R. C. "Group Size: A Determinant of the Quality and Stability of Group Decisions," *Sociometry*, 1957, **20**, 165–173.

43.   COMMUNICATION STRUCTURE, DECISION STRUCTURE AND GROUP PERFORMANCE *

Mauk Mulder

In the classical Bavelas-Leavitt research on communication structures in task-performing groups it was found that so-called wheel or star groups (cf. Figure 1) worked faster, needed a smaller number of messages and made less errors than circle groups (2, 8). Results were exactly similar in a replication of Leavitt's experiment by us with Dutch subjects (10). In these experiments the task of the group was to identify by means of written communication a symbol, held in common by all group members.

The topological structure determines, according to Leavitt (8), the better performance of the wheel groups. "Centrality," as a measure of "closeness" of an individual position to all other positions in the structure, is also a measure of the "availability of all information," which is necessary for the solving of the group problem. The most central position in the wheel, closest to all other positions, is most likely to get the answer first. This answer-getting potential is very different from the one in the circle, where all members have an equal opportunity to collect all information and to solve the problem.

Quite contrary, however, were experimental results found by Shaw (12, 13). When solving "simple" problems (Leavitt-type) his wheel groups required less time than the circle groups (although the difference failed to reach

significance). But his circle groups were faster than the wheel groups for so-called "complex" problems (for an example, see below).

In his theoretical explanation Shaw suggests that the differences found between the structures are due to the "availability of information" (with regard to simple problems) and to the "possibility of contributions" from all members of the group (complex problems).

"When simple problems are to be solved the availability of information is of primary importance. Thus, the wheel should be faster than the circle because the wheel pattern has the effect of designating which S will perform the function of identifying the common symbol. As the complexity of the problem increases, however, the possibility of contributions from all members of the group becomes much more important. This is true because some S's are more capable than others of solving such problems quickly, and because part solutions can be delegated to various positions, thereby compensating in part for the effects of "saturation." With complex problems, then, the wheel should be slower than the circle because the *central person becomes saturated* (i.e. because the optimal output level is exceeded) and because it sometimes forces the weakest person in the group to function in the leadership role" (13; cf. also 4).

However, the difference between the so-called simple and complex problems is a difference in degree rather than

* Reprinted from *Sociometry*, 1960, 23: 1–14, with permission of the author and the American Sociological Association.

in kind and does not prepare us beforehand for the complete reversal appearing in Shaw's results. Is it then possible to explain the seemingly quite contrary findings of Leavitt and Shaw in one theory, without using the "substantial" concepts of "complexity" and "simplicity" of problems as basic in such a theory?

A characteristic common to the theories of both Leavitt and Shaw seems to be that too much emphasis is laid on the *topological* structure. "Availability of information," "contributions from all members" and "saturation" are *directly* derived from the networks (wheel and circle). However, the topological structure does not determine what really happens, but only what is possible.

Predictions (on "time" and "amount of communication") derived from the topological structure are not validated by the data reported by Leavitt and, for a comparable task, by Heise and Miller (8, 7). Furthermore Guetzkow and Simon, and Flament demonstrated that in different topological structures the developing organization determines the speed of groups when solving Leavitt-type simple problems (5, 6, 3).

This paper attempts to demonstrate that the decision structure, not the topological structure, determines the task performance of a group.

THEORY

Decision Structure

In task-performing groups there is exchange of information items. But besides that, several decisions by individual members have to be made. Among these are the decision to collect all needed information before passing it on; the decision to make a problem solution for one's self, and so forth. We introduce the construct "decision structure" as referring to: "who makes decisions for whom," and hypothesize that *groups with a more centralized decision structure will be capable of better group performance, because the contributions of the individual group members can be integrated by the person in the central "position" (the leader position)*. The theory is restricted to situations in which two or more persons perform a *group task*, as in our experiment in which information, initially divided over all members, must be used to solve the problem.

In contrast to the topological structure, which does not change in time and whose parts are never modified by each other, the decision structure must *develop*. This is only logical, but a very important consequence hereof may be clarified.

A *more centralized structure* is in general characterized by "*vulnerability*." In the case of a centralized interaction structure (referring to "who interacts with whom") a high proportion of the total interaction goes through one of the group members. A disturbance in the functioning of this central position will have a radical effect, because this effect will be spread quickly through the total group and it will be very difficult to send the information flow via other positions.

The manifestation of vulnerability will be a result of the pressure exerted on the central position and its resistance against this pressure.

By *pressure* we mean heavy input and output requirements, such as requests for information or for explanation, by peripheral group members. The capacities, motives and access to resources of the central person determine whether he accepts the "imperatives" in these messages, or opposes them. By *resistance* we mean this relative degree of opposition which may be mobilized versus attempted inductions. An example would be the central person's refusing to send the requested separate information and instead collecting information until he can make the problem solution. Thus would begin the centralization of the decision processes.

It is our opinion that negative effects of vulnerability will become manifest when a centralized interaction structure fails to sufficiently develop toward a strongly centralized *decision structure*. In experiments such as Leavitt's and Shaw's, newly formed groups start new tasks. If they fail to develop centralized decision structures we expect that, in the beginning of the "work phase," groups with a more centralized interaction structure (wheel groups) will perform no more effectively and eventually may perform less well than do less centralized (circle) groups. Now Shaw's experimental group tasks differ in an essential way from those of Leavitt and Guetzkow. While the latter groups solved fifteen problems, the former performed only three or four tasks.[1] The opportunity for the centralized decision structure to develop itself is considerably smaller in Shaw's experi-

[1] Another crucial difference concerns the size of the groups (number of positions): Shaw's groups are smaller. This variable has been studied by the present writer in an experiment, reported in 11. In this publication it is also explained why the three-position circle and other totally interconnected structures are inadequate for testing Shaw's participation-theory.

ments because of the smaller number of problems (which also leads to a shorter work period).

There is support for this theory in reported data. In Shaw's experiments half, or less than half, of the wheel groups develop into strongly centralized decision structures in which a central person makes the solution and sends it out, while in the experiments by Leavitt, Guetzkow and the present writer all wheel groups develop into such "central" groups. In the temporal analyses of these latter investigators and others, the weak start of wheel groups is apparent (8, 5, 9, 10).

With regard to the seemingly controversial results for "simple" and "complex" problems, it does *not* seem correct to state that "the wheel allows for better performance with simple problems, the circle with complex ones," but that the more centralized decision structures, which developed in Leavitt's groups solving 15 problems, enabled a better performance. Furthermore, the *gradual* difference between simple and complex problems has the effect, simply, that the development of the more centralized decision structure takes more time (that is, problems) with the complex problems than with the simple ones.

An operational definition of the decision structure is as follows.

In the experimental groups a person (for example, the central person in the wheel) may function as a mere "relayer" or as an "integrator." In the latter case he may make the decision not to pass the messages he receives, but to withhold them till he himself can make the problem solution and then he may (a) send the solution to other group members or (b) send the solution plus all necessary information in one message to other group members or (c) send all necessary information in one message to other group-members.

The "centrality index," which measures the degree of centralization of the decision structure, is based on communication acts of these three "types," all of them referring to decisions which have consequences for other group members.

The "decision centrality index" (D.C.I.) is computed in this way: As a first step, for each person in the group, it is necessary to compute how many persons are supplied by this person with messages of type (a), (b) or (c). This is done by a precise analysis of the communication-content.[2] Second, the scores of all "positions" in the group are summed up. Third, the *proportion* of every "position" is calculated by dividing his individual score by the total score. The last step is to calculate the *difference* between the "position" with the highest proportion and the "position" with the next highest. Thus the "decision centrality index" (D.C.I.) gives a measure of the centralization of the decision structure on *one* "position" (the "leader"). It may vary from 0 to 1.00.

Hypotheses

The theory is laid down in the following hypotheses.

1. To the extent that the decision

structure of groups is centralized, the groups will give a better performance in their group tasks.[3]

The specific hypotheses to test in the present experiment are:

1a. To the extent that the decision structure of groups is more centralized, the group task will be performed faster.

1b. To the extent that the decision structure of groups is more centralized, the quality of the task performance will be better.

1c. To the extent that the decision structure of groups is more centralized, the group task will be performed more efficiently.

Performance per time-unit is measured by the time the group needs to solve its problem. The quality of performance is defined here by the number of errors made by the group during the task accomplishment. Efficiency is defined by the number of messages the group needs to solve the problem.

2. To the extent that a structure is more centralized, it is characterized by a greater "vulnerability." The vulnerability will manifest itself when the pressure exerted on the central position of the structure is greater than its resistance.

In our experimental design, the wheel groups start with a centralized *interaction* structure, but they do not immediately develop a centralized decision structure. We expect then that, during the beginning of the work period, the resistance of the center will be

[2] In this operation type (b)- and (c)-content, although *in principle different*, are given the same weight (=1), because when all information is put together on one sheet, the solution of *this experimental task* can be read off easily. Type (a)-content is weighted double (=2) because here the person who sends out the solution does not allow for *any* participation in the solution by the "receiver."

[3] It is understood that the groups accept as their task to work as fast as possible. Should the group goal be: "to work slowly and badly," more centralized groups should perform this task "better."

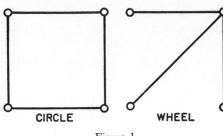

Figure 1

agreement with the vulnerability hypothesis, so the specified hypothesis can be formulated:

> 2d. To the extent that the interaction structure is more centralized, the "corrective power" of the group will be smaller.

PROCEDURE

smaller than the pressure on it. Specific hypotheses:

> 2a. To the extent that the interaction structure in groups is more centralized, the group task will be performed relatively more slowly during the beginning period of the work.
>
> 2b. To the extent that the interaction structure in groups is more centralized, the quality of the group task will be relatively poorer during the beginning period of the work.
>
> 2c. To the extent that the interaction structure in groups is more centralized, the group task will be performed relatively less efficiently during the beginning period of the work.

These hypotheses can be tested in the experiment, by comparing the performance of more centralized (wheel) groups and less centralized (circle) groups, during the first part of the work-period (for instance, in the first two problems) and in the last period of the work (last two problems).

Shaw has found that the "corrective power" (determined by comparing the number of corrected errors with the total number of errors) is smaller in wheel than in circle groups. This is in

The Experimental Groups

In the present experiment two topological structures of four positions are investigated: wheel and circle. (cf. Figure 1.)

Twenty-six groups were run, 13 for each "structure." The subjects were students of Leiden University in their first year. They were naive in this type of experiment and were instructed to work as a group as fast as possible. Subjects of a given group were not acquainted with each other prior to the experiment; instructions for the experiment were given them after they were seated together. They were told who could communicate with whom, but the structure was not made explicit.

The Experimental Situation

The subjects were told that we wanted to investigate how fast groups can solve certain abstract problems. Five problems had to be solved; the writer would have preferred more problems, to allow for the complete development of the decision structure, but this was the maximum possible in the time the subjects had available. The problems were the "complex" ones Shaw had used. The following is an example:

A small company is moving from one office-building to another. It must move four kinds of equipment: (a) chairs, (b) desks, (c) filing-cabinets and (d) typewriters. How many trucks are needed to make the move in one trip?

The eight items of information needed to solve the problem are that the company owns a total of 12 desks, 48 chairs, 12 typewriters, 15 filing-cabinets, and that one truckload can take 12 typewriters, or 3 desks, or 5 filing-cabinets, or 24 chairs.

The statement of the problem was typed completely on each of four separate cards and each of the eight items of information was typed on a separate card. Each subject was given one of the problem cards; the information was equally divided over the group members. For completion of the group task each subject has to know the problem solution.

The subjects were seated around a circular table, so that each was separated from the next by a vertical partition from the center to the table's edge. The partitions had slots permitting subjects to push written message cards to the persons on either side of them.

To allow for communication to the other members of the group, a four-layered quadrilateral box was placed at the center of the table. The box was placed so that the partitions just touched each of the four points of the quadrangle. Each of the four resulting work spaces was painted a different color. The subjects were supplied with blank message cards whose colors matched those of their work spaces. Any message sent from a booth had to be on a card of the booth's color.

Measurement

When the group had solved the problems, each subject was asked to fill out a questionnaire, in which mainly measurements of satisfaction and leadership were made. The most important data in this experiment, however, were time scores, communication units and errors. These could be directly observed during the session or analyzed from the material afterwards.

RESULTS

First we will report results of analyses of circle versus wheel data, bearing especially on the "development hypotheses" (2a., 2b., 2c.) but also on 1a., 1b. and 1c.

Then we will report results of analyses based on the degree of centralization of the decision structure during the last phase of the work. Only hypotheses 1a., 1b., and 1c. will be tested in these analyses.

With regard to the development of the group structure, the decision centrality index of the wheel groups during the last two problems is .51; that of the circle groups is .24. This difference is significant (Mann Whitney U Test: $p < .01$ one-tailed test).[4] For the *first* phase of the work period, no such difference occurs. Each position's proportion of the total *interaction* remains the same during the work period, both in the wheel groups and in the circle

---

[4] Since the data satisfied few of the assumptions of normal-distribution methods, only "distribution-free" methods have been used. Results will be stated for a one-tail test, since they test directional predictions. For more details on this study cf. 11.

TABLE 1. MEAN TIME PER PROBLEM (FOR TOTAL GROUP) IN MINUTES *

	First Problem	Second Problem	Third Problem	Fourth Problem	Fifth Problem	All Problems
Circle	13.95	8.70	6.60	6.55	7.25	8.61
Wheel	16.27	9.92	6.13	5.85	5.88	8.81
Circle minus Wheel	−2.32	−1.22	+0.47	+0.70	+1.37	

* Note: 13 circle groups are compared with 13 wheel groups. The interaction between structure and problem sequence is significant (Kendell's Tau = 1.0, p = .01).

groups. Thus the interaction structure does not appear to develop in wheel or circle groups.

Wheel versus Circle

In Table 1, data on the speed of the work performance are reported.

The increase in "superiority" of the wheel appears clearly from the data in the last row. In the beginning of the work period, the circle groups are faster than the wheel groups, but the difference decreases. In a later phase the relation is reversed, and then the difference increases. Thus hypothesis 2a is strongly supported.

Hypothesis 1a is not confirmed. Although the wheel groups are faster in the fourth and fifth problems, the difference fails to reach significance.

In Table 2, data on the quality of the performance are reported.

It appears that 60 percent of all wheel errors are made in the first two problems, 19 percent in the last two. For the circle these figures are, respectively, 40 percent and 44 percent. This difference between wheel and circle groups is large and significant. Hypothesis 2b is thus strongly supported by these findings.

The same holds for hypothesis 1b. In the last phase of the work period, the wheel groups make fewer errors than the circle groups.

With regard to errors, hypothesis 2d is also strongly supported by the data. In the circle groups, 29 errors are corrected from a total of 57 errors; in the wheel, only 13 are corrected from a total of 53. The difference is significant (Chi-square: p < .01).

In Table 3 data on the efficiency of the task performance are reported.

Again the superiority of the wheel

TABLE 2. ERRORS PER PROBLEM *

	First Problem	Second Problem	Third Problem	Fourth Problem	Fifth Problem	All Problems
Circle	9	15	8	7	18	(57)
Wheel	20	12	11	4	6	(53)

* Note: The difference between wheel and circle in the 2 x 5 table is significant at the .05 level (likelihood ratio test of the independence hypothesis).

The differences between wheel and circle in the fifth problem and in the fourth and fifth problems together are significant at the .05 level (Chi square, with correction for continuity).

TABLE 3. MEAN NUMBER OF MESSAGES, PER PROBLEM, PER POSITION *

	First Problem	Second Problem	Third Problem	Fourth Problem	Fifth Problem	All Problems
Circle	8.20	7.08	5.88	5.75	6.28	(6.64)
Wheel	7.15	5.68	3.63	3.43	3.38	(4.65)
Circle minus Wheel	+1.05	+1.40	+2.25	+2.32	+2.90	

* Note: The interaction between structure and problem sequence is significant (Tau = 1.0, p = .01).

The difference between wheel and circle is not significant in the first problem; it is significant at the .01 level in the last problem (Mann Whitney U test).

increases steadily from first to fifth problem. Hypothesis 2c has found strong support.

While the difference is not statistically significant in the first phase of the work period, it increases to such an extent that, in the later phases, it is large and significant. Thus hypothesis 1c also is strongly supported.

D.C.I. in Last Phase

We now turn to the second set of analyses, based on the degree of centralization of the decision structure achieved by the groups in the last problem. For every group, the decision centrality index during the last problem was calculated; then the wheel groups were divided in two classes, containing the six more-centralized and the six less-centralized wheel groups; the same was done with the circle groups.

Results of these analyses are reported in Table 4.

It will be noted in Table 4 that the sub-classes of wheel and circle groups varied substantially in degree of centralization of decisions. The less centralized six among both wheel and circle groups

TABLE 4. DECISION CENTRALITY INDEX, SPEED, QUALITY, AND EFFICIENCY, ON LAST (FIFTH) PROBLEM *

	n (1)	D.C.I. (2)	Time to Solve (3)	Errors (4)	Messages per Position (5)
More-centralized wheel groups (W_1)	6	.85	4.01	0	2.46
Less-centralized wheel groups (W_2)	6	.17	7.88	5	4.21
More-centralized circle groups (C_1)	6	.54	5.79	4	4.88
Less-centralized circle groups (C_2)	6	.07	8.84	12	7.46

* Note: Within the table, differences in D.C.I., time and messages are tested with the Mann Whitney U test. The difference in errors is tested with Fisher's exact test.

Results are for one-tail test, except the D.C.I.-comparison of W_2 versus C_1.

Significance of differences:

	$P < .01$	$P < .05$
W_1—W_2,	Col. 2, 3, 5	
W_2—C_1,	2	Col. 3
C_1—C_2,	2, 5	3
W_1—C_2	3, 4, 5	

achieved only a low level of centralization, while the more centralized six achieved a substantial level, even among circle groups. Indeed, the C_1 groups show a significantly higher level than the W_2 groups.

The time data are according to prediction on the basis of the decision centrality index: groups with a more centralized decision structure are faster, as is apparent from the large and significant differences between W_1 groups and W_2 groups, C_1 and C_2 and W_1 and C_2. The most important datum, however, is that the circle groups with a more centralized decision structure (C_1) needed considerably less time than the less centralized wheel groups (W_2). From these findings it may be concluded that the decision structure is the primary determinant of the speed of performance. The more centralized the decision structure, the faster is the group's performance. Hypothesis 1a is thus strongly supported by these experimental results.

The number of errors decreased with increasing decision centrality index (Tau: $p < .05$) but some differences are extremely small. Only the difference between the most centralized groups (W_1) and the least centralized ones (C_2) was significant. These results give support to hypothesis 1b.

With regard to number of messages, a large difference exists between W_1 and C_2. Also, within the topological structure, an increasing decision centrality index leads to a decreasing amount of communication. But C_1 groups did not need fewer messages than W_2 groups. Hypothesis 1c is supported, but the degree of centralization of the interaction structure also exerts some influence on the *amount* of communication.

Some of our data on the distribution of communication over the different "positions" within the group are very relevant in connection with Shaw's concept of "saturation." In the wheel groups, the central person sends out a mean of 8.7 messages per problem, the "peripherals" 3.3 One may question whether the central person does not exceed the optimal output level. He may do so in the beginning (mean number of messages $= 13.6$) but definitely does not at the end (mean $= 6.2$). Here his communication activity is not different from that of circle members (cf. Table 3). Table 5 presents further crucial data bearing on this problem.

Persons in the center position of the decision structure in W_1 *send out* fewer messages than central persons in W_2 (and less than circle members, although this difference is not significant). The number of messages they receive is made up of the number the peripherals send. Thus it appears from the table that the central persons in W_1 also *receive* fewer

TABLE 5. MEAN NUMBER OF SENT MESSAGES, PER POSITION, IN LAST PROBLEM *

Central position $W_1 = 4.67$	Peripheral positions $W_1 = 1.72$
Central position $W_2 = 7.17$	Peripheral positions $W_2 = 3.22$
Circle position $\quad = 6.17$	

* Note: Differences are tested with Mann Whitney U Test (one-tail test).

The difference between central positions in W_1 and central positions in W_2 is significant at the .05 level. The difference between peripheral positions in W_1 and peripheral positions in W_2 is significant at the .01 level.

messages than central persons in W_2. These relations do not change when a correction is made for time differences. Thus the communication activity (input and output) of the central position even decreases when centralized decision structures develop, and the saturation hypothesis must be rejected.

DISCUSSION

In early studies in this field, stress was laid on the topological structure as a determinant of group performance. Guetzkow and Simon, and Flament, however, already demonstrated that, when *simple* problems are solved, the *speed* of the group's performance is determined by the organization which the group develops.[5]

A theory by Shaw states that "availability of information" determines the performance of groups when simple problems are solved, but that for more complex problems the possibility of contributions from all members becomes much more important. Groups which allow for participation of all group members should perform complex tasks faster than groups where this is not the case. Shaw tested this theory by a comparison between groups with a topological circle structure and groups with a wheel (star) structure. The latter structure may be called a centralized interaction structure, since all interaction is "to" or "from" a central position. The former structure should permit more participation of all members.

The present theory is quite the reverse. It states that a high degree of centralization of the decision processes leads to better group performance.

Shaw assumes a sharp, "substantial" difference between simple and complex problems. This difference, however, is one of gradation. In our opinion the essential point is that, irrespective of the complexity of the problem, *integration* of the group process is necessary. When two or more persons work on the same task, so that the work of each of them is only a part of the "total," the integration of their contributions is a basic condition for a good end performance. When decision structure refers to "who makes decisions for whom," integration is secured to an optimal degree by a strongly centralized decision structure. The central person can then integrate the contributions of all individual members.

The theory is confirmed by the experimental results. In a number of our groups, a centralized decision structure develops during the work period, even though it was relatively short. These groups performed their tasks with more speed, fewer errors and more efficiency than groups where centralization of the decision processes did not develop to such an extent.

In Shaw's participation theory it is hypothesized that, as a consequence of centralization processes, the central person would become "saturated" because the optimal output level would be exceeded. Our data, however, demonstrate that, in groups where a more centralized decision structure develops, the central position is not characterized by a greater communication input or output, but rather by a smaller one. Thus the saturation hypothesis proves to be incorrect.

---

[5] Simon and Guetzkow refer to "optimal organizations." In their *conclusions* they do not distinguish the decision structure from the interaction structure (cf. 6 and also for more elaboration on this point 11).

The data also demonstrate that the development of a centralized decision structure (and, consequently, a better group performance) is to a very considerable degree independent of the topological structure or the interaction structure. But *if* the centralized decision structure develops on the basis of a centralized interaction structure, this leads to some special consequences. More centralized structures are in general characterized by a greater "vulnerability." By this is meant that a disturbance in the functioning of the central position will quickly disturb the functioning of the total group. Now we hypothesized that in groups with a centralized interaction structure (as the wheel groups in the experiment) such disturbances in the functioning of the central positions should occur *in the beginning* of the experimental sessions. Then the input and output requirements of the central position would be such that he could not meet them. This would lead to negative results for the group's performance.

This hypothesis, which may explain some of Shaw's results, is also confirmed by our results. The more centralized interaction structures demonstrate a greater vulnerability at the begining of the work, which leads to negative performance results. The development of centralized decision structures appears to cancel these initial negative effects radically.

SUMMARY

This paper reported a laboratory investigation testing two hypotheses about group structure and group performance. The first hypothesis was that the more centralized the decision structure of groups, the better will be the group's performance in regard to speed, quality and efficiency. The second hypothesis stated that more centralized structures are generally characterized by "vulnerability," which leads to negative performance results as long as centralized *decision* structures have not developed. These hypotheses were confirmed by the results of an experiment in which groups of four persons solved so-called complex problems.

REFERENCES

1. BAVELAS, A.   "A Mathematical Model for Group-Structures," *Applied Anthropology*, 1948, 7, 16–30.
2. BAVELAS, A.   "Communication Patterns in Task-Oriented Groups," in D. Cartwright and A. Zander (Eds.), *Group Dynamics*, New York: Harper & Row, 1953, 493–506.
3. FLAMENT, C.   "Changements de Rôles et Adaptation à la Tâche dans les Groupes de Travail Utilisant Divers Réseaux de Communication," *L'Année Psychologique*, 1956, 2, 411–431.
4. GILCHRIST, J. C., M. E. SHAW, & L. C. WALKER.   "Some Effects of Unequal Distribution of Information in a Wheel-Group Structure," *Journal of Abnormal and Social Psychology*, 1954, 49, 554–556.
5. GUETZKOW, H.   "Organizational Development and Restrictions in Communications," Dittoed paper, Carnegie Institute of Technology, 1951, (108 pp.).
6. GUETZKOW, H., & H. A. SIMON. "The Impact of Certain Communication Nets Upon Organization and Performance in Task-Oriented Groups," *Management Science*, 1955, 1, 233–250.
7. HEISE, G. A., & G. A. MILLER. "Problem Solving by Small Groups

Using Various Communication Nets," *Journal of Abnormal and Social Psychology*, 1951, 46, 327–335.

8. LEAVITT, H. J. "Some Effects of Certain Communication Patterns on Group Performance," *Journal of Abnormal and Social Psychology*, 1951, 46, 38–50.

9. LUCE, R. D., J. MACY, L. S. CHRISTIE, & D. H. HAY. "Information Flow in Task Oriented Groups," Technical Report No. 264, 1953, Research Laboratory of Electronics, Massachusetts Institute of Technology.

10. MULDER, M. "Groepsstructuur en Gedrag," *Nederlands Tijdschrift*

voor de Psychologie, 1956, 11, 85–133.

11. MULDER, M. "Group-Structure and Group-Performance," *Acta Psychologica*, 1959, 16, 356–402.

12. SHAW, M. E. "Some Effects of Unequal Distribution of Information Upon Group Performance in Various Communication Nets," *Journal of Abnormal and Social Psychology*, 1954, 49, 547–553.

13. SHAW, M. E. "Some Effects of Problem Complexity Upon Problem Solution Efficiency in Different Communication Nets," *Journal of Experimental Psychology*, 1954, 48, 211–217.

44. INTERDEPENDENCE, DIFFERENTIAL REWARDING, AND PRODUCTIVITY *

L. Keith Miller and Robert L. Hamblin

Cooperation and competition are basic processes of social life which have important consequences for diverse aspects of group behavior. This is an investigation of the effects on group productivity of two interacting dimensions of competition and cooperation: differential rewarding and task interdependence.

THEORY

Since at least 24 studies have been conducted to determine the relative effect of cooperation and competition on group productivity,[1] this relationship must rank as one of the more intensively investigated social phenomena. Yet, one is struck by the ambiguity of the results. In 14 of these studies competition resulted in greater group productivity than did cooperation. while in ten others, cooperation resulted in greater productivity than did competition. Why such ambiguity? To find the answer is the purpose of the present investigation. Three explanations may be offered.

First, since most of the studies did involve small groups, one might point to these contradictory results as another example of the inadequacy of small-group research. We shall evaluate this

---

[1] Martin M. Grossack, "Some Effects of Cooperation and Competition Upon Small Group Behavior," *Journal of Abnormal and Social Psychology*, 49 (July, 1954), pp. 341–

* Excerpted from *American Sociological Review*, 1963, 28: 768–778, with permission of the senior author and the American Sociological Association. This study was conducted under a contract [Nonr 816(11)] from the Office of Naval Research, Group Psychology Section.

possibility later. Second, the ambiguity may have arisen because many of the studies were conducted before statistical tests came into vogue. Yet, random fluctuations apparently do not account for the ambiguous relation of group productivity to competition and cooperation. Taking the results of statistical tests where they are available, and calculating the appropriate statistical tests where the raw data were published, we find that the null hypothesis is rejected at better than the 5 percent level in 20 of the studies.

A third possibility is that the concepts of competition and cooperation as they have been operationalized in past studies are not a unidimensional phenomenon, but instead, involve two orthogonal dimensions. If this is the case, then these two dimensions may interact to produce the inconsistent effects on group productivity. An examination of the experimental situations used in this study suggests that this is the case. Co-operative and competitive situations in these studies may be differentiated by two dimensions: (1) the presence or absence of differential rewarding for relative achievement of group members, and (2) the presence or absence of task or functional interdependence. It is possible that the contradictory results occur because the differential rewarding under conditions of low task interdependence has one effect on productivity, whereas differential rewarding under conditions of high task interdependence has quite another.

In classifying past investigations, experimental situations involving problems such as the discussion of a human relations problem were placed in the high interdependence category because the resolution of such a problem does involve a mutual exchange of ideas and information as well as the give and take required to make a group decision. On the other hand, experimental situations involving problems such as reading,

---

348; Morton Deutsch, "An Experimental Study of the Effects of Co-operation and Competition upon Group Process," *Human Relations*, 2 (July, 1949), pp. 199–231; L. Keith Miller, *The Effect of Interdependence on Small Group Interaction*. Unpublished Master's thesis, University of Illinois, 1959; Alexander Mintz, "Nonadaptive Group Behavior," *Journal of Abnormal and Social Psychology*, 46 (April, 1951), pp. 50–159; Anthony J. Smith, Harrison E. Madden, and Ronald Sobol, "Productivity and Recall in Cooperative Discussion Groups," *Journal of Psychology*, 43 (April, 1957), pp. 193–204; Peter M. Blau, "Cooperation and Competition in a Bureaucracy," *American Journal of Sociology*, 59 (December, 1954), pp. 530–535; Julius B. Maller, "Cooperation and Competition—An Experimental Study," *Teachers' College Contributions to Education*, 384 (1929); Beeman N. Philips, "An Experimental Study of the Effects of Cooperation and Competition, Intelligence and Cohesiveness on the Task Efficiency and Process Behavior of Small Groups," *Dissertation Abstracts*, 14 (1954), p. 635; George Forlano, "An Experiment in Cooperation," *Journal of Education Research*, 25 (February, 1932), pp. 128–131; Verner M. Sims, "The Relative Influence of Two Types of Motivation on Improvement," *Journal of Educational Psychology*, 19 (October, 1929), pp. 480–484; Pitirim A. Sorokin, Mamie Tanquist, Mildred Parten, and Mrs. C. C. Zimmerman, "An Experimental Study of Efficiency of Work Under Various Specified Conditions," *American Journal of Sociology*, 35 (March, 1930), pp. 765–782; Irving C. Whittemore, "The Influence of Competition on Performance," *Journal of Abnormal and Social Psychology*, 19 (October-December, 1924), pp. 236–253; W. Moede, *Experimentelle Massenpsychologie*, Leipzig: S. Hirzel, 1920; Alice J. Philp, "Strangers and Friends as Competitors and Cooperators," *Journal of Genetic Psychology*, 57 (December, 1940), pp. 249–258; Richard deCharms, "Affiliation Motivation and Productivity in Small Groups," *Journal of Abnormal and Social Psychology*, 55 (September, 1957), pp. 222–226.

adding numbers, and carrying sand, were placed in the low interdependence category, since these problems could be solved without the help of other individuals in the group.

In Table 1, the studies listed above the dividing line all involve high interdependence situations, whereas those below the line involve low interdependence situations. Note that the results of these studies as plotted in Table 1 are much less ambiguous. In the high interdependence situations, the results of all six of the studies indicate that differential rewarding for relative achievement decreases group productivity. The results in the low interdependence category also become clearer. Fourteen studies indicate that differential rewarding increases productivity while only four studies show the inverse relationship. These four exceptions may mean that in the low interdependence situation, the positive relation between group productivity and relative differential rewarding is extremely weak, or they may mean that there is still another confounding variable. To check these two possibilities, and in general, to confirm or disconfirm this *ad hoc* analysis of

TABLE 1. OUTLINE OF STUDIES CONCERNING THE EFFECT OF REWARD DIFFERENTIATION ON GROUP PRODUCTIVITY

Authors	Relationship [a]	Type of Group	Task
Crossack	—	Experimental	Discussion problem
Deutsch	—	Class	Discussion problem
		Class	Puzzle problem
Miller	—	Experimental	Leavitt-Puzzle
Mintz	—	Experimental	Withdrawing cones from jar
Smith	—	Experimental	Discussion problem
Maller	+	Class	Adding numbers
	+	Sex groups	Adding numbers
	—	Teams	Adding numbers
	+	Partners	Adding numbers
Phillips	+	Classes	Twenty questions
Forlano	+	Classes	Cancellation of letters
	+	Teams	Cancellation of letters
	—	Sex groups	Cancellation of letters
Sims	+	Classes	Substitution of letters
	+	Classes	Reading
Sorokin	+	Partners	Carrying objects
	+	Partners	Sorting different objects
Whittemore	—	Friends	Mechanical printing
Moede	—	Unknown	Hand grip
Philp	+	Friends	Transferring marbles to box
Philp	+	Strangers	Transferring marbles to box
deCharms	+	Experimental	Arithmetic
	+	Experimental	Scrambled words

[a] A "+" indicates a positive relation between differential rewarding and productive efficiency, that is, the differentially-rewarded groups were more productive, and a "−" indicates a negative relation.

previous data, we designed our own experiment to test the following hypotheses:

(1) Under conditions of high task interdependence, the amount of group productivity varies inversely with the degree of differential rewarding for relative productivity.

(2) Under conditions of low task interdependence, the amount of group productivity varies directly with the degree of differential rewarding for relative productivity.

EXPERIMENTAL METHODS

The Sample

Ninety male students from Washington University were used in the experiment. These students were formed into 30 three-person groups, five groups in each of six cells of the experimental design. The students were selected from all university class levels, all curricula, and from both on and off campus residencies.

The Experimental Procedure

Each subject was seated in an isolated booth that was connected to the booths occupied by the other group members and the experimenter by an electrical system of lights and switches. After being placed in their booths, the subjects were given instructions explaining the experiment. As a trial session, they solved five problems in a row, and in so doing learned how to send and receive messages using the experimental apparatus. Further instructions indicating the goals and the reward structure

were then given. Next, after receiving the ground rules which structured the situation as one of either high interdependence or low interdependence, the subjects proceeded with two additional practice problems to become acquainted with the implications of the reward and interdependence conditions under which they were operating. Finally, they were given the ten sequential problems which were used to determine the effect of differential rewarding for relative achievement on productive efficiency in the two interdependence conditions.

The task was to determine which one of 13 numbers had been selected by the experimenter. It was considered completed only when each group member knew the answer. As a clue, each subject was privately informed of four numbers that had *not* been selected by the experimenter. Furthermore, these clues were different for each subject so that they could pool their clues (by the electrical system) and thereby determine the correct answer. The task was used in all of the 17 trials, but each trial had a different solution.

The Experimental Manipulations

A three-by-two factorial design was used for the manipulations. Three variations of rewarding were set up in each of two variations of interdependence.

Rewarding

Rewards for group members were based both upon their own efforts and upon the efforts of the group as a whole. For example, each group started with 90 points, and one point was subtracted for every second that elapsed before all members had solved the problem. Thus, if a group took 60 seconds, 30 points were awarded. Since the group could not win points after 90 seconds, the trial was automatically terminated if the group had not reached a solution by that time.

The group's points were then distributed to its members in shares proportionate to their rank order in solving the problem. In the equally rewarded variation, each subject received one-third of the group award. At the other extreme, in the high differential variation, the subject who solved the problem first received two-thirds of the group reward; the second, one-third; and the third, none. In addition, a third, medium-differential variation was used in which the subject who finished first received one-half of the group's points; the subject who finished second, one-third; and the subject who finished third, one-sixth. These three conditions can be described in terms of difference in proportions between the shares of total points received by subjects in adjacent ranks. These differences are .00 in the equally rewarded variation; .17 in the medium-differential variation; and .33 in the high-differential variation.

Interdependence

This variable was manipulated by varying the way in which the subjects could solve the problem. In the high-interdependence situation, guessing was discouraged by a substantial penalty. This meant that the subjects had to communicate with each other in order to obtain the missing information; they were therefore highly interdependent. In the low interdependence situation, subjects were encouraged to guess by the absence of a penalty; since the problem could be solved much faster by guessing than by communicating, the absence of a penalty always resulted in a high rate of guessing and the total absence of communication. Consequently, the subjects were not dependent upon one another for information: the problem could be solved by each subject alone without any exchange of information.

Measurement

In this experiment, individual productive efficiency was measured by an automatic electric timer simply as the length of time it took the individual to obtain and send the correct solution to the experimenter. Group efficiency was measured by calculating the average of individual efficiency.

RESULTS

The Basic Results

Here we can focus on three relatively distinct questions: (1) What is the effect on productive efficiency of interdependence alone? (2) What is the effect of differential rewarding alone? (3) What is the combined effect of interdependence and differential rewarding on productive efficiency?

The data show that our manipulation of interdependence was extreme, that the relation between interdependence and productive efficiency was significant in all three reward conditions. In fact, the relationships were so large as to be distracting. Therefore, we will ignore the independent effect of interdependence and arbitrarily eliminate it in the various tables by equating the means of the high and low interdependence variations. The answers to the

TABLE 2. ANALYSIS OF VARIANCE SHOWING THE EFFECT OF DIFFERENTIAL
REWARDING AND INTERDEPENDENCE ON PRODUCTIVITY SCORES

Source of Variance	Sums of Squares	Degrees of Freedom	Mean Squares	Variance [a]	Dx [b]
Interdependence	00	1	—	—	—
Differential rewarding	7,776	2	3,888	275.0	.14**
I × R	7,583	2	3,791.5	530.7	.28*
Between	15,359	5	—	—	—
Residual	27,363	24	1,138	1,138.0	.58

    * Significant beyond 6 percent level by F-test.
    ** Significant beyond 5 percent level by F-test.
    [a] This is an unbiased estimate of variance associated with each source, derived from fixed constants components of variance model. See Quinn McNemar, *Psychological Statistics*, New York: John Wiley, 1955, p. 306.
    [b] The "coefficient of determinancy," Dx, indexes the strength of impact which the source has on the dependent variable by measuring the proportion of the variance of the dependent variable attributable to that source. The coefficient is numerically comparable to the square of the correlation coefficient.

other two questions regarding the effect of differential rewarding itself, and the combined effect of differential rewarding and interdependence on productive efficiency, are unchanged by this equation.

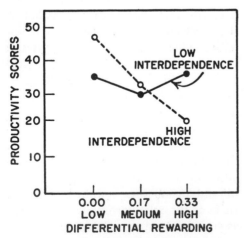

Figure 1. Mean productivity scores by differential rewarding in high and low interdependence conditions

    [a] Productivity scores equal 90 (maximum solution time allowed in seconds) minus average solution times (in seconds).

As can be seen in Table 2, both differential rewarding itself and the combination of differential rewarding and interdependence account for some of the variance of productive efficiency. By itself, differential rewarding explains 14 percent of the variation in productive efficiency. However, the interaction, or combined effect of the two variables, is significant and reasonably strong, explaining 28 percent of the variance. When the interaction is significant, it means that the relation between one of the two variables and the dependent variable is a function of the other— precisely as was postulated. In the introductory analysis, we assumed that the effect of differential rewarding might vary, depending upon the task interdependence of the social system in question. However, the data in Table 2 do not furnish the necessary details to confirm or disconfirm our original hypotheses. To obtain these necessary details, the data for the groups from the high and low interdependence variations were separated, and Figure 1 was prepared to

TABLE 3. LINEAR REGRESSION ANALYSIS OF THE RELATION BETWEEN DIFFERENTIAL
REWARDING AND PRODUCTIVITY SCORES UNDER HIGH AND LOW INTERDEPENDENCE [a]

Inter-dependence	Source	Sums of Squares	Degrees of Freedom	Mean Squares	Variance	Dx
High	Linear regression of differential rewarding	14,062.5	1	14,062.5	1,397.6	.467*
	Deviations from linearity [b]	86.5	1	86.5	00.0	.000
	Between	14,149.0	2	—	—	—
	Residual	19,037.0	12	1,586.6	1,586.6	.533
	Total	33,186.0	14	—	2,984.2	1.000
Low	Linear regression of differential rewarding	3.6	1	3.6	00.0	.000
	Deviations from linearity [b]	1,203.4	1	1,203.4	101.9	.128
	Between	1,207.0	2	—	—	—
	Residual	8,326.0	12	693.8	693.8	.872
	Total	9,533.0	14	—	795.7	1.000

* Significant beyond 2.5 percent level by F-test.
[a] Both Bartlett's and Cochran's tests reveal a fairly serious lack of homogeneity of variance. This casts doubt upon the results of the analysis of variance, as well as this regression analysis, as significance may arise from real difference, inhomogeneity of variance, or a combination of both. Analysis of transformed data, fourth root of the inverse, deduced by Kendall's method (*The Advanced Theory of Statistics*, London: Griffin, 1948, Volume II), confirms the existence of real and strong effects almost identical to those revealed by the non-transformed data. Thus, the significance tests were based on transformed data.
[b] Estimate derived from Linear Model presented by F. Acton, *Analysis of Straight Line Data*, New York: John Wiley, 1959, p. 108.

determine more about the relation between differential rewarding and productive efficiency for each of the two variations. For the high-interdependence variation, the results are clearly consistent with the first hypothesis. As differential rewarding increases, productive efficiency decreases—and it does so rather sharply with 32 percent in the medium and 57 percent in the high differential rewarding conditions.[2]

[2] In the calculation of these percentages, the productivity scores in Figure 1 were not used, as the zero point is somewhat arbitrary. Rather, these percentages were calculated directly using an increase in solution time as the negative indication of a decrease in productivity.

In Table 3, a statistical analysis of these same data is provided. Based on a linear regression analysis, the relation in the high-interdependence condition between differential rewarding and productive efficiency is both significant and strong, involving 47 percent of the variance. Both this and the graphic analysis in Figure 1, then, provide strong support for the first hypothesis.

In the low interdependence condition, however, the relation between differential rewarding and productive efficiency is evidently very weak. As indicated in Figure 1, productive efficiency is slightly lower in the medium than in either the low or the high differential rewarding conditions. Furthermore, the data in Table 3 (in the deviations from linearity line) indicate that differential rewarding accounts for 13 percent of the variation in productive efficiency in the low interdependence condition when a nonlinear relationship is assumed. Even so, this nonlinear relationship is not significant statistically. Furthermore, when a linear relationship is assumed, as it evidently was in hypothesis 2, it turns out that none of the variance of productive efficiency is explained in the low interdependence condition. Therefore, the second hypothesis is not supported by the data; productive efficiency apparently does not increase with differential rewarding in low interdependence situations. We will check the generality of these results and their implications in the next section.

Generality of the Results

One weakness of much experimental work is that its generality is either taken for granted or ignored. Actually, the generality of any results should be regarded as problematic and worthy of attention. Other things being equal, the more general a hypothesis, the more widespread are both its theoretical and applied implications.

One way to determine the generality of a hypothesis is to test it systematically under a number of different conditions. For example, in the case of the present experiment, most sociologists would feel that it is desirable to repeat the study in a natural setting; others might feel that the study should be repeated using different age groups; others might want to use larger groups; others might want the task to last a much longer time;

others might want to vary the type of task; and still others might want to use groups of friends instead of strangers.

Although such a set of replications was beyond our patience, our interests, and our budget, we did find a way of obtaining somewhat comparable information. Since the previous studies of cooperation and competition have been conducted under widely varying conditions, they may be regarded as replications of the present experiment under these respective conditions. Even though one might wish that additional conditions were available for a comparison, this may be taken as a beginning.

The procedure followed in examining the previous results is quite simple. First of all, the studies were segregated into the categories of high and low interdependence, and, where there was sufficient statistical information available in the original article, measures of association were computed. Then, using one control dimension at a time, the studies were segregated into the two or three categories along that dimension and the average strength of the association between differential rewarding and productivity was calculated for each of them. For example, all studies were categorized as either "laboratory" or "field." Means for the strength of association between differential rewarding and productivity were then calculated for the high interdependence laboratory groups and compared with those calculated for the high interdependence field groups. If the average association turned out to be about the same, then we assumed that laboratory versus field conditions had little effect, and consequently, that the studies in the laboratory may be generalized to field situations.

The basic data appear in Table 4,

TABLE 4. DETERMINANCY (DX) OF PRODUCTIVITY FROM REWARD DIFFERENTIATION FOR PAST STUDIES CONDUCTED UNDER DIFFERENT CONDITIONS

Author	Dx[a]	Age of Subjects	Size of Groups	Type of Reward	Conditions			
					Type of Task	Type of Group	Duration	Composition
High interdependence situations:								
Smith	−23.3[b]	17–21	5	Honor	Mental	Experimental	Short	Strangers
Mintz	−63.8[c]	17–21	17	Honor	Manual	Experimental	Short	Strangers
Deutsch	−36.8[b]	17–21	5	Grades	Mental	Classroom	Long	Acquaintances
Deutsch	−42.8[b]	17–21	5	Grades	Mental	Classroom	Long	Acquaintances
Low interdependence situations:								
Maller	+00.4[b]	8–17	37	Honor	Mental	Classroom	Short	Acquaintances
Sorokin	+06.0[b]	3–6	4	Toys	Manual	Experimental	Short	Acquaintances
	+00.2[b]	5–6	4	Toys	Mental	Experimental	Short	Acquaintances
	+06.4[b]	13–17	3	Money	Manual	Experimental	Short	Acquaintances
Philp	+17.6[b]	4–6	2	Toys	Manual	Experimental	Short	Strangers
	+12.2[b]	4–6	2	Toys	Manual	Experimental	Short	Friends
deCharms	+07.0[b]	17–21	5	Honor	Mental	Experimental	Short	Strangers
Forlano	+08.0[b]	12	11	Books	Mental	Classroom	Short	Acquaintances
	+02.2[b]	12	5	Books	Mental	Classroom	Short	Acquaintances
	∓17.3[b]	12	5	Books	Mental	Classroom	Short	Acquaintances
Whittemore	−01.7[b]	21–31	4	Honor	Manual	Experimental	Long	Friends

[a] A plus or minus was added to these coefficients of determinancy to indicate the nature of the relationship obtained. Dx measures the ratio of uncertainty in a variable that is controlled by an independent variable to the total uncertainty in the variable.

[b] Derived from analysis of variance; the ratio of between-sums-of-squares to total-sums-of-squares yields a slightly biased estimate of Dx.

[c] Derived from contingency table. In this case, Dx is the "coefficient of restraint" which is the ratio of "transmitted information" to total uncertainty, as both are defined by Shannon and Weaver. For further information, consult W. J. McGill, "Isomorphism in Statistical Analysis," in Henry Quastler, Editor, Information Theory in Psychology, New York: Free Press, 1955, pp. 56–62.

and the results of the cross-tabulation in Table 5. The first question to be asked of these data is: Are the results of our experiment representative? In the low interdependence situations, the average explained variance in past studies is .04, as compared with .00 in the present experiment. In the high interdependence situations, the average explained variance in past studies is .42, whereas in the present experiment, the explained variance was .47. Thus, the overall correspondence between the findings from the past studies and those from the present experiment is quite striking, suggesting that we may place a good deal of confidence in the results of the present experiment.

The second and main question to address to these data concerns the generality of these findings: Do the other variables influence the strength and possibly the nature of the relationship between differential rewarding and productivity? For those experiments involving low interdependence situations, none of the control variables appears to influence greatly the strength of the relationship between differential rewarding and group productivity. Apparently,

TABLE 5. AVERAGE DETERMINANCY (DX) OF PRODUCTIVITY FROM DIFFERENTIAL
REWARDING UNDER DIFFERENT CONDITIONS

	Interdependence			
	Low		High	
	Dx	N	Dx	N
A. Interdependence	+3.7	(11)	−41.7	(4)
B. Type of group studied				
Experimental	+6.8	(7)	−43.6	(2)
Non-experimental	−1.7	(4)	−39.8	(2)
C. Size of group				
Big (over ten)	+4.2	(2)	−63.8	(1)
Small (under ten)	+3.6	(9)	−34.3	(3)
D. Duration of experimental period				
Long	−1.7	(1)	−39.8	(2)
Short	+4.3	(10)	−43.6	(2)
E. Composition of group				
Friends	+5.3	(2)	−	
Acquaintances	+0.8	(7)	−39.8	(2)
Strangers	+12.3	(2)	−43.6	(2)
F. Nature of the rewards				
Objective	+4.4	(8)	−39.8	(2)
Subjective	+1.9	(3)	−43.6	(2)
G. Age of subjects				
Grade school	+3.6	(8)	−	
High school and college	+6.7	(2)	−41.7	(4)
Adult	−1.7	(1)	−	
H. Type of task				
Mental	+0.1	(6)	−34.3	(3)
Manual	+8.1	(5)	−63.8	(1)

the size of the group, the duration of the task, and the nature of the reward make very little, if any, difference. However, the association might be slightly stronger in a laboratory situation where the task involved is manual rather than symbolic, and where the groups are composed of strangers who either are high school or college students. Note, too, that these are the very conditions that obtained in the low interdependence variations in our experiment where the explained variance was .00. Consequently, these differences are probably of such small magnitude as to be unstable.

In high interdependence situations, it makes little difference whether the investigation occurred in a laboratory or in a field situation, whether the subjects were acquaintances or strangers, whether the competition was over a short or a long period, or whether the rewards were objective or subjective. On the other hand, the negative relationship between differential rewarding and productive efficiency is *apparently* strengthened considerably when the competition is among a larger as opposed to a smaller number of individuals, or when the task is manual rather than mental or symbolic. It is difficult to tell, however, whether both, only one, or perhaps neither of these latter variables (that is, size and type of task) influence the strength of the negative relation between differential rewarding and productive efficiency. The results with respect to both of these variables involve the same four experiments cross-tabulated in exactly the same way. The Mintz experiment,[3] which involved a large number of individuals in a manual task, also involved a third, complicating factor, since it was a task where it was extremely difficult to avoid blocking. Consequently the above-noted differences in productive efficiency probably reflect the effects of increased interdependence— an increased necessity of cooperation and the resulting increase in the probabilities of blocking—rather than the effects of size or type of task. Note in this case that the conditions of the present experiment were biased against the hypothesized results. These data, then, give an important indication that the negative relation between relative differential rewarding and group productivity in high interdependence conditions evidently may be generalized into many naturally occurring situations.

[3] Mintz, *op. cit.*

10

Personality Influences in Social Situations

45. DOMINANCE AS A FACTOR IN ACHIEVEMENT AND PERCEPTION IN COOPERATIVE PROBLEM SOLVING INTERACTIONS *

William T. Smelser

The first part of this study relates different pairings of dominant and submissive males, interacting under various role assignments, with their joint achievement in a cooperative problem solving situation. The second part investigates the relationship of these different pairings to the perceived dominance of the self and the partner.

The thesis is advanced that different combinations of dominant and/or submissive individuals achieve more or less successfully according to the pair-combination as well as the conditions of assignment of dominant or submissive roles, and that it is possible to predict differential success among these permutations according to hypotheses derived from personality theory.

The hypotheses are derived from

Sullivan's (1953) general assumption that a person's modes of relating to others are functional in that they enable him to maintain anxiety at a minimum. Interpersonal situations that permit, or encourage, the use of a salient interpersonal technique, such as dominance or submission, give rise to less anxiety than situations that do not. The experiencing of anxiety disrupts cognitive functioning and leads to a less effective performance in a task. Hence, there should be greater achievement when persons are permitted or encouraged to assume habitual modes of relating.

In spite of the explicitness and theoretical importance of this reciprocal aspect of interpersonal theory, few experimental studies have been concerned with it. Leary (1957), employing dom-

* Reprinted from *Journal of Abnormal and Social Psychology*, 1961, 62: 535–542, with permission of the author and the American Psychological Association.

TABLE 1. PAIRINGS OF DOMINANT AND SUBMISSIVE SUBJECTS AND CONDITIONS
OF ROLE ASSIGNMENTS
(10 pairs in each group)

Group	Description of Interaction	Code
A	Dominant subject assigned dominant role; submissive subject assigned submissive role.	D:d–S:s
B	Dominant subject and a submissive subject interact with no role assignment.	D:x–S:x
C	One dominant subject assigned dominant role; other dominant subject assigned submissive role.	D:d–D:s
D	One submissive subject assigned dominant role; other submissive subject assigned submissive role.	S:d–S:s
E	Two dominant subjects interact with no role assignment.	D:x–D:x
F	Two submissive subjects interact with no role assignment.	S:x–S:x
G	Dominant subject assigned submissive role; submissive subject assigned dominant role.	D:s–S.d

inance as one of his central variables, posits a reciprocal theory of interaction. In Mann's (1959) review of the studies of the relation of personality and performance in small groups, he did not report any studies considering the relationship between interacting individuals differing in dominance and the influence of this relation upon either the nature of group achievement or mutual perception. Tuma (1955) found that dissimilarity in dominance between therapist and client, regardless of the direction of the difference, correlated highly with rated improvement in a counseling situation.

The following four hypotheses are based on a theoretical prediction of differences, among different pairings of male subjects under specified conditions of role assignment, in achievement in a cooperative task situation. Table 1 describes the seven different groupings and the interaction and the role assignments, when such assignments were made. The predicted rank orders of achievement of the groups involved in each of the four hypotheses are presented in Table 2.

Hypothesis 1 compares Groups A, B, and G. Following Sullivan (1953), the pairings in Group A perform the most productively, since each member of the pair has a salient inter-personal technique explicitly requested by the experimenter as well as "pulled for" by the behavior of the partner. The pairs of dominant and submissive subjects comprising Group B interact under somewhat less optimal conditions, since these pairs lack the congruent role assignments of the pairs in Group A. The pairs of dominant and submissive subjects in Group G interact with an assignment of roles contrary to their preferred modes, which arouses anxiety and disrupts achievement.

TABLE 2. HYPOTHESES OF RANK ORDER
OF ACHIEVEMENT OF GROUPS

Hypothesis	Predicted Rank Order of Achievement
1	A > B > G
2	B > E > F
3	C > D > E > F
4	A > B > C > D > E > F > G

Hypothesis 2 compares Groups B, E, and F. Paired dominant subjects (Group E) do not interact under as optimal conditions as do the pairs in Group B, since each member of the paired dominant subjects interacts so as to induce submissive behavior in his partner, who is also a dominant subject. The paired subjects in Group E were predicted to perform more successfully than the paired submissive subjects in Group F, since dominant subjects are hypothesized to behave in the pursuit of satisfaction rather than security, and thus to be more at ease with each other and themselves than the paired submissive subjects. Sullivan (1953) considered the power motive as one of the pursuits of satisfaction, rather than security. Individuals lacking in dominance may have found it necessary to dissociate the expression and/or awareness of this motive.

Hypothesis 3 compares Groups C, D, E, and F. The prediction involves the differential achievement of two different pairings (two dominant subjects interacting and two submissive subjects interacting), each under two conditions (no role assignments and assignment of the dominant role to one subject and assignment of the submissive role to the partner). The predicted rank order of achievement, by groups, is C, D, E, and F, since it was hypothesized that pairings with role assignment perform more successfully than comparable pairings with no role assignment, and further, that the paired dominant subjects would perform more succesfully than paired submissive subjects under comparable conditions. For a dominant subject to relinquish a dominant role should produce less anxiety than for a submissive subject to assume a dominant role. In Sullivan's (1953) terms, it is less disruptive to modify a mode of attaining satisfaction (dominant role) than it is to modify a security operation (submissive role).

Hypothesis 4 is not independent of the other three hypotheses, but compares achievement among all seven groups. The predicted rank order corresponds to the alphabetical ordering of the groups, i.e., Group A is predicted to be the most successful and Group G the least successful. Hypotheses 1 and 3 are independent, since their predictions do not involve any common groups. Hypothesis 2 has one group (Group B) in common with Hypothesis 1 and it has two groups in common with Hypothesis 3 (Groups E and F).

METHOD

The subjects were all male volunteers enrolled in either Military Science or Air Science at the University of California, Berkeley. Since enrollment in the university armed forces training program is compulsory, this group afforded a broad sampling of university undergraduate men. The total number of subjects who volunteered was 748. Participation in the experiment was credited as an excuse from one military drill period.

Before requesting volunteers, the students were administered a short form of Gough's California Psychological Inventory (CPI), which contained the Dominance (Do), Social Responsibility, and Self-Control scales (Gough, 1957). A vocabulary test (Thorndike & Gallup, 1944) was administered at the conclusion of the personality test. The subjects for the experiment were selected from the extremes of the distribution of the Do scores. The mean of this distribution was 28.5 (*SD*, 6.5) which is quite similar to Gough's (1957) standardization group mean of 28.5 (*SD*, 6.0). A subject scoring 34 or above was defined as dominant; a subject scoring 23 or below as submissive. The raw scores of 34 and 23 correspond to Gough's T scores of 110 and 92, respectively, on a scale with a mean of 100 and a standard deviation of 10.

Experimental Situation

The interaction of the paired subjects involved the joint operation of two model railroad trains. The apparatus was that employed by Ghiselli and Lodahl (1958). The main track was 6 feet in diameter, and had two bypass sidings by which the two trains could leave and enter the main track. The two subjects sat on high stools to operate their respective control panels, which were 3 feet high, on the same level with the tracks. The left half of each control panel contained switches that supplied power to different numbered sections of the track. The right half of each control panel contained several controls: direction and speed of the trains, switches to and from the sidings, and a master control switch. The subjects were thus able to control the speed, direction, and route of each train. Carelessness by either subject in operation of his switches could obstruct the efforts of the partner in operating his train.

Procedure

Before the instructions for operation of the trains, the subjects were introduced, both as a matter of social convention, and also to determine whether the subjects were acquainted with each other. Subjects previously acquainted were not included in the results. Subjects from Military Science and Air Science were not mixed in the pairings. The instructions for operation of the two trains were given during the first 20 minutes. Both trains were operated by the experimenter at this time, and both control panels were equally employed for demonstration. The subjects were permitted to ask questions during the demonstration. They were allowed 3 minutes to discuss the operation of the trains before the first trial.

The role assignments, when given, were given just prior to the first trial. In the following example, "X" is assigned the dominant role and "Y" is assigned the submissive role.

Mr. X, your train will be the passenger train, and Mr. Y, your train will be the freight. Mr. X you are the dispatcher and you will arrange and order the solutions to the problem, and Mr. Y, your task is to carry out, on your board, Mr. X's directions. Remember, Mr. X, you are to plan and organize the solutions, while both of you are to carry out the operations of the trains on your respective boards. Mr. Y, your function is to carry out as well as you can the directions of Mr. X. You are permitted to make suggestions, but the final decision rests with Mr. X. Do you have any questions?

Task

At the start of the first trial, the passenger train was on one siding, pointed so as to move counterclockwise around the track. The freight train was on the main track, pointed so as to move clockwise around the track. The prescribed route for the passenger train was different from the route for the freight, so that the subjects frequently operated the switches to the sidings. Each subject was responsible for the operation of the assigned train. The subjects' task was to complete as many mutually complete trips as possible around the track in a 3-minute trial period. There were six 3-minute trials, with a 1-minute rest period between each trial. The trains were not run simultaneously. The subjects were free to communicate with each other during the entire procedure, but could not ask the experimenter for directions once the first trial had begun.

The achievement score for a given trial was the number of *mutually* complete trips around the track, for example, if one subject made 8 trips and his partner made 5, the achievement score for that trial was 10. The maximum

possible score for a given trial was 32. After the last trial, each subject checked Leary's (1957) Interpersonal Check List (ICL) twice: as he saw himself and as he saw his partner. This 128-item check list can be scored for dominance. The entire procedure lasted one hour.

RESULTS

Achievement

Groups A through G were first compared on age, the Responsibility and Self-Control scales of the CPI, and verbal intelligence. No significant differences between any of the seven groups on any of these variables was found. The means and standard deviations of achievement scores for Groups A through G on Trials 1 through 6 and the sums of trials are presented in Table 3.

Table 4 contains the results of testing Hypothesis 1. The analysis of vari-

TABLE 3. MEANS AND STANDARD DEVIATIONS OF ACHIEVEMENT
FOR TRIALS 1 THROUGH 6 AND SUMS OF TRIALS

Group		1	2	3	4	5	6	Sums
A	M	18.9	23.9	26.8	29.8	30.3	30.8	160.4
	SD	7.0	5.3	5.4	2.1	2.8	2.0	19.0
B	M	14.1	19.8	25.7	26.2	26.7	28.7	141.2
	SD	6.7	5.5	4.0	6.0	5.5	4.4	20.1
C	M	15.4	23.2	27.4	27.7	28.8	30.8	153.3
	SD	7.5	5.6	4.3	6.5	5.4	1.6	18.7
D	M	13.6	20.4	22.5	26.4	29.2	30.8	142.9
	SD	7.7	7.0	8.1	4.5	3.0	2.0	22.8
E	M	12.0	20.3	20.7	26.9	26.6	29.2	142.0
	SD	8.7	6.8	3.5	4.2	6.0	3.3	23.0
F	M	10.0	18.1	21.2	24.1	27.3	29.5	130.2
	SD	6.9	6.7	4.0	7.8	4.4	2.5	13.8
G	M	7.3	14.8	15.9	22.4	27.6	28.4	116.4
	SD	5.7	4.9	7.0	5.1	2.4	4.9	13.5

Trials

TABLE 4. ANALYSIS OF VARIANCE FOR HYPOTHESIS 1

Source	df	MS	F
Between Groups A, B, G	2	811.02	13.91***
Between Trials 1 through 6	5	1,081.78	47.85***
Trials × Groups	10	56.56	2.50**
Between subjects in same group	27	58.31	
Pooled subjects × Trials	135	22.61	
Total	179		

** $p = .01$.
*** $p = .001$.

ance employed was that recommended by Edwards (1950) when there are repeated measurements of the same subjects. Before any of the analyses of variance were performed, Bartlett's test of homogeneity was performed, which proved to be insignificant in all cases.

There is a highly significant difference in achievement between Groups A, B, and G. Inspection of Table 3 shows that Group A was more productive than Group B, which in turn was more productive than Group G. The significant mean square between trials indicates a marked increase in performance across trials for all three groups. The significant interaction of trials by groups reflects the initial higher achievement and greater rapid improvement in perform-ance of Groups A and B over Group G. The analysis of variance confirms Hypothesis 1.

The results of another simple analysis of variance to test Hypothesis 2 are presented in Table 5. The hypothesis was not confirmed, since the mean square between Groups B, E, and F was not significant, and the empirical ordering by achievement was E, B, then F, instead of B, E, then F as predicted. Thus paired dominant subjects (Group E) outperformed paired dominant and submissive subjects (Group B), who in turn outperformed paired submissive subjects (Group F). The mean square between trials was again highly significant, a finding attributable to the increasing achievement with successive trials for all three groups.

TABLE 5. ANALYSIS OF VARIANCE FOR HYPOTHESIS 2

Source	df	MS	F
Between Groups B, E, F	2	72.47	1.04
Between Trials 1 through 6	5	1,175.57	41.40***
Trials × Groups	10	19.96	.70
Between subjects in same group	27	69.72	
Pooled subjects × Trials	135		
Total	179		

*** $p = .001$.

A complex analysis of variance was performed to test Hypothesis 3, since the two variables of pairings and role assignments were each varied in two ways. The results are presented in Table 6. The empirical rank order of the four groups was C, D, E, then F, which corresponds to the predicted rank order. The mean squares between pairings and between role assignments were both significant. The results confirm Hypothesis 3. The mean squares between trials was again significant.

Hypothesis 4 predicted the rank order in achievement of all seven groups. The predicted rank order was alphabetical, A through G, while the empirical rank order was A, C, D, E, B, F, and G. The rank order correlation between predicted and empirical rank orders was .78, significant at the .05 level (Table P in Siegel, 1956). This empirical rank order is based on the sums of trials. The rank order correlations, on the other hand, between predicted and empirical rank order calculated separately for Trials 1 through 6 were: .96 ($p = .01$), .64, .61, .75 ($p = .05$), .39, and .55, respectively.

A frequency count of the subjects' spontaneous requests for the maximum possible score shows that 59 of the total N of 70 dominant subjects made such a request, while 12 of the total N of 70 submissive subjects made this request (chi square is 55.6, $p < .001$). Also, 15 additional dominant subjects operated the trains without a partner, as did 15 additional submissive subjects. An F test between the achievement of these two groups was significant at the .05 level, with the dominant subjects achieving more than the submissive subjects. In Mann's (1959) review of the relation of personality and performance in small groups, dominance is found to be positively related to the number of task contributions.

Perception

Since each subject checked the ICL as he perceived himself and as he perceived his partner, it was possible to determine the subjects' own definition of the situation in terms of dominance of self and partner. The ICL dominance scores are presented in Table 7.

TABLE 6. ANALYSIS OF VARIANCE FOR HYPOTHESIS 3

Source	df	MS	F
Between pairings (Groups C, D vs. E, F)	1	205.35	5.68*
Between roles (Groups C, E vs. D, F)	1	240.00	6.50*
Between Trials 1 through 6	5	1,570.95	43.48***
Trials × Pairings	5	44.95	1.24
Trials × Roles	5	8.88	.25
Pairs × Roles	1	.81	.02
Pairs × Roles × Trials	5	3.66	.10
Within groups	216	36.13	
Total	239		

* $p = .05$.
*** $p = .001$.

TABLE 7. INTERPERSONAL CHECK LIST DOMINANCE SCALE MEANS AND STANDARD
DEVIATIONS OF PAIR COMBINATIONS FOR CHECK OF SELF
AND CHECK OF PARTNER
(N = 10 for each pair combination)

Group	Pair Combination	Self M	Self SD	Partner M	Partner SD
A	D:d	64.4	3.8	55.8	4.3
	S:s	49.6	9.6	61.2	6.8
B	D:x	62.7	2.9	60.1	6.7
	S:x	49.0	8.5	58.3	7.7
C	D:d	62.9	3.1	60.8	4.7
	D:s	61.7	5.3	61.5	5.9
D	S:d	53.1	8.2	54.3	8.5
	S:s	51.3	7.1	54.1	8.7
E	D:x_1	59.0	3.8	58.9	8.6
	D:x_2	62.6	3.7	57.7	3.8
F	S:x_I	49.8	9.9	57.4	5.9
	S:x_2	49.2	8.1	53.9	8.8
G	D:s	58.0	3.9	56.7	3.5
	S:d	52.1	6.9	57.5	7.0

The *intra*group differences in perceived dominance are considered first. The test employed was the Wilcoxon matched-pairs signed-ranks test (Siegel, 1956). Differences that attained statistical significance are presented in Table 8. Inspection of Table 7 shows that for every group which includes a dominant subject, the dominant subjects' self-check mean is always higher than the check of his partner mean. This difference attains statistical significance within Groups A and B. Thus in terms of a comparison of group means, the submissive subjects consistently perceived themselves as less dominant than they perceived their partners and the dominant subjects as more dominant, regardless of the roles assigned and regardless of whether the partner was a dominant subject or a submissive subject.

In those groups were a dominant subject and a submisive subject interact (Groups A, B, and G), the dominant subjects' mean check of their partners was always higher than their partners' mean self-checks. This difference attains statistical significance in Group B. In Groups A, B, and G, the submissive subjects' mean self-check was consistently lower than the dominant subjects' mean self-check. This difference is statistically significant in Groups A and B.

Several *inter*group comparisons were made, employing, for the most part, the data as presented in Table 7. The standard deviations of the submissive subjects' self-checks are significantly greater than the standard deviations of the dominant subjects' self-checks ($p <$ .01), employing the Wilcoxon matched-pairs signed-ranks test (Siegel, 1956).

Thus in their self-checks, dominant subjects are a more homogeneous group than are the submissive subjects. The standard deviations of the dominant subjects' self-checks are significantly greater ($p < .05$) than the standard deviations of the dominant subjects' checks of their partners. Dominant subjects are less uniform in their perceptions of their partners than they are of themselves. This relationship is not true of the submissive subjects.

A comparison of the self-check of the dominant subjects interacting with submissive subjects under three different conditions of role assignment (Groups A, B, and G) shows that the dominant subjects assigned a dominant role (Group A) perceived themselves as more dominant than the dominant subjects assigned no role (Group B), who in turn perceived themselves as more dominant than the dominant subjects assigned a submissive role (Group G). These three groups are significantly different ($p < .02$), employing the Friedman two-way analysis of variance (Siegel, 1956). A similar (statistically insignificant) rank order holds for the submissive

subjects' check of their respective dominant partners in Groups A, B, and G, that is, the submissive subjects in Group A rated their own dominant partners as more dominant than did the submissive subjects in Group B rate their own partners. The submissive subjects in Group B in turn rated their dominant partners as more dominant than the submissive subjects in Group G rated their own dominant partners.

DISCUSSION

The general pattern of the achievement of the seven groups tends to validate the hypotheses, both in statistical significance of the differences between groups and in the direction and ranking of the predicted differences. The failure of the results to support Hypothesis 2 is due largely to the unpredicted high achievement of Group E. Group C also achieved higher scores than predicted in Hypothesis 4. Both of these groups have paired dominant subjects. The greater achievement of these two groups is in part due to the higher aspiration level

TABLE 8. STATISTICALLY SIGNIFICANT INTRAGROUP DIFFERENCES IN INTERPERSONAL CHECK LIST DOMINANCE

($N = 10$ for each pair combination)

Group	Pair Combination With Higher Dominance [a]	Pair Combination With Lower Dominance [a]	p
A	D:d (s)	S:s (s)	.006
B	D:x (s)	S:x (s)	.006
A	D:d (s)	D:d (p)	.006
E	D:x_1 (s)	D:x_1 (p)	.05
A	S:s (p)	S:s (s)	.01
B	S:x (p)	S:x (s)	.02
B	D:x (p)	S:x (s)	.01

[a] (s) denotes self-check; (p) denotes check of partner.

of the dominant subjects, as previously noted.

With the exception of Group G, the assignment of dominant and submissive roles to any of the pairings resulted in an increase in achievement. The greatest absolute increase in achievement as a result of assignment of roles was between the dominant subject with a submissive subject pairings (Group A compared with Group B). The assignment of roles to paired dominant subjects or paired submissive subjects resulted in virtually the same absolute increase in achievement, that is, the difference between Group C and Group E is similar to the difference between Group D and Group F. The assignment of roles gave a structure within which the subjects were able to function more effectively than the comparable pairings without role assignment.

There was a rapid rise in achievement across trials for all groups, so that by Trial 6 all groups were performing at virtually the same level. This similarity of level of performance by Trial 6 is in part an artifact of the task, since the top possible score for a trial was 32. Group G made the greatest absolute gain from Trial 1 through Trial 6. However, this is due in part to the low initial performance on Trial 1. If there had been, for example, only three trials instead of six, the differences in achievement would have been greater and in the same direction. The major differences in achievement between groups appeared in the initial trials. The effect of the relative dominance of the partners as well as the assignment of roles is greatest here.

The ICL results indicate that the subjects' definition of the situation in terms of dominance closely reflected both the selection of the subjects high and low in personal dominance as well as the assignment of dominant and submissive roles. The degree of dominance ascribed to the partner, relative to the subjects' own dominance, is a function of the subjects' personal dominance. These findings are in accord with those of Leary (1957) and Naboisek (1953). The degree of dominance ascribed to the self and the partner varied in the direction of the assigned role.

These relationships between the subject's own dominance and the degree of dominance he ascribes to others are in contrast to a study (Altrocchi, 1959) employing the same pool of subjects as the present study, where the dominant subjects did not ascribe less dominance to others than the submissive subjects. One critical difference between these studies is that Altrocchi's subjects observed movies of social objects before rating them, whereas the subjects in the present study interacted before rating each other, thus both communicating as well as evoking cues (Bruner & Tagiuri, 1954) of dominance or submissiveness.

Both the dominant and submissive subjects attributed considerable dominance to their partners, regardless of the partner's personal dominance. This finding may be attributed in part to the cooperative nature of the task as well as the fact that dominance is an approved trait for males, so that attributing dominance to another is a way of indicating social desirability (Edwards, 1957).

Generalizations from the achievement and perceptual findings are restricted in that the subjects were males chosen from a rather restricted socio-economic-educational stratum of society as well as from the extremes of the distribution of dominance. However, the task is representative (Brunswik, 1947) of many life experiences, where two individuals work together in the pursuit of some objectively mutual goal under circumstances requiring a good deal of communication and cooperation.

SUMMARY

This study related different pairings of dominant and submissive males, who interacted under various role assignment conditions, to their joint achievement in a cooperative problem solving situation. Predictions of differential achievement were derived from the thesis that the productivity of a pair depends upon the degree to which conditions permit each member to utilize his habitual patterns of interpersonal behavior.

A personality inventory was administered to 748 male university undergraduates. Volunteer subjects scoring very high or very low on a dominance scale were selected for participation in the cooperative task situation. The task was the operation of two model railroad trains for a series of six 3-minute trials. All groups were homogeneous with respect to age, and score on social responsibility, self-control, and vocabulary tests.

Of four predictions concerning the relative achievement of the seven interaction groups, three were confirmed. The most productive group was composed of pairs in which the dominant subject was assigned the dominant role and the submissive partner the submissive role. The least productive group was composed of these pairings with the roles reversed. Paired dominant subjects were more successful than paired submissive subjects, and both of these pairings achieved more when assigned roles. All groups showed significant increases in performance across trials.

The degree of dominance attributed to others was a function of the subjects' personal dominance. Dominant subjects perceived their partners as less dominant than themselves and submissive subjects perceived their partners as more dominant than themselves. The degree of dominance ascribed to the self and the partner varied in the direction of the assigned role.

It was concluded that congruence of role and habitual pattern within the subject and complementarity of patterns as between subjects were major determining variables in cooperative achievement. Sullivan's (1953) personality theory was employed in theoretical consideration of these results.

REFERENCES

Altrocchi, J. C. Dominance as a factor in interpersonal choice and perception. *J. abnorm. soc. Psychol.*, 1959, 3, 303–308.

Bruner, J. S., & Tagiuri, R. The perception of people. In G. Lindzey (Ed.), *Handbook of social psychology.* Cambridge, Mass.: Addison-Wesley, 1954. Ch. 17.

Brunswik, E. *Systematic and representative design of psychological experiments, with results in physical and social perception.* Berkeley: Univer. California Press, 1947.

Edwards, A. L. *Experimental design in psychological research.* New York: Holt, Rinehart and Winston, 1950.

Edwards, A. L. Social desirability and probability of endorsement of items in the Interpersonal Check List. *J. abnorm. soc. Psychol.*, 1957, 55, 394–396.

Ghiselli, E., & Lodahl, T. M. Patterns of managerial traits and group effectiveness. *J. abnorm. soc. Psychol.*, 1958, 57, 61–66.

GOUGH, H. G. *Manual for the California Psychological Inventory.* Palo Alto, Calif.: Consulting Psychologists Press, 1957.

LEARY, T. *Interpersonal diagnosis of personality.* New York: Ronald, 1957.

MANN, R. D. A review of the relationships between personality and performance in small groups. *Psychol. Bull.,* 1959, 56, 241–270.

NABOISEK, H. Validation of a method for predicting role expectations in group therapy. Unpublished doctoral dissertation, University of California, 1953.

SIEGEL, S. *Nonparametric statistics for the behavioral sciences.* New York: McGraw-Hill, 1956.

SULLIVAN, H. S. *The interpersonal theory of psychiatry.* New York: Norton, 1953.

THORNDIKE, R. L., & GALLUP, G. H. Verbal intelligence of the American adult. *J. genet. Psychol.,* 1944, 30, 75–85.

TUMA, A. H. An exploration of certain methodological and client-counselor personality characteristics as determinants of learning in the counseling of college students. Unpublished doctoral dissertation, University of Maryland, 1955.

46. QUALITY AND ACCEPTANCE OF PROBLEM SOLUTIONS BY MEMBERS OF HOMOGENEOUS AND HETEROGENEOUS GROUPS *

L. Richard Hoffman and Norman R. F. Maier

In an earlier article Hoffman (1959) reported that higher quality solutions to problems were produced by groups whose members had dissimilar personalities (heterogeneous groups) than by more homogeneous groups. On the other hand, the reported satisfaction of the members with the solutions (acceptance) was quite similar in the two types of groups. Since only two problems were used, however, the generality of the superior problem solving ability shown by the heterogeneous groups may be questioned.

Might homogeneous groups do better on other problems? Problems that emphasize differences among group members, and thus strain the ability of heterogeneous groups to work together effectively, may provide conditions advantageous for homogeneous groups. Even if the quality of solutions to such problems by heterogeneous groups should not be impaired, the members' satisfaction with the solutions may be reduced.

In addition to the two problems used in the original study, the present study employed three new ones that involved conflicts in values, personal conflicts, and the distribution of a bonus. With the same experimental design the

* Reprinted from the *Journal of Abnormal and Social Psychology*, 1961, 62: 401–407, with permission of the senior author and the American Psychological Association. The major part of the research reported herein was supported by Project Michigan, a Department of the Army-sponsored project of the University of Michigan in the field of combat surveillance. The contract (DA-36-039 SC 52654) is administered by the Signal Corps. The final report was written in conjunction with USPHS Grant No. M-2704 from the National Institute of Mental Health, United States Public Health Service.

original study was thus extended to determine whether heterogeneous groups would produce higher quality solutions to such varied problems without sacrificing acceptance.

METHOD

Four-person homogeneous and heterogeneous groups were constructed in the eight laboratory sections during two semesters of an undergraduate psychology course in human relations. The Guilford-Zimmerman Temperament Survey (Guilford & Zimmerman, 1949) was used as the measure of personality, and profile correlations (Kendall's tau) were computed between the 10-score profiles of all pairs of students in each section. Originally 16 homogeneous groups (high positive tau's) and 25 heterogeneous groups (either near-zero tau's or high negative and positive tau's) were formed in the third week of the semester and interacted weekly thereafter in case discussions, problem solving, and role playing.

Periodically, test problems were introduced into the laboratory sessions. Solutions to four of these problems could be scored for their objective quality; one was a problem purely of fairness, having no external standard of quality. Of the problems that could be scored for quality, solutions to three (Mined Road, Student Assistance Fund, and Painter-Inspector Argument) were graded quantitatively according to systems of content analysis that assigned increasing numbers of points to solutions of higher quality. On the fourth quality problem—Change of Work Procedure —new-modified and, especially, integrative solutions were considered to be of high quality.

The Mined Road Problem, used in the earlier study, (Hoffman, 1959) requires the group to develop a method for permitting five men to cross a heavily mined road. It was administered in the first meeting of each group. The major problem for the group here is to recognize and solve all facets of the problem in the safest possible way.

The Student Assistance Fund problem, a role playing case developed for the present study, was administered in the fourth meeting. Each subject was assigned the role of a different student who was deemed qualified for financial assistance from a university fund. Each "student" was told that he qualified on one or more attributes. Each also was told that he needed $1,500 for the next academic year, but the total fund was only to be $3,000 this year. The group had to decide on how to allocate the money this year and to recommend a method for allocating money in the future. Conflict was induced by the provision that the total amount of money was less than that needed by all group members combined and not enough for any one member if they divided the money evenly. The chance of reaching agreement was reduced further by giving the subjects opposing standards for allocating money among themselves. Only the method developed for allocating funds among students in the future was scored for quality.

The Painter-Inspector Argument problem (adapted from Maier, Solem, & Maier, 1957), another role playing case in which a leader was assigned randomly within each group, was administered in the sixth laboratory session. A painter, an inspector and rough primer, a shop steward, and a foreman meet to settle an argument between the painter and the inspector. The argument reflects a basic conflict in the entire shop, but few groups were able to get beyond the initial argument and identify the total shop problem.

The Change of Work Procedure problem (Maier, 1952), administered in somewhat modified form in the eighth session, is also a role playing case, with a foreman appointed to lead the discussion, and was repeated from the earlier study. The discussion centers around a request by the foreman that each of the three workers work in his best position rather than rotating among three simple jobs. The problem is usually approached as a choice between the increased pay of the fixed-position method (New solution) and the relief from boredom offered by rotation (Old solution).

The Point Distribution problem was administered in the tenth session, immediately following the return to the class members of the third of four course examinations. Each group was given 19 points to distribute among its members as a bonus for participating in the experiment. The points were to be used to raise the final grade of the student. Each subject knew his own position in the class relative to the tentative cutting points for grades indicated by the instructor. The groups were given 40 minutes to arrive at a decision, and were told that no fractional or negative points were to be given and that failure to agree would give each subject four points. Since no objective standard of quality could be applied to the solutions, this problem was one of fairness or acceptance.

Following each problem solving session, the subjects completed two Likert-type five-point questions concerning their satisfaction with the solution reached and with the amount of influence they had over the solution. Values from 1 to 5 were assigned to each response, with 1 indicating "very dissatisfied" and 5, "very satisfied."

RESULTS

Quality of Solutions

The overall findings of the present study support those of the earlier one. On the various problems, the solutions by heterogeneous groups either were scored as significantly superior in quality to those of the homogeneous groups, or did not differ in quality. Never were the homogeneous groups better than the heterogeneous groups.

Table 1 presents a comparison of the results on the three quantitatively-scored problems that had a quality component—Mined Road, Student Assistance Fund, and Painter and Inspector—for the homogeneous and heterogeneous groups. For the Mined Road problem the results combining the data of the present and earlier studies are also presented. The proportion of high quality solutions to both the Mined Road and Student Assistance Fund problems by heterogeneous groups was substantially greater than by homogeneous groups. (The means are not very different as a result of a few very high scoring solutions by homogeneous groups.) The Painter and Inspector problem was the only one in which no differences were found between the two types of groups. The generally low scores on this problem (an average of about 15 out of a possible 45 points with less than 20 percent of the groups achieving scores of 30 or more) point to the restrictive

TABLE 1. QUALITY OF SOLUTIONS BY HOMOGENEOUS AND HETEROGENEOUS GROUPS

	Present Study		Combined Studies	
	Homo-geneous	Hetero-geneous	Homo-geneous	Hetero-geneous
Mined Road Problem				
Percentage above median [a]	30%	57%	21.7%*	52.6%*
M	55.9	65.3	45.9*	64.3*
SD	34.6	29.9	32.1	29.3
Number of groups	10	21	23	38
Student Assistance Fund				
Percentage above median [a]	36%*	80%*		
M	44.2	50.9		
SD	17.5	12.8		
Number of groups	14	20		
Painters and Inspectors				
Percentage above median [a]	54%	56%		
M	16.5	15.1		
SD	10.5	13.9		
Number of groups	13	16		

[a] The median score was determined from the results of all four-person groups, including residual groups not assigned to either the homogeneous or heterogeneous types.

* Percentage or mean difference significant at the .05 level.

character of this problem. Even heterogeneity of personality was insufficient to force the groups to consider other than the immediate problem of settling the personal dispute.

The results in Table 2 for the Change of Work Procedure problem again show the superiority of the heterogeneous over the homogeneous groups. Whereas 65 percent of the heterogeneous groups in the present study produced new-modified or integrative solutions—the higher quality solutions—only 21 percent of the homogeneous groups' solutions were of these types. This difference is statistically significant at the .05 level. Furthermore, the percentage of integrative solutions—the highest quality solution—produced by the heterogeneous groups in both the present and earlier studies was significantly greater than the percentage produced by homogene-

ous groups (indicated in parentheses in Table 2).

Thus on three of the four problems that could be scored for quality, substan-

TABLE 2. SOLUTIONS TO THE CHANGE OF WORK PROCEDURE PROBLEM BY HOMOGENEOUS AND HETEROGENEOUS GROUPS

Type of Solution	Homogeneous	Heterogeneous
Integrative	0 (7.7%)[a]	5 (35.3%)[a]
New-modified	3*	6*
New	7	4
Old	4	2

[a] The numbers in parentheses are the percentages of Integrative solutions obtained from each type of group in the combined studies. This percentage difference is statistically significant at the .05 level.

* Chi square test comparing Integrative and New-Modified with Old and New solutions is significant at the .05 level.

tially more of the heterogeneous than of the homogeneous groups produced better solutions. On the fourth problem there was no difference between the group types, most solutions being of poor quality.

The Point Distribution problem was designed to place strain on the heterogeneous groups by exaggerating the differences among the group members. The problem demands agreement on the criteria to be used in assigning points to the several group members. Greater conflict was anticipated in the heterogeneous than in the homogeneous groups on the grounds that in the former groups the differing personalities would use different standards to determine the appropriate method of awarding points. Thus the heterogeneous groups were expected either to allocate the points nearly equally, reflecting an inability to resolve the conflict, or to distribute the points widely, reflecting some agreed-upon systematic method of awarding the points.

The data tend to support this prediction. Since all groups arrived at some conclusion, the standard deviation of points awarded in a group was computed and used as the measure of outcome. Small scores represent nearly equal distributions of points and large scores represent diverse distributions. Although the mean standard deviation scores for the two types of groups were approximately equal (3.06 for the homogeneous groups and 4.08 for the heterogeneous groups), the standard deviation of these scores for the heterogeneous groups was significantly greater than for the homogeneous groups (2.95 for the heterogeneous and 1.72 for the homogeneous groups). In the heterogeneous groups either points were awarded nearly as equally as possible or they were almost all given to one or two members. The distribution of points by homogeneous groups tended to be more moderate, being negatively correlated, in general, to the class standing of the members on the three previous examinations. Thus the problem appears to have created greater conflict in the heterogeneous than in the homogeneous groups, but certain heterogeneous groups were able to resolve the conflict.

Interaction of Sex and Personality Composition

Using the combined data of the present and the original studies, the interaction of sex mixture and personality composition was studied in its effects on solutions to the Mined Road and the Change of Work Procedure problems. Mixed-sex as distinct from all-male groups involve another type of heterogeneity. The results indicate that the interaction of sex and personality mixture was not the same for the two problems and suggest important differences in the requirements that the problems placed on the groups.

The results for the Mined Road problem are presented in Table 3 for groups in three categories of sex composition: All Male, One Female, and Two or Three Females. Although the means and percentages above the median for the heterogeneous groups were larger than for the homogeneous groups in all three categories of sex composition, the only significant difference occurred between the All-Male groups. The differences between the homogeneous and heterogeneous groups successively diminished as the proportion of women in the group increased. (Unfortunately,

TABLE 3. HOMOGENEOUS-HETEROGENEOUS DIFFERENCES IN SOLUTION QUALITY
TO THE MINED ROAD PROBLEM IN GROUPS OF DIFFERENT SEX COMPOSITION
(Combined data: 1959 and present studies)

	All Male		One Female		Two or Three Females		Total	
	Homo-geneous	Hetero-geneous	Homo-geneous	Hetero-geneous	Homo-geneous [a]	Hetero-geneous	Homo-geneous	Hetero-geneous
Percentage above median [b]	12.5*	66.7*	0.0	33.3	50.0	72.7	21.7*	52.6*
M	34.8*	75.1*	37.7	54.1	64.1	72.2	45.9*	64.3*
SD	35.8	31.3	11.3	24.4	35.3	31.9	32.1	29.3
Number of groups	8	9	7	18	8	11	23	38

[a] Data from one homogeneous group in the 1959 study that consisted of four women are included in the two or three women category.

[b] The median score was determined from the results of all four-person groups, including residual groups not assigned to either the homogeneous or heterogeneous types.

* Mean or percentage difference between homogeneous and heterogeneous groups is significant at the .05 level by *t* test or chi square test, respectively.

only one group of all females was obtained in the 2 years' data.)

The results for the Change of Work Procedure problem, presented in Table 4, are divided only into All Male groups versus groups with One or More Females. For this problem the major difference between the homogeneous and heterogeneous groups occurred in the mixed-sex groups. Proportionately more new-modified or integrative solu-tions—high quality solutions—were produced by Mixed-Sex heterogeneous groups than by Mixed-Sex homogeneous groups. The proportions in both types of All-Male groups were approximately equal and were like those of the Mixed-Sex homogeneous groups. In the present study, moreover, all five of the integrative solutions were produced by Mixed-Sex heterogeneous groups (see Table 2).

TABLE 4. HOMOGENEOUS-HETEROGENEOUS DIFFERENCES IN QUALITY OF SOLUTIONS
TO CHANGE OF WORK PROCEDURE PROBLEM IN GROUPS OF DIFFERENT
SEX COMPOSITION
(Combined data: 1959 and present studies)

	All Male Groups		One or More Females	
Type of Group	Old or New Solutions	New-Modified or Integrative Solutions	Old or New Solutions	New-Modified or Integrative Solutions
Homogeneous	7	5	11*	3*
Heterogeneous	5	3	9*	17*

* This relationship is significant at the .05 level by chi square test.

TABLE 5. SATISFACTION WITH SOLUTIONS IN HOMOGENEOUS AND
HETEROGENEOUS GROUPS

	Homo-geneous [a]	Hetero-geneous
Mined Road Problem		
M	4.47	4.22
SD	0.37	0.43
Percentage unanimously satisfied [b]	80%	57%
Number of groups	10	21
Student Assistance Fund		
M	4.28	4.21
SD	0.67	0.67
Percentage unanimously satisfied [b]	71%	70%
Number of groups	14	20
Painters and Inspectors		
M	4.00	4.05
SD	0.70	0.57
Percentage unanimously satisfied [b]	54%	50%
Number of groups	13	16
Change of Work Procedure		
M	4.09	4.05
SD	0.81	0.44
Percent unanimously satisfied [b]	50%	35%
Number of groups	14	18
Point Distribution		
M	4.19	4.39
SD	0.69	0.41
Percentage unanimously satisfied [b]	50%	59%
Number of groups	16	17

[a] None of the differences between group types is significant at the .05 level.
[b] To determine unanimity of satisfaction a person was considered satisfied if he checked either "very satisfied" or "quite satisfied."

The results suggest that heterogeneity of personality may be sufficient to produce high quality solutions where, as with the Mined Road, the problem presents no restraints on possible alternative solutions. The group must generate its own potential solutions to this type of problem and then decide on the best one. Where, however, as with the Change of Work Procedure, alternative choices are presented in the problem, the addition of sex mixture to the personality mixture may be required to produce high quality solutions. To arrive at a solution of high quality to this type of problem, the group must recognize that the given alternatives are inadequate and "invent" a better solution. Mixing sexes and personalities appears to have freed these groups from the restraints of the solutions given in the problem.

Acceptance of Solutions

Although on three of the four quality problems a higher proportion of heterogeneous groups produced good solutions than did the homogeneous groups, the reported member satisfactions with their solutions showed no consistent differences between the two types of groups (see Table 5). Both the mean satisfaction ratings and the percentages of groups in which all members were satisfied were closely similar on all the problems except the Mined Road problem, on which satisfaction was somewhat (but not significantly) higher for the homogeneous groups. Thus the somewhat higher quality of the heterogeneous groups' solutions was not obtained at the sacrifice of acceptance by the group members.

As might be anticipated from this result, the correlations between quality of solution and mean member satisfaction were generally rather low. These are shown for the four quantitatively scored problems in Table 6. Although all of the correlations are positive, only two of the eight achieve statistical significance.

A more important variable than quality of solutions in determining member satisfaction with the group's solution is suggested by the high correlations between the subjects' satisfaction with the amount of influence they had over the decision and their satisfaction with the solution. Table 7 shows that, with two exceptions, these correlations, both at the individual and the group levels, are all significantly positive. The correlations between the subjects' satisfaction with the solution and their actual amount of influence over the decision (as rated by the other group members) were significantly different from zero in only 3 of the 10 instances and were, in every case, smaller than the corresponding correlation between satisfaction with solution and satisfaction with influence. These correlations suggest, then, that the subjects are satisfied with the decision their group reaches if they feel that their perceived amount of influence over the decision has coincided with some self-determined level of expectation concerning the amount of influence they should have.

TABLE 6. CORRELATIONS BETWEEN QUALITY AND MEAN SATISFACTION WITH SOLUTIONS

	Homogeneous		Heterogeneous	
Problem [a]	r	Number of Groups	r	Number of Groups
Minded Road Problem	.01	10	.33	21
Student Assistance Fund	.49*	14	.24	20
Painters and Inspectors	.35	13	.63**	16
Point Distribution	.29	16	.26	17

[a] A Pearson coefficient could not be computed on the Change of Work Procedure since the solutions were not scored quantitatively. The fourfold contingency tables formed in each group type by combining Old and New solutions against New-Modified and Integrative and taking the number of groups above against below the median mean satisfaction showed only slight positive relationships.

* Correlation significantly different from zero at .05 level.
** Correlation significantly different from zero at .01 level

TABLE 7. CORRELATIONS BETWEEN SATISFACTION WITH SOLUTION AND SATISFACTION WITH INFLUENCE OVER DECISION

| | For Individuals | | For Group Means | |
Problem	Homo- geneous	Hetero- geneous	Homo- geneous	Hetero- geneous
Minded Road Problem	.54** (40)[a]	.48** (84)	.47 (10)[a]	.49* (21)
Student Assistance Fund	.63** (56)	.55** (80)	.66** (14)	.73** (20)
Painters and Inspectors	.62** (52)	.48** (64)	.74** (13)	.80** (16)
Change of Work Procedure	.46** (56)	.46** (68)	.46* (14)	.06 (17)
Point Distribution	.37** (64)	.65** (68)	.59** (16)	.88** (17)

[a] Numbers in parentheses are the number of individuals or groups on which each correlation is based.
* Correlation significantly different from zero at .05 level.
** Correlation significantly different from zero at .01 level.

DISCUSSION

The results of this study confirm, for a wider sampling of problems, the findings of the earlier one that heterogeneous groups are relatively superior to homogeneous groups in problem solving ability. Even on problems designed to produce emotional conflict, the heterogeneous groups produced solutions that were better than or at least as good as those of the homogeneous groups.

The similar personalities of members of the homogeneous groups may have provided them with similar perspectives on each problem. Common to all of the homogeneous groups was the fact that all the members of each group had very similar self-perceptions. To the extent that similarity in self-perceptions is accompanied by similarity in the perceptions of problems and social situations, the number of different "directions" (Maier, 1930) available to each homogeneous group was much less than

the number available to each heterogeneous group. With fewer directions available the likelihood was reduced that homogeneous groups would develop high quality solutions to these complex problems. In the heterogeneous groups, moreover, the conflict resulting from opposing viewpoints may have caused more complete solutions to emerge or new ones to be invented. Thus we might conclude that, although one can think of unreasonably extreme exceptions (for example, people who do not speak the same language, adults and children), given relatively equally able people, the greater the differences in perceptions among the group members, the higher the quality of their problem solving.

Although other interpretations of these results are possible, the interactive effects of heterogeneity with respect to sex and personality on the solutions of the Mined Road and Change of Work Procedure problems seem to provide further supporting evidence for this view. Mixing sexes in the groups enhanced the quality of solutions to both problems, although in somewhat different ways for each problem.

The differing results of sex and personality mixture for the Mined Road and Change of Work Procedure problems suggest that differences in perspective are most important where the task is restrictive in its nature. But even where the problem is relatively unstructured, where the solutions must be developed by the group, the greater the differences the higher is the quality of group problem solving.

The data indicate that the higher quality of solutions associated with group heterogeneity were not obtained at the sacrifice of their acceptance by the group members. It would appear, moreover, that the very process by which the quality of group problem solving is improved, namely, the complete expression of such differences, is likely to enhance the acceptance of solutions. Having shown that a member's satisfaction with his group's solution to a problem is a function of his satisfaction with his amount of influence over the decision, we can conclude tentatively that, where differences in perspective are present among group members, the group's solution will be of highest quality and will have the most acceptance where these differences are expressed and finally utilized in making the final decision. This does not mean that each group member must have an equal amount of influence over the final decision. Rather, all divergent viewpoints must be given what the member perceives as a fair hearing by the group and be employed in making the final decision to the extent that they are seen as relevant. Not every group member has to participate actively in the discussion, as has sometimes been suggested (for example, Coch & French,

1958). Each group member must participate, however, if he is dissatisfied with the decision as it appears to be forming and he has some alternative approach or modification to offer.

By separating the factors important for quality and acceptance of solutions in this way, one can understand how group members may be satisfied with very poor group solutions or dissatisfied with very good ones. In the first case the group may have only a few directions available among its members, but these have been expressed completely to the group's satisfaction. In the second case a variety of directions may have been available but only those which led to the correct solution were heard. Dissatisfaction with the group's decision stems from the members' feeling that their alternative viewpoints were not evaluated fairly by the group.

SUMMARY

A wider variety of problems was used to test the generality of Hoffman's (1959) earlier finding that groups composed of people heterogeneous with respect to personality were superior in solving problems to groups composed of people with homogeneous personalities. Sixteen homogeneous and 25 heterogeneous four-person groups were initially formed in the laboratory sections of an undergraduate course in the psychology of human relations. Homogeneous groups consisted of people with high positive profile correlations among their scores on the Guilford-Zimmerman Temperament Survey, heterogeneous groups of people with near-zero or negative correlations. The group members interacted weekly in case discussions, problem solving, and role playing.

Five different problems were used to test the relative abilities of the two types of groups, four with some component of quality and one only involving acceptance. The subjects were also questioned about their satisfaction with the solution and with their influence over the solution for each problem.

The following results were obtained:

1. Heterogeneous groups produced a higher proportion of high quality solutions than did homogeneous groups to three of the four problems with quality components. On the fourth problem, there was little difference and both types of groups produced poor solutions for the most part.

2. Mixed-Sex groups tended to produce higher quality solutions than did All-Male groups.

3. Satisfaction with the problem solutions was about the same in the homogeneous and heterogeneous types of groups.

4. Satisfaction with the solutions was shown to be more strongly correlated with the members' satisfaction with the amount of influence they had over the solution than with the objective quality of the solutions or with

the members' actual amount of influence.

It is suggested that solutions with high quality and high acceptance can be obtained from groups in which the members have substantially different perspectives on the problem, and in which these differences are expressed and used by the group in arriving at the final decision.

REFERENCES

Coch, L., & French, J. R. P.   Overcoming resistance to change. In Eleanor E. Maccoby, T. M. Newcomb, & E. L. Hartley (Eds.), *Readings in social psychology.* (3rd ed.) New York: Holt, Rinehart and Winston, 1958. Pp. 233–250.

Guilford, J. P., & Zimmerman, W. S. *The Guilford-Zimmerman Temperament Survey.* Beverly Hills: Sheridan Supply, 1949.

Hoffman, L. R.   Homogeneity of member personality and its effect on group problem solving. *J. abnorm. soc. Psychol.,* 1959, **58,** 27–32.

Maier, N. R. F.   Reasoning in humans: I. On direction. *J. Comp. Psychol.,* 1930, **10,** 115–144.

Maier, N. R. F.   *Principles of human relations.* New York: Wiley, 1952.

Maier, N. R. F., Solem, A. R., & Maier, A. A.   *Supervisory and executive development.* New York: Wiley, 1957.

47.   A NOTE CONCERNING HOMOGENEITY OF MEMBERSHIP AND GROUP PROBLEM SOLVING *

Marvin E. Shaw

Homogeneity of group members with regard to individual differences has long been recognized as an important variable in group behavior (Hemphill, 1950). In a recent article, Hoffman (1959) reports results supporting the

* Reprinted from *Journal of Abnormal and Social Psychology,* 1960, 60: 448–450, with permission of the author and the American Psychological Association.

TABLE 1. THE RELATION OF MEMBER HOMOGENEITY TO GROUP
PERFORMANCE AND SATISFACTION

Homogeneity Variables	Structural Conditions	N	Group Process Variables		
			Trials to Target	Time Scores	Ratings of Satisfaction
Intelligence (Shaw, 1959a)	Power:				
	Centralized	20	+.07	+.38	−.49*
	Decentralized	20	−.07	+.08	+.21
	Communication:				
	Centralized	24	—	.00	+.21
	Decentralized	24	—	+.26	+.30
Acceptance of Authority (Shaw, 1959a)	Power:				
	Centralized	20	−.11	−.17	−.08
	Decentralized	20	+.48*	+.53**	−.59**
	Communication:				
	Centralized	24	—	.00	+.02
	Decentralized	24	—	+.27	−.11
Individual Prominence (Shaw, 1959b)	Power:				
	Centralized	22	−.22	+.06	−.18
	Decentralized	22	−.08	−.26	+.20

Note.—Signs of correlations have been adjusted so that a positive correlation indicates increasing efficiency or satisfaction with increasing homogeneity.
* $p < .05$.
** $p < .01$.

hypothesis that homogeneity results in less efficient problem solving than does nonhomogeneity of membership. Citing the findings of Pelz (1956) to support his view, he suggests that ". . . the results reported in the present study are probably generalizable well beyond the limited population of college students who supplied the data." (Hoffman, 1958, p. 31.) It was this statement which motivated the writer to report some of his own observations of relations between homogeneity and group effectiveness.[1]

During the past few years, the writer has conducted a series of experiments attempting to study the joint effects of group structure and composition upon group efficiency in problem solving situations (Shaw, 1959a, 1959b). While not related to the primary purpose of the investigations, the data were analyzed systematically to determine the relationship between various estimates of homogeneity and problem solving effectiveness under varying structural conditions. The results of these analyses are given in Table 1. The measure of homogeneity used in computing the correlations reported was the average deviation of scores earned by members of the group on measures of intelligence (the verbal scale of the Scholastic Aptitude Tests), acceptance of author-

[1] The purpose of this note is not to criticize Hoffman's excellent report, but only to offer a word of caution regarding the generalizability of the results and a word of encouragement to others who may be interested in this problem.

ity, and individual prominence. Essentially the same results were obtained, however, when other indices of homogeneity were used, such as range and standard deviation. Measures of group process variables were number of trials to criterion, total time required by the group to complete the assigned task, and average ratings of satisfaction by group members.

A number of comments may be made in connection with the results reported in Table 1. First, there seems to be no systematic relation between homogeneity and group efficiency and satisfaction. Degree and direction of correlations vary with the group structure and the particular characterisic under consideration.

Second, most of the correlations fail to meet the usual requirements for statistical significance. This may be due to the small number of cases in each sample, to the fact that the homogeneity estimate is based upon a single characteristic rather than a profile as were Hoffman's measures, or to the fact that no relation exists. It is interesting to note, however, that the one condition yielding uniformly significant correlations (acceptance of authority in a decentralized power structure) is precisely the one where such a relation might be expected on a priori grounds.

Third, centralized structures appear consistently to produce correlations that differ from those found in decentralized structures, although these differences are mostly unreliable.

These findings point to the difficulties in generalizing the results of a single study or even several studies beyond the limits imposed by the experimental situations. It may be, of course, that the effects of profile homogeneity will prove to be unchanged by such extraneous variables as group structure, group task, and the like; however, it seems far more likely that the effects of homogeneity, like so many other variables in group behavior, will be found to vary with the particular conditions under which its effects are measured.

The general problem of homogeneity as a variable in group behavior is a tremendously important one and deserves extensive investigation. The limited evidence reported here, along with the findings of Hoffman (1959) and Pelz (1956) indicates that the results of such studies will richly repay the investigator for his efforts.

REFERENCES

Hemphill, J. K. The measurement of group dimensions. *J. Psychol.*, 1950, **29**, 325–342.

Hoffman, L. R. Homogeneity of member personality and its effect on group problem-solving. *J. abnorm. soc. Psychol.*, 1959, **58**, 27–32.

Pelz, D. C. Some social factors related to performance in a research organization. *Administrative Sci. Quart.*, 1956, **1**, 310–325.

Shaw, M. E. Acceptance of authority, group structure and the effectiveness of small groups. *J. Pers.*, 1959, **27**, 196–210. (a)

Shaw, M. E. Some effects of individually prominent behavior upon group effectiveness and member satisfaction. *J. abnorm. soc. Psychol.*, 1959, in press. (b)

48. TRUST, TRUSTWORTHINESS, AND THE F SCALE *

Morton Deutsch

This study is part of a series of experimental studies (Deutsch, 1957, 1958) that have investigated some of the determinants of trusting behavior. In this brief paper, some striking findings relating trusting behavior to scores on the F scale (Adorno, Frenkel-Brunswik, Levinson, & Sanford, 1950, p. 260) are reported.

Our experimental work has utilized a two-person non-zero-sum game (see Figure 1) in which the gains or losses incurred by each person are a function of the choices made between two alternatives by one's partner as well as the choices made by oneself. Person I has to choose between Rows X and Y; Person II has to choose between Columns A and B. The amount of (imaginary) money each person wins or loses is determined by the box they get into as a result of their respective choices. For example, if Person I chooses Row X and Person II chooses Column A, they get into the AX box and they each win $9.

If you examine the possibilities of choice for Person I, you will notice that he can win most and lose least by choosing Y. Similarly, Person II can win most and lose least by choosing B. However, if Person I chooses Y and II chooses B, they both lose $9. Both can win only if they end up in the AX box. If Person I is reasonably sure that Person II is going to choose A, he can win more by choosing Y. Analogously, if Person II is confident that Person I is going to choose X, he can win more by choosing B rather than A.

The essential psychological feature of the game is that there is no possibility for "rational" individual behavior in it unless the conditions for mutual trust exist. If each player chooses to obtain either maximum gain or minimum loss for himself, each will lose. But it makes no sense to choose the other alternative, which could result in maximum loss, unless one can trust the other player.

In the study reported here, Ss were drawn from an introductory psychology course at a local university. Several weeks prior to the experiment, they had filled out the F scale. During the experiment, the instructions to the Ss about the game were such that they fully understood the implications of any combination of choices that they and the other person might make and they knew that the other person had a similar knowledge of the game. Unlike some of our other experiments (in which the Ss were induced to assume a cooperative,

	A	B
X	(+9, +9)	(−10, +10)
Y	(+10, −10)	(−9, −9)

Person I chooses between Rows X and Y, Person II between Columns A and B. Person I's pay-offs are the first numbers in the parentheses, Person II's are the second numbers.

Figure 1. Two-person nonzero-sum game

* Reprinted from the *Journal of Abnormal and Social Psychology*, 1960, 61: 138–140, with permission of the author and the American Psychological Association. This research was conducted under a contract with the Office of Naval Research.

individualistic, or competitive orientation), the Ss were given no motivational orientation. They were allowed to assume whatever orientation they wished to assume vis-à-vis the other person, about whom they were given no information. The S did not know the identity of the other person and knew that the other person did not know his identity (except that each S knew that the participants in the experiment were all students in the same psychology course).

Ss played the game twice, each time in a different "position" and each time, presumably, with a different person. In the First Position, S made his choice first and his choice was presumably announced to the other person before the other made his choice. In fact, the other person was "fictional" and, hence, the S was not informed what the "other person" chose after the S made his choice. In the First Position the S was faced with the decision of trusting the other person or not. In the Second Position, the S chose second after he knew the choice of the other person. Here, too, the other person was "fictional" and the actual S was always informed that the "other person" had chosen Row X (that is, had trusted). Hence, in the Second Position, the S was faced with the decision of being trustworthy or not.

RESULTS

Table 1 presents the data concerning the relationship between choices in the two positions. It is clear that the Ss who were "Trusting" when they chose first tended to be Trustworthy when they chose last; on the other hand, the Ss who were "Suspicious" when they chose first tended to be Untrustworthy when they chose last.

Before the Ss made their choices in the first position they were asked to indicate what they expected the other person to choose. Of the 24 Ss who chose Row X in the first position and Column A in the second position, 21 indicated that they expected the other person in the second position to choose Column A; of the 22 persons who chose Row Y in the first position and Column B in the second position, 17 indicated that they expected the others in the second position to choose Column B. Thus, predominantly a choice of Row X was a "trusting" rather than "masochistic" choice and a choice of Row Y was correlated with an expectation of "untrustworthiness" rather than of "masochism" from the other person.

When the Ss were in the second position they were asked to indicate what they thought the other persons (who were then in the first position) expected them to choose. The results indicate that 95 percent of the Ss who were Trusting and Trustworthy in their own choices and who had also expected trustworthy choices from the other (that is, a choice of Column A) thought the other person would be trusting (that is, would expect a choice of Column A from the S); only 35 percent of the S who were Suspicious and Untrustworthy in their own choices and who had also

TABLE 1. RELATIONSHIP
BETWEEN CHOICES IN THE FIRST
AND SECOND POSITIONS

First Position Choice	Second Position Choice	
	Trustworthy (A)	Untrustworthy (B)
Trusting (X)	24	5
Suspicious (Y)	4	22

TABLE 2. RELATIONSHIP BETWEEN BEHAVIOR IN THE GAME SITUATION AND F SCALE

| Game Behavior | F Scale Score | | | N |
	Low (1.2–2.2)	Medium (2.3–3.3)	High (3.4–4.4)	
Trusting and Trustworthy	12	10	2	24
Suspicious and Untrustworthy	0	13	9	22
Suspicious but Trustworthy	0	4	0	4
Trusting but Untrustworthy	2	3	0	5

expected untrustworthy choices from the others (that is, a choice of Column B) thought the other person would be suspicious (that is, would expect a choice of Column B from the S). This finding suggests that the Ss who were Trusting and Trustworthy expected Trustworthiness and Trusting from the others while the Ss who were Suspicious and Untrustworthy predominantly expected an exploitative orientation from the others (that is, they expected the other persons to be trusting but not trustworthy). Hence, it is not surprising that, in the Second Position, these latter Ss would respond to a Trusting choice from another by "taking advantage" of the other.

The data presented in Table 2 indicate a significant relationship between the S's game behavior and his score on the F scale.[1] Almost all of the Ss with relatively low scores made Trusting and Trustworthy choices, almost all of the Ss with relatively high [2] scores made

Suspicious and Untrustworthy choices, while the Ss with medium scores tended to choose one way or the other equally often. It is interesting to note that 7 of the 9 Ss who were inconsistent in their choices in the two positions (that is, they were Trusting but Untrustworthy or Suspicious but Trustworthy) were in the medium range of the F scale scores for their class.

DISCUSSION

The data of Table 1 provide a striking demonstration of the symmetry of the S's behavior in his two complementing roles vis-à-vis the other person. *His behavior toward the other is congruent with what he expects from the other, and also, what he expects from the other is congruent with his behavior toward the other.*[3] The Ss tend to be trusting and

[1] The point biserial correlation between the scores on the F scale and the two most frequent categories of game behavior indicated in Table 2 is .50 ($p < .001$). The mean of the F scores for the Trusting and Trustworthy Ss was 2.38; the mean for the Suspicious and Untrustworthy Ss was 3.37.

[2] It is evident that the "highs" are high only in comparison with the other Ss in their class; the high scores in this group are similar to the mean scores reported in other groups (Adorno, Frenkel-Brunswik, Levinson, & San-

ford, p. 266). When using the F scale as a personality measure, we believe it makes most sense to consider the individual's score in relationship to the scores of others within his cultural milieu.

[3] It is apparent that the Ss were not behaving in accordance with the ethical injunction of "do unto others as you would have others do unto you," but were rather guided by the dictum of cognitive consistency "do unto others as you expect others to do unto you and expect others to do unto you as you do unto them."

trustworthy or suspicious and untrustworthy in this essentially ambiguous situation with unknown others. This result suggests that the personality predispositions tapped by the experimental game are not simply one-sided internalized orientations toward another or internalized expectations from another but are instead internalizations of a *reciprocal* pattern of interrelationships with another. In other words, what appears to be internalized is a *system* of interrelations between oneself and the other, including the norms which prescribe *both* what to expect from the other and how to act toward the other. A similar conception of the nature of personality predispositions is advanced more fully by such authors as Mead (1934) and Parsons (1955).

The F scale data indicate that the game behavior was related to personality predispositions and that it was not determined by "accidental" orientations assumed during the course of the experiment, except in the special sense that vulnerability to "accidental" factors was itself influenced by the personality predispositions measured by the F scale.

The mass of research on the F scale, surveyed in Christie and Cook (1956), indicates that there are consistent differences between Low and High scorers in their behaviors in social situations and in their responses to various questionnaires. The High as compared with the Low scorers tend to be more authoritarian, less intellectually sophisticated, less liberal in their political views, more cynical concerning human nature, more prejudiced toward minority groups, and to have experienced and to favor stricter child rearing practices. The present results suggest that in addition, one may say that in an ambiguous situation involving the choices of trusting or not and of being trustworthy or not, Low scorers are more likely to be Trusting and Trustworthy while High scorers are more likely to be Suspicious and Untrustworthy (exploitatively oriented). These results are obviously concordant with the description of what the F scale was intended to measure and with the conception of the "antidemocratic personality" as advanced in *The Authoritarian Personality* (Adorno *et al.*, 1950).

However, it is not necessary to posit as do the California authors (Adorno *et al.*, 1950) that the characteristics of the authoritarian personality are to be

Understood as expressions of a particular kind of personality structure within the personality. The most essential feature of this structure is . . . that the conscience or superego is incompletely integrated with the self or ego. . . . There is some reason to believe that a failure in superego internalization is due to weakness in the ego, to its inability to perform the necessary synthesis. . . . (p. 234)

An alternative viewpoint would be that the personality differences between High and Low scorers on the F scale do not necessarily reflect *structural* differences in personality so much as *content* differences in the values that have been internalized as a result of the individual's reaction to his socialization experiences in a particular social milieu, characterized by a given value pattern. This latter viewpoint suggests that Highs and Lows, Trusting people and Suspicious people do not necessarily differ in superego integration or in ego weakness (a common synonym for "psychopathology"). As we have indicated more fully elsewhere (Deutsch, 1957), there are characteristic forms of pathological trust (for example, "gullibility") as well as of pathological suspicion (for example, "paranoia"). Presumably, the pathologies of trust and suspicion both reflect internal conflict and ego weakness, both of which may be found in individuals who have internalized widely differing values.

tended to be Trusting and Trustworthy while Ss with High scores tended to be Suspicious and Untrustworthy in their game choices.

SUMMARY

Ss played an interpersonal game which, in one position, required them to choose between being trusting or suspicious of another and, in a second position, required them to choose between being trustworthy or untrustworthy toward another. There was a striking tendency for Ss who were trusting to be trustworthy and for Ss who were suspicious to be untrustworthy. F scale scores correlated significantly with game behavior; Ss with Low scores

REFERENCES

ADORNO, T. W., FRENKEL-BRUNSWIK, E., LEVINSON, D. J., & SANFORD, R. N. *The authoritarian personality.* New York: Harper & Row, 1950.

CHRISTIE, R., & COOK, P. A guide to published literature relating to the Authoritarian Personality through 1956. *J. Psychol.*, 1958, **45**, 171–99.

DEUTSCH, M. Conditions affecting cooperation. *USN tech. Rep.*, 1957, NONR-285(10). (Mimeo.)

DEUTSCH, M. Trust and suspicion. *J. conflict Resolut.*, 1958, **2**, 265–79.

MEAD, G. H. *Mind, self, and society.* Chicago: Univer. Chicago Press, 1934.

PARSONS, T., & BALES, R. F. *Family, socialization, and interaction process.* New York: Free Press, 1955.

11

Social Behavior in Stressful Situations

49. ANXIETY, FEAR, AND SOCIAL AFFILIATION *

Irving Sarnoff and Philip G. Zimbardo

In his recent monograph, Schachter (1959) reports that anticipated exposure to a painful external stimulus determines the degree to which persons wish to affiliate with each other: the greater the anticipated pain, the stronger the desire to await the onset of that pain in the company of others in the same predicament. In attempting to account theoretically for this finding, Schachter mentions such motivational forces as the subjects' needs for reassurance, distraction, escape, and information. However, among the various possible explanations, Schachter appears to favor one derived from Festinger's (1954) theory of social comparison processes. Adapting that theory to the phenomena under investigation, Schachter postulates that the arousal of any strong emotion evokes a need for comparison. Emotions are assumed to be quite unspecific states of affect. Hence, persons can only evaluate the quality, intensity, and appropriateness of their emotions properly by comparing their own reactions with those of others. Moreover, novel emotion producing stimuli should induce a greater tendency to affiliate than familiar stimuli. By definition, a novel stimulus is one that is more difficult to fit into a person's established frame of reference for emotive states. Accordingly, the individual is more obliged to seek out others in order to define the emotional effects of novel stimuli.

The explication of Schachter's (1959) results in terms of the theory of social comparison processes is appeal-

* Reprinted from *Journal of Abnormal and Social Psychology*, 1961, 62: 356–363, with permission of the senior author and the American Psychological Association.

ingly parsimonious. However, it requires the assumption that *all* emotive states have the same effect on affiliative behavior. Thus, Schachter, like many contemporary psychologists, does not deal with the possible conceptual distinctions between fear and anxiety. Yet, it seems to us that, by adopting an alternative assumption about the psychological properties of emotions, to be presented briefly below, it is possible to formulate predictions concerning affiliative responses that could not have been derived from the theory of social comparison processes. Indeed, by employing Freud's (1949a, 1949b) conceptual distinctions between fear and anxiety, we are led to predict a tendency toward social isolation—rather than affiliation—as a consequence of certain conditions of emotional arousal.

The present experiment was, thus, undertaken with two objectives: to assess the empirical validity of conceptual differentiation between fear and anxiety, and to evaluate the extent to which the theory of social comparison processes may be applied to the relationship between all emotions and affiliative behavior. In order to implement these objectives, we have conducted an experimental investigation of the differential effects of fear and anxiety upon social affiliation.

Functional Relationship between Emotions and Motives

The guiding assumption of our experiment holds that all emotions are consciously experienced epiphenomena of motives.[1] When our motives are

aroused, we experience subjective reactions to which we learn, over time, to attach commonly agreed upon labels that signify the various emotions.

Motive, on the other hand, is defined as a tension producing stimulus that provokes behavior designed to reduce the tension. Each of our motives (innate or learned) requires the performance of a *different* response for the maximal reduction of its tension.

Fear and Anxiety Viewed as Motives

The motive of fear (which Freud called objective anxiety) is aroused whenever persons are confronted by an external object or event that is inherently dangerous and likely to produce pain. Only one type of overt [2] response can maximally reduce our fear: separation from the threatening aspects of the feared object, accomplished by flight from the object, at one extreme, and conquest, at the other. In the case of fear, then, one's energies are mobilized toward dealing with the external stimulus; to eliminate, through some mode of escape or attack, the threat that is clearly and objectively present in the stimulus.

If we examine the consequences of anxiety (which Freud termed neurotic anxiety), we see no such correspondence between the internal disturbance of the person and an objectively harmful environmental stimulus. Instead, anxiety is typically aroused by stimuli which,

[1] The concept of motivation which we have chosen to employ has been elaborated elsewhere (Sarnoff, 1960a).

[2] Space limitations do not permit a consideration of the two types of covert (ego defensive) responses, denial and identification with the aggressor, which persons may employ in their efforts to cope with external threat. A full discussion of these ego defenses is presented by Sarnoff (1960a).

objectively considered, are *innocuous*.[3] For example, in the case of the classical phobias, harmless objects possess a special motivational significance for certain people. These objects activate some motive other than fear, and this other motive, in turn, arouses the consciously perceived motive of anxiety. Hence, the emotional reaction of the anxious person is inappropriate to the inherent characteristics of the external stimulus.

Regardless of their content, the motives whose arousal evokes anxiety share a common property: they are all *repressed*. These repressed motives continue unconsciously to press for the reduction of their tensions; and anxiety signals the threat of possible expression of these repressed motives. Consequently, the person develops a number of additional ego defenses that function to safeguard the initial effects of repression. If the ego defenses do their work effectively, the motives are kept under repression, the inner danger passes and the individual's anxiety is reduced.

Implications of the Motives of Anxiety and Fear for Affiliative Behavior

It follows from the foregoing discussion that, when their anxieties are aroused, people are more inclined to become preoccupied with the reasser-

[3] In fact, since anxiety arousing stimuli are often related to unconscious libidinal motives, they may be regarded by most people as intrinsically pleasurable, rather than in any way painful. For example, owing to the manner in which their heterosexual motives have been socialized, some men may tend severely to repress their sexual cravings for women. Hence, when such men are shown photographs of voluptuous nudes, stimuli which might be quite evocative of pleasurable fantasies among most of their fellows, they are likely to experience anxiety (Sarnoff & Corwin, 1959).

tion of inner self-control than with modes of dealing with the anxiety evoking external object. Because the anxious person tends to be aware of the element of *inappropriateness* in his feelings, he is loath to communicate his anxieties to others. To avoid being ridiculed or censured, he conceals anxiety aroused by stimuli which he guesses do not have a similar effect upon others, and which, he feels, ought not so to upset him. Thus, when anxiety is aroused, a person should tend to seek isolation from others. On the other hand, when fear is aroused and he is unable to flee from the threatening object, he welcomes the opportunity to affiliate. Since the usual responses to fear, flight and fight, are restricted in the experimental situation, the subject seeks other fear reducing responses. Therefore, the probability of affiliation increases because it mediates fear reduction through the potentiality for catharsis and distraction as well as the emotional comparison offered by interpersonal contact.

We are led, therefore, to the hypothesis that the motives of fear and anxiety should influence social affiliation behavior differently: the greater the fear aroused, the more the subjects should choose to be together with others while they await actual contact with the fear arousing object. Conversely, the greater the anxiety elicited, the more the subjects should choose to be alone while they await contact with the anxiety arousing object.

METHOD

The experiment was presented to the subjects as a physiological investigation of the cutaneous sensitivity of various parts of the body. A 2×2 design was used in which two levels of fear and of anxiety were experimentally aroused. The dependent variable of social affiliation was measured by having the subjects state whether they preferred to spend an anticipated waiting period alone or in the company of others.

Subjects

The subjects were 72 unpaid, male undergraduate volunteers from six introductory psychology classes in Yale University. An additional 36 subjects were used to pretest the manipulations and measuring devices, and an additional 13 subjects were excluded from the analyses because they did not qualify as acceptable subjects, that is, were friends, misunderstood the instructions, did not believe the rationale.

Procedure

Background information was collected by an accomplice alleged to be from the counseling program of the Student Health Department. A questionnaire was designed to obtain background information on the subjects and also their preferred mode of defense mechanism. The latter data were in response to four Blacky cards. As in a recent experiment by Sarnoff (1960b), each card was accompanied by three alternatives that were to be rank ordered according to the subjects' reaction to the theme of the card (sibling rivalry, achievement, and two of sucking). The alternatives reflected predominantly an acceptance of the motive, projection of the motive upon others, or a reaction formation against the motive.

About one month later, the experimenter was introduced to the psychology classes as a physiological psychologist studying physiological responses to sensory stimuli. The subjects were subsequently recruited individually, and randomly assigned to the four experimental treatments. The specious purpose of the experiment and of the conditions of waiting were further established by marking the experimental room "Sensory Physiology Laboratory" and two nearby rooms "Waiting Room A" and "Waiting Room T." Because of absentees, the size of the groups tested varied from three to five, and was usually composed of four subjects. In order to avoid the development of superficial friendships during the experiment, and eliminate the possibility that the subjects might react to cues from each other or from the experimenter, the subjects were isolated in adjacent cubicles, no communication was allowed, and the tape-recorded instructions were presented through earphones.

The experimental conditions and instructions common to all subjects will be presented first. After rolling up their sleeves, removing their watches from their wrists, and gum or cigarettes from their mouths ("They interfere with the recording electrodes"), the subjects were told:

> Our experiment falls in the general area of physiological psychology. As you may know, one branch of physiological psychology is concerned with the reactions of the sense organs to various kinds of stimulation. Our present experiment deals with the skin [or mouth] as an organ of sensation. We are interested in studying individual differences in response to particular stimuli applied to it.
>
> There has been a good deal of

controversy about the relative sensitivity of the fingertips [lips] as compared to the palms [tongue], and upper surface of the hand [palate]. Our experiment will help to provide data upon which we may be able ultimately to draw a detailed map of the cutaneous sensitivity of the human hand [mouth].

In order to measure your physiological reactions, we are now going to attach some instruments to your arm and finger [corner of your mouth]. These instruments are electrodes which are connected to a machine which records exactly the strength of your response to each stimulus. . . . Electrode jelly will be applied first to the area to insure that we get a good electrical contact. (The electrodes were then attached by a female laboratory assistant of middle age.)

In order to provide a reasonable basis for asking the subjects to wait in other rooms (and, thus, for making the choice of affiliation or isolation), the subjects were told that it was necessary to assess their basal rates of responding prior to the application of the actual stimuli. They were led to believe that their individual sensitivities were being recorded while they viewed a series of slides of a typical subject who had participated in the experiment. They anticipated that a waiting period would come after the slides, and then in the second —and purportedly major—part of the experiment their direct reactions to the actual stimuli would be measured. Accordingly, they were told:

Now that your basal rates have been recorded on our polygraph recorder, it will take us about 10 minutes while we tally the data and reset our measuring instruments so that they will be geared to your individual basal rates as you are run one at a time through the rest of the experiment. While we are doing these things, we are going to ask you to wait in other rooms which are available to us. We will come to get you when it is your turn to go through with the experiment. Incidentally, we have found that some of our subjects prefer to do their waiting alone, while others prefer to wait together with other subjects. Therefore, we are going to give you your choice of waiting alone or with others. In either case, you will be ushered to a comfortable room furnished with adequate reading material.

After indicating their preference of waiting alone or together with others, the subjects also indicated the intensity of this preference on an "open-ended" scale in which 0 represented a very weak preference and 100 a very strong preference. On this relatively unstructured scale there was as much as 175 points of difference between subjects (from "75-alone" to "100-together").

Presentation of the slides during the experiment served two purposes in addition to the one previously mentioned. The content of the slides (appropriate to each experimental treatment) served to reinforce the subjects' differential expectations of the nature and severity of the stimulus situation. Furthermore, the subject seen in the slides became a focal point for measuring the effectiveness of the experimental manipulations. It was assumed that a direct attempt (by means of a scaled question) to appraise the level of the subjects' fear or anxiety would be likely to: sensitize them to the true purpose of the experiment; yield unreliable results since the subjects might neither be consciously aware of, nor able to verbalize, their anxiety reaction; and evoke resistance since some subjects might not want to admit to being anxious or fearful, calling their masculinity into question.

Therefore, it was necessary to use an indirect, disguised measure to evaluate whether the experimental inductions had actually aroused two levels of both fear and anxiety. Immediately after the slides had been shown (but before the affiliation choices had been made), the subjects were told:

As you may know, an individual shows his physiological reaction in a variety of behavioral forms. We are interested in seeing whether it is possible to estimate how ill-at-ease or upset individuals are at the prospect of receiving the stimulation in this experiment. Recalling the subject whom you just saw in the slides, how upset or ill-at-ease did he seem to you? Please assign a number anywhere from zero to 100 to indicate your feeling. (Zero = unconcerned, at ease; 100 = extremely concerned and ill-at-ease.)

Since the subject in the slides was a posed model instructed to remain poker faced throughout, it was assumed that there was no objective difference in his expression. Thus, any systematic difference in ratings between groups should reflect a projection of the subjects' own motives upon this screen.

However, because the content of the slides was not identical for every group but rather "tailored" to each specific treatment, it was possible that the model may have actually looked more fearful in the slides shown to the subjects in the High Fear than in the Low Fear condition. As a control check on this possibility, four additional introduc-

tory psychology classes ($N = 108$) served as judges. They were told that the slides were of a typical subject in a recently completed experiment, and their task was to estimate how ill-at-ease and concerned he appeared (on the same scale used by the experimental subjects). Two of the classes saw only the face of the model (the rest of the slide was blacked out) and were told only that he was a subject in a physiological experiment in which stimuli were applied and responses measured. The other two classes saw the entire stimulus field of the slides and were given the same complete description that the experimental subjects received. Since each class of judges rated the slides for all four experimental treatments, the order of presentation was counterbalanced.

After the projective measure of motive arousal and the measure of affiliation, the electrodes were removed and a measure taken of the subjects' reasons for choosing to affiliate or be isolated. This was done with the rationale that a social psychologist had become interested in the fact that some of our subjects preferred to be together while others preferred to be alone, and he had asked us to get some information for him about the reasons underlying this preference.

The questionnaire, designed by Gerard and Rabbie (1960), contained both open-ended and structured questions asking for reasons for the affiliation choice. Finally, the subjects noted whether or not they wished to continue in the experiment. Only one subject (in the High Fear condition) refused to remain for the "stimulation" part of the experiment.

The true purpose, hypothesis, design, and reasons for the various deceptions (and, at a later time, the results) were explained fully to each subject.

High Fear

A high level of fear was induced by leading the subjects to anticipate a series of painful electrical shocks. Although they expected to endure each of the shocks for 2 minutes, the subjects were assured that the shocks would not cause damage or injury.

The female assistant (dressed in a white lab coat, as was the experimenter) then attached electrodes to each subject's arm and fingertip and strapped his arm onto a cotton-padded board. The leads from the electrodes appeared to go to a polygraph recorder, which also was seen in the series of slides of the typical subjects. Another slide showed an enormous electrical stimulator, and the implication was that it was behind a curtain in the experimental room. It was called to the subjects' attention that:

The four dials shown in the upper right-hand corner of the stimulator enable us to regulate automatically the frequency, duration, delay, and intensity of the shock you will get.

The other slides portrayed the subject with earphones and electrodes attached (like the subjects themselves), "listening to the instructions," and then "about to receive his first painful shock," administered by the experimenter, who could be seen in the background manipulating the dials on the stimulator. A final situational factor that may have enhanced the effectiveness of the High Fear manipulation was that the experimental room housed electrical generators which made a continuous buzzing sound, a cue interpreted by the High

Fear subjects as the electrical stimulator "warming up," but unnoticed or quickly adapted to by the other subjects. An unobtrusively posted sign reading "Danger/High Voltage," present only for the High Fear subjects, gave further credence to this notion.

Low Fear

In the Low Fear condition the word "shock" was never used, and all cues in the situation associated with shock, fear, or pain were removed; that is, no white lab coats, arms not strapped to boards, and so on. The expectations of these subjects were guided by instructions stating that our methodology was to apply a 10-second stimulus of very low intensity that would be just sufficient to elicit a measurable physiological response.

In the series of slides viewed by these subjects, the imposing electrical stimulator was replaced by a small innocuous looking apparatus (actually a voltmeter), and the experimenter was seen not in the active role as an agent of pain, but in the passive role of recording data from the polygraph recorder.

High Anxiety

Anxiety was manipulated by arousing a motive that was assumed to have been repressed by most of the subjects. In Freudian terminology, the motive might be called "oral libido," a desire to obtain pleasurable gratification by sucking on objects that are clearly related to infantile nursing experiences. The female breast is, of course, the prototype of such objects, but others include nipples, baby bottles, and pacifiers. Thus, to arouse this oral motive and, hence, the anxiety that should follow its arousal, subjects in the High Anxiety condition were led to believe that they would have to suck on a number of objects commonly associated with infantile oral behavior. They were told that their task would be to suck on these objects for 2 minutes while we recorded their physiological responses from the skin surfaces stimulated by the objects. In clear view in front of the subjects were the following items: numerous baby bottles, oversized nipples, pacifiers, breast shields (nipples women often wear over their breasts while nursing), and lollipops.

The same variety of stimulus objects was shown arrayed in front of the subject in the slides. He could be seen, tongue hanging out, lips puckered, about to suck his thumb (as one of the objects of stimulation) or one of the other objects. Subjects were told that the contact taped to the mouth recorded the direct reaction to the oral stimulation, while the arm contact recorded peripheral reactions.

Low Anxiety

The instructions to the Low Anxiety subjects did not mention "suck," nor any stimulation that they would receive from putting the objects in their mouths. Moreover, they were led to believe that they would keep each object in their mouths for only 10 seconds. The stimulus objects were not in immediate proximity to the subjects while their electrodes were being attached. The stimulus objects which they anticipated putting in their mouths were shown in the slides: whistles, balloons, "kazoos," and pipes. Since these objects do not require sucking (but rather, in general,

blowing), the model's tongue was not seen as he prepared to use the stimuli in the slides.

RESULTS

Evidence of the Effectiveness of the Experimental Manipulations

In using the subjects' estimates of the degree to which the model seen in the slides was upset by the prospect of receiving the stimulation in the experiment, it was assumed that the subjects would tend to project their induced level of fear and anxiety. Table 1, which presents the mean projection scores for each experimental treatment, offers evidence that this assumption was valid and the manipulations effective. The High Arousal subjects perceived the model to be significantly [4] more upset, concerned, and ill-at-ease than did the the Low Arousal subjects.

Our theoretical distinction between fear and anxiety, and the way these concepts were operationally defined in this experiment, lead to the prediction that, assuming similarity of past experience, persons facing the same clearly, objectively present threat should react in a relatively homogeneous fashion. This close correspondence between stimulus and response is not assumed to hold for anxiety. We have already noted that a stimulus that produces anxiety for some persons is not an anxiety producing cue for many others. Since the significance of the stimulus depends upon its symbolic and generally idiosyncratic associations, one would expect that a stimu-

[4] All *p* values reported throughout the paper are based on two-tailed tests of significance.

TABLE 1. MEAN PROJECTION SCORES
FOR EACH EXPERIMENTAL TREATMENT

| Motive | Level of Arousal | | p value |
	Low	High	
Fear	24	42	<.01 $(t = 3.05)$
Anxiety	14	31[a]	<.01 $(t = 2.95)$
	ns	ns	

Note.—The larger the score, the greater the degree of projection.

[a] Variance greater than in High Fear group, $p < .10$; SD for High Anxiety = 24, for High Fear = 16.

lus which elicited anxiety for persons with relevant predispositions (repressed motives) would have less effect on those who had more adequately resolved the conflict over the expression of the same motives. Thus, one way of determining whether our experimental manipulations produced two different motives, fear and anxiety (rather than only two levels of one motive), is to compare the variability in response between treatments.

The heterogeneity of response in the High Anxiety group is, as predicted, greater than in the High Fear and the Low Arousal conditions. The same difference in response variability between the High Anxiety group and all other groups is manifested as well in the dependent variable of social affiliation. The questionnaire data to be presented in a later section offer further support to the distinction between fear and anxiety.

Before presenting the major results, it is necessary to account for two possible sources of artifact in the just reported data on projection. They are: by chance sampling, the High Arousal groups could have contained more subjects who characteristically used projection as a mechanism of defense than the Low Arousal groups; and the subject seen in the High Fear and High Anxiety slides was objectively more upset and concerned than he was in the Low Fear and Low Anxiety slides. If either of these alternatives were true, then the projection measure would not be a reflection of differences due to the experimental arousal of levels of fear and anxiety.

The pretest data of the subjects' mode of defense preference on the Blacky Projection test show no initial significant difference between any of the groups in their tendency to use projection.

Among the groups of neutral judges who evaluated all the slides shown in the study, from 68 percent to 98 percent reported perceiving either no difference in the degree to which the model appeared upset, or a difference opposite to that reported in Table 1. This result holds for both fear and anxiety, and regardless of the order of presentation or amount of the stimulus field seen (model's face only or entire slide). Thus, it appears that the projection measure can be used as an index of the efficacy of the experimental conditions and manipulations.

Effects of Fear and Anxiety on Social Affiliation

The results bearing upon the hypothesis of the study are presented in Table 2, where for each condition the mean intensity of desire to affiliate, as well as the number of subjects choosing to affiliate and to be alone, are presented. It is evident that there is a strong positive relationship between fear and

TABLE 2. RELATIONSHIP OF MOTIVE
TO SOCIAL AFFILIATION

		Number of Subjects Choosing	
	Mean Affiliation Strength [a]	Together	Alone or "0-Together"
Fear			
Low	34.0	12	3
High	51.0	19	1
Anxiety			
Low	27.0	11	4
High	8.0	10	12

Interaction: (Motive × Level) $p < .05$,
$t = 2.30$, $df = 68$.

[a] The larger the score, the greater the affiliation tendency; isolation intensity score subtracted from affiliation intensity score.

the index of affiliative tendency, but a strong negative relationship between anxiety and affiliation, so that as fear increases affiliation also increases, while an increase in anxiety results in a decrease in affiliation. Thus, our prediction of an interaction between kind of motive and level of arousal is clearly supported by the data. While some 95 percent of the High Fear subjects chose the "together" alternative (with more than 0 intensity), only 46 percent of the High Anxiety subjects chose to wait together. The marked mean difference between these groups in intensity of choice (51.0–8.0) is significant well beyond the .01 level ($t = 3.63$). The large mean difference in affiliative tendency between the High and Low Fear groups ($p < .07$, $t = 1.96$) represents a replication of Schachter's (1959, p. 18) results. While the mean difference between High and Low Anxiety was even larger than that

between the Fear conditions, it only approached significance ($p = .16$, $t = 1.46$) due to the marked heterogeneity of variance of the High Anxiety group.

Reasons Given for Affiliation Choice

The final measure taken was a questionnaire that explored the reasons the subjects gave for choosing to wait together with others or to wait alone. The 11 structured items on the questionnaire each presented a possible motive for affiliation; and each was accompanied by a 70-point scale on which the subject indicated how important he thought the motive was in determining his choice. The highly significant interaction between experimental treatment and questions ($p < .001$, $F = 3.74$, $df = 30.570$) on a repeated-measurement analysis of variance justified a search for those questions (motives for affiliation) that differentiated the groups.

Since there were too few subjects choosing the alone condition, the analysis is limited to those wanting to affiliate. The motives for affiliation that were most important for the High Fear subjects and most distinguished them from the Low Fear subjects were (the lower the mean, the greater the importance; 10 = extremely important):

1. I am not sure whether I am reacting in the same way as the others to the prospect of getting shocked and would like to compare my reactions to theirs. [Emotional comparison] High Fear $\bar{x} = 38$, Low Fear $\bar{x} = 54$, $p < .001$.

2. I feel worried about getting shocked and would like to know to what extent the others are worried too. [Extent of comparison] High Fear $\bar{x} = 40$, Low Fear $\bar{x} = 61$, $p < .001$.

3. I want to be distracted in order to take my mind off the prospect of getting shocked. [Distraction] High Fear x̄ = 44, Low Fear x̄ = 59, $p < .01$.

4. I am worried about the prospect of getting shocked and felt that talking with someone about it would get it off my chest. [Catharsis] High Fear x̄ = 50, Low Fear x̄ = 59, $p < .05$.

The reasons for affiliation given spontaneously to a single open-ended question also reflect the importance of these same considerations. Among High Anxiety subjects choosing to be alone, the major reason given spontaneously and supported by the scaled questions is the desire "to be alone to think about personal affairs and school work."

Curiosity as to "what the others were like" was important, but equally so across all conditions. Of least importance among all subjects are the following motives for affiliation ("oral stimulation" substituted for "shock" for Anxiety groups):

"It would be clearer in my own mind as to how I feel about getting shocked if I could express my reactions to someone else." "I anticipated that the others would offer reassuring comments." "I want to be with others to reassure myself that I am not the only one who was singled out to be shocked." "I feel that perhaps together we could somehow figure out a way to avoid getting shocked."

There are several large differences between the High Fear and High Anxiety groups; with the former finding the following motives as significantly more important: emotional comparison, extent of comparison, distraction, catharsis, and the physical presence of others ($p < .05$ in each instance). Similarly, an internal analysis of the High Fear

group reveals these same motives (especially catharsis and emotional comparison) to be more important for those subjects who chose to affiliate most strongly than for those below the group median in affiliation strength.

Ordinal Position and Its Relation to Affiliation

While the reasoning used in the planning of the present study did not include predictions of the effects of ordinal position upon affiliation, data relevant to this question was nevertheless obtained, to check on Schachter's (1959) finding that affiliation tendencies increased with emotional arousal only among first- and only-born children. This finding is duplicated in the present study. First-born children want to affiliate significantly more than later-borns under conditions of high fear, but not when the level of fear is low. While the mean affiliation intensity for the first-born High Fear subjects was 62, it was only 23 for the later-born High Fear subjects ($p = .05$, $t = 2.10$). This same general finding holds for the High Anxiety group, but again the within-group variability does not permit the large mean difference obtained (16 for first-borns and −3 for later-borns) to be statistically significant.

DISCUSSION

Since our basic hypothesis has been supported, our results lend credence to the previously drawn conceptual distinction between fear and anxiety. In view of the fact that our anxiety arousing stimulus was specifically designed to tap only one kind of repressed motive, it of course remains an empirical question whether or not the evocation of other types of presumably repressed motives also leads to social isolation.

In order to predict the consequences of the arousal of a motive, therefore, it is necessary to know which responses are required to reduce its tension. The probability of the social comparison response is, thus, a function of: the kind of motive aroused, the intensity of the motive, the degree of novelty of the emotional experience, the response hierarchy associated with the specific motive, and certain attributes of those with whom the person is to affiliate.

We do not question the assumption that the need for some kind of cognitive-emotional clarity and structure is a basic human motive. However, we feel that the need for self-evaluation is not the *most* salient motive aroused in the experimental situations that Schachter (1959) and we employed. We do not view the cognitive need to structure a vague emotional state as the primary motive in these experiments; we see social comparison not as an end in itself but merely as one of the several responses that are *instrumental* in reducing the tension associated with the situationally more salient motives of fear and anxiety.

Strict application of the theory of emotional comparison processes to the present experimental situation should lead one to predict greater affiliation tendencies for the High Anxiety subjects than the High Fear subjects, since the Anxiety situation was more unusual than that of Fear, and the emotion aroused was probably more novel and vague. The opposite prediction, supported by the results, demands an approach, such

as the one followed here, that specifies the probability of the response alternatives evoked by the dominant motives aroused.

As the emotional experience becomes very novel and unusual, the need for comparison of one's reactions with others should increase, and, hence, intensify affiliation tendencies. The induction of esoteric states of consciousness by "anxiety producing drugs" (being studied presently by Schachter) may be the kind of situation in which emotional comparison theory offers the best explanations and predictions. Under such circumstances, it may be possible to create emotional states that are epiphenomena of motives whose neurophysiological bases had never previously been set into motion. A more natural counterpart of this novel emotional experience occurs the first time a person experiences the emotions associated with the death of a loved one.

The predictive importance of knowing the specific responses appropriate to the motive aroused is clearly illustrated by the following examples. If a person's guilt is aroused, his response to feelings of guilt should be to seek out others only if they could be expected to punish him and, thus, to expiate his guilt,, but not to affiliate with individuals perceived as unable to fill this role. Similarly, if repressed homosexual anxieties are aroused, isolation should generally be preferred to affiliation, as with oral anxiety in the present study. However, affiliation tendencies should increase if the subject is allowed to wait with females, but not if he can wait only in the company of males.

While our questionnaire data offer support for the importance of emotional comparison, they also point up the role of other motives such as need for catharsis and distraction. The marked difference in the importance of the reasons given for affiliation between the High Fear and High Anxiety groups is perhaps the most substantial evidence that the experimental manipulations have indeed led to the arousal of two quite different motives.

A final point of interest concerns the data about ordinal position. The finding that firstborn children show greater affiliation tendencies than laterborn children when either fear or anxiety are aroused supports Schachter's (1959) results. Theoretical and experimental attempts to uncover the dynamics underlying this "static" variable should prove interesting and fruitful.

SUMMARY

This experiment tests the utility of the psychoanalytic distinction between fear and anxiety for making differential predictions about social affiliation. It also assesses the breadth of generalization of Schachter's (1959) empirical finding of a positive relation between emotional arousal and affiliation. Seventy-two subjects were randomly assigned to four experimental treatments in which low and high levels of fear and anxiety were manipulated. The success of these inductions was established by a projective device and questionnaire data. The dependent variable of social affiliation was measured by having the subjects choose to await the anticipated exposure to the stimulus situation either alone or together with others.

The results show that, while the desire to affiliate increases as fear increases (a replication of Schachter's, 1959, results), the opposite is true for anxiety; as anxiety increases the desire to affiliate decreases. Thus, as predicted, our findings lend empirical support to the theoretical distinction between fear and anxiety. At the same time, our results suggest that the theory of social comparison processes may not be adequate to account for the general relationship between emotions and affiliative tendencies.

REFERENCES

FESTINGER, L. A theory of social comparison processes. *Hum. Relat.*, 1954, 7, 117–140.

FREUD, S. *Inhibitions, symptoms, and anxiety.* (Originally published 1936) London: Hogarth, 1949. (a)

FREUD, S. *New introductory lectures on psychoanalysis.* (Originally published 1933) London: Hogarth, 1949. (b)

GERARD, H. B., & RABBIE, J. M. Fear and social comparison. Unpublished manuscript, Bell Telephone Research Laboratories, 1960.

SARNOFF, I. Psychoanalytic theory and social attitudes. *Publ. opin. Quart.*, 1960, 24, 251–279. (a)

SARNOFF, I. Reaction formation and cynicism. *J. Pers.*, 1960, 28, 129–143. (b)

SARNOFF, I., & CORWIN, S. M. Castration anxiety and the fear of death. *J. Pers.*, 1959, 27, 374–385.

SCHACHTER, S. *The psychology of affiliation.* Stanford: Stanford Univer. Press, 1959.

50. PROPHECY FAILS AGAIN *

Jane Allyn Hardyck and Marcia Braden

On July 4 of a recent year, a group of 135 men, women, and children vanished from their homes in a small southwestern town. Their homes were sealed; the windows were covered with newspapers; the cluster of houses was deserted. The only message they had left was a sign on the door of their church, reading "Gone for two weeks, camp meeting."

The neighbors of the group and the town officials soon discovered where the members of the Church of the True Word [1] had gone. In response to prophecies of a forthcoming nuclear disaster, the group had for many months been building and stocking underground fallout shelters, with as much secrecy as possible. On July 4, one of their prophets received a message, "The Egyptians are coming; get ye to the safe places," and they immediately obeyed what they believed to be a command from God. They were huddled in their shelters, awaiting the nuclear catastrophe. For 42 days and nights they remained there, in expectation of imminent disaster. While they stubbornly sat underground, the authors walked around the hot, dusty desert town piecing together the history of the

group from interviews with townspeople and the few group members who, disillusioned, left the shelters.

The Church of the True Word is an evangelical Christian church associated with the Pentecostal movement. Its members believe in the Bible as the literal word of God and accept as operating today the gifts of the Holy Spirit delineated in First Corinthians of the New Testament, Chapters 12 and 14. These gifts include speaking and interpreting tongues, personal prophecy, and healing by faith. The titular head of the group, a Mrs. Shepard, is their minister and chief prophet, although important decisions are made only after she has consulted with two of the group members, Peter Jameson and David Blake, both of whom are also ordained ministers.

The "colony," as they call themselves, springs from two main sources. Mrs. Shepard established a following about 5 years ago in the small southwestern town, and soon began work on the present church building. In this, she had the help of Jameson and Blake, who at the time were missionaries to Central America from two congregations in the Middle West. The second source of members of the Church of the True Word was these midwestern churches.

---

[1] This is a fictitious name which, we believe, captures the flavor of the actual name of the group. All other names and places used in this paper have been similarly disguised.

* Reprinted from *Journal of Abnormal and Social Psychology*, 1962, 65: 136–141, with permission of the senior author and the American Psychological Association. The investigation was carried out during the tenure of a Predoctoral Research Fellowship from the National Science Foundation to the first author and a Predoctoral Research Fellowship from the National Institute of Mental Health, United States Public Health Service, to the second author. The collection of data was undertaken in cooperation with the Studies in International Conflict and Integration, Stanford University, directed by Robert North.

Even in the early days of her ministry, Mrs. Shepard was preaching preparedness for nuclear attack, and almost 4 years ago a prophecy was received in the Midwest to the effect that "in fewer years than I have fingers on my right hand" there would be nuclear devastation. The more recent history of the Church of the True Word began with another prophecy. On November 23, 8 months before the group finally went underground, a prophet in the Midwest received word that "you have 6 months to prepare." On receiving this message, Blake, Jameson, and various others packed up and moved to the Southwest and about February began to build fallout shelters and homes.

The shelters were built "through the inspiration of God," according to the specifications of Civil Defense, which is, for these people, "the Noah's Ark of today." They were not designed as bomb shelters, since the group believed that their town would receive only fallout from a direct hit on Desert City, which lay 50 miles to the west. There were probably five large shelters under houses and four smaller ones dug in an open field nearby. The larger ones were quite livable, although far from luxurious, as they lacked modern plumbing and were rather badly ventilated. The shelters were stocked with canned and dehydrated food, large cans of water, and other necessities, and were provided with generators for use when public power failed.

For the group to make such careful and extensive preparations, they must have had a rather clear and specific idea of what was to happen. Indeed they did. From a particular interpretation of portions of the book of Revelation, they believed that about one-third of the population of the earth would be wiped out by nuclear warfare and that injuries and sickness would be widespread among the survivors. The members of the Church of the True Word also expected that after the disaster they would receive special powers from God so that they might perform miracles of healing beyond what they were already able to do, and might be enabled to spread the gospel to all nations within the short space of about a year. It was the necessity of saving themselves for this purpose that dictated that they must keep their preparations secret. They feared that if the location and nature of their shelters were generally known, they would be unable to prevent others from breaking in at the time of the attack, thus creating a situation in which no one could survive.

From February until the "deadline" of May 23, many more families from the midwest congregations arrived to join in the preparations. There were also, of course, several families from the local community who were members of the church and who helped in the work. The shelters were not finished by May 23, and much apprehension arose among the members of the group. In an anxious flurry of preparations they waited until July 4, when they received the message, we believe through Mrs. Shepard, "The Egyptians are coming; get ye to the safe places." They then entered the shelters —29 families, about 135 men, women, and children.

Hypothesis to Be Tested

Our interest in the True Word group arose because of their apparent similarity to the "doomsday groups" discussed by Festinger, Riecken, and

Schachter (1956) in *When Prophecy Fails*. The historical accounts of such groups as well as an empirical study of a more recent group, the Lake City group, suggest that the failure of the members to confirm their pessimistic predictions led them to increase in fervor of belief and in proselyting. Festinger et al. state five conditions that they feel must be met for this to occur:

1. A belief must be held with deep conviction and it must have some relevance to action, that is, to what the believer does or how he behaves.
2. The person holding the belief must have committed himself to it; that is, for the sake of his belief, he must have taken some important action that is difficult to undo. In general, the more important such actions are, and the more difficult they are to undo, the greater is the individual's commitment to the belief.
3. The belief must be sufficiently specific and sufficiently concerned with the real world so that events may unequivocally refute the belief.
4. Such undeniable disconfirmatory evidence must occur and must be recognized by the individual holding the belief.
The first two of these conditions specify the circumstances that will make the belief resistant to change. The third and fourth conditions together, on the other hand, point to factors that would exert powerful pressure on a believer to discard his belief.
5. The individual believer must have social support. It is unlikely that one isolated believer could withstand the kind of disconfirming evidence we have specified. If, however, the believer is a member of a group of convinced persons who can support one another, we would expect the belief to be maintained and the believers to attempt to proselyte or to persuade nonmembers that the belief is correct (p. 4).[2]

[2] From: *When Prophecy Fails* by Leon Festinger, Henry W. Riecken, and Stanley Schachter, University of Minnesota Press, Minneapolis. Copyright 1956 by the University of Minnesota.

These five conditions define a situation in which the believer has two sets of cognitions that clearly do not fit together. That is, he is experiencing a great deal of dissonance between the cognitions corresponding to his belief and the cognitions concerning the failure of the predicted event to occur. This situation, however, is one in which it is almost impossible for the individual to reduce his dissonance. He cannot give up his strongly held beliefs, and he cannot deny that the predicted event has failed to occur. He is also unable either to reduce the importance of his commitment to his beliefs or to make the disconfirmation irrelevant to them. Therefore, the believer who holds to his belief under these conditions has but one recourse if he is to reduce the dissonance; he must seek new information consonant with his beliefs. One of the best sources of new consonant cognitions is the knowledge that others' beliefs are the same. The authors suggest, then, that the need for new supporting cognitions will lead the believer to try to convince others of the validity of his beliefs.

Suitability of the True Word Group for a Test of the Hypothesis

Our purpose in learning about the history and beliefs of the True Word group was to determine whether the group met the conditions enumerated in *When Prophecy Fails* and thus would provide a test of the hypothesis under consideration. The first condition is that the group members must hold their belief with deep conviction and that the belief have some relevance to action. It is quite clear that the members held their general religious belief system with deep conviction. Many were originally ministers or missionaries actively engaged in Christian work, and most of the members to whom we spoke would refer to "gifts" they themselves or members of their families possessed. Also, as far as we were able to discover, Mrs. Shepard was respected by all of the congregation as a truly exceptional prophet. Thus, since the prophecy probably came from her and was closely tied to their belief system, it seems clear that it would be very strongly believed by the majority of the congregation. The obvious fact that the group had acted on their belief by building and entering the shelters is the strongest evidence for their belief in the prophecy and also, of course, proof that the belief had relevance for action.

The second condition is that the person holding the belief must have committed himself to it by some action difficult to undo. For the Midwest contingent, the commitment was extreme. They had given up their jobs, had picked up and moved over a thousand miles, and had invested a great deal of time, effort, and money in the building and stocking of homes and shelters. Those from the local area had perhaps given up less, but in several cases they also had lost jobs and had invested considerable sums of money. The things that they have done they cannot undo; the money is spent and the jobs are lost. Most important, none of them can deny or take back the fact that he spent 42 days in hot, humid, crowded shelters and he did this because of his belief.

The third condition, that the belief must be sufficiently specific and sufficiently concerned with the real world so that events may unequivocally refute it, is also quite easy to document. At the time that the group went into the shel-

ters, they believed that a nuclear attack was imminent, and that they would not come out of the shelters until that attack had occurred. That is, they expected to return to a world that had been devastated.

The fourth point, that "undeniable disconfirmatory evidence must occur and must be recognized by the individual holding the belief," is also clearly met. No nuclear attack occurred while the group was in the shelters, and they did not return to a devastated world. Thus, we must conclude that the True Word group suffered the unequivocal disconfirmation of a specific prediction.

The last condition that must be met in order that the True Word group may provide an adequate test of the hypothesis is that the individual believer have social support. This was so clearly the case that it hardly needs documentation. The members of the group had been living together as a separate, rather isolated community for several months prior to July 4. Indeed, some of the members had known each other for years and many were related by blood or marriage. During the time of the disconfirmation, social support was not only present, it was unavoidable. There were as many as 35 people in each shelter, and the shelters provided absolutely no privacy. Furthermore, the shelters were organized in such a way that each contained at least one very strongly convinced member who could hold his group together, and all of the shelters were connected by an intercom system so that the leaders could be consulted in case any members should begin to weaken.

It can be concluded, then, that the five conditions enumerated by Festinger et al. (1956) are met by the True Word group. Therefore, if the theory as specified is valid, we should expect to observe an increase in fervor of belief, a greater openness to publicity, and strong attempts to proselyte upon their emergence from their shelters. This, of course, follows from the postulated need for the group members to reduce their dissonance and their inability to do this by any means other than by gaining new cognitions consonant with their belief.

Behavior of the Group Following the Disconfirmation

In the very early morning of August 16, the 103 "faithful" who had remained in the shelters for the full 42 days received the word to come out. At about 9 A.M. they held a joyous reunion in the church, led by their pastor, in which they were asked, "Did you have victory?" In unison came the reply, "Yes, praise the Lord!!!" Mrs. Shepard spoke of how their faith had not been shaken, "The Lord has brought the people closer to Him, there is not division, there's a fellowship here and we are the holiness people." Many other church members gave testimonies as to how their stay in the shelters had both strengthened their Christian fellowship and increased their belief.

The information concerning this first meeting was obtained from reporters who had been present. During the following week, the authors were able to speak with almost all of the members of the group, to attend their frequent church services, and to interview many of the members, including the leaders, Jameson, Blake, and Mrs. Shepard, quite intensively.

It is clear from our observations that the beliefs of the group remained intact. The group members did have a reinter-

pretation of the purpose of their stay in the shelters that served as an explanation for the failure of the prediction. They had discovered by looking back over all of their messages that it had never been stated that an attack was imminent; they had simply misinterpreted God's purposes. Really, God had just been using them to warn a world that was asleep, while at the same time He was testing their faith. They passed the test and thus proved themselves even more worthy to be among God's elect. We further discovered that they all continued to believe that an attack would come soon. Thus, the group members should be suffering from dissonance; the reinterpretation may have lessened it somewhat, by giving them some reason for having sat so long in the shelters. But their prediction had been shown to be wrong, and they still believed; they should, then, seek publicity and attempt to proselyte.

This did not occur; one must look very hard to uncover even the slightest indication that the members of the Church of the True Word wished to find new converts to their beliefs. The prayer meeting on the morning of August 16 was a golden opportunity if the group wanted to seek new believers. The press was there en masse, including several reporters, cameramen, and TV representatives. One newsman, who had kept in close touch with the group from the beginning of their stay in the shelters, did report that the group was a little more friendly to the press than formerly. Blake asked the press to print certain passages from the scriptures in their reports, and these passages, which speak of widespread destruction, are clearly intended as a warning to the world. Also, Mrs. Shepard, at this time and later, spoke favorably of all the free publicity they had gained for the Lord by the worldwide coverage of their activities. However, the group members were relatively indifferent to the attempts of Civil Defense officials to contact them and turned away curious tourists who asked to see their shelters. Furthermore, they made no immediate attempts to interest the townspeople in their church services. There is no indication from the behavior of the group when they first emerged or from our observations of them during the following week that they had any intentions of going out to seek new believers on a large scale.

DISCUSSION

The True Word group meets all of the criteria for a test of the theory as set forth in *When Prophecy Fails*, and yet their behavior following the disconfirmation does not conform to the expectations derived from that theory. Clearly, either the theory is wrong,[3] or it is incomplete in the sense that it specifies insufficiently the variables determining the predicted proselyting. We have two suggestions to make concerning differences between the True Word group and those previously studied that might have affected the differences in behavior that were observed.

The first difference that we wish to consider is that of the amount of social support present within the group. It is stated in *When Prophecy Fails* that one of the conditions necessary for proselyting to occur is the presence of social support for the believers. That is, a certain minimum amount of support is needed so that the individual believer may maintain his beliefs against the dis-

[3] Leon Festinger, personal communication.

confirmation. But what might be the effect of additional amounts of social support? We would like to suggest that the more social support an individual receives above the minimum he needs to maintain his belief, the less need he will have to proselyte.

For this suggestion to be acceptable, it must be assumed, first, that there is some limit to the amount of support that is useful to an individual in his attempts to reduce his dissonance. For example, if only a few of your friends agree with a cherished belief of yours, you may be tempted to seek support by convincing others that you are right. On the other hand, if everyone with whom you associate agrees with you, you will feel very little need to go out and attempt to influence others in order to gain more support for your belief. Second, it must be assumed that a person will choose that means of reducing dissonance that is least likely to introduce new dissonance and most likely to reduce that which already exists. In the situation faced by the True Word group, and by other such groups, talking to other already convinced group members could not introduce new dissonance. In fact, interacting with others who had survived the same disconfirmation and who had emerged with their beliefs unshaken would be the best sort of support an individual could have. On the other hand, talking to the skeptical would be very likely to introduce new dissonance, since the person approached would probably reject one's attempts at influence and counter with arguments of his own. Thus, one would expect that, if at all possible, a person would choose to interact with those who agree with him rather than with the unbelievers.

In a group such as the True Word group with strong social support and a strongly shared belief system, the believer can turn to any other member for confirmation of his beliefs. Following our two assumptions, then, a member of such a group would first choose to talk to other members in his attempts to reduce his dissonance. If in this way he is able to garner new cognitions consonant with his belief up to the limit that he can use, he will then feel no need to seek further support by proselyting. On the other hand, a believer who is a member of a group such as the Lake City group, in which there is less support and more disagreement with regard to the belief system, would be much less likely to encounter sufficient support from his fellows. Thus, he may well have to resort to the otherwise less preferred means of gaining new consonant cognitions, that of proselyting.

It is easy to document the fact that the Lake City group did not provide social support to a degree that even approached that provided by the True Word group. First of all, the Lake City group was not well under way until about 5 months prior to the predicted date of the catastrophe; on the other hand, many members of the True Word group had worked together for several years. Further, the Lake City group had never lived as a community separated from the rest of the world as did the True Word group. This close association present in the True Word group should, one would think, foster a degree of trust in and understanding of the other members that far exceeded that which developed in the Lake City group.

With regard to shared beliefs, there was often disagreement among the members of the Lake City group. For example, the messages received by the two primary leaders of the group often contradicted each other. In contrast, the members of the True Word group were unanimous in their support of Mrs. Shepard, as far as we were able to observe. There was one leader, and one coherent set of beliefs shared by all of the group members. In conclusion, the Lake City group seems to have been characterized by only a minimal degree of social support, and we are suggesting that this degree of support was far from sufficient to reduce the dissonance suffered by the members as a result of the disconfirmation. As a result, the members, in search of further support, felt the need to proselyte. In contrast, the True Word group was very close and had a strongly shared belief system. Thus, they may well have had as much support within the group as they could utilize to reduce their dissonance and consequently felt no need to proselyte.

An interesting, although almost anecdotal, further piece of support for this suggestion comes from a very short article written by a Dutch psychologist, Van Peype (1960), in a Dutch newspaper. He briefly visited a group called the "Communita," who had gathered together near the top of Mont Blanc in expectation of a flood that would destroy the world on July 14. They had existed as a group for over 4 years, and many of the members had lived in the lodge on Mont Blanc for several months, separated from the other people living in the area. They had one prophet, one coherent body of beliefs, and, as far as Van Peype reports, a feeling of community and fellowship. When their prediction was disconfirmed, the leader announced to the waiting reporters, "You should be happy that we made that error. Our faith does not waver . . . Amen" (p. 3). He said no more to the assembled crowd and was reluctant to talk to Van Peype. The members had, then, not given up their belief and yet they showed no indications of a desire to proselyte. In the apparent degree of social support that was present, this group resembles the True Word group much more than it does the Lake City group, and their behavior following disconfirmation was essentially the same.

A second difference between the True Word group and the Lake City group that may have affected the amount of proselyting we observed lies in the amount of ridicule the groups received from the outside world. It would seem reasonable that if a group is receiving considerable ridicule from nonmembers, one way of reducing dissonance that would be apparent to them would be to convince these "unbelievers" that the group is right. If, however, the group is not receiving this sort of treatment from outsiders, this means of reducing dissonance would tend to be a great deal less salient to them. Furthermore, ridicule from others adds more dissonance to that which the group suffers from the disconfirmation. Thus, a very direct way of actually reducing part of the dissonance would be to eliminate the source of ridicule by converting the scoffers.

As far as we were able to determine, the True Word group received very little ridicule from townspeople and the press, considering the unusual step they had taken. The greatest amount of censure the group received seemed to come from other evangelical churches rather than from people in general. In talking to the local townspeople we often encountered statements such as "Yes, we knew they were building bomb shelters. We believe in doing that, too." The Civil Defense officials in the area even presented the group with an award for "the service which they have performed for the pub-

lic." After the group had left the shelters, the Mayor of the town was quoted in the newspaper as saying, "I sincerely hope no one ridicules them for their beliefs." Newspaper accounts of the group were in general factual and did not make fun of the group.

The treatment (Festinger et al., 1956) the Lake City group received was very different. Again, the news stories were generally factual and straightforward. But the headlines were cruel. In response to the announcement of the prediction, one paper headlined, "Tuesday—That Sinking Feeling," and another reported, "World Won't End, but Boy It Sure Will Shake" (p. 137). Columnists and editorial writers were equally unkind. Thus, since the Lake City group suffered more ridicule than did the True Word group, it might be supposed that it was easier for the Lake City group to see proselyting as an effective way of reducing the dissonance they had after the disconfirmation.

Evidence from the Mont Blanc group [4] gives somewhat equivocal support for this second suggestion. Van Peype reported that the Communita was very well thought of by the people in the town near their lodge, and was never ridiculed by them. However, they did receive some ridicule at the hands of reporters.

In conclusion, the True Word group, who had suffered a major disconfirmation of an important prediction, held to their beliefs and yet did not proselyte for them. This fact is in clear contradiction to expectation derived from the theory set forth in *When Prophecy Fails*. However, since dissonance theory has received considerable

[4] W. F. Van Peype, personal communication.

support in laboratory situations, it seems unlikely that it is completely wrong. Thus, we have assumed that the specification of the conditions that must obtain in the disconfirmation situation, in order that the predicted proselyting might occur, was insufficient. The two suggestions we have made for further conditions are that the group provide only minimal social support for its members and that the group receive ridicule from the outside world. It is, of course, impossible to know from the study of one group whether either of these has any relevance to proselyting. We can only say that there were clear differences on both these factors between the Lake City and True Word groups. We would like to suggest, then, that these two factors be considered and kept in mind by those investigating similar "doomsday groups" in the future.

SUMMARY

On July 4, 1960, a group of 135 men, women, and children began a 42-day stay in underground shelters in re-sponse to a prophecy of widespread nuclear disaster. Since their situation bore marked similarities to that of the group studied in *When Prophecy Fails*, their reactions to the disconfirmation of their prediction were observed in order to test the theory set forth in that book. Although the group members clung to their belief in the face of disconfirmation, and even seemed to increase in fervor, they did not attempt to proselyte for their belief. This result is contrary to expectations derived from the observations and the theory presented by Festinger et al. (1956). Two variables, the degree of social support available within the group and the amount of ridicule the group received, are suggested as possibly having effected this difference in behavior.

REFERENCES

FESTINGER, L., RIECKEN, H., & SCHACHTER, S. *When prophecy fails.* Minneapolis: Univer. Minnesota Press, 1956.
VAN PEYPE, W. F. Nu de wereld op 14 Juli niet is vergaan. *Vrij Ned.,* July 30, 1960, 3.

51. SOME EFFECTS OF SHARED THREAT AND PREJUDICE IN RACIALLY MIXED GROUPS *

Eugene Burnstein and Adie V. McRae

When members of a social system are threatened, marked changes seem to occur in social relationships (Jacobson & Schachter, 1954; Schachter, Nuttin, de Monchaux, Maucorps, Osmer, Duijker, Rommetveit, & Israel, 1954).

* Reprinted from *Journal of Abnormal and Social Psychology,* 1962, 64: 257–263, with permission of the senior author and the American Psychological Association. This research was supported in part by the United States Air Force under Contract No. AF 49(638)-460 monitored by the Air Force Office of Scientific Research of the Air Research and Development Command.

Where the consequences of the threat and the responsibilities for coping with it are shared, an increase in group cohesion and a reduction in disruptive antagonisms may occur (French, 1941; Leighton, 1945; Pepitone & Kleiner, 1957; Sherif & Sherif, 1953; Wright, 1943).[1] The application of this general finding to the study of particular social problems can have important consequences. If the social system in question is a society, community, or group containing distinct religious or racial subgroups, concern about a shared threat may lead to a decrease in the amount of hostility expressed toward these minorities.

In the first explicit attempt to test the hypothesis that shared threat reduced social prejudice, Feshbach and Singer (1957) presented a set of questions to individuals designed to provoke concern about dangers which confront the community as a whole, for example, floods, hurricanes, atomic attack. Immediately afterward a social prejudice

---

[1] A shared threat has also been observed to increase hostility among group members. In Nazi concentration camps, inmates went so far as to identify themselves with the source of the threat (Bettelheim, 1943; Cohen, 1953). At present it is not completely clear what are the necessary and sufficient conditions for a shared threat to reduce intermember hostility. However, a review of the literature suggests the important determinants are (a) the overwhelming nature of the threat, (b) the degree to which group action can ameliorate the threat, and (c) the degree to which members equally share the consequences of the threat and the responsibilities for coping with it. In the concentration camp the threat was quite overwhelming. Group action provided little amelioration; in fact, for many inmates a reduction in threat was only possible by dissociating themselves from the group. Treatment varied with the category of the inmate, and little role differentiation occurred other than imposed by the camp administration.

questionnaire was administered. Responses on the final questionnaire were compared to those the person made a month earlier. The authors reasoned as follows:

> Under the impact of a common threat . . . one's reference group may become the population that is subjected to the danger. If this reference group now includes both Negro and white, whereas under ordinary stimulus conditions the reference group has been primarily the white population, then the social distance between white and Negro should decrease, with a corresponding decrement in social prejudice (p. 412).

The results gave only weak support to the hypothesis. However, there are considerations which suggest the shared threat induced by this method may have been relatively weak.

Requiring people to think about a community-wide disaster does not insure that they view it as one in which the suffering and responsibilities are equally distributed among all community members. In a pilot study conducted by the senior author, 47 male students in the elementary psychology course at the University of Texas were administered the first four of the five "Flood and Hurricane Threat questions" from Feshbach and Singer (1957). In addition they were asked if such a disaster struck Austin, Texas, would all or nearly all socioeconomic levels, ethnic groups, or neighborhoods be equally affected. Only 27 percent thought this to be likely. Over 30 percent thought that there would be large differences among various groups in the degree to which they suffered from such disasters. Similar differences occurred in regard to the distribution of the burden for coping with the disaster. Therefore, given this method of induction, the extent to which the subjects perceived the threat to be shared is ambiguous.

Furthermore, in a highly complex social system such as a community, multiple group membership is the rule. During a disaster, the person may experience severe role conflicts. In spite of the perception that the threat is shared equally by all community members, the role of a father, neighbor, or plant manager may be more salient than that of community citizen. This phenomenon is vividly documented by Killian (1952) in his study of the Texas City explosion and of three tornado-torn towns in Oklahoma. Thus, even when a shared threat is perceived to exist in a community setting, it is uncertain whether the community as a whole or some subsystem will become the salient reference group. In the latter case, minorities within the community remain outgroups in terms of the social relations which are salient for the person at that time. Under such conditions, social prejudice may be unaffected.

In order to test the hypotheses that shared threat reduces the expression of hostility toward minorities either one of two general procedures can be used to minimize these processes which vitiate the threat induction: some method may be introduced to assure that the person faced by a community-wide threat takes the community as the salient reference group, or the threat may be induced in a simpler social system in which the number of group memberships available to the person is sharply reduced. Both procedures attempt to decrease the likelihood that roles or reference groups external to the threatened social system become salient. The present experiment

utilizes the second method. Members of racially mixed groups cooperate to solve a logical problem. In these groups, failure is clearly shared by all members. At the same time all members have a role in coping with the status loss that results from failure (Deutsch, 1953). The social system, furthermore, is simple enough so that under the threat of status loss few, if any, alternative roles are likely to become salient other than membership in the particular problem solving group.

Another source of variation in the expression of hostility toward an individual Negro that should be controlled is the attitude of the other members toward this racial group as a whole. The stronger the person's anti-Negro attitudes, the more likely is he to be hostile toward a Negro member of his problem solving group. Thus, in the present study anti-Negro attitudes as well as shared threat will be examined.

If the expression of hostility toward a Negro group member varies directly with the strength of anti-Negro attitudes and inversely with the degree of shared threat, then the following predictions can be made: (*a*) high prejudiced individuals under nonthreatening conditions will express the greatest amount of hostility toward the Negro member; (*b*) low prejudiced individuals under shared threat will express the least amount of hostility toward the Negro member; (*c*) high prejudiced individuals under shared threat and low prejudiced individuals under nonthreatening conditions will display an intermediate amount of hostility toward the minority group member. In the situation under study hostility may be manifested in evaluations made of the Negro, in the frequency with which the Negro is rejected from the group, and in the avoidance of communication with him during the problem solving interaction.

METHOD

Subjects and Confederate

Forty-eight male students in the elementary psychology course at the University of Texas were used as subjects. Participation fulfilled a course requirement. Several weeks before the experiment they were assessed as to their level of anti-Negro prejudice by means of Holtzman's D scale (Kelley, Ferson, & Holtzman, 1958), in the form of a "Student Attitude and Opinion Questionnaire." This was administered by the instructors in a number of the sections of the course. The distribution of prejudice scores was split at the median; subjects falling above the median were considered high in prejudice, those below the median, low in prejudice. In order to minimize the possibility of prior acquaintanceship, the four subjects used in each experimental group were drawn from separate sections.

A Negro confederate was paid to serve as a member in all experimental groups. The four other members were, in one half of the groups, all high prejudiced subjects, in the other half, all low prejudiced subjects. The confederate participated in several pilot groups to attain maximum familiarity and skill with the type of problem to be used in the experiment. It was necessary to tell him about all phases of the experiment and its objectives. The only information that was witheld from him was the extent of prejudice of the subjects with whom he was to work.

Procedure

Six groups were run with low prejudiced subjects and six with high prejudiced subjects. Within each of these two conditions of prejudice, shared threat was induced in half of the group, while a nonthreatening or successful state of affairs was induced in the other half. The design, therefore, consisted of three groups of four subjects, plus the confederate, under each of the following conditions: High Prejudice, Nonthreat (HPNT); Low Prejudice, Nonthreat (LPNT); High Prejudice, Threat (HPT); and Low Prejudice, Threat (LPT).

Communication among the subjects occurred around a table similar to that used by Leavitt (1951). The subjects were seated so that each was separated from the next by a vertical partition extending from a post in the center of the table. The center post had slots allowing subjects to push written messages to other members. Direct communication was permitted among all members. Messages were written on colored cards corresponding to the color of the cubicle from which each subject operated.

As each subject arrived he was given a seat in front of his cubicle. When all subjects had taken their places, they were asked to stand and see who the other members were but not to engage in any conversation. A copy of the instructions was given to each member and they were asked to follow as the experimenter read them aloud. In summary form, the instructions were as follows:

The purpose of this procedure is to evaluate how groups work together in solving problems when communication is limited to written messages. It has been found that a procedure such as this can be used to single out groups with different levels of skillfulness, efficiency, and creativity. The university recently has become quite interested in estimating how productively undergraduates can work together in groups. They have suggested that the Psychology Department initiate this program of evaluating groups of students with respect to these qualities. Thus, a record will be kept for the university administration of the performance of the group participating in this preliminary testing. Skillful, efficient, and creative group problem solving will be reflected in the time that it takes the group to solve the problem, that is, how long after starting before every member has the correct answer. Each member will receive a grade that is based on how well his group performs in solving these problems. This means, of course, that everybody in the group gets the same grade. The grade a group receives will depend on how its performance compares to that of a large number of other groups of college students in Texas who have worked on the same type of problem in the same type of situation.

During the reading of the instructions the subjects were standing facing each other.

All groups were given four successive problems to solve—Leavitt's (1951) "common symbol" problem. They were instructed that each member had been given a different set of symbols and that their task, as a group, was to discover the symbol that was common to all members. When a member knew what

this symbol was, he was to put it on a white slip and place it on top of his section of the center post. The group was considered to have completed the problem when all members had placed their white slip on the center post.

At the conclusion of Task 2, subjects were told to stand, stretch their legs, but not to converse. They were seated and given an evaluation of their performance. Half of the high prejudiced groups and half of the low prejudiced groups (HPNT and LPNT) were told that their performance was well above average. The remaining high prejudiced and low prejudiced groups (HPT and LPT) were informed that they had performed poorly compared to the average performance of similar groups. The experimenter reinforced these evaluations by making two or three positive or negative statements about the group's performance during or immediately after both Tasks 3 and 4. At the end of Task 4, the experimenter similarly evaluated the groups with respect to their overall performance. While the final evaluation was made subjects were standing in front of their cubicle facing each other.

Immediately following the final evaluation a post-questionnaire was administered. On six-point scales, subjects rated the experimenter in terms of his "competence as a psychologist" and in terms of their "liking" for him. Similarly, the test situation was rated for its "fairness," its "worthwhileness" and its "interest." To partially assess the success of the threat induction, subjects were asked to rate how "depressed" they felt at the results of the test. Three items allowed subjects to evaluate the other four members. Two of these items involved ranking members in terms of their contribution to the solutions and in terms of who the subjects liked best. The third item required subjects to rate other members for their estimated "communciation and problem solving skill in everyday life." At the end of the questionnaire subjects were given a sheet which asked if they wished to replace one of the present members with a new one from the subject pool at the next testing session. If they did desire to do so, they were to indicate the rejected member by encircling one of the four listed colors which corresponded to the color of his cubicle.

After completing the questionnaires, subjects were given a full explanation of the nature of the experiments.

RESULTS

An analysis of variance of the mean times required for task completion by the four experimental groups indicates that completion time decreases significantly over trials ($F = 8.06$, $p < .001$). This is in accord with Leavitt's (1951) findings regarding improvement in performances over successive tasks.

To assess the success of the threat induction, two t tests were made, one on the self-ratings of depression as a result of the test, another on the subjects' ratings of themselves and other white members for their communication and problem solving skills in everyday life. The tests indicated that threatened subjects felt more depressed than nonthreatened subjects ($t = 2.82$, $p < .01$). Similarly, threatened subjects graded themselves and other white members significantly lower in everyday communication skills than nonthreatened subjects ($t = 3.67$, $p < .001$).

There were no reliable difference as a function of threat in regard to the subjects' evaluations of the experimenter and of the test situation.

To determine differences in hostile expression resulting from shared threat and prejudiced attitude, t tests were run on the post-questionnaire items in which the subjects ranked the confederate in terms of contribution to task solutions, liking for him, and in which they estimated his everyday communication and problem solving skill. It was predicted that maximum hostility would be expressed in HPNT conditions; the least in the LPT conditions; while HPT and LPNT subjects would express an intermediate amount. In Table 1 the mean rank for contribution to the solutions given to the Negro confederate are presented. A rank of 1 indicates the greatest contribution, a rank of 5, the least contribution. The order of these mean ranks correspond exactly to the predicted order. However, only the differences between HPNT and HPT and between HPNT and LPT are statistically reliable. The difference between HPNT and LPNT approaches, but does not reach an acceptable level of significance ($p < .10$). For the mean rank given to the Negro confederate in regard to "liking," a score of 1 indicates the greatest relative liking for the confederate, 4 indicates the least liking. The Negro would be expected to be ranked lowest in the HPNT condition, highest in the LPT condition, and intermediate in the LPNT and HPT conditions. The results show the order of mean ranks once again conform to what was hypothesized. Only the differences between HPNT and HPT and between HPNT and LPT are significant. On the third

TABLE 1. EVALUATION OF NEGRO CONFEDERATE

	Mean Task Contribution Rank		Mean Likability Rank		Mean Skill Ratio	
	Shared Threat		Shared Threat		Shared Threat	
	Present	Absent	Present	Absent	Present	Absent
Prejudice						
High	2.58	4.33	2.60	3.25	1.02	1.37
Low	2.42	3.25	2.58	2.83	.91	1.17
Difference tested	*t*		*t*		*t*	
HPNT vs. HPT	3.12****		2.57***		2.50***	
HPNT vs. LPT	3.42****		2.16**		2.52***	
HPNT vs. LPNT	1.85*		1.02ᵃ		—	
LPT vs. LPNT	1.28ᵃ		—		1.33ᵃ	
LPT vs. HPT	—		—		—	

ᵃ Not significant.
* Significant at .10 level.
** Significant at .05 level.
*** Significant at .02 level.
**** Significant at .005 level.

item, subjects were required to estimate their fellow members' everyday communication and problem solving skill. In the context of this item, hostility may be expressed toward the Negro by rating him lower than the other group members. Ratings of group members, however, were shown to be biased by the presence or absence of threat. This is corrected by using a ratio of the rating given to the Negro by each subject over the mean rating given by the subject to all other members. A high degree of similarity between the Negro's rating and the mean rating is indicated as the ratio approaches 1. A ratio greater than 1 means that the confederate is considered less skillful than the average group member, less than 1 indicates he is considered more skillful than the av-

erage. Once again the obtained order fits the prediction exactly. However, only the differences between HPNT and HPT and between HPNT and LPT are significant.

With respect to the more general hypothesis that shared threat reduces the expression of hostility toward the confederate, responses to the above three items were analyzed by *t* tests for subjects exposed to shared threat and those not exposed, regardless of prejudice. The mean ranks given to the confederate on the first two items and the mean ratio given on the last item by threatened individuals were 2.50, 2.54, and 0.96, respectively. The same means for nonthreatened subjects were 3.70, 3.04, and 1.27, respectively. The difference between threatened and nonthreatened subjects on the first item was significant at the .005 level; the difference on the second item was significant at the .05 level; and the difference between the ratios was significant at the .01 level.

If they wished, subjects were given the opportunity to vote privately on rejecting a member from the group. In the HPNT condition 9 of the 12 subjects decided to reject a member. Of these 9 rejections, 6 were of the Negro confederate. With 9 subjects making use of their privilege to reject 1 of the 4 members in their group, it is highly improbable that as large or a larger number of these rejections would be directed toward one member by chance ($p < .01$). In the LPNT condition, 8 subjects wished to reject another member. The confederate received 3 of these rejections. Both in the HPT and LPT conditions 9 subjects decided to reject another member; and in each of these conditions 2 rejections were directed toward the confederate. In none of the latter three conditions did the frequency of rejecting the confederate depart significantly from what would be expected by chance alone. Thus, only under the HPNT condition, where the strongest expression of hostility toward the confederate was expected to occur, is the Negro rejected more frequently than chance.

Another significant source of information concerning the orientation of the members toward the Negro is the proportion of the task messages sent to him during the course of the problem solving interaction. Earlier studies have shown that interpersonal dislike can be coordinated to an increase in the barriers to communication (Festinger, Cartwright, Barber, Fleischl, Gottsdanker, Keysen, & Leavitt, 1948; Festin-ger, Schachter, & Back, 1950; Potashin, 1946). Thus, it is reasonable to expect that the amount of task communication with the Negro would vary inversely with the degree of hostility felt toward him. The total number of messages each subject sent to all other subjects was counted. The percentage of this total which the subject sent to the confederate was then computed. This was done only for those tasks following the initial induction of shared threat, i.e., Tasks 3 and 4. The analysis of variance of these percentages indicates that only the F ratio (4.64) for prejudice is significant ($p < .05$). The differences between threat conditions and between tasks did not approach significance. Figure 1 shows that the low prejudiced subjects, both threatened and nonthreatened, sent a greater proportion of their messages on Tasks 3 and 4 to the confederate than subjects in either high prejudiced condition.

DISCUSSION

It appears that the expression of hostility toward a Negro group member varies directly with the strength of anti-Negro attitudes, and inversely with the degree of shared threat. Moreover, prejudice against Negroes as a group may be expressed through a reduction in communication to an individual Negro. This is similar to Schachter's (1960) observations regarding communication to a persistent deviant. Of course, since there could be no question of the Negro changing his "deviant" position, that is, his status as a Negro, there was no initial rise in communication to the confederate as was found by Schachter during the early phases of interaction.

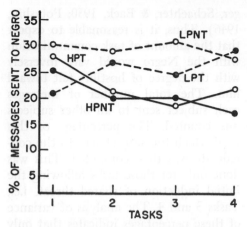

Figure 1. Percentage of messages sent to Negro confederate by Low Prejudiced, Nonthreatened (LPNT) groups, High Prejudiced, Nonthreatened (HPNT) groups, Low Prejudiced, Threatened (LPT) groups, and High Prejudiced, Threatened (HPT) groups over the four tasks

Moreover, it is interesting to note that avoidance of communication with the Negro by high prejudiced subjects occurred in a situation where messages were of an impersonal, task oriented nature and where the Negro member possessed information of value to other members in solving the problem.

The prediction that shared threat would inhibit tendencies to avoid communication with the Negro was not confirmed. No difference in communication to the confederate appeared as a function of shared threat. There are a number of possible explanations as to why shared threat reduced the expression of hostility toward the Negro in terms of direct evaluation on the postquestionnaire, but had no effect on the tendency to avoid communication with him. The first bears on the procedure used to induce the threatening and nonthreatening conditions. It will

be recalled that the evaluations of the group's performance by the experimenter, which was the means whereby threat was induced, was not made until after the second task. This was relatively late in the problem solving process. The reorganization of the person's initial attitude toward the Negro may take some time. Thus, attitude change may not have occurred in time to appreciably affect task communication. This explanation loses some of its force when one notes in Figure 1 that the differences in communication to the Negro as a function of prejudice occurs more markedly in the second two tasks than on the first two. An ongoing attitude change process should at least prevent such a difference from becoming more pronounced. Nevertheless, it might still be argued that with partitioned cubicles, a relatively long period of time is required before subjects become impressed with the fact that one member is a Negro; and still later, more time is needed for failure and status loss to sink in. Thus, the experiment may have obtained a sample of behavior when the subjects had fully noted the presence of the Negro but before the shared threat had an appreciable effect on communication. On this basis it would be predicted that if more than four tasks were given, subjects in the HPT condition would eventually begin to increase communication with the confederate.

A second line of reasoning assumes that avoidance of communication is a less direct form of hostile expression than rating the person as poor with respect to certain valued attributes. It also focuses on what is being affected by the induction of shared threat. Are prejudiced attitudes being remolded, or are the expressions of hostility stemming from such attitudes being inhibited without any underlying attitude change? If attitude change had occurred under shared threat, less overall hostility, direct and indirect, should be expressed toward the confederate. This did not occur. If, however, shared threat served to inhibit direct aggression without modifying prejudiced attitudes, our expectation would be quite different. In this case, it would be anticipated that high prejudiced individuals confronted by a common threat would express a smaller amount of direct hostility toward a minority group member than equally prejudiced but unthreatened individuals. Both groups, nevertheless, would be expected to express a similar amount of indirect hostility (avoidance of communication with the Negro) which would be greater than that manifested by less prejudiced individuals.

Finally, discriminatory behavior based on cultural norms and the affective orientation toward Negroes may under certain conditions be uncorrelated. One can follow the discriminatory practices of one's group without necessarily entertaining feelings of hostility. This suggests a third possible interpretation. Since about 75 percent of the items on the prejudice scale used in this study concern appropriate behavior toward Negroes, a high anti-Negro prejudice score may indicate that the person has strongly internalized the discriminatory behavior patterns of Texas culture. The strength of these norms regarding behavior may not be appreciably modified by a momentary event in a temporary group. Thus, the shared threat induced may have produced a positive change in the affective orientation toward the Negro group member while having no influence on conformity to cultural patterns which stress avoidance of equal status interaction.

SUMMARY

The purpose of this experiment was to test the relationship between shared threat and the expression of prejudice hypothesized by Feshbach and Singer (1957). Forty-eight subjects, varying with respect to anti-Negro prejudice, were placed under conditions of shared threat or nonthreat, in task oriented, cooperative work groups. A Negro confederate was a member in each group.

It was found, as hypothesized, that under conditions of shared threat a reduction in the expression of prejudice occurs in terms of direct evaluation of the Negro by other group members on a post-task questionnaire. No significant differences in the amount of communication to the confederate occurred as a result of the threat induction. However, significantly fewer messages were addressed to the Negro by the high prejudiced subjects, regardless of the presence or absence of shared threat.

REFERENCES

BETTELHEIM, B.   Individual and mass behavior in extreme situations. *J. abnorm. soc. Psychol.*, 1943, 38, 417–452.

COHEN, E. A.   *Human behavior in the concentration camp.* New York. Norton, 1953.

DEUTSCH, M.   The effects of cooperation and competition upon group processes. In D. Cartwright & A. Zander (Eds.), *Group dynamics research and theory.* New York: Harper & Row, 1953. Pp. 319–353.

FESHBACH, S., & SINGER, R.   The effects of personal and shared threat upon social prejudice. *J. abnorm. soc. Psychol.*, 1957, 54, 411–416.

Festinger, L., Cartwright, D., Barber, Kathleen, Fleischl, Juliet, Gottsdanker, Josephine, Keysen, Annette, & Leavitt, Gloria. A study of a rumor: Its origin and spread. *Hum. Relat.*, 1948, 1, 464–486.

Festinger, L., Schachter, S., & Back, K. *Social pressures in informal groups: A study of a housing community.* New York: Harper & Row, 1950.

French, J. R. P., Jr. The disruption and cohesion of groups. *J. Psychol.*, 1941, 36, 361–377.

Jacobson, E., & Schachter, S. (Eds.) Cross-national research: A case study. *J. soc. Issues*, 1954, 10(4), 5–68.

Kelley, J. G., Ferson, J. E., & Holtzman, W. H. The measurement of attitudes toward the Negro in the South. *J. soc. Psychol.*, 1958, 48, 305–317.

Killian, L. M. The significance of multiple-group membership in disaster. *Amer. J. Sociol.*, 1952, 57, 309–314.

Leavitt, H. J. Some effects of certain communication patterns on group performance. *J. abnorm. soc. Psychol.*, 1951, 46, 38–50.

Leighton, A. *The governing of men.* Princeton: Princeton Univer. Press, 1945.

Pepitone, A., & Kleiner, R. The effects of threat and frustration on group cohesiveness. *J. abnorm. soc. Psychol.*, 1957, 54, 192–199.

Potashin, R. A sociometric study of children's friendships. *Sociometry*, 1946, 9, 48–70.

Schachter, S. Deviation, rejection, and communication. In D. Cartwright & A. Zander, (Eds.), *Group dynamics research and theory*. New York: Harper & Row, 1960, Pp. 223–248.

Schachter, S., Nuttin, J., deMonchaux, Cecily, Maucorps, P. H., Osmer, D., Duijker, H., Rommetveit, R., & Israel, J. Cross-cultural experiments on threat and rejection. *Hum. Relat.*, 1954, 7, 403–440.

Sherif, M., & Sherif, C. *Groups in harmony and tension.* New York: Harper & Row, 1943.

Wright, M. E. The influence of frustration on the social relations of children. *Charact. Pers.*, 1943, 12, 111–122.

52. SOCIAL PSYCHOLOGY AND DESEGREGATION RESEARCH *

Thomas F. Pettigrew

What one hears and what one sees of southern race relations today are sharply divergent. Consider some of the things that occur in interviews with white Southerners.

"As much as my family likes TV," confided a friendly North Carolina farmer, "we always turn the set off when they put them colored people on." But as the two of us were completing the interview, a series of famous Negro entertainers performed on the bright, 21-inch screen in the adjoining room. No one interrupted them.

A rotund banker in Charleston, South Carolina, was equally candid in his remarks: "Son, under no conditions will the white man and the black man ever get together in this state." He apparently preferred to ignore the government sponsored integration at his city's naval installation, just a short distance from his office.

Another respondent, this time a

* Excerpted from the *American Psychologist*, 1961, 16: 105–112, with permission of the author and the American Psychological Association.

highly educated Chattanooga business-man, patiently explained to me for over an hour how race relations had not changed at all in his city during the past generation. As I left his office building, I saw a Negro policeman directing downtown traffic. It was the first Negro traffic cop I had ever seen in the South.

The South today is rife with such contradictions; social change has simply been too rapid for many Southerners to recognize it. Such a situation commands the attention of psychologists—particu-larly those in the South.

There are many other aspects of this sweeping process that should com-mand our professional attention. To name just two, both the pending vio-lence and the stultifying conformity at-tendant with desegregation are uniquely psychological problems. We might ask, for instance, what leads to violence in some desegregating communities, like Little Rock and Clinton, and not in others, like Norfolk and Winston-Salem? A multiplicity of factors must be relevant and further research is des-perately needed to delineate them; but tentative early work seems to indicate that desegregation violence so far has been surprisingly "rational." That is, violence has generally resulted in local-ities where at least some of the author-ities give prior hints that they would gladly return to segregation if disturb-ances occurred; peaceful integration has generally followed firm and force-ful leadership.[1]

Research concerning conformity in the present situation is even more im-portant. Many psychologists know from

personal experience how intense the pressures to conform in racial attitudes have become in the present-day South; indeed, it appears that the first amend-ment guaranteeing free speech is in as much peril as the fourteenth amend-ment. Those who dare to break consist-ently this conforming taboo must do so in many parts of the South under the intimidation of slanderous letters and phone calls, burned crosses, and even bomb threats. Moreover, this paper will contend that conformity is the social psychological key to analyzing deseg-regation.

It is imperative that psychologists study these phenomena for two rea-sons: first, our psychological insights and methods are needed in understand-ing and solving this, our nation's pri-mary internal problem; second, this process happening before our eyes offers us a rare opportunity to test in the field the psychological concomitants of cul-tural stress and social change. Thus I would like in this paper to assess some of the prospects and directions of these potential psychological contributions.

ROLE OF SOCIAL SCIENCE IN THE DESEGREGATION PROCESS TO DATE

The role of social science, particu-larly sociology and psychology, in the desegregation process has been much publicized and criticized by southern segregationists.[2] Many of these critics

---

[1] Clark (1953) predicted this from early border-state integration, and a variety of field reports have since documented the point in specific instances.

[2] For instance, once-liberal Virginius Dab-ney (1957, p. 14), editor of the *Richmond Times-Dispatch*, charged that "the violence at Little Rock . . . never would have happened if nine justices had not consulted sociologists and psychologists, instead of lawyers, in 1954, and attempted to legislate through judicial decrees."

apparently think that sociology is synonymous with socialism and psychology with brainwashing. In any event, their argument that we have been crucially important in the Supreme Court desegregation cases of the fifties is based largely on the reference to seven social science documents in Footnote 11 of the famous 1954 *Brown vs. Board of Education* decision. It would be flattering for us to think that our research has had such a dramatic effect on the course of history as segregationists claim, but in all truth we do not deserve such high praise.

In making their claim that the 1954 decision was psychological and not legal, the segregationists choose to overlook several things. The 1954 ruling did not come suddenly "out of the blue"; it was a logical continuation of a 44-year Supreme Court trend that began in 1910 when a former private in the Confederate Army, the liberal Edward White, became Chief Justice (Logan, 1956). When compared to this backdrop, our influence on the 1954 ruling was actually of only footnote importance. Furthermore, the language and spirit of the 1896 *Plessy vs. Ferguson*, separate-but-equal decision, so dear to the hearts of segregationists, were as immersed in the jargon and thinking of the social science of that era as the 1954 decision was of our era. Its 1896, Sumnerian argument that laws cannot change "social prejudices" (Allport, 1954, pp. 469–473) and its use of such social Darwinism terms as "racial instincts" and "natural affinities" lacked only a footnote to make it as obviously influenced by the then current social science as the 1954 ruling.

A final reason why we do not deserve the flattering praise of the segregationists is our failure to make substantial contributions to the process since 1954. The lack of penetrating psychological research in this area can be traced directly to three things: the lack of extensive foundation support, conformity pressures applied in many places in the South that deter desegregation research, and the inadequacy of traditional psychological thinking to cope with the present process. Let us discuss each of these matters in turn.

A few years ago Stuart Cook (1957) drew attention to the failure of foundations to support desegregation research; the situation today is only slightly improved. It appears that a combination of foundation fears has produced this situation. One set of fears, as Cook noted, may stem from concern over attacks by southern Congressmen on their tax free status; the other set may stem from boycotts carried out by some segregationists against products identified with the foundations. In any case, this curtailment of funds is undoubtedly one reason why social scientists have so far left this crucial process relatively unstudied. Recently, however, a few moderate sized grants have been made for work in this area; hopefully, this is the beginning of a reappraisal by foundations of their previous policies. And it is up to us to submit competent research proposals to them to test continually for any change of these policies.

It is difficult to assess just how much damage has been done to desegregation research in the South by segregationist pressures. Probably the number of direct refusals to allow such research by southern institutions outside of the Black Belt has actually been small. More likely, the greatest harm has been rendered indirectly by the stifling atmosphere which prevents us from actually testing the limits of research opportunities. Interested as we may be in the racial realm, we decide to work in a less controversial area. Perhaps it is less a matter of courage than it is of resignation in the face of what are thought to be impossible barriers. If these suspicions are correct, there is real hope for overcoming in part this second obstacle to desegregation research.

In some situations, there should be little resistance. In racially integrated veterans' hospitals, for instance, much needed personality studies comparing Negro and white patients should be possible. In other situations, the amount of resistance to race research may be less than we anticipate. Since Little Rock, many so-called "moderates" in the South, particularly businessmen, have become more interested in the dynamics of desegregation. This is not to say that they are more in favor of racial equality than they were; it is only to suggest that the had publicity, the closing of schools, and the economic losses suffered by Little Rock have made these influential Southerners more receptive to objective and constructive research on the process. It is for this reason that it is imperative the limits for the southern study of desegregation be tested at this time.

Finally, psychological contributions to desegregation research have been restricted by the inadequacy of traditional thinking in our discipline. More specifically, the relative neglect of situational variables in interracial behavior and a restricted interpretation and use of the attitude concept hinder psychological work in this area.

The importance of the situation for racial interaction has been demonstrated in a wide variety of settings. All-pervasive racial attitudes are often not involved; many individuals seem fully capable of immediate behavioral change as situations change. Thus in Panama there is a divided street, the Canal Zone side of which is racially segregated and the Panamanian side of which is racially integrated. Biesanz and Smith (1951) report that most Panamanians and Americans appear to accommodate without difficulty as they go first on one side of the street and then on the other. Likewise in the coal mining county of McDowell, West Virginia, Minard (1952) relates that the majority of Negro and white miners follow easily a traditional pattern of integration below the ground and almost complete segregation above the ground. The literature abounds with further examples: southern white migrants readily adjusting to integrated situations in the North (Killian, 1949), northern whites approving of employment and public facility integration but resisting residential integration (Reitzes, 1953), etc. Indeed, at the present time in the South there are many white Southerners who are simultaneously adjusting to bus and public golf course integration and opposing public school integration. Or, as in Nashville, they may have accepted school integration but are opposing lunch counter integration.

This is not to imply that generalized attitudes on race are never invoked. There are some Panamanians and some Americans who act about the same on both sides of the Panamanian street. Minard (1952) estimated about two-fifths of the West Virginian miners he observed behave consistently in either a tolerant or an intolerant fashion both below and above ground. And some whites either approve or disapprove of all desegregation. But these people are easily explained by traditional theory. They probably consist of the extremes in authoritarianism; their attitudes on race are so generalized and so salient that their consistent behavior in racial situations is sometimes in defiance of the prevailing social norms.

On the other hand, the "other directed" individuals who shift their behavior to keep in line with shifting expectations present the real problem for psychologists. Their racial attitudes appear less salient, more specific, and more tied to particular situations. Conformity needs are predominantly important for these people, and we shall return shortly to a further discussion of these conformists.

One complication introduced by a situational analysis is that interracial contact itself frequently leads to the modification of attitudes. A number of studies of racially integrated situations have noted dramatic attitude changes, but in most cases the changes involved specific, situation linked attitudes. For example, white department store employees become more accepting of Negroes in the work situation after equal status, integrated contact but not necessarily more accepting in other situations (Harding & Hogrefe, 1952). And *The American Soldier* studies (Stouffer, Suchman, DeVinney, Star, & Williams, 1949) found that the attitudes of white army personnel toward the Negro as a fighting man improve after equal status, integrated contact in combat, but their attitudes toward the Negro as a social companion do not necessarily change. In other words, experience in a novel situation of equal status leads to acceptance of that specific situation for many persons. Situations, then, not only struc-ture specific racial behavior, but they may change specific attitudes in the process.

One final feature of a situational analysis deserves mention. Typically in psychology we have tested racial attitudes in isolation, apart from conflicting attitudes and values. Yet this is not realistic. As the desegregation process slowly unfolds in such resistant states as Virginia and Georgia, we see clearly that many segregationist Southerners value law and order, public education, and a prosperous economy above their racial views. Once such a situation pits race against other entrenched values, we need to know the public's hierarchy of these values. Thus a rounded situational analysis requires the measures of racial attitudes in the full context of counter-values.[3]

CONFORMITY AND SOCIAL ADJUSTMENT IN SOUTHERN RACIAL ATTITUDES

Evidence of the importance of conformity in southern attitudes on race has been steadily accumulating in recent years. The relevant data come from several different research approaches; one of these is the study of anti-Semitism. Roper's (1946, 1947) opinion polls have twice shown the South, together with the Far West, to be one of the least anti-Semitic regions in the United States. Knapp's (1944) study of over one thousand war rumors from all parts of the country in 1942 lends additional weight to this finding. He noted that anti-Semitic stories constituted 9 percent of the nation's rumors but only three percent of the South's rumors. By contrast,

[3] A popular treatment of this point has been made by Zinn (1959).

8.5 percent of the southern rumors concerned the Negro as opposed to only 3 percent for the nation as a whole. Consistent with these data, too, is Prothro's (1952) discovery that two-fifths of his white adult sample in Louisiana was quite favorable in its attitudes toward Jews but at the same time quite unfavorable in its attitudes toward Negroes. But if the externalization function were predominant in southern anti-Negro attitudes, the South should also be highly anti-Semitic. Externalizing bigots do not select out just the Negro; they typically reject all out-groups, even, as Hartley (1946) has demonstrated, out-groups that do not exist.

Further evidence comes from research employing the famous F Scale measure of authoritarianism (Adorno, Frenkel-Brunswik, Levinson, & Sanford, 1950). Several studies, employing both student and adult samples, have reported southern F Scale means that fall well within the range of means of comparable nonsouthern groups (Milton, 1952; Pettigrew, 1959; Smith & Prothro, 1957). Moreover, there is no evidence that the family pattern associated with authoritarianism is any more prevalent in the South than in other parts of the country (Davis, Gardner, & Gardner, 1941; Dollard, 1937). It seems clear, then, that the South's heightened prejudice against the Negro cannot be explained in terms of any regional difference in authoritarianism. This is not to deny, however, the importance of the F Scale in predicting individual differences; it appears to correlate with prejudice in southern samples at approximately the same levels as in northern samples (Pettigrew, 1959).

The third line of evidence relates conformity measures directly to racial attitudes. For lack of a standardized, nonlaboratory measure, one study defined conformity and deviance in terms of the respondents' social characteristics (Pettigrew, 1959). For a southern white sample with age and education held constant, potentially conforming respondents (that is, females or church attenders) were *more* anti-Negro than their counterparts (i.e., males or non-attenders of church), and potentially deviant respondents (that is, armed service veterans or political independents) were *less* anti-Negro than their counterparts (that is, nonveterans or political party identifiers). None of these differences were noted in a comparable northern sample. Furthermore, Southerners living in communities with relatively small percentages of Negroes were less anti-Negro than Southerners living in communities with relatively large percentages of Negroes, though they were *not* less authoritarian. In short, respondents most likely to be conforming to cultural pressures are more prejudiced against Negroes in the South but not in the North. And the percentage of Negroes in the community appears to be a fairly accurate index of the strength of these southern cultural pressures concerning race.

Thus all three types of research agree that conformity to the stern racial norms of southern culture is unusually crucial in the South's heightened hostility toward the Negro.[4] Or, in plain language, it is the path of least resistance in most southern circles to favor white

[4] Similar analyses of South African student data indicate that the social adjustment function may also be of unusual importance in the anti-African attitudes of the English in the Union (Pettigrew, 1958, 1960).

supremacy. When an individual's parents and peers are racially prejudiced, when his limited world accepts racial discrimination as a given of life, when his deviance means certain ostracism, then his anti-Negro attitudes are not so much expressive as they are socially adjusting.

This being the case, it is fortunate that a number of significant laboratory and theoretical advances in the conformity realm have been made recently in our discipline. Solomon Asch's (1951) pioneer research on conformity, followed up by Crutchfield (1955) and others, has provided us with a wealth of laboratory findings, many of them suggestive for desegregation research. And theoretical analyses of conformity have been introduced by Kelman (1958, 1961), Festinger (1953, 1957), and Thibaut and Kelley (1959); these, too, are directly applicable for desegregation research. Indeed, research in southern race relations offers a rare opportunity to test these empirical and theoretical formulations in the field on an issue of maximum salience.

Consider the relevance of one of Asch's (1951) intriguing findings. Asch's standard situation, you will recall, employed seven preinstructed assistants and a genuine subject in a line judgment task. On two-thirds of the judgments, the seven assistants purposely reported aloud an obviously incorrect estimate; thus the subject, seated eighth, faced unanimous pressure to conform by making a similarly incorrect response. On approximately one-third of such judgments, he yielded to the group; like the others, he would estimate a 5-inch line as 4 inches. But when Asch disturbed the unanimity by having one of his seven assistants give the correct response, the subjects yielded only a tenth, rather than a third, of the time. Once unanimity no longer existed, even when there was only one supporting colleague, the subject could better withstand the pressure of the majority to conform. To carry through the analogy to today's crisis in the South, obvious 5-inch lines are being widely described as 4 inches. Many Southerners, faced with what appears to be solid unanimity, submit to the distortion. But when even one respected source—a minister, a newspaper editor, even a college professor—conspicuously breaks the unanimity, *perhaps* a dramatic modification is achieved in the private opinions of many conforming Southerners. Only an empirical test can learn if such a direct analogy is warranted.

Consider, too, the relevance of recent theoretical distinctions. Kelman (1958, 1961), for example, has clarified the concept of conformity by pointing out that three separate processes are involved: *compliance, identification,* and *internalization.* Compliance exists when an individual accepts influence not because he believes in it, but because he hopes to achieve a favorable reaction from an agent who maintains surveillance over him. Identification exists when an individual accepts influence because he wants to establish or maintain a satisfying relationship with another person or group. The third process, internalization, exists when an individual accepts influence because the content of the behavior itself is satisfying; unlike the other types of conformity, internalized behavior will be performed without the surveillance of the agent or a salient relationship with the agent. It is with this third process that Kelman's ideas overlap with authoritarian theory.

We have all witnessed illustrations of each of these processes in the acceptance by Southerners of the region's racial norms. The "Uncle Tom" Negro is an example of a compliant Southerner; another example is furnished by the white man who treats Negroes as equals only when not under the surveillance of other whites. Identification is best seen in white Southerners whose resistance to racial integration enables them to be a part of what they erroneously imagine to be the Confederate tradition. Such identifiers are frequently upwardly mobile people who are still assimilating to urban society; they strive for social status by identifying with the hallowed symbols and shibboleths of the South's past. Southerners who have internalized the white supremacy dictates of the culture are the real racists who use the issue to gain political office, to attract resistance group membership fees, or to meet personality needs. Southerners with such contrasting bases for their racial attitudes should react very differently toward desegregation. For instance, compliant whites can be expected to accept desegregation more readily than those who have internalized segregationist norms.

On the basis of this discussion of conformity, I would like to propose a new concept: *the latent liberal*. This is not to be confused with the cherished southern notion of the "moderate"; the ambiguous term "moderate" is presently used to describe everything from an integrationist who wants to be socially accepted to a racist who wants to be polite. Rather, the latent liberal refers to the Southerner who is neither anti-Semitic nor authoritarian but whose conformity habits and needs cause him to be strongly anti-Negro. Through the processes of compliance and identification, the latent liberal continues to behave in a discriminatory fashion toward Negroes even though such behavior conflicts with his basically tolerant personality. He is at the present time *illiberal* on race, but he has the personality potentiality of becoming liberal once the norms of the culture change. Indeed, as the already unleashed economic, legal, political, and social forces restructure the South's racial norms, the latent liberal's attitudes about Negroes will continue to change. Previously cited research suggests that there are today an abundance of white Southerners who meet this latent liberal description; collectively, they will reflect on the individual level the vast societal changes now taking place in the South.

SOME SUGGESTED DIRECTIONS FOR FUTURE PSYCHOLOGICAL RESEARCH ON DESEGREGATION [5]

We are in serious need of research on the Negro, both in the North and in the South. Most psychological research in this area was conducted during the 1930's and directed at testing racists' claims of Negro inferiority. But the most sweeping advances in American Negro history have been made in the past generation, requiring a fresh new look—particularly at the Negro personality.

Two aspects of this research make it complex and difficult. In the first place, the race of the interviewer is a complicating and not as yet fully understood factor. Further methodological study is needed on this point. Moreover, special problems of control are inherent

[5] For other suggestions, see the important analysis of desegregation by Cook (1957).

in this research. Not only are there some relatively unique variables that must be considered (for example, migration history, differential experience with the white community, and so on), but such simple factors as education are not easy to control. For instance, has the average graduate of a southern rural high school for Negroes received an education equal to the average graduate of such a school for whites? No, in spite of the South's belated efforts to live up to separate-but-equal education, available school data indicate that the graduates have probably not received equivalent educations. Yet some recent research on Negro personality has been based on the assumption that Negro and white education in the South are equivalent (for example, Smith & Prothro, 1957).

Fortunately, the Institute for Research in the Social Sciences at the University of North Carolina has embarked on a large study of many of these content and methodological problems. It is to be hoped that their work will stimulate other efforts.

Some of the most valuable psychological data now available on desegregation have been collected by public opinion polls. But typically these data have been gathered without any conceptual framework to guide their coverage and direction.

For example, one of the more interesting poll findings is that a majority of white Southerners realize that racial desegregation of public facilities is inevitable even though about six out of seven strongly oppose the process (Hyman & Sheatsley, 1956). The psychological implications of this result are so extensive that we would like to know more. Do the respondents who oppose desegregation but accept its inevitability

have other characteristics of latent liberals? Are these respondents more often found outside of the Black Belt? Typically, we cannot answer such questions from present poll data; we need to build into the desegregation polls broader coverage and more theoretical direction.

The third direction that psychological research in desegregation could usefully take concerns measurement. Save for the partly standardized F Scale, we still lack widely used, standardized field measures of the chief variables in this realm. Such instruments are necessary both for comparability of results and for stimulation of research; witness the invigorating effects on research of the F Scale, the Minnesota Multiphasic Inventory, and the need achievement scoring scheme. Mention of McClelland's need achievement scoring scheme should remind us, too, that projective and other indirect techniques might answer many of these measurement requirements— especially for such sensitive and subtle variables as conformity needs.

Finally, the definitive interdisciplinary case study of desegregation has yet to be started. Properly buttressed by the necessary foundation aid, such a study should involve comparisons before, during, and after desegregation of a wide variety of communities. The interdisciplinary nature of such an undertaking is stressed because desegregation is a peculiarly complex process demanding a broad range of complementary approaches.

Any extensive case project must sample three separate time periods: before a legal ruling or similar happening has alerted the community to imminent desegregation, during the height of the desegregating process, and after several years of accommodation. Without this longitudinal view, desegregation as a dynamic, ongoing process cannot be understood. This time perspective, for instance, would enable us to interpret the fact that an overwhelming majority of Oklahoma whites in a 1954 poll sternly objected to mixed schools, but within a few years has accepted without serious incident integrated education throughout most of the state (Jones, 1957).

A carefully selected range of communities is required to test for differences in the process according to the characteristics of the area. Recent demographic analyses and predictions of the South's school desegregation pattern (Ogburn & Grigg, 1956; Pettigrew, 1957; Pettigrew & Campbell, 1960) could help in making this selection of communities. Comparable data gathered in such a selected variety of locations would allow us to pinpoint precisely the aspects of desegregation unique to, say, a Piedmont city, as opposed to a Black Belt town.

Compare the potential value of such a broad research effort with the limited case studies that have been possible so far. Low budget reports of only one community are the rule; many of them are theses or seminar projects, some remain on the descriptive level, all but a few sample only one time period, and there is almost no comparability of instruments and approach. A comprehensive case project is obviously long overdue.

This has been an appeal for a vigorous empirical look at southern race relations. Despite segregationists' claims to the contrary, social psychological contributions to desegregation research have been relatively meager. There are, however, grounds for hoping that this situation will be partly corrected in the near future—particularly if psychologists get busy.

Foundations appear to be re-evaluating their previous reluctance to support such research. And we can re-evaluate our own resignation in the face of barriers to conduct investigations in this area; the tragedy of Little Rock has had a salutary effect on many influential Southerners in this respect.

Recognition of the importance of the situation in interracial behavior and the full exploitation of the attitude concept can remove inadequacies in the traditional psychological approach to the study of race. In this connection, an extended case for considering conformity as crucial in the Negro attitudes of white Southerners was presented and a new concept—the latent liberal—introduced. One final implication of this latent liberal concept should be mentioned. Some cynics have argued that successful racial desegregation in the South will require an importation of tens of thousands of psychotherapists and therapy for millions of bigoted Southerners. Fortunately for desegregation, psychotherapists, and Southerners, this will not be necessary; a thorough repatterning of southern interracial behavior will be sufficient therapy in itself.

REFERENCES

Adorno, T. W., Frenkel-Brunswik, Else, Levinson, D. J., & Sanford, N. *The authoritarian personality.* New York: Harper & Row, 1950.

Allport, G. W. *The nature of prejudice.* Cambridge, Mass.: Addison-Wesley, 1954.

Asch, S. E. Effects of group pressure upon the modification and distortion of judgments. In H. Guetzkow (Ed.), *Groups, leadership and men.* Pittsburgh: Carnegie, 1951.

Biesanz, J., & Smith, L. M. Race relations of Panama and the Canal Zone. *Amer. J. Sociol.,* 1951, **57**, 7–14.

Clark, K. B. Desegregation: An appraisal of the evidence. *J. soc. Issues,* 1953, 9, 1–76.

Cook, S. W. Desegregation: A psychological analysis. *Amer. Psychologist,* 1957, **12**, 1–13.

Crutchfield, R. S. Conformity and character. *Amer. Psychologist,* 1955, 10, 191–198.

Dabney, V. The violence at Little Rock. *Richmond Times-Dispatch,* 1957, **105**, September 24, 14.

Davis, A., Gardner, B., & Gardner, Mary. *Deep South.* Chicago: Univer. Chicago Press, 1941.

Dollard, J. *Caste and class in a southern town.* New Haven: Yale Univer. Press, 1937.

Festinger, L. An analysis of compliant behavior. In M. Sherif & M. O. Wilson (Eds.), *Group relations at the crossroads.* New York: Harper & Row, 1953.

Festinger, L. A *theory of cognitive dissonance.* New York: Harper & Row, 1957.

Harding, J., & Hogrefe, R. Attitudes of white department store employees toward Negro co-workers. *J. soc. Issues,* 1952, **8**, 18–28.

Hartley, E. L. *Problems in prejudice.* New York: King's Crown, 1946.

Hyman, H. H., & Sheatsley, P. B. Attitudes toward desegregation. *Scient. Amer.,* 1956, **195**, 35–39.

Jones, E. City limits. In D. Shoemaker (Ed.), *With all deliberate speed.* New York: Harper & Row, 1957.

Kelman, H. C. Compliance, identification, and internalization: Three processes of attitude change. *J. conflict Resolut.,* 1958, **2**, 51–60.

Kelman, H. C. *Social influence and personal belief.* New York: Wiley, 1961.

Killian, L. W. Southern white laborers in Chicago's West Side. Unpublished doctoral dissertation, University of Chicago, 1949.

Knapp, R. H. A psychology of rumor. *Publ. opin. Quart.,* 1944, **8**, 22–37.

Logan, R. W. The United States Supreme Court and the segregation issue. *Ann. Amer. Acad. Pol. Soc. Sci.,* 1956, **304**, 10–16.

Milton, O. Presidential choice and performance on a scale of authoritarianism. *Amer. Psychologist,* 1952, **7**, 597–598.

Minard, R. D. Race relations in the Pocahontas coal field. *J. soc. Issues,* 1952, 8, 29–44.

Ogburn, W. F., & Grigg, C. M. Factors related to the Virginia vote on segregation. *Soc. Forces,* 1956, **34**, 301–308.

Pettigrew, T. F. Demographic correlates of border-state desegregation. *Amer. sociol. Rev.,* 1957, **22**, 683–689.

Pettigrew, T. F. Personality and sociocultural factors in intergroup attitudes: A cross-national comparison. *J. conflict Resolut.,* 1958, **2**, 29–42.

Pettigrew, T. F. Regional differences in anti-Negro prejudice. *J. abnorm. soc. Psychol.,* 1959, **59**, 28–36.

Pettigrew, T. F. Social distance attitudes of South African students. *Soc. Forces,* 1960, **38**, 246–253.

Pettigrew, T. F., & Campbell, E. Q. Faubus and segregation: An analysis of Arkansas voting. *Publ. opin. Quart.,* 1960, **24**, 436–447.

Prothro, E. T. Ethnocentrism and anti-Negro attitudes in the deep South. *J. abnorm. soc. Psychol.,* 1952, **47**, 105–108.

Rabb, E., & Lipset, S. M. *Prejudice and society.* New York: Anti-Defamation League of B'nai B'rith, 1959.

Reitzes, D. C. The role of organizational structures: Union versus neighborhood in a tension situation. *J. soc. Issues,* 1953, **9**, 37–44.

Roper, E. United States anti-Semites. *Fortune,* 1946, **33**, 257–260.

Roper, E. United States anti-Semites. *Fortune,* 1947, **36**, 5–10.

Rose, A. M. Intergroup relations vs. prejudice: Pertinent theory for the study of social change. *Soc. Probl.,* 1956, **4**, 173–176.

SMITH, C. U., & PROTHRO, J. W. Ethnic differences in authoritarian personality. *Soc. Forces,* 1957, **35,** 334–338.

SMITH, M. B., BRUNER, J. S., & WHITE, R. W. *Opinion and personality.* New York: Wiley, 1956.

STOUFFER, S. A., SUCHMAN, E. A., DeVINNEY, L. C., STAR, SHIRLEY A., WILLIAMS, R. M., JR. *Studies in social psychology in World War II.* Vol. 1. *The American soldier: Adjustment during army life.* Princeton: Princeton Univer. Press, 1949.

THIBAUT, J. W., & KELLEY, H. H. *The social psychology of groups.* New York: Wiley, 1959.

ZINN, H. A fate worse than integration. *Harper's,* 1959, **219,** August, 53–56.

Author Index

Subject Index

Ability
of group members, 391, 409–416
of leader, 390–395
and self-evaluation, 272–274
Acceptance
of communication, 158, 162, 163
of influence, 287–294
of problem solution, 458–468
Achievement, need for, 60, 63, 277–287, 349–357, 516
Achievement training, 85–87
Adaptation level, 12
Affect
and attitude, 107–133
and belief, 111–119, 121, 122
and cognitive structure, 121–133
and drive, 9, 11, 12
and emotion, 477
and language, 96, 99
Affective-Cognitive consistency, 123, 124
Affiliation, need for, 477–489
Aggression, 59, 63, 64, 90, 422, 507
Anxiety
and affiliation, 477–489
in child training, 85–87
and cognitive functioning, 447
and congruency of role assignment, 449
defined, 477, 478
and fear, 477–489
in interaction, 447, 448
and social distance, 212
Arousal
cortical, 48
of emotions, 477, 478, 482, 488
inconsistency, 121–133
of motives, 11, 13, 477, 478, 486
Aspiration, level of, 350, 375, 455
Assimilation, 179, 359, 360
Attitude
and affect, 107–133
and authoritarianism, 39, 512, 513, 516
and belief, 107–119, 121, 122
change, 27–41, 70, 71, 118, 121–133, 153–185, 371, 374, 375, 380, 506, 512
and cognition, 27–41, 107–133

components of, 107–110, 115, 123, 126, 127, 133
cross-cultural comparison of, 95–106
defined, 101, 107–109, 111, 123
dynamics, 118, 125–133
internal consistency of, 27–29, 31–33, 123–133
measurement, 95–106, 108, 109, 113–116, 122, 165, 166, 169, 511, 512
polarization of, 103, 104
and social influence, 70, 71, 371, 374, 375
and voting behavior, 134–143, 174
Attraction
and agreement, 222–224
constancies in, 218
interpersonal, 31, 217–228
of roles, 349–357
Augmentation, 69–79
Authoritarianism
and attitude, 39, 512, 513, 516
and conformity, 294–296, 298, 299
and consistency in personality, 39
and interpersonal attraction, 220, 225, 226
and social distance, 212, 216
and socialization, 474
and trusting behavior, 471–475
Autokinetic phenomenon, 294–299, 309–321
Aversive behavior, 7, 11

Balance theory, 27–41, 218, 219, 221, 224, 227–229, 231, 232, 374
assumptions underlying, 29
and communication, 231–234
defined, 29–31, 218, 219, 228
and interpersonal attraction, 218–228
and interpersonal choice, 228–234
and social influence, 374
See also Congruity theory; Consistency; Dissonance theory; Strain toward symmetry
Behavior, of organisms, 50–56
Behavioral commitment, 263–277
Behavioral intention, 110, 111, 116
Behavior theory, 6, 7, 10, 48, 50–56, 57, 116
Belief
and affect, 111–133

527